4332

High Financier

NIALL FERGUSON

High Financier

The Lives and Time of Siegmund Warburg

THE PENGUIN PRESS

NEW YORK

2010

For Charles S. Maier
colleague and friend

THE PENGUIN PRESS
Published by the Penguin Group
Penguin Group (USA) Inc., 375 Hudson Street, New York, New York 10014, U.S.A. •
Penguin Group (Canada), 90 Eglinton Avenue East, Suite 700, Toronto, Ontario, Canada M4P 2Y3
(a division of Pearson Penguin Canada Inc.) • Penguin Books Ltd, 80 Strand, London WC2R 0RL, England •
Penguin Ireland, 25 St. Stephen's Green, Dublin 2, Ireland (a division of Penguin Books Ltd) • Penguin Books Australia
Ltd, 250 Camberwell Road, Camberwell, Victoria 3124, Australia (a division of Pearson Australia Group Pty Ltd) •
Penguin Books India Pvt Ltd, 11 Community Centre, Panchsheel Park, New Delhi – 110 017, India •
Penguin Group (NZ), 67 Apollo Drive, Rosedale, North Shore 0632, New Zealand (a division of
Pearson New Zealand Ltd) • Penguin Books (South Africa) (Pty) Ltd, 24 Sturdee Avenue,
Rosebank, Johannesburg 2196, South Africa

Penguin Books Ltd, Registered Offices:
80 Strand, London WC2R 0RL, England

First published in 2010 by The Penguin Press,
a member of Penguin Group (USA) Inc.

1   3   5   7   9   10   8   6   4   2

Copyright © Niall Ferguson, 2010
All rights reserved

ISBN 978-1-59420-246-9

Printed in the United States of America

The ego, this mysterious conception, hypothetical motor of human beings, is a clear unity only in the physical sense but a mixture of many different and contradictory elements . . .

Siegmund Warburg, 1965

The main argument for such an autobiography is the great variety of activities in which I have been involved in my life – as a man born and educated in Germany, who started his career there but had later to establish his home and professional basis in England; as a man who lived in a way several lives, that of a German scholar, of an international banker, of an adherent to Judaism and above all of an ardently enthusiastic citizen of Britain, his country of adoption.

Siegmund Warburg, 1976

Contents

List of Illustrations

Acknowledgements

This book has been a dozen years in the making. Despite being delivered late, however, I believe its publication is timely.

The idea that I should write a biography of Siegmund Warburg was first suggested to me by George Warburg and Hugh Stevenson in March 1998. My first thanks are therefore due to Siegmund's children, George and his sister Anna Biegun, closely followed by Hugh and the other Trustees of Sir Siegmund Warburg's Voluntary Settlement, notably Christopher Purvis and Doris Wasserman. They all showed superhuman patience as I allowed myself to be sidetracked by no fewer than six other books, four television documentaries, transatlantic migration and a host of other distractions. The subject of this biography would surely not have been so forbearing.

A number of people closely associated with Siegmund Warburg kindly allowed me to interview them. I would like to thank Ken Costa, Sir John Craven, Peter Stormonth Darling, Geoffrey Elliott, John Goodwin, Martin Gordon, Sir Ronald Grierson, Bernard Kelly, Oscar Lewisohn, Nick McAndrew, Renate Popper, Lord Rothschild, Sir David Scholey, Joshua Sherman, Andrew Smithers, Peter Spira, George Steiner and James Wolfensohn. Among those I interviewed, a number have regrettably not lived to see the finished product: Raymond Bonham Carter, Henry Grunfeld, Robin Jessel and Eric Roll. I would also like to thank James and Mark Lewisohn, Simon McGuire, Jill May, Diego Pignatelli, David and Mark Seligman and Jens Tholstrup. Additional thanks are also due to all those named above – especially Joshua Sherman – who either supplied me with documents in their private possession or generously read and commented on the book in manuscript. Gene Dattel also read some of the manuscript.

In the course of my research, I had invaluable assistance from three former students, Hannah-Louise Clark, Glen O'Hara and Andrew Vereker. More recently, Jason Rockett and Thomas Weber helped me dot the last 'i's and cross the last 't's. Cecilia Mackay helped with the pictures. Thanks are also due to Ellie Warburg for her exceptional hospitality in Middletown.

I would like to thank the archivists and staff at the following institutions: the Leo Baeck Institute, New York; the Baker Library, Harvard Business School; the Bank of England; the Bundesarchiv Koblenz and Potsdam; the Churchill Archive Centre, Cambridge; the Columbia University Oral History Collection; the London School of Economics; the Federal Reserve Bank of New York; the Herbert Hoover Library, Iowa; the Jacob Rader Marcus Center of the American Jewish Archives, Cincinnati; the John F. Kennedy Memorial Library, Boston; Number 100 Hatton Garden, London; the Franklin D. Roosevelt Library, New York; the Rothschild Archive, London; the Sterling Library, Yale University; M. M. Warburg & Co., Hamburg; the University of Warwick Modern Records Centre, Coventry; and the Yale University Library.

I have been superbly well served, once again, by my agent, Andrew Wylie, and by my editors Ann Godoff and Simon Winder. It was a pleasure to work once again with the peerless Peter James, my copy-editor. Richard Duguid managed the book's production with his customary *sangfroid*. Thanks are also due to Penelope Vogler and Lauren Hodapp, who deftly handled publicity. Lawrence Slattery may dimly recall his work on the original book contract, for which I remain grateful.

No academic historian can find the time to write a book like this without considerable institutional support. I would therefore like to thank all my colleagues and the staff at the Belfer Centre for Science and International Affairs; Harvard Business School; the Harvard History Department; the Hoover Institution, Stanford; Jesus College, Oxford; Lowell House; the Minda de Gunzburg Center for European Studies and the Weatherhead Centre for International Affairs. Of all my friends in the United States, none has provided more inspiration – as a mentor, a teacher and a scholar – than Charles Maier. I dedicate this book to him.

Finally, let me pay tribute to all the friends and family members who have supported me over the past twelve years, and especially in the final, hardest year. In particular, I want to thank my children, who grew up as this book took shape; and Ayaan, who provided the inspiration at long last to finish it.

Cambridge, Massachusetts, March 2010

Preface

*We should not deceive ourselves into thinking that when we die
we shall be remembered intensively for more than a limited
number of days – except by a very few people to whom we are
bound by the closest ties of friendship and emotional attachment.*

Siegmund Warburg, 1974[1]

I

For better or for worse, the City of London today is the world's pre-
eminent international financial centre. Along with Wall Street, it is a
place synonymous with the ascent of money. Where other sectors of
the British economy languished after the Second World War, finance
thrived, latterly to the point of dangerous preponderance. This was not
foreordained. In 1945 London was to all intents and purposes dead as
a financial centre, its business 'catastrophic', in the words of one banker,
its grand Victorian counting houses one-third destroyed.[2] The era of
'gentlemanly capitalism' appeared about as likely to revive and endure
as the British Empire the gentlemanly capitalists had so loyally served.
That the City rose, literally as well as phoenix-like, from the ashes left
by the Blitz was a historical surprise harder to explain than would have
been its irrevocable demise, had that in fact occurred. This is a biography of the man who, more than any other, saved the City.

From the moment he hit the headlines with the first ever hostile
takeover bid in 1959 until his death in 1982, Siegmund Warburg was
the City's presiding genius, a brilliant exponent of high finance – *haute
banque*, as he liked to call it – who saw with unrivalled prescience the

possibilities of global financial reintegration after the calamities of the Depression and two world wars. He was the architect of that transformation of economic institutions which led the Western world back to the free market after the mid-century excesses of state control. Beating down the barriers that had been erected to limit the international flow of capital, Warburg made possible the resurrection of London as the world's principal centre for cross-border banking. His career illuminates nearly all of the most important historical questions about the role of finance in shaping modern Britain:

- Why was it that bankers of Jewish origin played such a leading role in British financial history?
- Did the gentlemanly capitalism of the City of London undermine the performance of the economy of the United Kingdom and accelerate Britain's decline as a manufacturing power?
- Did the City, in alliance with the 'gnomes of Zurich', thwart the ambitions of the Labour Party to modernize Britain's economy in the 1960s?
- Why did financial deregulation end up benefiting foreign banks more than British banks in the period after Warburg's death?

Yet these questions are not the best arguments for this biography. For Warburg was also, as he himself put it, 'a man who lived in a way several lives, that of a German scholar, of an international banker, of an adherent to Judaism and above all of an ardently enthusiastic citizen of Britain, his country of adoption'.[3] He was a scion of one of the great German-Jewish banking dynasties. He was also a politician *manqué*. Few figures in modern financial history have simultaneously played such an influential political role, albeit largely behind the scenes. As a young man, Warburg had intended to go into politics. The rise of Hitler shattered his ambitions. Yet even as an exile in 1930s England he retained his passion for politics. He was among the most outspoken City opponents of the policy of appeasement. And, after the war, he emerged as a highly influential proponent of European integration. Indeed, the part Warburg played in what has hitherto been the secret history of European unification – the process whereby Europe was financially as well as politically integrated – is among the most historically significant revelations of this book. Bankers, it now becomes clear, were as important as bureaucrats in propelling forward the project for a united Europe, and no banker did more to advance this cause than Siegmund Warburg. He consistently sought to accelerate the process whereby European institutions, in both the public and the private sector, were linked together across national borders. And he strove for decades to overcome the resistance of the British Establishment – the political and civil service elites of Westminster and Whitehall – to the idea that Britain should be a fully fledged member of a European Union.

At the same time, Warburg remained a committed Atlanticist, seeing no contradiction between Europe's economic integration and its strategic dependence on the United States. Despite the fact that he had opted for the City over Wall Street, he never lost sight of his lifelong goal of transatlantic financial integration and spent as much of his working career in New York as in Frankfurt, Hamburg, Paris and Zurich combined. His attempts to salvage Kuhn, Loeb & Co., once one of the titans of Wall Street, is one of the hitherto unwritten chapters of American financial history.

Bankers, it is often said, are the real powers behind the scenes of politics. But how in practice could a banker like Warburg exert power in the post-war world? Part of the answer lies in his pioneering role in corporate finance, which put him at the very heart of successive governments' efforts to resuscitate the ailing British economy. It was the emergence of S. G. Warburg & Co. as the masterminds of the takeover bid – beginning with the contested bid for British Aluminium – that transformed Warburg from an outsider, cold-shouldered by the snobbish old boys' network of the City, into one of the key insiders of 1960s politics. To an extent not previously realized by historians, Warburg became one of Harold Wilson's most trusted confidants on economic questions during the latter's first term as prime minister. In their regular meetings, about which other Cabinet members knew little, Warburg steered Wilson in the direction of EEC membership and strove, vainly as it proved, to avert first the devaluation of sterling in 1967 and then the descent of Britain's economy into the financial maelstrom of the mid-1970s.

Though eternally grateful to England for the opportunities it gave him, Warburg retained a lifelong suspicion of the English social elite, attributing many of the country's post-war problems to the deadening influence of the socially exclusive public schools and the mandarins of the senior civil service. A compulsive traveller, Warburg came to regard his own identity as multinational. Though he had been relatively swift in discerning the evil of Nazism, he never lost his attachment to German culture, and especially to the literature of the eighteenth and nineteenth centuries. In the years after 1945, few if any refugees from the Third Reich worked harder to bring about the economic and political rehabilitation of West Germany – to the extent of working closely with men who had played less than edifying roles under Hitler. At the same time, he became keenly interested in the fate of the state of Israel, first as a defender of the Zionist cause in the late 1960s, and later as a bitter critic of the Israeli government's policy of settling Jews in the occupied territories of the West Bank and Gaza. 'In its entirety,' as George Steiner* justly remarked, Warburg's 'background and career enacts one of the crucial chapters – at once brilliant and profoundly tragic – in the history of the Diaspora, and of German Jewry in particular.'[4]

What makes Warburg such a fascinating figure is not just his combination of economic power and political influence, however. There is also the extraordinary complexity of his personality. He was certainly among the best-read bankers of all time. Steeped not only in classical and romantic German literature and philosophy, he was also a devoted student of the great Central European modernists from Nietzsche to Freud. An intellectual whom fate rather than free will had made into a financier, he was always more interested in the organizational challenge of running a firm than in the bottom line of the business itself. Indeed, he was one of the great unsung innovators of modern management, a pioneer of open-plan offices and of corporate democracy. A gifted amateur psychologist, he evolved an idiosyncratic but apparently effective system for assessing the personalities of those around him, using graphology to complement his own psychoanalytical insights. The intensity of both his affections and his aversions made him devoted as a friend but unforgiving as a foe, as those unlucky protégés who passed from one category to the other found to their cost.

In writing this book, I have frequently wished for just a fraction of the literary talent of Thomas Mann, Warburg's favourite writer. For, if

* Warburg gave the Cambridge-based literary scholar Steiner the longest and most detailed interview of his life in a series of meetings in 1976.

the Warburg family were in some respects like a Jewish version of the Buddenbrooks, and in others like modern reincarnations of Joseph and his brothers, Siegmund himself resembled one of Mann's later protagonists, pursuing an elusive perfection like the composer Adrian Leverkühn in *Doctor Faustus*. Certainly it would take a Mann to do full justice to the hawk-eyed, sleek-haired, subtly theatrical German Jew in the immaculately cut Savile Row suit – as sensitive as a human tuning-fork, as intolerant of lapses as a Prussian martinet, a volatile compound of *feu sacré* and *élan vital*: sacred fire and vital impetus, two favourite Warburg phrases.

II

Biographers choose their subjects in response to a mixture of stimuli: authorial preoccupations, publishers' prejudices, readers' tastes, the lure of lucre. It might be said that the chroniclers of the lives of others are almost as much attracted to fame as the readers of glossy magazines devoted to the lives of celebrities. Wicked dictators are especially attractive to biographers. Search for 'Hitler' in the online catalogue of the British Library's General Reference Collection and you will find 478 results (though admittedly not all are straight biographies). There are 311 books about Stalin, 172 about Mussolini and 115 about Mao. Happily, a few democratic leaders have comparable appeal. Winston Churchill beats Il Duce with 298 results, as does Abraham Lincoln with 270. Not far behind are the royals. There are ninety books on the subject of Henry VIII, England's most celebrated king, and thirty-nine about Diana, Princess of Wales. But film stars are also in contention. There are thirty-eight books about Marilyn Monroe. Perhaps not surprisingly, writers especially love to write the lives of writers, despite the fact that these are usually quite dull. The number of books about Shakespeare exceeds two thousand. Even Jesus Christ cannot match that (1,613 results).

This is a book about someone less famous. Indeed, many quite well-informed people have never even heard of Siegmund Warburg. This is not, as has sometimes been suggested, because he was averse to publicity, though he frequently claimed to be, or contemptuous of the press, which he most certainly was. In 1944, for example, he was approached by the London *Evening Standard*'s City editor, whom its proprietor Lord Beaverbrook had sent in search of a story. Warburg told the journalist:

that I was in principle against any publicity for bankers and particularly Jewish bankers, and he said he was very sorry about that. In order to console him I told him that if we should do any specific transactions in the future I should be very glad to give him information in advance. But it would always then be publicity about firms we finance, but never about ourselves. He repeated how sorry he was about my reaction because Lord Beaverbrook had expressed himself extremely interested in the New Trading [as Warburg's firm was originally known] having heard about us that we were one of the really active and at the same time sound firms in the City (who should be 'a bit advertised').[5]

When it suited his business purposes, in other words, Warburg was prepared – 'happy' would be the wrong word – to give interviews to journalists.[6] City editors and correspondents lunched regularly at the offices of S. G. Warburg & Co.; indeed, at the height of the so-called Aluminium War, Warburg personally briefed the *Financial Times* almost daily, and subsequently recruited the long-serving author of the Lex column. The reason he is not more celebrated today is not that he eschewed publicity, but simply that he was a banker.

To be sure, there are some biographies of bankers and, more commonly, banking dynasties. There is, indeed, already one life of Siegmund Warburg,[7] and several books about his family.[8] On the whole, however, biographers prefer monarchs to money-changers, film stars to financiers. This preference may be intelligible in the sense that the activities of a banker are less exciting to write or read about than the antics of a demagogue or a diva. Whether he is making a loan or taking a deposit, buying a stock or selling a bond, declaring a dividend or counselling a client, the banker is not a man of action in the conventional sense. There may be battles, but they take place in boardrooms and lack the pandemonium and the pathos of real warfare.

Yet the neglect of bankers by biographers cannot be justified on the basis of their relative historical unimportance. In any serious assessment of the way the world works – and especially the modern world since the Italian Renaissance – finance has surely been as important as government or war in the evolution of Western civilization (and a great deal more important than the movie business).[9] How could Western economies have scaled the heights of industrial and post-industrial prosperity without banks and bourses to channel savings from the thrifty to the entrepreneurial? What great war of the past century could have been waged, and what welfare bill enacted, without the bond market to pay for it? Any reader who doubts the historical importance of finance should reflect on recent events. Which group contributed most to the great financial crisis that struck the world in 2007 and plunged it into the nearest thing to a Great Depression we have experienced since the early 1930s? In their folly, the bankers – some of them, at least – have unwittingly laid bare their importance. If we now blame all our economic troubles on the men who so grotesquely mismanaged Royal Bank of Scotland or Citigroup, can we simultaneously deny that financial deregulation and innovation contributed at least something to the great upswing in global economic activity that characterized the previous quarter-century?

Bankers may not be famous. But they are important. And nothing illustrates this distinction better than the career of Siegmund Warburg.

III

Though at least four other members of his family wrote memoirs,[10] Siegmund Warburg himself elected not to write his own autobiography. He was also deeply hostile to all attempts by outsiders to write the history of the Warburg family. He disliked even the staid and semi-official history of the Hamburg bank written by two former employees, Eduard Rosenbaum and Joshua Sherman.[11] He vainly tried to 'kill' David Farrer's attempt (as Warburg put it) to 'apply his mental magnifying glasses to the Warburg bug', arguing that a book about the Warburgs was 'something nonsensical inasmuch as the collective conception of "The Warburgs" . . . was a distortion of both the historical and genealogical facts'.[12] He would have been no more enthusiastic about Ron Chernow's better-researched attempt at a family history, though he might have enjoyed his insightful essay on the 'death' of the 'relationship banker'.[13] As for Jacques Attali's portrayal of him as the ultimate *homme d'affaires*, Warburg might possibly have been flattered by the author's verdict that he 'blended political power, financial innovation, creativity and morality', but he would have been dismayed by the book's (and associated television film's) numerous inaccuracies and even more by the implication that he wielded power in a somewhat mysterious way.[14] On balance, I suspect he would also have derived more pain than pleasure from the various volumes of autobiography by former Warburg directors who were at various times his subordinates.[15]

The difference between this volume and all previous work is twofold. First, this is the first study of any sort to be based on Warburg's extensive collection of private papers, as well as other archival materials, together comprising nearly 10,000 letters, memoranda and diary entries. Secondly, this is the first serious attempt to set Warburg's multiple lives in the proper historical context of his time. This is the story of a man whose life began in the golden glow of imperial Germany, who came of age in the febrile atmosphere of 1920s Berlin, who became an exile in the age of dictatorship, war and genocide, and who rose to a position of real historical significance during the Cold War. At a time when historians are striving to recast the history of the twentieth century in a more global framework, Warburg provides a valuable and in some ways a corrective focal point. He was the quintessential *homo atlanticus*, criss-crossing the ocean from London to New York, progressing from Cunard liners to Concorde. A member of the Pilgrims Society, founded in 1902 'to promote good-will, good-fellowship, and everlasting peace between the United States and Great Britain', he was also an occasional attendee at the Bilderberg Meetings, the annual conference of politicians and captains of industry launched in the Netherlands in 1954 to promote transatlantic understanding. Yet he was also a lifelong European, as much at home in Germany or Switzerland as in England and allergic to much of the 'modern barbarism' of American life. He was intrigued by Japan and had a love–hate relationship with Israel. The rest of the world scarcely interested him – except insofar as he was repelled by the Soviet Union. Warburg's world was emphatically the Western world – indeed, a north-western corridor running from Manhattan to the River Main.

With his extraordinarily clear and articulate vision of international financial reintegration, Siegmund Warburg more than any other contemporaneous figure deserves the title of 'prophet of globalization'. Yet with his deeply ingrained pessimism, scarred as he was by the experiences of the 1930s, he was an ambivalent prophet, whose hopes for the world economy were always qualified by Cassandra-like forebodings. Much that happened in the last decade of his life, between 1973 and 1982, vindicated Warburg's pessimism.

As I write, the world finds itself emerging, tentatively, from an even bigger financial crisis, one which can in large measure be blamed on the conscious abandonment by a new generation of bankers of Siegmund Warburg's *haute banque* ideal – financial service based on the primacy of the client relationship rather than the speculative transaction. In the eyes of the public, the City of London's reputation has sunk low indeed. If ever there was a time to learn from a true high financier, this is surely it.

Warburg family tree

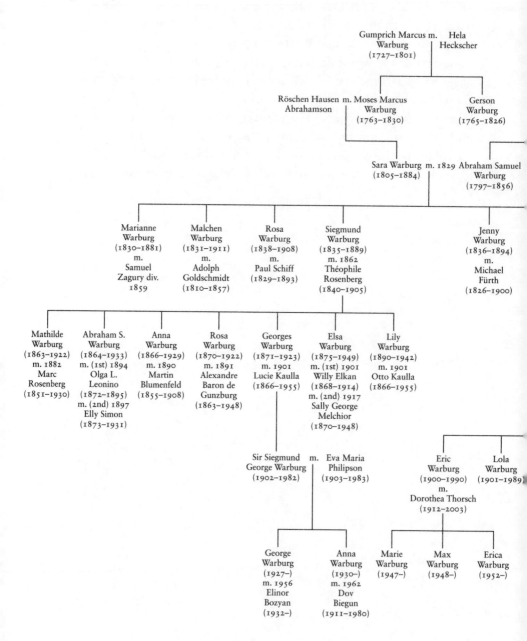

Gumprich Marcus m. Hela
Warburg   Heckscher
(1727–1801)

Röschen Hausen m. Moses Marcus   Gerson
Abrahamson   Warburg   Warburg
(1763–1830)   (1765–1826)

Sara Warburg m. 1829 Abraham Samuel
(1805–1884)   Warburg
(1797–1856)

Marianne   Malchen   Rosa   Siegmund   Jenny
Warburg   Warburg   Warburg   Warburg   Warburg
(1830–1881)   (1831–1911)   (1838–1908)   (1835–1889)   (1836–1894)
m.   m.   m.   m. 1862   m.
Samuel   Adolph   Paul Schiff   Théophile   Michael
Zagury div.   Goldschmidt   (1829–1893)   Rosenberg   Fürth
1859   (1810–1857)   (1840–1905)   (1826–1900)

Mathilde   Abraham S. Anna   Rosa   Georges   Elsa   Lily
Warburg   Warburg   Warburg   Warburg   Warburg   Warburg   Warburg
(1863–1922) (1864–1933) (1866–1929) (1870–1922) (1871–1923) (1875–1949) (1890–1942)
m. 1882   m. (1st) 1894 m. 1890   m. 1891   m. 1901   m. (1st) 1901 m. 1901
Marc   Olga L.   Martin   Alexandre   Lucie Kaulla Willy Elkan Otto Kaulla
Rosenberg   Leonino   Blumenfeld Baron de   (1866–1955) (1868–1914) (1866–1955)
(1851–1930) (1872–1895) (1855–1908) Gunzburg   m. (2nd) 1917
            m. (2nd) 1897   (1863–1948)   Sally George
            Elly Simon   Melchior
            (1873–1931)   (1870–1948)

Sir Siegmund m. Eva Maria   Eric   Lola
George Warburg   Philipson   Warburg   Warburg
(1902–1982)   (1903–1983)   (1900–1990) (1901–1989)
                                                m.
                                                Dorothea Thorsch
                                                (1912–2003)

George   Anna   Marie   Max   Erica
Warburg   Warburg   Warburg   Warburg   Warburg
(1927–)   (1930–)   (1947–)   (1948–)   (1952–)
m. 1956   m. 1962
Elinor   Dov
Bozyan   Biegun
(1932–)   (1911–1980)

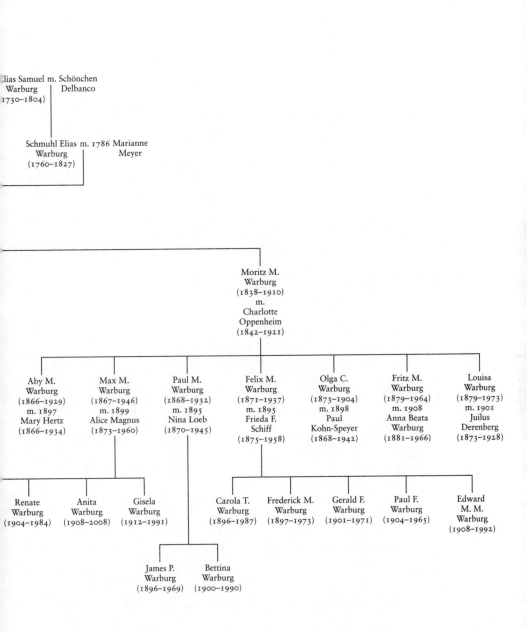

Elias Samuel m. Schönchen
Warburg   Delbanco
(1730–1804)

Schmuhl Elias m. 1786 Marianne
Warburg   Meyer
(1760–1827)

Moritz M.
Warburg
(1838–1910)
m.
Charlotte
Oppenheim
(1842–1921)

Aby M.
Warburg
(1866–1929)
m. 1897
Mary Hertz
(1866–1934)

Max M.
Warburg
(1867–1946)
m. 1899
Alice Magnus
(1873–1960)

Paul M.
Warburg
(1868–1932)
m. 1895
Nina Loeb
(1870–1945)

Felix M.
Warburg
(1871–1937)
m. 1895
Frieda F.
Schiff
(1875–1958)

Olga C.
Warburg
(1873–1904)
m. 1898
Paul
Kohn-Speyer
(1868–1942)

Fritz M.
Warburg
(1879–1964)
m. 1908
Anna Beata
Warburg
(1881–1966)

Louisa
Warburg
(1879–1973)
m. 1901
Juilus
Derenberg
(1873–1928)

Renate
Warburg
(1904–1984)

Anita
Warburg
(1908–2008)

Gisela
Warburg
(1912–1991)

Carola T.
Warburg
(1896–1987)

Frederick M.
Warburg
(1897–1973)

Gerald F.
Warburg
(1901–1971)

Paul F.
Warburg
(1904–1965)

Edward
M. M.
Warburg
(1908–1992)

James P.
Warburg
(1896–1969)

Bettina
Warburg
(1900–1990)

Note: This is not a complete family tree. I have given preference to individuals who feature in this book.

I

Siegmund and his Cousins

In Joseph's home the past . . . had become tinctured with the future and with prophecy.

Thomas Mann, *Joseph and his Brothers*

I

In 1933 the first volume of Thomas Mann's *Joseph and his Brothers* was published – a tale, according to the author, of 'love and hate, blessing and curse, fraternal strife and paternal grief, pride and penance, fall and rise'.[1] An early admirer of the work was a young German banker named Siegmund Warburg, who read it while sailing from Hamburg to London – a journey into exile not dissimilar from the one Mann himself made later in the same year. Warburg, it has been suggested, was struck by the parallel between his own family and Joseph's, with whom he himself closely identified.[2] Of course, the parallel was not exact. Unlike Joseph, Siegmund Warburg had no brothers; nor was he being driven into exile by members of his own family – rather, by a regime bent on the expulsion and ultimately the destruction of all the descendants of Jacob. Nevertheless, even a cursory glance at the genealogy of the Warburg family indicates why the parallel might have occurred to him.

Like the Abraham of the book of Genesis, Siegmund's great-grandfather Abraham Warburg* had married Sara – also a Warburg

---

* Like many German-Jewish families, the Warburgs derived their name from a town. In the sixteenth century their ancestor Simon had established himself in the town of Warburg as a *Schutzjude* (protected Jew) under the patronage of the Prince-Bishop of Paderborn.

– and had two sons. Like Jacob and Esau, the sons did not have an easy relationship. Arguments between the pious Siegmund and the worldly Moritz were 'a daily occurrence', a great-grandson was told. 'Regularly, once or twice a week, there were quarrels which echoed down the whole Ferdinandstrasse,' the street in Hamburg where the family bank was located.[3] As in the Bible, there was a parting of ways in the next generation. In 1864 Moritz Warburg married Charlotte Oppenheim, who gave him, in addition to two daughters, five sons: Abraham (usually known as Aby M.), Max, Paul, Felix and Fritz.[4] These five brothers – in particular the confident and charismatic Max – would come to dominate both the family and the family firm. The other side of the family was overshadowed. Following the elder Siegmund's death in 1889, his widow left Hamburg for the French Riviera with her two youngest children Elsa and Lilly. Although their elder brother Abraham (Aby S.) did become a partner in the family firm, the other, Georges, was considered so mentally feeble* that he was encouraged to leave Hamburg altogether. This explains why Georges' son Siegmund was not born, like so many other Warburgs, in Hamburg's thriving commercial metropolis, but in the somnolent South German countryside. He was thus, from the very outset, an outsider whose upbringing differed fundamentally from that of his clannish Hamburg relatives. And that was precisely why the story of Joseph and his brothers had such significance for him. Though there was nothing like the violent antagonism that existed between the biblical Joseph and his brothers, Siegmund was always conscious of a certain unbridgeable divide between himself and his Hamburg cousins.

Of course, internecine strife is a perennial and universal theme. The hatred of the biblical Gad and Asher for their half-brother, the precocious favourite Joseph; the intense affection between Joseph and his young brother Benjamin; the ambivalent feelings of Reuben, the first-born; the violent confrontation and final reconciliation between the brothers – some at least of these relationships would have their parallels in the experience of most large families. However, for a variety of reasons, such themes had a particular resonance in late nineteenth-century Europe, and especially within the educated and propertied middle class. To begin with, this was a period of marked demographic

---

* He suffered from headaches and an enthusiasm for history.

change, in which the size of the average family fell sharply. As late as 1910, more than 40 per cent of German households had five or more members (including parents); one in ten still had upwards of eight. By 1930, however, fewer than a fifth of families had four or more children; while the percentage settling for two or less had risen from 29 per cent to 65 per cent.[5] In just three decades, growing up with several siblings went from being the experience of the majority to being that of a minority. At the same time, the late nineteenth-century generation had the advantage of improving nutrition and public health. Male life expectancy rose from thirty-five years to fifty-five on average; in Hamburg in the two decades after 1893, the mortality rate fell from 25–35 per thousand on average to 15–20 per thousand.[6] The wealthy were especially likely to enjoy longer life. Infant mortality, typhus, tuberculosis: all were lower in the wealthy Harvestehude or Rotherbaum areas on the west side of the Alster Lake, where wealthy families like the Warburgs tended to live. During the 1892 cholera epidemic the mortality rate in the higher income brackets (above 10,000 marks) was one sixth of that suffered by those on less than 1,000 marks.[7] Aby M. survived typhoid fever at the age of six, while his mother Charlotte overcame an equally severe illness the following year. Max Warburg – who remained in Hamburg throughout the cholera epidemic – had good reason to feel, as he put it, 'certain . . . that I was immune'.[8] Only one of his siblings died prematurely: Olga, in childbirth. The brothers lived to be sixty-three (Aby M.), seventy-nine (Max), sixty-four (Paul), sixty-six (Felix) and eighty-three (Fritz). In short, their generation was unusual in being both numerous and long lived. As an only child, born in 1902, Siegmund belonged to another era in more ways than one.

A large and wealthy family like the Warburgs could – and in the work of Aby M.* self-consciously did – liken themselves to the Medici. They

---

* With the financial support of his brothers, Aby M. dedicated his life to the study of art history and is remembered today as the founder of the London-based Warburg Institute, which houses his huge collection of books on art. An expert on the Florentine Renaissance, he was deeply influenced by a visit to the United States, where he encountered the art of American Indians in Arizona, Colorado and New Mexico. Anticipating ideas later made famous by Walter Benjamin, Warburg argued that the mechanical reproduction of artworks led to a kind of cultural inflation. Among his many essays, perhaps the best known is the study of Domenico Ghirlandaio's fresco in Santa Maria Novella in Florence.

thought in dynastic terms, tracing their genealogy back to the sixteenth century, and their business back to the 1640s, when their ancestor, the money-changer Jacob Samuel, had moved from the town of Warburg to Hamburg.[9] Over the years, the Warburgs had developed a system of familial organization, the central principle of which was that, whatever the procreative fortunes of the family, and whatever the individual inclinations of its members, a certain number of male members should always pool their inherited wealth and treat it as the capital of the family firm. This put a premium on harmonious fraternal relations, since it was as a partnership between brothers that the firm was run – a tradition dating back to the three sons of Jacob Samuel (d. 1668) and continuing through the four sons of Samuel Moses (d. 1759), the two sons of Gumprich Marcus, the two sons of his brother Elias Samuel and the two sons of Abraham.[10] As Gumprich Marcus solemnly urged his two sons Moses Marcus and Gerson in his will, it was vital that they should 'maintain brotherly peace, solidarity and cooperation'.[11] When the two drew up a formal partnership contract, they stressed the significance of this brotherly tie: 'We brothers wish to take one another at his word, and demand no form of oath one from the other.'[12] A generation later, relations between the brothers Siegmund and Moritz were likewise regulated by an elaborate contract devised by their formidable mother Sara.[13] There was thus nothing new in Charlotte Warburg's efforts to instil a sense of fraternal harmony in her five sons. When Max, Paul and Felix were aged between five and nine, they were expected to assist one another with reading and writing. On the inside of Max's desk Charlotte engraved the opening lines of Psalm 133: 'Behold, how good and pleasant it is for brethren to dwell together in unity!'[14] The risk of fraternal conflict was somewhat mitigated by migration. Of the sons of Samuel Moses Warburg, one moved to neighbouring Altona and another to London, leaving the younger brothers to take over their father's business; one of Elias Samuel Warburg's two sons later settled in Sweden.[15] This pattern was repeated in the early 1900s, when Paul and Felix Warburg both emigrated to the United States. Such dispersion had the added advantage of establishing the family in other strategically important commercial centres.

One consequence of the importance of fraternal ties was that there was little room for the traditional figure of the bourgeois patriarch.

Power was shared within each generation, and the older generation could do little more than seek to ensure the smooth transition to the next.* The only period when a single figure dominated the bank was during the 1830s and 1840s, and then it was a matriarch, Sara.[16] That brief interlude points to the importance of the second vital mechanism for maintaining the continuity of family and firm: intermarriage within the business community. When the brothers Gerson and Moses Marcus both failed to produce even a single son, the preferred solution was for Sara, the latter's daughter, to marry Abraham, their cousin Samuel Elias's son – a form of endogamy that was common in nineteenth-century business families.[17] More adventurous matches proved possible in the next generation: Sara's daughter Rosa was married to Paul Schiff, who went on to become a director of the Vienna Creditanstalt, Rosa's brother Siegmund's bride Théophile Rosenberg was a relative of the Russian Gunzburgs, while their sister-in-law Charlotte Oppenheim was the product of a union between the Frankfurt Oppenheims and Goldschmidts.[18] The sickly Georges Warburg's marriage to a member of the Kaulla family continued this tradition; more or less simultaneously his sister Lilly married Otto Kaulla. The Kaullas were in fact a rather more distinguished family than the Warburgs, having risen to eminence in South Germany some time before the Warburgs had ascended in Hamburg.[19] Such marriages brought benefits in terms of dowries and business connections when sons were marrying, though they could also bring substantial costs when it was daughters that were being disposed of.

How far did the five sons of Moritz and Charlotte Warburg live up to the family ideal of fraternal harmony? The brothers were temperamentally very different, as indicated even by the contrasting and characteristic mottoes they adopted,† but there is no question that there were close affective ties between them, particularly between Max and

---

* The familiar picture of the vengeful patriarch's threat of disinheritance has to be set alongside the son's threat not to follow in his father's footsteps. Contemporary literature (for example, Mann's *Buddenbrooks*) shows how much leverage this gave sons. Fathers had to be careful not to alienate their heirs.

† Compare the scholarly 'Der liebe Gott steckt im Detail' (Aby M.) with the bold 'En avant' (Max), the selfless 'In serviendo consumere' (Paul), the cheerfully Americanized 'Let me do what I have to do today; I might not come this way again' (Felix) and the fatalistic 'Man muss aus allen Blüten Honig saugen' (Fritz).

Paul.[20] There also appears to have been unlimited tolerance of the unstable and sometimes demanding Aby M., as well as a sympathetic relationship between the elder brothers and the less handsome, less self-confident youngest, Fritz. As in the past, however, harmony continued to depend on a satisfactory division of responsibility, and here the first signs of a centrifugal tendency manifested themselves. At the age of thirteen, Aby M. resolved not to avail himself of his opportunity to enter the family firm, choosing instead to pursue his passion for art history.* His brother Felix showed practically no interest in business, devoting himself throughout his life to a combination of leisure and philanthropy.[21] Max wanted to become a cavalry officer, so greatly did he enjoy his military service in Bavaria. The academically inclined Paul considered studying science. It was only with difficulty that he and Max were persuaded by their parents to take the traditional route of apprenticeship and ultimately partnership within the family firm. Fritz alone compliantly followed his parents' advice to put aside his love of German literature and study law; he became a partner in the family firm when his brother Paul emigrated to the United States.[22]

The story was somewhat similar with respect to the five brothers' (and two sisters') marriages. Conventionally enough, Max married the daughter of a distantly related Swedish family, Alice Magnus, while his sister Olga married Paul Kohn-Speyer of the London metals firm of Brandeis Goldschmidt.[23] Fritz married a Swedish cousin, Anna Beata Warburg.[24] However, the other brothers all incurred family disapproval in one way or another. Although it proved a mutually beneficial match, Felix apparently defied both families in wooing the daughter of the German-American banker Jacob Schiff, the chief of the investment bank and railroad finance specialists Kuhn, Loeb & Co.[25] Paul compounded this offence by falling for Frieda Schiff's aunt, Nina Loeb, whom he met at his brother's wedding.[26] The most radical break with tradition was made by their eldest brother, Aby M., when he married Mary Hertz, the artist daughter of a Protestant Hamburg shipowner – a match that appears to have fuelled his youthful revolt, not so much against his

---

* As his brother Max recalled, however, he gave up his birthright not for the biblical mess of pottage but for a guarantee that his brother would buy all the books he would require during his life. The Frankfurt grandparents vainly urged Aby to become a rabbi, the traditional path for an academically inclined son.

Jewish background, as against the Hamburg bourgeoisie as a whole.[27] However, if their parents regarded at least some of these as *mésalliances*, they did not do irreparable damage to the fabric of familial relations. On the contrary, despite the brothers' divergent choices of career and consort, the members of the family remained warmly attached to one another. Each summer the seven siblings, their spouses and children would converge on Moritz and Charlotte's idyllic villa, Kösterberg, nine miles west of the city centre at Blankenese on the northern bank of the River Elbe. There they would engage in elaborate amateur dramatics while great cargo ships sailed by.[28]

In all of this, of course, the Warburgs were very far from being exceptional. The list of Jewish families in which groups of brothers played a decisive role, whether in the early days of building up a business, or later, when paths began to diverge, is a long one: Mayer Amschel Rothschild's five sons; the four sons of Moritz Deutsch; the five sons of Salomon Benedikt Goldschmidt (not to mention the six sons of Benedikt Salomon Goldschmidt and the five of Benedikt Hayum Goldschmidt); the three sons of Meyer Kaufmann; as well as the five Tietz brothers.[29] Similar patterns of endogamy and dynastic intermarriage can also be seen in other Jewish genealogies: not only the Goldschmidts, with their links in the space of six generations to at least twelve other more or less eminent Jewish families, but also the more endogamous Hirsch family and the Oppenheim–Mendelssohn–Warschauer–Simson network.[30] Indeed, it seems certain that in the way they conceived of themselves – particularly the emphasis they laid on fraternal harmony – the Warburgs were quite self-consciously modelling themselves on by far the most successful Jewish family of the nineteenth century, the Rothschilds. It was not lost on the five sons of Moritz Warburg that the five sons of Mayer Amschel Rothschild had made their family's legendary fortune two generations before.[31] Nevertheless, it should be borne in mind that such patterns of fraternity and marriage were not peculiarly Jewish. They could also be found among non-Jewish families, particularly in the Hanseatic ports. A case in point is that of the Amsinck family, members of which arrived in Hamburg from the Netherlands in the sixteenth century. In successive generations, one son would generally be trained as a lawyer, paving the way for a career in the city's government, while the others would go into business, or occasionally one of the other professions. The Amsincks married almost exclusively members of other comparably grand merchant families.[32] A similar story emerges in the case of the Schramms and the O'Swalds.[33] As Percy Schramm recalled of the social life of Hamburg society around 1900: 'How one was interrelated, what the name of the father's firm was, how well born the mother was – naturally, these were the things one had to know.'[34]

The large family, in short, was one of the essential building blocks of late nineteenth-century bourgeois society. And, as the case of the Warburgs illustrates, the period offered unique opportunities to Jewish and Gentile families alike. Five brothers, all turning out to live long lives, could pursue careers in an unprecedented range of occupations and countries. They could make marriage decisions more freely than any previous generation. Yet through their connections as brothers they could keep these different spheres in harmony – a harmony which was represented pictorially in the numerous photographs taken when the family gathered together each summer at the Kösterberg, veritable tableaux of bourgeois achievement.

There was nevertheless a transient quality to all of this. At the start of the new century, at least some contemporaries were aware that the peculiar circumstances that had nurtured clans like the Warburgs could not last – an awareness perfectly captured in Thomas Mann's first novel, *Buddenbrooks: Decline of a Family*, published in 1901. Partly based on his own Lübeck relatives, the Buddenbrooks are the archetypal Hanseatic merchant family. Grown prosperous in the eighteenth century, they reach the peak of their achievement with the election to the Lübeck Senate of Thomas Buddenbrook, the eldest of the third generation depicted in the novel. But the seeds of decline have already taken root. The family produces too few sons and, when there is more than one, the brothers quarrel. The significance of such fraternal conflict is clearly spelt out early on: 'This bitter feud with my brother [is] . . . like a crack in the house . . . A family should be united . . . It must keep together. A house divided against itself will fall.'[35] (The sale of the family house is preceded by the most violent fraternal quarrel in the book.) At the same time, the family is miserably unsuccessful in marriage; Thomas's sister Tony marries first a bankrupt and then a Bavarian boor, while her daughter weds a crook and even Thomas himself makes an unsuitably exotic match (with a Dutch violinist). Mann nevertheless identifies more profound roots of malaise than these missteps. The Buddenbrooks' family firm declines along with the decline of the family's entrepreneurial spirit. There is also a hint of the social threat to the merchant elite, symbolized by Consul Johann's confrontation with the revolutionary mob in 1848. Above all, there is a philosophical decline, from the robust rationalist outlook of Johann the elder, through the exaggerated piety of his son, the self-indulgent romanticism of Thomas and, finally, the abject decadence of Hanno, the last of the line. These deeper themes explain why *Buddenbrooks* had sold 60,000 copies by 1911, finding its way into the library of Max Schramm[36] as well as Siegmund Warburg. For this was not merely the decline of *a* family, but an intimation of the decline of *the* family – a charge sufficiently close to the bone to prompt overt denials, like Percy Schramm's description of his mother's family as 'Buddenbrooks in reverse'.[37] The Warburgs too can hardly have been oblivious to Mann's point; Max Warburg's first taste of business responsibility involved bailing out his cousin Rosa's near-bankrupt in-laws; meanwhile, his eldest brother read Schopenhauer, succumbed to the arts and only narrowly survived typhus.[38] In short, even before the great storms of the twentieth century broke, the great merchant families had an inkling of their vulnerability. A devoted reader of Mann all his life, Siegmund Warburg was himself not untainted by symptoms of decadence: above all, his extreme bookishness. His reverence for the Warburg name was always strangely ambivalent; the name was sacrosanct, but the wider tribe that bore it was, as we shall see, another matter.

II

The Warburgs had regarded themselves as bankers since 1798, when the family firm had been formally established as M. M. Warburg & Co.[39] However, until the late nineteenth century, the bank was of little more than local significance. In the great pan-European financial network established by the five Rothschild brothers after the Napoleonic Wars, the Warburgs played only a minimal role, despite periodic efforts by the family to manoeuvre itself into the place occupied by

Salomon Heine as the principal Rothschild agent in Hamburg.[40] Although they finally achieved this in 1865, it was not until Max Warburg emerged as the dominant partner just before the turn of the century that the family can be said to have entered the same league as the Rothschilds. Max Warburg himself had served part of his financial apprenticeship at the Rothschild banks in Paris and London – a sign in itself that the Warburgs had risen in the Rothschilds' estimation. By the late 1890s M. M. Warburg & Co. was for the first time acting as the principal Hamburg issuing house for international government loans floated by the Rothschilds, such as the Chilean bond issue of 1896. Although Max Warburg later insisted on 'how large a role chance plays in the development of such a business' as a bank, in the early 1900s he made his own luck. He aggressively diversified beyond the bank's traditional business of arbitrage and commercial bill-broking into international bond issuance and German industrial investment. He also took a leading role in the rapid expansion of Hanseatic shipping as, under the leadership of his close friend Albert Ballin, the Hamburg-America Line (Hapag) rose to become the biggest passenger shipping line in the world.[41]

To the elderly and by now somewhat complacent Rothschilds in London and Paris, Max Warburg seemed an insufferable self-promoter. 'Warburg at Hamburg', grumbled the London Rothschilds in 1906, 'resembles the frog in the fable & is swollen up with vanity & the belief in his own power to control the European markets, & interest all big houses in any & every syndicate.'[42] But Max's thrusting style proved highly effective. Between 1895 and 1913 the firm's balance sheet grew nearly fourfold, from 30 million marks to 118 million marks.[43] In these terms, it is true, the three major joint-stock banks in Hamburg (the Norddeutsche Bank, the Commerz- und Diskonto Bank and the Vereinsbank) were substantially bigger, and played a more important role in the rapid industrial development of Hamburg and its environs after 1880.[44] But M. M. Warburg & Co. was a family-owned merchant bank, focused more on the international bond market than on attracting deposits or advancing credit to German industry.[45] Crucially, Max and his brothers were able to establish what had always eluded the Rothschilds – an effective transatlantic financial alliance. With Felix and Paul linked by marriage to the Schiff family, the Warburgs became partners in one of the most successful Wall Street firms of the pre-1914 era: Kuhn, Loeb & Co., founded in 1867 by Abraham Kuhn and Solomon Loeb, and after 1885 firmly under the control of Loeb's son-in-law Jacob Schiff.[46] This not only gave them access to the rapidly growing US economy – in particular, to the huge market for American railroad bonds. It also ensured that when the Japanese government entered the international financial markets at the time of the Russo-Japanese War, the Warburgs were able to steal a march on the Rothschilds, who were slower to see Japan's potential than the strongly Russophobic Schiff, whose attitude was shaped by the Tsarist regime's discrimination against Jews and tolerance of anti-Semitic pogroms.

In one sense, Max Warburg was indeed lucky. The period from the mid-1890s until 1914 was one of rapid growth throughout the world economy. A bold young man with his innate optimism was bound to do better in these boom years than the elderly and conservative Rothschilds. Moreover, Hamburg was the biggest port of the fastest-growing European economy. This was what has justly been called the 'first age of globalization', in which markets for commodities, manufactures, labour and capital were being integrated as never before. The volumes of goods flowing in and out of great ports like Hamburg were growing every year. It was not only M. M. Warburg & Co. that thrived in this period. Nearly all Hamburg's merchant houses and banks prospered in what contemporaries later looked back on as a golden age. Nevertheless, a number of developments already posed a threat to the prosperity of the traditional family firm as an institution. The first was the emergence of what the socialist theorist Rudolf Hilferding called 'organized capitalism'. True, the great joint-stock banks, integrated industrial concerns and producers' cartels exercised less monopolistic control over markets than Hilferding implied. Nevertheless, it was already evident that, in most fields of business activity, they were capable of much larger-scale operations than the traditional family partnership. By issuing shares, they could raise much more capital; by limiting liability, they could protect their proprietors from complete ruin; by separating ownership and management they could avoid the economic consequences of 'Buddenbrooks syndrome'. The most that could be said in defence of the old merchant houses was that they remained better suited to the variegated demands of international import and export business than the new corporations. M. M. Warburg could claim to offer clients more exclusive access to the international *haute banque* network than relative newcomers like the Deutsche Bank and the Disconto-Gesellschaft or their Hanseatic counterparts, the Commerzbank and the Vereinsbank.

The second important development of the early 1900s was the growth of the public sector. The mid-nineteenth century had seen the high tide of laissez-faire economics, with its promise of free markets and a minimal, nightwatchman state. By the turn of the century, that tide had turned. Again this should not be exaggerated; the German Reich before 1914 was a very long way from being an interventionist state. Even the limited tariffs introduced in the late 1870s and increased in the 1890s were fiercely opposed by the Hamburg business community, which remained as devoted to free trade as the most ardent British liberal of the time. Still, the expansion of public expenditure and public borrowing, particularly at the level of the state and municipal government, was rapid. In this process Hamburg played a leading role, spending heavily on infrastructural improvements in order to avoid a repeat of the public health crisis of the early 1890s. The simultaneous growth in the importance of employers' and employees' associations – particularly of trade unions – was also marked in Hamburg, where the working conditions on the waterfront were almost as conducive to unionization and collective action as those to be found in the heavy industrial heartland of the Ruhr. With the advent of these new bureaucracies in both the public and the private sector, the power of the family firms that had traditionally dominated the Hamburg economy was bound to diminish.[47]

It was, needless to say, decisive for their family's history that the Warburgs were and remained Jews. To the casual observer, this was a fact that mattered much less in 1904 than it had in 1804, or even 1874.[48] The common interests of *Besitz* and *Bildung* (property and education) appeared gradually to have dissolved earlier barriers of belief and observance. In 1871 around three-quarters of Hamburg's Jewish population had still lived in the crowded and insalubrious inner-city areas of the Altstadt, Neustadt, St Pauli and St Georg; by 1914 the majority lived in the West End, predominantly in the Rotherbaum area and the

elegant Harvestehude on the banks of the Alster.[49] The dominant
Warburg branch lived at Mittelweg 17; the other resided on the Alsterufer. In 1897 over a quarter of Hamburg Jews paid tax in the top two
tax brackets, compared with 11 per cent of the population as a whole.[50]
This was at a time when the Jewish community was in relative demographic decline. In 1811 just under 5 per cent of the population had
been Jewish; by 1910 that figure had fallen to 1.2 per cent, reflecting
the relatively low Jewish birth rate and the paucity of new Jewish
settlement in Hamburg.[51] Although many East European Jews passed
through Hamburg on their way to England and America, few stayed.
The established Jewish community meanwhile grew more and more
assimilated. The grandparents and parents of the five Warburg brothers had been strict in their observance of the Sabbath;[52] the next
generation, with the exception of Max's youngest brother Fritz, was
significantly less pious. Max's own attendance at the synagogue was
formal rather than faithful, while his eldest brother Aby M. ceased to
keep kosher at university.[53]

At the same time, bastions of bourgeois associational life such as
the elite Harmonie Club, the masonic lodges and the Hamburg Rowing
Club began to admit Jewish members.[54] Significantly, such associations
were explicitly designed to transcend social and confessional differences
by asserting an ideal of fraternity between members. 'Burdensome titles'
were replaced by the appellations 'brother' and 'friend' and the informal pronoun *Du* – a practice adopted by cardplayers (*Skatbrüder*),
skittleplayers (*Kegelbrüder*), singers (*Sangesbrüder*), marksmen
(*Schützenbrüder*) and oarsmen (*Alsterbrüder*).[55] The motto of the Lied-
ertafel Fraternity of 1859 – 'Joy, Accord, Brotherliness' (*Freude,
Eintracht, Brüderlichkeit*) – can be regarded as typical of the mid-
century conception of brotherhood by voluntary association.[56] In this
climate, it was relatively easy for Jews to rise to prominent positions
in commercial and professional associations like the Hanseatic Lawyers
Chamber or the Chamber of Commerce, and to play prominent roles
in the city's politics and administration.[57] A further indication of the
rapidity and extent of integration was the rising proportion of mixed
marriages in the city. By the mid-1920s, half of all Hamburg marriages
involving at least one Jewish partner were mixed, while only 66 per
cent of Jewish marriages were ritually formalized; a marriage like Aby

M. Warburg's was becoming normal.[58] Socially, there was now scarcely anything to distinguish the Warburgs from the Gentiles of the Hamburg Establishment. Bürgermeister Johann Georg Mönckeberg was happy to allow his daughter Mathilde to stay with Aby M. and Mary Warburg in Florence in 1900; Max Schramm was proud to count himself among their friends.[59]

Yet it would be wrong – even if one knew nothing of what lay ahead – to regard this process of assimilation as complete or irreversible before 1914. Religious toleration, particularly for Jews, had developed only slowly in Hamburg, and was far from complete even after the successive legal reforms enacted between 1842 and 1884. There remained subtle divisions even on the west side of the Alster, where the area of Rotherbaum between Bundesstrasse and Rotherbaumschaussee was known as 'Klein-Jerusalem' because of the high concentration of Jewish residents.[60] Nor was Adolphine Schramm alone in taking the view that there were four types of unsuitable husband for well-bred Hamburg girls: officers, nobles, actors – and Jews.[61] Max Warburg himself continued to believe that there was anti-Semitism in Hamburg society; in his experience it was simply 'latent'.[62] Whereas the Hamburg working class expressed its dissatisfaction with the manifest inequalities of the industrial age by flocking to join and vote for the German Social Democratic Party, many members of the Hamburg *Mittelstand* turned to political anti-Semitism to express their distinctive discontents – an age-old phenomenon which became politically organized in the 1890s with the formation of the Anti-Semitic People's Party, the German Social Reform Party and the German National Commercial Clerks' Association.[63] Fraternity in the old, universal sense had no place in associations of this sort, which defined brotherhood in a strictly racial sense.

Partly in response to such radical pressures from below, the Hamburg elites, Jewish and Gentile alike, were naturally drawn towards more conservative forces at the level of national politics – a phenomenon summed up in the term 'Prussianization' – so that its traditional cosmopolitanism yielded in some measure to the chauvinism of the new German nation-state.[64] Before around 1870, pro-Prussian or *kleindeutsch* nationalism had been the enthusiasm of only a minority of liberals like Johannes Versmann or Eduard Schramm.[65] The majority of Hamburg families remained staunchly attached to Hamburg's status as an independent city-state and suspicious of Prussian expansion. But after Otto von Bismarck's string of diplomatic and military victories and his epoch-making proclamation of the German Reich at Versailles, the old patriotism of the urban republic was subsumed in a new nationalism. At the city's exclusive secondary school, the Johanneum, there were military parades to mark Sedan Day and the Kaiser's birthday. Hamburg businessmen not only submitted to military training (which the previous generation of Warburgs had paid to evade)[66] but were positively proud to serve as reserve officers. Some were even ennobled, notably the Schinckels, Schröders and Berenberg-Gosslers.[67]

Yet 'Prussianization' does not quite do justice to a process that had more to do with the emergence of a new German empire than with the preservation of the old Prussian monarchy. Moreover, embracing the new regime in Berlin made at least some business sense. Close links with Bismarck were important when it came to establishing military protection for the Hamburg business community's growing trade with Africa, while influence at the court of Kaiser Wilhelm II might encourage Berlin to move away from agrarian protectionism towards a more commercially oriented *Weltpolitik* (world policy).[68] Nor did the Kaiser's enthusiasm for a German navy hurt the Hamburg docks, where a substantial portion of Admiral Tirpitz's famous battle fleet was built. Lobbying in Berlin was also a rational response to the old merchant elite's gradual loss of political representation; by 1890 all three of the city's Reichstag seats were in the hands of the Social Democrats. In any case, lobbying – whether for lower tariffs, more colonies or bigger battleships – was not the same as exercising real power.

It is against this background that Max Warburg's role in Wilhelmine politics needs to be understood.[69] Though he preferred to call himself a Free Conservative rather than a National Liberal, and sat among the 'Rights' after his election to the Hamburg assembly (Bürgerschaft) in 1903, there is no question that Warburg was fundamentally a classical liberal in his politics.[70] On one occasion he even referred to himself mischievously as 'an old democrat'. Warburg himself later likened his support for Germany's colonial policy to the party-political contributions habitually made by British and American bankers, though the historian Alfred Vagts preferred to see it as an attempt to counter the influence of the radical right in Berlin.[71] Whatever his motive, Warburg's activities after 1900 undoubtedly entitled him to claim that 'no banking house in Germany has interested itself so determinedly for Germany's activity in the colonies as ours'.[72] He was heavily involved in the attempt by the German Foreign Minister Alfred von Kiderlen-Wächter to challenge the growing French dominance of the Moroccan economy. It was a close business associate of M. M. Warburg, Wilhelm 'Guido' Regendanz, who furnished the German Foreign Office with the claim that there were valuable copper deposits in the south of Morocco, which it was alleged the French were seeking to monopolize.[73] In the last few years before the First World War, Max Warburg and his partners also joined the German Colonial Office's new syndicate for colonial loans; raised money for a number of German companies with colonial interests; negotiated with the British Bank of West Africa to establish a new Anglo-German Bank of North-West Africa; and participated in a German–Portuguese Colonial Syndicate set up by the Colonial Office to facilitate the penetration, if not takeover, of Portugal's colonies in Africa.[74] All these efforts were clearly motivated by something other than economic self-interest. Indeed, Warburg himself admitted that his labours for German *Weltpolitik* brought 'little return'.[75]

Perhaps for just this reason, Max Warburg gradually came to have doubts about the viability of *Weltpolitik*. His critique was based on the identification of two basic structural weaknesses in Germany's position relative to its overseas rivals. The first was fiscal. Quite simply, the German Reich lacked a tax base large enough to match British, French or Russian expenditures on armaments. As a result, according to Warburg, Germany had to rely too much on government borrowing, and this in turn led to problems of crowding out by pushing up German long-term interest rates. The second weakness Warburg detected lay with the German balance of payments. Late nineteenth-century imperialism rested above all on capital exports. But Warburg argued that Germany did not export sufficient capital to exert the kind of leverage in foreign markets that could be exerted by Britain and France. As a member of the Reich Loan Consortium from 1905, he was only too well aware of the high level of government borrowing necessitated by rising armaments spending and the growth of social expenditure at the state and local level. In the years after 1908 he and his friend Ballin became convinced that Germany could not (in the latter's words) 'afford a race in dreadnoughts [state-of-the-art battleships] against the much wealthier British'.[76] In 1909 Warburg persuaded the Hamburg Chamber of Commerce to lend its support to the newly founded Hansa League's campaign for more progressive Reich taxation. At the time of the financial wrangles that helped topple Prince Bülow from the Reich chancellorship, he drafted a memorandum on Reich fiscal reform entitled 'How can we avoid a solution to the Reich's financial crisis that [simply] leads to a financial crisis among the federal states?' This document denounced the fiscal stalemate in the Reichstag in remarkably prescient terms: 'If we carry on our financial policy in this way, we will be guilty of financial asset-stripping; and, one fine day, we will find that we can make good the damage only with the greatest possible sacrifice – if we can make it good at all.'[77] Unfortunately, these arguments fell on deaf ears in high places. When Warburg attempted to broach the subject of financial reform with the Kaiser, he merely provoked the shrill response that it was Russia rather than Germany which was 'going bust'.[78]

Yet it was not just Germany's fiscal weakness that perturbed Warburg. It was also the vulnerability of German financial markets to outflows of foreign capital in the event of political crises. This was a phenomenon he noted as early as 1905, in the wake of the first Moroccan Crisis, when Germany vainly sought to challenge the status of Morocco as a quasi-colonial sphere of French influence.[79] It was, he later declared, 'financial influence that supported French policy in Algeciras . . . The success [of that policy] was more a victory of French financial strength than a victory of French diplomacy.'[80] In September 1907, at the annual conference of the Central Association of German Banks, Warburg asked his audience whether, in view of this vulnerability, Germany was adequately prepared to weather the financial consequences of a major European war.[81] Provocatively, he entitled his speech 'Financial Readiness for War' and startled his audience by estimating the annual cost of a major European war at 22 billion marks,[82] a higher figure than most other commentators anticipated (although still an underestimate, as it turned out). The strong implication was that Germany was not in the least bit ready for such a war.

To some contemporaries, the second Moroccan Crisis seemed, as it unfolded in 1911, to expose the relative weakness of the German capital market compared with those of Britain and France. In Albert Ballin's view, it was the 'collapse of the bourse' that was to blame for the failure of German policy.[83] Warburg was more positive in his assessment, arguing that 'Germany had withstood the test well in financial terms'.[84] However, he never had any doubt that it would be a different story if Germany were to risk a confrontation with Great Britain. As early as 1912 he could see the possibility that an Austrian clash with Russia over the Balkans could lead to 'further complications (Germany *contra* France and England)'.[85] Despite the failure of Lord Haldane's unofficial mission to Germany to improve relations with Britain (which they helped to arrange),[86] he and Ballin continued to pin their hopes on small-scale colonial agreements as the basis for a broader Anglo-German understanding. Indeed, Warburg's three visits to England in February, April and June 1914 to discuss German involvement in Portuguese Angola and other overseas markets led him to hope that 'an extraordinary amity between the Germans and England [had] broken out'.[87] Needless to say, none of this had an enduring influence in either London or Berlin. Warburg was astonished when, at a gala dinner held in Hamburg on 21 June 1914, the Kaiser outlined to him the case for a preventive war against, implicitly, Britain, France and Russia: 'He [the Kaiser] was worried about the Russian armaments [programme and] about the planned railway construction; and detected [in these] the preparations for a war against us in 1916. He complained about the inadequacy of the railway links that we had at the Western Front against France; and hinted . . . [at] whether it would not be better to strike now, rather than wait.' Warburg 'advised decidedly against' this:

[I] sketched the domestic political situation in England for him ([Irish] Home Rule), the difficulties for France of maintaining the three year [military] service period, the financial crisis in which France already found itself, and the probable unreliability of the Russian army. I strongly advised [him] to wait patiently, keeping our heads down for a few more years. 'We are growing stronger every year; our enemies are getting weaker internally.'[88]

This advice, as we know, was ignored. In the wake of the assassination of the heir to the Austrian throne at Sarajevo, the German government deliberately connived at the outbreak of a general European war, according to the fateful maxim of the Chief of the General Staff: 'The sooner the better.'

III

Siegmund Warburg was nearly twelve years old in the summer of 1914. Compared with his 'uncle' Max* – in so many ways an archetypal figure of the Wilhelmine era – Siegmund was a very different kind of German. Born in another century, on 30 September 1902, he was also born in another land: the German south, specifically in the university town of Tübingen. He grew up more than 400 miles away from the bustling streets of Hamburg and the corridors of power in Berlin, amid the green hills and clear streams of the Swabian countryside, on a small estate near the spa town of Bad Urach. If Max Warburg embodied the soaring ambition of one of the great nineteenth-century German-Jewish dynasties, Siegmund Warburg was the product of a quite different milieu. It was in many ways as unpropitious a point of origin for a future financier as could be imagined.

His father Georges was, as we have seen, the Warburg family under-achiever. Because of his susceptibility to debilitating headaches, which were thought to be exacerbated by the Hamburg climate, he had been sent to school in Konstanz, near Stuttgart, and had remained in the south to study agriculture at Hohenheim in Swabia. With his mother's help, he then purchased a somewhat dilapidated property in that region by the name of Uhenfels, a partly forested, partly arable estate that had once belonged to the Royal Marshal of the King of Württemberg.[89] The main farmhouse had no running water and only the most primitive heating, but with the help of his sister Elsa, who helped him to furnish it, and a fellow student from the agricultural college, who took over the management of the estate, Georges was able to live there in reasonable comfort.[90] In December 1901, at the age of thirty, he married – or rather was married, since it seems doubtful that either he or his

---

* Technically Siegmund was not Max Warburg's nephew but his first cousin once removed. However, as he often referred to him as 'Uncle Max', I have used this term throughout for the sake of clarity.

bride had much say in what was almost certainly an arranged match.[91] She was Lucie (or 'Luz') Kaulla, the daughter of a Wiesbaden lawyer and a member of one of southern Germany's leading Jewish families. They led the quiet life to a fault. A gifted pianist with a keen intellect and handwriting as meticulous as her husband's was sloppy,[92] Lucie was forced to give up playing because of her husband's chronic headaches. Often cut off by snow in winter and reliant on kerosene lamps for light, the couple lived surrounded by sheep, assisted only by their estate manager, a couple of maids and a St Bernard dog.[93] Their social circle, as the surviving Visitors' Book makes clear, was largely confined to their relatives: Gunzburgs, Kaullas, Rosenbergs, Rosenthals and Warburgs.[94] In these somewhat claustrophic circumstances, it was perhaps not entirely surprising that Lucie Warburg found a channel for her energies in the education of her one and only child.

Little appears to have survived of correspondence between mother and son. It is clear, however, from numerous family photographs and a great deal of later testimony that she doted on her 'Bubi', and he adored her in return. By the standards of their time and class, they spent a great deal of time together both before and after Siegmund went to school, for the establishment at Uhenfels was small. If there was ever a nurse or nanny, she made no impression on the boy. Nor does his invalid father seem to have played any significant part in Siegmund's upbringing; he seldom if ever alluded to him in later life.* It was his mother, and only his mother, who made him.

What was it that Lucie Warburg taught her son? 'Probably the strongest influence in my life', he later recalled, 'has been a basic idealism which has been infused into me by my mother . . . who felt that, to use mother's sentence – happiness in life consists in fulfilment of duties and not of desires.'[95] Her own duties were twofold: first to educate her son, secondly to nurse her ailing husband. In a moving memoir he wrote shortly after his mother's death, Siegmund recalled what a hard taskmaster she had been. Often she reduced him to tears when he failed to recite a poem he had been asked to learn by heart, or when a written exercise contained even the most trivial error. Not that she scolded him or lost her temper; she merely made it clear, gently but firmly, that he had disappointed her.[96]

* Georges suffered a stroke in 1921, deteriorated gravely in May 1922 and died in October the following year.

The essence of his mother's philosophy, as Warburg put it, was that 'what had to be done must be done with the utmost thoroughness; what had to be thought over must be thought through to its ultimate consequences; and what had been identified as the right objective, must be pursued with uncompromising tenacity.'[97] Systematically, she instilled in her son an extraordinarily potent combination of self-discipline and intensity of feeling, encouraging him to derive pleasure from perfectly performed duties rather than from mere sensual stimuli.[98] This perfectionism was something her pupil took to heart; it never left him. Nor did the content of his maternal lessons. Many years later, he could still quote with ease her favourite lines of Goethe:*

> Gathering all your forces
> For the offensive,
> Never submitting,
> Showing yourself to be strong:
> Thus summon the arms
> Of the gods to your side!

> (Allen Gewalten
> Zum Trutz sich erhalten,
> Nimmer sich beugen,
> Kräftig sich zeigen,
> Rufet die Arme
> Der Götter herbei.)[99]

As Siegmund well knew, his mother's keen sense of moral rectitude owed as much to religion as to the Enlightenment. However, as he later recalled, her faith was 'wholly non-conformist':

Neither the Jewish religion nor that of any other sect had an important meaning to my mother. She had a strong feeling for the Jewish tradition and for the moral elements of Judaism, but her religiosity absorbed elements of belief from the most diverse religions and philosophies, though above all [elements] from her beloved Goethe; she decidedly repudiated any form of dogmatism. She once said to me

---

* The lines come from his 1777 play Lila. They were often quoted by the father of Hans and Sophie Scholl, members of the White Rose group of students at Munich University who printed and distributed anti-Nazi leaflets during the Second World War. Hans carved Goethe's words on the wall of his jail cell shortly before his execution.

that ecclesiastical forms often seemed to her to stand in direct opposition to true belief . . . In her view, the most important thing in religious things was to believe in a great power above the earthly world and to remain in constant contact with this power through daily prayer and one's daily conduct.[100]

Significantly, the principal function of prayer, in her eyes, was to foster self-criticism. Up until he was thirteen, she prayed with Siegmund every night before he went to sleep, telling him on the eve of his bar-mitzvah:

From now on, my dear boy, you must pray alone in the evening, and you must always ask yourself before you pray what mistakes you have made during the preceding day, or what you could have done better. If a whole number of mistakes or omissions do not at once occur to you, then you must look deeper into yourself, until you have attained the necessary self-knowledge. We all make many mistakes every day, and the most important thing is to be critical of your own mistakes in the most unsparing way. That is the only way to arrive at honest prayer.[101]

It seems unlikely that Warburg kept up the habit of nightly prayer, but he never lost the habit of searching self-criticism. The aim was to learn from even the slightest lapse; only that way could one get closer to perfection. This pursuit of perfection was by no means confined to the life of the mind; it could also apply in the material world. Of all his mother's maxims, the one he repeated most frequently was: 'Some call it disappointment and get poorer; others call it experience and get richer' ('Die einen nennen's Enttäuschung und werden ärmer, die anderen nennen's Erfahrung und werden reicher').

Besides asceticism, perfectionism and self-criticism, his mother drummed one other vital quality into Siegmund Warburg: an aversion to social snobbery. She often told him that she found people who were not part of society preferable to those who were and, when she encountered snobbery, her reaction was exasperation: 'I really do not understand why grown men and women should waste so much of their precious time on such stupid unnecessary things as snobbery.'[102] This too was an attitude Warburg retained all his life; the only snobbery to which he was prone was intellectual snobbery. Yet this dislike of social snobbery had an important implication for his relations with the rest of the Warburg clan. For his mother left him in no doubt that snobbery was one of their least commendable traits. As he told George Steiner in an interview in 1976, 'My mother did not attach any importance to names and even talked often about her husband's Warburg relations as stupid, conceited people. When I first came across people in Hamburg who were impressed by the name it surprised me greatly. My mother always stressed that one should be respected for what one did but not for one's name. My mother was one of the least snobbish people and had a contempt and distaste for snobs.'[103] Before he had come into regular contact with his Hamburg relatives, and long before he had met his American cousins, Siegmund's mother had instilled in him a suspicion of them. Many years later, he made a revealing remark on the subject to Jacob Rothschild, another product of a powerful Jewish dynasty:

I, who had grown up in a very closely knit family circle, have gradually and increasingly come to the conclusion that the desirable relationships are what Goethe called 'Wahlverwandschaften', i.e. selected relationships in contradiction to blood relationships. This, of course, does not exclude the possibility – though a very rare one – that a selected relationship may coincide with a blood relationship.[104]

Despite regular visits to and by members of the extended Warburg kinship group, Siegmund never felt wholly comfortable among his own folk.

What his mother taught him was reinforced at school. Perhaps the most striking thing about Siegmund's formal education was its strongly Protestant character. After attending the Humanistische Gymnasium in Reutlingen, he spent two years as a 'guest student' at the Urach Seminar; indeed it was there that he obtained his *Abitur* (the German school-leaving certificate). Looking back, Siegmund saw the 'South German puritanism' he was exposed to there as a further encouragement 'to serve the community in whatever individual place one occupies and to give to such service the utmost of one's intensity and enthusiasm and [to look upon] all other elements of life such as aesthetic, material or subjective considerations . . . as being of inferior quality'. His teachers, he recalled, shared his mother's view that 'play of any kind was a waste of time and concentration on self-improvement was the priority in life':

Such self-improvement meant a continuous advance in the development of one's talents and the acquisition of further knowledge in various fields which might be useful to the community and which would prepare one for professional competence. To become acquainted with the artistic aspects of life – music being possibly the art valued above all others – was not excluded but was considered as definitely secondary to adding to one's intellectual efficiency and perception.[105]

His academic performance was excellent, particularly in the classics and history, though his strongest memories were of reading the poets of the romantic *Sturm und Drang* (storm and stress) movement, Friedrich Schiller and Friedrich Hölderlin, and the Swabian lyricist Eduard Mörike.[106] If he made friends there, the friendships were not enduring,[107] though it is perhaps worth remarking that it was almost certainly at school rather than at home that Siegmund picked up the slight Swabian accent with which he always spoke German.

Siegmund's, then, was in some ways an austere upbringing, in which love took the form of an encouragement to self-denial, and education was a preparation for the performance of arduous duties. Only occasionally – when his more worldly relatives visited – did shafts of a more colourful light enliven the picture. It was his paternal great uncle, the art historian and bon vivant Marc Rosenberg, who introduced the scholarly young man 'to a new world, by introducing me to the aesthetic values in life whilst previously I had been surrounded only by the ethical values'.[108] It was probably at around the same time that Siegmund discovered Friedrich Nietzsche, the most influential of all late nineteenth-century German thinkers, who 'threw into the melting pot all my early religious and philosophical concepts, based on Judaic idealism, on Goethe and on the Romantics'. 'Could it not perhaps be otherwise?' he found himself wondering for the first time in his life.[109] Political events were about to confirm that it could indeed.

IV

To be a boy growing up in Germany during the First World War, as Sebastian Haffner has written, was to be at once consumed by and excluded from the greatest of all contests – and then to be shattered by its wholly unforeseen outcome.[110] Siegmund Warburg was five years older than the young Berliner, but still young enough to miss being called up. Like Haffner, he experienced the war as a remote spectator, 'reading voraciously the War news and . . . following the progress of the War with a mixture of elation and concern'.[111] And, like so many Germans who were confined to the home front, he realized only slowly that his country might not only be in the wrong but might also be defeated.

In a way which today in retrospect seems to me almost lunatic [he later recalled], we felt that Germany's cause was the cause which deserved to win and it did not seem to enter the minds of anyone that the enemies could have even a particle of justice on their side. My chief worry at the time was that being only 12 years of age I had no chance to enter the army and to fight for my country. I thought nothing better could happen to me than to sacrifice my life on what was then called 'the altar of the fatherland'.[112]

In short, his love of his country was 'blind'. He was 'convinced of the right of the German side'. 'I put up the German flag at school and, like my schoolfellows, thought [General] Ludendorff and [Field Marshal von] Hindenburg marvellous.'[113] Older members of his family – including his own father and his uncle Aby M.[114] – were less sure. This was partly because the war so immediately affected both the family and the family firm. On 3 August 1914 Fritz Warburg's sister-in-law arrived in Hamburg from London to visit the family, but had to return by the next ship because of the British declaration of war.[115] For more than four years, the Warburgs were cut off from their British relations, just as they would be from the American family members from the spring of 1917.[116] As Paul Warburg put it in May 1917: 'My two brothers in Germany . . . naturally now serve their country to the utmost of their ability as I serve mine . . . As in the Civil War, brother must fight brother, each must follow the straight path of duty.'[117] Moreover, the war plunged the Hamburg economy into a profound slump.[118] A quarter of the city's trade had been with Britain alone; with the blockade of the North Sea, that ceased. The merchant fleet was devastated, foreign investments lost and relatively little in the way of war contracts came to Hamburg. Siegmund's uncle Max – who as early as 1912 had feared the possibility of war – did what he could to make a financial contribution to the German war effort, particularly with regard to negotiating credits for strategically vital imports from Sweden. As he himself admitted, however, the extent of the bank's dependence on the Reich was peril-ous. 'If Germany should lose the war', he commented with bleak humour, 'and should the Reichsbank find itself unable to honour its obligations to us', there would be no alternative but to place an obitu-ary notice in the press: 'Payments suspended in the field of honour: M. M. Warburg & Co.'[119]

Max Warburg was not immune to the febrile patriotism that swept through bourgeois Germany during the First World War. For example, he argued repeatedly in the course of 1916 for the creation of German colonies in the Baltic territories of Latvia and Courland, assuming a German victory in the east.[120] As late as May 1918, he continued to envisage imposing reparations on the other side of up to 100 billion marks.[121] But the economic disadvantages under which Germany laboured as a result of the sea blockade made him much less certain of victory against the Western powers.[122] Mounting pessimism about Germany's chances of victory explain Warburg's involvement in the efforts to win new allies for Germany (Italy, Romania, Bulgaria, Sweden), and his advocacy of a separate peace with England.[123] It also explains why – uniquely in the Hamburg business community – he opposed the lifting of restrictions on submarine warfare, which prevented German U-boats from attacking neutral shipping, on the ground that, however great the impact on British food supplies, the risk of alienating the United States was too grave.[124] As he put it in January 1917, 'If we end up at war with America, we will face an enemy with such moral, financial and economic strength that we will have nothing more to hope for from the future; that is my firm conviction.'[125] But the restrictions on submarine warfare were again lifted, and in just over two months the United States declared war on Germany. To be sure, the collapse of Russia and the military victory on the Eastern Front gave fresh impetus to those who opposed negotiation. Indeed, it was the publication of the Treaty of Brest-Litovsk in March 1918 that helped torpedo an attempt by Warburg (acting on government instructions) to hold back-channel talks about the post-war status of Belgium with the American ambassador in Holland.[126] But Max Warburg had little doubt that this victory in the east would prove illusory. He denounced the peace with Russia as 'thinly veiled annexation, with an all-too-trans-parent façade provided by the right of national self-determination',[127] and increasingly gravitated towards pacifist writers such as Martin Hobohm and Walther Schücking.[128]

His young relative in Bad Urach may well have been influenced by his example. Siegmund Warburg later recalled that, 'when the question of the so-called unrestricted U-Boat warfare, which was a decisive event politically during the War, arose, I gradually became a member of the opposition and very radical at that'. So passionately did he feel on the subject that when the government went ahead and lifted the restrictions he 'cried for days and was in a state of despair for more than two months.' Rightly, he too recognized 'that this decision would involve the defeat of Germany because it would bring America into the war'.[129] It was in this period of inner upheaval that he turned to new and more politically engaged writers: the sociologist Max Weber, the theologian Ernst Troeltsch, the historian Friedrich Meinecke, as well as Thomas Mann, Hermann Hesse and (perhaps most importantly) the Austrian Stefan Zweig, all of whom came in their different ways to question the rationality of the war.[130] Like many Germans traumatized by the prospect of defeat, he also read Oswald Spengler's darkly apocalyptic *Decline of the West*, but the fundamental direction of his thinking as the war drew to its ignominious conclusion was 'a slow conversion from an utterly narrow German nationalism towards an international outlook which up to then had been completely foreign to my thinking'. It took, as he later put it, 'a great amount of inner suffering . . . to discard that strange mixture of brutal chauvinism and naive idealism which [had] formed the basis of my nationalistic feelings'.[131] It was an inner revolution that would very shortly be overtaken by a world revolution.

2

The First World Revolution

*The First World Revolution brought with it more inner spasms
and more anarchic and destructive tendencies than any previous
upheaval.*

*It is part of the First World Revolution that the roles of the
revolutionaries have been reversed. Those who consider themselves as radical revolutionaries are the reactionaries while the
more moderate forces are the real revolutionaries. On the one
side is the most pronounced and also the most sophisticated
materialism that has made its appearance in the world's history
so far and on the other side are the citadels which were built
up since the Renaissance as centres for maintaining a collective
life of freedom tenuously blended with order and being the
most precious asset of the Western community.*

*When we look at the multitude of battles which result from
the First World Revolution it is quite clear that these battles are
part of an enormous undeclared war between reactionary forces
masquerading as revolutionaries and fighters for freedom who
are the real revolutionaries.*

Siegmund Warburg, 1976[1]

I

It was 'the First World Revolution', in Siegmund Warburg's striking
phrase. 'Up to the beginning of the First World War,' he observed in
an interview nearly sixty years later, 'there [had] been many revolutions affecting bigger or smaller sections of the world but . . . the first

revolution which had an impact on considerably more than half of the world began in 1914.' It was a revolution about which he always felt ambivalent. On the one hand, 'it did away with old empires which had become fossilized and it began to create new nation states out of previous dependencies of colonial and semi-colonial character. However at the same time many sound structures of the previous order were torn to pieces and with them an infinite number of institutions and other centres which had been safeguards of freedom.'[2]

The revolution may be said to have begun in exhausted peasant regiments; it swiftly spread to miserable industrial cities. Its root causes were defeat and deprivation. Demoralized armies, beginning with the Russian, simply disintegrated in waves of mutiny, desertion and mass surrender. Military failure in turn caused fatal crises of legitimacy in four of Europe's great empires – the Romanov, the Hohenzollern, the Habsburg and the Ottoman – two of which broke up into their component parts, never to be reassembled. At the same time, the hardships of more than four years of total war precipitated riots, rebellions and revolutions in cities the world over. Events in Petrograd and Moscow were echoed, with varying results, not only in Berlin, Budapest, Munich and Vienna but also as far afield as Glasgow and Seattle – even Buenos Aires. In November 1918 Max Warburg and his brother Fritz found themselves conducting tense negotiations with a would-be Lenin named Heinrich Lauffenberg, who had proclaimed a soviet republic in Hamburg. It was only with difficulty that they dissuaded him from abolishing the city's established institutions of government and defaulting on the state debt.[3] Sporadic violence persisted for months, as armed bands of mutineers and radical socialists roamed the city centre.[4] Even after the arrival of troops loyal to the moderate socialist republic that had been proclaimed in Berlin, the city remained a powder keg. There were serious outbreaks of political violence in every year from 1918 until 1923.

Though a revolution was scarcely to be expected in sleepy Bad Urach, the momentous character of events was immediately obvious to the sixteen-year-old schoolboy. In the wake of the Bolshevik coup in Russia, he had begun to read the German Social Democrat writer Rudolf Hilferding. 'I was generally much more leftish than my co-schoolfellows,' he later recalled. 'I disagreed with the old-fashioned capitalist ideas of my father and his family, more in a way beyond political matters in terms of human and social aspects.'[5] Yet the more Warburg saw of revolutionary violence (in Stuttgart and later in Hamburg and Berlin), the more he inclined towards the distinctly defensive liberalism espoused by the sociologist Max Weber and the industrialist Walther Rathenau, both of whom the war and the revolution had galvanized into political engagement. As leading lights of a new German Democratic Party, Weber and Rathenau aimed to contain the revolution by working in tandem with the moderate Majority Social Democrats. While Weber sought to preserve bourgeois society through a presidential constitution, Rathenau sought to preserve capitalism through a parallel set of corporatist institutions. Warburg met Weber at the latter's home in Heidelberg in the spring of 1919, shortly before the elections to the constituent National Assembly, and was profoundly impressed by his host's almost 'fanatical' style of argument. (Rathenau, whom he met later in Berlin, struck him as a much colder though no less admirable personality.) The young man was soon immersed in the heated political debates of that year, which were as much within German liberalism as against socialism. How American should the new German constitution be? How progressive should its tax system be? As he later remembered: 'I did not feel that communism or socialism were at that time questions with which I had to confront myself. It was more the inner compulsion to think about the way in which the mixed economy and the new tax systems should work and be adjusted to an economy which had to overcome the devastation of the First World War. A confrontation with socialism did not play a very big role with me at that time.' Warburg's assumption was that 'a sort of . . . socialist *cum* leftish Liberal coalition' would emerge and would survive.[6] By 1920 he was a member of a Democratic Party youth committee, and was seriously considering a political career. At eighteen, he was a liberal idealist – though with a realist's eye for influential patrons.

II

Politics was an option Warburg's uncle Max also had to consider. Even before the revolution broke out, as the Wilhelmine regime made its belated and abortive bid for constitutional reform, the last imperial

Chancellor, Prince Max of Baden, offered him the post of finance minister. Warburg declined. A month later, Prince Max tried again, suggesting that Warburg become his economics minister. There was even an attempt to appoint him as Germany's sole delegate to the anticipated peace negotiations.[7] Warburg's reason for declining all these invitations shows his awareness of the threat already posed by the radical right to his position: 'The current combination is emerging as democratic/social democratic,' he wrote, 'but ought not to be tinged capitalist-Jewish.'[8] As he later recalled: 'I knew the Germans, and knew that they would never accept a Jewish Finance Minister. On the other hand, the Social Democrats would see me as a representative of capitalism.'[9] A reminder of the persistence of anti-Semitism had already come during the war with the narrow (and evidently unexpected) defeat of his candidacy for the Hamburg Senate in 1917; despite being proposed as first choice by the Senate, his nomination was rejected by the lower house, the Bürgerschaft.[10] With this experience in mind, he declined to stand as a candidate in the post-war Bürgerschaft elections, and withdrew his name from the list of possible German People's Party candidates for the 1920 Reichstag elections, the first held under the new constitution drawn up at Weimar the previous year (hence the name 'Weimar Republic').[11] Nevertheless, Warburg was willing to play a significant political role behind the scenes. 'Reticence' was his watchword throughout the 1920s, though it is clear that he felt frustrated at having to maintain a low profile. 'Ah, dear God!' he exclaimed in a letter to his wife shortly after the Versailles peace conference: 'If I weren't a Jew I really would put myself in charge now!'[12]

In Max Warburg's eyes, constitutional reforms were of secondary importance. Under the terms of the armistice, as he often said, Germany was 'an object, not a subject'. The paramount question was therefore the form that the peace treaty would take. It was with that in mind that he consented not only to attend the Versailles conference in early 1919 as a financial adviser to the German financial delegation, but also to let his business partner, the brilliant Carl Melchior, serve as one of the official German representatives.[13] Warburg and Melchior had shrewd ideas about how Germany could best exert pressure on the Allies from a position of weakness; the arguments they put forward at Versailles were cogent and compelling. If the Allies confiscated Germany's overseas assets and merchant fleet while at the same time imposing an open-ended reparations burden, they reasoned, it would be impossible to stabilize the German currency. The resulting depreciation would lead to dumping of German exports, while the social upheaval caused by the Allied measures would lead to the spread of Bolshevism into Germany.[14] The influence of these arguments on John Maynard Keynes (who attended the conference in his capacity as a wartime Treasury civil servant) is clear from his immensely influential tract *The Economic Consequences of the Peace*.[15] Between 1919 and 1923, Max Warburg and Melchior consistently reiterated their position, insisting that the German currency could not be stabilized until reparations had been reduced from the total of 132 billion marks set in 1921 and an American loan to Germany had been floated.[16] Warburg's significance in these years has often been underestimated by historians precisely because of his public reticence.[17] Although his view of Germany's international position had much in common with Rathenau's, his emphasis on the financial leverage Germany could exert through currency depreciation was both original and influential.* Nor was his revisionism narrowly nationalist. He also developed his wartime commitment to international institutions:

It is the [principal] question of the next fifty years. How can international economic agreements be devised which will ultimately make racial and national borders of secondary importance, and make it possible, under the auspices of the League of Nations, for the individual national parliaments to send delegates to a 'super-parliament', in which fundamental global issues can be settled in a more consensual fashion than hitherto? . . . In this [way] . . . I hope that we will be able to kill off secret diplomacy, militarism [and] navalism . . .[18]

A remarkable example of his vision was his outline of a future world bank, managing international lending free from the constraints of the gold standard – an idea that would be realized only after another world war.[19]

Nevertheless, Max Warburg's strategy had serious flaws. His argument

---

* Like Rathenau, he interpreted 'fulfilment' to mean that Germany should demonstrate the impossible nature of the Versailles Treaty and the London schedule of payments by attempting (and failing) to fulfil them; and shared the idea that Germany should, at the same time, take advantage of its position between 'East and West', whether by threatening to succumb to Bolshevism or offering to facilitate Russia's economic reintegration.

that currency depreciation could act as a revisionist lever was not only economically mistaken (far from boosting German exports, German monetary laxity fuelled an import boom); it also played at least some part in the prolongation of German inflation after 1920. Although Warburg opposed the decision of his fellow Hamburg businessman Wilhelm Cuno to become chancellor at the end of 1922, he backed Cuno's decision to call the French bluff by suspending reparations payments – a move that led directly to the French occupation of the Ruhr – and he continued doggedly to resist currency stabilization up until October 1923.[20] Appealing though Warburg's arguments were, they gravely underestimated the dangers to the German economy of a complete collapse of the currency. It was all very well to say that Germany could not have a balanced budget or a stable monetary policy until reparations were reduced. But in practice this encouraged German politicians to increase government spending without making any serious attempt to raise matching taxation. Blithely blaming reparations for all Germany's problems, the early Weimar governments embarked on an astonishingly reckless spending spree, financing their spiralling deficits by printing ever larger quantities of banknotes. Warburg's hopes that the ensuing chaos would lead to a significant revision of the Versailles Treaty were unrealistic. The diplomatic gains were minimal; the economic, social and political costs of the descent into hyperinflation were far greater.[21]

These miscalculations can in part be traced back to the distinction between economics and politics that lay at the core of Max Warburg's thinking. 'The political fiasco currently to be seen in all countries', he wrote in early 1921, 'points to the need to divide economic policy from pure politics in future.'[22] Economic forces were working in Germany's favour, he believed, but were being impeded by the indecisiveness and incompetence of politicians. Although Warburg was not a democrat before 1918, his liberalism or 'free conservatism' (as he preferred) was of a sort that could sincerely come to terms with the Weimar system. When laying down conditions for representing Germany at Versailles, he had explicitly insisted upon 'the establishment of the Reich and the individual federal states on the broadest democratic basis [and] . . . the creation of a legally constituted parliament'.[23] Nor did the so-called 'Kaiser-Jew' show much regret at the passing of the monarchy; the first socialist Chancellor, Friedrich Ebert, whom he got to know during the war, was manifestly a more congenial head of state than Wilhelm II had ever been.[24] Warburg was also dismissive of political reaction, regarding the abortive military putsch led by the ultra-conservative Wolfgang Kapp in 1920 as 'idiotic'.[25] Yet his faith in the primacy of economics meant that his support for the Weimar Republic was not unqualified. His attitude to the proposed nationalization of the coal industry in 1919 had been cynical: 'In order to shove the demands of the workers and clerks down to a tolerable level, it may well be necessary to allow [their] representatives a look at the accounts . . . Of course, this must not impede the entrepreneurial spirit.'[26] When it became clear that the efforts of successive Weimar governments to extend the role of the state in the economy might impede precisely that, he did not spare his criticism:

It will be our mission, wedged between the old Western and the new Eastern worldview, to find the correct foundations for the new economic and political order [he wrote in October 1920]. [But] today an experimental councils system, tomorrow a trial socialization, at the same time decapitalization through taxation – no people can prosper in this fashion.[27]

A growing and by no means unjustified conviction that the Weimar system led to wasteful and economically damaging public expenditure on social policy meant that throughout the 1920s Warburg toyed with schemes for constitutional reform designed to limit parliamentary influence over the economy. In 1919 he briefly contemplated full-scale centralization of the Reich to curb the over-spending of the federal states.[28] In August 1923 he and the industrialist Hugo Stinnes discussed the possibility of a 'finance directorate' (*Finanzdirektorium*) – a triumvirate with dictatorial powers over finance – with the objective of 'depoliticizing the money supply so that the economy [would] function independently of the current state form and holders of power'.[29] 'The parliamentary system in this form', he commented three months later, 'is not the right solution for difficult times.'[30] In short, Warburg accepted the liberal core of Weimar, but his economic priorities made him critical of its socialist and social-welfare elements, and willing to countenance constitutional changes. This was to underestimate the danger of a more radical constitutional change that might not only end the parliamentary system but also impose a dictatorship intent on subordinating the economy to the goals of a hypertrophic nationalism.

III

His uncle's considerable if covert political influence was a crucial factor in Siegmund Warburg's fateful decision to leave Uhenfels and join the family firm in Hamburg. It was, of course, this decision that launched Warburg's career as a banker. However, it should be understood that his original intention was to launch his career as a politician. For what better starting point for a political career could there be than to work for Max Warburg, the financial *éminence grise* behind the misleadingly named policy of 'fulfilment' of the Versailles Treaty? As Siegmund later recalled, his 'chief ambition' had been:

to go into politics whether on the stage or behind the scenes. It was rather common among many of the older generation under whom I grew up that entry into politics did not at all exclude but rather fit well with other activities, be it the profession of a lawyer or an industrialist or a banker or an academic . . . When I went into business in 1920 – immediately after leaving school – I looked upon this as nothing but a stepping stone towards politics.[31]

There was an additional and perhaps more pressing reason for going to Hamburg; it was economically essential. It should be remembered that the inflation did not hit all German families equally hard. The working classes benefited in relative terms because inflationary policies maintained German employment at artificially high levels. They were also protected by rent controls and were better able to secure wage increases through collective action. Businessmen, too, could protect themselves, whether by investing in real assets or in hard currencies. Thus M. M. Warburg & Co. fared relatively well in the inflation years; although the bank's assets at the end of 1924 were around 28 per cent lower than before the war, that was a comparatively good showing compared with many other Hamburg firms.[32] The real losers were those bourgeois families who relied on salaries or the income from their savings. Max Warburg was painfully aware of what was happening to the wider society of which he was a part: 'Periodicals, learned associations, cultural activities of all kinds . . . have had to be given up. . . . Sons and daughters can no longer be educated to the standard that had formerly been taken for granted. Fine houses and old family heirlooms are having to be sold off. It is an unobtrusive kind of impoverishment we are witnessing . . .'[33] Among the victims of this process were Siegmund's parents. By the time he died in October 1923 – at the very height of the hyperinflation – Georges was in serious financial difficulties, as was Siegmund's uncle Otto Kaulla, whose savings had been wiped out. That put paid to any academic ambitions that Siegmund may have nurtured to study at university. As he later put it, 'I was actively employed in banking, because I had to earn money to support my family.'[34] Indeed, it took him at least a decade to resolve the economic problems he inherited from his father.[35] The fear of another great inflation remained with him all his life – as would the conviction that inflation was a primarily political phenomenon caused by 'governments [who] do not have the courage either to reduce their expenditure or to cover it by taxation'.[36] The German hyperinflation, he later remarked, had been 'an economic consequence of a political disaster'.[37] As he later summed up the lesson he had learned so painfully: 'Badly controlled Government expenditures have all over the world been the chief sources of inflation for as long as economic history can be observed.'[38]

The idea that Siegmund Warburg should join M. M. Warburg & Co. was his uncle Max's, who proposed it to the young man's parents when they paid a visit to Hamburg in June 1920. Though professing surprise at his uncle's 'big offer', Siegmund immediately accepted. 'It was . . . clear to me', he wrote to his beneficent relative in evident excitement, 'that I could never, ever refuse, but that I must and could consciously and confidently say yes':

For if there is one thing in particular that has recently made school tedious for me, it has been above all the fact that I am inwardly more and more driven to do something real, something [that lies] beyond the individual sphere. There is most certainly the opportunity to do that in this case. Naturally, my decision depends on the consent of my parents. But that seems likely, given the fact that I have here the prospect of a field of activity which is laden with so many family traditions, and which involves so many dear relations – such as you, Uncle Aby and Uncle Fritz.[39]

36

With the 'world situation so unclear', his uncle replied, it made good sense for Siegmund to work for at least the next two years in the tried and tested surroundings of the family firm. He could always opt later for an academic career or the management of the Uhenfels estate.[40]

Hamburg in the early 1920s was as stimulating a place as wartime Bad Urach had been soporific. The young Swabian had no intention of letting his duties as an apprentice banker inhibit his enjoyment of big-city life. He attended lectures at Hamburg University. He continued his involvement with the Democratic Party, befriending like-minded young liberals like Ernst Kocherthaler, an economist close to Walther Rathenau, and Arnold Bergstraesser, one of Max Weber's protégés. 'We talked politics,' he later recalled, 'but also discussed philosophy and *Weltanschauung* [worldview] and our talks lasted often well into the night.' As a member of the liberal Free German Youth organization, he spent weekends on hiking expeditions, sometimes rambling (in both senses) from dusk until dawn.[41] At the same time, he sought to establish scholarships for 'young socialists and young workers' to go to university.[42] On business trips to Berlin he took every opportunity to attend the capital's theatres, especially relishing the innovative productions of Max Reinhardt. Like Sebastian Haffner, he also seems to have enjoyed the new sexual freedom that was such a distinctive feature of the time. 'There were moments and many periods of suffering,' he remembered, 'but others of joy and ecstasy.' His lifelong friend Edmund Stinnes – son of the supreme inflation profiteer Hugo Stinnes – recalled an affair Siegmund had with the Viennese actress Ida Roland, who would go on to marry Count Coudenhove-Kalergi, the founder of the Pan-European Movement.[43] Another Viennese 'elective affinity' was to Elisabeth Schiff, a distant relation whose plainer sister Theodora would later introduce him to the art of graphology (see Appendix). Warburg was young. He was good-looking. He was smart. And as a favoured employee of the most successful merchant bank in Germany's second city, he was not short of money. If anyone was in a position to enjoy the fleeting pleasures of Weimar's brief period of relative stability, it was Siegmund Warburg. And if there was a time when the strict puritanism of Warburg's upbringing yielded to the temptations of the flesh, it was during the years of inflation, when all values – and not merely monetary values – were on the slide.*

Yet, as time passed, family and firm came to predominate. This may have come as something of a surprise to Siegmund Warburg, who, as we have seen, had been brought up to view his Hamburg relations with some disdain and to regard politics rather than business as his vocation. One important reason for this was the powerful influence on him of Carl Melchior. Cool, clever, meticulous and hypersensitive, Melchior played the role of Max Warburg's alter ego at M. M. Warburg & Co., his sangfroid counterbalancing the senior partner's ebullience. Melchior struck the young Siegmund Warburg as a twin soul. To be sure, he was at first intimidated by Melchior's reserved air of authority:

Soon, however, there revealed themselves behind these qualities of authority a human understanding and inner tranquillity that decidedly encouraged [me] to speak out in Carl Melchior's presence and frequently to ask his advice. In . . . [the] many conversations that followed over the years, the strongest impression that Carl Melchior's personality made on me rested on his moderate, factual and objective attitude . . . He had the highest form of objectivity, which he strove to achieve with passion and through hard inner struggle. It consisted of constantly educating himself, in a way that bordered on masochism, with the goal of overcoming his own instinctive subjectivity, without [at the same time] repressing the intensity of his own feelings. Examples are more effective than good exhortation. The example of objectivity [and] of moderation . . . which Carl Melchior set remained an enduring inspiration for all who really knew him. Combined quite naturally with [this] objectivity was his feeling for justice, and this was perhaps the strongest motor of his being. Reserved as he generally was, it was impossible for him silently to accept unjust deeds or unjust words. Righteousness was not a formal thing for him, but a matter of seeking after truth, in accord with the French motto: 'Justice is truth in action.'[44]

These were in many ways the same qualities that so struck John Maynard Keynes when he met Melchior at Versailles. Keynes, for his

---

* In a 1928 lecture, his uncle Aby M. drew a revealing parallel between the inflation and the baroque, a cultural inflation in which the 'gold reserves of suffering' inherited through images from the art of antiquity were devalued by the printing press. For Aby Warburg the twin shocks of military defeat and revolution were too much: he suffered a nervous breakdown and had to be hospitalized in Ludwig Binswanger's Swiss sanatorium.

part, felt an almost sexual attraction to Melchior.[45] For Siegmund, however, Melchior was a role model. He proved that the rigorous perfectionism that had been instilled in him as a boy could perfectly well be applied in the world of high finance.

The other strong influence on Warburg during his banking apprentice-ship was Max Warburg's brother Paul. Although he had not become an American citizen until 1902, seven years after his marriage to Nina Loeb, Paul Warburg had played a leading role in the establishment of the Federal Reserve System and, as a founding member of the Federal Reserve Board, became a close adviser of President Woodrow Wilson.[46] Accord-ing to Benjamin Strong, the first Governor of the Federal Reserve Bank of New York until his untimely death in 1928, the Federal Reserve System was Paul Warburg's 'baby' – a response to the 1907 financial crisis, which had revealed that the sole lender of last resort in the US financial system was J. P. Morgan – though Warburg's original scheme (loosely modelled on the German system) had to be substantially altered in order to pass a wary Congress. However, after the American entry into the war in 1917, anti-German feeling had led Wilson to prevaricate about renewing Warburg's Federal Reserve appointment, stinging him into resigning.[47] It did not help that Jacob Schiff, the senior partner at Kuhn, Loeb & Co., had been identified as pro-German by proponents of US intervention in the war, a slur that his Anglophile colleague Otto Kahn had to work hard to efface.[48] After the war was over, Paul Warburg also made no secret of his sympathy with the land of his birth. He was the driving force behind the Amsterdam Bankers' Memorandum of October 1919, which called for a review of the financial provisions of the Versailles Treaty. Although he insisted that he was helping 'in the formulation of a purely American point of view', it is clear that his sympathies lay with his brother Max, whose views on domestic and foreign issues he tended to echo, and hence with Germany.[49]

To Siegmund, who met him for the first time after the war, the fifty-year-old Paul Warburg seemed the 'outstanding' member of his generation of the Warburg family. The younger man was awed by his mastery of German literature, the subject that dominated their first conversation. He was also intrigued by Paul Warburg's transatlantic existence and identity. A partner of both M. M. Warburg & Co. in Hamburg and Kuhn Loeb in New York, he was also the founder, in

1920, of one of the first authentically international financial institutions, the International Acceptance Bank, the founding shareholders of which included (besides the two banks of which Warburg himself was a partner) some of the leading merchant banks of London, Amsterdam and Zurich. With the Federal Reserve System, he had imported the German model of a federal central bank to the United States; with the IAB he sought to import the European model of merchant banking based on the acceptance of bills of exchange.[50] Finally, Siegmund was struck by his uncle's cautious, even pessimistic, temperament, which stood in marked contrast to the indefatigable optimism of Max Warburg. He likened the relationship between Paul and Max to that between Tonio Kröger and his friend Hans Hansen in Thomas Mann's novella *Tonio Kröger*. The former is cerebral and literary, the latter muscular and sporty. Paul Warburg, Siegmund later recalled,

was very far-seeing but his tragedy was that he never carried out his good instincts. In 1921 he already warned his brother Max that the Hamburg firm should no longer continue as an 'offene Gesellschaft' [unlimited liability partnership] but this good advice was not heeded by Max Warburg whose enormous charm overcame the better instincts of Paul. Paul considered Max much too optimistic and enterprising in those troubled times.[51]

These forebodings were to prove all too prescient.

IV

To be truly *haute banque* was to be international in both outlook and mode of operation. At their zenith, the Rothschilds had branches in Frankfurt, London, Paris, Vienna and Naples. The Warburgs had pretensions to play a similar role in the early twentieth century, but with their principal bases in Hamburg and New York. These pretensions did not, as might be thought, imply that the Warburgs were rivals to the Rothschilds. By the 1920s it had long been clear that relatively small family-controlled firms like N. M. Rothschild & Sons and M. M. Warburg & Co. could operate effectively only by collaborating together – most obviously by floating international loans in *ad hoc* syndicates. At a more mundane level, banking families like the Rothschilds and the Warburgs collaborated in the education and training of potential future partners. Thus it was that in 1926, after only one foreign business trip as a junior (to Vienna and Budapest), Siegmund Warburg was sent to England to continue his apprenticeship, and to learn the very different *modus operandi* of the City, at New Court, St Swithin's Lane, home of the London house of Rothschild.[52] It was his first visit to Great Britain.

In view of the fact that within a matter of a decade Warburg would settle in England, it might be expected that his first impressions of the country would be favourable. They were not. Before entering the hallowed precincts of New Court, he spent six chilly months at Cambridge University, attending lectures of which the most memorable were by C. W. Guillebaud, Alfred Marshall's nephew and co-author of the *Principles of Economics*, and C. K. Ogden, the psychologist, linguist and translator of Ludwig Wittgenstein's *Tractatus*. As Melchior's protégé, Warburg was able to secure an interview with Keynes, by now established as the university's leading media don, writing regularly for the British press on contemporary questions of economic policy, ranging from the impossibility of collecting punitive reparations from Germany to the folly of returning Britain to the gold standard. The great economist made a poor impression on his young German visitor, who found him disconcertingly 'bohemian'. Keynes was certainly like no German professor Warburg had ever met:

It was after 11 a.m. and he received me in red slippers – for a conventional German this caused me much surprise. I had heard that he was a very great man but I did not like him at all at our first meeting. There was something effeminate, something 'schnoddrig' [irreverent] about him. He dealt with serious matters in what seemed to me a facetious way . . . [He] personified for me a rather typically English combination of intellectual cynicism and . . . [the] highest standards in evaluating human thoughts and actions. Keynes could be almost sadistic in demolishing the arguments of people, however well meaning they might be, if he could detect the slightest flaw in their thought processes.[53]

His reaction to the gentlemanly capitalist ethos at N. M. Rothschild was not a great deal more positive. Once the epicentre of the global financial system, by the 1920s the London house of Rothschild more closely resembled a gentleman's club than a bank. One senior clerk seldom came to work before noon, went to lunch at one o'clock and at 2.30 set off again for home. As a junior clerk, Ronald Palin 'rarely arrived much before 10.30 in the morning and could always count on two free days at the weekend'. Warburg's colleagues seemed to have stepped from the pages of P. G. Wodehouse. 'This, my boy,' he was told, 'is the best club in London. We really ought to be paying a subscription instead of receiving a salary.'[54] The puritanical visitor from Germany was appalled. Despite his junior status, he was surprised to find himself entrusted with much of the work of arranging an £835,000 bond issue for the Prussian province of Westphalia. 'My first impression of that firm', Warburg later commented, 'was that compared with the way in which one worked in Hamburg it was lazy, easy-going, and even sloppy.'[55] By the time he left England, Siegmund had begun to suspect 'that the British Empire had completely passed its zenith and that the political skill that had once been peculiar to the English was in a state of severe degeneration'.[56] The man who most impressed him during his stay was in fact another German: an aspiring young banker from the Rhineland named Hermann Josef Abs.

Not long after Siegmund Warburg returned to the continent, on 8 November 1926, he put his bachelor days behind him. He was twenty-four. The woman he married was a Swede, Eva Maria Philipson, the daughter of the head of the Svenska Handelsbanken in Stockholm, Mauritz 'Malle' Philipson. The reception for more than 170 guests was lavish, with an eight-course dinner – including supreme of sole Monte Carlo and saddle of venison Montmorency, all washed down with 1919 Pol Roger Brut and 1916 Mouton-Rothschild and accompanied by Swedish folksongs, Strauss waltzes and an excerpt from *Madame Butterfly*. Fortunately, the couple proved to be a happier match than Pinkerton and Butterfly.

'It is a pity', Siegmund Warburg once remarked, 'that so many specially fine men have hysterical wives.'[57] This was never a problem with which he himself had to contend. Eva Warburg was throughout his life a source not only of love, but of emotional stability and cool good sense. In the words of two of the many aphorisms he liked to collect: 'To love someone – and to be loved in return for no other reason except because of what one is – this happens so rarely that when it occurs it is almost like a miracle . . . To be in love with another human being, and to be in love with life – these two loves united into one great single love is the greatest gift that can come to us.'[58] By the standards of the early twenty-first century, their relationship was, of course, in many respects an unequal one. He had been much better educated than her. During their first transatlantic voyage together, she asked him to give her lessons in philosophy.[59] He worked and travelled – was very often far away from home for prolonged periods – while she was usually left to the more mundane chores of the home. For a time, she even took up typing in the hope of being able to accompany him on business trips. (If it was ever tried at all, this was a short-lived experiment.) Her husband was a self-confessed flirt who had at least one affair, with the Russian ballerina Alexandra Danilova, during the 1930s.[60] Siegmund and Eva's sexual relationship almost certainly suffered when she had to undergo a mastectomy after she was diagnosed with breast cancer following the birth of their daughter, Anna, in November 1930.[61] Yet it would be a mistake to conceive of Eva as some kind of docile accessory. As Siegmund Warburg later observed, 'the most difficult aspects for the two partners in a marriage are that they must make a continuous effort to combine independence and interdependence (to use for individual relations these terms which are considered nowadays so appropriate to international relations).'[62] His relationship with Eva was never one of unconditional domination. Eva was able to compel Siegmund to end his relationship with Danilova by threatening to leave him.[63] For by now, despite his infidelity, he had come to depend on his wife in a host of other ways. As their son recalled, she was:

quite indispensable (and, fortunately, wholly devoted) to the management of her husband's life, on the emotional as well as the practical level. As he brought his business concerns home with him and discussed them with her, she even played a part in many of his more troublesome non-family decisions. For a man who never learned to drive a car, boil an egg or change a lightbulb . . . Eva saw to the efficient management of his family life and to unwelcome tasks outside the office. She had a strong sense for the aesthetic, and created the unshowy all-round comfort in which he revelled at home. She had a natural cheerfulness that helped offset his inclination to melancholy . . . But, far above that, for a volatile romantic like Siegmund, the steadier and in some ways worldly-wiser Eva was a vital counter-balance. She constantly sought to protect him (not always, of course, successfully) from his passionate inclination 'to fall in love' with people he met, and he clearly valued her sober, perceptive (usually sterner than his) judgements of character.[64]

From the outset, theirs was a marriage of equals on the question of religion. Although the Philipsons were originally a Jewish family bearing the name Jeremias – the bride and groom in fact shared a common great-great-great-grandfather in Elias Samuel Warburg – Eva was brought up as a Protestant. She and Siegmund were married in a private ceremony with a rabbi and a Protestant clergyman both present. As Warburg explained to his father-in-law, 'We want with complete self-consciousness to build our married life in a simultaneously Protestant and Jewish spirit and to raise our children to revere both.' The couple agreed that, 'given the character of their name and all the things associated with it', their children should be received into the Jewish faith. This required Eva to convert to Judaism, which she subsequently did. For the wedding, Siegmund went out of his way to find a liberal rabbi who would bless their wedding regardless of, and without referring to, her Christianity.[65]

In 1937, a time of perils for all Jews that had been scarcely conceivable when they married, Siegmund wrote Eva a letter that she was to open only in the event of his death. In it he passionately avowed his devotion to her:

Please never forget, that I have loved you as much in all the time of our life together as it is possible for one human being to love another. Even when there have been shadows, as is unavoidable with such intense people, it's true that our love was also occasionally overshadowed, but it always came forth out of the shadow and into the light with new strength. Looking back I am happy to say it: We have had a splendid time of it together – at once a great feeling of shared life and shared love.[66]

His marriage brought Siegmund Warburg an additional boon. He quickly formed a firm friendship with his father-in-law, who appears to have provided precisely the kind of worldly patriarchal figure that

Siegmund had lacked in his own youth. 'Malle' Philipson was a hard-nosed businessman, a pillar of the Stockholm commercial community, whose marriage to a Lutheran, Ingrid Horngren, in some ways prefigured Siegmund's to Eva.[67] Pragmatic, quick-tempered and fond of a cigar, Philipson increasingly supplanted Max Warburg as the young banker's mentor. Significantly, Warburg began all his letters to Mauritz with 'Dear Father'. 'You really make me happy', he wrote in 1927, '. . . with the truly paternal interest and understanding that you give me . . . I am so happy with the many fine hints and pieces of advice that you gave me the last time we were together, which invariably hit the nail on the head in a way that one almost never encounters in this cold world – not even from one's nearest and dearest.'[68]

In May 1927 Siegmund and Eva Warburg left Hamburg for the United States, where he was to continue his financial training. Rather than begin work at once with his uncle Paul at Kuhn Loeb, Warburg elected to learn the principles of American accounting at the Boston-based firm of Lybrand, Ross Brothers & Montgomery. Leaving behind the plush Upper East Side residences of his New York relatives, he and Eva rented a modest apartment in the Brookline area of the city. He worked from 9 until 5; she did the housework (surely the first time in her life she had been without an establishment of servants). It was here, in September that year, that their first child, George (significantly not Georg or Georges), was born.[69] They strove, in short, to conform to the stereotype of middle-class American newlyweds.

Like countless European newcomers before him, Siegmund Warburg sought to understand the United States by comparing and contrasting it with Europe. In the usual fashion, his first impressions were somewhat condescending. Americans were very alike; there was a disconcerting 'uniformity' about them.[70] 'Here', he wrote home to a Hamburg friend, 'you may not expect too much in the way of subtle understanding.'[71] People were friendly but shallow. The 'long earnestly conducted conversations about golf' – a game to which Warburg developed a lifelong aversion – were symptomatic of this.[72] To be sure, Americans were gripped by a 'remarkably strong vibration of energy and freshness'. The tempo of life was quicker (much quicker than in London) and social intercourse more 'democratic'; there was also a 'remarkable general mutual good will and an enormous social energy'.[73] Yet there was:

a lack of some of the intellectual subtlety that Europeans are so proud of. Fate has made it easier for the Americans than for Europeans to keep worries and bitterness at a distance, but it must be admitted that the Americans have consciously and deliberately wanted to make life more comfortable than have Europeans. The Americans confine themselves to those pleasures that don't require too much effort, in contrast to Europeans, who attach the most value to those pleasures which call for painstaking care.[74]

He also detected a certain over-sensitivity to criticism, which he had not encountered in London.[75] Yet, as Warburg delved more deeply into the literary, political and economic life of the United States, he gradually revised his opinion. At work, he was especially struck by the greater efficiency of American accounting, a function in turn of the remarkable standardization of American business practice. Balance sheets had to be drawn up according to strictly prescribed models.[76] He began to wonder, as he compared the American system with the European, if the former was in fact a model which the latter would sooner or later have to adopt.[77] In the offices of a Boston accounting firm, he saw the economic future, and it seemed to work. So dynamic did the American economy appear that he was moved to draw a parallel with one of the high points of European history. Perhaps the lack of subtlety that had first struck him was simply the 'necessary obverse' of:

the grandiose entrepreneurial spirit that prevails here. It seems to me as if one must compare the present epoch here in certain respects with the Renaissance. Both epochs had the same huge, restless energy, which expressed itself more in the aesthetic direction in the Renaissance, but which in contemporary America expresses itself in a social and technical direction. Both epochs were and are accompanied by much cynicism . . . injustice and harshness, and both epochs produced and produce similar sharply chiselled, hard-formed faces.[78]

The problem, as Warburg rapidly realized when he and Eva moved to New York, was that this economic Renaissance appeared to be passing the American Warburgs by.

As we have seen, Siegmund Warburg had found much to admire in his uncle Paul Warburg when they had met in Germany immediately after the war. He was also touched by the warmth of the welcome he and Eva received from Paul's brother Felix and his exuberant wife Frieda. It was not long, however, before he began to find the gregarious hospitality of his numerous relations 'more of a hindrance to our lives than a help'.[79] Their Fifth Avenue palaces,* bedecked with Rembrandts, seemed to him the abodes of parvenus.[80] More than perhaps he had expected, he was ill at ease with the next generation of American Warburgs. Some had studied at Harvard or Yale. All seemed more devoted to golf and sports cars than to literature or, for that matter, business. To his mind, they conformed uncannily to the stereotype of the wealthy WASP playboy that F. Scott Fitzgerald was already portraying so ambivalently in his fiction. Even the enthusiasm with which his relatives celebrated Christmas bemused him.[81] They seemed, in short, to have become as excessively American as an earlier generation of Warburgs had become excessively German, with wealth taking the place of nobility as the basis for snobbery, and football the place of fencing as the substitute for intellectual activity.[82] As he confided to his father-in-law, 'Of all my many American acquaintances, my own family – with the exception of Paul Warburg – please me the least . . . Their whole circle is so boring, vacuous in both spiritual and human terms and suffocating in money . . .'[83] This was bad enough socially, but it was potentially disastrous for the future of Kuhn, Loeb & Co.

When Siegmund Warburg arrived in New York, Kuhn Loeb was still regarded as one of Wall Street's most important banks. However, it was heavily dependent on servicing the needs of an industry that had passed the peak of its expansion, namely the American railway network. True, with total proprietary shareholdings that gave it a stake in nearly 60 per cent of the country's long-distance routes, Kuhn Loeb could count on substantial dividend and interest income. True, the firm had a number of big industrial clients – among them American Smelting & Refining and United States Rubber. Yet

---

* A good example is Felix and Frieda Warburg's mansion at 1019 Fifth Avenue and 92nd Street, designed by the architect C. P. H. Gilbert in the early Renaissance French style usually known as François I, and built in 1908. It now houses New York's Jewish Museum. The house was just up from Jacob Schiff's at 965 Fifth Avenue and Schiff's son Mortimer's at 932. Directly opposite, at number 1100, was Otto Kahn's house.

Mortimer ('Morti') Schiff, the most dominant of the bank's five partners after his father Jacob's death in 1920, seemed uninterested in diversification. Warburg could not interest him in financing the new generation of public utilities, among the most dynamic economic sectors of the 1920s. Nor was Schiff much concerned to rebuild the bank's overseas activities, which had collapsed during the war because his Russophobe father Jacob had refused to finance the Allied war effort against Germany, leaving the field open to J. P. Morgan. 'K.L. & Co. today is still a splendidly shining star,' Warburg reported in a confidential letter to his father-in-law, 'but I fear it is a star that is steadily and rapidly losing its radiance. For the various partners . . . it is not a sober, businesslike entrepreneurial spirit that is decisive, but personal vanity, hobbies and snobbery.'[84] He was dismayed by 'an often astonishing ignorance and mismanagement of people, combined with a remarkable enthusiasm for arguments inside and outside the firm'.[85] Indeed, he came to think that the bank was actually run 'by the clerks, despite the partners'.[86] Kuhn Loeb was not by any means doomed; on the contrary, its vast capital, its standing in New York and its links to American industry gave it 'enormous, unexploited possibilities'.[87] Without more enterprising leadership, however, these would ultimately go to waste. The vision of a rejuvenated Kuhn Loeb would tantalize Warburg for many years to come; it first came to him as early as 1928.

At first, Warburg was more impressed by the International Acceptance Bank. It was, after all, his uncle Paul's creation.[88] However, power over the IAB was now wielded by his cousin James ('Jimmy') and the latter's 'clique of semi-idiotic Harvard Society halfwits'.[89] Jimmy struck him as 'a fearful bluffer, more a dialectician than a person of real ability, and remarkably unpopular wherever people have got to know him'.[90] Siegmund's instructions from Max Warburg were to cultivate good relations with both Kuhn Loeb and the IAB, but this was far from easy. As Warburg tried to explain to his uncle, a fundamental tension had arisen between Morti Schiff and Paul Warburg. The former, insofar as he interested himself in foreign business at all, felt no strong loyalty to the Hamburg Warburgs. By 1928 he was doing significantly more business with Jakob Goldschmidt of the Darmstädter und National ('Danat') Bank.[91] Paul Warburg, by contrast, had intended the IAB to become the main conduit for transatlantic business, permanently linking Kuhn Loeb, M. M. Warburg and the other shareholding banks.[92] It was not Paul Warburg's style to seek a confrontation on the issue, but his son Jimmy seemed intent on a showdown with Schiff. It was in vain that Siegmund Warburg warned his uncle Max of the 'whispering, exaggeration and feelings of mistrust' between Kuhn Loeb and the IAB.[93] By the time he returned with his wife and son to Germany in the middle of 1928, his early enthusiasm for the pace and scale of America's economic possibilities was giving way to a more sombre pessimism about transatlantic financial – and especially familial – relations.

In the space of ten years, Siegmund Warburg had experienced both revolution and relocation. In Germany he had glimpsed a political future – of a social democratic republic in which he hoped to play a leading role. In the United States it was an economic future that flashed before him – of a revitalized Kuhn Loeb, modernizing its business under his direction. Intriguingly, the latter vision led him to re-examine the former. At the time of the German revolution, he explained to his friend Ernst Kocherthaler, it had seemed obvious that the younger generation had known better than the older. Until now, he had 'always had a strongly antagonistic feeling towards the present older generation, whose roots lay in the pre-war era and in a more or less weak liberalism, whereas I saw in the younger generation a strong perhaps partly fascistic desire for organization'. But that had been true only for Europe. In the United States, by contrast, the relationship between the two generations was quite different.

The aims the older [American] generation set themselves were [as in Europe] based on a liberal utilitarianism with a thin idealistic veneer, whereby the European 'Live and let live' was translated into 'A chance for everybody'. But on the part of the younger generation here there is not even a reaction against their elders, just a complete emptiness . . . I once heard an aphorism that went something like this: 'That generation which has not had a period of revolutionary . . . fire is worthless' . . . I believe there has seldom been as big a collection of mediocre hearts and minds or as big an over-supply of philistines as there is among the present younger generation in America.[94]

It was for this reason that Warburg left the United States with a sense of foreboding – a fear that 'catastrophic things' would sooner or later befall this vacuous generation of young Americans. It was January 1928. He little knew how soon those catastrophes would begin.

3

The Degeneration of a Republic

*Every morning a circa two-hour-long principals' conference of
circa 8 people, where continually different views are [expressed],
and which mostly come to more or less fruitless conclusions.
The consequence [is] something like a system of intrigues internally and a zig-zag course externally, and it is continually getting
worse as a result of the sclerosis of the arteries now discernible
in the conduct of Max M. W[arburg]. That the performance of
the firm is still stable should be attributed not to the skill of its
chief, but to the truly mysterious nimbus that surrounds the
[family] name.*

Siegmund Warburg, May 1927[1]

I

The decline and fall of the Weimar Republic used to be understood as
a consequence of class conflict and associated party-political division.
Yet in many ways generational conflict was just as important, perhaps
more so. Formally, Weimar politics was supposed to operate along class
lines. Many of the most important parliamentary disputes of the 1920s
were between the Social Democrats, who thought of themselves as
representing the organized working class, and the People's Party, which
– despite its name – tended to be identified with industry. The National
People's Party was seen as the party of the Prussian aristocracy, while
the Democratic Party represented civil servants. Even the Centre Party
could be understood in class terms; although ostensibly a Catholic
party, it was disproportionately a party of peasants and artisans. Yet

on closer inspection the parties were not quite so neatly aligned with sociological strata. A large section of the working class (not forgetting a considerable number of intellectuals) were Communists. Middle-class Germans – businessmen, academics, professionals – could be found in all the so-called bourgeois parties; in itself, the fact that there were at least four of these suggests that class was not their organizing principle. Indeed, the striking thing about the sociological middle of German society in the 1920s was its political disintegration; a host of ephemeral splinter parties was one of the symptoms of Weimar's political malaise. When these political fragments were absorbed or supplanted by an altogether new kind of political party after 1929, it too defied class analysis. Calling itself a National Socialist German Workers' Party (NSDAP), it succeeded in attracting support from virtually every social group, including workers (only Catholics proved disproportionately resistant to the potent new political religion it purveyed).

To many contemporaries, this was one of the most attractive things about the Nazis – their ability to transcend social division. Another was their ability to mobilize new voters. Germans born after 1900 were significantly more likely to vote for Hitler in the decisive elections of 1930 and 1932 than those born before. Among the most potent leit-motifs of Nazi propaganda was that of Hitler as the youthful leader of a generational revolt against a senescent, degenerate system. It was a theme that resonated with many Germans in their twenties, who felt that altogether too much of the old, discredited Wilhelmine system had survived into the Weimar era. Though he recognized earlier than most what Nazism really signified, that theme undoubtedly struck a chord with Siegmund Warburg.

Perhaps Germany's generational conflicts would not have become so intense if the Weimar Republic had been able to deliver economic stability. It was not. There was an illusory quality to the relative stabilization of the mid-1920s in Germany. For one thing, the legacy of inflation was a lop-sided edifice of under-capitalized banks and over-capacity in heavy industry. German agriculture shared the pain of global deflation from the mid-1920s as prices of plentiful primary products drifted downwards. German industry found its profits eroded by rising labour costs as a highly unionized and politically protected workforce resisted downward shifts in nominal wages. The public sector was also constrained; national and international financial markets demanded high-risk premiums when they lent money to all levels of German government because of the persistent fear that new deficits might lead to another bout of inflation. Local authorities, for example, found it increasingly difficult to fund the public housing programmes that were such an important source of economic stimulus throughout inter-war Europe.[2] This made it much harder than many on the left ever grasped to realize their ambitious schemes for a Weimar welfare state.

For the central government in Berlin, the fiscal position was further constrained by the reimposition of reparations under the 1924 Dawes Plan, named after the American banker and later vice-president Charles G. Dawes. Although this rescheduled the payments Germany had to make, thereby reducing the short-term pressure on the budget, it did not reduce the total due, so that Germany remained saddled with a very large total debt burden. True, the annual reparations payments Germany had to make were not unmanageable as percentages of national income; on average they amounted to just 2 per cent between 1924 and 1930. However, relatively generous expenditures on domestic programmes and public sector salaries, combined with a general reluctance to raise taxation to pay for reparations, meant that the transfers had to be financed in large measure by borrowing. If the private sector had run a current account surplus, that might not have been too difficult. But throughout the 1920s, with continuing foreign discrimination against German manufactures, imports exceeded exports and, in the absence of any significant income from international investments, that meant that the German economy was dependent on foreign capital. In effect, the German government was paying reparations with hard currency borrowed from abroad.[3] With the new Reichsmark currency firmly pegged to the restored gold standard – in effect, tied inflexibly to an exchange rate of 4.20 Reichsmarks to the dollar – foreign investors were supposed to feel confident about putting their money into Germany. Only a few contemporaries understood that, if their confidence were for any reason to ebb, the German authorities would have to choose between deflation and default. They might even end up with both.

This nightmare might never have become a reality if German industry had managed to achieve sustained productivity growth, especially if this had translated into a rise in German exports (in particular to the United States). But businessmen felt weighed down by high taxes, high interest rates and high wages. They preferred to take refuge in price-fixing cartels or to plead for government subsidies or tariff protection. True, the 1920s saw a wave of industrial rationalization, in the form of mergers and other steps towards greater horizontal integration. Unfortunately, this tended to reduce competition rather than to enhance efficiency. Foreign investors started out with high hopes of rapid economic recovery based on the impressive pre-war performance of German industry. It dawned on them only gradually that the German economy of the 1920s was fundamentally sick. Long before the Wall Street Crash, which is usually seen as ushering in the Great Depression, the Weimar economy was ailing.[4]

It was therefore to a troubled Germany that Siegmund Warburg returned in early 1928.[5] He had left behind in New York a disquieting combination of family dissension and economic under-achievement. Unfortunately, what he found in Hamburg was worse. Inside the elegant panelled offices of M. M. Warburg & Co., Weimar's generational conflict would play itself out in microcosm.

Siegmund Warburg was not wholly pessimistic about Germany's chances of sustained recovery, despite the handicap imposed by reparations. Although 'occasional critical side-effects' were inevitable, he wrote in August 1927, he had confidence that Germany could 'in the long run further consolidate itself and make progress, and in the process continue to have the important help of foreign, particularly American, loans. Just as before the war the surplus of European money found an outlet in America, so today it will work the other way around between America and Europe.'[6] He had confidence in the Dawes Plan, because of its emphasis on currency stability; he simply could not conceive of circumstances in which 'collisions over reparations payments would be allowed to endanger the fulfilment of the obligations on the loans that Germany has concluded in the course of recent years with American and other foreign investors'.[7]

Yet Warburg was well aware that American confidence in Germany was in part a function of ignorance. In New York he had been struck by how 'remarkably optimistic' people were about the German currency; there was no real appreciation of the economy's underlying weaknesses. As he saw when he returned to Germany, 'the tax burdens [had] grown so enormous' that 'an accumulation of capital and thus of new means of production' had become 'practically impossible'; businessmen thought themselves lucky if they could just keep their heads above water.[8] In particular, Warburg worried about the mounting short-term foreign debts of German local authorities.[9] He was convinced that 'the profligate policy of the gentlemen currently in charge of the German Finance Ministry' would sooner or later 'lead to a grave crisis'. In his view, the German government would be much more likely to persuade the Western powers to reduce the reparations burden by cutting its own domestic expenditures, and aiming to pay reparations wholly out of budget surpluses. A policy of parsimony would make German pleas for reparations reduction 'plausible',[10] while at the same time providing encouragement to German business. 'The only people who would not welcome [such a policy] would be the particularistic beer-bench politicians who admittedly still rule Germany today, as logically corresponds to the political aptitude of the German nation.'[11] He pinned his hopes, in short, on a change in the direction of Reich fiscal policy.

As we have seen, it had been Warburg's hope that he would himself be able to contribute to this political change of direction. But increasingly his time was taken up by what amounted to a struggle for power within the family firm. The more serious the economic situation within Germany became, the more uneasy he felt about his uncle Max's leadership, which seemed to him altogether too optimistic in its assumptions and reckless in its direction. The problem was that Warburg was not in a strong position to mount a challenge against his uncle. He was, after all, the poor relation whom Max had, out of the goodness of his heart, invited to join the family firm. From the outset, he was treated as junior to Max's own son, Erich, who was promoted to the position of *Einzelprokurist* (in effect, senior manager) in 1927 and made a full partner in 1929. Siegmund was allowed to follow at a respectful distance, being appointed *Einzelprokurist* himself in 1929 and made a partner the following year.[12] Although he got on well with other senior managers at the bank – in particular Ernst Spiegelberg – nothing could overcome this subordination to the Hamburg branch of the family.

Siegmund Warburg's complaints about his uncle Max's managerial style prefigure much that he would later say about other institutions in the City of London; indeed, it is impossible to understand the later evolution of his own managerial style without appreciating what it was that he disliked about his uncle's (see the epigraph to this chapter). Previously, Carl Melchior had acted as a check on Max Warburg, but he was now increasingly preoccupied with political matters, and Spiegelberg was no substitute. Neither Aby S. nor Fritz was willing or able to stand up to the domineering Max. Nor was the anointed heir, Erich – 'a nice fellow', in Siegmund Warburg's opinion, 'but indescribably superficial'.[13] Among the senior managers, he had potential allies in Ludwig Rosenthal and Rudolf Brinckmann, but he regarded the more senior Hans Meyer as a mere sycophant who earned his generous bonuses simply by flattering the dominant partner. The result was an autocracy: the rule of 'Kaiser Maximilian'. Worse, it was an autocracy that remained fixated on the 'principles of the pre-war era . . . concentration on Hamburg and friendship with K[uhn] L[oeb]'.[14] This refusal to recognize that times had changed struck Warburg as the first sign of senility.[15] 'Kaiser' Max's 'grandiose words and gestures' were matched only by those of his intemperate nephew Jimmy ('Pasha James'), his 'parallel figure' in New York.[16]

The main bone of contention between Siegmund and Max Warburg was the question of whether to open a permanent office of M. M. Warburg & Co. in Berlin. In the younger man's view it was futile to deny the relative decline in Hamburg's importance as a financial centre, which the war had significantly accelerated. The biggest banks in Germany – the Deutsche Bank, the Disconto-Gesellschaft (which merged with the Deutsche Bank in 1929), the Dresdner Bank, the Danat Bank and the Berliner Handels-Gesellschaft, as well as the state-owned Reichs-Kredit-Gesellschaft – had, for all practical purposes, their head offices in Berlin. So did the biggest German industrial concerns. As a result, it was to Berlin that the American bankers interested in Germany sent their representatives. Warburg had encountered the same centralizing tendencies in both London and New York; they seemed to him irresistible. To carry on as before would therefore condemn M. M. Warburg & Co. to marginalization:

No amount of travelling back and forth will suffice, since as long as it is the peculiar pleasure of the Hamburg *Herren* to reduce the number of hours they spend in Berlin to a bare minimum, no really intimate relationship with the Berlin market can develop. Contact with a city is possible only if one really settles there for a certain amount of time and establishes a network there. Anything else is a half-measure, and half-measures are often worse than doing nothing at all.[17]

After much wrangling, Warburg was able to persuade the other partners to establish a Berlin office and to put him in charge of it. Yet his uncle continued to regard Hamburg business as the firm's principal concern, despite the fact that much of it was not even profitable. Meanwhile, he evinced more interest in Paris (where the bank maintained an expensive and, to the younger Warburg's mind, superfluous office) and in Amsterdam (where a subsidiary firm called Warburg & Co. had been set up after the war) than in Berlin. By 1930 Warburg was beside himself with frustration. In two strictly confidential letters to Lucien Nachmann at the International Acceptance Bank in New York, he denounced his uncle's mismanagement of the Hamburg firm in the strongest possible terms. Not only was the firm losing money on its core business; it urgently needed to sell its metal trading division and to increase the equity of the junior partners (he, Erich and Spiegelberg had just 5 per cent apiece). It was, he lamented, now essential:

to change our entire business policy, which unfortunately also means that Max M. W. must allow his personal thoughts of a dynastic character to recede somewhat into the background. Many of the changes . . . which I have discussed time and again with him and the other partners and which long ago could have been implemented, have been thwarted by him [alone]. Time and again he has taken it upon himself to grant new Hamburg credits, and opposed a reduction in the amount of securities we hold, despite the fact that we all have a larger portfolio of shares than corresponds to the firm's capital, so that we are practically maintaining part of it with borrowed money (which in my view is not a legitimate way of conducting business).[18]

Perhaps the most frustrating thing of all, from Warburg's point of view, was that he himself was actually making money for the firm, simply 'by refusing any second-class business and any long-term commitments' and concentrating on routine, short-term transactions with first-class Berlin clients such as Siemens.

Siegmund Warburg wrote this extraordinary indictment in September 1930.* By that time, however, it was already too late to avert disaster. Even before the Wall Street Crash which began on Black Thursday – 24 October 1929 – the German economy had already moved into recession. Unemployment had been rising since mid-1928. By September 1929 the German trade unions estimated that 14.5 per cent of German workers were jobless; a year later the unemployment rate stood at 24 per cent. Financial institutions had already been rocked by a stock-market slump as early as May 1928. In the course of that year there was a sharp drop in the rate of growth of currency in circulation, which turned negative in the third and fourth quarters. Events in the United States thus merely accelerated and exacerbated a German recession that had already begun.

II

It seems at first sight as if the present boom in America were due to last forever, but if one looks at it more closely, one discovers a lot of elements which contain several dangerous possibilities. As everyone knows, the resources of this country are enormous but I am afraid the skyscrapers of economical and financial kind which have been and are being built on the basis of these resources, are, in the long run, too high, and the top floors are being too heavily loaded. For instance, I think the loans given to the stock market are – even considering the American size of things – too big as such and in a much too large extent given simply for gambling purposes, both these points causing a situation which might easily lead to serious developments in the stock and money market.[19]

It was 26 December 1927 when Siegmund Warburg wrote those lines to Samuel Stephany, the general manager of the Rothschild bank in London. His fear that the stock-market boom he was witnessing was in fact a bubble that might end by bursting with 'volcanic' force was, as we know,

* The letter is so damning in its criticism of Max Warburg that as late as 1982 the bank's authorized historian thought it best to suppress it.

more than justified.[20] The difficulty, as he recognized, was to work out exactly when that crisis would come. 'It almost seems to me', he told his cousin Erich, 'as if the American economy, with the momentum generated from its huge reserves of resources and manpower, [could] roll on at the same tempo for some time, until, in a few years, it over-reaches itself . . .'[21] Nor was it easy to say what might prick the bubble, which was as inflated in the real estate market as it was in the stock market. During his time in the United States, Warburg carefully monitored a variety of different sectors and indicators for some harbinger of the crisis he feared. Might the tightening of restrictions on immigration perhaps be the fatal catalyst for a crash, by pushing up American labour costs?[22]

Siegmund was not the only Warburg to feel disquiet about the US economy in the late 1920s. Paul Warburg, too, foresaw the coming crash; indeed, Siegmund's own views in late 1927 were almost certainly an echo of his more experienced uncle's. In May 1929 his uncle Paul again voiced his anxiety about what he called 'the present orgy of speculation'. The Federal Reserve Board, he warned, was 'giving the country a demonstration of deplorable incapacity'. 'One cannot disregard every sound principle and practice of central banking', he declared, 'without ultimately paying the price for it. A system [that is] politically controlled and primarily governed by the desire to preserve business prosperity at all times is bound to lead to a disaster such as we have never witnessed before.'[23] Yet it was one thing to prophesy doom and urge a change of ways on his successors at the Federal Reserve; it was quite another to protect his own firm from the impending calamity. Although Paul Warburg reduced the exposure of the International Acceptance Bank somewhat in the course of 1929, it proved to be too little, too late. Siegmund Warburg later recalled the vital lesson he learned from his uncle Paul's hesitancy at this time. 'He became a great influence on me', reflected Warburg, 'not only for what he taught me consciously but even more for the fear instilled into me that I might share his fate and not follow my own good instincts.'[24]

As in the United States, so in Germany, it was the collapse of the banking system that transformed a deep recession into a catastrophic great depression. Historians generally date the German banking crisis from the summer of 1931, when the Danat Bank failed. That is certainly true with respect to the great banks centred in Berlin. However, there was a crisis before the crisis in Hamburg, and its principal victim was M. M. Warburg & Co.

It used to be assumed that the German banking crisis was caused by external pressures.[25] Some historians argued that it was the repatriation of American capital to the United States that was to blame; others that financial contagion spread to Germany from Austria following the failure of the Vienna Creditanstalt to publish its annual accounts – an effective admission of insolvency – in May 1931. However, more recent research has revealed that the German banking system was brought low as much, if not more, by internal factors. Investors in Germany – foreigners and Germans alike – had to weigh up three quite different but interrelated risks. The first was that the Reich government would be unable to meet its reparations payments, thereby precipitating an international crisis. The second was that the Reichsbank would be unable to maintain the convertibility of the German currency into gold, thereby trapping assets in marks that might one day be worthless. The third was that some or all German banks would be unable to repay money which had been deposited with them in any currency. It was far from easy to separate these dangers from one another.

According to one interpretation of what happened, the German banks themselves were vulnerable throughout the 1920s because their ratios of capital to assets were too low and their liquidity positions were too weak. Their balance sheets having been depleted by hyperinflation and currency reform, many banks had sought to restore their positions with short-term foreign currency deposits (from Germans as well as foreigners). By the end of June 1928, such dollar deposits accounted for 42 per cent of all deposits at the German credit banks.[26] The most reckless institutions in this regard were the big Berlin banks, especially those with countrywide networks of branches, which seem to have regarded themselves as too big to fail (in other words, they counted on the Reichsbank to bail them out in a crisis).[27] It was the withdrawal of a large proportion of their foreign deposits in the spring of 1931 that proved fatal. Initially this reflected fears of currency devaluation (the suspension of dollar convertibility) more than fears of bank insolvency. The Danat Bank was worst affected simply because it was most exposed to notoriously under-performing sectors like textiles, in particular the bankrupt Nordwolle company, and German municipalities. Although it was big, it turned out not to be too big to fail; the Reichsbank simply could not rescue it because its own hard-currency reserves had effectively run out; indeed, the drain on its reserves forced it to raise its discount rate, intensifying the already severe monetary squeeze. Only if the government had abandoned dollar convertibility at once – say on 4 July, rather than 15 July – could the Danat Bank have been saved. (Alternatively, only if the Reichsbank had ceased its preferential treatment of the big banks much earlier – in 1930 – might the dollar peg have been saved.) In other words, it was a general run on the German currency that led to a crisis affecting specific banks.

But what was the trigger for the crisis? Some have emphasized the German government's reparations declaration of 6 June 1931, which stated bluntly 'that the limits of what the German people can tolerate have been reached'.[28] Others have pointed to bad news about the Reich's fiscal position, which surfaced on 9 June.[29] Still others have blamed domestic political events, beginning with the governmental crisis of July 1930 and the election results two months later, which strengthened the power of the extremist parties in the Reichstag, and encouraged Chancellor Heinrich Brüning to pursue a more confrontational foreign policy.[30]

What has generally been overlooked is the fact that there was a dress rehearsal for the crisis that sank the Danat Bank in 1931, and it took place in Hamburg in the autumn of 1930. This should not surprise us. Private banks had been even more energetic than the great Berlin branch banks in accumulating foreign currency deposits; in December 1929, some 58 per cent of private bankers' total deposits were foreign.[31] Though precise figures are lacking, it seems likely that M. M. Warburg was in the vanguard of this trend. When bad political news in the second half of 1930 sent some foreign deposit holders scurrying for their money, M. M. Warburg was especially badly affected. In the last week of 1930, a run on the bank forced the repayment of 80 per cent of its foreign and 50 per cent of its domestic deposits. It became clear very quickly indeed that the Hamburg bank could not survive without substantial assistance from Max Warburg's American relatives, specifically Paul and his son Jimmy. By October, Max was planning a visit to New York where he evidently intended to appeal for fraternal assistance. Before he could set off, however, Paul's son Jimmy arrived in Hamburg. It seems reasonable to assume that he knew at least something of what Siegmund had told Nachmann in his letter of the previous month.

For Siegmund Warburg, it was vital to exploit the weakness of his uncle Max's position to impose long-overdue changes on the Hamburg bank. 'What makes this difficult to achieve', as he put it revealingly, 'is that in this case we face the challenge of bringing about reassessments without letting those who are supposed to make these reassessments realize that they have been persuaded to make them by the younger generation, or one member of it.'[32] No less problematic was the fact that so much responsibility now devolved on Jimmy, in whom Siegmund had relatively little confidence. He tried to explain to the American what he saw as the key reforms needed at M. M. Warburg:

1) Concentration of our firm on the big industrial transactions, which means e.g. sending, if possible, two partners to Berlin
2) Hiving off the metal business and Paris office etc. [and] clearer division of responsibilities
3) Somewhat less of a dynastic style and rational capitalist expansion.[33]

In the few moments the two young men had alone together, Siegmund sought to reassure Jimmy that Germany and the family firm were not lost causes. In particular, he endeavoured to convince him of the 'enormous strength in terms of life and ideas that there is still in Germany, which, if all post-war questions are finally nearing a solution, will give Germany even more of a leading role in Europe than in the past'.[34] It seems doubtful that Jimmy was persuaded by this. For reasons that are unclear, Siegmund chose this moment to leave Hamburg for a family holiday in his beloved South Germany. In the diary that he began writing in the tranquillity of Heilbronn, on the banks of the River Neckar, Warburg reiterated his conviction that 'the younger generation' at the bank was 'significantly better able to deal with the situation than the older'. But he worried that 'under the pressure of the current nervousness something over-hasty might be done,' because 'the firm's nervousness is typically momentary rather than long term.'[35]

Whatever was agreed between Max and Jimmy during Siegmund's

absence, it did not suffice. The collapse of the Creditanstalt five months later was very nearly the last straw for M. M. Warburg. It is true that, on the whole, financial links between Austria and Germany were limited. But Max Warburg was on the Creditanstalt's supervisory board.[36] As we have seen, his bank had long been a part of the Rothschilds' European network, of which the Creditanstalt was a major offshoot. The Austrian government's rescue operation, which effectively nationalized the Creditanstalt, could not prevent the Warburg bank from suffering substantial losses. Nor was this the bank's only problem. When Jimmy Warburg returned to Hamburg in June 1931 – the month before the collapse of the Danat Bank – he found a cumulative deficit of more than $3.5 million (15 million marks), with bad debts ranging from loans to the bankrupt Karstadt department store to a 5.8 million mark credit to the Hamburg state that seemed unlikely to be repaid.[37] According to his calculations, the Hamburg firm required $7–9 million (29–38 million marks) to clear all its debts.[38] Although the American was inclined to let his uncle Max go under, blaming him for irresponsible management, the situation was saved by the German government, which offered a payment of 30 million marks to avoid what it feared might be a collapse of the entire Hanseatic banking system.[39] Had this not been done, in other words, the German banking crisis would have begun a month earlier, with the collapse of M. M. Warburg.[40]

Why was it possible to save Max Warburg but not Jakob Goldschmidt? Viewing events from New York, Jimmy Warburg could not understand why the government did not intervene to bail out Goldschmidt's Danat Bank as it had rescued the Warburg bank.[41] In his memoirs, he claimed that his father had offered to assist the German government in bailing out the Danat, but this offer was declined by Chancellor Brüning, for fear of revealing the fact that one of the bank's biggest non-performing loans was to Oskar von Hindenburg, the son of the Reich President.[42] However, evidence to support this claim is scanty. A more straightforward explanation is that the Danat Bank, far from being too big to fail, was too big to save once the Reichsbank's dollar reserves began to run out in July. The Hamburg bank survived because its crisis came while the Reich was still in a position to finance a bailout. It was also (like the Creditanstalt in Vienna) able to call on the resources of wealthy foreign relations; just as the London and Paris

Rothschilds saved the Creditanstalt (and the Vienna Rothschilds, who might otherwise have gone down with it), so Paul and Jimmy Warburg's International Acceptance Bank helped to keep M. M. Warburg afloat. In any case, it is hard to believe that Paul Warburg was in a position to help rescue the enormous and insolvent Danat Bank. For his own firm, the International Acceptance Bank, was itself in serious difficulties by 1931. As Siegmund Warburg later recalled, his uncle found himself in the position of many banks engaged in international trade in the summer of 1931; he could not find buyers for a large portfolio of commercial bills he had discounted. As a result, he had to 'go cap in hand to the Chase National Bank to ask them to take his acceptances into their portfolios'. For such a proud and rigorous man it was 'the gravest possible humiliation'. He suffered a stroke that same summer, the first of a succession that finally killed him in the winter of 1932. 'I had never seen a sadder person than Paul Warburg in the last months of his life,' Siegmund Warburg recollected many years after the event. 'His lasting legacy to me is that his example made me much more stubborn in not allowing myself to be talked around by others.'[43]

Siegmund Warburg's verdict on the events that very nearly destroyed his family's financial empire was not untypical of the era. The crisis, he came to believe, was a consequence of the self-indulgence of the older generation. Writing in the diary that he kept intermittently during the upheavals of the early 1930s, he was unsparing in his criticism. Once, in the early 1920s, he had 'looked forward with proud confidence to having a significant career in the firm that bore [our] name, always regarding the firm not as an instrument for making money, but as an important and constructive part of the German and world economy and community'. Only gradually had 'shadows' fallen on this brilliant and inspiring vision:

On one side these shadows consisted of the inability of the older generation to adjust to the altered circumstances, an inability that became ever more apparent to me, the more the deepening crisis caused by Brüning's deflationary policies affected the firm; on the other side the shadows consisted of the symptoms of decadence . . . of the wider family, particularly those branches of it that were closely linked to the firm.[44]

In particular, Warburg condemned the 'mixture of personal, familial matters with objective business matters' which had led to 'the wrong measures and the wrong policy for the firm for purely personal reasons, misplaced respect out of family piety [and] unnecessary interference from dissatisfied women' (it is not clear which of his female relatives he had in mind): 'In short, a combination of all the bad characteristics of a decadent dynasty: Byzantinism, lack of reverence for honesty and honour ... the success of flattery, bogus sympathy with hollow weakness, theatricality and insincerity, artificiality and a hothouse atmosphere.'[45]

Yet the principal cause of the firm's downfall, Warburg came to believe, was nothing more or less than his uncle Max's jealousy. Again, he drew a parallel between Max Warburg and the last Kaiser, 'particularly in his weakness for petty flatterers, in his way of linking everything to his own personality and vanity, in his superficial optimism'.[46] Unlike Wilhelm II, however, 'Kaiser' Max was afflicted by a 'boundless jealousy' – a suspicion of any challenge not only to his own dominance but also to the intended succession of his son Erich. As Warburg now realized, he himself had posed just such a challenge:

Over the years I had built an increasingly strong position in the firm. After I had, with so much difficulty, extricated myself from Hamburg and secured the expansion of the Berlin office, many important negotiations tended to pass into my hands, including ultimately the expansion of our foreign network once Berlin had become the decisive support for Hamburg. While all this was happening, Max struggled painfully to retain the leadership of the firm for himself and his son, without noticing that it had long ago slipped away from him. The son, by temperament reliable and good-humoured but ineffectual, was pushed by his father and as a result developed into a twisted individual, who wanted and tried to do great things that were beyond his abilities ... All of this within a dynasty whose decadence also manifested itself in the way that all employees had lost the drive of their own, independent personalities.[47]

This was a damning judgement on the relatives who had plucked him out of Swabian obscurity.

Warburg's critique of his own family was certainly heartfelt; but was it fair? In effect, he was blaming nearly all the bank's difficulties on his uncle's character defects. That surely underestimated the role of the immense political and economic shocks that had been inflicted on the entire German banking system. Warburg had the young man's confidence that he could do a better job. Yet he would never again, in all his long career, have to contend with a financial crisis on this scale. It is far from certain that M. M. Warburg would have come through 1930 unscathed even if the leadership had been concentrated entirely in his hands.

III

The German banking crisis killed not only the Danat Bank; it also killed the post-war system of reparations. On 20 June 1931 President Herbert Hoover proposed a moratorium on all war debts and reparations claims. A month later, an international conference in London recommended a freeze on all foreign loans to Germany; by September, 'standstill agreements' had been concluded with Germany's principal creditors.[48] To those who believed that reparations were the Weimar Republic's biggest problem, these developments should have constituted a major victory. Yet the government's diplomatic success was far outweighed by the economic havoc that deflation was now wreaking. As consumer prices plummeted – the rate of annual inflation reached minus 12 per cent in the summer of 1932 – so too did output and employment. German industrial production in 1932 was less than 60 per cent of its 1929 level. New housing construction was down by 56 per cent, shipbuilding by 83 per cent. By July of that year, 49 per cent of trade union members were unemployed. Using a standardized measure that allows cross-country comparisons, the unemployment rate in Germany for the entire civilian workforce was around 37 per cent, even higher than in the United States (34 per cent). This was why getting rid of reparations did not save Weimar. Indeed, the dismantling of the economic provisions of the Versailles Treaty turned out to make the destruction of the Republic easier. As Harold James has put it, reparations turned out to have been a kind of 'bracket' that had been holding German democracy together. With reparations gone, those who called for repudiation of *all* the provisions of the Versailles Treaty gained credibility.

Was the catastrophic deflation of 1931 and 1932 inevitable? Perhaps.[49] However, it has also been suggested that alternative policies might have mitigated the crisis. If the government had not tried to balance the budget with tax increases and swingeing cuts in expenditure, but had instead run large deficits, demand might have fallen less steeply. Alternatively, if the government had abandoned the gold standard earlier, the Reichsbank might have been able to act more effectively as lender of last resort to the banking system.[50] This was Siegmund Warburg's position at the time. Just as he felt he could have managed the affairs of M. M. Warburg & Co. more effectively than his older relatives, so too he believed that he could have managed the German economy better than Chancellor Brüning and his ministers. For Warburg had not lost sight of his political ambitions in the course of the 1920s. Indeed, one of the reasons he pressed so hard to establish a Berlin branch of M. M. Warburg was to give himself more time in the capital, whither political life had returned after the brief revolutionary interlude in sleepy Weimar. During the tumultuous years between 1929 and 1933, he was in frequent contact with the Republic's leading politicians: not only Chancellor Brüning himself, but also Hermann Müller, the Social Democrat whom Brüning had replaced in March 1930; Gustav Stresemann, the long-serving People's Party Foreign Minister whose untimely death in October 1929 was such a heavy blow to the Weimar system; his successor Julius Curtius; and Gottfried Treviranus, who served as Brüning's minister for the occupied territories and then his minister for transport. 'I am convinced', he later recalled, 'that if . . . Germany had developed as a healthy republic I would have gone into politics. As late as 1932 and the first weeks of 1933 I would say that I still saw myself as a young man [he had only just turned thirty] preparing to enter politics.'[51]

What exactly were Warburg's politics at this critical time? He appears to have favoured the shift to presidential government that occurred with the appointment of Brüning as Reich chancellor, since he 'wrote several memoranda at that time advocating the necessity of a Presidential rather than a Parliamentarian constitution for the Weimar Republic'.[52] He understood very well that the more Brüning invoked the President's emergency powers to enact legislation, the less parliamentary the Weimar system became. He was enough of a Weberian not to worry about this. Nevertheless, he was critical of the specific measures Brüning chose to adopt. Warburg had, in his own words, 'very definite views as to those who were dealing with matters at the top, and . . . strongly criticized [Finance Minister Hermann] Dietrich as being much too slow in applying the necessary remedies'. In his diary entry for 30 September 1930, Warburg spelt out what he had in mind: 'The government could now do much to calm the situation – and even to build up its popular support – by enacting measures that were speedy, forceful and far-sighted (in this respect the Soviet 5-Year Plan is a brilliant model, given the current popular mood), even if some of these measures . . . should actually prove to be harmful from an object-ive standpoint.' However, he went on, 'the bureaucracy does not know the necessary tone of political fanfare, and unfortunately Brüning is also a bad trumpeter, with no sense of direction or pathos.'[53]

If that seems remarkably strident language for a liberal banker, the next day's entry was more moderate, and even technocratic in tone. Contemplating the government's latest fiscal proposals, he complained that they made the mistake 'common to all German politics at the moment of only doing the absolutely necessary, only seeking to mitigate evils, rather than wanting to create something new'.[54] Why was the government cutting civil servants' salaries by 20 per cent (for senior civil servants) and 6 per cent (for their juniors), instead of by 25 per cent and 10 per cent respectively? His fear, as he told his father-in-law in a letter written three weeks later, was that these measures, combined with the loan that had been secured from the US bank Lee Higginson, would provide the government with only a temporary reprieve from its fiscal problems – only a 'bridging loan, that once again stops a hole in our budget, but without coming to grips with the various kernels of the evil'. This seems very different from the 'rather Keynesian' recommenda-tions he subsequently claimed he had made to the Reichsbank President Hans Luther.[55] In short, Warburg was acutely aware of the weakness of the Brüning government's position, while at the same time sharing that growing thirst for radical measures which was manifesting itself through-out German society, not least among younger voters. As he put it, ominously: 'Only when the highly unpopular laws for the reduction of the civil servants' salaries and the separation of the unemployment insur-ance fund from the Reich budget come to the Reichstag in the course of December will it be decided how far the parliamentary system will endure.'[56] The inability of the government to secure a parliamentary majority for its measures forced it to rely, with increasing frequency, on the power of the President, under article 48 of the Reichstag constitution, to promulgate laws as emergency edicts.

The puzzling thing is that Warburg nevertheless remained remarkably confident – even complacent – about the possible consequences of a shift from parliamentary rule to presidential rule. As he later recalled,

... I saw the crisis as one which would leave the political organism relatively unchanged and I certainly did not expect the degree of change which did ensue ... I imagined that the Weimar Republic would come through all these crises and that there would be a reformed Republic similar to that of France. I realized the dangers but probably indulged in easy optimism. I did not conceive that the Nazis would be totally victorious.[57]

In later life, he would be scathing in his condemnation of the politicians of the late Weimar period, not least Brüning. He later referred to the 'Brüning time' as a period of 'half-hearted compromises [by] the young leading minds who did not want to take decisions either in the interest of national unity or in order to prevent worse things happening – with the result that they compromised themselves and what was worse compromised the whole cause for which they stood'.[58] The Weimar era, he remarked in 1974, was a time when Germany was 'led by a mixture of well-meaning mediocrities and weak-minded crooks and above all when the aims which were pursued were based not on a cold, sober assessment of the facts but on wishful thinking or, one should rather say, on wishful non-thinking'.[59] Yet, as we shall see, he himself was not immune to the temptations of radical solutions at this time. In his private diary, he lamented what he saw as 'patently obvious degeneration in the intellect and above all the character of the German bourgeoisie'.[60] 'The middle is too moderate,' he reflected, paradoxically. 'It is lacking, not in insight and certainly not in subtlety, but in radical will':

Unfortunately ... National Socialism has by contrast the strongest radical will, combined with an equally large lack of insight and subtlety. How well the middle ground and fascism could complement one another, and yet how much they block one another's way! It is the recurrent tragedy of life, that polar opposites could complement one another so well, but so seldom produce strong sparks of power from the fruitful tension between them.[61]

Such dialectical reflections were soon to be exposed as mere whimsy, as Germany was pushed, step by fateful step, from presidential rule to lawless dictatorship. His dissatisfaction with the shortcomings of the older generation had led Warburg to underestimate disastrously the 'radical will' that was Adolf Hitler.

4

Exile

*One often heard his voice on the radio. He seemed to me to be
a strange mixture of a sadist and a fanatic of the worst kind, a
man incorporating narrow-mindedness, a madman, and it was
incomprehensible to me that he would have such a following.
I knew no-one who belonged to the Nazi party. After he had
come to power ... and been in office a few weeks I had a sudden*
volte face, *but most of my friends and colleagues did not wake
up to the dangers until much later in the thirties. Indeed I was
the only one in the Hamburg firm to do so.*

Siegmund Warburg, 1976[1]

I

On 4 March 1933 Siegmund Warburg was struck by a remarkable
political coincidence. On the same day that Franklin D. Roosevelt
delivered his first inaugural address as president in Washington DC,
another newly elected political leader gave a speech to another nation
mired in the depths of the Depression. The second leader was Adolf
Hitler and his speech – a pre-election broadcast on national radio –
though in some respects surprisingly similar to Roosevelt's in its content,
differed profoundly in its tone. Warburg was struck by the 'peculiar
contrast between Hitler's sentimentality and pathos, on the one hand,
and Roosevelt's matter-of-fact way of speaking' on the other. Perhaps,
he reflected, 'this contrast at the same time revealed something about
the differing characters of the [American and German] people's communities [*Volksgemeinschaften*]'. Strangely, he found himself wondering

whether or not '*sub specie aeternitatis* the sentimentality of a Hitler was superior to the prosaic style of a Roosevelt'.[2]

Given all that we know about what happened after 1933, it may seem extraordinary that a highly educated German Jew could even pose such a question or, for that matter, unconsciously adopt the terminology of National Socialism in doing so. But this merely illustrates how very hard it is to recapture the profound uncertainties felt by contemporaries as the Nazi seizure of power was unfolding in Germany. With the benefit of hindsight, we can see that Hitler's appointment as Reich chancellor was an event pregnant with future calamity not just for Germany but for the world – and particularly for the Jews of Europe. And we can see that, for all the radicalism of Roosevelt's rhetoric (which explicitly blamed the Depression on unscrupulous financiers and threatened to override the power of Congress to combat the economic emergency), his New Deal posed no meaningful threat to individual liberty in the United States. At the time, however, it was not so easy to anticipate the profound difference between New Deal and New Order. Even those who stood to lose the most from Nazi rule – wealthy German Jews like the Warburg family – did not grasp immediately the threat that Hitler represented. On the contrary, they believed their wealth, social status and, above all, their sincere patriotism would protect them.

In electoral terms, the rise of the Nazis was truly meteoric. In the last general election before the Depression struck, held in May 1928, the National Socialist German Workers' Party had won a meagre 2.4 per cent of the popular vote, entitling it to just twelve Reichstag seats. In September 1930 the Nazis won 18.5 per cent of the vote and 107 seats. Less than two years later they won just under 38 per cent of all the votes cast and became at a stroke the biggest party in the Reichstag with no fewer than 230 seats. At this point it became very difficult indeed to deny them the opportunity to form a government, though the cabal around President von Hindenburg strove for the rest of that year to do precisely that. By January 1933, however, all the available alternatives appeared to have been exhausted. The successive attempts by Heinrich Brüning, Franz von Papen and General Kurt von Schleicher to govern without Reichstag majorities on the basis of presidential emergency powers had foundered. On 30 January 1933 Hitler was finally sworn in as chancellor at the head of a coalition government of Nazis and German Nationalists.

Historians traditionally see the Depression as the principal cause of this political earthquake. Between 1929 and 1932, as we have already seen, German economic output fell by around 23 per cent in real terms. The inflation rate plunged from around 4 per cent to minus 12 per cent. Employment fell by 37 per cent. The number of registered unemployed soared from less than one and a quarter million to more than six million.[3] In the face of this economic earthquake the Weimar system had seemed impotent. Indeed, the deflationary policies that were adopted merely served to worsen the crisis. The democratic system itself began to crumble under the strain, so that more and more legislation after 1929 was enacted by emergency decree; it might be said that Hitler's was the fourth dictatorial government since 1930. Yet the historical puzzle remains: why did the Depression in Germany produce the Third Reich, while other countries which were just as hard hit managed to retain democratic government and the rule of law? The rate of unemployment was nearly as high in the United States as in Germany in 1932; yet Americans voted for Roosevelt, who passed only two minor constitutional amendments in his twelve years as president, while Germans voted for Hitler, who overthrew not only the Weimar constitution but also the longer-established rule of law, deprived Germans of their political and civil rights, persecuted the Jews and other minority groups to the point of exterminating them and unleashed the most destructive war of modern times.

One clue to why the German reaction to the Depression was so much more radical than the American is offered by the remarkable private diary kept by Siegmund Warburg during the decisive period of the Nazi seizure of power. The diary is a tantalizing document because at some time after its composition an unknown hand carefully removed certain lines and sometimes entire paragraphs with a knife or scalpel. Yet enough has survived to provide a unique insight into the Nazi takeover of power as it was experienced by a highly intelligent and articulate member of the German-Jewish elite.

II

It might be thought that Siegmund Warburg had ample reason to be pessimistic about the implications of Hitler's appointment as chancellor. Repeatedly during the 1920s, proto-Nazi organizations in Hamburg like the German Popular (Deutschvölkische) Party, the Hammer League (Hammerbund) or the League for Protective and Offensive Action (Schutz- und Trutzbund) had attacked his uncle Max for his role in the Versailles peace negotiations.[4] As early as May 1919, there had been a scuffle at the Hamburg Stock Exchange when a member of the Schutz- und Trutzbund began handing out anti-Semitic leaflets.[5] Max Warburg was driven to sue two right-wing newspapers for libel – one of them the Nazi *Völkischer Beobachter* – but this brought scant redress. In 1922 his name appeared on a list of prominent Jews drawn up by the merged German Popular Protection League (Deutschvölkische Schutz- bund), along with those of the Foreign Minister Walther Rathenau, who was shot dead as he drove through the streets of Berlin that July, and the journalist Maximilian Harden, who only narrowly survived an assassination attempt.[6] Max Warburg was advised by the police to move house and was provided with a bodyguard, but thought it best to withdraw from public life altogether and go abroad, first to Holland (under an alias) and then to the United States, where he spent several months lying low.[7] Although there was little Hanseatic support for the National Socialists' abortive coup (the so-called Beerhall Putsch) launched in Munich on 8 November 1923,[8] Max Warburg was suffi- ciently concerned once again to leave Hamburg for New York until the crisis blew over.[9] He gave up attending the synagogue, confining himself to private worship.[10] It is against this background that we should understand Siegmund Warburg's resolve to enter politics. It was a brave ambition.

For most of the 1920s support for the radical right was confined to relatively small social groups. Yet from an early stage there were signs that National Socialist ideas were also capable of penetrating the main- stream Weimar parties. In Hamburg the Pan-German League and the newly formed German National People's Party (DNVP) both adopted anti-Semitic stances in the hope of attracting votes.[11] When Max

Warburg appealed to Friedrich von Loebell, the founder of the conservative Reich Citizens' Council (Reichsbürgerrat), to resist anti-Semitism
in the DNVP, Loebell demurred, arguing that 'a clear position against
anti-Semitism could easily call forth opposition and division . . . among
us.'[12] Although the Hamburg branch of the German People's Party
(DVP) was prepared openly to disavow anti-Semitism, Warburg could
not persuade the party's leader Gustav Stresemann to make a similar
statement at the national level because of anti-Semitic tendencies in
the party's South German branches.[13]

At a meeting of Hamburg business associations in March 1919,
Max Warburg insisted that a 'nationally minded' Jew could 'uphold
German national identity [*das nationale Deutschtum*]' while at the
same time 'striving for a cosmopolitan bourgeoisie, compatible with
this national identity', though he gave some ground to the right by
accepting their 'clear distinction between the German Jews resident
here' and *Ostjuden* – Jews who had immigrated to Germany from
Eastern Europe.[14] This was not a distinction that greatly interested the
extreme right. In the immediate aftermath of Rathenau's murder,
Warburg struggled to make sense of their undifferentiated hostility to
all Jews:

All the dissatisfied, indeed desperate circles, in whom only need and hopeless-
ness are visible, are becoming desperadoes. It is this desperation . . . which
brings forth such acts. In the parental home, hatred is preached; the family
has ceased to be a place of tranquillity, but [has become] the source of false
doctrine. Into all this anti-Semitism comes naturally, since the misguided desire
to help [matters], to change [matters] and to agitate all too readily turns on
the minority. Finally of course there is the Peace of Versailles – but that is
merely a secondary factor – [and] the demagogy of [Karl] Helfferich and
comrades [on the right wing of the DNVP], who turn the heads of the young.

It was not just, he told his friend Lili du Bois-Reymond, 'the security
of the individual which is at stake, but [also] the danger that, unless
there is not now a decided change, Germany will permanently sink
into the second class, the class of pogrom countries'.[15] In a public letter
of protest, he stressed the link between anti-Semitism and 'the barbar-
ity of the East', warned against 'the mentality of civil war' and
painstakingly sought to dispel anti-Semitic myths like the 'stab in the

back' legend, which blamed Germany's military defeat in 1918 on Jews who had fomented revolution at home.[16]

The difficulty about mobilizing opposition to anti-Semitism outside the relatively small Hamburg Jewish community was that the radical right simply did not pose a direct threat to the non-Jewish majority of the Hamburg Establishment. When anti-Semitic gangs invaded the city's wealthy West End in 1932, vandalizing the Rotherbaum synagogue,[17] it seemed much less alarming to rich Gentiles than the proletarian invasion of Harvestehude they had experienced during the socialist revolution of late 1918. In any case, the bitter arguments over war aims and peace aims between 1914 and 1918 had already brought Gentile Hamburg businessmen like Richard Krogmann, Hermann Blohm and Max von Schinckel into contact with proto-fascist elements in the newly created Fatherland Party.[18] Similarly, whereas Max Warburg had taken a more or less accommodating attitude to the events of 1918–19, for the likes of Krogmann, Blohm and Schinckel there could be no question of compromise with the 'November criminals' of Weimar. Their exclusive Hamburg National Club of 1919 was an explicitly counter-revolutionary, ultra-nationalist entity.

In many ways, it is true, the elite right and the petty-bourgeois right remained distinct. The local Nazi Party regarded itself as, and in many ways was, an anti-bourgeois party, seeking to mobilize the young and the unemployed, as well as workers, public employees, shopkeepers and artisans, against 'the present liberal-capitalist economic way of life, personified by the entrepreneur'.[19] Although the Nazis secured a high percentage of votes in the wealthy neighbourhoods of Harvestehude and Rotherbaum,[20] close scrutiny reveals that most of the West End's Nazi votes came from lower-income groups living on the less prosperous periphery of the relevant electoral districts. However, the Nazi leadership soon learned to temper the radicalism of the party's rank-and-file activists in order to woo Germany's social elites. As early as 1924 the Hamburg Pan-German League joined electoral forces with the NSDAP. Two years later Hitler was invited for the first time to speak at the National Club.[21] When he addressed the Club again in 1929 he made a point of portraying the party as a 'force for order'. There is evidence that donations began to be made to the Nazis by a number of Hamburg firms at around this time.[22] More importantly, the Hamburg elite began to take the Nazis seriously as potential political partners. The Hapag director and ex-Chancellor Wilhelm Cuno hoped that Hitler would help him relaunch his own political career.[23] In 1932 four members of the Hamburg Chamber of Commerce came out openly in support of Hitler, arguing for a power-sharing agreement between him, Hindenburg and the DNVP leader Alfred Hugenberg.[24] This idea of co-opting the Nazis into a conservative government (in the expectation that power would temper their radicalism) seems also to have motivated another group of Hamburg businessmen who joined Wilhelm Keppler's circle of economic advisers to Hitler.[25] These men do not seem to have been committed Nazi Party members; rather they saw themselves as dealing with the 'counter-revolution', much in the way that the business community had dealt with the 1918 socialist revolution, seeking as far as possible to insulate Hamburg's economy from the vagaries of popular politics. For others, however, support for the Nazis, particularly once Hitler became chancellor, was more than instrumental. Many, particularly in the younger generation, saw the regime change as an opportunity to return to Hamburg's pre-war glory days of navy-building and colonial trade.[26] Some hoped for a restoration of the Wilhelmine social order; others looked forward to a Nazi cultural revolution that would rejuvenate Germany more than it would turn the clock back. Only a tiny minority within the Hamburg Establishment correctly discerned that the 'national revolution' of 1933 posed a much more serious threat to the city's traditional polity than had the socialist revolution of fourteen years before.[27]

III

Especially in view of his uncle's experiences in the early 1920s, Siegmund Warburg might have been expected to be among the members of that prescient anti-Nazi minority. But he was not. Indeed, the fascinating thing is to find how far – albeit only for a brief period – he was actually tempted to join his Gentile contemporaries in the business community in welcoming the Nazi victory. As early as September 1930 (having won a bet on the outcome of that month's general election), Warburg argued that it would be 'right to let the "Radikalinskis" of the right into the government, as did the Labour Party so much good in England. Once they are in government, they will immediately become, first, more sensible and, secondly, once again less popular.'[28] Warburg believed 'entirely in the possibility of slowly making the National Socialists more sensible. Our Social Democrats were also once irresponsible demagogues and have today nearly all become bourgeois and willing to compromise.'[29] He did not readily abandon these deeply misleading analogies. As he later admitted, though he had read *Mein Kampf*, he 'did not think it contained a possible programme for Germany'. He had been 'foolish and complacent' enough to believe that the regime 'would not last'.[30]

To be sure, Warburg understood well enough that Hitler's appointment as Reich chancellor was a moment fraught with peril, not least for German Jews. It was on 27 February 1933 – less than a month after Hitler had been sworn in and just a week before the new election called by the self-styled Führer – that Warburg decided to begin keeping a diary of 'the huge political upheavals of the last few weeks, which must be especially moving for a Jewish German and above all for one such as myself, who feels his entire being to be inextricably rooted in Germandom'.[31] That very night a deranged Dutch Communist bricklayer named Marinus van der Lubbe set fire to the Reichstag building. Alleging that this arson attack had been the opening gambit of a Communist coup, the Nazis swiftly proclaimed a state of emergency and rounded up the leaders of the German Communist Party, while at the same time imposing a two-week ban on all left-wing newspapers, including the Social Democrats'. This meant that the elections of 5 March were far from free and fair.[32] Under the terms of the sweeping emergency decree to which Hindenburg gave his assent, the NSDAP and their brown-shirted auxiliaries were able to intimidate their opponents with impunity, while at the same time dominating the German media. Warburg knew full well that Hitler was already abusing his power as chancellor. He never lost sight of the key question: 'How will things turn out with the anti-Semitism of the new leadership?'[33] Yet to a remarkable extent he was willing to give the new regime the benefit of the doubt. Why was this?

On the evening of 4 March 1933 Warburg heard Hitler speak (possibly for the first time) on the radio. His reaction was revealingly ambivalent. The first half of the speech struck him as 'demagogic, attacking his opponents, basely polemical to the point of sadism'; but the second was 'cleanly idealistic, powerfully proactive, delivered with authentic inspiration and an unbounded will for action'.[34] It is evident from other diary entries at this time that some elements of Hitler's message were ringing true with Warburg, who had become preoccupied with the need for radical reform in Germany to address the manifest defects of inter-war capitalist society. His reaction to the Nazis' election victory was also ambivalent. Historians are inclined to be dismissive of the result, which gave the Nazis just under 44 per cent of the popular vote, as if nothing short of an absolute majority could be regarded as a true victory (particularly given the advantages enjoyed by the government parties). But by Weimar standards, as Warburg noted, this was a victory 'beyond all expectations'. Admittedly, it was 'a victory which had unfortunately been achieved with many abuses and acts of terror, with lies and evil promises to [the] masses'. Yet it was also 'a victory in which one must acknowledge the idealistic forces which above all have brought it about'. And 'the idealistic forces [had] proved to be stronger in the Nazi movement than the petty, human admixture':

If one were to seek a deeper historical explanation for this election result, it is the struggle between the dynamism of one side and the sluggishness of the others. Youth and ardour were on the side of dynamism – the bourgeoisie of the trade unions, the post-war bureaucracy and the business barons stood on the other side. The bourgeoisie in their indolence wanted [to preserve] their interests, their money, their comfort; they had prudence and experience on their side, but neither the decisive analysis nor the self-sacrificing will to fight evinced by their opponents. Dynamism has won and now must show what it can do. The prospects are good . . .[35]

In other words, the Nazis' promise of a social revolution resonated with Warburg, who had for so long been frustrated by the complacency of Hamburg's bourgeois society, exemplified by the older members of his family.

Remarkably, Warburg even discerned a possibility that the new regime might allow the German Jews to set their own house in order, just as it was shaking up middle-class Germany as a whole. Had not the Jews been among the leading lights of the 'decadent German bourgeoisie', who had relished bourgeois society precisely because it allowed them to combine 'an aptitude for accommodation with . . . spiritual glibness and eclecticism' – because it allowed them to answer questions 'not with "yes" or "no" but with the proverbial "maybe"?'[36] Might not this change of regime be an opportunity for those other Jews (Warburg evidently had himself in mind) who were 'capable of sharply distinguishing between "yes" and "no", between avowal and denial'?

Perhaps the coming man is now precisely this type among both Aryan and Jewish Germans – a Jewish German of this type can therefore rightly say that he would be a Nazi if it weren't for the Nazis' anti-Semitism. And at the same time he is almost thankful for this very anti-Semitism, because it purges those around him of pride, frivolity and equivocation, it creates what we need more than anything else – a dynamism among those people who have had enough of played-out problems and exhausted strength.[37]

For Warburg, the 'national revolution' seemed like an opportunity for the 'socially critical, socially revolutionary, energetic and idealistic' individuals among German Jews to distance themselves from the 'bourgeois, liberal opportunists' who seemed to predominate in their community.[38]

Above all, what Warburg found hard to resist was Hitler's fervent promise of national redemption. The Nazis understood well how to cast Hitler as the heir to Bismarck and, harking back even further in German history, to cast themselves as the harbingers of a new Reform Era. To anyone whose youth had been steeped, as Siegmund Warburg's had been, in the overblown nationalism of the late Wilhelmine period, this was powerfully attractive. In the days after the election, Warburg read with approval Arthur Moeller van den Bruck's seminal book *The Third Reich*, applauding its appeal for the 'extension of the national ethos as the basis of all life as opposed to thoughts of the individual or humanity as a whole'.[39] He eagerly speculated about 'fascistic rather than bourgeois' solutions to, for example, the vexed question of Franco-German relations.[40] And what of the Nazis' anti-Semitism? National Socialism, he mused, was a political parvenu and 'even from the best parvenu one should not demand good manners to begin with, but simply vitality, strength, a willingness to advance and construct'. Hitler's racism was like the vulgarity of a social parvenu, a phase that would pass.[41] Here, as in so many other ways, Warburg (and the circle of kindred spirits with whom he shared such ideas) fundamentally misunderstood the nature of the new regime. He hoped for a generational revolt of the young and dynamic against the old and stuffy, whereas the principal role Hitler had in mind for German youth turned out to be that of cannon fodder. Warburg hoped for a new era of European peace on the basis of balanced strength, whereas Hitler was from the outset bent on war and the exorcism of the demons of 1918. Warburg hoped that anti-Semitism was an epiphenomenon of Nazism, whereas racial hatred lay at its dark heart. When, in later life, he accused others of 'wishful non-thinking' he cannot wholly have forgotten his own self-deception about Hitler.

Others would labour under these delusions for another five years. Towards the end of March 1933, however, Siegmund Warburg suddenly grasped the truth about the Third Reich with a swiftness that was remarkable in the light of his early ambivalence.[42] 'We have fascism,' he wrote in his diary on 21 March, 'but the big question remains whether it will be a good German fascism, in other words a fascism that wants to be orderly and just, akin to the Italian [sic], or a fascism closer to that of Moscow, a fascism that leads to arbitrariness and communism, to brutality and intolerance.' Having initially been optimistic on this score, he now regarded himself as a pessimist.[43] In the succeeding days, weeks and months, Warburg's pessimism deepened – so much so that before long he was contemplating leaving Germany altogether.

What brought about this abrupt change of mind? The simple answer is: events. It is important to bear in mind how authentically revolutionary the 'national revolution' of early 1933 was, in the sense that the most radical elements in the Nazi movement – particularly the brownshirted members of the Sturmabteilung (SA) – seized the opportunity presented by victory to settle scores not only with their political rivals on the left but also with the Jews, long the objects of their most violent animosity. During the torch-lit parade staged in Hamburg by the SA and other right-wing paramilitary groups on the night of 6 February, there were chants of 'Death to the Jews'. According to one eyewitness, some of the marchers openly 'sang of the blood of the Jews which would spurt from [the wounds inflicted by] their knives'.[44] Such words were not immediately translated into action, it is true, though there were some attacks on Jewish businesses in Hamburg even before the nationwide boycott ordered on 1 April.[45] But the policy of excluding Jews from public, civic and economic life began at once. As early as 14 March – even before national legislation had been passed expelling all Jews from the civil service – Max Warburg was ousted from the Hamburg Finance Deputation by the new mayor Carl Vincent Krogmann, son of the nationalist shipowner Richard. A number of Hamburg companies followed Krogmann's lead, requesting that Warburg resign his place on their supervisory boards.[46] This followed what amounted to a coup in Hamburg, as local Nazis with the support of the new government in Berlin demanded that the Senate hand over control of the Hamburg police to the NSDAP – part of that process of 'synchronization' (*Gleichschaltung*) of all the Reich's regional governments which predated the termination of parliamentary rule at the political centre. With the belated passage of the crucial Enabling Law by the Reichstag on 24 March – an event slowed down by the need to secure a two-thirds majority – Hitler was at last freed to rule entirely by decree, without reference to either the Reichstag or Hindenburg. Among the first fruits of the new dictatorship was a string of measures drastically curtailing the civil rights of Jews. Between April and October 1933 they were prohibited from working as civil servants, as patent lawyers, as doctors or dentists in state-run insurance institutions, as public employees in any capacity, as directors of cultural institutions or as journalists.

It is against this background that Siegmund Warburg's apparently abrupt decision to leave Germany needs to be understood. The combination of violence and systematic discrimination shattered almost overnight his fleeting illusions about the nature of Nazi rule. He was not the only family member to respond this way. Siegmund was followed into exile by Fritz Warburg's daughter Ingrid.[47] Others reacted more desperately to the same realization. In December 1933 Carl Melchior suffered a fatal stroke, possibly brought on by his fear of arrest by the Gestapo.[48] Paul Wallich, a director of the Deutsche Bank who had been born a Jew but had been baptized and who had married a Gentile, committed suicide in 1938 rather than endure further discrimination, just one victim of the wave of suicides that swept through the German-Jewish community after 1933.[49]

IV

According to Siegmund Warburg's own account, his decision to go into exile was the result of a Damascene conversion – a moment of revelation that took place in the unlikely setting of the German Foreign Office in Berlin. On 9 March 1933, as he later told George Steiner, he had a meeting with the Foreign Minister, Konstantin von Neurath, a career diplomat appointed by Papen who was to remain in office for nearly five years under Hitler:

I said I was very worried about events and he asked me what I thought should be done. I replied (having prepared myself very carefully for this interview) that although Hindenburg was an old man he was not a Nazi and if people like von Neurath were to say to Hindenburg that he should get rid of Hitler he would do so and would be backed by the Army. Indeed there was a paragraph in the Weimar Constitution permitting the President to take this action if the Chancellor committed a breach of the *Grundrechte* [fundamental laws]. Neurath replied: 'You are quite right. I am fully aware that Hindenburg has complete confidence in me and I could influence him as you suggest, but this is risky and I cannot do it. *Ich werde nicht für national zuverlässig betrachtet* [I am not regarded as reliable from a national standpoint].' These words of von Neurath were like a mystical experience for me. I woke up. I took a taxi home and told my wife to pack. 'If von Neurath admits I am right but says he can do nothing, what more can I do?'[50]

Later writers have repeated this vivid story. Yet it is not borne out by any document that has survived. Warburg's diary makes no mention of a meeting with Neurath, though there is no reason to doubt that it occurred: the Swabian aristocrat was a near-neighbour of Warburg's parents who had often paid visits to Uhenfels during Warburg's childhood. Rather, the evidence suggests that the conjuncture of a business trip to New York and mounting anti-Semitic agitation in Germany persuaded him to send his wife and children abroad, to stay with Eva's parents in Sweden. This happened nearly three weeks after the meeting Warburg recollected having with Neurath.

On 27 March 1933 Warburg wrote at length about his efforts to counter the now rampant anti-Semitism in Germany, which included a meeting with Max Naumann, a pro-Nazi Jew who had set up a new Association of National German Jews. Criticizing as 'half-hearted' a statement on the subject that had been issued by the older Central Association of German Citizens of the Jewish Faith, Warburg sought to persuade Naumann and the few other people he knew within the Nazi movement of the 'practical impossibility of . . . radical anti-Semitism (impossibility to make racial diagnoses, impossibility to implement a racial detection, falsehood of every hypothesis of racial purity (there are no pure races . . .), morally intolerable virtue of establishing a communal life on the hypothetical elements of blood instead of a strength-filled ethos and inner vitality)'.[51] Given the evidently muted support this argument elicited, Warburg readily welcomed his uncle Max's decision to send him to New York for meetings with their relatives and colleagues at Kuhn Loeb. However, he felt uneasy at the thought of leaving his wife and children in Germany without him, given the threat that Nazi 'excesses', if they escalated any further, might pose to their safety. This, along with Eva's desire to visit her invalid mother, explains her and the children's departure for Stockholm a few days later. Warburg also persuaded his mother to leave Germany, dispatching her to stay with relatives in Switzerland.

Warburg understood perfectly that these hasty arrangements might represent a major parting of the ways. He wondered 'whether or not we will return to find Germany, our home and our way of life there as we left it':

No injury or wrong done to one can damage the sense of being at home in Germany, but when one's employment, personal freedom and personal dignity are taken away, then perhaps one must draw [the logical] conclusions, just as the greatest German patriots in the middle of the last century did when they left their fatherland, not in order to relinquish their fraternal tie to it, but on the contrary with joy and renewed strength to work for the fatherland and its rebirth.[52]

This allusion to the revolutionaries of 1848 was in some measure ironic; Warburg was scarcely following in the footsteps of Karl Marx as he booked his first-class cabin to New York. In any case, he was also attracted to America by the possibility of being able to mobilize the American side of the Warburg clan – particularly Jimmy, whom he had identified as a possible ally during the 1931 crisis – against his uncle Max's management (in Warburg's view, mismanagement) of the Hamburg firm.[53] Nevertheless, he made it clear to his father-in-law that his prime motive for leaving Germany was political. The elections had exposed the weakness of the conservative right in Germany, while accentuating the 'sadistic mood' among the 'radical elements', increasing the probability of a 'Danton–Robespierre development (Hitler=Mirabeau, Danton=Göring, Robespierre=Goebbels)'. Much as he had previously criticized the 'failure of the [German] bourgeoisie, its indolence, materialism and cowardice', he had been deeply disillusioned since the election by the 'crassness and brutality of the great mass of the German people', and in particular by the anti-Jewish boycott, something no 'conscious Jew could tolerate psychologically or materially'. 'I already have begun to think of emigration,' he confessed.[54] The news that the Nazis intended to regulate overseas travel for German citizens only added to his growing sense of 'shame' at what was happening in his homeland, and his conviction that self-imposed exile – before flight became necessary – was the only possible response. 'It may take a long time before Hitler's barbarian horde has expended its fury,' he reflected on the transatlantic voyage. 'In the interim the best patriots . . . will do more for their fatherland by working for it abroad.'[55]

But emigration where? The United States was the obvious option, the most dynamic of the world's economies in the 1920s and the foreign country where Warburg had spent by far the most time. It is not clear if he explicitly discussed the possibility of moving to New York after his arrival there on 6 April, but it seems highly probable.[56] Mortimer Schiff may even have offered him a partnership or at least employment at Kuhn Loeb. Just as his trip was drawing to a conclusion nearly five weeks later, his assistant called from Prague, where he had gone to escape Nazi telephone-tapping, to urge him 'not to come home'.[57] The problem was that, as long as they continued to have substantial assets frozen in Germany under the terms of the 1931 standstill agreement, which had suspended repayment of foreign credits granted to Germany before the Depression, neither Jimmy Warburg nor any of the other Kuhn Loeb partners wanted to see Siegmund relinquish his post in Germany. He was the one member of the German firm in whom they now had confidence; the man they hoped would be able to do business with the new regime, not least with Hjalmar Schacht, now reinstalled as Reichsbank president (a post he had earlier resigned in protest against the Young Plan for rescheduled reparations, named after the American businessman and presidential adviser Owen D. Young). If Siegmund emigrated, all such hopes evaporated. Even as things stood, his assistant warned, 'Schacht was being undermined during his absence . . . the bolshevistic part of the Nazis was getting stronger by the minute, and . . . if American banks could sell any German credits for cash, even at a 60 or 70% discount, during the next week, he strongly urged them to do so.' (Jimmy Warburg grimly described this as 'a cheerful bit of news!')[58]

A second possibility was Sweden. Before leaving for New York, Siegmund had explicitly asked his father-in-law if there might be an opening for him in Stockholm. 'Malle' Philipson's reply was as frank as it was couched in flattery. Under the circumstances, with economic shadows lengthening over Sweden, there was nothing suitable for 'a man with your qualifications and with your brilliant connections especially in New York and London'. A third possibility was, of course, England. In view of Siegmund Warburg's later successes in London, it may seem surprising that this was his third choice of destination – perhaps even his fourth after Amsterdam (see below). Even more remarkable is the possibility that he had to be talked into considering London by his father-in-law. As Philipson presciently argued, during a brief visit by Warburg to England in May 1933, Warburg had just the 'qualities that could bring you the same kind of success [that was] achieved by so many of your gifted immigrant fellow countrymen in previous periods':

You understand very well the peculiar English mentality as it manifests itself in business life. Making swift decisions in business matters suits you, and you are familiar, I think, with the unwritten Codex of fairness and a certain measure of generosity . . . Although you are no sportsman, you have always been respected and liked by your friends in the City. That you are a German Jew will not be forgotten either to begin with or later, but I have the inner feeling you could be one of those whose connections, experience and shrewdness in foreign matters [the English] would willingly make use of and certainly would not undervalue, and also one of those who would very quickly find himself well received in the best circles of society.[59]

Just a few days after receiving this letter, as if to personify the dilemma he faced, Warburg found himself travelling in a train from London to Harwich, en route to the continental ferry in the improbable company of Marlene Dietrich and none other than Schacht himself. The Reichsbank President sought to reassure Warburg that Germany's new leaders, for all their present 'bigotry and barbarism', would come to 'see reason'. But Schacht's enthusiasm for Hitler merely confirmed Warburg's impression that he was, for all his 'freshness and dynamism', nevertheless 'extremely unreliable'.[60] Only 'very bad experiences', Warburg now believed, would 'bring the Nazis to their senses or waken up their followers', and he expected this to take '4–8 years'. He must certainly emigrate, therefore. But must it really be to London rather than to New York? 'England is, as always, marvellous in its inner tranquillity, solidity and security,' he wrote as the train clattered eastwards across the monotonous East Anglian landscape, 'but America is healthier and stronger, while it is precisely in terms of strength and health that England in recent years has surely lost ground.'[61] Neighbouring continental Europe, meanwhile, was on the road to economic and political 'Balkanization'. While it was unclear how this tendency would affect the British Empire, it seemed obvious that the principal beneficiaries would be 'the three big empires outside Europe, namely the United States, Russia and Japan'.[62]

Romantic though his own later account of an overnight emigration may have sounded, Warburg did not in fact leave Germany for another year. In the intervening months he was almost incessantly on the road – twice in London, twice in Berlin and once apiece in Frankfurt, Berne, Basle, Zurich and Paris. Yet he continued to be based in Hamburg.[63] As late as March 1934 he was still weighing up the pros and cons of fascism:

A fascist dictatorship . . . has a great appeal on the surface: good streets, punctual trains, few beggars, clean houses, fine uniforms, impressive parades, good marching rhythms. The façade is good and catches the eye, and that is why fascism is so good at winning popularity among the superficial majority. But the dictators do not ask what will come after them and their supporters marvel at the successes of the moment, without asking how high the price will be that ultimately has to be paid for them. Hence so often [the result is] an economy with expenditures uncovered by revenues and a constitution with one leader, many led, but no leadership in between.

What Warburg foresaw for Germany was 'a steep decline not only in the material but also in the spiritual standard of living', which could ultimately lead to 'moral anarchy – even war?'[64] The question mark was significant. Nevertheless, the more he observed the pace of German rearmament, and particularly the speed with which the new German air force was being built up, the more convinced he became that war would prove to be the final destination of a Germany led by Hitler, whom he now likened to Genghis Khan – 'a man who created and ruled a world empire solely on the basis of organized violence, without any finer spiritual qualities'. Already Warburg discerned what a risk-taker Hitler was. The key question was: would the Western democracies bow to Hitler before the German economy broke down under the strain of high-speed rearmament?[65] The most likely outcome, he shrewdly concluded, would be a war initiated by the Nazi regime as a way out of its own self-inflicted economic crisis, an adventure which must inevitably end in 'catastrophe'.

Meanwhile, the Nazi regime's anti-Semitism showed no sign of abating; on the contrary, by 1935 it seemed to be moving in the direction of what Warburg called 'anti-Semitic Communism'.[66] Hitler's will, he came to see, was to 'destroy Judaism' and to that end he could count on popular support.[67] Although Warburg officially became a resident alien of the United Kingdom in April 1934, it was only some months after that date that he and his wife finally made up their minds to emigrate; and even at this stage their destination was still undecided. Eva Warburg evidently preferred the idea of Paris. Her husband, however, was now more and more attracted to the idea of establishing himself in London, where – rather against his own expectations – he now found himself spending as much as 'forty per cent' of his time.[68]

V

In choosing a new home for himself and his family, the crucial question in Siegmund Warburg's mind was where the best business opportunities would lie in what promised to be turbulent times. It was at around this time that Warburg had one of the most important insights of his entire career. His frustration with his uncle Max and the other senior executives at M. M. Warburg & Co. by this stage knew no bounds. He had

given up all hope of reforming the way things were done in the Ferdinandstrasse; in any case, with Germany embarked on the road to ruin,
there seemed less and less point in pressing the case for reform. Working for M. M. Warburg essentially meant toiling to reduce the chronic
illiquidity of its balance sheet – the enduring legacy of the 1931 crisis
– work which was both literally and metaphorically thankless. By
contrast, he began to understand, there was a very different kind of
business to be done in both Amsterdam and Paris, which arose from
the very complexity of the post-Depression international monetary and
financial system. With capital and exchange controls proliferating
around the world, and a bewildering tangle of blocked accounts and
fiat currencies, established corporations were struggling to go about
their traditional business. What they required above all else was financial expertise and advice – what Warburg called *Vermittlung* or
'mediation' ('meaning mediation in a large and constructive sense', he
hastily added, no doubt anticipating the scepticism of those at Kuhn
Loeb, who continued to see securities issuance as the core of the banking business). What was needed was to establish an institution that
would 'go prospecting for such business abroad'. This would require
experienced people rather than substantial sums of capital. 'Highly
qualified mediation activity' was the way Warburg summed up the
business model he had in mind. It was to prove a mould-breaking
model in the moribund world of European finance.[69]

The challenge was to find a viable vehicle for this model – one that
would be able to exploit the Warburg brand and network without
being once again beholden to the old guard in Hamburg. Here again
Warburg was ingenious. First, he sought to weaken if not to sever the
ties between M. M. Warburg and its Amsterdam-based affiliate Warburg
& Co.[70] At the same time, he tried to find ways to leverage the new
position which had arisen in London as a result of attempts by the
Hamburg firm to create an offshore safe haven for a portion of its
assets. At the end of 1933, in partnership with Paul Kohn-Speyer, the
chairman of Brandeis Goldschmidt (and widower of Max's deceased
sister Olga), the Warburgs had established Merchants & General Investment Corporation, a small London-based trust with a capital of just
£84,000, which was intended to act as an offshore 'liquidity reserve'
and pied-à-terre for the Hamburg firm.[71] Formally it was to be an

investment arm of Warburg & Co. Amsterdam, although, because of its underlying purpose, it was obliged to pursue a fairly passive investment strategy. By 1935 a good deal of Warburg's time was being spent managing the Merchants & General portfolio as a kind of 'reserve savings bank'.[72] Yet this alone, though necessary, was not sufficient. In 1934 a new company was established in Amsterdam by Warburg & Co. in partnership with the Berliner Handels-Gesellschaft: the Dutch International Corporation. This firm in turn created a second London affiliate – 'a new and more active financial mediation firm' – which would be jointly owned with a small group of English investors. In order to avoid 'calling forth anti-foreign feelings', Warburg at first merely acted as an advisory 'delegate' for all the firms concerned.[73] But it is clear that his intention was to be the driving force in this new financial mediation firm, which was given the almost perversely unglamorous name of the New Trading Company (the second and third words a literal translation of the Dutch *Handelsmaatschappij*).[74]

This was the moment of conception. The firm that would grow from this fertile idea would come to be regarded by contemporaries as a merchant bank in the traditional sense, and did indeed come to conduct merchant banking transactions. But its kernel was, in effect, a high-quality financial consultancy, a firm that would troubleshoot for corporate clients as they struggled to cope with the myriad complexities of the over-regulated international economy of the mid-twentieth century.

The New Trading Company was not only a modestly named enterprise. It was also modestly housed, in two small offices in Brandeis Goldschmidt's premises in King William Street, that central City thoroughfare which runs between Bank and Monument. At first, the firm did whatever business it could, including trading shares on its own account, trying to place the shares of UK companies in the United States, organizing a cotton syndicate to buy up supposedly undervalued textile company shares and managing the assets of various Warburg relations. Warburg's American cousin Jimmy was frankly sceptical about the new arrangement. 'You should be either in Amsterdam working for the firm there and be paid by it,' he wrote to Siegmund in October 1938, 'or you should be in London and work for the New Trading Company and be paid by it.' In his view, 'the present status was both bad from your point of view and [from] the firm's point of view', and he had said as much to Max Warburg. 'I went further,' he admitted to Siegmund:

I . . . said that I thought your enterprising spirit required a different type of organization than that of a family firm and that the historical development clearly showed that a hook-up such as the present hampers you on the one hand in the exercise of your talents and on the other hand provides too little control over your enthusiasms. I said that I considered you an admirable co-worker in a well organized and well disciplined organization, but a rather dangerous fellow when out on a string by himself in London with an undisciplined organization.[75]

This candid critique was half right. Siegmund Warburg was indeed eager to free himself from the dead hand of his Hamburg family. But he was very far from being 'dangerous' as an independent operator. On the contrary, with memories of his uncle Max's nemesis in 1931, he was caution personified. Aware that the goodwill of the Rothschilds was an invaluable asset, he was careful not to 'stand on the toes of potentially hostile third parties'.[76] At the same time, he insisted on keeping the firm's capital 'very liquid', despite the costs that entailed. His aim was to have 'a service business without any considerable risks and, therefore, with sound but not exciting profits'.[77] Above all, from the firm's very inception, Siegmund prided himself on keeping its expenses to a bare minimum. There was to be no ostentation. Dividends were paid in only one of the pre-war years; earnings were ploughed into hidden reserves. After the Swiss firm of Brettauer & Co. had been persuaded to invest £60,000 in the company in 1935, its authorized capital was set at £250,000, of which just under £170,000 was paid up – around £52 million in today's money,* a not inconsiderable sum for such a start-up enterprise. (For the sake of comparison, the long-established merchant bank Kleinwort, Sons & Co. had partners' capital of £3.2 million in 1935.)[78] Warburg's risk-averse policy meant that, when the London stock market unexpectedly slumped in 1937, the firm's losses were limited to £12,000.[79]

* In order to arrive at meaningful equivalents in today's pounds, I prefer to calculate sums as shares of nominal gross domestic product, rather than using price indices. For an excellent online guide to such calculations, see http://www.measuringworth.com.

VI

For all his love of Germany and uncertainty about England, Warburg was in one respect an eager emigrant. His deep-seated asceticism was strongly attracted by the idea of shedding accumulated possessions and beginning a new and simpler life. He welcomed the end of the 'hitherto existing bourgeois order'. Throwing 'material comfort overboard' would be a blessing, since – provided one's idealism were strong enough – it would lead to 'an increase and renewal of spiritual values'. 'We should joyfully and resolutely prepare ourselves', he had declared in 1933, 'for a good kind of communism (not the Hitler Bolshevism of the philistines and under-achievers).'[80] The time of 'great capitalist individualization and huge class differences' was gradually coming to an end; it would make way for 'a socialistically mitigated petty capitalism'.[81] He looked forward eagerly to 'a new development of the spirit in a new religious community, away from the old ways of politics, away from the old ways of conventional valuations, away from the old ways of the churches – to a new simplicity and inwardness'.[82] Yet in two respects this was something of a fantasy. First, as we shall see, the Warburgs can scarcely be said to have lived in penury when they moved to England, though there is no doubt that they lived more modestly than they had been accustomed to doing in Hamburg, Berlin or, for that matter, New York. Secondly, prior to 1939, this was an exile that did not preclude regular contacts with the land of Warburg's birth. At no point before the outbreak of war in 1939 did Siegmund Warburg entirely cut his links to Germany. He remained in touch, for example, with Hermann Abs of the Deutsche Bank and made regular visits to Hamburg and Berlin on business.[83] There is no evidence that he suffered harassment by the regime on these trips.

What did Warburg think of those former business associates who now acted as, in effect, Hitler's economic auxiliaries? In an important memorandum drafted in 1941, he attempted to make sense of the 'intermediate position' of so many German businessmen under the Nazis, a position summed up by the readiness of 'important exponents of the capitalist strata to throw overboard the content of their own liberal tradition in their determination to maintain their material and social position'. Those in whom this tension between liberalism and self-interest was unconscious Warburg acidly dismissed as political 'hermaphrodites' (*Zwitterfiguren*), even more dangerous precisely because of their outward respectability than the Nazi 'criminals' themselves: 'Thus have many German economy leaders [*sic*], precisely those who do not regard themselves as Nazis, become the most effective accomplices of the Nazis.' In particular, he singled out the industrialist Albert Vögler, director of United Steelworks (Vereinigte Stahlwerke), Hermann Bücher, director of the AEG (Allgemeine Elektrizitäts-Gesellschaft), Kurt Schmitt of the Allianz Insurance Company, August Diehn of the Potash Syndicate and the steel magnate Friedrich Flick. These men had one thing in common, Warburg observed. In their words, they had sometimes distanced themselves from the crimes of the Nazis during the 1930s; in their business dealings, however, they did nothing whatever to hinder the regime – quite the contrary. By contrast, Warburg could almost forgive Fritz Thyssen, who had generously financed the Nazis before 1933, only to realize too late the nature of the tyranny Hitler intended and then openly to break with him.[84]

VII

Between 1933 and 1939 somewhere in the region of a quarter of a million Jews emigrated from Germany – some, like Siegmund Warburg, to England, many more to the Americas, Palestine, the Far East and other destinations. Almost as many remained behind, however. Max Warburg stayed, determined not to leave his beloved Germany and deeply critical of Siegmund's decision to do so. For his part, the latter had the greatest difficulty in persuading his relatives that the Warburg family had no future in Germany. Max Warburg spent nearly five years vainly trying to resist his own exclusion from German economic life, as he was ejected one by one from the many company boards on which he and other M. M. Warburg directors served, including the chemical company Beiersdorf, the department store Karstadt, the Hapag shipping line and the shipyard Blohm & Voss.[85] He was forced to withdraw from the Chamber of Commerce. The firm of M. M. Warburg & Co. was ejected from the Reich Loan Consortium. Finally, in 1938, he

bowed to the inevitable. Two senior Gentile employees – Rudolf Brinckmann and Paul Wirtz – became legal proprietors of the bank, along
with a group of German and foreign institutions, though it was not
until 1941 that the firm was actually renamed Brinckmann, Wirtz &
Co.[86] From Siegmund Warburg's point of view, the wrangle over
'Aryanization' was a vindication of his earlier argument for selling the
Warburg bank to the Berliner Handels-Gesellschaft in the wake of the
1931 crisis, when its international contacts and goodwill had still been
worth something.[87] To all intents and purposes, the bank was now
being sold off at a lower price than it would then have fetched.* As
far as Siegmund was concerned, the more important thing now was to
secure the independence of the Dutch-based Warburg & Co.; privately
he had written the Hamburg firm off.[88] In December 1938 he submitted – no doubt with much inner heartache, but without any recorded
expression of bitterness – to the sale of his boyhood home at Uhenfels.
His mother had by now moved to the safety of a Swiss sanatorium;
she would subsequently join her son and his family in England.

It turned out that Warburg had made his move at the right time.
Those members of the family who chose to outstay their welcome in
Nazi Germany paid a heavier emotional price – as young George
Warburg saw for himself in 1942, when his father took him to meet
his uncle Otto Kaulla, who had finally fled Germany in 1939. Once a
judge, Kaulla had been beaten up by Nazi youths, adding new wounds
to the duelling scars from his university fraternity days. 'Pathetically
dazed . . . he shuffled along absent-mindedly, broken' by the prospect
of exile from his beloved Germany.[89] For his part, Max Warburg post-
poned departure until the last possible moment. It has often been said

---

* Even as late as 1933 it still had capital of 18 million Reichsmarks and a balance sheet
of 120 million Reichsmarks. In the Aryanization process, the firm was said to have net
assets of 11.6 million Reichsmarks (less than $5 million), but the actual sale proceeds
were reduced to 6.4 million Reichsmarks. A further 3 million Reichsmarks were retained
as a notional 'sleeping contribution' to the firm (which was soon liquidated), 850,000
Reichsmarks were deducted to pay the Reich Flight Tax, 1,000,000 Reichsmarks to pay
the costs of Aryanization, 1,221,000 Reichsmarks to pay the Jewish Property Levy and
450,000 to pay the Emigration Levy. A further 1,200,000 Reichsmarks were transferred
into a blocked German account in the Netherlands and subjected to a 90 per cent fee.
The total deductions actually exceeded the firm's stated net worth. Around thirty German-
Jewish private banks suffered a similar fate; many more were liquidated altogether.

that he stayed in Germany out of naivety, believing against all the evidence that he would be able to preserve his firm's independence through his influence with Schacht.[90] Indeed, Warburg himself gave this impression in his own published memoirs.[91] Certainly, he was one of those Jewish business leaders – along with Emil Herzfelder of the Victoria Insurance Company, Rudolf Loeb of the Berlin private bank Mendelssohn & Co. and Hans Schäffer of the Ullstein publishing house – who were willing to devise some kind of plan to moderate the Nazis' campaign of anti-Jewish economic discrimination.*[92] At an informal meeting with Otto Wagener, Hitler's economic adviser and briefly Reich Commissar for the Economy from April to June 1933, Warburg even expressed his support for the prohibition of further Jewish immigration from Eastern Europe and the gradual exclusion of Jews from German government service.[93] In August 1933 he asked Emil Helfferich, the younger brother of Karl Helfferich and pro-Nazi chairman of the Hapag board, whether:

it would be possible to arrive at some agreement with the NSDAP. He completely understood that the Jews could no longer be active in the administration and could no longer lead the large enterprises, but one still had to grant them some rights. The misery in Jewish circles would be quite extraordinarily large ... One ought to try at least once to bring about a discussion with the leading National Socialists. He thought that the Jews would now be ready for comprehensive concessions.[94]

In August 1937 Max Warburg met with SS Standardtenführer Wilhelm Stuckart, Under-Secretary of State at the Interior Ministry and an ardent anti-Semite, to discuss ways of 'promoting the emigration of the Jews from Germany', a subject on which he wrote a succession of memoranda for Stuckart.[95] To do Warburg justice, however, his prime motive as chairman of the Aid Association of German Jews (Hilfsverein der Deutschen Juden) was to try and help other German Jews extricate themselves and their savings from Germany. He helped finance the

---

* This group met twice in the early summer of 1933 with a number of non-Jewish businessmen: Carl Bosch of BASF, Gustav Krupp von Bohlen und Halbach, Carl Friedrich von Siemens, and Albert Vögler of Vereinigte Stahlwerke. They had also hoped to involve Kurt Schmitt of the Allianz Insurance Company, but his appointment as economics minister put paid to the initiative.

Palästina-Treuhandstelle, which transferred the funds of emigrants to Palestine under the 1933 Haavara Agreement between the Nazi regime and the Anglo-Palestine Bank.[96] In 1935 he and his brother Fritz had proposed a 'liquidation bank' to allow German Jews wishing to emigrate to take at least some of their savings with them (net of punitive Nazi taxes) in return for helping to finance German exports.[97] This scheme foundered on American opposition and German second thoughts. Thanks to their continued efforts, however, several thousand German Jews were able to bring as much as 50,000 marks (around $20,000) with them to Palestine during the first six months of 1936.[98] In remaining in Germany the two now elderly brothers* ran a considerable risk, when they might quite easily have joined their American relations. Max Warburg was in fact visiting his daughter Renate in the United States when Hitler and Goebbels unleashed the pogrom that would come to be known as *Reichskristallnacht* (9 November 1938) after the broken glass from synagogues and Jewish businesses that littered the streets of Berlin and other German cities the next morning. He was dissuaded from returning to Germany only when Fritz Warburg was himself arrested and sent to Fuhlsbüttel prison near Hamburg. Thanks to the intervention of Cornelius von Berenberg-Gossler, whose family had long been linked both economically and socially to the Warburgs, Fritz Warburg was released after two weeks' incarceration and in May 1939 was allowed to emigrate to his wife Anna's native Sweden.[99]

Thus were destroyed the bonds of influence and investment, affection and philanthropy, that had for so long tied the Warburgs to Germany, and particularly to Hamburg. To be sure, none of Siegmund's close relatives was murdered by the Nazis, thanks to timely emigration; in that respect they were more fortunate than millions of other European Jews. On the other hand, it was abundantly clear to Siegmund Warburg long before 1939 that Germany under Hitler's leadership was certain to plunge Europe into a new war. And he understood sooner than most what such a war would mean for the Jews not just of Germany but of all Europe. Three months after Hitler's notorious Reichstag speech of January 1939, in which the dictator

---

* Max was seventy-one in 1938, Fritz fifty-nine.

prophesied the destruction of the Jewish race in Europe in the event of a war, Warburg drafted a remarkable memorandum warning that 'The efficiency of propaganda and the unfirm [sic] direction of a nation of more than 80 millions are behind Hitler's will to destroy Judaism':

Whenever national-socialism feels that a country has a tendency towards anti-Semitism the Institute [for the Investigation of the Jewish Question, based in Munich] supplies free of charge pseudo-scientific arguments, adapted especially for each country, all presuming that the rise or restoration of these countries depends only on the elimination of the Jews from the population. Such was the case in Hungary and in Rumania, and so it will happen in every country to be included in Hitler's sphere of influence . . . Today there are 1,250,000 Jews directly under German pressure, tomorrow it might be 4,200,000 more (Rumania and Poland). And the Jewish question in Russia with its 2,450,000 people appears like the Sphinx, like Russia itself.[100]

Warburg had not been especially prescient in 1933, though he had been unusually quick to correct his initial misapprehensions about Hitler's regime. But to anticipate the magnitude of the Holocaust in 1939 – to take Hitler at his own murderous word – was far-sighted indeed.

5

Trading against the Enemy

How to be an Alien
> Title of a book published by the Hungarian humorist
> George Mikes in 1946

I

Siegmund Warburg became a naturalized British subject in April 1939, less than five months before the United Kingdom faced the gravest military threat in its history – a threat posed by the country of Warburg's birth. His was an ambivalent adoption. Britain adopted him, and ultimately honoured him, and yet always considered him in some measure an outsider, a breaker of the unwritten rules of the City club. He adopted Britain, and yet always considered it a country past its prime, an empire in denial about its own decline.[1] When considering where to emigrate, as we have seen, he initially favoured America over England. The old country might have an admirable 'inner calm, poise and security', but the United States was 'healthier and stronger'.[2] He could not take seriously the largely symbolic role of the monarchy in Britain, fleeing London to avoid the coronation of George VI because, as he put it, he felt 'altogether very tired of old Europe and of all the unnatural conventions and obligations by which we are surrounded'.[3] Warburg never entirely lost his sense that he had moved to a decadent society.

He was certainly impressed by 'the wonderful pluck and discipline of the British people' during the war.[4] He marvelled at their self-control in the face of bereavement, which was not 'due to a lack of sentiment but to a certain religious discipline which accepts the inevitable'.[5] Nevertheless, these strengths were outweighed by two grave weaknesses, of which the first was chronic inefficiency.[6] From a very early stage, he was deeply suspicious of what a later generation would call the British Establishment: the country's ruling elite, so many of whom conformed to 'that rather awful type who enjoys enormously to boast and to pose and who have neither brain nor heart, but only one asset, if that by itself is an asset at all, namely correct manners'.[7] Time and again in his wartime diary he lambasted 'the wide-spread paralysis of will-power in high places'.[8] There was, he complained, 'still too much deadwood in Government Offices, the Services, important industrial firms, transport organizations, local administrations and many other quarters of national life'. What was lacking was 'sufficient appreciation of the paramount importance of speed and boldness'. Closely associated with its inefficiency was the Establishment's clubbishness, which manifested itself as an 'extraordinary weakness and lack of courage towards personal or social connections which might be hurt by strong and ruthless actions'.[9] It was this old-boy network that Warburg most disliked about his adopted home:

A certain group of men is in control of a number of key institutions and whenever one of these men gives up his function because of death or for other reasons his position is being filled by his colleagues co-opting somebody who fits into the set. This system can of course not be described as corruption, because no monetary bribery is involved, but a cobweb of connections result[s] in a machinery where it is extremely difficult for young and progressively minded persons to obtain responsible positions. Instead those types who from the point of view of old insiders are most convenient, namely persons who are inclined to go the way of appeasement or least resistance, have the best chance of a successful career.[10]

On more than one occasion, Warburg identified these traits of inefficiency and 'insiderism' as the principal defects of the British civil service. However, he was just as critical of the private sector institutions he encountered in the City of London. It was entirely characteristic that by 1942 he was recommending a radical reform of the governance of the Bank of England itself:

The Governor and the directors of the Bank of England . . . should be appointed by the Treasury and should not be chosen preferably from representatives of the City. The Board of the Bank of England should of course contain a number of experienced bankers, but the majority should consist of industrialists, trade unionists, accountants and economists. The result would be that the Bank of England would be a centre of British economic life which would stimulate commercial and social progress instead of being a bulwark of reaction as it is today to a considerable extent . . . As to the actual policy of the Bank of England, its chief aim should be to prevent inflation in times of prosperity and deflation in times of depression. Unfortunately during the twenty years before the war the Bank of England did usually just the opposite, namely in times of prosperity they allowed over-investment, and in times of depression they accentuated the crisis by restricting the flow of credit.[11]

There was an element of self-interest in this critique. We are all inclined to resent social elites that exclude us from membership. On the other hand, as we shall see, Warburg was less of an outsider in the City than he liked to suggest, and for that reason stood to gain less from root-and-branch reform of the Establishment than might be assumed. The ambivalence he felt towards England was not that of a parvenu or an upstart, ill at ease in foreign surroundings, but rather that of an admirer who is disappointed to find the object of his affections on the slide. As Isaiah Berlin put it, many years after the Second World War, Warburg 'remained a deep anglophile, but at a certain stage . . . he gave up all hope of rescuing this country from its inevitable, slow and dignified but still inevitable, decline. That he used to say to me over and over again.'[12]

II

For all Siegmund Warburg's doubts about his adopted homeland, the New Trading Company bore for some years a distinctly British stamp. The company's first chairman was Sir Andrew McFadyean, an Oxford-educated Treasury official and politician who had become an expert on German finance during the 1920s as, successively, secretary to the post-Versailles Reparation Commission, secretary to the Dawes Committee and commissioner of controlled revenues based in Berlin. Knighted for his public service in 1925, McFadyean had emerged as one of the leaders of the rump National Liberal Party and remained a staunch Liberal throughout his life.* Here was British respectability, allied to intelligence and industry – even if Warburg came privately to mistrust his 'liberalistic . . . outlook which in a strange way combines decency, broad-mindedness, laziness and wishful thinking'.[13] Equally important in giving New Trading a solidly British aspect was the firm's managing director Harry O. Lucas, a Jew by birth like Warburg – his mother was a Goldsmid – but an Old Etonian by education and in manner. Until the outbreak of war, when Lucas resigned to work for the Ministry of Economic Warfare, the company employed (as Warburg disdainfully put it) several other 'school-tie individuals'.[14] So snobbish was Lucas's conversation at one New Trading lunch that it provoked a protest from the sober Scot McFadyean.[15]

Behind this Establishment façade, however, the firm was developing a strongly Central European core of kindred spirits far closer in their attitudes, if not their personalities, to Siegmund Warburg. A crucial moment in Warburg's life was his first encounter with the thirty-one-year-old Heinrich Grünfeld. Henry Grunfeld, as he renamed himself after settling in England, was a somewhat unlikely recruit to the City of London. Born in Breslau in the Prussian province of Silesia, but educated in Berlin, he had worked for a decade in the German steel industry after taking over the operations of his father's company, A. Niederstetter, at the age of just twenty. A manufacturer of steel tubes and structural steel, the company was part of a network of Grünfeld family firms in Silesia, including the huge Bismarckhütte steelworks. In 1926 the young man made his reputation by successfully defending Bismarckhütte when its rivals Mannesmann and Thyssen sought to exploit the introduction of customs duties between Germany and Poland, where most of Bismarckhütte's assets had ended up following the cession of eastern Upper Silesia under the terms of the Versailles Treaty. This wrangle revealed Grünfeld's exceptional talent as a negotiator; he subsequently represented the steel industry in negotiations with the Brüning government over its policy of mandatory price reductions. In 1932 Grünfeld was sufficiently well regarded outside Germany

* A committed pan-European, McFadyean may have come to Siegmund Warburg's attention as the translator of two of Count Coudenhove-Kalergi's books. He may also have inspired Warburg's privately expressed preference for the Scots over the English.

to be appointed Spanish consul, though the Nazis refused to ratify this appointment.[16]

The decisive event in Grünfeld's life, as he himself often said, was his arrest by the Breslau Gestapo in April 1934, which 'radically changed' his views 'on what is and what is not important in life'. ('Having witnessed the lack of courage of many who had until then professed to be my friends,' he later wrote, 'I never again judged people at their face value.')[17] Almost as soon as the Nazis won power, he and his father had come under political pressure to surrender control of their firm; as in Hamburg, the process of Aryanization was driven by opportunistic Nazis among the firm's own employees. At first, the pressure was more intense in Berlin than in Breslau, encouraging Grünfeld and his father simply to move the centre of their operations to Silesia. However, in the revolutionary atmosphere that prevailed in many parts of Germany between the Nazi seizure of power and the purge of the SA known as the Night of the Long Knives (30 June 1934), they found themselves at the mercy of the local Gestapo. On 20 April Grünfeld was arrested and held in prison for three days, narrowly avoiding deportation to a concentration camp. Never were his negotiating skills more vital to him. Insisting on his rights as Spanish consul, he managed to secure a hearing before a judge, who ruled that he should be released. Now a married man with a young son, Grünfeld did not waste time. Having retrieved his passport, which the Gestapo had confiscated, he travelled to London – just as Warburg had done before him – in search of alternative employment, but returned to Breslau after six weeks, having drawn a complete blank. It was a friend of a friend, Horst Ulrich Wagner von Kaltenborn, the manager of a minor Berlin bank, who came up with the answer. Through Wagner von Kaltenborn, Grünfeld was introduced to Alfred Honigmann, the chairman of the Dutch International Corporation, one of the original shareholders of the New Trading Company. Having heard that New Trading needed to hire someone with industrial experience, Honigmann invited Grünfeld to meet Warburg in The Hague, at the Hotel des Indes.* The date was 17 March 1935.[18]

---

* Ten years later – by one of the many dark ironies of that time – Wagner von Kaltenborn and his Berlin boss would both be dead, having served in the Waffen-SS on the Eastern Front, while Honigmann would be in Allied custody, having been convicted of collaboration during the German occupation of the Netherlands.

Grünfeld had no desire to play second fiddle to Warburg. His preference was to set up his own firm in London. But he lacked the international financial contacts of a Warburg. His family's wealth was entirely concentrated in Germany and therefore subject to the ruthless depredations of the Nazi regime. In 1934 it was made clear to Grünfeld just how little of this wealth he would be able to take with him if he emigrated. First, under the Aryanization programme, he and his father were bought out on the basis of the 1898 book value of their firm's assets. Then the 25 per cent Reich Flight Tax had to be paid. After that, the remainder was converted into so-called blocked marks, which could be converted into foreign currency at around 10 per cent of the official exchange rate. All that remained, as Grünfeld later recalled, was '7.5 per cent of the value of the company 35 years earlier'. Once again he had to negotiate. Finally, after months of procrastination, the authorities in Berlin agreed to allow him to realize around £5,000 by buying machine tools with his German blocked marks and exporting the merchandise to England. After paying a commission to an experienced machine-tool exporter, Grünfeld was left holding precisely £4,000. With a small family to support, he felt unable to risk more than half of that money as the capital of his new company.[19] Initially, therefore, he and Warburg did no more than pool their meagre resources. New Trading invested £200 in 10 per cent of Grünfeld's company; he and Warburg squeezed into tiny adjoining offices at Brandeis Goldschmidt. On the advice of Lucas and the discount broker Richard Jessel, a British-sounding name was devised for Grünfeld's firm: Portman Hill & Co. Grünfeld himself became Grunfeld. Only after two years of doing whatever new business he could devise did he agree to merge his firm with New Trading. Without Warburg's contacts, an independent existence was simply too tenuous.

Despite their not dissimilar backgrounds in the German-Jewish business community, and their shared experience of enforced exile, Grunfeld and Warburg were outwardly very different men. Grunfeld's role at New Trading was initially a combination of risk manager and credit controller. Soon, however, he established himself as the resident expert on corporate restructuring. Here his experience of German industry during the Depression was critical. 'There was not much I had not seen with regard to restructuring and refinancing insolvent companies,' he later reflected. Such experience was much less plentiful in Britain, where the Depression had caused many fewer business insolvencies.[20] Grunfeld, in short, became Warburg's troubleshooter: the man to whom all eyes turned when the firm had to contend with bad debts and insolvencies; the negotiator who could be relied upon to clear up a deal that had gone wrong. Grunfeld was the stickler for detail, Warburg the artist with the broad brush; Grunfeld the impassive calculator, Warburg the actor-manager. (Grunfeld once faintly praised his friend for 'the refreshingly temperamental way in which you express your disagreement'.)[21] What united them (besides a shared faith in graphology) was their propensity to regard business as an almost religious calling, requiring a combination of industry, rigour and rectitude. 'A fairly strong sense of duty', Grunfeld once reflected, 'was drummed into me from my earliest childhood – so much so that it became and still is a kind of compulsion.'[22] 'You have developed into a supreme perfectionist,' Warburg once told him, in terms he might equally well have used of himself. 'Whilst you have increased continuously over the years your thoroughly perceptive sense of the realities and have discarded any comforting illusions, you have simultaneously maintained and enhanced your adherence to the highest standards of integrity and justice.'[23] When Warburg came to look back on their partnership in the years ahead, he was unstinting in his praise of Grunfeld. 'I look upon you as my greatest pillar of strength,' he wrote on the occasion of the latter's fiftieth birthday, 'apart from the most intimate members of my family.'[24] Theirs had evolved into 'a complete partnership'. 'I realize well', he told his partner, 'that whatever I have been able to accomplish would have been utterly impossible without your inner strength and your amazing sense of justice and proportion.'[25] Shortly before his own death, Warburg paid his old friend a memorable tribute: 'You couldn't have done it without me and I couldn't have done it without you.'

No other colleague ever won such praise from Siegmund Warburg. Yet New Trading and its successor was never a two-man band; it was from its earliest days a team, and Grunfeld was only one of several refugees from Central Europe who joined in the late 1930s. In marked contrast to Grunfeld the master negotiator, Erich Körner was a master salesman. Born in Marbach, in Austria, but Viennese to his fingertips,

Korner (he too soon dropped the umlaut, as well as the 'h' in 'Erich') brought to New Trading the self-assurance of a former Habsburg officer and the bonhomie of a compulsive networker. His great talent was his ability to place securities, no matter how unappetizing, with investors. His focus, throughout his career in the City, was to be on the sales side of the stock market. 'Whenever we had a problem with placing an issue,' Grunfeld later recalled, 'we would say "Where's Korner?" On hearing the problem, he would say, "Leave it to me. Forget about it." An hour later he would come back and say "It's all done."'[26] The third émigré to join the firm was the Berliner Ernest Thalmann (originally Thälmann), who was lured to New Trading in 1943 to act as Warburg's all-round handyman.[27] Finally (though he did not join the firm until after the war), there was another Austro-Hungarian Jew, Karl Spitz, who had known Warburg since the mid-1920s, when he had worked for the firm of A. E. Wassermann in Berlin. Unlike his colleagues, Spitz elected to Anglicize his name entirely to Charles Sharp, mainly to protect his daughter from ridicule (as 'Spits') at school. Every royal court needs its licensed jester, and this was to be Sharp's role throughout his career, though he was a jester who was always deeply loyal to his sovereign.[28] Following Harry Lucas's death from tuberculosis in early 1945, the way was clear for these new and distinctly German employees – who would later be known affectionately as 'the Uncles' – to move into positions of greater responsibility.

III

In addition to deciding how to live, immigrants must also make up their minds where to live. After a brief period of lodging in Selsdon, near Croydon in the Surrey commuter belt, the Warburg family's first home in London was 25 Gayfere Street, an elegant Georgian row in Westminster, a short walk from the Houses of Parliament.[29] It was the first of a succession of temporary addresses. By the outbreak of war they had moved to Great Missenden, a village in the Chilterns between Amersham and Wendover. Neither town nor country quite agreed with Warburg. The former entailed too much socializing, the latter too much commuting – and too much gardening. With petrol and servants both in short supply, they moved once again in early 1943, this time to a modern flat in Roehampton Lane, near Richmond Park in the leafy suburbs to the south-west of London (and therefore a great deal more convenient for a City commuter).[30]

The question of where to educate two growing children now posed itself. George (born in 1927) was first sent to Hillbrow Preparatory School, a somewhat austere establishment in Rugby best known for having educated the poet Rupert Brooke. From the outset, his father felt ambivalent about the effects of English public schooling. Unsure whether the boy should proceed to Eton or Rugby, Warburg fretted that the headmaster of Hillbrow was 'somewhat too conventional in his educational outlook'. 'The whole atmosphere in the school', he complained after a visit there in 1939, 'is very clean, but terribly narrow-minded and rather cowardish [sic] both mentally and morally. This is of course symptomatic of the upper and upper middle-classes of our time.' By the end of 1940 he had determined not to send George to a major public school but to keep him 'entirely out of the old school tie surroundings' by sending him to Merchant Taylors' School in Northwood, on the ground that it was better 'in view of changed conditions in this country . . . to educate a boy from the point of view of a life where thorough work is more important than social life'.[31] Merchant Taylors' had the advantage of being a day school, thus keeping George at home in case the war took a turn for the worse. However, as fears of a German invasion receded, George was sent to board at Westminster School.[32]

Already Warburg detected in his son a fundamental difference of temperament which English schooling would do nothing to lessen. 'There is no question of his tenderness and kindness,' mused Warburg in his diary, 'but he should have more initiative and more feeling of responsibility.'[33] On New Year's Eve 1939 the twelve-year-old boy had this message drummed into him in the course of a 'long speech' from his father containing three stern injunctions:

1. Now that he is entering the year when he will be 13 he must become conscious of his own responsibility. His parents will continue to help him in everything, but he must become more and more used to taking a substantial part in the decisions of his life.

2. He must take a much less important view of the unimportant things like food, play and all sorts of exterior comforts. All these things are particularly unimportant now in view of the serious developments of our time. He must be particularly careful not to lose his temper about unessential things (he is quite allowed to lose his temper about essential things). I suggest to him that in cases when he is in danger to lose his temper over unessential things his mother and father will just try to help him in getting over such temper by saying a specific word for which I propose 'my very young boy'.

3. Dreaming is . . . quite necessary, but it should not just be empty dreaming. He should try to watch his dreams and make them directed towards real aims. In accordance with the Boy Scouts prescription he should think every morning about the good deed which he would want to do and possibly about several good deeds and in the evening before sleeping he should ask himself whether he has done a sufficient amount of good deeds.[34]

It is a mistake fathers easily make; in essence, Warburg was putting pressure on his son to become as far as possible a junior version of himself, despite the fact that he was quite different not only in his situation but also in his innate character. At the age of thirteen, George found himself working in his father's office during the school holidays, 'performing certain messenger duties, copying, calculations, etc'.[35] If the son intended to please the father, he succeeded: George was 'much keener on business than I was at his age', Warburg proudly reported to his uncle Fritz.[36] He nevertheless remained suspicious that Westminster was encouraging George to have 'a too high valuation of masculine and a too low valuation of feminine characteristics'.[37]

The pressure on George's younger sister Anna was less intense. She was, he wrote in June 1940, a 'very happy and kind-hearted young woman with a healthy tendency to flirt and tease in a moderate way'.[38] Within a couple of years, however, he had revised his assessment upwards. 'Anna', he told his uncle Fritz, 'is very much the type of my family, very active and enterprising and enjoying life greatly whilst being very sad on rare occasions, when things do not develop in accordance with her wishes. George on the other hand has many similarities with the family of Eva's father. He is very tidy and exact, in a way more thorough than active, not as quick as Anna, but very keen on putting his heart into special hobbies or duties.'[39] It was Anna, Warburg felt, who had inherited his own zealous temperament, though he occasionally worried about her 'too easy going attitude'.[40] She evidently relished her father's inclination to treat his children as young adults, playing bridge with them and even allowing her to puff on his cigar. When London was menaced by the V-1 flying bombs and later by the V-2 rockets, he noted admiringly, she remained with her parents 'and took it very calmly'.[41] She attended St Paul's Girls' School and later read modern languages at Oxford. Typically, her father accompanied her to the interview. 'I have been very active during these last years in many matters concerning politics and business,' he told his father-in-law in 1945, 'but however much energy I have spent on these matters I have given far more effort to the education of the two children . . . I consider at present my chief job in their education [is] to counteract certain school influences.'[42]

If there is an enigma at the heart of Warburg's correspondence it is the character of the most intimate relationship in his life: his marriage. There is no question that Eva provided Siegmund Warburg with domestic stability. If she ever complained about his working habits – the hours of dictation and telephone calls at weekends, the many absences abroad – the complaint has gone unrecorded. If she ever regretted her husband's regular losses of temper, albeit over 'essential things', that too was never committed to paper. She was, it can be said, a stoical wife, uncomplainingly listening to his 'long lectures' on the subject of grand strategy and post-war politics, even when they were supposed to be on holiday; acquiescing in her husband's wartime enthusiasm for Russian lessons.[43] It is possible that the tribulations of the war reforged the tie between husband and wife, who thereafter presented the world with a united front of marital harmony and equanimity. There was nevertheless a revealing edge to Warburg's joke that in their household there were two aristocrats – Eva and George – and two proletarians – Siegmund and Anna.[44] Many years later, Anna summed up her mother's predicament as that of someone who had gone 'from the frying pan into the fire':

From a very strict father, who demanded absolute obedience, she married a husband who demanded her absolute and constant cooperation. Their relationship was romantic, from their secret courtship in Hamburg and throughout their life together . . . When there were disagreements or rifts in harmony Siegmund was unable to ignore them until they were set right. Although in her role she was subservient . . . she was the emotionally stronger one, and knew it . . . She was no less bounden to her duty than he was to his. In her role, which she played to perfection, there was no room for a life of her own, but she did have satisfaction in the knowledge that her contribution was essential and valued.

Despite her long struggle with cancer, Eva Warburg was determined to outlive her husband, in the belief (as she later said) that 'he could never have managed without me'.[45]

IV

Siegmund Warburg's naturalization petition was sponsored by members of the City's leading banking families: the Rothschilds, the Barings, the Hambros and the Samuels.[46] As we have seen, he became a naturalized British subject in April 1939, having completed the required five years of legal residence. Even before this, however, he had started to take a native's passionate interest in British politics. He was, perhaps predictably, an ardent opponent of the policy of appeasement towards Nazi Germany. 'It is utter illusion', he wrote to Harry Lucas after a trip to Zurich in February 1938, 'if people . . . think that one can educate Hitler and his friends by kind words or kind actions. From historical experience and actual psychology it should be clear that the radical Nazis will finally decide in favour of military actions if they do not feel that the forces with which they are confronted are so superior that they have no chance against them.' According to his sources in Berlin, Göring was 'rather in favour of a swift war before other countries particularly Great Britain have made further progress in the armament race'. Hitler might hesitate to take 'the critical decision on war', but in the end he would be 'swayed . . . by his radical followers and also by Goering'. The proponents of appeasement underestimated at their peril 'the lunatic and reckless spirit which prevails at present in some of the leading circles of the German Government'.[47]

Having correctly forecast the *Anschluss* (annexation) of Austria, and having concluded that Czechoslovakia would not long be spared despite the cession of the Sudetenland imposed on the Czechs under the deal struck between Chamberlain and Hitler at Munich, Warburg warned that Hitler might turn his attention next to the question of Germany's former colonies, threatening Britain and France with air strikes if they were not restored. The only remedy was 'rearmament and propaganda and a change in the atmosphere from the ambiguous "laisser aller" to definite constructive statements of policy which (with or without [the] League of Nations) would immediately rally behind the British Empire a front of nations . . . formidable enough to frighten the dictator countries'. Frustrated by the British Prime Minister Neville Chamberlain's apparent pusillanimity, Warburg began to fantasize about 'the formation in Great Britain of some sort of all party-organisation, which would try to wake up people at home and abroad'. He even devised a name for this entity, the British Democratic Union, and sketched what its programme might be:

1. Safety of British Empire,
2. close co-operation with U.S.A. and France, the two great sister democracies,
3. disarmament, but not on [a] unilateral basis,
4. so long as no disarmament possible very energetic rearmament especially as regards Air Force and Air Defence.[48]

In all of this Warburg was very much at odds with majority sentiment in the City, where a significant number of firms had assets frozen in Germany that they stood to lose in the event of war.[49] In the financial press, only the *Economist* shared his staunch hostility to appeasement.

When war finally came, Warburg instinctively knew where to look for a new direction in British policy. 'May God deliver us soon from Chamberlain's stupidity,' he exclaimed in his diary; Churchill, by contrast, was 'inspiring' and 'very clever'.[50] His abiding fear during the months of the Phoney War and throughout the calamities of 1940 was that the Chamberlainite spirit of appeasement might still prevail over the Churchillian spirit of resistance. 'When will the governing circles here recognize that the British Empire is on its final trial . . . [?]' he asked himself on 6 October 1939. 'So far there has been no indication of any constructive measures for facing this trial, but only belated and feeble attempts to deal with problems as they arise or arose.'[51] Like Churchill, he discerned the indispensability of co-operation with the Soviet Union if Germany were to be defeated, lamenting 'the prejudice of Chamberlain and his clique against the Russians'.[52] His response to Chamberlain's resignation was one of 'relief' – though he could not help but admire the dignity in defeat of the architect of appeasement.[53] In the dark days that followed Dunkirk, Warburg remained 'grateful to the depth of our hearts that we have at this moment such a grand leader who is as great as the famous leaders of ancient times'.[54] He even drafted a 'Magna Carta of the British European Commonwealth', to serve as a Churchillian analogue to Woodrow Wilson's Fourteen Points during the First World War. Yet he continued to worry about 'the feebleness of the Foreign Office' and the 'many "dead wood" people in leading places', dreaming of a new 'Minister for Democratic Efficiency . . . [who] should be told about all cases of inefficiency in this country, investigate those cases and punish ruthlessly or dismiss those who are guilty'.[55] 'During the first eight months of the war,' Warburg remarked in May 1940, the month Churchill became prime minister, 'one had often the feeling that many of the Conservatives were more in favour of keeping their Party Government intact than of winning the war.'[56] Such impressions left Warburg with an enduring prejudice against both the Tory Party and the higher echelons of the British civil service.[57]

Never content to confine his political opinions to the pages of his diary, Warburg soon began expressing them to eminent members of the British political Establishment. In September 1939 he impressed the Conservative MP Leo Amery* with his complaints 'about the incompetence of the economic warfare department and generally about our seeming incapacity even to begin seriously going to war'.[58] He also became friendly with Violet Bonham Carter and her mother Margot, Lady Oxford (the widow of the late Prime Minister Herbert Asquith),

---

* A staunch opponent of appeasement and defender of the British Empire, Amery's education at Harrow and Oxford and his rapid rise through the Tory press and party ranks allowed him to gloss over the fact that his mother was a Hungarian Jew. In 1939 Warburg, who had met Amery only once many years before, persuaded him to become chairman of a new company intended to purchase goods from neutrals, though he had to resign the post on his appointment as secretary of state for India.

both of whom became regular correspondents.* It was Lady Oxford who introduced him to Sir Frederick Leith-Ross, the director-general of the new Ministry of Economic Warfare.[59] Another new contact was the press baron Gomer Berry, Lord Kemsley, owner of the *Daily Sketch* and other titles.[60] The leader of the rump Liberal Party, Sir Archibald Sinclair, found himself being assured by Warburg of 'the enormous danger of Nazism and of the shocking inefficiency which was both on the top and going through the rank and file of the whole Chamberlain administration'.[61] Through Amery, Warburg secured an introduction to Harold Nicolson, another eminent Churchillian who had been given wartime employment at the Ministry of Information.[62]

No doubt the hyperactive young immigrant ruffled some feathers as he pressed his unsolicited advice upon the great and the good. Yet the high quality of the advice meant that, over time, the doors in the corridors of power opened with less pushing. In January 1941, for example, Warburg was invited to brief Lord Halifax prior to his departure for Washington DC as ambassador.[63] Five months later he had a lengthy audience with the former Prime Minister David Lloyd George, whose pessimism about the war often exceeded Warburg's own.[64] He briefed the Air Ministry on German morale.[65] He endeavoured to persuade Anthony Eden that 'collaborators and advisers who were exponents of appeasement' should be purged from the Foreign Office and, later, that Churchill should cease to combine the offices of prime minister and minister of defence.[66] At the other end of the political spectrum, he assiduously cultivated Sir Stafford Cripps after the latter's missions to Moscow and India, discussing with him the possibility of a change of premiership ('smashing up the whole government' and perhaps replacing Churchill with Cripps himself) during the crisis unleashed by the loss of Tobruk.[67] Nor was Cripps the only man of the far left Warburg befriended during the war; another was Emanuel ('Manny') Shinwell,

* Warburg was having tea with Violet Bonham Carter in October 1943 when her son Mark quite suddenly and unexpectedly appeared, fresh from his escape from an Italian prisoner-of-war camp and a 400-mile walk to freedom. Warburg was deeply impressed by the understated greeting the young man received from his father, who did not shake his hand or kiss him but said simply: 'Well, well, really!' This struck their guest as quintessentially British – as did Lady Oxford's bon mot: 'Rather bombed in London than bored in Scotland.'

chairman of the Labour Party, who had made his political reputation as a firebrand on Red Clydeside.

Not all exiles from Germany were as uncompromising as Siegmund Warburg in their determination to see Hitler defeated. When his uncle Max visited him in London in the autumn of 1939, the older man sought to persuade the younger one that 'though all German Jews are interested in fighting Hitlerism there should be [a] certain inhibition amongst them to hurt their friends who are still in Germany whether Non-Aryans or Aryans'. His nephew replied that he had 'the intention to do everything in my power without any inhibition or restriction whatsoever to help in fighting Germany as long as the Hitler régime is in power'.[68]

These were not empty words. Previous accounts of Warburg's life have suggested that he confined himself to such business activity as wartime controls allowed. But this is not the case. From the outset, he offered his services to the British government with respect to 'propaganda in Germany and contacts with Germany'. He was full of ideas for the content of British propaganda towards Germany, suggesting ways in which the BBC's German-language service might be improved and even drafting speeches that he felt Churchill ought to make.[69] As a British subject, he was also able to act as an intermediary between the various groups of German exiles in London. At first, Warburg toyed with the idea of establishing a kind of German government in exile. But Hitler had driven too diverse a group of people into exile for such a monolithic entity to be feasible. Warburg found it particularly difficult to endure Hermann Rauschning, the former president of the Danzig Senate, who had himself been a Nazi before deciding that Hitler was in fact a dangerous revolutionary.* The economist Fritz Demuth was a more congenial figure. He, Warburg and others founded a Council for Freedom and Justice to promote ideas for 'propaganda, economic warfare and even handling of relations with a IV. [Fourth] Reich [that is, a new regime in Germany] if it should come' (a prospect that struck Warburg as distinctly remote).[70] A special economic committee was set up to discuss possible ways of undermining the German war economy.[71] At the same time,

* As the work of a supposed Nazi insider, Rauschning's books The Revolution of Nihilism (1939) and Hitler Speaks (1940) attracted rather more attention than they deserved in both Britain and America.

Warburg suggested using his business links to neutral countries like Holland, Sweden and Switzerland to gather intelligence from firms with links to Germany.[72] He bombarded officials at the Ministry of Economic Warfare with memoranda, sketching ways the British government could reduce German imports from the neutrals.[73] He had long regarded trade as a potential lever for foreign policy. Now he advocated large-scale British imports from the major neutrals as well as from as yet unaligned Southern European states like Yugoslavia, if only to deprive the Germans of raw materials like Swedish iron ore.[74] He consistently urged 'greater ruthlessness & less scruple' in the conduct of economic warfare.[75] Although such suggestions were initially dismissed by officials like Leith-Ross, Warburg went ahead regardless, setting up (along with the merchant bank Robert Benson & Co.) a new company, the Mercantile Overseas Trust, with this kind of trade in mind.[76]

Warburg also made several wartime journeys to the continent – to France and Switzerland in October–November 1939 and to Switzerland, Belgium and Holland in January 1940 – to gather economic intelligence on Germany. Among the Germans he met with were Fritz Thyssen, the steel magnate who had been one of the Nazis' earliest business supporters but had broken with the regime and moved to Switzerland when war broke out. Others – like Hermann Röchling, another leading figure in the iron and steel industry – had remained loyal to Hitler, but were still prepared to talk to the newly minted Englishman.[77] By early 1940 evidence in Warburg's papers indicates that he was buying intelligence from such sources, on one occasion using Treasury funds to purchase gold smuggled out of Germany.[78] He was also involved in Gero von Schulze-Gaevernitz's abortive attempt to ship Schacht to the United States with an unofficial peace proposal.[79] Later in the war, when his continental travel became impossible, he continued to circulate information he was able to glean from Swedish businessmen like Marcus Wallenberg.[80]

Warburg's intelligence was good. One of his German sources informed him in late December 1939 that 'a military attack on a gigantic scale, probably through Belgium and Luxemburg and possibly through Holland, should be expected any time between the end of January and the end of March'.[81] Another source warned on 6 May 1940 of an impending attack on Belgium and Holland followed by 'a large scale air attack against Great Britain'.[82] Few of those whose views he canvassed held out hope of a domestic crisis in Germany, much less a regime change, so long as Hitler's war was going well. On the contrary, Warburg's worry was that one of Hitler's peace offers might sap British morale.[83] Thus, unlike his cousin Erich – who in September 1939 bet him £5 'that Hitler will not be alive by September 10th, 1940, and [that] Germany will have lost [the] war by that time'* – Warburg was a realist about the likely duration and uncertain outcome of the war.[84] Nevertheless, he never thought seriously of leaving England, despite the numerous relations he had in the United States. Great Britain, he told an American correspondent, was now 'the citadel of civilization'.[85] Even with German troops in Paris, he and Eva agreed that 'it would be neither right to leave this country nor of any use to run away from what we cannot evade anyhow anywhere in the world if our fight in this country should fail.' There was no alternative but to 'fight on', realizing 'that we have not yet had to sacrifice anything like the sacrifices which have to be made before the fight is to be given up'.[86]

Warburg was clear in his own mind what he would do in the event of a Nazi victory. 'In case the in my opinion still improbable happens and Hitler should get control over this country,' he told his mother in May 1940, 'I would much rather make a voluntary end of life both of myself and of those who are near me than to live in slavery.'[87] Such Churchillian sentiments were a powerful affirmation of Anglicization. (It is no coincidence that at more or less the same time Harold Nicolson was pledging to do away with himself and his wife Vita in the event of a successful German invasion.) Warburg and his wife also decided against sending their children to America, 'feeling as we do that British people, and particularly British Jews, should not try to obtain in these times any special favours either for themselves or their children'.[88] On the contrary, Warburg felt a strong obligation to intercede on behalf of the many German exiles interned as enemy aliens in the crisis months

---

* This was not the only such bet Warburg took during the early part of the war – a reminder of the uncertainty contemporaries felt about its likely duration, and the quite widespread underestimation of Hitler's ambitions and Germany's capabilities. Even Warburg himself suggested (in the spring of 1940) that the war could be won by 1941. He was right, however, that such a victory would be won 'only after absolute destruction and exhaustion of the whole European continent'.

of 1940, most of whom were as hostile as himself towards Hitler, and many of whom had an important role to play in the war economy.[89] (Henry Grunfeld lived for months in fear of internment as an enemy alien, rising early and walking around Hyde Park in the belief that the police tended to round up suspects between 8 and 9 a.m.)[90] While recommending the evacuation to Canada of 'those people who are not able to help in defending the [British] fortress', Warburg would never have regarded himself as belonging to that category.[91] He unabashedly asserted New Trading's importance to the war effort when applying to defer his call-up for military service.[92]

For a businessman, Warburg was remarkably sensitive to the importance of propaganda and morale in wartime. Early in the war, he argued for a Churchillian version of the Fourteen Points precisely because he grasped the need to outbid Goebbels in the contest for international support. He struggled to persuade Amery that the British Empire could 'do to a very large extent what the League of Nations failed to achieve for the world: peaceful, liberal and constructive cooperation between different countries and nations', provided the government was prepared 'unreservedly [to] declare the equality of the native races throughout the Empire'.[93] Warburg's early – and, for a born German, remarkable – support for the bombing of civilian centres in Germany also rested on his belief that German morale needed to be weakened. 'Once the terror of the British bombers exceeds the terror of the Gestapo,' he argued in 1941, 'British bombers will replace the Gestapo as masters.'[94] Nevertheless, in Warburg's eyes, the Second World War would ultimately be decided by economic factors – and it was this that stopped his habitual pessimism from sliding into despair in 1940. He saw trade as the best magnet for attracting undecided countries to the Allied side.[95] He stressed the importance of limiting German and Italian access to strategic raw materials, by fair means or foul. The Allies would win the war, he believed, so long as they 'destroy[ed] . . . Axis strongholds in Africa in order not to lose the Mediterranean', exceeded Axis aircraft production and maintained 'the oil blockade of the European continent, which cannot live on home produce, Roumanian and Russian oil'.[96] He grasped the decisive character of the Battle of the Atlantic against the German U-boats and the vital importance of keeping American imports flowing,[97] just as he appreciated the significance of the German attack on the Soviet Union (which he accurately predicted would happen between 15 June and 7 July 1941).[98] He was right, too, that a Second Front could not be opened by landing troops in Western Europe earlier than 1944.[99] Only occasionally did he err, as when he exaggerated the impact of Allied air superiority and Soviet military strength in May 1942, to the extent of imagining the war over by the end of that year – an illusion shattered by the fall of Tobruk.[100]

Far from disliking the relative hardships of wartime England, Warburg positively relished them. There were fewer parties to attend ('all the stupid society business'), fewer trips to the theatre and, alongside the roses, the garden was planted with potatoes. After their move to Roehampton the family continued to manage with a single servant, their cook. All this appealed to the ascetic young financier. He worked six days a week, sometimes even seven. Cut off from the continent, he travelled widely in England for the first time in his life, visiting the industrial areas where future business opportunities might lie. For him, as for others on the so-called Home Front, wartime austerity was in some measure mitigated by lofty visions of what peace might bring. The later war years saw a remarkable burst of political creativity in Britain as the key institutions of the post-war utopia were hurriedly devised: Labour's long-promised state appropriation of key sectors of the economy, William Beveridge's welfare from cradle to grave and Keynesian demand management. Warburg, ever the radical, was attracted to all this. Indeed, he believed drastic change was essential if post-war Britain were to avoid the fate of the Weimar Republic, which had failed so dismally to live up to its revolutionary promises to the working class.[101] When the Labour election landslide swept Churchill from power at the very moment of Allied victory, Warburg's reaction was characteristically contrarian: 'Most people in the City are frightened of the new Labour Government, and it gives me particular pleasure to shock them by telling them that the new government will probably bring a lot of fresh air into many frustrated channels.'[102]

In international relations, too, Warburg foresaw revolutionary changes after the war. As early as June 1940, he pointed out the risk that 'the downbreak [sic] of Germany after this war might be of such nature that a large part of Germany would without resistance fall into the hands of Russia, so that there might be a division of Germany between Russia and the Allies similar to the recent division of Poland between Germany and Russia'.[103] Indeed, he regarded large-scale territorial concessions to the Soviet Union as the necessary price of Stalin's defection to the Allied side, without which, he felt sure, the defeat of Germany could not be achieved.[104] Anticipating a second American retreat from the European scene and at the same time fearing that Stalin might also covet Western Europe, he began to devise grand post-war designs for a British-led West European Association or European Commonwealth of Nations.[105] He also felt certain that 'in preparing for the solution of post-war problems [Britain] has to link-up more closely with the Dominions and with the West-European countries and cannot rely on the U.S. at all.'[106]

V

It might well be asked what kind of business an obscure trading company could find to do in the midst of a global conflagration that was causing an even steeper decline in global trade than the Depression before it. As economic warfare intensified after 1939 it became extremely hazardous to take on any overseas credit risk in the absence of appropriate collateral in London. Instead, the company involved itself in a wide range of relatively small loans and investments, mostly involving British companies. In February 1940, for example, Warburg was able to list total credits worth just under £140,000, distributed between twenty-eight different firms.[107] Three months later he drew up a highly restrictive set of eleven rules to govern the scale and duration of all such transactions.* These rules may have been inspired by the debacle of New Trading's involvement with the brilliant Hungarian-born film director Alexander Korda, whose brainchild Denham Laboratories was supposed to give England up-to-date facilities for developing celluloid films in Technicolor. Korda was one of the most commercially successful directors of the 1930s, with a string of hits to his name including *The Private Life of Henry VIII* (1933), *The Scarlet*

---

* For example, the net share of New Trading in any participation in the unquoted securities of an industrial or commercial firm was not to exceed £18,000 (that is, 10 per cent of the firm's paid-up share capital).

Pimpernel (1934) and *The Four Feathers* (1939). His earlier creation, Denham Studios, enjoyed the financial backing of United Artists and the Prudential Assurance Company. Persuaded by Korda's charm more than by his figures, Warburg and his colleagues organized a private placing of his new company's equity with the Prudential and a number of other blue-chip investors. But Korda's expectations proved to be over-optimistic and, despite the installation of a new managing director, Denham Laboratories slid rapidly towards insolvency.[108] Warburg was prostrate, taking to his bed with a temperature and a throat infection that rendered him literally speechless. It was Grunfeld who stepped into the breach and, after a meeting with lawyers that lasted from 9 a.m. until midnight, persuaded Denham Studios to take over the ailing subsidiary in its entirety.[109]

In March 1941, at a time when much of the City lay idle, Warburg was able to give his uncle Max a confident report on the progress of New Trading. 'Quite in contrast to some other houses', the company had been able to 'earn its expenses with a decent margin', chiefly by means of 'credit transactions and financial advice and assistance to the continuously increasing number of our clients'.[110] Admittedly, most of its business either 'directly or indirectly serve[d] the war effort, i.e. financing imports, exports, and especially enterprises which [were] working for the supply departments'.[111] 'Roughly speaking,' Warburg explained in April 1942, 'New Trading's business is divided into two parts; 1. secretarial business and advising clients in whose business we are interested in some way or another, and 2. arranging for commercial credits with smaller or larger risk participations . . . The business . . . is not banking business in the old-fashioned sense but rather service and merchants business with the emphasis on trading and assistance . . . to trading rather than on the financing side.' A number of the firm's clients were companies formed by German-Jewish émigrés, such as B.K.L. Alloys, which had been set up by Rudolf Hahn,* a son-in-law of Max Warburg, and which proved a bigger source of headaches than

---

* Hahn had married Lola Warburg, Max Warburg's daughter. He was the brother of the educationalist Kurt Hahn, who in 1934 founded the famously spartan Gordonstoun School after his emigration from Germany, where he had earlier established the innovative Schloss Salem School. Former pupils include the Duke of Edinburgh and his three sons.

of fees. Even more troublesome were the affairs of Ernest Minden's brainchild, Surrey Precision Tools. Less problematic enterprises in which New Trading had substantial interests included Lacrinoid Products Ltd, a button manufacturer, Newman's Slippers Ltd and the chemical engineers Sutcliffe, Speakman & Co.[112] The business was not glamorous, but it was lucrative. The war years, as Figure 1 shows, were markedly more profitable for New Trading than the pre-war years. The firm's substantially increased turnover was also important at a time when the overall volume of business in the City was much reduced. Had New Trading not been a demonstrably growing concern, Warburg himself might well have been called up.

Much more impressive, however, than the kinds of business the new firm was doing were the methods of business it was developing under Warburg's leadership (for during the war he was the sole full-time director). The 'Rules for Organization of Business' he drew up in May 1940 set a course from which, it can be said without exaggeration, he never deviated throughout his life. These rules merit examination, since

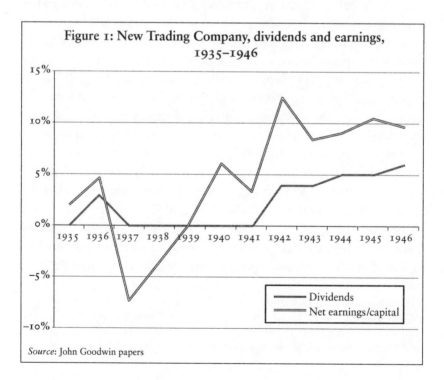

Figure 1: New Trading Company, dividends and earnings, 1935–1946

Source: John Goodwin papers

they offer such important insights into the highly original way Warburg conceived of management. Rule (a) stipulated that there should be a 'daily morning meeting in connection with [the] reading of [the] mail which can be attended by members of [the] Board and H[enry] G[runfeld] and E[ric] K[orner]'. This notion that the mail should be read collectively by the key directors and executives was revolutionary in its own right; no other City firm operated in this fashion (although daily morning meetings were introduced at Schroders after the war, inspired by Henry Tiarks's experience in the RAF). As with Warburg's credit rules, the paramount aim was control. There were to be 'no purchases of securities either for [an individual's] own account or in [his] own name . . . without consent of at least two members of [the] morning meeting'. The same applied to 'credits to new clients or to existing clients in excess of [the] line previously agreed upon'. There would be regular monthly reviews of investments in industrial companies and personnel matters. This control was to be maintained through a combination of collective responsibility and written records. 'Special memoranda' were to be written for the morning meeting 'concerning any important commitments'. A 'journal of commitments' was to be kept, 'on [the] instructions of one of the members of [the] morning meeting . . . such commitments to be initialled by [the] person who suggested [the] commitment at [the] morning meeting and one other member of [the] morning meeting'. Minutes were to be kept of the morning meetings themselves. According to rule (l), 'no specific suggestions for securities [were] to be made . . . without [a] . . . short note to be submitted to [the] morning meeting.'[113]

On paper, this seemed a recipe for a very Teutonic kind of bureaucracy. And indeed Warburg did see German organization as generally superior to British, which he found 'terribly primitive in statistical matters, filing, etc'.[114] Yet in practice the effect was not – as might have been feared – to stifle initiative, but rather to bind together the principals of the firm in a *modus operandi* that combined regular face-to-face contact with habitual record-keeping as an insurance against human error. Collective responsibility and *esprit de corps* were crucial. To be sure, the system depended for its effectiveness on the very small size of the New Trading Company itself. By 1939 it had grown sufficiently to require larger offices, which were duly found a stone's throw away at

82 King William Street, downstairs from the discount brokers Jessel Toynbee.* But with just twenty-three employees before the outbreak of war and around thirty by the end, it remained a tiny enterprise.[115]

The periodic loss of skilled staff to the armed forces was only one of the ways that the war made it hard for Warburg to live up to his own exacting business rules. In April 1941 a bomb hit the neighbouring offices, causing heavy damage to New Trading's premises and leaving him feeling like a 'combination between a banker and a charwoman'.[116] For a time the firm had to borrow office space from Robert Benson. On another occasion a nearby pub was hit, with gruesome results.[117] Yet the war also allowed Warburg to indulge his penchant for long working hours. During the Blitz, he and Grunfeld frequently sat up all night in the City on fire-watching duty, which enabled them to chew over financial 'problems which are as interesting as they are complicated'.[118] The principle of collective decision-making by means of protracted discussion was firmly established in the war years. Siegmund disliked it when he heard his counterpart at Merchants & General, the less successful of the two Warburg ventures in London, saying, 'when he negotiates business on behalf of the company . . . "I am giving this credit", "I am taking this participation", etc. At the New Trading Company we rather follow the principle of talking in the plural form of "we".'[119]

Of critical importance in the dark days of the war was Siegmund's talent for acquiring and cultivating powerful friends like Sir Louis Sterling, the former managing director of the record company Electrical and Musical Industries (EMI), whose new firm A. C. Cossor Ltd was a leading manufacturer of radio components and other electrical equipment. When Paul Kohn-Speyer died in late 1942, Warburg persuaded Sterling to replace him as the fourth director of New Trading.[120] The American-born Sterling was an unusually innovative figure

---

* It was here that the famous system of two lunches originated. The new offices were found to have a boardroom and an adjoining kitchen. As yet too parsimonious to be able to afford their own in-house dining, New Trading accepted a suggestion from Richard Jessel that they share the cost. Jessel Toynbee lunched between 12.30 and 1.15 p.m. The directors of New Trading started their lunch at 1.30 p.m. After the war, when S. G. Warburg moved to new premises at Gresham Street, the system of sharing with Jessel Toynbee was no longer practical, but two lunches continued to be served so that maximum use could be made of the dining room. On occasion Eric Korner was known to attend both lunches on the same day, but with different clients.

in wartime Britain: a pioneer successively of gramophone records and wireless radios, he was already deeply involved in the development of television. By contrast, the more contact Warburg had with other British manufacturing companies, the more struck he was by the poor quality of their directors and managers – and by the improvements that could be achieved with new personnel. 'I feel more than ever', he told his uncle Max in early 1943, 'that to find the right people for the right jobs is today more important than ever before . . . much more important than the conglomeration of material amounts and the technics [sic] of organization.'[121] Often, in these early days, the right person was Siegmund Warburg. It was he who joined the board of the chemical engineers Sutcliffe, Speakman & Co., after acquiring a controlling interest in the firm for a syndicate composed of New Trading, Robert Benson, the British Shareholders Trust, the Eagle Star Insurance Company and the Prudential. As the war progressed, however, there had to be some delegation. Warburg came increasingly to rely on Michael Richards, a young partner at the law firm of Ashurst Morris Crisp & Co., who often took his place at company board meetings.*

Nevertheless, there were limits to how innovative New Trading could be. Much, in the early days, depended on the patronage of N. M. Rothschild & Sons, where Warburg had served part of his banking apprenticeship in the 1920s. As hierarchical as New Trading was egalitarian, as Anglicized as New Trading was Germanic, Rothschilds nevertheless looked kindly on the fledgling firm, steering business Warburg's way (not all of it very lucrative, admittedly) and accepting bills on his behalf for a modest commission. It was only gradually that Warburg was able to move from the position of dependant to that of near equal. In 1939, for example, it was at the instigation of Anthony de Rothschild that New Trading was appointed to act as an intermediary between British importers of American goods and a consortium of acceptance houses to help overcome difficulties arising from the

---

* Richards had first come to Warburg's notice after his lawyers advised him against going to court when he had been caught travelling without a ticket on a train from Great Missenden. Having bought but lost the ticket, Warburg characteristically refused to plead guilty to the charge of fare-dodging. When Richards agreed to represent him – and won the case – he became New Trading's preferred lawyer.

American Neutrality Act.[122] It was a major breakthrough when, in 1943, Warburg was able to persuade Rothschilds and Robert Benson to join a share-issuing syndicate led by New Trading.[123] Also valuable in the firm's early years was its close relationship with Jessel Toynbee & Co., which extended beyond sharing a luncheon room. And, for all his criticism of the Bank of England, Warburg was at pains to forge a close relationship with George Bolton, the Bank's expert on exchange controls and the senior official who was closest to being a kindred spirit.[124] In short, New Trading did the very reverse of bursting on the City scene; it carefully insinuated its way into the London market, looking for unoccupied territory, no matter how lowly. Whenever he was asked if there had been a carefully worked-out strategic plan at the inception of New Trading, Henry Grunfeld invariably replied with a flat 'No':

The City had not exactly been waiting for us and as we started with practically empty desks, our thoughts were concentrated on two aspects: one, how to earn the expenses, and two, how to create new business; in particular business which would not compete with the business of the then very much larger and old-established City houses but would be complementary to their business so that we could hope for their cooperation.[125]

Even before the end of the war, then, Warburg had succeeded in establishing New Trading as a modestly profitable venture, offering new kinds of financial services while at the same time remaining firmly in the bosom of the old City. 'We have now around us some 15 to 20 industrial clients for whom we act not only as bankers, but also as advisers in general,' he reported to the M. M. Warburg veteran Ernst Spiegelberg. 'I think the internal organization has now finally arrived at such a solid state that the company can consider itself as well established in the conservative London sense, and I think it fills now quite a particular role as what I would call a general service and finance house.'[126] As early as 1943, he and Grunfeld were discussing how the business might be expanded after the war, perhaps by acting as a conduit for American investments in British industry, or by adopting a more inspiring name than New Trading, which Grunfeld had always regarded as an absurd misnomer (though 'Nutraco' was used as the nominee name for clients' holdings of securities for many decades to come).[127] But what name would best suit a company that had developed in the space of just ten years 'from a finance company into a house of Merchant Bankers'?[128]

<h1 style="text-align:center">VI</h1>

Victory, when it came, moved Siegmund Warburg as much as any man. He wept to hear the Dutch national anthem on the BBC following the announcement that British troops had crossed the frontier between Belgium and Holland.[129] Yet he also lost no time in seeking to travel to the Netherlands to revive the business of Warburg & Co., the former M. M. Warburg affiliate in Amsterdam.[130] He was equally eager to visit the United States and Canada to restore transatlantic business links, dispatching Eric Korner to New York even before the formal end of the war in Europe on VE Day.[131]

Strangely, no record survives of his reaction to the collapse of the Third Reich and the final unconditional surrender. Nor did he record for posterity his feelings as the horrific truth emerged from liberated Europe of the Nazis' crimes against the Jews – though he had certainly foreseen something like the Holocaust, and his daughter recalled that he made a rare visit to a synagogue shortly after the war. The land of his birth lay in ruins. The religious community of his ancestors had been all but obliterated. Yet he had distanced himself from both. He now spoke and wrote of Germany – in increasingly confident and very soon almost flawless (though never accentless) English – as a foreign country. 'The formation of the Bismarck Reich', he had written in 1940, was 'the really sad event in history because the political development which Bismarck forced on Germany . . . brought out the worst qualities of the Germans.'[132] This was uncannily close to the argument A. J. P. Taylor was to make in *The Course of German History*, published at the end of the war, and a classic expression of the view that German unity itself was a mistake. From Judaism, too, Warburg had grown still further removed. Though he encouraged them to pray, he gave his children no formal religious education and advised them, taking the phrase quite literally, to state their religion as 'Non-Conformist' on school forms.[133] It was as an Englishman, not as a German Jew, that Siegmund Warburg hailed the advent of peace. 'The people of this country', he told his father-in-law with unconcealed pride, 'have shown their best fibre perhaps even more than in normal times. Their aims, though it will always be impossible to reach them, are indeed good stars to lead one: to do the hard things with no more noise than the easy ones, to say yes without pomp, to say no with gentleness, to be firm and perseverant without being impatient and to accept the inevitable without withdrawing from any worthwhile battle.'[134] This was, of course, more than a comment on the dogged determination of the British people. It was also a concise statement of the ethos of the firm the Anglicized alien had built through peace and war – and which henceforth would bear his name.

6

Restoring the Name

A merchant banker's name is his most precious trading capital.
Ernest Bock, 1963[1]

*I recall once long ago . . . you said you had two personal ambi-
tions, to see Warburgs in London as highly regarded as Barings,
and to see it back in Hamburg.*
Eric Faulkner to Siegmund Warburg, 1970[2]

I

By the end of the Second World War, the Warburg family could no
longer credibly be regarded as a financial dynasty. Max Warburg spent
the last years of his life in the United States, devising pipedreams for
European reconstruction with his old friend Thomas Lamont.[3] He
never returned to Europe and died in 1946. Only the youngest of his
brothers survived him: Fritz Warburg, who lived quietly in Sweden and
then in Israel on his daughter's kibbutz, Netzer Sereni, for a further
sixteen years. Although Max and his four brothers had produced a
total of eighteen children, they were scattered across the globe. Of
Max's daughters, two had settled in England and one in Boston.[4] Paul
Warburg's only son Jimmy preferred politics to finance.[5] All four of
Felix Warburg's sons preferred their hobbies to banking: one bred
racehorses, the next played the cello, the third dabbled in diplomacy
and the fourth collected modern art.[6] Two of Fritz's daughters moved
to Israel after the war and married Zionists, while the eldest, Ingrid,
married an Italian former Communist.[7] After his father's death, Max's

son Eric – he dropped the 'h' on moving to the United States – was alone in thinking that the family business in Germany might be revived after the war.

As a banking brand, the name Warburg had been effaced as a consequence of the Nazi policy of Aryanization. No one could be sure in May 1945 what, if anything, remained of Brinckmann, Wirtz & Co., while Warburg & Co. in Amsterdam was no more than an empty shell. As far as Siegmund Warburg could see, 'for years to come' there would be 'no point in doing anything in Hamburg', while the most that could be contemplated in Amsterdam was a mere pied-à-terre.[8] Otherwise, there was only the fledgling Eric M. Warburg Inc., which Max's son had established in New York. For years, however, Henry Grunfeld and others had been arguing that the name New Trading Company was unsatisfactory, especially as the London firm was increasingly operating like a merchant bank. Siegmund Warburg himself had been 'personally . . . rather reluctant as to the change of the name'.* But (as he explained to Ernst Spiegelberg):

all my important friends have strongly advised me to take this step, not least my colleagues on the Board. The general view being that our Company having started as a general finance company has now developed into a real merchant banking house and should therefore in accordance with the Conventions of the City take on the name of one of the individuals chiefly connected with it.[9]

Warburg suspected that neither his uncle Max nor his cousin Eric would approve, but he made it clear that he regarded the views of his 'former partners' as all but irrelevant. After all, they had not consulted him before establishing Eric M. Warburg Inc. Nor had they shown much enthusiasm earlier in the year when Siegmund had first sounded them out about possible post-war initiatives. Sure enough, both Eric and his father vehemently objected.[10] But Siegmund was unyielding. Though he did not rule out 'future cooperation between the old partners of M.M.W. & Co.', he insisted that it should be on the basis of independent 'firms in the important financial centres, each of the firms doing constructive work at their places of domicile and in accordance with the *genius loci* and the requirements of the places of domicile'.[11] This

---

* Grunfeld suspected that his partner was still traumatized by the precipitous decline and fall of M. M. Warburg & Co.

was a polite way of saying, as one friend joked, that 'the skipper of a fast steamboat cannot stop long to pick up survivors'.[12] After much fruitless and increasingly acrimonious haggling, during which Warburg half seriously threatened to change his name to Warburg-Philipson, while his cousin urged him to rename New Trading after Andrew McFadyean – the name S. G. Warburg & Co. Ltd was formally adopted on 28 January 1946.[13] The initials, Warburg explained with thinly veiled irony, 'indicate that I do not want to involve any other member of my family who carries that same name in any mistakes that may or may not be made in my firm'.[14]

The renamed company was still small, but it was already much more than a one-man band. In addition to Grunfeld, Korner and Thalmann, Warburg increasingly relied on Hermann Robinow in the Investment Department. To counterbalance the Germanic tendency, but also to provide some expertise on post-war British industry, he recruited as a director Gerald Coke,* who before the war had been the deputy chairman of a steel company.[15] As Warburg made clear from the outset, the primary object of the newly renamed company in the post-war period should be 'giving service to British industrial firms'.[16] The firm, he explained to his father-in-law in early 1946:

does not do acceptance or deposit business but acts in the first place as a service house giving advice to its industrial and merchant clients, and in the second place as a placing and issuing house. In addition to the usual sort of general clients we have now around us a group of, say, 20 to 30 industrial and trading firms, for all of which we act as general advisers and some of which we control on behalf of syndicates led by us and consisting of firms like Prudential, Fleming's, Benson's, Rothschild's and ourselves. For those 20 to 30 firms we not only arrange the financial facilities that they require both in

---

* An Old Etonian with an undistinguished degree in modern history from Oxford, Coke had attained the rank of lieutenant colonel in the Scots Guards during the war and was an aficionado and collector of the music of Handel. He was, Warburg noted when he joined the firm, 'a strange race mixture, 75% Aryan and 25% non-Aryan; his grandfather on the fatherly side being the Earl of Leicester and his grandfather on the motherly side Lord Burnham (formerly Levy-Lawson of Daily Telegraph fame). He is married to one of the daughters of Sir Alexander Cadogan,' permanent under-secretary at the Foreign Office. However, he added pointedly (and perhaps not quite truthfully), 'I want to make it quite clear that he is not joining the Board of New Trading Company on account of his social connections, but because he is a remarkably nice and intelligent person.'

the way of long-term and short-term money, but we [also] advise them on problems of costing, marketing and management in general. We have made it a rule that the financial risks which we take never represent in any case more than a certain very limited percentage of the capital of the firm. Our chief risk lies in our overhead expenses which have to be relatively heavy considering that the sort of work we are doing depends on the highest possible quality of management.[17]

When Coke became a director of Rio Tinto in 1947 and chairman of the company nine years later, he established a valuable link between the new merchant bank and one of the biggest names in British and indeed global mining (though Rio Tinto never became a Warburg client, remaining unwaveringly loyal to N. M. Rothschild).

The context for relaunching the Warburg name was scarcely propitious. The City lay in ruins thanks to the ravages of the Luftwaffe. Wartime controls had all but killed the business of merchant banking. For at least one established firm, Kleinwort, Sons & Co., 'profits were so low that it was considered quite likely that we might shut down.'[18] A new Labour government, committed to nationalization of the 'commanding heights' of the economy and unprecedented redistribution of income and wealth, was hardly likely to look benignly upon a fledgling capitalist enterprise. Siegmund Warburg privately feared 'some political and economic unrest . . . and even slight upheavals'. But he was hopeful that the new government would do 'much constructive work which is badly needed'.[19] Not for the last time, Warburg rather enjoyed posing as the solitary socialist in the City. He renewed his wartime acquaintance with Sir Stafford Cripps, newly installed as president of the Board of Trade, discussing with him the implications of the new international monetary arrangements that had been agreed with the United States at Bretton Woods in 1944.[20] Warburg all but welcomed the cancellation of Lend-Lease (US wartime aid to Britain), accurately anticipating the 'very spartan peace regime' that would become inseparably associated with Cripps's name.[21] He was also impressed by a young Labour politician named Harold Wilson, who succeeded Cripps at the Board of Trade when the latter was appointed minister for economic affairs and then chancellor of the exchequer. Wilson shared Warburg's view of devaluation as 'particularly unreasonable and even immoral at the present time because it would give many people the impression as if it were a solution of our problems whilst at best it could only be a small short-term palliative'. The two men agreed that lowering the pound–dollar exchange rate would not necessarily alleviate Britain's balance of payments problems because of the limited American appetite for imports from the sterling area. Warburg also approved of Wilson's observation that 'gold was one of . . . many Freudian symbols which played such an undue role in this world'.[22]

Yet there were limits to Warburg's enthusiasm for the policies adopted by Clement Attlee's government. Taxes on business were high. Import restrictions and exchange controls remained in force, despite 'noisy lip service to multilateral trade and all round convertibility of currencies'.[23] There was altogether too much centralization. Cripps's plan to nationalize even the hotels at railway stations struck him as absurd. In any case, Warburg cultivated Cripps for his own reasons, subtly steering their conversations from the high ground of post-war planning to the lower terrain of the new Companies Act and its provisions regarding foreign-born directors, which Warburg considered discriminatory (not least against himself).[24] By the time of the September 1949 devaluation, which saw the pound's dollar value reduced by 30 per cent from \$4.03 to \$2.80, his wartime enthusiasm for Labour had waned significantly. Too many wartime restrictions were being maintained unnecessarily, he argued in a highly critical memorandum written in August of that year. The country was spending too much on defence. Profits and pay were 'on a much too high level'. People – management as much as employees – were not working long enough, hard enough or efficiently enough:

The employers indulge frequently in illusions as to the profits they make and their actions with regard to dividend policy, profit participations of management and management costs generally are only too often in accordance with these illusions. If proper replacement reserves were provided, many industrial companies would only be able to show much smaller profits or would not be in a position to show any profits at all. Inflation of profits or illusions of profits which actually do not exist – apart from many other unfortunate consequences – in many cases prevent the required reduction of overheads . . . The employees, often encouraged by artificially high profits shown by the companies which employ them, and above all under the influence of restrictive Trade Union practices . . . press simultaneously for shorter working hours and higher wages.

Most troubling of all, 'the two leading political parties . . . lack the courage . . . to tell the people of this country that in order to overcome the present crisis more of them will have to work very much longer hours and that those who will not work longer hours will have to be satisfied with definitely smaller real wages'.[25] Warburg saw no alternative to 'a reduced standard of living'. In economic terms, he believed, 'the position in this country today is perhaps even more serious than its military situation was at the time of Dunkirk'.[26] Not all modern students of the post-war British economy would accept that damning diagnosis. But few would deny that there was a significant gap between expectation and reality in post-war Britain.[27]

A major source of economic weakness, in Warburg's view, was the reluctance of the governing elite (regardless of party allegiance) to scale down Britain's overseas military commitments. The financial strain these imposed on a country already weighed down with external debts was indeed the country's principal macroeconomic problem, leading to repeated balance of payments crises.[28] With remarkable clarity of vision, Warburg saw little economic future in what was left of the British Empire after 1945. Admittedly, he expressed qualified support for his friend Leo Amery's idea of 'moulding as large a part as possible of the British Commonwealth into an economic unit which would be independent to a great extent of the fluctuations in the rest of the world'.[29] In practice, however, where others still saw opportunities, Warburg saw only overheads. He would have nothing whatever to do with South Africa's fascistic apartheid regime.[30] Tanganyika, too, was 'outside the scope of our interests'. Nor, as we shall see, did Warburg regard the transatlantic 'special relationship' as representing the sole key to Britain's post-war economic recovery. It was Western Europe to which Warburg always looked, in the belief that:

while there is so much talk about vast new developments in the so-called 'under-developed' countries of Africa and Asia, perhaps the biggest new developments will be among the old nations of the European continent . . . [which] have such an enormous fund both of old traditions and of forceful energy in highly educated and very industrious populations.[31]

Frustrated by the lack of direction of Labour's foreign policy, by 1950 he was looking to the Conservatives – notably Amery – to take some sort of lead.[32] He even lobbied the Liberal leader Clement Davies 'to say the unpopular things' about economic policy that he believed needed to be said.[33]

A critical factor in the firm's success was the attitude of the Bank of England in its capacity as the principal regulator of the City. The Bank, Warburg enthused to the Tory MP Bob Boothby, worked 'wonderfully' (in marked contrast to other nationalized institutions and indeed to the Bank before 1945, which Warburg had seen as a bulwark of reaction) because it had 'found a good balance between centralized policy and de-centralized administration' and 'a strong group of advisers who were superimposed above the executives'.[34] Not all Bank officials reciprocated.* 'A house by no means in the front rank' was one disdainful verdict passed in Threadneedle Street in 1951. 'They like to be described as merchant bankers but we prefer to look upon them as a finance or investment house. They are interested in various industrial and merchanting enterprises who no doubt keep deposits with them. They do a certain amount of placing and re-organizing and also do some Stock Exchange business on behalf of clients.'[35] Two years later, another senior Bank official voiced concern about 'the ever and rapidly expanding field of Warburg's interests', adding: 'His balance sheet looks strong but its strength depends on the firmness of his deposits and the soundness of his advances.'[36] 'It will be recalled', noted another official in 'historical notes' laced with snobbery and anti-Semitism, 'that throughout the war years and immediately afterwards the activities of the New Trading Co. Ltd., both here and in South America, were to say the least very strongly suspect':

He has established himself not only as a leading Jewish financier of international standing but partway to achieving his once proclaimed ambition of becoming 'the King Pin of Jewish international finance'. He acts as adviser

* 'His [Warburg's] circle is a little on the narrow side,' observed C. F. Cobbold to Sir John Woods, the Governor of the Bank, in the clubbish style of the day.

and depositary for a number of ex German Jewish banking families, including the Furstenbergs (Berliner Handels-Gesellschaft) and through his Swiss,
American, Canadian and Scandinavian connections has been able to salt
away fortunes out of Europe into America. He was in 1942 a depositary
for Dr. Edmund Stinnes in Buenos Aires. In November 1950 he wrote to
the Securities Control Office, Bank of England, re. a switch of his shares
from the Dutch International Corporation, this showed evidence of names
who were black-listed during the war . . . He is an international Jew to
whom no bounds of country or circumstance are known. He employs Jews
in his many operations which have often been askance to the Authorities.
He employs people of brains and Jewish acumen . . . and has climbed high
on their shoulders. He can be ruthless with his employees but never falls
foul of those of his own 'persuasion' who have helped him . . . to obtain
his present position.[37]

Such prejudices were remarkably widespread in the British Establishment of the post-war era.

However, at least one Bank of England official was prepared to
affirm that Warburg was 'a good fellow'.[38] George Bolton* held
Warburg in high esteem and declared himself to have been 'particularly
glad to give an affirmative answer when he had recently been asked
on two occasions whether we [that is, S. G. Warburg] were good for
two to two and a half million pounds'.[39] Bolton offered his 'full
support' to Warburg's request for an increase in his firm's capital above
the standard £50,000 annual limit imposed by the Treasury's Capital
Issues Committee.[40] He was also supportive of the idea that Warburgs
should secure a place on the prestigious and powerful Accepting
Houses Committee by acquiring an existing member of the Committee (see below).[41] In turn, Warburg told Bolton that he hoped 'to use
him as a Father Confessor to City bankers in the same way in which

---

* As adviser to and later executive director of the Bank, Bolton played a key role in
post-war debates about exchange control. Later, as chairman of the Bank of London
and South America (BOLSA) between 1957 and 1970 he worked closely with S. G.
Warburg & Co. on a wide range of transactions, particularly in the Eurodollar market
(see Chapter 8). Bolton was a strong proponent of the ROBOT scheme to make sterling convertible, rejected by Churchill in 1952. Unusually but presciently, he discerned
that the City of London could be rebuilt as a financial centre despite the weakness of
sterling as a currency.

the late Montagu Norman* acted for so many years'.[42] By the mid-1950s, relations between Warburgs and the Bank had become more harmonious, thanks in large measure to the former's punctilious deference to the Bank's authority (which had in truth been much reduced by nationalization).

Membership of the Accepting Houses Committee was necessary if S. G. Warburg & Co. were to make the transition from finance house to merchant bank – in other words, from being a 'very good house' to being 'good for any amount'.[43] Without membership, bills accepted (guaranteed) by the firm could not be taken to the Bank of England for rediscount, making them less liquid than those accepted by established City houses like Rothschilds.† First, however, Warburg was intent on strengthening his firm in other ways. In 1952 he proposed a merger of S. G. Warburg and Brandeis Goldschmidt, the metal-broking firm in whose London offices the New Trading Company had initially been based, on the ground that 'SGW & Co. today entirely control the direction of BG & Co. London and that it would be sound and logical to merge the two companies from the administrative point of view'.[44] This takeover was the culmination of a gradual process of fusion dating back

---

* As governor of the Bank from 1920 until 1944, Norman had been the dominant figure in the City of London between the wars. Despite his ginger beard and idiosyncratic manner, he was deeply orthodox on monetary issues and regretted the passing of the gold standard. His fondness for Brahms and friendship with Hjalmar Schacht had led him to give uncritical support to the policy of appeasement.

† A draft article approved by Warburg in 1961 concisely explained the acceptance system and its importance in his eyes: '[When] a merchant banker's name is . . . put to bills of exchange drawn by his customers, they are made acceptable currency at the Bank of England, and can be discounted at the finest rate by bill brokers borrowing for this purpose from the surplus funds of British deposit banks. This way, the time lag between delivery and payment of goods is bridged over which otherwise would have forced the productive process to move by fits and starts as and when funds become available. Acceptances are by far the cheapest form of finance: except for anything going wrong with them they do not involve the merchant banks' own resources as credits and overdrafts would do for it is not cash they lend but their name. For this service they charge a commission which was stated at the Bank Rate Tribunal to be between 1¼ and 1½ per cent in the case of first-class borrowers, others may have to pay-up to three per cent although this would be exceptional . . . One hesitates to single out any particular type of operation as of signal importance for [S. G. Warburg]. Yet the firm's spokesmen persist in underlining the expansion so far as their acceptance business [is concerned], thus bringing home the value they attach to its further increase.'

to the death of Paul Kohn-Speyer – a process which, in the eyes of his son Eddie Kohn-Speyer, recalled the behaviour of a cuckoo towards another bird's nest, but which the Bank of England saw as a sensible rationalization.* It was not until 1955–6 that the question of joining the Accepting Houses Committee was formally raised with the Bank. On learning that there would need to be a 'quarantine period' of at least a year before the Bank would be willing to rediscount bills accepted by Warburgs, and that only after that would they be admitted, Warburg and Grunfeld responded by taking over the small but venerable house of Seligman Bros., a long-standing member of the Committee.[45] Nor was Warburg content with (as the Bank's Hilton Clarke put it) 'the big prize which . . . was to have his bills taken by us and regarded as "prime bank"'; he also insisted that S. G. Warburg inherit the Seligman account at the Bank of England.[46] As the *Economist* noted, to gain admission to the 'inner sanctum of acceptance houses' within just over a decade of coming into existence as a bank was 'record-making progress'.[47]

To be sure, there were still those in Threadneedle Street who remained resistant to Warburg's charms, notably the Governor himself, Cameron Cobbold. It was to Cobbold that Reginald Seligman turned following the latter's forced resignation, complaining that he had been 'ill-treated' by Warburgs.[48] Others echoed Eddie Kohn-Speyer's charge of ruthlessness, notably the publisher and distant relation Frederic Warburg, who accused Siegmund of 'taking over' first New Trading from the other Warburgs and then Brandeis Goldschmidt from the Kohn-Speyers.[49] Yet for every foe there were two or more new friends. 'Sigismund' Warburg, as he was sometimes erroneously referred to at the Bank in the early days, had by 1959 become known more affectionately (though always behind his back) as 'Sigi'.[50] If Reginald Seligman soon tired of playing second fiddle to Warburg, the same could not be said for Geoffrey Seligman and his cousin Spencer ('Bobby'), who quickly adapted to the new regime.

Even as the British economy emerged from post-war austerity into mid-1950s prosperity, Warburg remained wary. The Conservative

---

* In May 1946 S. G. Warburg & Co. had joined forces with Rio Tinto to buy Brandeis Goldschmidt. Six years later Warburgs essentially bought out Rio Tinto in return for shares in Mercury Securities, the S. G. Warburg parent company.

Chancellor R. A. ('Rab') Butler was 'present[ing] the position to the country in much too favourable a light', he complained in late 1955. 'He tells the people that with monetary palliatives he can put things right instead of talking in Churchillian terms of "sweat and tears".'[51] The Eden government, he lamented on the eve of the Suez Crisis, was 'probably the most inefficient Government that Britain has had since the times of Lord North':

I wonder how many people outside the Government still think that purely monetary measures, such as the increase of the Bank Rate, can have a real impact on the ailments which have to be cured; I suppose only people who combine in such a unique way arrogance and inefficiency as the present Government can hold on obstinately to a point of view which has already been proved to be wrong, instead of taking the drastic measures which are required, such as export incentives, attempts at far-reaching agreements between employers and the unions, like a combined wage and dividend freeze, and going forward with a policy which puts its emphasis rather on increased productivity than on the negative and discouraging measures of monetary restrictions.[52]

If the British economy could manage to grow at only half the rate of the German, he observed, 'the argument about present British prosperity seemed to me . . . completely meaningless'.[53] These were harsher words than even the Labour leader Hugh Gaitskell felt were warranted.[54] But such cross-party complacency only deepened Warburg's gloom. 'There is a frightening amount of mediocrity and lazy conformism widely spread equally amongst trade union people and amongst their opposite numbers in the City and in industry,' he lamented to Lord Hailsham, the newly appointed Education Minister, in 1957. 'This lazy conformism is one of the big dangers of this country today and there should be a crusade against complacency.'[55] Warburg was dismayed by Harold Macmillan's insouciant claim, not long after he became prime minister in 1957, that people in Britain had 'never had it so good'.[56] In 1961, in a rare statement to the press, he warned of an imminent 'salutary downward trend in the trade cycle'.[57]

This perpetual apprehension of future trouble explains Warburg's almost compulsive risk aversion. At a board meeting in March 1952 he 'expressed great pessimism concerning our ability to earn our

expenses out of conventional banking business during the next years
... in a period of business contraction as was to be expected during
the coming years and probably for a very long time'. To survive, the
firm would need 'to cultivate increasingly activities other than the usual
and conventional banking business'.[58] He bet and lost £5 to Robinow
that 'the figures of SGW & Co. for the year ended 31st March 1953
would be ... worse than those for the previous year.'[59] Two years later
Warburg confessed to Bolton that his 'chief worry at the moment was
that personnel was increasing too much and quality of work on the
top level was bound to suffer from too big a quantity in regard to the
general scope of our activities'.[60] He was also a great believer in accumulating hidden reserves. 'Because the profitability of international
private banking business nowadays seems to me a very fragile matter,'
he explained in 1959, 'substantial reserves are to-day required more
than ever for a private banking business such as ours.'[61]

Yet these were growing pains, not serious problems. Regardless of
which party was in power, and regardless of the travails of the UK
economy, the ascent of S. G. Warburg & Co. in fact continued apace.
'Forget, for once, the sorrows of this world,' exclaimed his cousin Lola
on Warburg's forty-sixth birthday, 'and contemplate your shining gifts
... At King William Street ... Grunfeld, of perceptive vision and efficiency; Korner, full of flair, who charms the golden springs of
participations from the dry rock of European capital; E[rnst] T[halmann]
whose great cool brilliance illuminates the wisdom both of his judgement and his execution ... All these, and many others, grow faithfully
in the rich flowerbeds of S.G.W. & Co.'[62] It was true. The financial
performance of S. G. Warburg in the 1950s was impressive. In 1949
its paid-up capital had been just £2.75 million. Thirteen years later its
market capitalization was £20 million (around £1 billion in 2008
terms). As the *Sunday Times* pointed out in 1961, someone who seven
years before had bought 100 shares in Mercury Securities, the Warburg
parent company (see below), would have invested just over £237:

For that money he would now have 274 shares at £18, and his investment
would be worth £4,930, 20 times the cost ... In this period the company's
earnings have multiplied six times, and the dividend nine and a half times.
This means that the original holder would now have a dividend yield of 42½

per cent on the original cost of his investment, and an earnings yield of no less than 145 per cent on the same basis.

It was, as the newspaper noted, a 'phenomenal rate of growth' (see Figure 2).[63] It was especially remarkable in a period when the transition from wartime controls to a somewhat amateurish Keynesian demand management was marked by considerable economic volatility: the notorious 'stop–go' policies of the 1950s Conservative governments, which saw both monetary and fiscal policy being varied rather too frequently in response to the usually conflicting pressures of the balance of payments and the political business cycle.

II

Although British industry was supposed to be the primary post-war focus of S. G. Warburg & Co., the firm's leading figure lost little time in returning to continental Europe in search of the international busi-

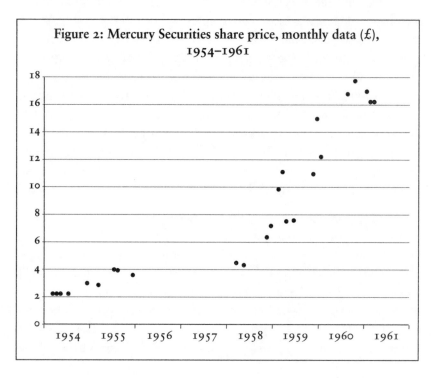

Figure 2: Mercury Securities share price, monthly data (£), 1954–1961

ness that was his true métier. In late 1945 he visited France and Switzerland, the latter as stable as the former appeared unstable. The following year took him to Sweden, where he sought to re-establish communications with the wealthy Wallenberg family and their Stockholms Enskilda Bank, as well as to Holland and Czechoslovakia (along whose frontier the Iron Curtain had yet to be drawn). Among Warburg's first post-war initiatives was to join forces with Robert Benson & Co. and the Banque Nationale pour le Commerce et l'Industrie (BNCI) to establish the British and French Bank, a London-based bank intended to focus on the French colonial empire.[64] In floating this scheme little more than a year after the end of the war and the election of a Labour government, Warburg was at pains to elicit the 'benevolent sympathy' of the Bank of England. Mindful of the hostility of elements in the government (and indeed the civil service) towards the rapid restoration of London as an international financial centre – implying as it did a relaxation of controls on capital movements – Warburg well understood the importance of the Bank as an official ally.[65] The Old Lady of Threadneedle Street was not unequivocal, expressing reservations about the proposed chairman and managing director of the new firm. At the same time, however, Bank officials gave Warburg to understand that they viewed the initiative 'with a benevolent eye' in principle, agreeing that 'it would be a pity if the connection were to be made in New York instead of in London'.[66] Here was an essential lever: the long-running competition between the principal financial centres, and the habitual desire of central banks to foster international business in their own backyards. It was a lever Warburg knew well how to use. In George Bolton he found a reliable and effective ally.[67] As Warburg later recalled, in an illuminating tribute, Bolton was:

among those who tried to fortify Britain's role in the creation of new instruments for international co-operation in the financial field. Whilst fully realizing the financial weakness of Britain in contradistinction to the overwhelming financial power of the United States at that time [that is, after the war], [he] fought with all his skill and persuasiveness to maintain a prominent position for Britain – not so much on the basis of Britain's material assets but of Britain's expertise and of Britain's function as a bridge between West and East . . . Besides working for the revival of close relations between the Central Banks of the

Western World, George Bolton gave much encouragement to private Houses in the City to build up international business from London notwithstanding foreign exchange regulations and many other impediments. His influence . . . always made itself felt in favour of individual endeavours as distinct from the more anonymous powers of the state machinery and those who tried to open new, privately based channels for international co-operation.[68]

Warburg grasped sooner than most that the revival of the City of London was not likely to be based, as its prosperity had been in the past, on the export of British capital. On the contrary, for the foreseeable future Britain would need to attract capital from abroad. Thus in February 1948 he sounded out a number of his Swiss contacts 'as to the possibility of Switzerland using part of its sterile gold reserves for sound financing of British or British Empire requirements'.[69] Four years later he was reviewing a number of possible projects 'for which . . . the United Kingdom could raise hard currency loans, mainly in the United States, but to a smaller extent also in Switzerland and in Canada'.[70] A recurrent theme of his work throughout the subsequent years was the desirability of attracting European and North American capital to Britain, not least to finance the modernization of British industry, but also to turn London into a conduit for international transactions.

It was not until 1949, however, that Siegmund Warburg returned to the land of his birth. Even before the end of the Second World War (and in marked contrast to Henry Grunfeld), Warburg had been keen to expedite the economic and political rehabilitation of Germany. This was not out of magnanimity, much less indifference to the horrors of the Third Reich, but out of pragmatism. Warburg drew a clear distinction between 'the chief gangsters' – by which he meant 'not only the political criminals, but also all businessmen who had no inhibition in profiting in every possible way from the Nazi regime' – and the 'relatively innocent people who only joined the Nazi Party in order to protect the lives of their families'. The latter, he believed, were being needlessly persecuted as a result of the highly mechanistic de-Nazification policy of the occupying powers, while the former – who deserved to be 'separated in forced camps' – were succeeding in ingratiating themselves with 'stupid military administrators'.[71] 'Most Germans these days', he commented acidly in 1949, 'consider it an offence against tact and good manners if somebody reminds them of all the awful things which have happened under the Hitler regime,' evincing 'the old typical and strange mixture of arrogance and naiveté'.[72] He had no objection to a 'final division of Germany into an Eastern and a Western Zone' and favoured French proposals for 'a separate administration of the Ruhr district under international control'.[73] Nevertheless, the paramount consideration in his mind was the rapid economic revival of western Germany. To achieve that end, he was prepared to turn a blind eye to the past conduct of at least one of those 'businessmen who had no inhibition in profiting in every possible way from the Nazi regime'.

On 8 July 1947 Hermann Abs – the disgraced former head of Deutsche Bank's Foreign Department – wrote what was surely one of the only begging letters he ever wrote in his long life. It was addressed to Siegmund Warburg and deserves to be quoted at length, not least for its surprisingly rough-hewn English and its (for Abs) uncharacteristic tone of humility:

It must be more than eight years when we last met in London [in] February 1939 and you can imagine that there are loads of things that I would like to discuss with you when only the opportunity would give me a chance. More than a year ago – It must have been in March – I dreamt of you in such a lovely way that ever since I feel I should write to you. How is Mrs Warburg and your folks [at] home? Tell me about them. Your boy must be a grown up one and he might go to a college by now. Often we talked of you all at home during these uneasy years.

Abs proceeded to recount the quiet life he was leading with his own family on a secluded farm near the Rhineland town (and recent battlefield) of Remagen. 'We all are happy to be reunited and to live in the country,' he insisted, before proceeding to the main business of the letter:

This country life has today enormous advantages and the daily troubles . . . help to forget at last sometimes the thoughts of unresolved problems which chase me. Even being dismissed from any activity in banking and finance one couldn't take away the sorrows and thoughts on the fate of Europe, on its own short comings and responsibility leading to the consciousness of the duty to do all one can to reconstruct and to rebuild where ever and whenever one is called.

There seems to be a difference of opinion about the usefulness of me so I have to remain patient. Patience is a great Christian virtue which to practise I use my best endeavours. It must be very difficult to form a just opinion on this country and I do not pretend that I have been able to judge it right. It is extremely difficult to put it in a letter what I would like to discuss with you one day . . . A letter from you would be a great joy[,] please remember me to Mrs Warburg.[74]

Warburg's reply was friendly but pointed, recollecting not their meeting in 1939 but 'those nice days which we spent together in London' in 1926, a time which now seemed 'like centuries ago'. He congratulated Abs ironically on his country life, 'which allows stoic consideration of life; whilst I still lead a hectic life in the City of London'. Referring to Germany as 'your country', Warburg dealt briskly with news of his wife and children and then came to the point:

I have been asked on one or two occasions to express an opinion about you and I was only too happy to say, whenever I was asked, that I have frequently experienced your emphatic anti-Nazi attitude which you have proved by courageous deeds on various occasions. I also offered to give evidence in this respect whenever required. Hence whenever you would like me to do anything on these lines just let me know. My old friendship and high respect for you is unchanged.[75]

There can be no question that Warburg was sincere in the admiration he often expressed for Abs as a businessman. How far he took seriously Abs's claim that he had an 'emphatic anti-Nazi attitude' during the 1930s is another question. Although never a member of the NSDAP and not prosecuted for war crimes, Abs had played a prominent role in the Aryanization of Jewish-owned firms such as Mendelssohn & Co. and Adler & Oppenheimer.[76] He had led the Deutsche Bank takeover of the Austrian Creditanstalt and energetically built up a network of affiliated financial institutions in occupied Europe.[77] Indeed, a quarter of his forty-five directorships during the war had been of companies in annexed or occupied territory. Moreover, Abs had been on the supervisory board of IG Farben, the chemicals company that built the synthetic-rubber factory adjoining the Auschwitz death camp. And he had been closely involved in Deutsche Bank's acquisition of gold plundered from the Jews of Europe.[78] Nor had Abs given any meaningful support to the active opponents of the Nazi regime, though he was certainly approached by Adam von Trott zu Solz, Helmut James von Moltke and Peter Graf Yorck von Wartenburg. The only real risk Abs had taken during the war was to accumulate a gold hoard in Switzerland as a hedge against Germany's defeat.*

We cannot be sure that Abs knew that Deutsche Bank's gold came in large measure from victims of the Holocaust. Nor do we know how far Warburg believed Abs's protestations of innocence. What is beyond doubt is that, despite the cloud of suspicion that hung over Abs's head – he was in fact arrested and held in custody by the Americans immediately after the war, but never prosecuted – Warburg did whatever was in his power to expedite his rehabilitation† so that by the end of that same year the German was back in business and tutoring Warburg's son George – now training as an accountant, having been turned down by both his chosen university and the armed services – on the technicalities of a bond issue for the Reconstruction Loan Corporation (Kreditanstalt für Wiederaufbau), of which Abs had been appointed deputy head.[79] Warburg's aim was clear: to use Abs as a liaison officer between London and the German economy, the post-war prostration of which Warburg felt confident would not long endure.[80] Abs, he assured Jean Furstenberg, was 'by far the best man available in Germany for any new finance organisation, and . . . would be the chief attraction from our point of view if we did anything there at all'.[81] There were, he once noted, 'very few people in the business world who combine realism and imagination to the extent to which he does'.[82] Realism and imagination, indeed – Abs had these qualities in abundance, and they very soon elevated him to a position of unique influence in the Federal Republic: adviser to Konrad Adenauer, the first Chancellor of the new Germany, and chairman of Deutsche Bank's board and later of its

* The 307 kilograms of gold bars remained in Switzerland, even after the Deutsche Bank's assets were unfrozen under a 1952 treaty between Germany and Switzerland. Abs persistently refused to consider selling or even moving them. When, after his death, the gold was finally sold, it fetched 5.6 million DM ($3.8 million). Wisely, Deutsche Bank gave the money to Jewish charitable organizations.

† Surprisingly, Abs's biographer, Lothar Gall, overlooked his relationship with Warburg and the important role Warburg played in his rehabilitation. In his memoirs, Ian Fraser depicted Warburg later sycophantically trying to ingratiate himself with the imperious Abs, but the boot was plainly on the other foot in the immediate post-war years.

advisory board. For Warburg, helping Abs paid handsome dividends for decades. But it entailed turning a blind eye to the German banker's conspicuous lack of civil courage between 1933 and 1945.

Abs was not the only German businessman with whom Siegmund Warburg re-established communications.[83] Yet it was significant that Frankfurt and Düsseldorf rather than Hamburg were Warburg's first ports of call when he returned to Germany. To begin with, he was resolved to be unforgiving towards the beneficiaries of the Third Reich who continued to manage the former M. M. Warburg & Co. as Brinckmann, Wirtz & Co. In Warburg's eyes, the only legitimate basis for a restoration of the family firm in Hamburg was to re-establish 'the entire status quo ante 1938 . . . at least in principle' – in other words to reverse the bank's so-called Aryanization. He was willing to help Brinckmann during the de-Nazification period, but not his partner Paul Wirtz, whom Warburg regarded as having been a more ardent Nazi, as opposed to a mere opportunist.[84] However, by the time Warburg returned to the Ferdinandstrasse in December 1949 – after a long, meditative walk around the Alster Lake – his attitude had softened. The bank seemed to be well run. 'Rio' Brinckmann was as charming as he was efficient, entertaining Warburg with a 'very enjoyable' dinner in his own home.[85] To be sure, Warburg could not help but be unnerved by the sight of so many familiar faces among the bank's staff, faces he had not seen for some fifteen years. 'Coming to Germany', he reflected, made him feel as if he was (once again) 'sitting on the edge of a sort of volcano'. Yet he could not deny that 'as far as Hamburg is concerned life on the volcano is not only remarkably active but also quite cheerful and cosy'.[86] He endorsed the laboriously negotiated *modus vivendi** that a 'Warburg group' would take a 25 per cent share in Brinckmann Wirtz, with a five-year option to increase the stake to 50 per cent (an option that was not, however, exercised).[87] Of that quarter-share, 47 per cent went to Max Warburg's heirs, 26 per cent to Fritz Warburg and 9 per cent

---

* According to an internal memorandum of the Bank of England, 'There was a secret and personal agreement between the Warburg family and Brinckmann that, in the event of conditions becoming less unfavourable to Jewish banking in Germany, the family would have the right to take over 25% of the business and to restore the name.' Brinckmann initially stated that, while he was still willing to abide by this agreement, his partners were not, and that the most he could offer was 10 per cent. Eventually, however, he was persuaded to honour the agreement.

apiece to Siegmund, Eric Warburg and Ernst Spiegelberg. When the bank published its first deutschmark balance sheet after the 1948 currency reform, it declared capital of DM 3.1 million and assets of DM 25.5 million. In effect, Siegmund Warburg was to receive stock worth DM 75,780 (around £7,500) for his share in the bank that had been stolen from his family.[88]

It is not immediately obvious how Warburg's change of attitude is to be explained; suffice to say that it was not a change that lasted long. By 1950 he was discussing with Eric the need to recruit new executives to Brinckmann Wirtz and proposing the restoration of the old firm name, provided Eric were prepared to spend at least a third of the year in Hamburg.[89] 'If he [Brinckmann] should get in touch with you,' he counselled his son in 1950, 'please . . . be Prince Charming . . . Below his arrogant and frightfully egocentric surface there is a good dosis [dose] not only of shrewdness (not to be valued too highly, of course) but also of real kind-heartedness and of a – though somewhat subdued – subtle oriental wisdom.'[90] A year later, however, he dismissed Brinckmann as 'very inclined towards egocentricity and laziness'.[91] By 1952 he was pressing to restore the old name, to bring in at least one other new partner and to convert the bank into a limited company, all in order to dilute Brinckmann's influence.[92] A visit to Hamburg that summer confirmed Warburg's sense of alienation:

Brinckmann appeared to me in an even worse 'Pasha' and 'Prima donna' mood than I have ever found him before [an allusion to his Turkish mother]. I have experienced several instances when he was neither open nor honest in the statement he made, and I noticed very uncomfortably how he looked at every single question only from the point of view of his personal 'Geltungsbeduerf-nis' [that is, need for status]. (It is significant that there is no word in the English language into which this unfortunately very expressive German word can be translated.) Thus, all that happened in Hamburg was 'Gedibber' [chat-ter] without conclusions, and I have nothing worthwhile to add to this description until we meet again. In the meantime I have drawn a definite conclusion, namely that I will in future have as little as possible to do with B.W. & Co.[93]

It was, perhaps unfortunately, a resolution he proved unable to keep. As he observed in early 1953, he found himself having to spend 'a great deal of time' on Brinckmann Wirtz 'only so as to prevent anything very undesirable happening'.[94] For a time he thought he had persuaded his cousin Eric to accept the idea that S. G. Warburg should establish some new institution in Germany in which Brinckmann Wirtz might have a small stake.[95] By the second half of 1954, however, Warburg was advising Eric to consider selling his stake in the Hamburg bank, arguing that a partnership with the Deutsche Unionbank or an altogether new Düsseldorf-based 'instrument' would be preferable to continued involvement with Brinckmann Wirtz.[96] He was mystified when Eric resolved to make Hamburg his main base and to devote his energies increasingly to the former family firm, in return for being made a partner in succession to Hermann Schilling.[97] Indeed, he contemplated selling Eric his share in Brinckmann Wirtz.[98] When the Hamburg firm invited Siegmund to join its finance committee, he made his acceptance conditional on the reinstatement of the name M. M. Warburg and the appointment as partners of 'a few younger people of real calibre', conditions which were both rejected by Brinckmann, who now seemed intent on bequeathing the firm to his two sons.[99] Here was another moment when the ways might have parted. But still Warburg found it impossible to let go. He finally agreed to join the firm's finance committee, despite Brinckmann's continued refusal to accept his two conditions.[100] After all, he still remained 'closely attached . . . to the dear old Hamburg firm' – and even on occasion feigned amity towards 'Brinkie', while remaining privately contemptuous of his egotism and deeply suspicious of his nepotistic tendencies.[101]

To Siegmund Warburg, the solution seemed clear: restore the old name and revitalize the firm as a (but not, as we shall see, the) West German partner for S. G. Warburg & Co. But his every move in this direction was checked by Brinckmann. In 1960, for example, Warburg proposed by way of a compromise that the firm be renamed M. M. Warburg, Brinckmann & Co. He went so far as to imply that Brinckmann's resistance might be based on 'regard for German sensitivities with respect to Jewish names'.[102] When Eric countered with Brinckmann, M. M. Warburg & Co., Siegmund threatened to resign from the finance committee.[103] Brinckmann then proposed that his thirty-two-year-old son Christian be made a partner, to which Warburg retorted that 'in our time crown prince nepotism was more inadvisable than ever before, and that [his] suggestion to make his son a partner right away seemed to me entirely wrong'.[104] Brinckmann's position now was that the time to revert to the old firm name had been in the immediate post-war years; by the mid-1950s it was too late.[105] 'Having become much too much used in the last fifteen years to being surrounded by yes-men,' Warburg told his less assertive cousin, Brinckmann was 'inclined to take the attitude that anybody who does not agree with him is unfriendly, or "treulos" [disloyal], or lacking in kindness':

> It is no longer good for you and me to be only on the defensive. I think the time has come when Brinckmann has to be attacked for his egocentricity – which I am afraid nowadays shows not only signs of viciousness but of senility – and that he has to be told how much he owes to the old partners of MMW & Co. They put into his hands in 1938 not 'a torso' – what an incorrect word for him to use – but a firm which in spite of the Nazi situation had maintained a wonderful name, an excellent earning power and very important reserves . . . He should not forget that he owes most of it to the old partners and also to the way in which you and the other members of our group supported him after the war.[106]

Brinckmann was 'trying to establish a Brinckmann dynasty in Hamburg'; it was, moreover, 'a scandal that the old name had not been restored prominently'.[107] The result was a compromise: Brinckmann's son became a partner, but at the same time so did Hans Wuttke, formerly of Daimler-Benz, who enjoyed Siegmund Warburg's full support and repaid his confidence with his 'strong and independent views' – independent, that is, of Brinckmann.[108] In truth, by the early 1960s the Hamburg firm's relative economic importance had waned so much that the financial stakes had diminished. It had become, Warburg complained, a 'very provincial affair', focused entirely on commercial credits and all but absent from the commanding heights of German industrial finance. Yet he continued to manoeuvre to dilute Brinckmann's influence and, as we shall see, never lost sight of the ultimate goal of restoring the Warburg name in Hamburg.[109]

In all of this, Warburg was clearly not actuated by narrow self-interest. With S. G. Warburg in the ascendant, he would have stood to gain if the bank had remained Brinckmann Wirtz, without the illustrious

Warburg name. It is impossible to escape the conclusion that his principal motivation in the protracted battle over the Hamburg firm was
retrospective. Quite simply, it was a matter of principle that the nomenclature imposed in the name of Aryanization should not stand. By the
same token, Warburg regarded Eric Warburg's use of the family name
in New York as an intolerable dilution of what would now be called
the Warburg brand. When he heard that Eric was contemplating a
stock-market flotation of his firm as E. M. Warburg & Co., Siegmund
immediately wrote insisting that the firm should give up the family
name if Eric no longer had a majority of votes; not to do so would
constitute 'a sort of prostitution of the name'.[110] He made no secret of
his disapproval when Eric sold half his New York company to Lionel
Pincus, and welcomed it only grudgingly when the firm changed its
name to E. M. Warburg, Pincus & Co.[111]

To Siegmund Warburg, control was everything. Who, after all, could
be sure that Pincus would add lustre to the Warburg name rather than
detract from it? As we have seen, he had recognized even before the
Depression the limits of the private partnership, the simplest structure
for a family-controlled firm. S. G. Warburg & Co. would be organized
quite differently. In 1954 more than 99 per cent of the ordinary shares
of S. G. Warburg & Co. were acquired by a holding company called
Mercury Securities, the renamed Central Wagon (Holding) Co., a shell
company left over from railway nationalization. This company was
then floated on the London Stock Exchange.[112] The rationale of taking
the bank public in this way was threefold. First, there was the chance
to draw in outside capital. Secondly, the holding company vehicle facili-
tated diversification. As Warburg told Grunfeld, 'We must have more
than one subsidiary [besides S. G. Warburg], because banking business
was risky.'[113] From the outset, Mercury Securities also acquired and ran
non-financial businesses, beginning with Brandeis Goldschmidt, the
metal trader, and continuing to diversify so fast that by 1960 Warburg
could speak of 'our insurance broking business, our advertising agency
business and our real estate development business'.[114] Thirdly, the holding company structure ensured that Warburg retained control over the
Warburg name. 'In no circumstances must the name of the public
company be Warburg,' Grunfeld recalled his partner saying. 'Because
... you never know.' In 1956 Mercury shares were distributed between

272 individual shareholders; only a fifth of them were owned by directors of the parent company and its subsidiary. Warburg himself owned
just 6.29 per cent.[115] On the other hand, through the so-called founder
shares – which had three times the total votes of the two classes of
ordinary shares put together – S. G. Warburg & Co. was controlled by
another company, Warburg Continuation Ltd, which was 52 per cent
owned by Warburg, his wife and their two children (the remainder being
divided up among senior Warburg directors).[116] This structure was far
from straightforward, but it seemed to work, combining the tradition
of family control with the market discipline of a Stock Exchange quotation and the defence mechanism of diversification.

III

Siegmund Warburg's mother died in October 1955. His relationship
with her had always been intimate and intense. It had been Lucie who
had provided the better part of his education as a boy, drilling him in
literature more rigorously than any schoolmaster. It had been she who
had instilled in him her own distinctive ethos: an idiosyncratic mixture
of puritanical self-denial and Jewish self-criticism, which simultaneously
inspired asceticism and anxiety – a sense of belonging to the Elect, but
also a sense that membership might be withdrawn if a single line were
misquoted or a single word misspelled. No one, in short, had a greater
influence on Warburg. The stringent sense of duty, the incessant perfectionism, the love of aphorism, the contempt for social snobbery – these
were just a few of the qualities he inherited from her.[117]

It might have been expected that his mother's death would weaken
somewhat his attachment to Germany, where he had spent his formative years so much in her company. On the contrary, Warburg remained
as keenly interested as before in the fate of his former homeland.
Throughout the 1950s, wrangling over the future of the old Hamburg
firm was in many ways a distraction from the opportunities being
generated for the new London firm by the extraordinary West German
Wirtschaftswunder (economic miracle). With a remarkably modern
capital stock despite the devastation wrought by Allied bombing, a
highly educated workforce reinforced by German expellees from the

East, and plentiful export orders stimulated by the Korean War boom that began in 1950, the economy of the fledgling Federal Republic grew at rates never previously seen in European history. The performance of German industry, especially after the currency reform of 1948, was, as Warburg noted in June 1951, 'amazing'.[118] Admittedly, he retained a lifelong ambivalence towards the Germans from a political standpoint, decrying their 'lack of political ability and . . . want of . . . moderation and objectivity', but he never underestimated their aptitude for (among other things) 'technical and industrial organization'.* His relationship with Hermann Abs generated myriad business opportunities: the financing of the Hamburg shipyard Deutsche Werft, the rejuvenation of the management of Metallgesellschaft and the sale of shares in the engineering firm Mannesmann. It was to Abs that he turned in 1952 with the idea of 'a British and German Bank similar to the British and French Bank'.[119] It was to Abs he turned again in 1953 with the idea of 'a Canadian/German finance instrument in Canada'.[120] By the following year Warburg was able to inform his cousin Eric that 'our closest connection in Germany today was the Deutsche Bank group'.[121] The initiative to issue shares for major German companies on the London Stock Exchange came jointly from Warburg and Abs.[122] The same was true of the attempt to bring German money into the Commonwealth Development Finance Company Ltd.[123] In 1957 it was Abs whom Warburg sought to establish as 'a sort of intermediary for bringing about an understanding between the Bank of England and the Bank deutscher Länder' (the forerunner of the Bundesbank).[124] 'As you know,' he told Abs in January 1958, 'I make it a principle never to deal with any important business transaction in Germany without trying to cooperate with you and at least without informing you about it, even when it is a question of embryonic matters.'[125] It was therefore uncomfortable for Warburg when first East German sources and then a number of Western authors, notably Tom Bower, began to reveal the extent of Abs's complicity with the Hitler regime.[126]

---

* '[The Germans] have been great in music, poetry and metaphysics and likewise in matters of technical and industrial organisation, but the things between heaven and earth, like diplomacy, art of living, political balance and the practice of political justice, have at most times been outside the province of their aptitudes and predilections' (SGW VME/CL/CZ../2, Warburg to Hans Schaeffer, 16 July 1951).

Nevertheless, it would be misleading to portray the relationship between Warburgs and Deutsche Bank as in some sense exclusive. It was not. As more and more German companies sought to issue shares in London (and New York), there were multiple opportunities for Anglo-German co-operation and Warburg worked with more than one partner. In 1959, for example, he raised the possibility of acquiring 'a substantial block of shares' in the Bayerische Vereinsbank.[127] At the same time, he was exploring with Jean Furstenberg the possibility of 'the establishment of a closer link between SGW & Co. and Berliner Handels-Gesellschaft'.[128] It was also possible for Warburgs to act independently, as in the case of the 1960 placement in London of a tranche of shares in the August Thyssen steel company, the first Stock Exchange quotation for a continental company since the war.[129] Indeed, Warburg went so far as to offer Abs a London listing for Deutsche Bank.[130]

By the early 1960s, it was clear to Warburg that neither Brinckmann Wirtz nor Deutsche Bank could offer him the kind of presence in the West German market that he sought. Accordingly, in 1964 S. G. Warburg & Co. (in partnership with the Bank of London & South America) bought the Frankfurt bank Hans W. Petersen, renaming it S. G. Warburg & Co. KG (Kommanditgesellschaft), and seconding Gert Whitman, formerly of the US investment bank Lee Higginson, to run it alongside its founder, Petersen, and his partner Richard Daus.[131] In his more sanguine moments, Warburg imagined the new firm repeating the success of the London firm 'immediately after the war when the training and the moulding together of the right kind of team proved in the end the primary factor of long term prosperity'.[132] Characteristically, however, he also hoped that this initiative would serve to weaken Rudolf Brinckmann's position – perhaps even to force his hand on the question of the Hamburg firm's name.[133] But such hopes were stymied by the sharp decline in the German stock market that commenced more or less simultaneously with the creation of the new Frankfurt firm and continued until the end of 1966.[134] Instead, the Frankfurt and Hamburg firms ended up collaborating as both Hans Wuttke and Eric Warburg joined the Frankfurt board.[135] By 1967 Warburg had become disillusioned with the new venture, quarrelling with both Wuttke and Daus, whom he accused of suffering from 'complexes' about his status within the firm.[136] In 1969, fearful that the Frankfurt branch might be over-extending itself,

Warburg combined it with the J. M. Voith-controlled Deutsche Effecten-
und Wechselbank to form Effectenbank-Warburg AG, ousting Daus in
the process.[137] By this time Warburg had found a new German ally in
Paul Lichtenberg of the Commerzbank, who increasingly took the place
of Abs after the latter stepped down as chairman of Deutsche Bank in
1967.* Brinckmann, meanwhile, remained in Hamburg, incorrigible
and seemingly immovable.[138]

Despite the extent of his West German business activities, it would
be a mistake to conclude that Siegmund Warburg had entirely forgiven
and forgotten the Germans' past misdeeds. He frequently expressed
his doubts about West German politicians (though never the Federal
Republic's founding father, Konrad Adenauer). The Social Democrat
Carlo Schmid struck him as 'arrogant and obstinate'.[139] The strengths
of the Federal President, Theodor Heuss, did 'not lie in the field of
political strategy or tactics'.[140] The Vice-Chancellor and architect of
the economic miracle, Ludwig Erhard, was 'a kind, brilliant, but rather
uninhibited rascal'.[141] Sometimes, too, he went beyond such *ad
hominem* criticisms. Warburg distinguished between convinced Nazis
and the mass of Germans, whose role in the Third Reich he did not
regard as exceptionally malignant. 'About Nazism,' he noted revealingly in his collection of aphorisms: 'How easy it seems to be to seduce
even good and reasonably mature people.'[142] As he put it in a letter to
Paul Mazur of Lehman Brothers:

I feel that the bulk of human beings all over the world do not have the courage to stand up to bullies who possess overwhelming instruments of power
and have no hesitation to use such power ruthlessly. Moreover I am afraid the
terrible cruelties perpetrated by the Nazis – though much larger in numbers
– were not worse in monstrosity than the cruelties which were committed over
the centuries by the criminal and perverted elements which are to be found in
any national community – indeed no worse than cruelties which are at present
being committed in various corners of the world. The special horror of the
Nazi cruelties was that their power for evil was organized with the application
of the scientific methods of our time.[143]

* Rather surprisingly, Abs's successor declined to undertake a private placement of
Mercury Securities shares in Germany. Undaunted, Warburg sought to patch up the
relationship with Deutsche Bank, arguing for a triangular partnership with Commerzbank.

However, for this very reason, he was a good deal more critical of the role played by Germany's elites. 'I am afraid the words "Befehl ist Befehl" [an order is an order] apply today as much as ever to German mentality as far as most of the people in the upper and middle classes are concerned,' he told an English friend in 1956.[144] While many Germans 'had really learnt from the experience of the Hitler period', he observed in 1959, the same could not be said for 'a large number of the leaders of the heavy industry who are as pompous and arrogant as they ever were'.[145]

On the other hand, he was unfazed by the short-lived surge in support for the radical nationalist National Democratic Party in the 1960s, rightly seeing it as an aberration. As far as Warburg was concerned, the democratic foundations of the new Germany were sound; Jews had more to fear from anti-Semites in Egypt or, indeed, the racist regime in South Africa.[146] He told one correspondent in 1967 that 'the resurgence of a nationalistic and expansionist Germany' was a lesser danger than 'the extravagant and completely irresponsible ambitions of the Middle East potentates'.[147] Moreover, unlike in the 1920s, the German right had no hope of mobilizing support on the issue of lost territory or reunification. Under the conditions of the Cold War, there was no way that reunification could be achieved other than through a sacrifice of West German freedom – the price-tag attached to all Soviet proposals to end Germany's division.[148] The real trouble with the new Germany was not that it remained the same, but rather that it had changed rather more than Warburg liked. There was now, he told his son in 1960, 'too much complacency and too much pride of a rather materialistic character – after too much intensity in self-pity now too much intensity of the opposite kind'.[149] He continued to monitor the German political scene closely for any signs of anti-Semitic recidivism, never doubting that there were still 'people with the national-socialist mentality', but with little expectation of a serious Nazi revival.[150] Even the abrasively conservative Bavarian Christian Socialist Franz-Josef Strauss, though he might 'indulg[e] in noisy exhibitionism with almost as much vulgarity as Hitler did', was clearly no Nazi.[151]

Inevitably, there were those who criticized Warburg for the energy with which he promoted the economic rehabilitation of post-war Germany. Among these was the former M. M. Warburg executive Hans

Meyer, now based in New York. When Warburg heard that Meyer was objecting that two 'Jewish houses' (Warburgs and Rothschilds) were handling the Thyssen share issue in London, he responded with barely contained anger. Accusing Meyer of being 'both hypocritical and superficial', he reminded him that:

Soon after the first weeks of the Hitler regime I strongly advocated with all partners of MMW & Co. and W[arburg] & Co. that we should get out of Germany as quickly as possible, not only for our own sake but above all as an example to other German Jews and as an action of exhortation and support to them, and that any contact with the people who were then masters of Germany should be avoided as far as possible. You took another view at that time. I emphatically expressed my disagreement to you and others who shared your views but I did not question the soundness of your motives from a moral or quasi moral perspective.

Just as I felt in the years of the Hitler regime that we should keep away from that regime at all costs, I feel today that, with a decent and very statesmanlike regime being at the head of German affairs, businessmen in London or in New York or anywhere else – whether Jewish or non-Jewish – should deal actively with sensible business propositions emanating from Germany and should not be ashamed of identifying themselves with such matters. It seems to me better to strengthen people who are decent – although they may have been weak – and who want to start by turning over a new leaf after a bad past [did he perhaps have Abs in mind?], rather than to appease bullies. In other words, I prefer to deal with decent German industrialists under the Adenauer regime rather than to deal with such people under the Hitler regime.

This was not simply a matter of economic pragmatism. It also reflected Warburg's understanding of the Western integration of Germany as a strategic imperative:

From the very first when I started negotiations last year in regard to the Thyssen matter I was, of course, fully aware in my mind that if we did a transaction of this sort we might be criticized by various circles, not least amongst certain parts of the British Jingo Press. However, I thought we ought not to be frightened by the reactions which we might encounter with such groups who in the six years before the second world war were much less anti-German than they are now. On the contrary if we want to serve the cause of strengthening the

Atlantic Community, to my mind the foremost political and social cause of the present time – everything we can do to effect and encourage transactions between the German business community and other business communities in the western world appears to me of considerable importance . . .[152]

IV

The reality was, of course, that in many respects Siegmund Warburg remained throughout his life an uprooted German. 'Siegmund is very German', his old friend Paul Ziegler once observed, 'and . . . very XIX century German at that, plus a strong dose of Nietzsche, and then Hitler came and made him "heimatlos" [without a homeland] for ever – I was always surprised how utterly unenglish he remained . . . And so his business became his only Heimat.'[153] That was why he could not bring himself to give in on the question of the Hamburg firm's name, regardless of how insignificant the financial implications were. And, in the end, he succeeded. In 1969, as Brinckmann turned eighty, Warburg was able to force through an agreement to rename the firm M. M. Warburg-Brinckmann, Wirtz & Co. in the context of a DM 6 million increase in its capital.[154] The announcement in January 1970 represented one of the hardest-fought victories of Warburg's entire career. 'I do not deny', he told his cousin Eric, 'that I worked hard for this end and sometimes found the nature of the obstacles with which I had to contend almost unbearable.'[155] As Eric Faulkner, the chairman of Lloyds Bank, recalled, Warburg had once declared his two personal ambitions to be to put the name Warburg on a par with Baring in London and to see the family name restored in Hamburg. The second had taken at least ten years longer to achieve than the first.

The same sense of affinity with his German past led Warburg to accept an invitation to a reunion at his old school at Urach in 1968.* He had, he told another former pupil, 'always resisted the thesis of so-called German collective guilt, as generalizations of any sort are a

---

* Most of his fellow former pupils had become Protestant pastors. With ineffable Swabian parochialism, they were most impressed by the fact that Warburg had retained so much of his hair.

great sin against intellectual and moral justice'.[156] He made a second visit to Urach in 1977 and even contemplated buying back the old estate at Uhenfels where he had spent so much of his youth.[157] In a somewhat less forgiving spirit, he belatedly set about trying to obtain compensation for his mother's movable property, which the Nazis had prevented from being transported to England and which had been destroyed during the war in an air raid in Stuttgart.[158] His reconciliation with his former *Heimat* was complete in 1973, when the government of Willy Brandt awarded him the Grosse Verdienstkreuz, the Order of Merit of the Federal Republic. As he told the German ambassador in 1973, his loyalties were twofold: 'to his old fatherland, and to his new fatherland'.[159]

Anglo-German reconciliation was not, however, his primary objective, though it was without question an objective he favoured and fostered. In the words of one of his oldest German friends, Edmund Stinnes, Warburg had once confessed on the telephone that it was his 'life's mission to consolidate WORLDWIDE the place of the name WARBURG in "haute finance", from London to New York, from Zurich to Frankfurt'.[160] This rings true, even if the bombastic capital letters were Stinnes's rather than Warburg's. To achieve that goal, it was plainly not enough merely to restore old ties to Germany. Of equal, if not greater, importance was the reconstruction of financial relations across the Atlantic to New York. Here, too, pre-war family ties would play a major – and not always helpful – role.

7

Atlantic Unions

As you know, I strongly believe that nothing is more important to our Western world than Anglo-American co-operation in every field of activity including the business spheres.

Siegmund Warburg, 1952[1]

Up to that time the [British] Establishment felt that any radical change in management in any of the big enterprises was wrong . . . This complacency was shattered by the British Aluminium war, complacency which was a mixture of wrong pride and of laziness . . . Michael Berry, a partner of Robert Fleming and one of the then leading City bankers, said to me: 'If it can happen that somebody can buy shares and obtain influence in a company and then change the management, which member of the management can sleep quietly in his bed?' I replied to the effect that there was no reason for someone to sleep quietly in his bed if he was not doing a good job.

Siegmund Warburg, 1976[2]

I

Back in 1927, Siegmund Warburg had called the Wall Street investment bank Kuhn, Loeb & Co. 'a splendidly brilliant star but, I fear, a star that is steadily and rapidly losing its lustre'. He had found the senior partners there (to whom he was distantly related since the marriages of his 'uncles' Felix and Paul into the Loeb and Schiff families) more interested in 'personal vanity, hobbies and snobbery' than in 'practical, businesslike entrepreneurship'.[3] 'The more time I spend at Kuhn, Loeb,' he had told his uncle Max, 'the more impressed I am with the wonderful charm and the splendid structure of the firm, above all with the vast, unexploited possibilities which lie within it. The exploitation of these possibilities would not require artificial [means] or an exceptionally big effort. It depends solely upon the various partners taking an interest in business again.'[4] For the next thirty years or more, Siegmund Warburg clung to his dream of reviving Kuhn Loeb and restoring the dynamism that appeared to have died with Jacob Schiff in 1920. Grown fat before the Depression on the profits of issuing US railway bonds and stocks, then excluded (along with other investment banks) from commercial banking by the 1933 Glass–Steagall Act, Kuhn Loeb had become chronically complacent and risk-averse, seemingly indifferent to the new business opportunities that opened up in the United States after the war.[5] The firm still possessed one of the most revered names on Wall Street, second only to Morgan. Its client list was a Who's Who of American big business, from Anheuser Busch to Westinghouse. Asked how many people worked there, however, one partner famously answered: 'About half.'

This probably explains why, on his first trip to New York after the war, in February 1946, Warburg was mainly concerned with the possibility of establishing an independent pied-à-terre for S. G. Warburg & Co., rather than reforging his old ties with Kuhn Loeb. Indeed, he went out of his way to tell Paul Mazur 'that we were in no way bound to . . . Kuhn, Loeb & Co.'.[6] When he was offered the use of an office at the Bank of Manhattan, he readily accepted. Warburg's first impression of the new leadership at Kuhn Loeb – which comprised John Schiff, Sir William Wiseman, Ben Buttenwieser and John Meyer – was that 'we should not expect them to be flexible or subtle enough for dealing with complicated international propositions'.[7] The most he was prepared to contemplate at this stage was a 'platonic friendship'.[8] This feeling was strengthened when the US government issued an indictment against Kuhn Loeb and other leading Wall Street issuing houses, alleging anti-competitive practices.[9] As far as Warburg could see, there was a glaring discrepancy between the 'wonderful name and the enormous wealth of the firm' and the 'most incredible muddle' of its management structure.[10] Warburg was more impressed by his former German associates Ernst Spiegelberg and George Spitzer, both of whom seemed to be eager to seize the new opportunities of the post-war world. Warburg therefore decided to reduce his firm's stake in the Mercantile Overseas Trust, which had ceased to be profitable during the war, and to focus instead on a new entity, American European Associates Inc., which was intended to be 'a pure finance and holding company' under Spiegelberg's direction.[11]

Warburg made a succession of visits to New York in the late 1940s, returning in June 1947, in November of the same year and again in January 1949. This was no small undertaking at a time when it was still usual to cross the Atlantic by sea.* To compensate for the brevity of these trips, he crammed an extraordinary number of meetings into each day, limiting each one to thirty minutes.[12] Yet the initial results were disappointing. By the end of 1948, he and his colleagues had made no fewer than fourteen journeys to the United States. But the amount of business that had been generated had been 'extremely poor'.[13] In its first year, AEA produced 'nothing but either a sort of collection of Zufalls-transactions [accidental transactions] or a kind of Kleinkraemer [junk] shop . . . classes of business . . . not suitable for bankers' or professional investors' investments'.[14] 'A.E.A. has been of no use to SGW & Co.,' concluded Warburg bluntly in January 1949. 'Notably no investment propositions of any special value have been produced for A.E.A.'s own account or for SGW & Co. . . . No earnings have been achieved and A.E.A. has not been able to contribute even to the expenses which have been incurred by various members of SGW & Co. on the occasion of their journeys to the Western side of the Atlantic.'[15] In short, the firm was proving to be 'a weed allotment suffering from too little humus and too many gardeners and stones'. So disillusioned was Warburg that by 1950 he had concluded that there was significantly more worthwhile business to be done in London than in New York.[16] When Wiseman explicitly offered to replace Rothschilds

---

* Warburg always found these Atlantic crossings a challenge because of the enforced socializing they entailed. 'I would have had still more relaxation', he wrote to Eric Korner after returning to London in October 1951, 'if there had not been so many acquaintances of mine on board who all have a strange hesitation in going to bed at normal hours . . . In most of these cases there is a strange arithmetic relationship between the deficiency of sleep and the number of glasses of whisky consumed.'

with Warburgs as the 'European and particularly British chief connection of K.L. & Co.', Warburg politely declined.[17] This, however, by no means signalled the end of his interest in the United States – or in Kuhn, Loeb & Co.

II

Although, as we shall see, Siegmund Warburg was a lifelong proponent of European integration, he never saw this as incompatible with a staunch Atlanticism. He could indeed claim to have inspired the Atlantic Charter which formed the basis of the wartime and post-war relationship between the United Kingdom and the United States. Shortly before Lord Halifax took up the British ambassadorship in Washington in 1941, Warburg had recommended that he propose 'a new Magna Carta [for] the world' – and not just for the Commonwealth – at his first US press conference.[18] The alternative to the Anglophone alliance was all too clear. As early as 1940 Warburg saw with remarkable prescience that the fall of France might ultimately mean 'a further extension of Russian power', conceivably as far as the Rhine.[19] This fear that Hitler's defeat would be achieved only at the expense of handing the continent to Stalin haunted him throughout the war and laid the foundation for his firmly anti-Soviet outlook during the Cold War. 'The Communist Party may have its good sides,' he observed in 1942, at the high tide of pro-Soviet feeling in Britain, but 'it is and will always be an anti-democratic party.'[20] Though prone, like many in the Labour Party, to moments of wartime sentimentality about the 'realism, fearlessness and sense of purpose' of the Soviet Union – which was, after all, shedding vastly more blood than the Western democracies in pursuit of victory – Warburg never lost sight of the underlying threat to freedom posed by Stalin's regime.[21] Though at times a little too ready to consign Eastern Europe (in particular Poland)* to the Soviet sphere of influence, he had no illusions about the consequences for those on the wrong side

---

* Significantly, Warburg assumed that Czechoslovakia would not be consigned to the Soviet bloc, and visited Prague in June 1946 with a view to resuming business there. But he was disquieted by the Communist penetration of organized labour and the deleterious effects of post-war nationalization of the economy.

of the coming 'Chinese Wall' across Europe.[22] The more aggressive Soviet policy became – particularly at the time of the 1948–9 Berlin blockade – the more vehement Warburg became in his denunciations of Stalin's 'totalitarian' and 'bellicose' regime.[23] He was hypersensitive to anything that could remotely be construed as 'appeasement' of Moscow.[24] He consistently refused to have any dealings whatever with Communist governments.[25]

It is easy today to forget the cloud under which the generation of the Cold War had to live once the Soviet Union succeeded in acquiring its own atomic capability. From 1949 until 1987 the possibility never wholly disappeared of a devastating superpower confrontation that would have dwarfed the Second World War in its destructiveness. 'If the Russians really have the atomic bomb on any worthwhile scale,' Warburg wrote to his friend William Schubart in October 1949, 'then I am quite sure they will be able to carry it as far as the United States . . . No geographical distance is today any protection. The only relatively safe places today are probably [those] . . . which are comparatively remote from centres of population and of industry':

Talking on this subject I am reminded of the story of the refugee from Central Europe who came to England in 1938 or so, and worried as to the next place to which he should move on, and could not make up his mind. He was asked 'Where do you really want to go?' and he answered 'Far, far away.' He was again asked 'Far away from where?' He answered 'Far away from everywhere.'

A point of view such as this is today more widespread than at any previous time. It is a sign of the both futile and hysterical attitude which is the accompaniment of the moral, social and economic disintegration which started in our world with the First World War and which has made steady progress almost ever since in spite of short interruptions by brighter spells. In the face of this disintegration most of those who are not prepared to be subdued by hysterical complexes can either act in accordance with Voltaire's prescription 'Il faut cultiver le [sc.notre] jardin' or lead an active life in accordance with the 'as if' philosophy, namely act and behave as if there were no disintegration around us.[26]

There is an important sense in which Warburg did indeed have to live the rest of his life 'as if' the world were neither so dangerous nor so decadent as he inwardly knew it to be.

Yet Warburg was intuitively right about the magnitude of the risk of nuclear war, just as he was quick to grasp the stabilizing implications of deterrence and what came to be known as mutually assured destruction.[27] Even at the height of the Korean War, when General Douglas MacArthur's combination of extreme belligerence and political ambition suggested a disquieting parallel with the German First World War general and early Hitler supporter Erich von Ludendorff, Warburg still understood that a full-scale 'hot' war between the superpowers was less likely than 'a continuation of the cold World War [sic] accompanied by a few isolated hot wars as in Korea and Indo-China': 'I even visualize the possibility that in due course we may start to consider the cold war as a sort of normal habit for the next one or two decades and we may then gradually settle down to it in a less nervous tension than prevailed hitherto.'[28] Indeed, as early as 1951, Warburg ventured to look ahead to a time of what would later be called détente and even convergence between the superpowers:

If one is prepared to indulge in particularly optimistic anticipations, one might even visualise that after ten years or so of further cold wars, East and West may get used to a co-existence in a spirit which will be a strange mixture of mutual suspicion and mutual tolerance. It is an old experience of psychology that, although there is, abstractly speaking, a conflict between suspicion and tolerance, in reality a good dose of suspicion mixed with a good dose of tolerance results in quite a sound spiritual catalyst in settling relations between contrary mental attitudes; this applies alike to individuals and nations. Thus, after a long interval, East and West may slowly adopt a more peaceful attitude towards one another and at the same time the East may tend to develop in a less totalitarian and less centralized direction, whilst the West may become organised on a wider regional basis and on a more socialist pattern.[29]

What produced this somewhat uncharacteristic optimism was Warburg's gradual realization that Western leaders were not about to repeat the mistakes of the appeasement era. 'Compared with the autumn of 1938 or the spring of 1940,' he told one correspondent,

the Western World is today, although still in great danger, much more awake than was the case at that time. By the way, a slight strengthening of my optimism results from the fact that almost all those who pooh-poohed my convinced forebodings of the Second World War during the years 1933–1939 are the ones who now accept the third World War as just around the corner. The Neville Chamberlains who believed in 1938 and even in 1939 in 'Peace in our time' are now the gloomy [ones] prophesying imminent disasters.[30]

The key to the stabilization of the Cold War was the emergence of the North Atlantic Treaty Organization as a credible guarantor of the security of Western Europe. As early as May 1950 Warburg had become convinced that the security of the West depended on 'a real defence and currency union between North America and Western Europe'.[31] He even proposed the formation of a bipartisan association – Friends of the Atlantic Union – which was intended to rally 'Industry, City and Trade Unions' behind the emerging Western alliance.[32] Interestingly, Warburg described this venture as 'immensely more important than the various associations which try to further the purposes of the United Nations, of Federal Union and of European Union'.[33] As he explained to Paul Mazur – who feared that 'Russia would profit from . . . isolated hot wars' and that 'the only possibility of beating Soviet Russia [lay] in a Third World War' – Warburg was confident that 'a well-concerted policy of the Western Powers and their friends [would] weaken Russia continuously without leading to a Third World War'.[34] Among those he invited to join the new organization were the former Foreign Secretary Lord Halifax, his fellow banker Francis Glyn and the economists James Meade and Lionel Robbins.[35] Later recruits to the cause were the Labour leader Hugh Gaitskell, the Liberal leader Jo Grimond, the former Attorney-General Hartley Shawcross and the novelist Rebecca West.[36] The agreed objective was to deepen the existing Atlantic defence alliance by instituting, 'as a minimum, regular meetings of a Council of Ministers, served by a common secretariat'.[37]

At the same time, Warburg appreciated that the Soviet Union was an antagonist different in character from Nazi Germany. 'In the case of Nazi Germany,' he observed in a letter to the military historian Basil Liddell Hart, 'there was never any readiness for co-existence, only passion for world domination. In Soviet Russia, however, the situation is different from what it was in Nazi Germany':

There are despots in the Kremlin as ruthless as were the Hitlerites, but besides these despots there are some very shrewd and constructive thinkers who are trying to get the upper hand of the tyrants. Nobody can foresee, of course, how this fight between the reasonable and unreasonable elements in the Kremlin will be resolved but there is at least a chance that the East–West conflict may end in . . . coexistence. The only ways to achieve this are, first, by continuously building up the strength of the Western allies, second, raising the standard of living in the East (particularly in South-East Asia), and third, by a relaxation of tension . . .[38]

Warburg was also quick to grasp how easily the apparently monolithic Communist bloc might fracture. If Yugoslavia could break with Stalin, what was to stop China one day breaking with his successors? This important point was first suggested to him in 1954 by the ambitious Labour frontbencher Harold Wilson.[39] He came to see Eisenhower's abrasive Secretary of State, John Foster Dulles, as partly responsible for throwing 'the Chinese and the Russians into one another's arms'.[40]

The Cold War might on more than one occasion have escalated into a hot war. Indeed, it became a hot war in a number of countries – not only Korea and later Indo-China, but also Guatemala, Cambodia and Angola, the principal theatres of the 'Third World's War'. Yet in Warburg's eyes it was fundamentally a contest between two somewhat similar military-industrial – and bureaucratic – complexes. In 1955 he was intrigued to hear Harold Talbot, the then US Secretary for Air, 'talk about the American Air Force as against the Russian Air Force . . . like the managing director of one industrial company talking about another industrial company'.[41] If American politicians seldom impressed him, at least they were less likely to make the 'very serious mistake' that Warburg foresaw Nikita Khrushchev making. 'The fact that the collective dictatorship of the important post-Stalin period has now given way to individual dictatorship will have, I think, the consequence that Khrushchev, like Hitler and Mussolini before him, will over-play his cards,' he predicted in April 1958. 'I think it will be the old story of a dictator who is not being properly informed by his underlings because they do not want to tell him unpleasant news and who, due to being supplied with insufficient intelligence service, will draw wrong conclusions.'[42] He deplored Khrushchev's 'disgusting and bullying' behaviour in 1960 – epitomized by his intemperate shoe-banging denunciation of the 'American imperialists' at the United Nations on

12 October – and correctly foresaw a crisis over Berlin ('even less of a cause appealing today to . . . ordinary people in England, France or even the United States . . . than was the Sudetenland in 1938').[43] True, the new Soviet leader had signalled an end to domestic terror in his 'secret' speech against Stalin in 1956.[44] Nevertheless, superpower confrontations like the construction of the Berlin Wall (1961), the Cuban Missile Crisis (1962) and the escalation of American involvement in Vietnam thereafter gradually revived Warburg's earlier fear 'that we are faced today with a drift towards an atomic war'. Now, however, it was an accidental war that he feared: 'No-one really wants it, but no-one among the real powers . . . is prepared to take resolute steps to protect humanity from committing suicide.'[45] Incompetence generally struck Warburg as a bigger threat than malice.[46]

III

For all his commitment to the Atlantic alliance as a bulwark against Soviet expansion, Warburg was never an uncritical Americanophile. On the contrary, he was quite easily irritated by what he saw as the double standards of US foreign policy. He was especially irked by Congressman James P. Richards, whom he encountered at a dinner with the Welsh Labour MP Aneurin Bevan in September 1944:

Mr. Richards asked whether as a test case of the attitude of the British people of today towards Imperialism they would be prepared to renounce their possessions of Gibraltar and Malta in favour of an international authority. We all answered the question with 'yes' provided there would be a solution based on an international authority. Bevan said: 'Without any doubt the overwhelming majority of the people of this country would be prepared to renounce all the maritime key points in the world, for instance Gibraltar, Malta and the Straits of Singapore if the same would apply to say the Straits of the Bosporus, the Straits of Copenhagen and the Panama Canal.' Thereupon Mr. Richards said: 'All that would be alright, but of course the U.S. could not renounce their authority over the Panama Canal!' . . . Mr. Richards mentioned at great length that whilst it was criminal on the part of the British to maintain their regime in India, the attitude of the Americans towards the Negroes was entirely justified.[47]

One of the greatest blunders of the war, Warburg later reflected, had been Roosevelt's 'wrongly-reasoned resentment against so-called British imperialism', which had led him to 'sacrific[e] strategic key positions to Stalin . . . thus letting down his British and French friends in Western Europe'.[48] At times, Warburg could lapse into an almost Blimpish anti-Americanism: Americans did not converse with guests at lunch but cross-examined them, their railway stations were intolerably chaotic, their stock market was 'Monte Carlo without the fun of it'[49] – in short, they had 'jumped straight from trees into motorcars'.[50] 'I can summarize my impression', he wrote after his first post-war visit,

by saying, that most of the individuals I have met – even those who are outstandingly intelligent – change their views according to the movements of the Stock Exchange. What is even worse is a terrifying uniformity of opinions and reasoning of likes and dislikes. Sometimes I think that the uniformity and cessation of individualism here goes perhaps as far as it is supposed to go in Russia – only with this difference, that the penalty for nonconformity in Russia is death, while the penalty here is starvation or social ostracism.[51]

Unlike many more conventional Atlanticists, then, Warburg never thought of the Cold War in terms of a contest between Western (much less American) virtue and Soviet vice. 'I am afraid that this modern barbarism is spreading further not only east but also west of the Iron Curtain,' he wrote in a revealing letter on the very last day of the 1940s, 'and not only in the Western Hemisphere but also in Western Europe':

It looks to me as if the only parts of the world where good old Western traditions and culture will be preserved are some small, well-integrated sort of islands which will not be entirely submerged in this flood of modern barbarism. It will indeed be only a small number of compact units which have reached a very high degree of internal cohesion and balance and which are not suffering from the frustrating uniformity of overgrown, outsized and over-centralised units; the latter term certainly applies today to Soviet Russia and its satellites and might increasingly apply to the U.S.A., on the other hand, I include amongst those well-integrated islands, Great Britain and some of the Dominions (not South Africa!), Switzerland, the Scandinavian countries and perhaps a few others.[52]

The superiority of the West lay in the continued existence of these few 'islands' of traditional values, rather than in the caricature of 'Western

Civilization from Plato to NATO' purveyed in American universities in the Cold War years.

Warburg's economic critique of the post-war transatlantic order was more profound. He had two objections. First, the Bretton Woods system devised by British and American experts in 1944 retained a link to gold, in that the dollar remained convertible into specie. Secondly, Bretton Woods envisaged continued restraints on the international mobility of capital as the corollary of fixed exchange rates and more or less independent national monetary policies. Neither arrangement struck Warburg as desirable. From 1940, at the latest, he was a convinced opponent of any semblance of a return to gold, arguing facetiously that the best use of the vast US gold reserve after the war would be to manufacture ashtrays to sell to tourists.[53] From 1942 onwards he argued that the wartime policy of Lend-Lease, whereby the United States extended large-scale credits to its allies to equip them with matériel, should be prolonged into peacetime, though preferably through some kind of private, non-profit corporation. As he envisaged it, this entity had much in common with the International Monetary Fund devised at Bretton Woods by Keynes and his American counterpart Harry Dexter White.[54]

But Warburg's hope that after the war 'the Americans and the British [would] help one another in giving a joint lead to the world through . . . a combined Lease-Lend system' and 'industrial cooperation' was to be disappointed.[55] As Keynes had discovered at first hand in Washington, the Americans regarded the approaching peace as an opportunity to humble the British Empire, not to shore it up. By late 1943 Warburg had gloomily concluded 'that Britain in preparing for the solution of post-war problems has to link up more closely with the Dominions and with the West-European countries and cannot rely on the U.S. at all'.[56] What he saw as the 'aggressive economic policy of the U.S.' filled him with dismay.[57] The cancellation of Lend-Lease immediately after the cessation of hostilities confirmed that Britain would initially have to fend for itself,[58] and that the US might well commit more resources to the reconstruction of its former enemies than to that of its former allies.[59]

Anticipating no further US financial aid, Warburg turned his mind to what the private sector might be able to accomplish. 'Those who play some part in international banking', he more than once declared, 'should try as far as they can to contribute to a closer link-up between American finance and industry and British finance and industry.'[60] His initial idea was that American companies should establish 'manufacturing subsidiaries' in the UK, focusing on articles likely to be in short supply in post-war Britain, such as 'labour-saving devices for households and . . . cheap houses, furniture and textile goods'.[61] The difficulty was that the United States was insistent that exchange controls be lifted and sterling made convertible at the earliest possible date, something Warburg saw as impossible without the support of the Federal Reserve.[62] Matters were only made worse by domestic inflation in the United States, which was pushing up the cost of essential British imports from America.[63] At the same time – as British officials had made clear to him – American companies would be able to acquire only minority shareholdings in any UK firms. Despite much talk of 'multilateral trade and all round convertibility of currencies', the steps towards restoring free trade and capital flows across the Atlantic proved to be painfully slow.[64] This helps explain why, as we have seen, Warburg's efforts in post-war New York yielded such scant financial results.

Under these circumstances, it is hardly surprising that Warburg began to contemplate an alternative North American strategy – further north than the United States. Canada, he noted in September 1946, might offer at least 'two important advantages as compared with the U.S.'. For one thing, 'the pioneering stage in industry' was 'only beginning' in Canada, while Canadian administration was, in his view, 'far superior in competence'.[65] Canada also seemed to offer a more familiar business environment, complete with career rather than politically appointed officials.[66] At the same time, focusing on Canada accorded well with post-war hopes in Whitehall and the City of London that the old imperial ties could be economically revivified. As a result, a good deal of Warburg's transatlantic activity in the late 1940s and early 1950s was focused on Canadian rather than US companies. The first of these, Lomont Corporation, was a disastrous joint venture, whose managing director turned out to 'know all about Renaissance drawings, but as it turned out, not so much about banking'.[67] A happier venture was Triarch, established in Toronto under the leadership of Tony Griffin 'to provide from British and other sources finance and technical

experience for developing the natural wealth and expanding the industry and trade of Canada'.[68] Even more impressive on paper, though
less so in practice, was the Transoceanic Development Corporation,
which brought together a veritable 'galaxy' of London and New York
firms to make 'equity investments in countries other than the United
States and Canada'.[69] Yet Warburg was never firmly persuaded that
trade with Britain's erstwhile Dominions, colonies and other possessions offered a credible economic future for Britain itself. Indeed, he
later complained that he 'had to deal in Canada more than in any other
country with businessmen whose lack of courage in facing disagreements in a straightforward manner is of the same high degree as their
pretension of supreme virtue'.[70] A revealing moment came in 1955,
when Edmund de Rothschild sought to persuade him of the merits of
the British Newfoundland Corporation, in which N. M. Rothschild
had taken a substantial stake. Rothschild was forced by Warburg 'to
admit that, whilst there were immense opportunities in Newfoundland
of building a big power station, nobody could yet say who would buy
the power'.[71]

As it turned out, the incoherent and apparently self-centred policy
of the United States towards Western Europe in the immediate post-war
period was a fleeting aberration. With the intensification of superpower
rivalry in the eastern Mediterranean, Central Europe and the Far East
– and the increasingly strident tone of Soviet foreign policy – there was
a change of mood in Washington. Sudden alarm at the prospect of
Soviet dominos falling at either end of Eurasia galvanized the Truman
administration into an unprecedented (and since unmatched) peacetime
aid package: the European Recovery Plan, forever associated with the
name of Secretary of State General George Marshall though as much
the brainchild of his assistant and successor Dean Acheson, which gave
European governments a total of $11.8 billion between 1948 and 1952
and made available an additional $1.5 billion in the form of loans – a
transfer equivalent to around 1.1 per cent of US gross national product over that period and an average of 2.5 per cent of the recipients'
national income. It was not a huge sacrifice, to be sure; indeed, from
the vantage point of American exporters it was a fine example of
enlightened self-interest, since the dollars were spent partly on Amer-
ican-made capital goods. For the European recipients, however, that

was just the point: Marshall Aid alleviated the balance of payments problems that had been constraining post-war investment. None of this would have happened without fear of Soviet expansion and President Harry Truman's conversion to the strategy of containment formulated by the State Department's George F. Kennan. As Warburg put it:

Nobody has helped more in moving the United States away from isolationism than Mr Molotov [the Soviet Foreign Minister]. Great Britain and all the other nations of Western Europe would be entirely justified in presenting an address of thanks to Mr Molotov for whatever assistance they may receive through the Marshall Plan if presenting such an address of thanks were not contradictory to the rules of diplomacy.[72]

In absolute terms, it is often forgotten, Britain received the largest amount of Marshall Aid: in all just over $3 billion. Yet Warburg had no illusions that this would provide any more than a temporary respite from the grave structural problems that beset the UK economy. As we have seen, he urged Stafford Cripps (who was chancellor when the Marshall Plan was launched) to maintain his policy of austerity and to resist the temptation of currency devaluation as a quick remedy.[73] At the same time, Warburg continued to press for 'some sort of an economic union between the British Commonwealth and the United States' based on the 'growing coordination' of 'a narrowing dollar area with the strongest currency existing under today's conditions and on the other hand of a widening sterling area with a relatively weaker currency'.[74] His fear, by February 1949, was that 'people in America [were] generally too optimistic with regard to Britain's future':

I am afraid the attitude . . . is like one of those glamorous but quickly passing fashions of which one should not take too much notice. In a way it is even dangerous that people here are just now so impressed by the progress made in Britain, for they will be the more disappointed when the setbacks come which have to be expected. The gloom and despondency will then be just as exaggerated as the optimism is now.[75]

With the benefit of hindsight, we can see that Warburg was too pessimistic about the economic prospects of the Western world as a whole. His fears of 'alternating deflation and inflation scares' were certainly premature in 1949.[76] On the other hand, his concern that Britain's economy would struggle in the post-war years was all too well founded. With an average annual per capita GDP growth rate of 2.4 per cent between 1950 and 1973, the United Kingdom was the weakest of all the West European economies; growth in Germany was twice as rapid.[77] As we have seen, the drastic devaluation of sterling in 1949 – the first of many – did not impress Warburg because in his view 'the opportunity for using devaluation as a starting point for a new policy of harder work, decrease in Government expenditure, and liberalizing trading within Western Europe' had been 'entirely missed'. Despite the stimulus provided to British exports by devaluation, Warburg could 'well foresee that by the end of the year sterling will be . . . again at a discount and futile talk about devaluation will start again'.[78] This proved prescient. Nor did Warburg see much hope of salvation in a change of government, anticipating little 'difference between the policy of a future Conservative and a future Labour government'.[79] As he saw it, if the Conservatives were to win in 1950, 'we will have just as much austerity and we might even get more import currency restrictions'. The main difference between a Conservative and Labour government would be 'that a Conservative government will not nationalize the steel industry nor carry through any other nationalizing measures and that, paradox[ical] as it may sound, a Conservative government will carry on a less reactionary foreign policy than a Labour government'.[80] Anticipating the cross-party consensus that emerged over a wide range of policy issues in the 1950s, Warburg expected to see 'the extreme elements . . . rather pushed into the background' and a return to the 'last century's game of musical chairs between alternating Tory and Whig governments – fighting one another furiously, however not differing very much on basic matters of policy but mainly on points of emphasis'.[81] He was dismissive of R. A. Butler's efforts as chancellor of the exchequer ('an ardent appeaser in regard to international policy at the time of Munich and . . . now an appeaser in regard to financial matters'), condemning the 'completely anarchical' system of wage bargaining in Britain, which had wholly severed the relationship between pay and productivity.[82] 'I wonder how many people outside the Government still think that purely monetary measures, such as the increase of the Bank Rate, can have a real impact on the ailments which have to be cured,' Warburg wrote in February 1956. 'I suppose only people who combine in such a unique way arrogance and inefficiency as the present Government.'[83] Conservative and Labour chancellors alike, as Warburg foresaw, would struggle to achieve internal and external balance throughout the post-war period. The 1959 Radcliffe Committee on the Working of the Monetary System largely agreed with his view that traditional monetary policy was unequal to the task of managing Britain's overstretched economy.[84]

The best hope for Britain, in Warburg's view, was not devaluation but foreign capital, which might bring with it the superior managerial and industrial methods that were indispensable if British productivity were to be raised. In an important memorandum on 'economic–social defence' drafted in May 1950, he called for:

1. In the field of economic development . . . increasing productivity through technical improvements and through better management.
2. In the field of economic pooling . . . more efficient allocation of man-power and material resources between the various countries concerned through regional authorities and in other similar ways.
3. In the field of finance . . . stimulating and absorbing for great international purposes the saving power of the various countries concerned through joint international issuing transactions and through rational direction of investments.

Marshall Aid should be continued, Warburg argued, through a new Atlantic Finance Board, 'to assist those countries which would require financial outside help'.[85] If Bretton Woods were not overhauled, he warned, there would be no end to 'the present international carousel game of devaluations, revaluations and "letting currencies find their own level" (an especially ambiguous and dangerous term!)'.[86] Whereas others saw NATO as primarily a military alliance, Warburg was keen to give it a financial dimension, not least to alleviate the pressures on the British economy arising from the country's multiple overseas security commitments. To this end, he envisaged his Finance Board issuing a $30 billion loan 'guaranteed jointly and severally by the sponsors of the North Atlantic Treaty'.[87] Other schemes floated in this period included 'a possible New York organization for dealing with American armament orders to be given to European industrial firms' and 'an international loan for the purpose of reconstructing and modernizing the transport system of the United Kingdom and various countries of the European Continent'.[88] Warburg remained attracted throughout the 1950s to the idea of creating a 'NATO common market and a NATO common currency (without Turkey or Greece)'.[89] In short, he was convinced that Britain's economic problems were structural and could not be solved by currency devaluation alone. It was foreign capital that was needed, and that meant American capital.

Under these circumstances, it is hardly surprising that Warburg was dismayed by the breakdown in Anglo-American relations occasioned by the 1956 Suez Crisis. Sir Anthony Eden, who had finally succeeded Churchill as premier in 1955, was in fact an early private client of S. G. Warburg & Co., having opened a small investment account at the suggestion of Harry Lucas.[90] Since Eden's break with Chamberlain in the 1930s, Warburg had warmly admired him as a politician. He praised him for his efforts as foreign secretary at the 1954 conferences in Geneva and London,[91] and hailed his belated elevation to the premiership. He therefore tended at first to give Eden the benefit of the doubt during the Suez Crisis. Like Eden, Warburg was inclined to see the Egyptian leader Gamal Abdel Nasser as a Middle Eastern Hitler whom the Western powers had made the mistake of appeasing following the Egyptian military's seizure of power in 1952. 'Perhaps Nasser's overplaying of his cards may have a sobering effect on the people of this country and France,' mused Warburg five days after the Egyptian leader's nationalization of the Suez Canal. But he added the important caveat that 'in the United States . . . in an election year they are apt to take leave from international affairs'.[92] This was a shrewd observation, for the fatal flaw of Eden's strategy – a joint Anglo-French–Israeli operation to reclaim control of the Canal Zone – was his failure to forewarn the United States and secure at the very least its acquiescence, if not its support. Not only was the Eisenhower administration preoccupied with the impending presidential election; the simultaneous Soviet military intervention in Hungary also raised the nightmarish prospect of a full-scale confrontation between East and West, with the entire Arab world certain to take the Soviet side in reaction to what seemed like a recrudescence of European imperialism. After the intervention had ended in political disaster, Warburg's post-mortem followed his earlier logic:

For Britain and France to take unilateral action in the Middle East . . . was not wrong in itself, but . . . the methods applied – particularly lack of previous information to the members of the Commonwealth and the United States (not necessarily previous consultation) – were most unfortunate and above all it [was] a terrible mistake, once the military action had been undertaken, to break it off in the middle.[93]

In short, Eden's action had been a 'reckless adventure'. 'It has, of course, often happened before', Warburg reflected, 'that in times of conflict one country, either alone or with others, has blockaded another country, but I think Eden has achieved something unique inasmuch as under his leadership Britain has blockaded herself' – a reference to the Saudi oil embargo and the crucial American refusal to prop up sterling if the Anglo-French forces were not withdrawn in compliance with the UN General Assembly's 'Uniting for Peace' resolution.[94] It was not, in other words, the principle of Western intervention in the Middle East to which Warburg objected, but the ineptitude of Eden's policy. Two years later, when US forces were sent to Lebanon in the wake of the overthrow of the Iraqi monarchy,* he looked back with regret on the opportunity that had been lost:

How much better would be the situation for the West if the sort of resolute action now being taken in the Lebanon had been taken against Nasser two years ago, immediately on his nationalisation of the Suez Canal. Now it looks to me as if the best that can happen would be for the Americans and British to save the fringes of the Middle East.

If the American action in the Lebanon had been taken a week before, in all probability the upheaval in Iraq would not have happened. Here again it is a matter of too little too late . . .[95]

These sentiments were remarkably close to those Sir Winston Churchill contemplated expressing in what would have been his last speech to the House of Commons, had he spoken as he originally intended in July 1958.

* Operation Blue Bat was the first application of the Eisenhower Doctrine, which asserted the right of the United States to intervene anywhere in the world to check the spread of Communism. The aim was to bolster the pro-Western government of President Camille Chamoun against internal opponents who saw the change of regime in Iraq as a chance to align Lebanon with Egypt and Syria.

It seemed, in short, as if Anglo-American co-operation had broken down in the realm of foreign policy. Would it be more successful in the realm of finance?

IV

At the end of July 1951 the senior partners at Kuhn, Loeb & Co. made a remarkable proposition to Siegmund Warburg: that he become one of their number. What made this remarkable was the profound temperamental difference between Warburg and the senior Kuhn Loeb partner, Jacob Schiff's grandson John. A Yale- and Oxford-educated Navy veteran and philanthropic paragon of the Upper East Side, Schiff had two passions: thoroughbreds and the Boy Scout movement. Aside from their kinship, he and Siegmund Warburg had almost nothing in common.

Though flattered, Warburg declined at once, 'as it would involve my having to move from this country to the United States'.[96] It would also have required him to surrender control of his own firm to Kuhn Loeb, under the rules of the New York Stock Exchange. A year later, however, he and Wiseman reached an understanding 'to establish the intended cooperation in a happy and constructive spirit' by means of an ingenious and highly unusual compromise. Warburg would not be required to give up his existing role as chairman of S. G. Warburg & Co. or to make New York his primary residence. He would nevertheless be given a general power of attorney by Kuhn Loeb, granting him 'the right to commit them and draw on their accounts'. He would be compensated as an 'independent contractor' with an annual fee. This was, as Warburg noted, the revival of an idea that had first been contemplated as long ago as 1928.[97] It made him a Kuhn Loeb partner in all but name. Indeed, as John Schiff's lawyers pointed out, Warburg's powers 'would be much greater than those of the partners', since (as Warburg himself noted) 'the partners undertake in their Partnership Agreement to take commitments only after these commitments have been agreed by the partners on certain prescribed rules of procedure, whilst under my Power of Attorney I can commit the partnership without any reference to anyone'.[98]

Warburg's first task, at his own request, was 'to try to co-ordinate the work of the partners and of the chief executives' at Kuhn Loeb, while at the same time changing the firm's time-honoured policy of keeping its funds 'completely liquid, either in cash or in Government securities', rather than occasionally committing some capital to industrial concerns.[99] Warburg set to work with more energy than tact. After just three days in the Kuhn Loeb offices in February 1953, he had concluded that there was a chronic lack of 'co-ordination of work within the office and [of] guidance of many keen juniors who are neither sufficiently thorough nor sufficiently business-minded'.[100] In late April he set out an immodest 'ten-years' plan' for Kuhn Loeb. 'The important elements of a first-class private banking business,' he wrote, were:

1. Moral standing
2. Reputation for efficiency and high quality brain work
3. Connections
4. Capital funds
5. Personnel and organization

Of these five elements, Warburg went on, Kuhn Loeb possessed only 1, 3 and 4 'in a completely satisfactory way'. There was, by contrast, 'much room for improvement in regard to elements 2 and 5' because of a 'lack of proper coordination and internal discipline'. There were too many different departments, and too many of them were handled as watertight units. Too few employees knew what the various executives' responsibilities were. The senior executives were not sufficiently well informed about the incoming and outgoing mail. There was not enough 'progress-chasing' and following up with prospective clients. There were insufficient internal meetings, and no opportunity for junior employees to discuss 'pending propositions or long-term ideas'. Applying the procedures instituted years before at the New Trading Company, Warburg urged that a new 'junior [executive] committee' be formed to meet weekly with no more than two partners present; that all business-related correspondence should be listed, pooled and made available to this committee as well as to a new executive committee.[101] In November he proposed that this committee be empowered to make all business decisions (other than on 'matters of policy') without reference to the other partners, who would henceforth meet only on a monthly basis. 'The Committee' (as he suggested calling it) would consist of two general partners, Robert F. Brown and J. Richardson 'Dick' Dilworth, and – of course – Siegmund Warburg. The last of these would be designated 'the Managing Member', whose tasks would be:

1. To tighten the organization and to increase both the collective and the individual efficiency of the firm.
2. To give special attention to matters of promotion, remuneration, training and working discipline within the office.
3. To introduce procedures by which partners and chief executives are informed promptly and continuously about business conversations, business correspondence and important internal work.[102]

Complete with a complex flow chart, this was an audacious manifesto for revolution from within, if not an outright *coup d'état*. From afar, one unfriendly Bank of England official interpreted Warburg's new role at Kuhn Loeb as 'a further move to foster his ambition', adding: 'He is understood to be practically in control there, succeeding to his uncle's interest and having acquired by devious routes further monetary interest in that firm.'[103]

There can be little doubt that Kuhn Loeb's management structure required root-and-branch reform. Equally sclerotic was the firm's financial position. Of the firm's 1952 balance sheet of $15.2 million, no less than 79 per cent was invested in US government bonds (federal, state or municipal). More than two-fifths of the firm's liabilities were the partners' capital – $5 million – and personal accounts. The firm's gross income was almost entirely consumed by its overheads. Net profits in 1953 were less than $500,000, and nearly all of this was distributed to the partners as salaries and interest on their capital. In short, the firm was run as a low-risk cash-cow for its proprietors. The net profit figure implies a rate of return to them of around 9 per cent, but a third of this merely represented the interest on the bond portfolio.[104] Warburg was right that Kuhn Loeb was moribund. What is less clear is how realistic it was to attempt the radical reform he envisaged on a part-time basis.

Warburg believed he could push through his programme on the basis of a new transatlantic routine, whereby he would spend 'two months in the Spring and two months in the late Autumn in New York'. It was never going to work. When he returned to Manhattan in April 1954 he found 'the lack of organization and efficiency . . . unchanged' and 'even more than usual . . . too much futile talk and busy-body activity all round'.[105] Seven months later he felt moved to write another memorandum 'about some of the present problems of KL & Co.', enumerating the now familiar faults: 'dilettantism', 'superfluous talk in the office', inadequate internal communication, insufficient training of juniors, and so on. In places, significantly, this critique was almost identical to the memorandum he had written eighteen months previously, with the difference that he now recommended the appointment of 'a sort of managing partner' to act as 'chief of staff' to Schiff. Warburg all but admitted that his efforts had encountered obstruction, but he resolved to press on, even if it meant devoting as much as 'half my working time' to Kuhn Loeb.[106] Armed with the new title of executive director, he continued his campaign to improve internal communication and training, creating a unified Research Department (later merged with the Buying Department to create an Investment Research Section) and a new Stock Services Department. He was heartened by the smoothness with which the firm managed the move to new premises at 30 Wall Street.[107] Yet he continued to feel that 'direction from the top i.e. from the Partners' Room' was 'completely insufficient'.[108] By May 1955 Warburg and Schiff were considering whether or not to 'establish a closer identity of organisation and principles, even of names, between KL & Co. and SGW & Co.' – the first indication that some kind of merger might be Warburg's ultimate goal.[109] The following year Schiff proposed that Warburg become a full director and partner, an invitation that Warburg accepted, having come to the view 'that my two activities are complementary* and of considerable advantage to both firms'.[110] He remained chairman of Mercury Securities, the London parent company. It was agreed that he could continue to spend only part of the year in New York.

Yet by the summer of 1957 he had once again grown frustrated with the 'clear obstruction and procrastination' of other partners. Urging Schiff to press on with still more radical organizational changes (including the restructuring of the partnership itself and the fusion of the Buying and the Distribution Departments), he confronted him with three options:

---

* This was not strictly true, since 'in view of the strange rules of the New York Stock Exchange' he had to relinquish the chairmanship of Warburgs in order to become a full partner in Kuhn Loeb.

1. that KL would get rid of me or vice versa;

2. that I would remain a partner of KL, but only in charge of their foreign, particularly European business and without having any longer any part in the organisation of the firm;

3. that I would remain a partner, not only in charge of the firm's foreign business but also acting as a sort of charwoman in regard to the firm's organisation.[111]

In a letter to William Wiseman, written in the midst of the Aluminium War (see below) Warburg revealed the existence of another, equally rancorous conflict – one which was going on not only within Kuhn Loeb, but between two members of the Warburg family:

There is unfortunately still one very important element which stands in the way of our bringing about the kind of efficient organisation which I should like to see. You know this element; its arbitrary and moody actions as well as its lack of objectivity and of judgement in regard to human values and standards. If that element were one day eliminated, we would have the basis of a really good team and organisation and the firm could go places as in olden days.[112]

The rogue element in question was Frederick M. Warburg, the sixty-year-old son of Felix Warburg, whose flippancy (racehorses and doggerel verse were his forte) infuriated his German-born relation almost beyond endurance.[113] Worse, Siegmund Warburg's most important ally at Kuhn Loeb, Dick Dilworth, was lured away from the travails of Kuhn Loeb by the Rockefeller brothers – a 'somewhat dazzling prospect', as even Warburg had to admit, at a time when the five sons of John D. Rockefeller Jr seemed to bestride American business and politics with equal ease.[114] For a fleeting moment, it seemed that Dilworth's unexpected departure might galvanize Schiff into action. But, as Warburg complained to his wife, 'I never know whether or how far he [Schiff] will stick to his sound resolutions when I am out of immediate reach.'[115] When Fred Warburg (frequently referred to as 'X' by Warburg) accused him of wishing 'to gain control of KL & Co in various devious ways' – a reaction to the suggestion that Kuhn Loeb merge with the investment managers Wood, Struthers & Winthrop – Warburg was driven to submit his resignation to Schiff, angrily explaining:

I can only work in an atmosphere of complete mutual trust and I find that such an atmosphere does not exist at KL & Co. at present. In particular it has become evident to me, as far as I am concerned, that there is one partner – whom, for the sake of simplicity, I shall call X – who not only distrusts the integrity of my motives . . . but who also spreads poisonous tales about me amongst the partners. He does not give me an opportunity to justify myself against these tales. He had promised me that he would speak to me in the first place whenever he, X, had any criticism to express against me and that he would give me a fair chance of replying to such criticism before repeating towards anyone else his reproaches or suspicions against me. This promise was given by X only a few weeks ago after an unprovoked attack had been made by him against me and after he had subsequently apologized to me very emphatically. It is therefore clear that the promise given by X could not have been meant seriously. I must conclude reluctantly that the atmosphere of complete mutual trust which I consider essential does not exist at KL & Co. and hence there is no basis for real teamwork.[116]

This kind of explosion was Warburg's last resort, when both reason and charm had failed. It often worked, and came close to doing so on this occasion. Schiff hastily responded that 'he attached no importance whatsoever to what Fred said: why did I?'[117] Encouraged by Don Swatland, a senior partner at the firm's lawyers, Cravath, Swaine & Moore, Warburg hung on until the next partners' meeting, which agreed to appoint a new committee (of which, significantly, Fred Warburg was not to be a member) 'to work out the reorganisation of KL'.[118] He continued chipping away at the position of his rivals within the partnership, suggesting on one occasion 'that all the partners above the age of, say, sixty would become non-executive directors of a corporation or special partners of the existing partnership', if only to relieve the pressure on Schiff who was (he flatteringly suggested) 'Commander-in-Chief, Chief-of-Staff and Quartermaster-General of KL, all in one person'. 'A thorough independent cleaning of one's own stable' was still the option Warburg favoured, but a merger with another firm would have been another way of diluting the power of the existing senior partners.[119] The crucial thing was 'to remove the sources of frustration through your arranging for certain general partners to become special partners'. Perhaps it was even time for Warburgs and

Kuhn Loeb to merge (a proposal sometimes referred to in correspondence as 'Project X').[120] Again Warburg ventured to hope that 'the two firms between them' could become 'the sort of leading Anglo-American combination into which I hoped they would develop one day', building up 'a rather important position in regard to American issues for European borrowers'.[121]

The exchange of shareholdings successfully proposed by Warburg in 1958 might indeed have been the first step towards a Kuhn Loeb –Warburgs merger. Two obstacles stood in the way. As before, senior partners saw reform as a threat to their own comfortable positions. In particular, Percy Stewart (who acted, Warburg complained, as 'the Great God above the Waters') went on the offensive against the London firm.[122] The second obstacle was the New York Stock Exchange, which in April 1959 explicitly rejected Project X on the grounds that a non-American firm – one outside the NYSE's jurisdiction – could not have a significant interest in a Wall Street investment bank. Though reluctant to take no for an answer, Warburg was manifestly downhearted.[123] He continued to float his reform schemes, but sensed that his colleagues in New York were no longer listening.[124] By June 1959, for the first time, he felt the need 'to take a strong line' on the question of fees owed by Kuhn Loeb to Warburgs.[125] 'A certain harshness', as Warburg admitted to Wiseman, had now crept into the discussions, which he now delegated to Henry Grunfeld, to whom he often turned when even an explosion of temper had failed to achieve the desired objective.[126] For several more years, the Londoners continued to argue for change: for a reduction in the number of senior partners, for incorporation, for a redefinition of the relationship with the London firm – for anything, it seemed, that would jolt Kuhn Loeb out of its torpor.[127] Warburg continued to descend periodically on the New York offices like 'a somewhat feared headmaster'.[128] In his absence, the old problems instantly resurfaced.[129] Somewhat belatedly, he subjected Schiff to graphological analysis, as if seeking the key to the difficulty in the senior partner's psyche.[130] By 1963, however, after years of inconclusive wrangling, Warburg was finally driven to conclude that 'arrangements between American banks and London merchant banking houses do not make much sense'.[131] A year later, after more than a decade of trying to solve what Dilworth wryly called 'the perennial KL problem', Warburg resigned his partnership.[132] All that would remain was a vestigial arrangement to pool resources for certain transactions, mainly international government loans,[133] and continuing ties of friendship to younger Kuhn Loeb employees like Joshua Sherman and Yves Istel. 'I have to admit to you', Warburg wrote to his wife on returning to New York in 1965:

that your warnings over many years in regard to KL & Co were more than justified. Now, being detached from KL & Co., I see clearly how small minded and pedestrian these people were – with only very few exceptions – and how frustrating for me my association with them was. Perhaps it was necessary to lead the matter *ad absurdum*, perhaps my motive in sticking to KL & Co. so long was based on some [desire for] variety on my part. Be that as it may, I now enjoy a new freedom.[134]

If Warburg's aim had been to take over Kuhn Loeb – and it may very well have been – this was the takeover battle he lost.*

V

On 15 February 1956 Siegmund Warburg met with Olaf Hambro, chairman of Hambros Bank, to discuss British Aluminium. 'I informed Hambro confidentially', Warburg reported to his colleagues at S. G. Warburg, 'about the approach made to us [about British Aluminium] by [the] American Metal Co.' Hambro told Warburg that his firm was 'just now studying the financial problems of British Aluminium with a view to a large capital increase'. He was 'all for working on this whole

---

* For the rest of the 1960s, Warburg favoured a 'rather polygamic arrangement' with Wall Street firms, including White Weld and Lehman Brothers. Subsequent unhappy dealings with Kuhn Loeb prompted managing partner Nat Samuels to confess his firm's 'schizophrenic attitude towards SGW & Co. which was a strange mixture of love and hate'. Warburg gave the characteristic response that 'this was of course quite natural and analogous to a divorce, where the two sides which decided to separate were much more sensitive towards one another than would be the case if no intimate relationship had been in existence before'. Though John Schiff raised the idea of 'remarriage' in the mid-1970s, a merger once again proved impossible to implement. Kuhn Loeb merged with Lehman Brothers in 1977. The name vanished seven years later when Lehman was acquired by American Express.

matter jointly with us'.[135] As a result of this conversation, S. G. Warburg & Co. was subsequently 'offered a large underwriting in British Aluminium'.[136] Neither Warburg nor Hambro can have known that this was the first scene of a protracted drama that would not only pit the two men against one other but would also fundamentally transform the culture of the City of London.

The so-called Aluminium War is generally acknowledged to have been Britain's first ever hostile takeover, in the modern sense that a controlling shareholding in a public company was acquired on the open market with the conscious aim of ousting the company's management and board. According to Edmund de Rothschild, it dealt 'a decisive blow . . . to the unhurried, "gentlemanly" style of business'. 'For better or worse,' he reflected, 'the City never seemed to me to be quite the same again.'[137] To Lionel Fraser of Helbert Wagg – a key Warburg ally – it was 'a David and Goliath affair', with Warburg and his own firm in the role of David and practically the whole of the rest of the City as Goliath. Like Rothschild, Fraser saw the Aluminium War as a defining moment in modern British financial history:

Old citadels tumbled, traditional strongholds were invaded, new thought was devoted to City problems, there was a freshness and alertness unknown before, dramatic to watch . . . Everything has long since been tranquil and harmonious, nevertheless it is different. The merchant bankers are more on their toes, they vie with one another to give a better service to industry and their clients, some even advertise the facilities they can offer; there has been a girding of loins, resulting in more enterprise and competitiveness and less reliance on the 'old boy' idea. Of course these advances might have taken place anyhow, but I do not believe I am exaggerating when I say that most of them date from the British Aluminium episode.[138]

According to Peter Spira, then beginning his career at S. G. Warburg, it was 'a watershed'.[139] In this drama, Siegmund Warburg was either the subversive villain, acting duplicitously towards his fellow merchant bankers, or the revolutionary hero, outwitting the clubbish old-boy network that had dominated the post-war City. As Warburg himself recalled, 'A major factor in the bitterness was the aspect of the damned foreigner, the newcomer, the fact that I was not a member of the Establishment and held non-Establishment views.'[140] At one point, Sir

Charles Hambro accused Warburg of 'behaving extremely badly',[141] while the Governor of the Bank of England went so far as to refer to Warburg's 'monkey business'.[142] One Treasury official preferred the phrase 'jungle warfare'.[143] A leading stockbroker spoke of 'piratical ventures'.[144] Lord Kindersley, the chairman of the merchant bank Lazard Brothers, was heard to say that he would 'never speak to that fellow again', on the ground that Warburg had misled him.[145] For fifteen years, according to the Morgan group's historian, Morgan Grenfell refused to do any business with S. G. Warburg because of Warburg's allegedly 'monstrous and unforgivable' conduct.[146] Harold Macmillan, who had succeeded Eden after the Suez Crisis, summed up the Aluminium War as 'rather a "Gentlemen v. Players" affair'.[147] 'To the old City order,' in one historian's words, 'Warburg's victory was as welcome as King Billy's on the Boyne to the Ulster Catholics.'[148] Certainly, Warburg and his allies (Lionel Fraser and Ivan Stedeford) were self-made men, while among their principal opponents were the heirs of some established City names: Catto, Cunliffe, Hambro, Kindersley. In cricket, however, it is legitimate – indeed expected – for the players to beat the gentlemen. The crucial question is whether these players won by fair means or foul.

Founded in 1894 to exploit two technological breakthroughs that radically reduced the cost of producing aluminium, the British Aluminium Company had been one of the first UK firms to identify the Scottish Highlands as a source of hydroelectric power. Importing its ore from colonies like the Gold Coast (now Ghana), the company built a network of reduction works, smelting works and rolling mills that extended across the entire British Isles. However, post-war investments in Canada, British Guiana and Australia left it financially overstretched. At some point in 1956 it was identified by Warburg and his friend Hans Vogelstein of American Metal as a potential target for American investment.[149] To Warburg, it was a perfect example of the way UK industry could be recapitalized with US money – and a perfect example of the way his London firm could profit from his prolonged absences in New York, not least because American Metal could take up that part of the British Aluminium offering which Warburg had agreed to underwrite for Hambros. As he reported in March 1956 – long before the takeover battle began – Vogelstein:

[did] not want to make a purchase of British Aluminium shares for his company simply from the point of view of an investment, but would like to become in due course an inside industrial participant without, however, aiming at a controlling position. I explained . . . that in the circumstances . . . we could not guarantee that even a very large minority participation would secure for those who acquired such a participation an inside position in the company. However, I felt that if this matter were tackled in a careful diplomatic way there was a good chance . . . My suggestion was that we would inform Sir George Bolton [of the Bank of England] in the first place from the general foreign exchange point of view and that only after the American group had acquired say 55% of the share capital would we inform the board of the company about this investment. At that stage we would not ask for any representation on the board, but only say that the American group had bought this investment in view of the high opinion they had of the company's management and its possibilities and that without wishing to have anything like a controlling position the American group hoped to be able to be of help to the company in due course . . . Only some time later might we gradually go a step further when a suitable opportunity presented itself.[150]

From the outset, then, Warburg clearly intended to keep the Bank of England informed of the American acquisition of British Aluminium shares, but not necessarily to reveal that the plan was to establish a majority holding and thereby 'an inside position in the company', if not outright US control. Even before a deal was agreed with Vogelstein, Warburg instructed Kuhn Loeb and his own firm in London to begin 'accumulat[ing] a substantial block [of British Aluminium shares] for a group of clients'. Before the end of May 1956, the Canadian-based Transoceanic had bought up to $500,000 worth. By the end of the year, other Kuhn Loeb clients had agreed to buy hundreds of thousands of the shares.[151]

Not everyone was comfortable with what Warburg proposed. The President of Climax Molybdenum, whom Vogelstein had sought to involve as a partner in the deal, declared himself 'opposed to purchases of British Aluminium shares as long as the management of British Aluminium has not been informed and expressed a benevolent attitude'.[152] It was probably for this reason that by early 1957 Warburg was discussing British Aluminium with another American metals company, Reynolds Metals Co.* The aim now was to establish a predominantly American group, but with 'one strong British firm' to allay fears of a US takeover of a strategically important asset.[153] By early February 1957 Warburg had set a target: the group he was assembling should aim to buy 20 per cent of the shares in British Aluminium, up to a price limit of 80 shillings a share. It was only at this stage that Warburg approached the managing director of British Aluminium, Geoffrey Cunliffe, offering to assist with the company's financing difficulties. But he found Cunliffe 'remarkably slow in grasping anything unusual' and 'completely muddled both in his thinking and talking'. It struck Warburg as 'very depressing . . . that such an important British Company [was] under such bad management.'[154] As Warburg later succinctly put it, 'Cunliffe was upper class, received his job through good connections, but was not up to it although he was in no way conscious of his limitations.'[155]

It quickly became apparent that Warburg and Cunliffe fundamentally disagreed about British Aluminium's predicament. In Warburg's view, the funds the company planned to raise for its Canadian subsidiary were insufficient; indeed, so was the parent company's own share capital. He also found it 'entirely wrong for the company to give up their old traditional connection with Hambros' in favour of Lazards, which Cunliffe appeared to be contemplating.[156] Unmoved by Warburg's advice, Cunliffe went directly to American Metal and Climax Molybdenum, promising 'to take [them] at a later stage . . . into the confidence of the Board of British Aluminium' if they desisted from share purchases. To Warburg's dismay, the Americans seemed to be swayed. Only Richard Reynolds, encouraged by William Wiseman, seemed willing to press on with the agreed strategy.[157] Warburg now resolved 'to accumulate slowly and carefully a substantial block of British Aluminium shares for Reynolds, keeping the name Reynolds entirely secret for the time being'. At the same time, he initiated talks between Reynolds and another British aluminium producer, Sir Ivan Stedeford's Tube Investments. After Reynolds had taken a stake in one of Stedeford's aluminium rolling mills, TI was to become, in effect, the British front for the American takeover of British Aluminium.[158] Though this joint

---

* Although a large listed company, the firm was still run by the Reynolds brothers, of whom Richard Reynolds played the leading role in the events discussed here.

venture proved far from easy to broker, by 16 September 1957 agreement had been reached. Formally, if they gained control of British Aluminium, TI would hold 51 per cent and Reynolds 49 per cent. That meant, as Warburg well understood, that 'in any future approach to British Aluminium it [would] be impossible for British Aluminium to talk about the danger of an American take-over bid.'[159]

Warburg kept the Bank of England informed up to a point. On 20 June he had a meeting with the Governor, Cameron Cobbold, 'to tell him about our experiences in regard to purchases by American friends of ours of British Aluminium shares'. According to Warburg's account, Cobbold 'entirely agreed that it was quite wrong for anybody in the City to resent it if American groups should buy substantial minority interests in first-class British companies, and that, on the contrary, the active and financial cooperation of good American shareholders was very desirable'.[160] What Warburg did not spell out, however, was that the aim was to gain control of British Aluminium. Nor did he reveal his two-stage plan. Since most of the shares in British Aluminium were held in small quantities by multiple owners, he reasoned in October 1957, then 25 per cent could be regarded as a controlling interest if the holder of those shares were not wholly foreign. At this stage, the Warburg-led group already controlled 12 per cent of the company's shares. Once a quarter of the shares had been purchased, the Reynolds–TI group would insist on representation on the board of British Aluminium, after which a new Canadian-based company (formed by Reynolds–TI) would buy a majority of the shares and replace the old board entirely.[161] None of this was apparently spelt out to Cobbold, though George Bolton may well have been in the know.*

In other respects, too, transparency was emphatically not Warburg's watchword. 'In no circumstances', he wrote the morning after Reynolds and TI had reached a deal,

* Bolton's role in the episode has perhaps been overlooked. It was during the struggle for British Aluminium that he ceased to be an executive director at the Bank of England (though he remained a non-executive) in order to become chairman of the Bank of London and South America (BOLSA). This was a bank which had close links with S. G. Warburg. Indeed, just a few months after the end of the Aluminium War, at Bolton's suggestion Michael Lubbock of BOLSA became a director at Warburgs.

should any reference be made by anyone within this firm to the fact that Tube Investments have been buying or may buy British Aluminium shares. As we are not to have any official knowledge in this respect, if anyone should ever be asked the answer should be that we are not aware of Tube Investments having made any purchases of British Aluminium shares. It may happen that some time during the coming months something may leak out from America as to Reynolds having bought shares of British Aluminium . . . Even in this case we should officially disclaim any knowledge so far as we are concerned.[162]

This may explain why, when later asked by Kindersley if he was buying shares, Warburg allegedly replied with a blunt: 'No.' On 14 January 1958 Warburg informed Wiseman that Warburgs and Kuhn Loeb were still 'buying up carefully further British Aluminium shares' and that 'up to now no rumours about this have reached anybody'.[163] Small wonder, since no fewer than eleven nominee companies were used to make the share purchases.[164] Warburg's goal, as he outlined it six months later, remained a two-stage takeover, the first stage now to be achieved by increasing the Reynolds–TI share of British Aluminium from 8.3 per cent to 16.7 per cent. Once that had been achieved, 'the execution of the long term programme might begin with an approach to British Aluminium Co. to insist on Board representation for the [Reynolds–TI] group'. The underlying aim would nevertheless remain 'control of the whole Board of British Aluminium'.[165]

Stealth was of the essence. Having persuaded Stedeford that 'a take over bid for British Aluminium might become a practical proposition before the end of the year', Warburg warned against 'making love' to the British Aluminium board on the ground that 'with the mentality of Cunliffe it would be very dangerous to appear too soft'.[166] Inevitably, the other side got wind of some Warburg purchases of British Aluminium shares. However, when he was approached by a representative of Hambros and Lazards, Warburg declined to reveal on whose behalf he was acting, saying only that 'the people in question were first-class and were able to make a very important contribution to the financial and to the industrial strength of British Aluminium'.[167] The key, as Warburg repeatedly emphasized, was not to show the Reynolds–TI hand too soon; he consistently opposed all suggestions that the board of British Aluminium be approached directly.[168] 'The most important consideration must be to keep our plan completely confidential,' he told his colleagues at Kuhn Loeb time and again.[169] Even when the time came to reveal who was stalking British Aluminium, it should be done privately, 'on a confidential basis'.[170] When the identities of the buyers were finally revealed, it should be 'to as few people as possible in British Aluminium besides Portal [the chairman] and Cunliffe'.[171]

Yet if Warburg was being economical with the truth – a skill scarcely unfamiliar to the British Establishment, it should be noted – the board of British Aluminium was hardly a model of straight talking. These men were far from being the upper-class twits of City lore. The chairman of the board, Viscount Portal of Hungerford, was the former Chief of the Air Staff, a man who had played a key role in the development of the Allied strategic bombing campaign and had presided over Britain's atomic weapons programme. Sir Charles Hambro had been the executive chief of the wartime Special Operations Executive. These men knew how to fight, and not just cleanly. By late October, they were in negotiations with Alcoa, another longer-established US aluminium producer, which they saw as their natural American counterpart. When approached by Warburg, Stedeford and Joe McConnell of Reynolds on 3 November to discuss 'some kind of integration' of British Aluminium, Tube Investments and Reynolds, Cunliffe was himself evasive, saying only that British Aluminium was 'far advanced in other negotiations which really prevented him from talking about such a combination as had been mentioned by Stedeford and McConnell'. Much to Warburg's distaste, Cunliffe argued that:

To negotiate with two different sides at the same time . . . would be similar to something an acquaintance of his had done once. This man had had lunch with two girl friends at the Berkeley, with one in the grill room and with the other in the restaurant. He had arranged with the telephone operator to be called to the telephone every ten minutes so as to spend intermittently ten minutes with the one girl and ten minutes with the other.[172]

Warburg now advised writing at once to Portal 'making clear that Reynolds Metals and Tube Investments were prepared to make an offer to the shareholders of BA "well above market price"'.[173] When Portal procrastinated, Warburg turned to Hambros and Lazards, who admitted that it was 'not always easy to deal with the gentlemen at Norfolk House' – that is, British Aluminium.[174] However, H. N. Sporborg of Hambros immediately complained to Sir Frank Lee, permanent secretary at the Board of Trade, about the 'rather devious discussions' he had been having with Warburg and to make the case that some kind of 'close linking' with Alcoa was 'in the best interests of the company' because of Alcoa's superior resources.[175] Lee was personally inclined to support the association with Alcoa, as was the relatively untried Chancellor of the Exchequer, Derick Heathcoat-Amory, who had taken over the Treasury in January 1958 following the sudden resignation of Peter Thorneycroft.[176] Indeed, Heathcoat-Amory was himself a shareholder in British Aluminium and took the view that 'the link with Alcoa would be more in our own economic interest, and more in the interests of Commonwealth development than a link with TI/Reynolds'.[177] The Treasury's own portfolio of dollar securities also included some Alcoa shares.[178]

There was, however, a fatal flaw in Portal's counterattack. Alcoa was prepared to offer only 60 shillings a share for 4.5 million hitherto unissued British Aluminium shares; worse, it was willing to put only 4 shillings and 6 pence per share on the table immediately.[179] When the Reynolds–TI group offered to pay existing shareholders 78 shillings a share, Portal flatly declined to reveal the existence of the bid to British Aluminium shareholders, despite the fact that (as Sir Denis Rickett at the Treasury acknowledged) it was clearly a more attractive offer, not least from the point of view of earning foreign exchange from the sale of British assets,[180] and despite the fact that (as Stedeford bluntly told officials at the Bank) the offer could hardly be kept a secret from TI shareholders and therefore from the press.[181] On 3 December Stedeford told the joint permanent secretary to the Treasury, Sir Roger Makins, that he was prepared to call a meeting of British Aluminium shareholders to put the Reynolds–TI offer before them.[182] On 4 December he added the significant argument that even 'if TI were shut out here . . . the buying of B.A. shares from the United States would continue.'[183] When Makins expressed reservations about the idea of a special shareholders' meeting, Stedeford responded with a press statement informing British Aluminium shareholders of the terms of the Reynolds–TI offer.[184] In each of these moves the hand of Warburg was clearly legible.

Portal's underpricing of his own company and his vain attempt to keep the other side's bid secret were but the first of a string of misjudgements. He and Cunliffe went to the Treasury, claiming to have evidence (from the Transport and General Workers' Union) that Reynolds was 'not a happy' company. Heathcoat-Amory was unimpressed.[185] Portal requested a meeting with the Prime Minister; this, he was told, would be 'premature'.[186] Clumsily, he accused the government of 'wrecking' his efforts to protect British Aluminium from a covert American take-over and generally 'queering his pitch'.[187] He then ran a newspaper advertisement protesting rather too much that the board was not 'selling out to the Americans'. This played into Warburg's hands. A far from negligible role in the Aluminium War was performed by the press, which all but unanimously favoured the Reynolds–TI bid. Portal incurred widespread media ridicule when he accused Reynolds–TI of seeking to buy 'a powerful empire for the price of a small kingdom' – to which the *Economist* retorted that Alcoa seemed to be getting it 'for the price of a minor principality'. The *Financial Times*'s Lex column, in those days written single-handedly by Arthur Winspear, was especially devastating in its treatment of the British Aluminium board. This was all the more remarkable, since the *FT* and Lazards were both owned by the Pearson group, which says much for the independence of the editor, Gordon Newton, and Lord Drogheda, his powerful managing director.[188] Institutional investors (like the Prudential Assurance Company) were furious to read in the papers that their board had been seeking to sell the company so cheaply to Alcoa.[189]

This turning of the tide of opinion was far from fortuitous. By the beginning of December 1958, as Warburg reported to Wiseman, there was a new development in the story 'every few minutes . . . with lawyers writing opinions for their clients and with the clients writing letters to the Press'.[190] These efforts were orchestrated by none other than Warburg, who boasted to John Schiff that he now had at his disposal 'a little regiment of lawyers and public relations officers'.[191] Significantly, Stedeford disclaimed responsibility for the press campaign and at one point complained to Warburg about an article in the Lex column that he believed Warburg had inspired.[192] Henry Grunfeld was able to retort that it was the other side that was manipulating the press. During a break in a tense meeting at Portal's office, he had concealed himself behind a wall and spotted an employee from the financial printers Burrups, obviously there to collect an announcement for publication. Further inquiries by George Warburg revealed that Lazards had already booked space in the *Financial Times*, *Times* and *Telegraph*, with the intention of making public the Alcoa offer. Now it was Stedeford's turn to be shocked by Portal's ungentlemanly conduct. He could scarcely object as Grunfeld organized a Friday-night press conference to announce an improved counter-offer.[193] There was nothing illicit in any of this; it was just a game the 'gentlemen of Norfolk House' did not know how to play.[194] Warburg often expressed his aversion to publicity, but it was inevitable that the newspapers he had so expertly wooed later wrote him up as 'the slightly mysterious figure . . . without whom . . . the aluminium take-over . . . would never even have happened'.[195]

For all the appeal of the 'Gentlemen v. Players' analogy, however, it is important to emphasize that Warburg and his clients were far from isolated or marginal figures, stirring up the press against a monolithic Establishment. Neither the Bank of England nor the Treasury nor the Prime Minister, Harold Macmillan, ever unequivocally favoured the Alcoa deal over the Reynolds–TI offer. On the contrary, the Deputy Governor's view was that the British Aluminium board had 'very badly handled' the matter.[196] Officially, the Bank's position was neutral: it would be 'nice' if 'the best man' won.[197] Privately, officials preferred the Reynolds–TI bid.[198] Bolton positively encouraged Warburg, advising 'full show of compromise but no weakness'. The Treasury, too, declined to back Portal and Cunliffe, partly on the ground of national interest, partly on the ground of shareholder value.[199] With Heathcoat-Amory out of the decision-making process because of his conflict of interest, it was left to the Prime Minister to adopt a studied but insincere neutrality.[200] Despite his Chancellor's leanings towards the Alcoa deal – and despite the fact that he was seen to go shooting with Portal over the Christmas break – Macmillan understood that the Reynolds–TI bid was politically preferable, not least because (formally at least) it meant continued British control of British Aluminium.[201] Not long before, there had been a storm of Opposition indignation when Colorado Oil and Gas had sought to acquire Trinidad Petroleum Development, a bid blocked by the government on technical grounds.[202]

There was also good reason to fear that a successful Alcoa takeover of British Aluminium would have negative consequences for British shippers, who currently handled all British Aluminium's transatlantic exports.[203] As shadow chancellor, Harold Wilson was not slow to scent a political opportunity, hinting to Heathcoat-Amory that he might even demand an inquiry under the Companies Act.[204] Macmillan's decision to leave 'the choice between the two proposals . . . with the ordinary shareholder' therefore amounted to tacit support for the hostile bidders.[205] His principal worry as Christmas approached was that, for some reason, the shareholders might prefer the inferior Alcoa deal.[206]

There was therefore a certain lack of realism to Cobbold's appeal to both sides, on New Year's Eve, to accept some kind of two-month 'truce' to resolve 'a ridiculous situation, damaging to the City as a whole and to everybody concerned'.[207] Warburg momentarily alarmed his partners by appearing ready to bow to the Governor's wish.[208] But both he and Cobbold must surely have been aware that Reynolds–TI could not now withdraw their offer. It had been made clear already by Stedeford that, while he might agree to suspend purchases of British Aluminium shares, he could not bind Reynolds, who duly continued to 'buy like fury'.[209] When Cobbold appealed to the government to intervene 'for the sake of the City's general reputation', he was rebuffed by Macmillan, as was Portal when he again asked for a personal interview with the Prime Minister.[210]

By now, in any case, Portal was in a barely controllable rage, accusing Reynolds of aiming at 'an American "smash and grab" with a British front'. 'Any hope of a compromise', he declared, was now 'out of the question'.[211] In a last-ditch effort to avoid defeat, his bankers now sought to mobilize all their influence in the City to mount a more generous counter-offer. In a circular published on New Year's Day 1959, no fewer than fourteen City firms, including Hambros, Lazards, Morgan Grenfell, Brown Shipley, Samuel Montagu and Robert Fleming, affirmed their support for the Alcoa option and made an unconditional offer, worth up to £7 million, for British Aluminium shares at 82 shillings – more than a pound a share higher than Alcoa had offered to pay. (The intention was not to buy the shares for Alcoa, but to buy shares that might otherwise go to Reynolds–TI.) This was indeed an impressive list of names. But here, too, Warburg was less isolated than is often assumed. Significantly, Schroders were acting for TI, as were the stockbrokers Panmure Gordon and Joseph Sebag, while Rothschilds and Barings (arguably the most venerable names in the City) conspicuously failed to align themselves with either side.[212] Two leading stockbrokers, Rowe & Pitman and Cazenove, also sought to be neutral, though they were effectively bullied into line by Hambros and Lazards.[213] As Warburg was able to point out, 'those City houses who were not on the side of the City group represented an even bigger number than those in the City group . . . namely: Barings, Rothschilds, Kleinworts, Brandts, Erlangers, Arbuthnots, Gibbs, Philip Hill Higginsons, quite apart from the three houses representing the Tube Investments/Reynolds group.'[214] By contrast, the so-called City group seemed to Warburg 'a strange assortment of very important and rather insignificant names, mainly consisting of people who did not want to refuse an invitation from Lazards and Hambros'.[215]

When it came to the raw test of strength on the stock market, then, Warburgs and their associates had little difficulty out-buying the Hambros-led group, especially after the Reynolds–TI offer price was raised to 85 shillings. Here again Warburg's transatlantic ties proved a source of strength: Kuhn Loeb clients like Transoceanic could easily be persuaded to sell to Reynolds–TI. By way of a *coup de grâce*, Stedeford warned that, if the other side did not capitulate by cancelling its agreement with Alcoa, Reynolds might decide to act alone, raising the prospect of an all-American takeover. At the same time, magnanimous in victory, he intimated that there would not be an immediate purge of the British Aluminium board.[216] By 8 January the war was effectively over, since the Reynolds–TI group had by then acquired 65 per cent of the shares, though Warburg did not claim victory until two days later.[217] Despite Portal's expression of 'great distaste' when he finally saw Macmillan on 9 January, the government had little hesitation in approving the deal.[218] The outcome was confirmed the next day by the Financial Secretary to the Treasury, J. E. S. Simon, in his answer to questions in the House of Commons. Significantly, Harold Wilson declared 'that, despite the somewhat undignified performance of certain powerful interests in the City . . . we feel that the decision taken by the Treasury is the only decision to be taken in the circumstances'.[219]

Gentlemen are supposed to be good losers. The gentlemen in this case were anything but. There had been a lot of criticism of him in the City, Warburg admitted to Cobbold. Indeed, 'nearly everybody in the City was very angry.'[220] On 17 January Portal stormed round to 10 Downing Street 'in a rather excited and depressed state', to berate Macmillan and represent his rivals as 'a set of crooks'.[221] Olaf Hambro dashed off an indignant letter to *The Times*, lambasting the press for going 'against City opinion' (as if he and his associates *were* the City). As a young man contemplating a job offer from Warburgs, Peter Stormonth Darling was warned by a senior City lawyer: 'We don't know whether this firm with this thrusting Jew is going to make it here or not.'[222] 'In our old-fashioned way,' Evelyn Baring told an American reporter in 1961, 'we should not want to appear on a prospectus with them.'[223] In the highest dudgeon of all, as we have seen, Morgan Grenfell declined to work with Warburgs for the next fifteen years.

To all of this, the player Warburg was able to retort loftily that perhaps the press had 'felt principles of free enterprise were at stake in this controversy and that they were in favour of sound British/American industrial cooperation under British leadership . . . and, above all, in favour of protecting the rights of shareholders'.[224] The question therefore arises: was the Reynolds–TI takeover of British Aluminium truly a victory for free enterprise, Anglo-American co-operation and shareholders' rights?

It must be said that Siegmund Warburg knew little about aluminium or, for that matter, about any metal. He had read enough to persuade himself that global 'demand [for aluminium], based on increased penetration of volume markets, and aided by inventory re-accumulation, will probably be sufficient by the early 1960s to absorb all planned capacity'.[225] But that rough forecast proved optimistic. Nor does evidence survive of any attempt by Warburgs accurately to value British Aluminium's assets or its future revenues. Lionel Fraser certainly thought that Reynolds–TI had overpaid, as did Michael Verey, his colleague at Helbert Wagg. Louis Reynolds, too, suspected that his brother Richard had been duped into a deal that was too generous to shareholders (and, indeed, to Tube Investments).[226] To be sure, Reynolds' investment in the joint venture Reynolds–TI proved highly profitable, but its experience with British Aluminium was disappointing, despite improvements in the company's governance under Lord Plowden, who succeded Portal as chairman. Indeed, it could be argued that Reynolds simply stripped British Aluminium of its most valuable assets (the Canadian ones).[227]

There were in fact three real winners of the Aluminium War. The first were those shareholders, like the Church Commissioners, who sold their British Aluminium shares at inflated prices.[228] The second was the government, which removed itself successfully from the horns of a potentially embarrassing dilemma. The third and biggest victor was S. G. Warburg & Co., though it was probably only Henry Grunfeld who immediately understood this.* As UK shares rallied in a bull market that lasted from the summer of 1958 until the spring of 1961, there was a near doubling of new issues and mergers.[229] The Aluminium War made it abundantly clear to whom would-be corporate raiders should turn. As Peter Spira later noted:

It was a tremendous stepping-stone in putting Warburgs on the map. We were fairly gung ho-ish and there was a feeling of 'We've arrived. We are now a factor to be taken note of.' Many companies who had been contemplating buying other companies but were nervous of making hostile bids said, 'Maybe this is something we can do. Let's go and talk to Warburgs.' Warburgs became the leading experts in the hostile take-over field.[230]

In the immediate aftermath of the British Aluminium takeover, the firm found itself offering advice to a succession of companies contemplating possible mergers: Fisons and Spencer Chemical, for example, and then Fisons and Monsanto. The performance of S. G. Warburg and its parent company, Mercury Securities, confirms Spira's assessment. Net profits leaped by 94 per cent in 1960 compared with the previous year. The Aluminium War also helped attract two new media clients to Warburgs, namely the Canadian Roy Thomson, who was dazzled by Henry Grunfeld's ingenuity in organizing his bid for the

---

* As Warburg later told George Steiner: 'Without any question [the other side] could have won the battle. If Henry Grunfeld had been on the other side we would never have won . . . With the exception of Henry Grunfeld most of the seniors felt that we had won a Pyrrhic victory since all the goodwill which we had built up with great pains over the years had, in their view, been dissipated and they felt we would have to start all over again to create a feeling of goodwill in the City.'

Kemsley group of newspapers in 1958. In the next major takeover battle to make newspaper headlines – the contest for control of Odhams Press – the victor, namely Cecil King's Mirror Group, was once again advised by Warburgs (see Chapter 10). The chemicals company Laporte moved its account from Morgan Grenfell to Warburgs because the former seemed more interested in 'shooting and God knows what else' than in Laporte's latest results.[231] The reality, as Stephen Catto of Morgan Grenfell admitted, was that they and their allies had been 'outmanoeuvred and demoralized'.[232]

'I did not want the battle,' Warburg told a former employee shortly after winning the Aluminium War, 'but wanted rather a compromise – being, as you know, basically a pacifist and coward.'[233] 'I am reminded', he remarked more than once, 'of Churchill saying that the Second World War should be called "the unnecessary war". The British Aluminium battle [was] a similarly unnecessary battle.'[234] He was right in the sense that the board of British Aluminium might have been wiser to accept the Reynolds–TI offer when it was first made, rather than to seek a white knight in Alcoa. Hambros and Lazards might also have been wiser to accept Warburg's early invitation 'to work in this matter as closely as possible . . . as all three houses wanted to do everything possible to bring British Aluminium again into the position of leadership and power which the Company had enjoyed in rather long bygone days'.[235] They might also have been wise to accept the later truce offered by Warburg via David Robarts of Flemings.

Yet the Aluminium War was also necessary, in the sense that winning it did more than any other transaction to establish Warburg's reputation as the City's smartest player – the market leader in corporate finance. The worst that could be said of his conduct was that he was economical with the truth in the first phase of the takeover, before the identity of the Reynolds–TI group was revealed; and that he was aggressive in his use of the press in the second phase, when the battle lines were clearly drawn. There was certainly nothing improper done, unless propriety consisted of acquiescence in an arrangement – the one proposed by Portal and Cunliffe – that would have been against both the national interest and the shareholders' interest. If his rivals grumbled about Warburg, he too had every reason to lament 'the completely unreasonable and unbalanced attitude displayed by certain quarters in the City',[236] to say nothing of the 'hubris' exhibited by Portal, a man as accustomed to wielding power as he was inexperienced in managing a business.[237] The two brave academics who analysed the case even before the dust had settled got it right: 'Immersed in social and class, rather than economic, considerations, the leaders of the City took a view of the national interest that cannot be supported . . . As things turned out, it was probably the right side that won.'[238]

VI

Others might have paused to celebrate such a victory. Not Siegmund Warburg, who maintained that he 'hated every part of the British Aluminium affair'.[239] By the end of the 1950s, he had seen enough incompetence in the financial communities of both London and New York to feel deep disillusion. His vision had been of an Anglo-American transatlantic community, securely based on a combination of shared financial and strategic interests. Just as Reynolds would help modernize British Aluminium, so S. G. Warburg would help modernize Kuhn Loeb. Yet precious few people seemed to share his vision. 'Present developments in our Western business world', he confessed to Ernst Spiegelberg in March 1959,

give me very often the feeling as if the leaders and major or minor operators of the so-called capitalist community, are participating in a cruise on a super Cunard luxury boat which may go on for two, three or four years but which will end in the super Cunard boat hitting an iceberg. In the meantime practically all the passengers of the cruise enjoy to the full their cocktail parties, dinner parties and dancing parties and completely eliminate from their minds that there is bound to be a very unpleasant awakening from the orgies. While the aimless cruise is going on the East is making continuous progress in the Cold War.[240]

Warburg was assiduous in mending fences in the months after the Aluminium War, personally meeting with Anthony Hornby of Cazenoves, Richard Fleming and, finally, Olaf Hambro.[241] Nor, as we have seen, did he immediately abandon his doomed effort to turn around, if not to take over, Kuhn Loeb. But his dissatisfaction with the transatlantic nexus persisted. In particular, his doubts remained about the viability of the Bretton Woods system, doubts that merely increased as American investors hurried to snap up other European assets, conjuring up the troubling prospect of a dollar devaluation as capital left the United States.[242] As early as 1961 Warburg was looking ahead – ten years ahead, as it proved – to a world of managed but flexible exchange rates, unfettered by the dollar's 'ridiculous tie to those various lumps of gold stored at Fort Knox'.[243]

Large though London and New York loomed in Siegmund Warburg's mind throughout the 1950s and 1960s, it would nevertheless be a mistake to see his Anglo-American activities in isolation from his activities on the European continent. Certainly, he never lost his faith in the transatlantic strategic ties embodied by NATO, pouring scorn on those who pinned more hope on either the United Nations ('United Hypocrites') or a militarily autonomous Europe (which Warburg dismissed as a Gaullist chimera).[244] Yet Warburg's ultimate business objective was always to establish an optimal transatlantic triangle that would link together London, New York and a continental European financial centre, whether Hamburg, Frankfurt or Paris. In just the same way, at the political level, it was his assumption that 'a Continental Federation and North Atlantic Union' – both of which institutions he favoured – would be 'in many ways complementary'.[245] Warburg remained passionately committed to 'the strengthening of co-operation between Britain and North America and between Britain and the European Continent', in the belief that 'if we are not to lose the cold war, these two key aspects of the Atlantic Community seem to me to require the utmost effort, not least from businessmen with experience in the field of relationships within the Atlantic Community.'[246] By the beginning of the 1960s, however, his economic attention had clearly begun to shift from North America to Europe. If the 1950s had been Warburg's Anglo-American decade, the 1960s would be emphatically Anglo-European.

8

The Financial Roots of
European Integration

*The division between the Six [EEC members] and the Seven
[EFTA members] is potentially very disruptive and splits
Europe into two parts which, if the present trend is allowed to
continue, will not later merge. It was said that Great Britain
needs Germany as Marlborough needed Prince Eugene of Savoy
and Castlereagh needed Metternich. You are the unrivalled
master in business mergers. As the most prominent Anglo-
German you are the best qualified to work for the consolidation
of Europe. With your background, knowledge, and your
constructive, creative genius you should be successful in
completing this noble task of peace . . . [leading] towards the
unity of Europe, which I fervently hope will be realised.*

Fritz Oppenheimer to Siegmund Warburg,

24 May, 1966[1]

I

The economic integration of Western Europe after the Second World
War proceeded by a circuitous route. It began with the creation of a
Community to regulate the production and pricing of coal and steel
in six European states: Belgium, France, Holland, Italy, Luxembourg
and West Germany. The 1957 Treaty of Rome then created a Common
Market, formally prohibiting barriers on trade between these countries. Trade between them had been growing rapidly before the
formation of this European Economic Community; it continued to
grow thereafter – as did trade in the world as a whole. However, in

other respects economic integration proceeded slowly. In agriculture the development of an integrated market was hindered by the persistence of national subsidies until a Common Agricultural Policy superseded these. In manufacturing, too, national governments continued to resist pan-European competition by subsidizing politically sensitive sectors or by erecting non-tariff barriers. In short, European markets were not being integrated because they were not really being liberalized. Such practices were less frequently adopted in the case of services, but only because services in those days were less easily traded across national boundaries even under conditions of perfect free trade. The exception to this rule was financial services, one of which – the sale of long-term corporate and public sector bonds to relatively wealthy investors – became integrated in a quite novel way in the course of the 1960s.

The rise of the Eurodollar and Eurobond markets is often seen as an early step in the direction of financial globalization. Earlier accounts have emphasized the role of the Bank of England in liberalizing the London market for so-called offshore foreign currency transactions, at a time when most other financial markets were becoming more, not less, regulated.[2] But the birth of the Eurobond was also a major breakthrough in the history of European integration – though one largely unforeseen by the statesmen and technocrats Alan Milward has called the 'saints' of the European Union's formative years.[3] True, the Treaty of Rome envisaged reducing the restrictions on the free movement of capital between member states 'to the extent necessary for the proper functioning of the Common Market'.[4] However, the European Commission, the EEC's executive body, did not act as if it attached much importance to this. Its First Directive on capital controls aimed to liberalize only flows associated with trade within the EEC, direct investment or investment in listed shares.[5] Although the 1962 'Action Programme' aimed to relax capital controls by the end of 1965, the Second Directive on capital controls was an empty gesture and a Third Directive was stillborn.[6] National governments with few exceptions remained wedded to capital and exchange controls. The development of the Eurobond market was thus a largely spontaneous result of innovation by private sector actors, with some help from Britain's permissive monetary authorities. Within a few short years, the genesis and growth of this market transformed the European financial system, forging entirely new institutional links and networks across national borders. Nevertheless, it remains a largely unwritten chapter of post-war European history, rating literally no mention at all in most recent textbooks on the subject.[7]

For some of the bankers involved, no doubt the main objective was profit. Prestige was also a consideration; Eurobond league tables rapidly became an important measure of success. Yet there was an important political dimension, too. For in many ways the Eurobond market was as much a device for advancing Europe's political integration – and, in particular, reinforcing the case for British membership of the EEC – as a means of making money. Among the most powerful arguments against British membership was the legacy of sterling's historic role as a reserve currency. The accumulation in London of sterling balances by colonies and former colonies – a consequence of wartime loans by Commonwealth countries to Britain – made the British economy vulnerable to periodic crises of confidence, so long as the country continued to run current account deficits, as it did in thirteen out of thirty-four years between 1948 and 1982, and capital account deficits, as it did in all but two of those years. Britain had international reserves of foreign exchange and gold amounting to little more than £1 billion in the late 1950s and 1960s, but the sterling balances of other countries rose from just over £3 billion in 1958 to £6 billion ten years later.[8] Even when the current account ran a surplus, there was still the danger of increased capital outflows if confidence wavered, even if in practice it was not the sterling area countries that were responsible for such outflows. Britain's position in this regard was analogous to (though worse than) the contemporaneous American problem with the dollar: the providers of international reserve currencies had to run balance of payments deficits in order to supply the world with their currencies, but in so doing their currencies became vulnerable to crises of confidence. The French, convinced they were subsidizing the Americans because of the dollar's 'inordinate privilege', also feared they would end up having to prop up sterling if Britain joined the EEC, since membership was expected to worsen the UK balance of payments; this was a key reason for both of President Charles de Gaulle's vetoes of British membership in 1963 and 1967, in addition to the more political fear that the UK would act as an American Trojan Horse.[9] The counter-argument developed by the pioneers of the Eurobond market was that the French could not exclude Britain indefinitely if London re-established itself as Europe's principal financial centre for transactions in currencies other than sterling.[10] Part of the significance of the Eurobond market for proponents of British membership was that it turned the City of London from a liability into an asset.

If anyone could claim to be the father of the Eurobond market it was Siegmund Warburg.[11] Throughout his adult life, he was a convinced proponent of European economic and political integration. In the 1920s and 1930s, he and other family members had been generous supporters of the Pan-European Movement founded by that flawed visionary, Richard, Count Coudenhove-Kalergi.[12] To Warburg there seemed no necessary conflict between transatlantic financial integration, his principal preoccupation in the post-war decade, and European political integration. On the contrary, the experience of the 1920s seemed to suggest that they were complementary processes. It had been when capital was flowing across the Atlantic under the Dawes Plan that the prospects for Franco-German rapprochement had seemed rosiest. The breakdown of the global financial system in the Depression had been followed in short order by European disintegration. A second lesson Warburg had learned from the 1930s, however, was that explicit calls for European union were unlikely to succeed, no matter how benign the economic climate, because of the resilience of nationalism throughout the continent. That had been the fatal defect of Coudenhove-Kalergi's strategy. By the post-war period, Warburg had become convinced that the only way to advance the cause of European integration was by economic means – reversing Europeans into a united Europe through the back door of commercial and above all financial integration. Given his outlook and ambitions, it is not surprising that it was Warburg who was the driving force behind the creation of the Eurobond market. In its technical design – a supranational market that could coexist with continued national limitations on capital mobility – and its covert political function – as an aid to European confederation – it epitomized his *Weltanschauung*.

II

As a young man in the Germany of the 1920s, Warburg had been a convinced and optimistic pan-European. He believed, as he wrote to his friend Ernst Kocherthaler in 1927, 'that Europe has passed the culmination point of nationalism, or rather particularism, and is moving with very slow steps in the direction of consolidation'.[13] He discussed with Coudenhove-Kalergi ways of linking the latter's Pan-European Movement to the contemporaneous campaign for international disarmament. Among Warburg's proposals at this time was one for 'a central European ring of states united through a court of arbitration with pooled sovereignty in military matters and consisting of Germany, Holland and the Scandinavian states etc.'[14] Ten years later, with Hitler's dictatorship firmly established and radical nationalists in power all over Central, Southern and Eastern Europe, such notions had come to seem naive. But Warburg continued to assist Coudenhove-Kalergi – helping him, for example, to find an English publisher for his books. Even after the outbreak of war in 1939, Warburg clung to the idea of some kind of political union of Europe, seeing the wartime Anglo-French alliance as the potentially 'sound foundament [*sic*] for a new Commonwealth which should not be all embracing, but a nucleus for a really strong combination of people with European background . . .'.[15] France having been vanquished and with no end to the war in sight, he continued to toy with schemes for a 'West European Association', convinced that Britain's post-war future lay in developing its ties with Europe, not with the Empire.[16] In 1942 he urged Stafford Cripps 'to use the presence of all the refugee Governments residing here in order to declare the constitution of some sort of the United States of Europe in however fragmentary form it may be'.[17] A memorandum Warburg drafted for Cripps proposed a post-war 'Association of Western Europe under British Leadership' that would act as 'the nucleus for a European Commonwealth of Nations'. This Association, Warburg suggested, would have 'Supreme Authority' over '(a) Military affairs; (b) Transport and Communications; (c) Planning of Public Works [and] (d) Currency arrangements'. There was no use, he argued, in expecting the United States to make long-term commitments to Europe's post-war stability. Instead, the United Kingdom should take the lead in 'convert[ing] a temporary coalition and war alliance into a free but durable and far-going merger of economic interests and effective power'.[18] As in the 1920s, so in the 1940s, Warburg therefore remained committed to the idea of explicit political union. In a draft manifesto on the same theme, he explicitly called for an end to national sovereignty 'in the old legal sense', proposing that states in post-war Europe should 'have to delegate certain privileges so far embedded in their sovereignty to their respective Federation, which will delegate certain rights to common European Institutions'. In late 1942, he wrote an article entitled 'The Principles of Federal Union', which developed this line of argument further.[19] He continued throughout the later 1940s to hope that some kind of European union might emerge under joint Anglo-French leadership.[20]

Yet even at this early stage Warburg was already suggesting that these common European institutions would have primarily economic functions, such as the regulation of 'European traffic (railways, roads, waterways and air communications), and . . . European economical planning, money matters including currency, granting of credits and other European common institutions'.[21] Thus, when it became clear that the British government would not pursue the notion of a British-led European Association,[22] while the French government preferred to focus its attention on Jean Monnet's national economic plan, Warburg did not have to abandon his vision of European integration altogether. Governments might not be ready for a politically united Europe, but that did not preclude 'private efforts' like the regular meetings of British and French businessmen he envisaged to promote 'closer relations between the two countries'.[23] Travelling regularly across the Channel, Warburg began consciously trying to achieve in the realm of business, and especially finance, the kind of integration that seemed to be out of political reach. Although he remained involved in a variety of federalist initiatives,[24] from the late 1940s onwards he diverted an increasing proportion of his energies to economic integration, in the belief that this would lay an indispensable foundation for political union in the more distant future. In July 1950, for example, he discussed with Stafford Cripps, now chancellor of the exchequer, the 'advisability of starting West-European cooperation . . . with a unification [rather] of the West-European transport system than of West-European heavy industry as is proposed under the Schuman plan'.[25] The possibility that such a scheme could be financed with a loan 'issued jointly by the United Kingdom and various countries of the European Continent' seemed much more promising than Coudenhove-Kalergi's now outdated visions.*[26] When the idea for a Coal and Steel Community prevailed, Warburg overcame his initial scepticism and sought ways to develop the role of the ECSC's High Authority (the Community's executive, and hence the prototype of the future European Commission) beyond its initial, rather narrow remit. Some sceptics at Warburgs questioned the value of his regular trips to Luxembourg to cultivate his ECSC contacts, but Warburg reassured them: 'Just wait. Ultimately we'll get some business.'[27]

In Warburg's eyes, Britain's imperial days were over; for all his interest in Canada in the 1950s, he grasped earlier than most that trade with the Commonwealth countries could never be a substitute for full participation in European integration.[28] An early proponent of the idea of British membership of the European Economic Community, Warburg publicly supported the first campaign for British accession in 1956,[29] and refused to regard the European Free Trade Association (EFTA), founded in 1960, as a viable alternative to the EEC. Once again, however, he saw the need to build economic support for British entry on both sides of the Channel. A typical proposal was that:

an informal group of a few men in the City – perhaps together with some industrialists, trade unionists and politicians – might make a more active contribution to getting people from this country and from the Continent of Europe more closely together and to destroy some of the strong suspicions against British policy which have accumulated on the Continent.[30]

When the British position shifted towards seeking membership in 1960, Warburg gave little of the credit to 'official circles'.[31] Foreseeing insuperable differences between Britain and 'the Six', since the former saw

---

* Warburg's correspondence with Coudenhove-Kalergi in this period suggests a mounting impatience on the part of the former. As he observed caustically in February 1955: 'While I have always had and still have a great personal affection for Coudenhove I find that in recent years he has become a wishful thinker to an extent which is almost dangerous. He always sees the facts as he wants them and not as they are and as a result he has lost a great deal of his old reputation.'

membership as essentially a matter of trade policy, while the latter assumed that 'the creation of political structures would automatically solve the economic problems', he urged that the decision be referred to 'a small group of so-called "Wise Men"'.[32]

The fact that Warburg envisaged an American chairman for this group illustrates that he saw no contradiction between the North Atlantic alliance and European integration.[33] At times, indeed, he talked of the expansion of the Common Market grouping as a prelude to 'an Atlantic economic union'.[34] He opposed the idea of a European Defence Community, continuing to regard NATO as the only viable structure for West European security.[35] More importantly, Warburg recognized that European integration in the post-war period could proceed smoothly only with the assistance of American aid. As we have seen, American money undoubtedly helped European economies to finance the current account deficits they ran in the post-war period as they sought to re-equip their dilapidated industries. It may also have helped to avoid the kind of zero-sum industrial relations that bedevilled Europe in the 1920s.[36] From Warburg's standpoint, however, the key thing was that, in addition to priming the European pump with dollars, the American administrators of the plan positively encouraged European economic integration, pressurizing recipient countries to reduce trade barriers.

Warburg had argued in 1947 that a 'comprehensive programme of West-European reconstruction in which Great Britain would play the leading role would obtain [more] wholehearted and generous support in the U.S.A.' than 'the arrangement of a large number of Dollar loans to various European countries', as envisaged in the Marshall Plan.[37] But it soon became clear that dollar loans could themselves be used to encourage Europeans to co-operate. The most obvious example was the creation of the European Payments Union in July 1950, which linked together the international payments systems of the recipients of American aid. In the succeeding eight years of its operation, the EPU enabled the French and British economies to run substantial payments deficits with booming West Germany, and certainly contributed to the rapid growth of intra-European trade. To Warburg, however, this was merely a beginning. His ambition was to see an end to the kind of exchange and capital controls that persisted in all save the West German economy throughout the 1950s and 1960s. He encouraged the ECSC High Authority to enter the international capital market as a borrower, in the belief that this might enhance its standing as well as increasing its resources, while at the same time enticing American private investors to follow their government's lead in financing European recovery.[38] In 1957, after long and difficult negotiations, these efforts bore fruit with the issue in New York of a $35 million bond issue for the ECSC.[39] Another somewhat larger loan followed in 1958, a third for $25 million in 1960 and a fourth for the same amount in 1962.[40] Warburg also sought to encourage the European Atomic Energy Community (Euratom) and the European Investment Bank to raise funds on the New York bond market. He explicitly characterized such transactions as 'a small contribution' to the process of 'European integration'.[41]

It should be stressed that arguments of the sort Warburg put forward were not widely supported in the City, Westminster or Whitehall. In that sense, he was indeed fundamentally an outsider.[42] As late as 1979, he could still complain about the generally 'passive if not obstructive attitude of the City towards the European Economic Community'.[43] But he was not a completely isolated visionary. Others who (albeit with qualifications) shared his approach to the question of European integration included Sir George Bolton at the Bank of England and Sir Frank Lee at the Treasury. Abroad, a crucial supportive role was also played by Hermann Abs of the Deutsche Bank.[44] Another kindred spirit in Germany was the Christian Democrat politician and diplomat Kurt Birrenbach.[45] In the United States Warburg found an active sympathizer in John J. McCloy, who had been the US high commissioner for Germany during the creation of the Federal Republic before becoming chairman of Chase Manhattan in 1953.*

At first, it was the question of exchange rates that this group addressed. In theory the major European economies were all linked to the dollar, which was in turn linked to gold, through the system of pegged exchange rates that had been devised at Bretton Woods. In practice, their divergent economic trajectories necessitated periodic

---

* A Harvard lawyer and close associate of the Rockefeller family, McCloy had been Assistant Secretary for War between 1941 and 1945; he also served as the second president of the World Bank between 1947 and 1949. It was McCloy who was supposed to chair Warburg's committee of 'Wise Men' in 1960.

devaluations (of sterling and the French franc) and revaluations (of the deutschmark). As early as 1955, Warburg raised with Bolton 'the necessity of getting the European countries more closely linked in currency matters' with a view to achieving 'complete interchangeability of European currencies'.[46] Two years later he remained convinced that 'neither the common market arrangements nor the so-called free trade area arrangements will work unless there is a joint European stabilisation fund, which for all practical purposes means a joint sterling/D[eutsch] mark stabilisation fund.'[47] Abs, Birrenbach and he collaborated on an abortive project for an Anglo-German exchange rate stabilization fund, which Warburg at one stage conceived of as 'an Anglo-German currency alliance'.[48] There were obvious reasons for such a project. Nothing caused more disruption to post-war British economic policy than the recurrent sterling crises of the period, which were due as much to excessive overseas military spending as to the relative uncompetitiveness of British exports or the sterling balances.[49] At the same time, German policy-makers were increasingly concerned by the opposite tendency of their currency to appreciate. However, it proved impossible to take such schemes beyond the drawing board.[50] European monetary authorities preferred national or international solutions over European solutions, for fear of being committed to expensive interventions on behalf of their neighbours. As Warburg noted in 1960, the principal obstacle to monetary integration was the 'present completely unilateral policy adhered to by the German Central Bank and other authorities'.[51] Although the EEC's 1962 'Action Programme' had specified monetary union as a long-term objective, nothing more was heard of the idea until the Hague EEC Summit of 1969 and the report it commissioned by Pierre Werner, the Prime Minister of Luxembourg.

Instead, Warburg began to consider the possibility of integrating European capital markets rather than currencies. At first sight, this might seem a contradictory step. After all, it was precisely the lack of capital market integration in Europe that allowed the Bretton Woods system of fixed exchange rates to operate alongside more or less independent national monetary policies. However, we must distinguish here between full-scale capital market integration and the more limited form of integration Warburg had in mind.[52] At Kuhn Loeb, Warburg had seen at first hand how major American bond issues were managed by syndicates of Wall Street banks. This had also been a well-established practice in the days when London had been a major capital-exporting market. The discernible demand of European institutions and investors for the four ECSC loans issued in New York[53] made Warburg and others appreciate the possibility that similar syndicates could quite easily be created within Europe for dollar-denominated issues of bonds by European entities. Such syndicates could, under the right regulatory conditions, operate across European borders without violating existing rules on exchange and capital controls, not least because the loans in question were denominated in dollars. This fundamental insight was the basis for the birth and growth of the Eurobond market. It was, as Warburg had realized by 1958, hard to imagine a continuation of 'the present state of affairs in regard to the distribution of European dollar bonds . . . namely that the American issuing houses underwrite these dollar loans for European borrowers but that the European banks and banking houses place most of the bonds'.[54] It was equally hard to envisage European capital market integration proceeding on the basis of some kind of artificial 'currency of account', or 'multiple currency clause'.[55] The inference Warburg drew was that dollar-denominated bonds could be issued in European markets if an international market could be created there that circumvented the restrictions of national exchange and capital controls.

The necessary precondition for the Eurobond market was the existence of a large pool of liquid dollar deposits in European hands. These Eurodollars were a direct consequence of the American balance of payments deficits, which left a growing quantity of American currency in the hands of multinational companies, European commercial banks and central banks, as well as supranational entities like the Bank for International Settlements. There were also significant numbers of wealthy individuals who preferred to hold a portion of their assets in dollars.[56] Why were these dollars not simply deposited with American institutions in New York? The answer was that Regulation Q, introduced during the Depression, restricted the interest rate payable on short-term dollar deposits to 1 per cent in the case of thirty-day deposits and 2.5 per cent in the case of ninety-day deposits.[57] In addition, the Soviet Union and its client states had no desire to deposit their dollar holdings – which were not insignificant – in the United States, where they might be liable to confiscation in the event of a geopolitical conflict; they preferred to use the Banque Commerciale pour l'Europe du Nord, whose telex address EURBANK may have been the origin of the term Eurodollar.[58] When dollar interest rates in the London market rose significantly above American rates in mid-1955, the Midland Bank seized the opportunity to offer non-UK residents dollar deposit facilities.[59] At first this was a mechanism for channelling American deposits into the British economy, since Midland switched the funds into sterling and lent them on. But when it became clear that the Bank of England was prepared to tolerate such dollar deposits, other banks (including the rapidly multiplying London offices of American firms) were not slow to follow.[60] Soon most such deposits were being recycled as loans to companies and governments outside the UK. For example, the Kleinwort Foreign Exchange Department accumulated substantial dollar deposits and lent them on to German clients.[61] The Eurodollar market in London grew with extraordinary speed, from $12 billion in 1963 to $65 billion in 1969;[62] its annual growth rate peaked in 1969 at just under 50 per cent and was never below 10 per cent throughout the period from 1965 to 1979.[63] Yet this money was by its very nature hot money, on short-term deposit. That was what made other central banks so nervous about allowing Eurodollar markets to develop. The challenge was to use it as the basis for a new market in long-term securities.

III

By the end of the 1950s, Warburg was feeling distinctly disillusioned by the institutions that had been set up to promote European integration: the ECSC, Euratom and the EEC itself, to say nothing of the European Investment Bank. He feared that the continent was heading towards 'a time of renewed crisis in intra-European relations'.[64] He detected only 'inertia' and 'intrigues' in Brussels and Luxembourg.[65] These were intimations of the stagnation that was to afflict the official integration process throughout the 1960s. To be sure, as president of the European Commission between 1958 and 1967, Walter Hallstein strove energetically to implement the terms of the Treaty of Rome by enhancing the power of the Commission. But his efforts do not seem to have impressed Warburg. Even less encouraging was the diversion of the EEC's energies (and most of its resources) into what ultimately emerged as the Common Agricultural Policy, a system designed to protect French and German farmers from anything resembling the free play of market forces. With the French pressing for protective tariffs and the Germans pressing for artificially high prices, Europe embarked on the worst kind of economic integration, based on price supports, stockpiling and protection.

For a time, Warburg held out hope that the Macmillan government's decision to apply to join the EEC in 1961 might revitalize the existing European institutions; this, after all, was what he had been advocating for nearly twenty years. To help bolster the case for membership, he recruited the former British diplomat Lord Gladwyn (Hubert Gladwyn Jebb), who had just served for six years as Britain's ambassador to France, to become a dedicated campaigner for British entry into the Common Market in the capacity of a non-executive director at Warburgs. As in the 1940s, Warburg felt 'certain that if Britain joins the Common Market, and is represented in the various European organisations in the right way, the UK Government will be in a position to lead Europe and has no reason to fear that anything will be done which is strongly opposed by Britain as against the interests of the UK or the Commonwealth'.[66] He enthusiastically supported schemes for a Channel bridge or tunnel, as much for their symbolic as for their commercial potential.[67] Economic evidence by now strongly supported the case for British membership. The British economy was a sick man compared not just with West Germany but with all six members of the EEC. Meanwhile, the importance of Commonwealth markets to British trade was declining, while the importance of the European continent was growing. However, at a press conference on 14 January 1963, de Gaulle brusquely vetoed Britain's application for membership. It was all too obvious to the French that to admit Britain before a deal had been done on the Common Agricultural Policy would reinforce the proponents of (relatively) free trade, not least because Britain's farming sector was so much smaller than that of any EEC member. At the same time, the French had no desire to share responsibility for the chronic instability of Britain's dying reserve currency.[68] For his part, Warburg had grasped from an early stage that 'as regards the giving up of national sovereignty the French – and in particular de Gaulle – are even more hesitant than most of the people in this country.'[69] But he underestimated the lengths to which de Gaulle would be prepared to go to defend French national interests: not only rejecting British membership, but also boycotting European institutions in 1965 (the Empty Chair crisis) and insisting that member states should have a national veto when measures were referred to the Council of Ministers (the Luxembourg Declaration).[70] Disgusted,* Warburg accused de Gaulle of aiming to create 'a new Europe from Paris to Moscow under Franco-Russian leadership as a counterweight against what he considers Anglo-American preponderance in the Atlantic Community'.[71]

Warburg never entirely gave up hope of a belated British entry into the Common Market.[72] In the course of the 1960s, however, he became so disillusioned that he began to question whether or not Britain should continue to seek EEC membership 'now that that bus had been missed'.[73] At one point he even predicted a break-up of the EEC because 'most of the Common Market countries will rather join the Americans and the British than be dependent on the French'.[74] The EEC was 'a protectionist tariff club – in reality not a real European Community'.[75] In a memorandum of April 1968, he excoriated the degeneration and dissipation of the various EEC institutions:

A narrow-minded bureaucracy working in a kind of 'luftleerer Raum' [airless space] – a sort of meaningless vacuum unattached to any super national [sic] or national authority – has replaced what was a genuine and enthusiastic European organisation operating within a sound and efficiently functioning framework. What makes the present situation especially bad is the division of the European Commission into various sections, partly located in Brussels, partly located in Luxembourg. Whilst the Commission as such and its various industrial sections, in particular coal, steel, and energy[,] are operating from Brussels, the Finance Section and the Administration attached to the European Parliament are operating from Luxembourg, with the European Parliament

---

* Warburg's low opinion of the French political elite was not improved when Gladwyn sought to broker a meeting between him and the French Finance Minister Valéry Giscard d'Estaing. The latter initially asked 'who that strange fellow Monsieur Siegmund was' (though the meeting subsequently went ahead).

as such meeting in Strasbourg. In fact there are apart from the Luxembourg sections about thirty different sections or groups in Brussels which are badly co-ordinated or not co-ordinated at all and which are torn to pieces by intrigues either emanating from Brussels or caused from without through the Governments of the six EEC member countries.[76]

In his more sanguine moments, Warburg could still hope for a gradual rapprochement of the EEC and EFTA; this was what he advised Harold Wilson to aim for, and what Wilson actually attempted.[77] But so long as de Gaulle remained in power in France, his expectations remained low. 'Those who advocated the entry of Britain into Europe', he wrote in October 1964, 'should have admitted defeat in regard to the wider ranging aims and concentrated on a few very limited objectives.'[78] He seems not have taken much interest in the second British bid for membership in 1966–7. Not until the General's departure from office in 1969 did he regain his belief in the idea of British membership of the EEC, though only 'if we can be reasonably sure that the protectionist tendencies are restrained'.[79] As he explained in an interview in 1970:

Today the chief characteristic of the European Economic Community is clearly the tariff wall which is erected around it and which, of course, would be still higher if it had not been for the Kennedy Round [of the General Agreement on Trade and Tariffs]. Within the borders of this tariff wall little has been achieved towards the creation of common European endeavours in the field of helping under-developed areas or towards a European currency. Indeed the European Economic Community has at present more of an inward than of an outward-looking image. In these circumstances Britain has to be very careful about joining a movement which may be rather retrograde than progressive. Only if we should succeed in becoming members of a European Community in which the emphasis would be less on building up a joint tariff wall and on agricultural subventionism [sic] than on the constructive pooling of the great human resources of Europe in tackling big tasks both within and beyond Europe would I be in favour of Britain becoming part of the Common Market. Furthermore[,] if in the post-Gaullist period a more generous European spirit could be rekindled, I would return to my old enthusiasm with regard to Britain's role in Europe. Indeed, within the framework of a really outward looking Europe Britain could play a special role as a bridge builder between

Europe and the wider circle of the Atlantic Community as well as the under-developed countries, following in this way some of the best traditions of her old Commonwealth ties.[80]

Nevertheless, the stalling of official integration did not rule out the continuation of that *financial* integration that had first suggested itself to Warburg at the time of the second ECSC loan of 1958. The essential building blocks were to be the underwriting and selling syndicates of banks that were formed on an *ad hoc* basis for new dollar-denominated issues. In the 1950s these had been largely composed of the big Wall Street investment banks. As we have seen, however, the market for dollar-denominated bonds issued by European borrowers turned out to be larger in Europe than in the still domestically focused US market. This indicated that at least a portion of Eurodollar deposits in London might be available for investment in longer-term securities.[81] Increasingly, Warburg and other European financiers asked why it was that the American firms did the lucrative work of underwriting, leaving the European institutions to do the more lowly work of selling bonds to non-financial clients. In the words of Julius Strauss, of the stockbrokers Strauss Turnbull, 'the American houses got all the cream but did none of the work.'[82]

The very existence of the Eurodollar market in London reflected the predisposition on the part of the British monetary authorities to allow the City to act as a centre for offshore finance.[83] The Bank's position was one of tolerance in the interests of London's revival: 'However much we dislike hot money we cannot be international bankers and refuse to accept money.'[84] This was vital for the development of all the Euromarkets in London, since, other things being equal, they might more easily have developed in Switzerland or West Germany, where supplies of domestic savings for export were more plentiful than they were in Britain.[85] While other monetary authorities acted to restrict flows of hot money,[86] however, the Bank's policy was laissez-faire. The paradox was that London was in other respects a more heavily regulated market than Zurich or Frankfurt. Purchases of foreign securities by British subjects were effectively prohibited other than with strictly regulated 'investment dollars'. In 1957 the Bank of England also banned City firms from financing third-party trade in sterling; refinance credits were also banned.[87] Though these restrictions had been lifted by 1960, there remained a 4 (later 2) per cent stamp duty on new domestic issues and tax was deducted at source from interest paid to British bondholders. At the same time, the London Stock Exchange continued to list the sterling price of dollar securities as if the post-war depreciation of the pound had never happened. And exchange controls for residents remained in place until 1979. Yet it was precisely this dichotomy between the treatment of residents holding sterling and the treatment of non-residents holding dollars that made it possible to establish a completely separate and unregulated dollar bond market in London. As one market participant later recalled: 'The Bank could allow traffic in foreign currency securities on its capital market and activity in foreign currencies because it was completely isolated from the management of the domestic monetary mass.'[88] The mood in Threadneedle Street was changing. Already in 1960 the authorities had permitted Warburgs to arrange share listings for two continental companies in London: not only the German steelmaker Thyssen but also the Swedish telephone company L. M. Ericsson, a transaction organized in partnership with Deutsche Bank and the Banque de Paris et des Pays-Bas – the beginning of what was to prove to be a long and complex relationship with the latter.[89]

That said, the Bank still needed to be handled with care, and it was with some trepidation that George Bolton broached the subject with the recently appointed Governor, Lord Cromer, in June 1962. Bolton was now chairman of the Bank of London and South America (BOLSA), a pioneer in the Eurodollar market, and it was as a representative of the private sector that he now spoke to Cromer 'about a certain exchange of ideas that is currently taking place regarding the opening of the London market to a wide variety of borrowers for loans denominated in foreign currencies'. The exchange of ideas had involved representatives not only of Warburgs, but also of Barings and Samuel Montagu; Hambros became involved the following month. However, no one wished to 'proceed more actively unless the ideas have the general blessing of the authorities'. The aim, as Bolton explained, was simply to help 'restore London's function as a capital market': 'the restoration and revival of the London Market machinery to enable issues of foreign loans to be made [is] a matter of immediate importance to the Western World . . . The only centre that can help New York is London, as we are all uncomfortably aware of the isolation and inefficiency of the European capital markets.'[90] Cromer's reply was positive: 'We are sympathetic to this proposal,' he wrote, 'and will give it what practical support we can.'[91] The Bank particularly liked the fact that it might 'mop up some of the very volatile Eurodollars at present in London'.[92] Warburg's correspondence makes it clear, however, that he and his City associates were also seeking to convey a subtle threat to the Bank. 'Unless the Government was prepared to take action in regard to stamp duty and other measures which would make the London issuing market competitive with other foreign capital markets', they would go elsewhere – perhaps to Luxembourg.[93] Amsterdam was also investigated as a possible market.[94] Nor was the Bank the only regulatory authority that had to be squared away. The London Stock Exchange at first refused to list the bonds so that they could not be delivered (in settlement of a transaction) in Britain, and later insisted on quoting the dollar bonds in sterling at the pre-war exchange rate. British investors would have to buy the new bonds in Luxembourg with so-called investment dollars from the government-controlled pool of funds available for foreign currency purchases.[95] The Inland Revenue was no more helpful.

There were several possible candidates for the first true Eurobond issue. The Japanese government expressed an interest in such a loan.[96] There was also talk of a Norwegian loan for the city of Oslo. In his exasperation with the EEC, Warburg even contemplated a dollar loan for the Commonwealth Development Finance Company.[97] By April 1963, however, he and his colleagues had reverted to the more logical and familiar vehicle of the European Coal and Steel Community. This was how they explained their scheme to the Bank of England:

It would be a straightforward dollar loan with no currency options and . . . as far as the U.K. Exchange Control is concerned this would be a foreign currency security for which U.K. residents would have to pay a premium. Consequently they did not expect any subscriptions from this country. Nevertheless they would endeavour to get a quotation in London which could be regarded as a basis throughout Europe and thus encourage dealings through London.[98]

The Bank was attracted to the idea, despite fears that the Foreign Office might regard it as 'inappropriate in any way that a Common Market organisation should appear to be borrowing in London in the light of the Brussels breakdown' in negotiations over Britain's EEC accession. As the Bank's John Stevens explained to Sir Eric Roll, who had assisted Edward Heath in the negotiations for British Common Market entry, 'from the purely financial angle' such an operation would be 'welcome':

As the foreign bond market is not available for loans in sterling to the Continent, an operation of this type (of which there have been several before) keeps London alive as a financial centre even if the business is not done in Sterling. I would hope that you felt that sufficient time had elapsed since the Brussels breakdown. In fact it could be argued that there is a positive virtue in showing that at least there has not been a breakdown on the financial front and that this is an example of the intentions expressed after the breakdown that every step would be taken between ourselves and the Common Market to make it easy for the negotiations to be resumed.[99]

This view was endorsed by the Treasury and Foreign Office.[100] However, the need to secure approval from the finance ministers of all six EEC members, along with the hesitancy of Hans Skribanowitz, Director of the ECSC's Finance Division, led to months of delays.[101] As a result, the first Eurobond issue ended up being Italian.

At the suggestion of the Governor of the Banca d'Italia, Guido Carli, Warburgs had alighted on an Italian steel company, Finsider, a subsidiary of the giant state holding company the Institute for Industrial Reconstruction (IRI).* Once again, avoiding national taxation was crucial, so the bonds were issued in the name not of Finsider, which was legally obliged to deduct Italian taxation from any coupon payments, but of Autostrade, the Italian toll-motorway company, which had a special dispensation to pay coupons gross.[102] It was Ian Fraser and Peter Spira, assisted by the bond expert Gert Whitman, who did much of the hard toil of drawing up the path-breaking contract, working closely with the lawyers Geoffrey Sammons and Robin Broadley of Allen & Overy and the accountant Hugh Greenwood of Brown, Fleming &

---

* Two years before, Warburgs had already successfully placed a block of Finsider shares on the London Stock Exchange – 'further evidence', as the *Economist* remarked, 'of cross-fertilisation between the leading European stock markets'.

Murray. To avoid UK stamp duty, the bonds were formally issued at Schiphol Airport in the Netherlands. To avoid UK income tax, the coupons were payable in Luxembourg.[103] The transaction – a $15 million six-year loan – was managed by a consortium led by Warburgs and also consisting of Deutsche Bank, Banque de Bruxelles and Rotterdamsche Bank, underwritten by a syndicate of British and European banks led by Deutsche, and then marketed to investors through a wider network of associated intermediaries including Strauss Turnbull, White Weld and Credit Suisse.[104] It should be noted that despite the breadth of the distribution network that swiftly developed, Eurobond issues were not initial public offerings in the American sense, but widely sold private placements.[105] As Fraser put it, the Autostrade loan represented 'a compromise between a conventional London "placing" and a conventional New York "offering"'.[106] It was, as the *Economist* noted, not only 'the first foreign industrial loan floated in London for a generation' but also part of a 'new drive by the City of London to establish itself as an entrepôt centre in the international capital market'.[107]

Available in relatively small denominations (typically $1,000), with a 5.5 per cent coupon and an issue price of 98.5 per cent of par, the bonds were not hard to place. As bearer bonds they were anonymous and portable; they were also free from withholding tax. The typical investor was 'the only half-mythical figure of the Belgian dentist – a high-earning individual, living in a country with a bureaucratic tax system where domestic bonds were liable to tax at source, and where there was a limited choice of investment opportunities'.[108] As Fraser later observed:

The secret of these issues . . . was that the bonds must be totally anonymous, coupons must be paid without any deduction of tax and the bond at maturity paid off in full without any questions asked and that it must be possible to do this in several capitals . . . the main ultimate buyers of the bonds were individuals, usually from Eastern Europe but often also from Latin America, who wanted to have part of their fortune in mobile form so that if they had to leave they could leave quickly with their bonds in a small suitcase.[109]

European plans for a dollar-denominated bond market were thus already well advanced even before the US government proposed its Interest Equalization Tax in July 1963, the aim of which was to deter

American citizens and institutions from investing in Europe.[110] Indeed, if there had been no IET, the Eurobond market would still have developed because of the implicit subsidy provided by exemption from withholding tax.[111] There is no question, however, that this measure – and subsequent measures designed to restrict US capital export – gave a stimulus to the growth of the Eurobond market. Without the IET, the Austrian government would probably have gone ahead with a dollar loan in New York; instead, it raised $18 million in Eurobonds issued by Warburgs, Hambros, Rothschilds and the state-owned Creditanstalt. This loan paved the way for a succession of new issues in the course of 1964. By the end of the year, a total of forty-four foreign dollar issues had been made in Europe, raising a total of $681 million.[112] By 1967 more foreign securities were being issued on the Eurobond market than in the United States and five times more than in European national markets.[113] In 1968 the volume of new issues exceeded $3.5 billion; four years later the total was $5.5 billion.[114] Although public borrowers like the Austrian government and the cities of Oslo and Turin had initially predominated, from 1966 until 1973 the majority of issues were by private sector entities.[115] Gradually, too, a secondary market began to develop, which had been conspicuous by its absence at first (when most investors had adopted a 'buy and hold' strategy).[116] Purely transactional problems due to cross-border differences in delivery rules, methods of computing interest and allocation of costs were significantly reduced with the creation of two clearing systems, Euroclear and the Luxembourg-based Cedel.[117]

IV

Siegmund Warburg was understandably proud of the Eurobond market; he had no doubt that it was 'our [meaning Warburgs'] primary initiative'.[118] But what were his reasons for pushing its development forward? One obvious hypothesis is that the profit motive predominated – in other words, that the rise of the Eurobond was a straightforward case of product innovation designed to enhance S. G. Warburg & Co.'s bottom line. This was without doubt a factor. In the words of the South African John Craven, who joined Warburgs in

1967, 'Siegmund was clever enough to realize that if you quietly developed a [new] product, namely a Eurobond, which the other [City] houses would probably treat with a certain amount of disdain', then it was possible legitimately to approach their established clients. 'It was in fact a very clever ploy to get in the back door.'[119] Moreover, once the initial Autostrade issue had established a template, Eurobond issuance was comparatively easy. The fixed commissions that banks charged – conventionally o.5 per cent for managing banks and underwriters and 1.5 per cent for selling banks and brokers – reflected the fact that it was the lowly bond-salesmen who did the hard work. The commissions were not insignificant. A sterling issue for the Irish government in 1971 generated £200,000, a sum so large that Henry Grunfeld 'telephoned . . . from holiday and, in an unprecedented act, in an embarrassed way offered congratulation . . . quickly adding that of course we had "been very lucky"'.[120] There was effectively no downside risk to the underwriters since issues were either reduced or pulled outright if demand proved to be slack.[121] On the other hand, as so often is the case with financial innovation, entry barriers were low and 'first mover' advantage was short lived. At the weekly directors' dinners he held in the mid-1960s, Warburg warned his younger colleagues: 'Once a new line of business was invented, all the competing banks wished to have a share in it and the only result could be that profit margins for the banks went down or disappeared; this was bound to happen and it would soon happen with our Euro-bond business.'[122] So it proved. As more and more American and Swiss banks entered the market – the number of branches of foreign banks in London increased from 51 to 129 between 1962 and 1970 – the early dominance of Warburgs, Hambros and Rothschilds was challenged.[123] From 1967 until 1972 it was Deutsche Bank that led the rankings in terms of new Eurobond issuance; quite simply, the merchant banks lacked the capital base to compete.[124] Profit margins were also squeezed, just as Warburg had predicted. Though his bank did better than the other merchant banks in terms of the annual issuance rankings, we should not exaggerate how much money was actually being made from this line of business. As Warburg himself reminded his executive directors in October 1967:

however important Euro bond issues are, this must not be our first priority and . . . indeed our chief interest should be to look after our important industrial clients in this country, in the United States, and on the Continent of Europe. One fee which we earn from giving good service to one of our large industrial clients can be far in excess of what we earn in a whole year in connection with Euro bond issues.[125]

John Craven later confirmed that 'because SGW had no distribution powers at all . . . [w]e didn't make money, we never made serious money for years and years.' In Peter Spira's words, 'It was a wonderful prestige business,' rather than an especially profitable one.[126]

A second motive – the one most frequently cited in the existing literature – is that the architects of the Eurobond market shared the Bank of England's desire to rebuild London's pre-war position as an international financial centre. This certainly played a part in Warburg's calculations. It was his view that in any 'truly European capital market . . . London could and should play a leading role irrespective of the present division between EEC and EFTA'.[127] This also explains his passionate belief in the need to denominate the second wave of Eurobonds in European rather than American currency. As he explained to his colleagues, who complained that dollar bonds were easier to sell, 'Anyone who has studied the situation thoroughly and objectively must know that if we continue with the issue of foreign bonds expressed in dollars, the entire business will and should go to New York, and the London market will have no material part in it any longer. The only chance for the London market to participate in such issues is through arranging loans in other denominations than Dollars.'[128] The obvious European currency to choose was the deutschmark, not least because German long-term interest rates were trending below the European average in the course of the 1960s.[129] From Warburg's point of view, however, a purely deutschmark Eurobond market had little appeal, for the obvious reason that it would inevitably strengthen the already powerful position of the big German banks. In December 1963 he therefore proposed to Abs the idea of sterling bonds with a deutschmark option, combining – as Warburg explained to Cromer – the strongest EFTA currency with the strongest EEC currency.[130] Once the approval of the (admittedly uneasy) British and German monetary authorities had been secured – which was only after a 'fight' – it was this sterling–deutschmark model that was adopted for the £5 million loan issued in 1964 for the city of Turin.[131]

So excited was Warburg by this transaction that he took the exceedingly rare step of writing a series of newspaper articles for *The Times* on the subject, in which he was at pains to explain that it posed no threat to the stability of the British currency or balance of payments. London, he argued, was simply providing a service for foreign holders of Eurodollars and other liquid funds to buy European bonds. These could be denominated in whatever currency investors found attractive; hence the beauty of multiple-currency bonds.[132] Warburg did not expect such bonds to replace dollar-denominated Eurobonds in the near future, but he expressed the view privately that 'if European capital markets are gradually developed . . . European currencies or European currency units will have to be made more popular than they are at present.'[133] Peter Spira, for one, was dubious of such arguments at first, suspecting that the only reason Siegmund had devised the sterling–deutschmark bond was to ensure that 'a UK house could appear as lead manager' of what was essentially a deutschmark security.[134] When he successfully persuaded Imperial Chemical Industries to issue $100 million in sterling–deutschmark bonds, however, he changed his mind. To secure ICI as a Warburg client was a major breakthrough. 'This was it,' Fraser remembered Spira saying: 'We had got there.'[135] Warburg had in fact been angling for ICI's business since 1962, capitalizing on the bad publicity generated by its failed bid for Courtaulds.[136] From ICI's point of view, the appeal of S. G. Warburg lay partly in its continental European connections. ICI's management felt the company needed to 'go into the Common Market', yet there were still (as one director of the company told Ian Fraser in 1963), 'five people in ICI who could speak Hindi for every one who could speak any European language'.[137] However, it was not until Sir Peter Allen had replaced Paul Chambers as chairman that the Warburgs–ICI relationship really began to develop.[138] From 1971 ICI entrusted its international financial business to Warburgs, ousting Schroders from that role.[139]

The dual-currency bond was only one of a number of ways Warburg worked to secure London's position at the centre of the Eurobond market. In 1965, for example, Warburgs joined forces with Hambros and Rothschilds to lobby the Bank of England to exempt foreign bonds issued in London from stamp duty; at the same time, they pressed the Treasury to lift the requirement that income tax be deducted from the interest on bonds issued by UK-domiciled companies.[140] In a letter to *The Times*, Warburg and Jocelyn Hambro deplored:

the quite ludicrous situation that on the one hand the City of London is arranging long-term borrowing in Continental Europe for American oil companies, Italian nationalised industries and various Scandinavian quarters and on the other hand any attempt to perform the same service, even for British borrowers of the highest quality, is being frustrated by certain fiscal requirements which are without any practical substance and which could easily be eliminated.[141]

Not only did Warburg share the Bank's objective to resurrect London as an international financial centre; he was pressing the UK authorities to move even faster in the direction of liberalizing London's facilities for international investors.

Yet it would be quite wrong to see either his firm's profitability or the dominance of London as Warburg's prime motivation in devising and developing the Eurobond market. For he always conceived of it as simply a first step towards linking together the European capital markets and thereby advancing the wider project of European integration. Warburg intended the sterling–deutschmark bonds as securities designed for a *European* capital market. As he put it in April 1965:

The main motive force both for the creation of the EEC and EFTA . . . was the recognition that for its optimum scale modern industry required a larger market than could be supplied by any one European nation. As this policy bears fruit and industry becomes organised on a truly European scale, there will be an increasing need for a truly European capital market.[142]

Contemporaries were not slow to see this possibility. By 1969 it was possible for an academic economist to conclude: 'The Euro-bond market has grown to such a stature as to foreshadow a real European bond market.'[143] It was true, as René Larre noted that same year, that the borrowers and investors it brought together came not just from

Europe but from 'all over the world'; yet there was no doubt that the Eurobond market was making 'a significant contribution to the modernization of financial and banking practices in Europe'.[144]

Typical of the way Warburg saw the Eurobond market as a vehicle for European integration was his response to the minor teething troubles the market experienced in the later 1960s. For a time in 1966, there were so many new Eurobond issues that Warburg publicly warned of a glut.[145] Yields on some new issues rose above 6 per cent for the first time, reflecting the excess supply of new issues relative to demand as well, perhaps, as rising inflationary expectations. To Warburg, this suggested the need for some form of light regulation (meaning self-regulation by the financial markets). But he made it clear that this would need to be done at the European level, and not just in the City of London. In 1966 he argued that the Eurobond market should adopt the kind of queuing system used in Switzerland to prevent too many new issues happening at the same time. As Warburg remarked, it was 'obviously impossible to visualize the formation of a European capital issues committee which would have any legally enforceable powers'. But here was another opportunity for further unofficial European integration:

If[,] under the sponsorship of say the six or seven leading central banks of Europe, a small committee of representatives of these banks were established, it should be possible to arrange for the issuing houses concerned to register with such a committee the issues they are planning, and to be guided by the committee in regard to the timing and the maximum size of these issues.[146]

He returned to this theme in 1970, when the market threatened to be overwhelmed by an 'avalanche' of borrowing demands.[147] Now Warburg argued for the creation of a committee consisting of representatives from one issuing house in each of the principal European countries.[148]

The same kind of thinking underlay Warburg's response to the challenge posed by the invasion of Wall Street firms, which was simply to form larger European syndicates. In many ways, this was the most important kind of European integration that the Eurobond market encouraged. To begin with, many of the key decisions were taken as a result of regular consultation with Abs and a few others. As Warburg later recalled, he and Abs 'were continually in touch regarding the terms of the Euro issues on which we were working and were also checking with one another the attitudes of our . . . firms towards the Euro transactions done by our competitors on both sides of the Atlantic'.[149] In 1967 Warburg contemplated establishing an informal alliance between four of the biggest banks involved: Warburgs, Deutsche Bank, Banque de Paris et des Pays-Bas (Paribas) and Banca Commerciale Italiana.[150] This was typical of the kind of European financial structure Warburg aspired to build, foreshadowing his subsequent attempt to bring about a full-scale merger between Warburgs and Paribas. A similar initiative was the Transatlantic Bond Fund which linked together Warburgs, the Bank of London and South America, Banca Nazionale del Lavoro and the Stockholms Enskilda Bank.[151] By 1970 the group with which Warburgs liked to work had expanded to include the Dutch bank Amro, the German banks Commerzbank and Dresdner, and the French Société Générale.[152] British entry into the Common Market did not radically alter this pattern, contrary to the expectations of those who expected major structural changes in the banking world after January 1973.[153] As Warburg put it, 'with this new European background . . . major financial houses on the Continent and here in this country [would] become linked together . . . [b]ut linked in such a way that they do not lose their autonomous management, their autonomous style, their autonomous plans, their autonomous structure, including their separate close connections to many parts of the world.'[154] The next logical products of this process of financial evolution were the consortium banks that flourished in this period.[155]

Warburg was therefore perfectly sincere in conceiving of the Eurobond market as a stage in the process of European integration. This, rather than its inherent profitability or its advantages to the City of London, was his principal reason for pursuing it. A case in point was the spate of UK public sector issues proposed by Warburg in 1967 to coincide with the British government's second bid for EEC membership (see Chapter 10). Conversely, when his bank was left out of a Eurobond issue by the EEC in 1977, Warburg was incandescent not so much because of forgone commissions, but because it seemed to him a slight after his firm's pioneering role in creating and developing the Eurobond market.[156]

V

There were, nevertheless, practical limits to how European the Eurobond market could actually be. It is important to emphasize that the public and private sector entities that raised money on the new Eurobond market were not all European – nor, for that matter, were the European ones all based in the EEC. Between 1965 and 1970, some 37 per cent of Eurobond issues were for American companies; and 68 per cent were dollar-denominated.[157] Among the major issues handled by Warburgs in 1967 were three for Chrysler, the American car manufacturer; another was for Mobil Oil. Nor was it realistic to try to exclude the big American banks from this burgeoning new market. Although co-operation between European banks certainly increased as a result of Eurobond management and underwriting syndicates, American banks also featured prominently in the lists – so-called tombstones – of syndicate members that were published in the financial press on the occasion of each new issue. Moreover, it was often the Americans who pushed forward the innovation frontier. By 1969 a large syndicated loan market had emerged for short-term loans which, along with the certificates of deposit introduced in 1966, filled the middle ground in the term-structure of Euro interest rates between the Eurodollar and the Eurobond market.[158] The idea of floating-rate issues, though pioneered by Warburgs from 1970, was originally the brainchild of Evan Galbraith of Bankers Trust International.[159] Significantly, the $425 million loan organized on this basis for the Italian Electricity Authority ENEL (and hailed in the press as 'the largest finance transaction done by a private group in Europe') was managed by a syndicate that comprised not only Warburgs, Banca Commerciale Italiana and Credit Suisse but also Bankers Trust International and White Weld.[160]

A second difficulty was that, with the advent of floating exchange rates, the attractiveness of the Eurobond market was bound to diminish for corporations in weak-currency countries like Britain and Italy, which were unlikely to want to borrow in deutschmarks, Swiss francs or even dollars, even if loans in those currencies could be had at lower interest rates than were available on their domestic markets. Why would British Leyland want to saddle itself with deutschmark-denominated debt if the pound was going to continue sliding inexorably downwards against the German currency?[161] The case of the Italian company Finsider – which, as we have seen, had been behind the first Eurobond issue – is especially telling. By 1970 the company had accumulated Eurobond debts totalling $410 million, but was now desperate to repay them or convert them into lire because they were 'extremely gloomy over the future of the Italian economy and hence the strength of its currency'.[162] It was with this kind of problem in mind that Warburg discerned more and more the advantages of some kind of European monetary integration, beginning with the creation of a unit of account – Euro moneta – based on a basket of different national currencies (possibly composed of the six EEC currencies plus or minus the Swiss franc). A loan on this basis was briefly contemplated for the ECSC in 1968. As Warburg observed, such a transaction would not be one in which a British bank could play a leading role:

It will obviously be impossible for a British house to obtain a leading position in a High Authority issue based only on EEC currencies, and it will probably be impossible both from a political and currency angle to associate the Sterling currency with such an arrangement. However, if we make a worthwhile intellectual contribution to the present deliberations going on in the Finance Section of the European Commission (no longer the High Authority), such a contribution might not only be valuable for the sake of the good cause but might also justify our group in taking a part in a financial transaction which may ensue in due course.[163]

In practice, however, most issuers (including the ECSC) were put off by the complexities of such devices. The majority of Eurobond issues in the late 1960s and early 1970s were denominated in either dollars, deutschmarks (as the German government sought to encourage capital export) or Dutch guilders.[164]

There were limits, too, to the speed with which European financial integration would advance the more general economic integration to which Warburg looked forward. In an interview he gave to the *Sunday Telegraph* in January 1970, Warburg foresaw 'a new challenge in the field of establishing organic and integrating links between industrial firms in this country and on the Continent of Europe. There exist already several links of this nature and even if Britain does not join the

European Economic Community the combinations between industries on the two sides of the Channel will go on expanding.'[165] Three years later, he was still talking enthusiastically about the possible emergence of '"European" companies owning holdings in various "national" companies in Europe'.[166] The success of multinationals like Shell and Unilever implied more such entities. However, despite official encouragement for his idea of an EEC Industries Fund,[167] it proved much harder in practice to bring about the kind of pan-European mergers Warburg had in mind. At various times in the early 1970s he floated ideas for cross-Channel mergers in the automobile industry (British Leyland–Volkswagen, British Leyland–Daimler Benz), the chemical industry (ICI–Bayer) and the electrical engineering industry (GEC–Siemens, GEC–AEG). These schemes were far ahead of their time, not least because there was no very obvious benefit that first-class German companies could derive from taking over their less competitive rivals in the ailing UK market. For many years to come, most big European companies would continue to pursue sectoral integration through national rather than pan-European mergers.

Nevertheless, despite these limitations, it does not seem unreasonable to agree with Warburg that the creation and growth of the Eurobond market was a significant step in the process of European integration. By firmly establishing London as Europe's dominant financial centre, it undoubtedly helped to pave the way for British entry into the EEC. By revealing the costs of multiple floating currencies, it strengthened the case for some kind of European monetary co-ordination, pointing the way ahead to the European Monetary System, the Exchange Rate Mechanism and ultimately Economic and Monetary Union. Warburg never imagined that the goal of a single currency could be achieved in the way that the Eurobond market had been created, namely by private sector initiative. As he wrote to Gladwyn in October 1972, 'an economic and monetary union cannot be envisaged without a political union. I think it was Bismarck who always talked about "das primat der politik ueber die wirtschaft" [the primacy of politics over economics] and this is as true today as it was in his age.'[168] Throughout his life, however, he saw economic integration as a viable substitute when political union appeared to be log-jammed. That had seemed to be the case in the 1960s; the result was the Eurobond market.

On the question of Europe, Warburg was a lifelong idealist, as he made clear to George Steiner in 1976:

Today I feel that if we do not bring about a new European renaissance – going far beyond the Renaissance of 400 years ago – we will lose the last remnants of that specific element of freedom which was created by the Greece of Socrates and Sophocles and which since the Renaissance has expanded and spread in wider and wider circles throughout the private lives of Europeans, and throughout the European places of learning and teaching and research, as well as throughout European economic and political activities. It is a kind of freedom which in my opinion does not exist to the same extent anywhere else in the world; the freedom of conscious and adamant non-conformists who enjoy to produce perpetually different views and perspectives but at the same time are not only tolerant of differences but welcome a never-ceasing growth in the variety of attitudes.[169]

Yet he understood much better than most European idealists the interdependence between individual freedom and economic freedom. Though he liked to cast himself as a man of the left (and, as we shall see, he was certainly much closer to the Labour Party than any other City figure of his day), he never ceased to champion market liberalization and to see European integration as part of a wider project of international economic integration – what we would now call globalization. In the words of an article he co-wrote in the wake of the European currency crisis of late 1968:

Izvestia and *Pravda* repeat the Communist doctrine that such crises are inherent in the capitalist system. This is a total fallacy . . . The recurrent economic crises, just as the recurrent wars we have suffered since the beginning of this century, are the inevitable symptoms of the titanic clash between modern industrialism and technology on the one side and the outdated 18th-century political system of the sovereign nation states on the other side . . . The extraordinary evolution of science and technology and the ever-growing yearning of the masses for more consumer goods and luxuries, require production facilities and sales organisations covering increasingly wider areas of the world . . . but we insist that the economy, which is no longer a national but a world economy . . . should be developed within the outdated political framework of the sovereign nation-state structure which divides the world into smaller and smaller compartments.[170]

The thrust of this article was that Europe must ultimately have not only a common market, but also a common currency and ultimately a federal government. To be sure, little that had happened in the 1960s or the 1970s encouraged Warburg to expect that these goals would be attained in his own lifetime.[171] In the meantime, however, the creation of an integrated European capital market would do. It was no mean achievement.

Today Eurobonds comprise around 90 per cent of international bond issues.[172] The Eurobond market is 'one of the world's biggest and freest sources of long-term public funds'.[173] The fact that around 70 per cent of all Eurobond issuance and secondary trading is in London is no accident of history,[174] but the result of a conscious effort by Siegmund Warburg and his associates in the 1960s.[175] Though doubtless partly motivated by a desire to enhance their companies' profit and loss accounts and to re-establish the City of London as an international financial centre, the architects of the Eurobond market understood very well that they were simultaneously advancing, by financial means, the process of European integration.

9

The Rhythm of Perfection

For me the greatest interest and enjoyment were human relations . . . It was the human side, in practice the negotiating side, which attracted me to banking.

Siegmund Warburg[1]

The basic conception of our firm has always been founded on the following principles: success from the financial and from the prestige point of view, important and self-understood as it is, is not enough; what matters even more is constructive achievement and adherence to high moral and aesthetic standards in the way in which we do our work.

Siegmund Warburg[2]

The reputation of a banking firm for integrity, generosity and thorough service is its most important asset, more important than any financial item. Moreover, the reputation of a firm is like a very delicate living organism which can easily be damaged and which has to be taken care of incessantly, being mainly a matter of human behaviour and human standards.

Siegmund Warburg[3]

I brought something to England which was a little bit different because I was a damn foreigner, a German Jew.

Siegmund Warburg[4]

I

To outsiders, there was always something intimidating about the ethos of S. G. Warburg & Co. 'I don't think he [Siegmund] regarded there [as] being any other life but business,' commented Michael Verey of the merchant bank Schroder Wagg.* 'Jokes were not cracked at Warburgs – not more than once anyhow.' In his eyes, Warburg was 'an upsetter of the existing Establishment. He wasn't a member of it and he didn't like it and was trying to get rid of it. At the start, the Establishment was dismissive and he was regarded as a squirt, an upstart. Very few people would have regarded him as a personal friend. People took off his foreign accent.'[5] In the breathless prose of Fleet Street, Warburg was the man of mystery 'behind nearly every big City deal' – the 'invisible banker'.[6] Other papers characterized him variously as 'shrewd and able', 'ruthless yet sympathetic', 'cunning yet honest' and even 'thrustful' (the *Sun*).[7] According to 'people who have never worked there, but know someone who has', wrote one hard-pressed journalist, Warburg habitually used 'a sledgehammer to crack a nut' and liked to 'work . . . people very hard'.[8]

First impressions can be deceptive. As a man, Siegmund Warburg was not especially striking to behold, though 'always immaculately dressed, usually in a dark-blue suit with well-polished black shoes . . . If he wore an overcoat, it was black, and he sometimes had a Homburg hat of the same colour pulled down at a rakish angle.'[9] He was not a tall man; indeed, one contemporary found him 'quite short . . . [with] something of a hunchback' or stoop, a tendency exaggerated by his tendency to wear the waist of his trousers high, in the inter-war style.[10] The Warburg look was said to be 'a perfect expression of studied drabness'.[11] His hairstyle never changed: always neatly parted on the left with never a hair out of place. There was something old-fashioned in his manner too:

He was meticulous in preparation and precise both in speech and in writing . . . He was rarely late for an appointment, unless he was trying to make a point of putting some less than wholly welcome visitor in his place, and he

* Formed when Helbert Wagg and J. Henry Schroder merged in 1962.

was seldom early[;] he believed that arriving more than a minute before a meeting was due to start gave the impression that you didn't have enough to do.

Yet this almost clockwork figure evidently contained a passionate soul. His 'eyes seemed to penetrate right through you', recalled one colleague;[12] another found them 'snake like', though an American journalist was struck more by their 'melancholy' character.[13] His voice might be 'diffident, doubting, soft-spoken [and] . . . melodious',[14] but tales of his ferocious temper were legion. The right eyebrow sent the storm warnings: it rose sceptically when an interlocutor lapsed into error. Fear was said to stalk the corridors of his bank. Directors at longer-established firms noted with disdain that their Warburg counterparts dared not arrive at work later than eight o'clock, while they – true gentlemanly capitalists – could saunter into the office at ten. There was also, so it was said, 'a lot of backbiting' at the firm, which 'wasn't everyone's cup of tea'.[15] Warburg executives thought nothing of telephoning after hours: 'They'll call you at home in the evening and tell you you must make a commitment for $3 million or $4 million immediately.' In the event of a power-cut, Warburg employees were expected to stay at their desks and work by candlelight.[16] Other bankers had their suits made with two pairs of trousers. At Warburgs, you ordered two jackets from your tailor, so that one could be permanently draped over the back of your chair at work, suggesting that you had just stepped out, rather than gone home. In the City's most incorrigibly snobbish enclaves, Warburg and his employees were known simply as 'those shits'.[17]

It would have come as a shock to these and other outside observers to learn that, far from there being a prohibition on jokes at Warburgs, they were positively encouraged. Charles Sharp was not only a capable manager of the Investment Department; he was also a gifted humorist who periodically wrote comic sketches, which were typed up, copied and circulated among the directors (though apparently never performed). In one of the earliest of these that has survived, for example, Sharp made fun of the penchant of the firm's senior partners for premature and ineffectual retirement:

SIR GEORGE NELSON [of English Electric]: Does Mr Warburg still take an active interest in the firm's affairs?

E[RIC] K[ORNER]: Well – in a way – for instance, now when he is on holiday he receives copies of all incoming and outgoing letters and also of those that should have gone out but which for one reason or another have not yet been written, but apart from the usual routine matters and urgent propositions we let him relax . . .

SIR GEORGE: And Mr Thalmann? He is no longer an executive director?

EK: Oh no. You see we must give the younger people their opportunity. Thalmann is in charge of our Canadian Investment Trust, you know Toronto and London, and of Triarch of course, and of LNT but he lets the boys do whatever they like so long as they ask him before and obtain his consent.[18]

Many a true word is written in jest, and Sharp's sketches offer all kinds of invaluable insights into the distinctive culture of S. G. Warburg & Co. In the same sketch, for example, Sharp satirized the Investment Department's preference for 'clients whose securities are worth at least £50,000, who have a large credit balance and a large turnover without giving any work to our dealers . . . who do not bother us with their dividends, who never call at our office, who never phone and never write, who give us full discretion but do not depend on our advice'.[19] A running joke in the sketches was the desire of the senior directors somehow to get rid of the bank's too-numerous investment accounts.

In one especially fine piece of whimsy, an imagined archaeological report on the site of the bank's offices written in the year AD 5000, Sharp made fun of Siegmund Warburg's preference for written communication by imagining him inviting Henry Grunfeld to lunch by means of a dictated letter (copied to all the Warburg directors), despite the fact that they were sitting right next to each other. ('This note was carefully typed before being retyped, initialled and delivered and after HG had read it he did not simply say "yes" but called his secretary etc. etc.')[20] Sharp also regularly mocked the culture of overwork at Warburgs:

Attempts have been made to deduce from the discovered documents what kind of private lives those led who were responsible for the management of the Warburg affairs. Unfortunately this was not possible because those people had no private existence. Their life was a continual sequence of business meetings interrupted by meals which, however, were also business meetings. The only leisure time they occasionally got were flights in a Boeing plane from

London to New York. This leisure time was used to catch up with the reading of internal notes and external correspondence . . .

Mr Warburg himself . . . spent every day at least 8 hours in meetings, 4 hours with visitors, 3 hours at 3 different lunches, 3 hours in entertaining colleagues and business friends over dinner, 2 hours dictating letters, 1 hour reading letters, 4 hours in one aeroplane or another, altogether 25 hours on a conservative basis, to which have to be added 6 hours spent every Monday at the directors' dinner in the Connaught Hotel.[21]

At investment meetings, Sharp joked, 'everybody present was encouraged to give free rein to his views and the debates were conducted on democratic lines like the debates in the British Parliament with the difference, however, that all those present belonged to the Opposition.' So frequently did the initials 'HG' appear on company documents, he noted, that they were taken not to refer to a physical individual (Henry Grunfeld) but to 'some abstract entity, say for "Highest Guidance" or "Heavy Gun"': 'Never before or afterwards has the English language attained such a state of perfection. Many letters were discovered apologizing for accountancy mistakes, overlooking of dates or referring to errors in calculations, wrong decimal points etc. but the punctuation and spelling of the statements referred to was always impeccable.'[22] Few quirks of life at Warburgs – from malfunctioning computer systems to incompetent telephone receptionists – escaped the Sharp treatment.

Nor were other firms spared, though Sharp characteristically depicted rivals as allies and allies as rivals. 'We find . . . that whenever GWh [Gert Whitman] . . . turned up in, say, one of the Scandinavian capitals, there was always at once . . . at least one Hambro also there so that the conclusion cannot be avoided that there existed between these two houses such mutual sympathy and identity of views that whenever either of them wanted to do something the other wanted to do exactly the same thing at exactly the same time and vice versa.' By contrast, S. G. Warburg's 'bitterest foe was a New York firm called Kuhn, Loeb & Co.' whose partners made 'a tremendous effort . . . to persuade all prospective customers of the Warburg firm that nothing on earth would ever be so unpopular as a sterling or dollar bond sponsored by a London issuing house'.[23] Sharp especially enjoyed lampooning a small Swiss bank (Banque de Gestion Financière) that Warburgs acquired in the late 1960s:

Act I

STÜMPFLI [of Schäfli & Stümpfli in Zurich]: I wonder whether our firm would not lose its Swiss cachet and change in character if somebody like Sir Siegmund Warburg became a partner. Is he not a very dominating personality?

SCHÄFLI: (laughing) Not in the least. You would be astonished. Whenever he says something, he quickly adds: 'Subject, of course to my colleagues' consent' or 'I may be entirely wrong' or 'I know so little about it' – we shall have to give him a little bit more self-confidence . . .

Act III
One Year Later

The firm is now called Schweizerische Gesellschaft Warburg & Co. AG or, in the abbreviated form, S. G. Warburg & Co. AG . . . In order to emphasise the international character of the firm, all employees at the specific wish of Mr Schäfli, the Chairman, now speak only English in the office . . . Mr Stümpfli has left the firm and sought admission to a nursing home. Though all employees of age group over 50 have been sacked, there are now 60 people employed instead of 6. The firm occupies the whole building instead of one floor only and is on the look-out for a larger building.[24]

In other scenes, Eric Korner summoned the Austrian Cabinet to the Imperial Hotel to discuss the Vienna loan he had decided to float;[25] the French declined to participate in a Chrysler loan unless 'Chrysler corporation were a French company . . . the denomination of the bonds were in French francs [and] . . . the proceeds of the loan were earmarked for the payment of French exports exclusively';[26] Warburg inveighed against financial league tables ('Look up in the Thesaurus and write down all the synonyms for "stupid" and "lunatic"');[27] and the new *Who's Who* had to be published in two volumes to accommodate all of Eric Roll's multitudinous directorships.[28] Even the Eurobond market was mocked. In a report supposedly written by a visiting Midwestern banker, Sharp outlined with memorable irony the system for placing new bonds in Europe:

The lending body is headed by a leading sponsor who does not lend as much as a penny himself. In this he is supported by a small élite of co-managers. Next in the hierarchy is the list of underwriters who guarantee the success of the issue provided the guarantee becomes valid only after the issue has proved to be a success. Next in the rank comes the so-called selling-group who undertake to procure subscriptions by genuine investors. Amounts allotted to them are sold by them at the first possible moment. The last order by degree are the ultimate buyers who are to a large extent a secret society of numbered accounts and Liechtenstein nationals.[29]

But perhaps Sharp's best running joke was the chronic pessimism of Warburg and Grunfeld: 'It is always wrong to look at the bright side of the picture. One always risks being tempted into complacency – not you, of course – but some of our colleagues, if they see that for the last 25 years our non-recurring profits have each year recurred on an ever growing scale, may end up considering this as a normal state of affairs.'[30] Seldom can a financial institution have been so skilfully caricatured. When Warburg assured potential employees that they would have more 'fun' than at other banks, he was not deceiving them. Theatrical behaviour and wisecracks were almost routine. One day Warburg stepped into the office Sharp shared with Peter Stormonth Darling and said simply 'Good morning,' then slowly left. 'That's all very well, Mr Darling,' exclaimed Sharp, 'but when Mr Warburg says Good Morning what does he really mean?' As Ian Fraser observed, Warburg 'believed strongly that the firm could not prosper unless people working in it had "fun", a word he was fond of. As a result, the "sporting element" in the pursuit of a particular business transaction was always recognized and encouraged.'[31] David Scholey agreed. His friends thought him a masochist when he told them that working at Warburgs was 'fun'. But it was 'the internal sense of humor, the sense of the ridiculous, that never went outside the walls'.[32] The diary of Bernard Kelly, one of the leaders of the self-styled 'young Turks' on the Warburg board, abounds with jokes, often involving imitations of the older directors' German accents. At a festive occasion like Warburg's seventieth-birthday dinner, a play by Sharp was actually read aloud, amid much hilarity.[33] As another young director, Geoffrey Elliott, recalled: 'It was not work, more a life experience, a daily rerun of "The Persecution and Assassination of Jean Paul Marat as Performed by the Inmates of the Asylum at Charenton" mixed with [the wartime radio comedy show] ITMA [*It's That Man Again*].'[34]

II

The fun stopped, however, if it threatened to compromise S. G. Warburg's reputation as 'a first-class private banking business' or *haute banque* institution. As we have seen, such a bank had five defining characteristics: moral standing, efficiency, connections, capital and high-quality personnel.[35] Warburg was disparaging of other financiers who failed to live up to these exalted standards. One American (at First Boston Corporation) did 'not deserve to be called a banker but only a gambler'.[36] Warburg had no interest in what he regarded as mere Stock Exchange speculation. His damning verdict on Wall Street in the late 1940s was that it was 'a market of gamblers and not investors'.[37] In the eyes of at least one director of the bank, Warburg was 'a banking snob', who 'wanted Warburgs to be elitist, to be *haute banque*, to give well-thought-out objective financial advice to top-class companies and governments'.[38] The reality, however, was always in some degree at odds with this ideal.

The original *haute banque* of the nineteenth century had been a top tier of private banks, generally owned by dynasties over several generations. S. G. Warburg was never like that. As we have seen, it was only through its acquisition of the longer-established Seligman Brothers that Warburgs could claim a place on the exclusive Accepting Houses Committee.[39] Warburg himself still retained a controlling stake in the firm that bore his name through the family holding company Warburg Continuation. But with the creation of Mercury Securities in 1954, ownership of S. G. Warburg became public and quite widely distributed. Indeed, the bank became part of a remarkably diversified conglomerate. Such dilution was unthinkable at a classic family-owned partnership like Rothschilds.

The Warburg offices were also the very reverse of *haute banque*. The original offices at 82 and later 9–13 King William Street were modest to say the least. Expansion did not bring with it architectural distinction. In 1961 the firm moved to the 'hideous, plum-coloured box-shaped building' that was 30 Gresham Street, directly opposite the church of St Lawrence Jewry and the London Guildhall.* Those

* St Lawrence was martyred by being roasted on a gridiron – hence the shape of Sir Christopher Wren's weather vane atop the church spire. Junior employees liked half-

invited there saw none of the mahogany and gilt that adorned the premises of older establishments. As Peter Spira recalled, 'the offices were known for being spartan although they had good furniture and beautiful clocks . . . There were a large number of Chinese paintings [but] the significance of these was that there was not a single idle man in any picture.'[40] The corridors were white, with a conspicuous lack of 'ancestral portraits'.[41] Warburg himself occupied a modest and rather chilly office. The small room that lay between this and Henry Grunfeld's office, which had connecting doors on either side, was known revealingly as the 'nutcracker suite'.[42] When a new director complained about the size of his allotted office, Warburg insisted on swapping with him, in order to make the point: the firm was a monastic order, and all the monks' cells were equal, including the abbot's.[43] In practice most directors and senior executives shared offices, in compliance with the so-called rule of four, whereby 'in each important transaction four people must represent S. G. Warburg & Co. – one director and his deputy, and one chief executive and his deputy.'[44] This was designed not only to build team spirit but to ensure that no misunderstandings arose. It was the task of one of the juniors to memorize the negotiations (taking notes during meetings was frowned upon) and then to compose a memorandum for circulation. Often the whole team would listen in on crucial telephone calls. There was also an '"open-door" policy . . . i.e. in principle anyone could go into anyone else's room at any time'. Warburg had a strong aversion to the nineteenth-century style of 'counting house', with its 'combination of a corridor-labyrinth and prison cells'.[45]

In one respect, the outsiders had it right. What went on at S. G. Warburg was indeed primarily work. 'Bankers never get ill from overwork' was one of the founder's many maxims, 'but only either from bad organisation or bad business.'[46] Warburg drove himself hard and expected others to do the same. In Ian Fraser's words, working at S. G. Warburg meant being ready to 'give up evenings . . . [and] weekends . . . Above all it meant thinking about the problems of the bank morning, noon and night.'[47] When Peter Stormonth Darling divorced and

---

seriously to compare the experience of training at Warburgs with the saint's slow and painful incineration.

remarried, the wedding took place at lunchtime and he came into the office for meetings afterwards. Others worked even harder: Scholey and Spira were regarded as being '150% devoted to Warburgs'. After Michael Bentley narrowly escaped death in the 1975 Moorgate Tube crash, suffering two broken arms, four broken ribs and multiple broken fingers, one of his colleagues remarked: 'It had to be a Warburg director in the front coach, eager to get on.'[48] The Warburg work ethic manifested itself in a number of utilitarian practices that were, again, very far from *haute banque* traditions. The most famous was the practice of hosting two client lunches a day in the bank's offices, the first from 12.30 to 1.30 p.m., the second from 1.30 to 2.30. The origins of this custom have been variously explained. Warburg himself told a journalist that it was Eric Korner who began it, because 'there were so many people he wanted to have lunch with in a week.' In reality, as we have seen, the custom had its origins in the bank's early days in King William Street, when Warburgs had shared a kitchen with Jessel Toynbee.[49] The habit of having two sittings simply stuck, partly because it made sense as the firm expanded relative to its dining facilities, partly because Korner and others genuinely liked to maximize the number of clients they could entertain.[50] These occasions were in marked contrast to the prandial style at older City firms, where alcohol was plentiful and talking shop all but prohibited. At Warburgs only beer, cider and water were provided.[51] 'You get surrounded by people, half of whom are not eating because they've got a lunch after that,' grumbled one guest. 'So they all apologize for stomach trouble. And the lunch is conducted by a waiter flinging things in front of you, all very politely, but you get the message that by 1 o'clock [*sic*] you're supposed to be out.'[52]

Similarly functional was Warburg's approach to meetings, especially when he was abroad. In New York he was in the habit of telling lesser clients and counterparties that 'a propos length of meetings . . . I can only deal in 30 minute units.'[53] In the course of a typical trip in the late 1950s, he had separate meetings with fifty-seven individuals in the space of just two weeks.[54] Like a living time-and-motion study, it was reported, Warburg allotted himself just 'ten minutes a day of index-glancing for the perusal of the leading newspapers from England, the Continent and America'. He had a red light installed outside his office 'to keep people out when he is occupied with other matters, but he rarely uses the red light. People wander in and out all the time. Warburg interrupts his dictation, talks to the caller, makes a couple of telephone calls, turns back to his secretary, and continues to dictate his letters in the middle of the sentence, exactly where he had stopped.'[55] Yet his desk was always miraculously clear.

There was method in Warburg's workaholism. From as early as 1940, he had applied his mind to the question of how best to manage the firm he and his partners had created. His first surviving memorandum on this subject makes it clear that he intended to be an innovator in this regard, in two respects in particular. Among the rules he envisaged were that there should be a 'daily morning meeting in connection with reading of mail which can be attended by members of [the] Board and H[enry] G[runfeld] and E[ric] K[orner]'. A committee would review the performance of companies in which the firm had a controlling interest on the second Wednesday of every month at 4 p.m. Another committee of the senior directors would consider personnel matters at the same time on the third Wednesday of every month. Where necessary, 'special memoranda' should be prepared for the daily meetings in connection with the firm's principal investments. There should also be 'a journal of commitments to be kept . . . on instructions of one of the members of [the] morning meeting' and a similar 'journal for new accounts'. The two key features of these early 'business rules' was their emphasis on the regularity of directors' meetings and, even more importantly, the sanctity of written records.[56]

By the late 1950s a routine had been established. The 'inner circle' of directors arrived before eight o'clock each morning – the crack of dawn in the City of those days – so that they could 'read all the incoming mail, all the outgoing mail and the office memoranda of the previous day'. Between 9.15 a.m. (except on Mondays, when the meeting began five minutes late) and 10.00 a.m., the entire management met to discuss the day's business (a ritual referred to by younger directors as 'morning prayers'). The meetings were brisk but relatively informal, with junior directors taking turns to act as chairman-cum-secretary. (Although the other founding directors – the Uncles – were at these meetings, Warburg himself attended with diminishing frequency. By contrast, the firm's quarterly board meetings, which Warburg himself usually chaired, were highly formal and almost perfunctory, lasting less than an hour.)[57] The day then unfolded in a succession of internal and client meetings, including the two sittings for lunch (except on Mondays, when directors had to attend Mercury Group management meetings).[58] The pace could be frenetic, with colleagues regularly coming into offices in the middle of telephone conversations or ongoing meetings 'either to speak to us right away about a specific subject or to ask us to contact them when we are free'. For directors, the day typically continued in this fashion until 6.30 p.m.

Yet work did not cease when Warburg men left the office. From the early 1960s there were occasional (and after 1965 weekly) directors' dinners – usually at the Connaught, though occasionally in the Iolanthe Room of the Savoy Hotel – which frequently lasted until after midnight.[59] The atmosphere on such occasions was a distinctive mixture of Weimar and Winchester, as the Uncles sought to indoctrinate their public school protégés with German-Jewish wisdom,* not least Warburg's favourite injunctions that they should cry over spilt milk, that they ought to cross bridges before they came to them and that they should always eschew 'wishful non-thinking'. At weekends, those being primed for promotion were expected to join Warburg for:

weekend walks round Belgravia and talks in his flat [95 Eaton Square], not so much about the theory of this or that type of business, but more about individual banks, other companies and, above all, people: here was this German bank preoccupied with some particular industrial shareholding, there some American industrialist, convinced that to survive he had to acquire manufacturing bases in Europe, here again some subsidiary of a British

---

* Ian Fraser captured the atmosphere well: 'At my very first such dinner, Siegmund apologised for the absence of Uncle Ernest Thalmann . . . whose brother had just died. In fact he had committed suicide by jumping out of a thirtieth-storey window on Fifth Avenue in New York. Uncle Eric [Korner], who liked gory details, said that he had crashed through the awning of a sidewalk cafe and "made a terrible mess of the pavement". He had jumped because he had "gone short" of 10,000 Unilever shares hoping that they would go down but in fact they had gone up very strongly. Uncle Henry [Grunfeld] said, "Ten thousand shares is nothing. We could easily have helped him out." Uncle Eric wagged his finger and said, "Yes, but it was not Limited, it was NV." The Uncles nodded appreciatively at this intelligence because the shares of the Dutch parent of Unilever were ten times more valuable than the shares of the English subsidiary. "Ah yes, N.V. Zet is kvite anozzer matter."'

company that would do much better if it became part of a certain American group and so on.[60]

Warburg also liked to take his protégés with him on foreign trips, so that they could be introduced to important overseas clients and further schooled in the *haute banque* arts. With the advent of regular and faster transatlantic flights, the old limits on mobility fell away and senior employees were expected to take full advantage of this. In 1966, for example, Ian Fraser made a total of fifty-eight overseas trips in pursuit of new business for the bank. (This reflected Warburg's firm opposition to long-term overseas postings, which might tempt a man to go native, which in turn would diminish the Warburg reputation abroad.) Nor did holidays offer respite. The telephone might ring at any time of the night or day – even on Christmas Day or New Year's morning – with an inquiry from the great man.[61]

Yet for all the regularity of formal and informal meetings, and despite the frequency of the telephone calls, the Warburg system was based above all on the written word. Everything was recorded. Every meeting generated a memorandum, which was then circulated. Each afternoon a daily summary was circulated of every important communication received or sent, including telephone calls and internal memoranda. When directors left the office at night, they were given 'a cyclostyled twelve-page summary of all the day's letters and memoranda, just in case we had missed something'. In addition, Warburg (and to a lesser extent Henry Grunfeld) had a penchant for dashing off short memoranda for circulation. When the amount of toing and froing in the office grew intolerable, Warburg's solution was predictable: 'Life in our office would be made much easier if any specific subjects regarding which a discussion is required were either mentioned in memoranda dealing with the specific subject, or if I and others concerned were simply to receive a note that a discussion on a certain matter is desirable.'[62] In the same way, Warburg was driven to complain as early as 1959 that the 9.15 morning meetings were themselves being undermined by inadequate preliminary circulation of documents:

At the time when the institution of the 9.15 Meeting was started its chief purpose was thought to be that it should serve as a forum for discussion of matters calling for action and requiring the considered views of those attending the 9.15 Meeting,

with the understanding that such discussions would be based on a concise pres-
entation of the relevant facts in the form of notes previously circulated.

This primary purpose has been lost sight of at a number of 9.15 Meetings
in recent months. For instance, matters have often been brought up . . . which
were not urgent at the time and which, prior to the 9.15 Meeting, had not
been sufficiently clarified between the two or three people mainly dealing with
the proposition in question. Furthermore, notes were not circulated to a sufficient degree prior to the 9.15 Meetings: on the other hand, the 9.15 Meetings
have been wrongly used on various occasions as a convenient means of report-
ing on certain subjects, whereas the right procedure would have been the
circulation of notes.[63]

This soon became Warburg's standard response to a management problem. Were clients dissatisfied with the Investment Department? Then 'we
will put these cases in the form of short notes . . . to Mr Sharp.'[64] Were
new trainees being introduced in a haphazard way? Then 'a short memorandum should be prepared prior to the young [men] starting with us.'[65]
In general, he complained in 1959, 'much too much is done by way of
personal talks and much too little by way of notes . . . Too many people
find it more convenient to talk themselves to clarity rather than to put
their thoughts in writing.'[66] He reverted to the same theme four years
later, urging that 'wherever possible we should use for purposes of
communication letters or telegrams rather than the telephone.'[67]

The danger was of course that the firm would end up drowning in
paper. Yet here too Warburg was vigilant. Written records were essential, but only the essential must be recorded. Convinced that people
wrote more economically than they spoke, Warburg abhorred needless
prolixity and padding in any document. In a typical aside, he excoriated a ninety-eight-page draft prospectus for a Dutch bond issue as a
'stupendous accumulation of mainly irrelevant information, a document through which, apart from a few lawyers, no one, not even a
professional investor, can find his way, a statistical piece of work done
without any inspiration or any effort to distinguish between essentials
and non-essentials and, above all, a conglomeration of reading material
made up for the purpose of absolving the issuing house in question
from any material or moral responsibility'.[68] In contrast, the annual
reports of Mercury Securities were a model of concision, seldom covering more than ten pages, starkly black and white, bound in pale blue,

and conspicuously lacking the photographs and bar charts favoured by more ostentatious competitors.

Such a system could not have functioned without exceptionally skilled and industrious secretaries: Warburg's original secretary in London, Dinah Meyer (who later became the wife of the Labour MP Manny Shinwell), and, after 1962, Doris Wasserman. They and two others were on hand, day and night, to take dictation, to ensure the accurate copying and circulation of documents, to receive and place his telephone calls, to manage his hectic travel schedule.[69] Warburg never learned to drive; that would have been to waste valuable dictation time. A car collected him and a secretary each morning at 9 and he dictated as they were driven, the flow of words continuing without interruption even as they left the car, entered the office and waited for the elevator. Charles Sharp once elegantly complimented Warburg on 'the natural ease with which you always find enough time to do all you are doing as though time were something of which there can never be a shortage'.[70] But this appearance of effortless industriousness owed much to the patient labours of those hard-pressed women. Their lot was not an easy one. Trapped for long periods with their boss – especially when they accompanied him abroad – they frequently had to bear the brunt of his intolerance and irascibility. Yet Warburg was also capable of showing his staff real consideration. The unpredictable swings from anger to affection bred undying loyalty.[71]

The defining characteristic of the Warburg style – as his secretaries knew better than anyone – was an obsessive perfectionism. Just as the Viennese satirist Karl Kraus once remarked (in the 1930s) that a misplaced apostrophe was worse to him than the bombing of Shanghai by the Japanese, so Siegmund Warburg could treat a grammatical error in a memorandum (or, worse, an outgoing letter or, worst of all, a letter to the Bank of England) as comparable to the bankruptcy of a major corporation. Peter Stormonth Darling recalled a characteristic telephone call from the mid-1960s:

WARBURG: I do hope I'm not disturbing you.

DARLING: Oh no, Mr Warburg, not at all.

WARBURG: Well, it's about your note dated 22 December on the American stock market. Do you have a copy in front of you?

DARLING: Er, no, I'm afraid my copy is in the office.

WARBURG: Well, let me remind you of your second sentence in the fifth paragraph . . . I think there should be a comma after the word 'development'. . .[72]

This was on Christmas Day. A misprint in an article about the bank in a German newspaper; an excessive font size in an advertisement; a surfeit of jargon in a contract of employment; a stylistic inconsistency in the internal telephone directory; an excessive use of acronyms – such were the motes of error that appeared as beams to Siegmund Warburg. He was literally incapable of letting such errors pass, in the conviction that his vigilance alone stood between the firm and anarchy. As Charles Sharp observed, what Warburg cared about was:

Form (with a capital F) in all its aspects: in one's attitudes towards other people, in business manners, in the way one dresses, in one's behaviour at meetings, in writing letters where not only spelling, grammar, syntax and style were of vital importance, but also the correct addressing, the dating, the setting out of the individual paragraphs . . . the avoidance of errors and mistakes. In this respect Sir Siegmund was uncompromising to the point of losing self-control.[73]

To Warburg this was no mere pedantry. It was a way of enforcing excellence.

It is an interesting question where the Warburg business style came from. Many outsiders assumed that it represented a foreign importation from Germany. Yet it is clear from Warburg's papers that this was not the case. On the contrary, many of the management practices introduced at S. G. Warburg were the very opposite of those that had so infuriated him at M. M. Warburg in the 1920s and 1930s. Another negative influence was Kuhn Loeb in New York, which Warburg had spent so many years vainly trying to reform. Rather than arriving in London with an established German blueprint for managing a merchant bank, Warburg seems to have devised his own system in an attempt to learn from the mistakes of his relations. He frequently alluded to these, on one occasion reprimanding Gert Whitman for reverting to 'the old KL & Co habits of working through a great number of bilateral channels within the office'.[74] This was a managerial revolution based on familial trial and error.

*

The tension at the heart of Warburg's style of management was between his insistence on regular meetings and written records and his fear of bureaucracy as the enemy of individual initiative. '[The] big growth of administrative organisation throughout the world', he had written as early as 1942, 'has had the result of endangering individual initiative and individual sense of responsibility to a very dangerous extent. Large scale administrative organisation, whilst preventing mistakes and evasion of laws and rules, fails often to create the necessary conditions for creative work, quick decisions and courageous actions.'[75] From the mid-1950s onwards he fretted that the firm was growing unmanageably large. 'Personnel was increasing too much,' he told George Bolton in February 1955, 'and quality of work on the top level was bound to suffer from too big a quantity in regard to the general scope of our activities.'[76] Two years later he was arguing for a regular circulation of employees from department to department, on the grounds that:

our organisation is becoming bureaucratic and that we are losing some of the important qualities which should be the mark of a private banking house. We are becoming too departmentalized and many matters move slowly and cumbersomely from department to department. Too many members of our staff are only trained in one particular job and lack knowledge of any other part of the firm's business.[77]

For the next two decades, he seldom stopped harping on the theme that 'the personal character of a banking house is bound to suffer from inflation of personnel and of turnover'.[78] It should be borne in mind that in the early 1960s, four years after this memorandum was written, the bank still employed only 150 people.[79] His preoccupation with the diseconomies of scale helps explain why, despite its success, the bank grew only slowly over the next twenty years. In 1982, the year of Warburg's death, Mercury Securities still employed just 1,300 people.

A classic expression of Warburg's management philosophy was his lengthy 1964 memorandum lamenting that 'we can unfortunately no longer dispense with some rudiments of bureaucracy' and reminding his fellow directors not to lose sight of the firm's reputation for 'intensive . . . high quality personal service'. Warburg also thought he detected 'conceit' creeping into the office culture at 30 Gresham Street. Letters were no longer being answered punctually on the day of receipt. Clients were being kept waiting. Mistakes were being covered up. Foreign trips were being taken without sufficient preparation. Above all:

Many of my younger colleagues seem to forget that most of the substantial transactions which have been done by us are the result of the cultivation of contacts over very many years. It is of course important that the technical details of a transaction are dealt with in the most thorough and painstaking manner possible, but this should not make us forget that, however great the application to technical detail, this would be fruitless without human contact with the client in question. This aspect is nowadays often overlooked by some of my colleagues and it thus happens all too frequently that once a specific transaction has been concluded the client in question is immediately forgotten. I know of many cases when it would have been even more necessary to develop contact with the client after a transaction than before. In our kind of business the continuity of valuable connections overrides in importance the conclusion of any specific transactions.[80]

Here was as clear a statement as could be imagined of the difference between relationship banking and transactions banking. As Warburg saw it, the age of transactions lay in the past, when banking had consisted of 'channelling big sums of money from certain quarters which had a surplus to certain other quarters where there was a scarcity of funds. Today it is much more a matter of changing and adjusting management and capital structures of industrial and financial businesses to alterations in our environments than a question of trading in money and of moving funds.'[81]

Yet for all his obsession with administrative form, and for all his commitment to an open-door ethos within the firm's management, S. G. Warburg & Co. remained in the last resort a Renaissance principality, in which Siegmund was the Prince, retaining all the prerogatives of an absolute monarch. 'You know,' Kenneth Keith of Hill Samuel warned Eric Roll, 'you'll find that Siegmund's democracies are of a very special kind. Anything really important, he decides.'[82] This autocratic tendency manifested itself most clearly in his famous temper tantrums, eruptions that could sometimes be of 'truly volcanic proportions'. Opinions differ as to how far these were uncontrolled explosions or carefully crafted performances; it is probable that Warburg was capable of both. They were more often triggered by trivial lapses than by major blunders: an untidy desk in the firm's New York office unleashed a tirade of high-decibel, bilingual abuse at the female employee responsible which concluded: 'We are a banking house, not a butchers shop!' ('After what seemed an age,' Peter Stormonth Darling recalled, 'the office manager, still seated at her desk, pulled out a Salem filter-tipped cigarette, tapped it, lit it casually, blew out a long trail of blue smoke, looked him in the eye and said: "Gee, Mr Warburg, you gotta be insecure"' – insouciantly laying low the high financier.) Nor did Warburg confine himself to shouting when his in-securities boiled over into rage. Some of the objects of his wrath found themselves having to duck flying telephones or telephone directories, though these were seldom well aimed. There were nearly always witnesses to these rages, but only sometimes – after the victim had left the room – were others present asked conspiratorially: 'How did I do?'[83] This same trick could be performed in front of relatives as well as colleagues, nota-bly when a shop assistant in a shirt shop made the fatal mistake of smirking. 'How dare you smile when you tell me that you do not have the kind of shirt I want. This is not something about which a representa-tive of this shop should smile!' George cowered in embarrassment as his father thundered; Eva tried vainly to restrain her incandescent husband. Finally, Warburg stormed out, his wife and son following mortified in his wake. After the door had closed, he said slyly: 'Well, I think that made him think, don't you?'[84] Even Warburg directors could be the objects of his wrath. Geoffrey Seligman was perhaps the most frequent target, but none of the Uncles, including Henry Grunfeld, was exempt.[85]

It is worth adding that Warburg did not lose his temper exclusively with subordinates. After an hour of listening to the circumlocutions of the Czech-born financier Charles Petschek in 1947, during which he had 'repeated 56 times a platitude on the Marshall Plan as he saw it and 52 times a platitude on the British foreign exchange restrictions as he saw them', Warburg 'exploded and said that I really felt that we could not carry on sound business conversations in such a way, that it was no good talking around subjects and that, whilst he might afford to do that, I was not able to do so'.[86] By his own testimony, Warburg quite frequently confronted troublesome clients or business partners in this way: as he once put it, 'even wise elder statesmen respond to the roughest treatment.'[87] 'It seems impossible to stop the onrush of afterthoughts – especially on the part of the lawyers,' he reflected on another occasion, 'except by losing my temper in drastic outbursts.'[88] To say that he did not suffer fools gladly would be quite wrong, since many of those upon whom he heaped his opprobrium were very far from being foolish. Sir Eric Vansittart Bowater was the chairman of one of the biggest paper manufacturers in England, a formidable figure whom Warburg might have been expected to woo as a potential client. Yet when they met on a transatlantic crossing in 1954 Warburg was scarcely able to conceal his contempt. He was 'extremely charming to me', he told his wife, 'but his charm was like the blamange-top [*sic*] of a synthetic cake, mixed of second class sweets and spices. Amongst my many pompous City acquaintances I have rarely seen anybody even approaching this Bowater-animal in pompousness.'[89]

The obverse of this sometimes destructive behaviour was a paternalistic concern with the welfare of all the bank's employees, including its secretarial and menial staff. He worried about the health of one woman, who was a Christian Scientist and resistant to the modern medical treatment that she clearly needed.[90] He counselled another sick employee to rest and not to worry about work ('somewhat against my own convictions').[91] In 1960 he urged Geoffrey Seligman to beware of 'sheer over-conscientiousness' for the sake of his health.[92] He issued edicts in 1961 and 1964 not to overwork – or under-appreciate – secretaries.[93] He was especially incensed to hear reports of 'bullying' and 'intolerance' towards 'members of the organisation who might be slow or clumsy', calling for this to be 'eradicated lock, stock and barrel'.[94] It pained him when apparently promising recruits did not prosper at Warburgs, and he worried in at least two cases that his fellow directors had not shown 'benevolence and tolerance to the extent especially required towards younger men, shy by nature and not much inclined to use their elbows'.[95] As Doris Wasserman remembered, in the evening Warburg 'very often used to wander around [the office] . . . He'd go around and he'd sit and talk to people about what's going on today, how they're getting on, and he'd also very often during the day ring for the youngsters to come up.'[96]

No bank had ever been run this way before. As Ian Fraser recalled, the result was a distinctive combination of the authoritarian and the democratic, of the rigid and the flexible:

There was a formal hierarchy of Board members, executive and otherwise, general managers, etc., but this was supplemented and sometimes even supplanted by a sort of natural hierarchy of knowledge and experience in specific areas. Great stress was laid on two features: internal communication and the bringing up of the younger members of the firm . . . The spirit was a very special blend of democracy and speed of decision based on authority! 'Chains of command' were anathema as leading to blurring of responsibility rather than making it more precise, as well as to a loss of rhythm – a favourite word in the firm. Self-reliance was encouraged, but only in the sense that everyone was supposed to develop his own perception of when to consult and whom, thus leading to an almost natural hierarchy of importance of different decisions and to appropriate methods of reaching them. An especially heavy emphasis was placed on accuracy of a most meticulous kind to the point sometimes wrongly characterized as pedantry. Big errors of judgement – if they were recognized by those responsible – were more readily forgiven than small mistakes due to carelessness.[97]

III

More than one senior Warburg employee likened Siegmund Warburg to a teacher. According to Peter Stormonth Darling: 'He would have made a superb professional teacher . . . He taught us . . . a set of rules for the conduct of business, which could be copied with advantage by almost any business today.'[98] Ian Fraser too recalled that Warburg 'would have dearly liked to be . . . a teacher', albeit one whose introductory lessons were notably 'short but tough'.[99] The analogy may have said as much about the second generation of Warburg directors as about their boss himself. For, with few exceptions, the likes of Fraser and Darling were products of an educational system that tended to leave an indelible mark. The English public schools were from early on the breeding grounds for Warburg directors and they brought to banking at least some of the ethos of the old-boy network, an ethos fortified more than diluted by wartime experience. Fraser had been educated at Ampleforth and Magdalen, Oxford, and served with distinction in the Scots Guards (receiving the Military Cross for his part in an attack on a German position in Italy). Bernard Kelly studied at Downside School, was sent down from Magdalen, Oxford, after a term, served in the Royal Irish Hussars and married a Fitzalan Howard. Darling had attended Winchester and New College, Oxford. Though his family were originally Bavarian Jews, Ronald Grierson was another public school product who had been a member of the elite Special Air Service during the war. A somewhat later recruit, John Nott, had fought with the 2nd Gurkha Rifles in Malaya before going up to Trinity, Cambridge, where he became president of the Union.*[100] Martin Gordon was offered not only a job but also an above-average starting salary when he revealed that he was reading Greats at Oxford – classical languages, literature and philosophy.[101] Rugby blues were not in contention.[102]

Not everyone who won Warburg's confidence was in this mould, to be sure. Warburg remained ambivalent about English elite education, and on occasion blamed Grierson's 'beastly public school education' for his (allegedly) 'unaggressive and unpugnacious spirit' (a criticism that must surely have been ironic, in view of Grierson's famously pugnacious personality).[103] Though an Old Etonian (one of only two among all the executive directors), Peter Spira was a doctor's son from a middle-class Jewish background, and was already a qualified accountant when he joined the firm.† The crucial litmus test was not in fact class but literary taste. Warburg invariably asked potential recruits what they were reading. If the answer was Balzac, Dickens, Eliot, Tolstoy or Trollope, the candidate was almost certain to be employed, since a fondness for nineteenth-century European literature was a sure sign in Warburg's eyes that the precious *feu sacré* burned within. Best of all was to be a devotee of Thomas Mann, as both Ian Fraser and Joshua Sherman were. As Warburg explained in 1980, 'those with whom I am close in my firm are people with whom I can also talk about books, about music, about human beings, human problems . . . If a fellow would come to me and say his only interest is athletics, I wouldn't think he would stand a chance.'[104] He was also

---

* Before graduating, he wrote Warburg an impudent letter to the effect that 'you are the most distinguished banker of your generation and I am the most distinguished Cambridge undergraduate of my generation' and that therefore they should meet. Warburg was intrigued, saw Nott and hired him.

† Spira was recommended to Warburg by Garrett Moore, the Earl of Drogheda, managing director and later chairman of the *Financial Times*, to whose mother Spira's father had ministered during her final illness.

highly resistant to graduates of business schools and qualified econ-omists.* 'It is much better', he advised the father of one prospective recruit, 'for him to read good novels and interesting books on history rather than works on banking or economics in general. The young men who, I think, have the best future in banking are, as a rule, those who during their educational period have been good classical scholars.'[105] Signs of 'diffidence' in a Warburg interview were fatal, as was accept-ing a proffered cigarette.[106] 'You know, with people, it's like ties,' Henry Grunfeld once remarked. 'You don't buy a tie that you need one, you buy a tie that you like it [sic].'

In addition to impressing Warburg himself, however, any potential recruit in the 1950s and 1960s had to run the gamut of the Uncles. Ian Fraser's experience in 1953 was perhaps representative. Having revealed, over coffee with Warburg, a convincing familiarity with the German banking elite (based on his time in post-war Germany as a journalist working for Reuters), Fraser was handed on to Grunfeld:

He quickly established that I knew nothing of company law or of accountancy and very little about capital markets . . . 'Do you collect?' he shot at me. 'I'm sorry, I don't quite understand,' said I. 'Do you have a collection – silver, books or anything?' I said I had no money for collecting. I was then passed on to Hermann Robinow.

. . . 'Do you collect?' he asked. I was ready for it this time. 'No, unfortu-nately, I have no money. Not yet.' 'Aha, you will collect, I am sure. I collect silver, Grunfeld collects English furniture, Warburg collects fine bindings and Korner collects historical manuscripts.' I had not yet heard of Korner. 'Korner comes from Vienna; he originally had an umlaut on the o, but he changed his name like Sharp and Grierson,' Robinow said. I was beginning to get the flavour of Warburgs. Robinow then said that he was instructed to introduce me to another director, Hamburger. 'He is rather different from the rest of us; we are all Germans, he is a Russian.'

Sam Hamburger was rather less than five feet tall and very nearly as much round. He spoke English with a pure cockney accent.†

---

* Throughout his career, Warburg reserved a special contempt for graduates of Harvard Business School who, he asserted, 'combine[d] conceit and superficial sophistication with an excessive respect for organisation charts and all that this implies'.
† Hamburger had joined Warburgs from Kleinworts in 1957.

It was characteristic of the atmosphere in those days that both Warburg and Charles Sharp's wife suspected Fraser of having Jewish blood. So fluent was his German that they assumed his mother's maiden name, Grimston, must be an Anglicization of Grünstein.[107] He was in fact the grandson of Simon Fraser, thirteenth Lord Lovat, and of James Walter Grimston, third Earl of Verulam – a pedigree that manifested itself in the snobbish tone of much that he later wrote about his time at Warburgs.

The recruitment process at Warburgs was perhaps a little less idiosyncratic than Fraser's account suggests. He had proved himself not only in battle but also as a linguist. Grierson had done more than fight during his time in the SAS; he had also been seconded to the United Nations in Geneva as personal assistant to the Executive Secretary of the Economic Commission for Europe. Literary leanings were a desirable prerequisite, but not essential. Peter Stormonth Darling confessed to having none, but was employed nonetheless. Raymond Bonham Carter could scarcely have been better connected socially, as the grandson of the Liberal Prime Minister Herbert Asquith and son of Warburg's friend Violet Bonham Carter, but it was his experience as an adviser to the Bank of England that really recommended him.[108] Likewise, John Craven was already a qualified accountant as well as a Cambridge law graduate when he joined Warburgs in 1967. In practice, Warburg and his colleagues needed numeracy as well as literacy and most of those who prospered at the bank arrived with, or soon acquired, some accountancy training. ('It's all dead easy,' Frank Smith assured Fraser. 'Just read *Pitman's Accounting*, and ask me what you don't understand . . . Read the 1948 Companies Act but only the passages that I have marked . . . and read the *Financial Times* every day without fail from cover to cover.')[109] Finally, all recruits had to pass a graphological test before they could be employed, which was supposed to act as a check on subjective or superficial judgements (see Appendix). The real test, however, came in the first year. As one Warburgs veteran put it:

They give you a good period of knocking you about, finding out who you are, finding out how much tension you'll take . . . Will you work until four in the morning? Will you find the outrages inflicted by a director too much for your liking? Will you pop off at him? . . . The Anglo-German toughness is bred into you. You're constantly being vaguely insulted by the people around you, constantly having to defend yourself . . . Your qualifications as a banker, your education and your intellect are always under scrutiny.[110]

Nor was Warburg solely concerned to recruit youth, gilded or otherwise, to the firm. Experience was also at a premium, and particularly government experience. From 1960 onwards he made a concerted effort to recruit non-executive directors who had distinguished themselves either as ministers or as senior civil servants, with the obvious intention of improving access to the corridors of power at a time when the government's role in the realm of industrial policy was growing. Indeed, by the early 1970s Bernard Kelly was participating regularly in unofficial 'seven-a-side . . . City–Treasury dinners', the aim of which (on both sides) was 'getting to know each other and no doubt becoming known if either side has to find candidates for interesting jobs'. Contrary to the widely held belief that there was a close, even symbiotic relationship between the City and the Treasury, these meetings tended to expose a considerable gulf in terms of intellectual assumptions and material aspirations, which was not easily bridged. The strategy of outreach to Whitehall nevertheless paid some modest dividends.[111] An early prize in 1960, as we have seen, was the Eton- and Magdalen-educated Lord Gladwyn.* Unfortunately, despite their coincidence of views on European integration, relations between Warburg and Gladwyn did not develop well.[112] Also welcomed into the Warburg fold in 1966 was the dashing Earl Jellicoe,† who found himself without political

---

* Gladwyn Jebb had distinguished himself during the war as chief executive of the Special Operations Executive (SOE), and then head of the economic and reconstruction department of the Foreign Office. Appointed acting secretary-general of the United Nations in 1946, he was assistant (later deputy) under-secretary of state at the Foreign Office during the first post-war Labour government and served as British representative at the United Nations in New York between 1950 and 1953, before his appointment to the Paris embassy. 'Whatever you may say about Gladwyn,' Ernest Bevin was said to have remarked, 'he ain't never dull.'

† Son of the First World War victor at Jutland, a Wykehamist, a Trinity graduate and a war hero in the Special Boat Service, George Jellicoe's brilliant post-war diplomatic career had been cut short by an extramarital affair. His hereditary peerage allowed him to enter politics and by 1961 he was acting as government whip in Harold Macmillan's government. He held a succession of ministerial posts in subsequent years, notably first lord of the Admiralty between 1963 and 1964. His political career collapsed when, while serving as the leader of the House of Lords under Edward Heath, he was revealed to be having another affair, this time with a call girl. On hearing this news, Warburg

employment during the Wilson years.[113] In 1973 the bank hired Sir Denis Greenhill immediately after his retirement as head of the diplomatic service, the senior civil servant at the Foreign and Commonwealth Office.[114] A more successful appointment was that of Eric Roll, who had held a succession of mainly economic posts, ranging from the Ministry of Food to the British delegation to NATO, before being appointed permanent secretary at the new Department of Economic Affairs in 1966.[115] Perhaps it was Roll's Central European origins (he had been born Erich Roll near Czernowitz in the Habsburg province of Bukovina) that helped him to fit in at Warburgs more successfully than Gladwyn; perhaps it was his seven languages and 'ability to lip-read in both French and German'; perhaps it was his unrivalled network of international diplomatic contacts.[116] A fourth possibility is that Roll owed his ascent at Warburgs – which in 1974 took him to the chairmanship – to his unswerving subservience to Siegmund Warburg, a trait that earned him the soubriquet 'Sir Echo' from the firm's younger but more financially experienced directors.[117] David Scholey even saw him as Sancho Panza to Warburg's Don Quixote.[118] For Scholey's generation, it went against the grain that a bank that had once hired talented youngsters was now offering comfortable berths to fully fledged members of the Establishment. As far as Bernard Kelly was concerned, Roll was 'a mealy mouthed sycophant to Siegmund Warburg', despised not only for his sycophancy but also for his 'hardly ever originating a fee paying transaction'.[119]

IV

Warburg has often been portrayed as publicity-shy.[120] It would be more accurate to say that he was selective in his dealings with the press. Certainly, he had no great fondness for newspapers. 'The Press', he complained in 1951, 'puts almost everywhere quantity above quality and makes people inclined to swallow mental food which has been chewed and digested by others instead of choosing and absorbing their

---

– who was in New York – telephoned Jellicoe and told him: 'I am extremely sorry to hear of your predicament but I do not want you to go to bed tonight without knowing that there will always be a job for you at Warburgs if you so wish.'

spiritual nourishment by more personal and independent effort. As Erasmus said in 1523, "If possible there should be a check on the printing press." . . . The excessive growth of the products of the printing press is part of our modern barbarism to which we have to resign ourselves.'[121] He had a particular aversion to the *New Yorker*'s 'diarrhoea of words and constipation of thought'.[122] However, Warburg's 'resignation' to such 'barbarism' did not preclude flattering newspaper editors.[123] Indeed, he hired Arthur Winspear from the *Financial Times*'s Lex column after his positive coverage of the British Aluminium takeover and offered Geoffrey Crowther, editor of the *Economist*, a seat on the board of Mercury Securities. He also sought to lure Lord Drogheda away from the *Financial Times*, as well as Fredy Fisher, the paper's editor after 1972.[124] Warburg was perfectly willing to talk to journalists, though for most of his career he drew a distinction between stories about S. G. Warburg and stories about the bank's clients; 'publicity about firms we finance' was generally welcome, but 'publicity for bankers and particularly Jewish bankers' Warburg was 'in principle against'.[125] In principle, but not always in practice. His subsequent reputation as the mysterious 'invisible banker' was in fact the product of subtle media handling. Far from shunning the press, Warburg watched it like a hawk and gave considerable thought to the question of public relations.[126] He was ready to threaten legal action if he felt he or his firm had been libelled.[127] He would assist reporters with articles only on condition that he could have sight of a draft before publication.[128] He was even prepared to consider advertising the firm's services in the press, though he decided against doing so.[129] As a result, by the 1960s press coverage of Warburgs was nearly always positive. This was hardly surprising, considering the important role Warburg came to play in the finances of the British press (see Chapter 10). By the mid-1960s the supposedly publicity-shy Warburg felt confident enough to publish opinion articles under his own name.[130] He co-operated with Joseph Wechsberg when the journalist wrote a profile for the once-hated *New Yorker* in 1966 and gave a succession of interviews, notably to the *Sunday Telegraph* (1970) and the magazine *Institutional Investor* (1980).[131]

Some way beneath journalists in Warburg's hierarchy of humanity were economists, against whom he had a 'considerable prejudice' all his life.[132] 'The only people who are certainly wrong', he told Bob Boothby in May 1958, 'are those dogmatic economist–statisticians who prove with a terrific array of figures that certain definite things will happen at a certain definite date.'[133] 'This zoological genus', he wrote of economists in 1967, 'represents an exceptionally damaging component of present-day humanity, because with few exceptions they combine, in an almost perverted way, intellectual arrogance with a lack of natural human instinct.'[134] He had, he told George Steiner, 'a greater respect for [Keynes's] talent in formulating his thoughts than for the thoughts themselves, which often seemed to me rather too dogmatic and frequently impractical'. Likewise, 'Hayek's theory that there has been in history on the one hand sometimes a totally free economy and sometimes a completely watertight state economy on the other hand [was] in contradiction to the facts.'[135] Although he expressed a fleeting interest in Thomas Balogh and Nicholas Kaldor, two Hungarian émigrés who became influential over Labour Party policy in the 1960s, it was their personalities not their publications, much less their policy prescriptions, which (briefly) held his attention. He admired John Kenneth Galbraith, but primarily because of the clarity of his prose style.[136] Another notable exception to this rule was, of course, Eric Roll, a former professor of economics at Hull University and author of a widely read *History of Economic Thought*. Roll's appeal to Warburg was as an experienced civil servant and diplomat, however, not as an economic thinker.

Perhaps the greatest puzzle about Warburg's mode of operation, however, was his seeming indifference not to economics as a discipline but to the basic profitability of his own firm. 'The bottom line' was not a term Warburg liked to use, though he was certainly not above analysing the firm's profit and loss accounts.* 'Obviously I like to make money for my firm and myself,' he once told Jakob Goldschmidt, 'but this is not a decisive point.' As a businessman, he confessed, he suffered from 'too much superstition [and] too little respect for money' – to say nothing of

---

* See for example his complaint in 1960 about 'the complete disproportion between our income from current business and our expenses, and . . . [the] evidence of how few people have really contributed to what has been, during the above period, the chief income of SGW & Co, namely, the item to which I have given in the attached analysis the name "Fees from special transactions"' – meaning fees from the firm's corporate advisory business.

'an excess of frankness and too great an inclination towards pedantry'.[137] What did Warburg mean when (as he often did) he drew a distinction between 'constructive work', which was his primary concern, and making money, which was secondary?[138] An old friend outside the financial world, Paul Ziegler, thought he knew. To Warburg, managing relationships was an art form and Warburg was 'one of the very few good creative artists' he had ever known.[139] Warburg was much less interested in the money that came with success than with the success itself. Wealth was, as he put it to George Steiner, a 'by-product of high-class work'.[140] As Charles Sharp observed, Warburg was a 'capitalist by fate', who 'despised money-making for its own sake'.[141] 'Siegmund wasn't really interested in making money,' recalled Robin Jessel. 'I don't think he ever was. He was interested in the firm making money, which is different.'[142]

Certainly, Warburg seems to have been largely indifferent to his own personal wealth, leaving the management of his investments entirely to Sharp or Bob Arnheim. 'My personal experience', Warburg once observed, 'has been that if one expects miraculous results from investment management this is the best way to do badly and in the long run the most favourable achievements are obtained on the basis of modest anticipations and by way of policies which rather err on the side of being solid and pedestrian than original.'[143] Sharp did the solid and pedestrian job that was asked of him and the result – thanks in no small measure to the effects of the soaring tax rates, inflation and exchange controls of the late 1960s and 1970s – was as modest as Warburg had anticipated (see Chapter 13).

Part of the explanation for this was Warburg's own risk aversion. Always hanging over him like a cloud was the memory of the Depression, and particularly the crisis that had all but swept M. M. Warburg away in 1931. As he was fond of telling junior directors like Ian Fraser:

None of our generation had been through the financial crisis and depression of 1929 to 1931; we should remember what his Onkel Max had said in Hamburg, 'When disaster strikes, it always strikes from the most unexpected quarter.' We should keep the bank as liquid as possible and resist the temptation to lend money to property developers . . . Each generation believed that new banking crashes had been made impossible by a better understanding of their causes, but each generation had to learn from the beginning again. Once a new line of business was invented, all the competing banks wished to have a share in it and the only result could be that profit margins for the banks went down or disappeared; this was bound to happen . . .[144]

Expansion might seem attractive, but 'too much capital is a dangerous thing as it leads into temptation'.[145] Aside from the not inexpensive standby facilities which Warburgs maintained with other City firms (which were never actually used), the most frequently cited manifestation of this risk aversion was Warburg's scepticism about investment management, that is, the investment of clients' savings on their behalf.[146] According to Peter Stormonth Darling, Warburg 'always thought of investment management as a second-class activity only slightly better than stockbroking'. In Darling's view, this was partly a matter of snobbery.[147] That is not quite fair. As we have seen, Warburg viewed any expansion of the bank's payroll and balance sheet as dangerous hubris. He was probably right that many of the bank's early investment clients were mere minnows, whose commissions to the bank barely covered the running costs of their accounts.[148] When the Investment Department began to take off as a concern in the late 1960s, Warburg was mildly encouraging and approved the idea of providing it with new and separate premises (St Albans House, just around the corner from Gresham Street).[149] In 1969 it became a distinct subsidiary as Warburg Investment Management (later Mercury Asset Management).[150]

If Warburg had qualms about the investment business, he was even more leery of commodities trading. This was, of course, the life blood of Brandeis Goldschmidt, the metal brokers. Yet when he came face to face with the ethos of metals traders like Harry Green and his son Michael, he was manifestly appalled:

When I asked [Michael Green] about his interests outside business he said he especially liked to read 'popular best-sellers' but he did not read anything else; when I asked him what was his ambition in business he said that he liked trading in large amounts in a similar way as he liked playing bridge: the chief thing was to play for high stakes, to share decisions as little as possible with anyone else and also to share rewards as little as possible with anyone else.[151]

The volatility of profits at Brandeis Goldschmidt was to become a recurrent source of concern in the 1970s. Warburg felt a similar unease when the Eurobond business became the object of what struck him as unwarranted euphoria:

Personally, I am not interested in the waves of despondency and enthusiasm. These are appropriate for people who look upon matters purely from a Stock Exchange point of view, i.e. in a *'Boersianer* spirit'. However, if we want to succeed, we must make up our mind to follow a policy of establishing new values and new procedures rather than to act mainly as traders and sellers of securities which we find relatively easy to dispose of. In other words, we must be aware that we are primarily bankers and only secondarily Stock Exchange traders.[152]

He was equally wary of any strategy, no matter how lucrative, that exposed the firm to liquidity risk. When he discovered that the bank's recently created Frankfurt offshoot had entered into non-matching commitments in excess of its own modest capital, he issued a stern warning: 'As SGW & Co. London . . . are abstaining from non-matching commitments as a matter of well-considered policy, SGW & Co. Frankfurt with their much smaller capital should at least stick to an upper limit which should be below their capital . . . I am not impressed by profits earned in a business which carried undue liquidity risks.'[153] As one former director put it: 'Warburgs is always glad to risk its brains, but not its money.'[154]

All this should not be taken to mean that the firm of S. G. Warburg as a whole was indifferent to making money. Although Siegmund Warburg was unquestionably the dominant force at the bank that bore his name, he never sought to establish a completely homogeneous style of doing business. Each of the other Uncles had his own approach. In the case of Eric Korner, this was quite radically different from Warburg's. Although rules against insider trading had not yet been formalized in the City of the 1950s and 1960s, there was an in-house prohibition on the exploitation of inside knowledge for private gain.[155] As Ian Fraser recalled:

If it was thought likely that a client company was doing well we were encouraged to buy or if badly to sell; but if we as financial advisers knew the figures it was about to report or the dividend that it was about to declare, Frank Smith would put a stop on all staff dealings . . . The same applied to imminent takeover bids of which we had special knowledge through our advisory position.

However, Korner frequently circumvented these rules by placing orders in his wife's name with a Swiss private banker who managed the money he had received from the West German Restitution Law (for victims of the Nazis' racial persecution). As Ian Fraser recalled:

Whenever we, as a firm, learned that a client company was about to report higher profits, put up its dividend or receive a take-over bid, Uncle Eric would be on the telephone to Kaufmann. 'Kaufmann, hier Koerner. Bitte kaufen Sie mir zwanzig tausend Lonrho Ordinary Shares bestens.' Then he would look up and, seeing me standing in the doorway and uncertain whether or not I had heard his order to buy 20,000 Lonrho shares at the best price, would continue in German to instruct Kaufmann to book them in the name of 'Mrs Korner', adding as an afterthought 'Mrs Korner Joint Account'. This last twist meant that his wife was legally the buyer but she could not get hold of the proceeds without his agreement. Ten minutes later an order would come through from Zurich . . . to buy 20,000 Lonrho Ordinary Shares 'at best'.[156]

Frank Smith, who for many years ran the Corporate Finance Department, regarded it as quite normal to encourage younger executives by helping them play the stock market. 'You've been working on the deal,' he said to Peter Spira at the time of a share issue for Polycell. 'Would you like two thousand shares at one and threepence [the placing price]?' Spira replied that he would, but didn't have £125:

[Smith] picked up the telephone and asked the dealer to sell two thousand of his shares and wrote me a cheque for the difference between one and threepence and the market price of one and tenpence halfpenny . . . It was typical of the man – a way of saying, 'You've got your first foot on the ladder and now you're going up.'[157]

Today such a gift from a senior to a junior executive would be viewed as improper. But all this took place at a time when the rules and regulations governing financial services were in large measure unwritten. Insider trading did not become a criminal offence in Britain until 1980. Until then, companies like Frank Smith's Hermes – which acted as an investment vehicle to enable Warburg executives to buy favoured stocks – were regarded as legitimate. As Michael Valentine recalled, Warburgs staff were instructed never 'knowingly [to] breach the Companies Acts, the Takeover Code, or the Stock Exchange Regulations'. But the really important 'unyielding principles' were home-grown: 'If in doubt, ask someone else . . . do not commit the firm, for example to an underwriting or a fee, without agreeing this first with higher authority; and never do anything that would bring Warburgs into disrepute.'[158]

V

It was a distinctive feature of the history of S. G. Warburg & Co. that its founders felt themselves to be old men while the firm itself was still relatively young. Born in the first decade of the century as most of them were, the Uncles had been in some measure aged by the experience of enforced emigration and the need to start their business lives a second time almost from scratch. Warburg was always on the lookout for signs that people around him were going 'gaga', the classic symptom of which was an 'incapacity to distinguish between essentials and non-essentials'.[159] He and Henry Grunfeld took it in turns to exhort one another to work less, beginning as early as the latter's fiftieth birthday in 1954. 'You should now at the milepost of the fifty years', wrote Warburg, 'resolve solemnly to reduce the speed and the tension of your working rhythm, to restrain your perfectionism, to take with determination the risk of serious mistakes being made even under your very eye, to limit your duties, however much this may be against your nature, in other words to begin working like a wise older statesman and living as a young artist of life.' As Warburg admitted, the admonition might equally well have been addressed to himself.[160] Less than five months later, he made the first of what would prove to be many proposals for his own semi-retirement:

SGW & Co. was developing from a personal firm into something of a more institutional organisation, that I felt no longer able to control its operations as in former times and that we had to be very careful to preserve a personal, perfectionist and non-bureaucratic approach as far as possible. I raised the question of whether the time had come when I might change over from the position of Chairman to the position of senior adviser (with or without some such title as President).[161]

This preoccupation with imminent retirement was linked to Warburg's passionate faith in the vigour of youth. He was much taken with a phrase of Keynes's: 'that exuberant inexperience which is essential to success'.[162] It was his conviction that the firm must constantly be rejuvenated by younger men with that quality. 'I want to arrive in the near future at the stage of giving up my executive responsibilities on both sides of the Atlantic and of becoming a sort of senior adviser,' he explained to Grierson in 1958, 'whilst my younger associates are to reach the top of responsibility in full measure and with good tempo!'[163] Already that year he was telling John Schiff that 'in London the organization is now such that I am completely free from executive duties.'[164] It was time, he told Thalmann, to pass his executive duties 'to the younger members'.[165] At the end of 1959, still aged only fifty-seven, he formally announced his decision to become a non-executive director, along with Korner and Thalmann, so as not to 'stand in the way of their younger colleagues' – though he retained his position as chairman of the board of Mercury Securities until 1964.[166] He hoped, he told Grunfeld, 'to give a great deal of time . . . to various interests of mine in the field of literature, psychology and graphology'.[167]

Certainly, Warburg's greatest strength as a business leader was his ability to inspire the younger men around him. He wanted them, he once wrote, to think of 'what I call the S G W & Co. management team as a kind of family or clan comprising various generations and a great variety of brains and temperaments' and hoped:

that those who belong to this family or clan will always feel that they form a community of real friends and see in the firm and in the continuous development of its management team a cause which should transcend any kind of jealousies or vanities or considerations of personal financial advantage.

If we try to preserve and cultivate a spirit of this sort, we should be able to hand on from generation to generation far beyond our lifetime a torch of high aims which we are to pursue with good cheer through constructive work to be achieved by the firm in service to our country and to the Free World.[168]

A 'good human atmosphere' was more important than 'any professional success'.[169] On the surface, no doubt, Warburg practised what he preached about rejuvenation. Of the firm's ten executive directors in 1966, four were in their early thirties, making S. G. Warburg (as one journalist observed) 'the world's youngest merchant bank'.[170] As if to symbolize the passing of the torch, John Craven was promoted to a full directorship at the age of just twenty-nine, after only two years with the firm.[171] By 1970, twelve out of twenty-three executive directors were under the age of forty.[172] With Warburg spending an increasing proportion of his time away from London – first in Italy (where he and his wife bought a summer house at Roccamare on the Tuscan coast, opposite the island of Elba) and later in Switzerland (where they finally settled all the year round in Blonay, overlooking Lake Geneva) – it seemed that this younger generation had inherited the firm.

All that was needed to cement this generational transfer of power was some form of institutional change. In 1963 Warburg himself proposed the creation of a 'Steering Group consisting of four of the Executive Directors and one or two of our [non-]executives . . . [to] act as a kind of clearing house or central brain or . . . co-ordinating instrument within the firm's organisation'.[173] This body – sometimes known as the Operating Committee, sometimes as the Policy Group – was supposed to ensure 'a fast rhythm in decision-making', which Warburg acknowledged 'require[d] that ultimate power and responsibility . . . be concentrated with a small leadership team'.[174] (Ronnie Grierson had devised an alternative scheme, which would have divided the directors of the bank into four groups in order to reduce, as he put it, the 'great . . . strain on certain individuals', but this fell by the wayside.)[175] Yet these changes did not prevent Warburg from issuing a steady stream of written orders about the firm's future management structure, nor from spending long hours on the telephone telling the supposed executive directors what he thought they should do in this or that transaction. Throughout his four-month Italian sojourn in the summer of 1966, he kept one of his secretaries permanently on hand at a nearby hotel.[176] 'When Warburg is away from his London headquarters,' Joseph Wechsberg reported,

he receives every day a large envelope with two files. In each file there are several mimeographed lists. File Number 1 contains the Management Mail and Memoranda List which mentions every conversation and important telephone call inside the bank, every incoming and outgoing letter, cable and other communication, with initials indicating the names of the executives who were assigned to the case. The Management Mail and Memoranda List is the most important document of all. The file also contains Press clippings of the day; a list showing all bonds and stocks bought or sold; minutes of the daily 9.15 a.m. meeting; possibly the minutes of the weekly investment meeting; a list titled Secret Memoranda; the travel schedules of all directors and top executives who happen to be away from London; a list of all luncheons given at the bank, with names of guests; a list of all New Accounts; and the Daily Statement.

File Number 2 contains a list of Companies to be Kept Under Review; a list called Current Propositions (brief résumés of all pending matters); a list aptly titled Personnel Problems; a list of all Volunteer Trainees at the Bank . . . and, finally, a list of all Money Dealings.[177]

As Ernst van der Beugel, the Dutch economist and secretary of the Bilderberg Group, candidly told Warburg: 'In the present set-up . . . you are – in spite of the semi-retirement from the day-to-day business – still fully in charge.'[178] The executive directors in London became all too accustomed to injunctions from their distant founder (for example) to 'combine sufficiently the utmost discrimination regarding commitments with a readiness to have a multitude of irons in the fire in the pre-commitment stage'; to stop marking confidential notes 'not to be entered on the mail list', as opposed to 'not for circulation'; to 'use letters, telegrams, or telex communications instead of telephone calls'; to 'establish a progress chasing group . . . [to] deal with any complaints which anybody may have as to lack of sufficiently quick or competent procedure in the office'.[179] This was very far from an ideal arrangement, to say the least. One consequence was to make Warburgs, as Craven put it, a 'superbly political place':

We all had channels of communication – you couldn't have drawn an organizational chart, it would have looked like a map of European air routes! Some people liked certain people, others had worked together and had a better understanding of each other. Some people hated each other . . . I used to come home nearly pulling my hair with frustration because of the way the human relationships worked.[180]

Bernard Kelly's diary bears this out. Along with Craven, Nick McAndrew and Gianluca Salina, he constituted a group of 'plotters' or 'young Turks' who chafed at the dominance of the 'gerontocracy', also known as 'the old men'. Yet the divisions were not only between the generations. Kelly understood Ian Fraser's ambivalence about the firm's Jewish roots. When a potential client was turned down by 'the chairman-gang at the bank' on the ground that he was 'not top drawer' ('vos he not mixed up with something?'), Kelly was furious: 'this is irrelevant when it is a Jewish friend of theirs, but [if it is] an East End friend of Kelly, McAndrew and Fraser, then high principles are discovered.' On one occasion, Kelly observed revealingly that Warburg and Roll 'would both have benefited from a spell at a good English prep school rather than "Gymnasia" or whatever in Germany and Austria'.[181]

All kinds of gestures were made to placate the increasingly frustrated executive directors. In 1966 Warburg proposed that all 'directors who have reached the age of 65 should have to resign' – apart from those who had been executive directors 'for a long period'.[182] By this time Warburg himself was sixty-four, Grunfeld sixty-two and Korner a sprightly seventy. It was agreed that the three elder statesmen should move to separate offices on the fifth floor, 'to create – in a slightly detached way – a group of active but senior directors'.[183] But this too made no difference in practice. In 1967, after penning a long tirade against the 'serious weaknesses [that] have crept . . . into the workings of our firm', Warburg threatened to resign as a director altogether, becoming instead a consultant.[184] It did not happen. Within two years he was organizing after-hours meetings with all the senior employees in each department, in order to 'have an opportunity to discuss matters of the firm as well as personal subjects with those concerned'.[185] As Fraser observed, 'None of us noticed any evidence of Siegmund's retirement. Life went on as before, possibly even more so.'[186] Martin Gordon 'lost count of the number of times [Warburg] retired' during his long career at the bank. 'To those of us within the firm, it made no difference – if anything he got more active, developed a second or third wind, as he grew older.'[187]

VI

There was one side of Siegmund Warburg's mercurial personality that unquestionably caused more misery than fun. He had a capacity for falling out of love. 'He knew neither pity nor even compassion,' Pierre

Haas said of him. 'One lapse and one immediately saw his face close. If the fault was judged serious, it closed for ever. Average transgressions entailed a period of penitence lasting from three days to three months. For others, he was pitiless, an attitude of permanent suspicion on his part would drive the wrongdoer to resignation within a few weeks or a few months.'[188] An early victim of this cruel and seemingly capricious treatment was Michael Richards, who was frankly informed 'of the matters which had brought about a deterioration in your feelings towards me' in June 1951.[189] Ten years later it was Peter Spira's turn to be ticked off for a 'misunderstanding'.[190] As Spira later recalled, 'People were put in the doghouse for months and left to bite their nails without knowing why. Once, when I was in trouble with Siegmund, as I frequently was, I remember Eric Korner called me into his office and said, "Spira, you are still under a cloud. But it is no longer raining."'[191] No one was ever fired from Warburgs, one insider told the journalist Cary Reich. 'Instead, those who can't make the grade are simply "frozen out of the life of the firm".'[192] This would ultimately be Spira's fate. A rather different and more painful one awaited Warburg's own son, George.

It was an unspoken assumption at S. G. Warburg that the sons of directors and senior employees should be given at least a trial in the office. There was no obstacle, for example, to the rise of Henry Grunfeld's son-in-law Oscar Lewisohn, who joined the firm in October 1962, two months after marrying Louisa Grunfeld, and became a director in April 1969. However, Warburg was always clear that there could be no privileged treatment for family members in his firm. Grunfeld's own son Thomas was not considered suitable Warburgs material. In another break with Hamburg tradition, not even George Warburg could expect to inherit a directorship. 'Those who carry the name', his father declared, could 'maintain controlling positions [only] as long as they are sufficiently competent, imaginative, thorough and hard working'.[193] Warburg therefore encouraged George to study accountancy, despite being appalled by the 'inhumanly difficult but entirely futile' papers he had to study ('full of indigestible material on irrelevant tax and balance sheet matters').[194] To be sure, after learning the rudiments of business with the London & Scandinavian Metallurgical Co., George joined his father's firm in 1954 as 'the new junior partner', working in the Syndication

Department with sufficient distinction to be named a director in 1958. But problems surfaced within just a few years. Warburg does not seem to have approved of George's marriage in 1956 to an American of Armenian origin, Elinor Bozyan, the daughter of a professor of music (also the university organist) at Yale, presumably because a Jewish daughter-in-law would have been preferred. There was friction and frustration at work too. In January 1963, not for the first time, George announced his decision to leave the firm 'on health grounds' after a medical examination which, 'whether out of tact or tactics', he had asked his father to arrange.[195] But the reason he gave the *Daily Telegraph* was more credible. 'S. G. Warburg . . . [has] grown into a flourishing commercial empire,' he said, 'but some people prefer not so much the imperial life as doing something on one's own.' Relations with the 'empire' and its ruler deteriorated still further when George – in his father's view precipitately – resigned his position on the board of the meat-processing company Smithfield & Zwanenberg Group, a Warburgs client, after a dispute with its chairman and chief executive.[196] So bemused was Warburg by his son's conduct that he sent samples of his handwriting for graphological and 'psychological' analysis.[197] By 1967 their relationship was close to complete collapse.[198]

Siegmund's complaint, according to Paul Ziegler, was that George had allowed 'home' to 'interfere . . . too much with your job'; perhaps there was also frustration because 'the English education he let you have . . . was very alien to his own thinking and feeling'. Yet this was not the root cause of the trouble, as Ziegler shrewdly discerned:

A person like your father, especially after being forced by circumstance to create his own world, almost necessarily expects his son to be a replica of himself and hopes it'll be an improved one; the disappointment when it comes, as it is almost bound to do, is calamitous in proportion . . . His business had become your father's only *Heimat*, but naturally he also made it for you and through your entering it and continuing it, you would have taken it out of its artificial atmosphere, its surrounding empty space and linked it to reality. But then came the break between you and all that was left was to keep on turning the successful wheels, restlessly, more often than not exasperated with the mediocrity of the people one had to deal with and despising their shortsighted and grasping materialism.[199]

Warburg at first responded with ambivalence to the news that George and the former head of the Warburg Investment Department, Milo Cripps, were setting up their own bank, C.W. Capital (from 1973 Cripps Warburg).[200] The reality was that the inner circle of S. G. Warburg had by now become an ersatz family for him; George's secession represented the final separation between his natural family circle and the circle of *Wahlverwandschaften* (elective affinities) at work.[201] 'How is it that we get on so well?' Warburg once asked Doris Wasserman. She replied: 'It's very simple, because you can tell me to leave tomorrow, or today, and I can give you notice today or tomorrow. So we've got no bonds. So we come together because we get on well together. Whereas with your family or my family we're tied in. It's not easy.'[202] She understood him well.

The search for a surrogate son – someone with the qualities needed to be his successor – would preoccupy Warburg for many years. A succession of young men occupied the position of *spes regni*, sometimes for years at a time. In nearly every case Warburg's favour, which could verge at times on infatuation, was sooner or later forfeited or withdrawn. That was Peter Spira's experience; he was never wholly forgiven for a tactless request that he be allowed to take out insurance on Warburg's life to avoid potential estate-duty liabilities that might arise from a gift of Mercury Securities shares Warburg had made to him. To make matters worse, he then sold some of the shares to buy higher-yielding assets.[203] Ronald Grierson was at one time the favourite – to the extent of being considered, unbeknown to him, as a suitable husband for Anna Warburg – but by 1965 he appears to have lost Warburg's confidence.[204] The brilliant Australian James Wolfensohn, whom Warburg assiduously wooed, had the sense never to accept his standing invitation to join the firm, preferring instead to run Schroders' operation in New York.[205] For a time Jacob Rothschild was the apple of Warburg's eye, but in 1970 there seemed no chance whatever of his ever leaving N. M. Rothschild, least of all to join Warburgs. Gert Whitman rose briefly but mainly fell, as did Ira Wender in New York. Count Albrecht Matuschka was disgraced when one of his associates leaked details of Warburg pitches to US pension funds; Hans Wuttke and Tom Petschek (brother of Charles Petschek) also disappointed their mentor.[206] The only chosen one not to fall by the wayside (or to flee from Warburg's embrace) was David Scholey – but his coronation still lay in the distant future.

So long as no successor had emerged, Warburg's instinct was to delegate power to the man who in so many ways was his alter ego: Henry Grunfeld, whose star had been quietly in the ascendant since 1964, when he had succeeded Warburg as chairman of Mercury Securities. In September 1967, on the eve of a directors' dinner in London and in response to 'rumblings' by junior directors, Warburg wrote a memorandum to Grunfeld that effectively established him as *primus inter pares*. It was not possible with such a large board, Warburg argued, to aim for 'democratic unanimity [rather] than democratic leadership'. To do so would be to run the risk of 'excessive parliamentarianism and . . . bureaucratic bottlenecks'. Therefore:

Since I transferred a large part of my former responsibilities to you and until these responsibilities are transferred to others it is necessary that you have the ultimate authority and share this with others only to the extent to which you consider this right and appropriate.

I appeal to all directors, whether senior or junior directors, not to resent the authority which has to be exercised ultimately by one man, namely for the time being yourself, in the interest of the firm, and indeed to recognise and respect this authority to the utmost, whether or not it is exercised after consultation with, say, me or other senior directors or junior directors.[207]

This set a pattern that would endure for a dozen more years. By the late 1960s, in Darling's eyes, 'the reality was that . . . while he deferred to Siegmund on people decisions and overall direction, Henry Grunfeld ran the firm.'[208] Warburg still considered himself 'like the Head of a Government, who is responsible for all actions of his inner or wider Cabinet – even with regard to matters about which he has not been consulted and regarding which he may strongly disagree with the measures actually taken'.[209] A more accurate parallel would be with an absentee monarch, peripatetic and often away from his realm. With Warburg's resignation from the boards of both S. G. Warburg and Mercury Securities in January 1970, it was Grunfeld who was the increasingly powerful prime minister, if not grand vizier.[210] Now elevated to the supposedly symbolic and honorific position of president, Siegmund Warburg entered a new decade with neither power over nor responsibility for the firm he had created – or so it appeared.

Yet the reality was that his power had never been greater. And it was a power that now extended far beyond the offices of S. G. Warburg & Co. As the adviser not only to Britain's largest corporations but now also to the country's Prime Minister, Siegmund Warburg was at the zenith of his career.

10

Britain's Financial Physician

Harold Wilson . . . has been left with a terrible heritage, namely a domestic economy based on the assumption that the country, having lived beyond its means since 1914, could continue to do so for ever. Now at last the British people are slowly becoming aware of the realities . . . I think Wilson is carrying on a heroic fight against the restrictive practices both of the Trade Unions and of the employers and I have considerable hopes that he will win the fight. If he should fail, it will not be his fault but a sign of the decay of Britain. Indeed the real question for Britain is whether in the next ten to twenty years the strong and vital elements of the country will prove to be superior to the weak and morbid ones. Needless to say that the hotbed of the weak and morbid elements is mainly in the City of London . . .

Siegmund Warburg to Edmund Stinnes, 1 August 1966[1]

Sigmund [sic] Warburg had been Wilson's financial Rasputin. He had foisted some evil ideas on Wilson, who hadn't seen through them until too late.

Joe Hyman, 15 February 1968[2]

Show me trouble and I'll show you profit.

Siegmund Warburg[3]

I

'Is Britain becoming an underdeveloped country?' Siegmund Warburg asked himself in 1956.[4] His fear (as he made clear a year later) was that the economy of his adopted homeland was heading for that combination of low growth and rising prices which would indeed bring the United Kingdom to the brink of bankruptcy in the 1970s. When the short-lived Tory Chancellor of the Exchequer Peter Thorneycroft raised the possibility that Britain might need a loan from the International Monetary Fund, Warburg expressed the view that it was 'a gamble which would not come off and that we were in for a 1931 crisis, but this time with rising unemployment and rising prices simultaneously'.[5] This was certainly an exaggerated fear at a time when the unemployment rate was below 2 per cent and the consumer price inflation rate was below 5 per cent and falling (it briefly turned negative in 1959). Where Warburg was more prescient was in his choice of interlocutor. For the man to whom he expressed his forebodings was the Labour Shadow Chancellor Harold Wilson, the man who would come to dominate British politics in the 1960s and who would pay more heed to Siegmund Warburg than any other British prime minister. Theirs was a relationship that is largely absent from the official record – not surprisingly, given Wilson's earlier claims, directed against the Conservative government, that 'The real decisions affecting the well-being of the Queen's subjects were being taken outside the House [of Commons] . . . [They] were being taken by the Clores, Cottons, Lazards and Warburgs. The Government did not even hold the ring for these industrial giants; it abdicated.'[6] It comes as something of a surprise to discover that the man who coined the phrase 'the gnomes of Zurich' to express his disdain for foreign financial power came to rely so heavily for financial advice on a German-born merchant banker who would ultimately emigrate to Switzerland. On one occasion Warburg even arranged for Wilson to lunch with a Zurich banker – Edwin Stopper, head of the Swiss central bank – so that he could correct 'the misconception in this country of the gnomes of Zurich'.[7]

The reason Wilson turned to Warburg for financial counsel is not far to seek. In the early 1960s it was S. G. Warburg & Co. more than

any other City firm that appeared capable of helping British governments to address their recurrent financial problems. By the standards
of the twenty-first century, no doubt, the United Kingdom did not run
excessively large current account deficits in the 1960s (the largest, in
1964, was equivalent to just 1 per cent of gross domestic product,
compared with 4.9 per cent in 1989). Nor were net outflows on the
capital account especially large in relation to GDP (they totalled just
£174 million between 1960 and 1969). But because of the relatively
limited amount of international capital available at that time, compared
with the rapidly growing volume of international trade, these modest
imbalances could easily give rise to serious economic difficulties –
particularly for a country like the United Kingdom with expensive
naval and military obligations overseas and large foreign holdings of
sterling. Governments committed to maintaining fixed exchange rates
against the US dollar had to beware of any sharp decline in their hard
currency reserves. The 30 per cent devaluation of September 1949
(which had lowered the dollar–sterling exchange rate to $2.80) had
provided only temporary respite for the British currency. Long before
1967, the possibility of another devaluation was already in the air;
there were speculative attacks on sterling in July 1961, November
1964, July 1965 and July 1966.[8]

It was to address this problem that Warburgs advised the Macmillan
government to use the Treasury's holdings of shares in the Suez Canal
Company, British Petroleum and various US companies as collateral
for a foreign currency loan to be raised by the Commonwealth Development Finance Company or some new vehicle. 'Foreign, especially
North American and German, capital' would only be forthcoming for
investments in Commonwealth countries if there were an attractive
'nucleus of existing assets owned, directly or indirectly, by HMG'.[9] It
was, in Warburg's words, 'a sort of mixture of a finance transaction
with a demonstrative political gesture'.[10] On both occasions when
Warburg proposed such a scheme, however, the official reaction was
mixed. The Prime Minister himself was enthusiastic. As Macmillan put
it, this was 'the sort of thing a go-ahead merchant bank' could do more
readily than the Treasury or the Bank of England.[11] But the Chancellor
of the Exchequer was dubious, the Treasury sceptical and the Governor
of the Bank of England opposed.[12] A version of Warburg's proposal

was finally accepted, but no steps had been taken to implement it by the time the Tories left office.[13]

Having dominated British politics throughout the 1950s, the Conservative Party seemed played out by the early 1960s. The scandal surrounding the private life of the Secretary of State for War, John Profumo, served only to confirm Warburg's low opinion of the British Establishment.* Though as irreproachable as Profumo was tainted, the fourteenth Earl of Home did not impress Warburg when, as Sir Alec Douglas-Home, he succeeded Macmillan as prime minister in 1963; 'the fourteenth Mr Wilson' (as Home wittily called him) seemed an altogether more dynamic figure.[14] Warburg was by now 'very critical of the Conservative Party with its drifting policy . . . and . . . its antiquated image, reflecting [badly] on the British image altogether'.[15] Ministers like the famously relaxed Chancellor of the Exchequer Reginald Maudling had become 'complacent'.[16] The scene was set for a change of government. On 16 October 1964, having won the Labour leadership only the previous year and having secured a slim majority for his party in the House of Commons, Harold Wilson was appointed prime minister.

Warburg had been enthused, along with many others, by the new premier's bold assertion (at the 1963 Labour Party conference in Scarborough) that 'the Britain that is going to be forged in the white heat of this [technological] revolution will be no place for restrictive practices or for outdated measures on either side of industry'. This was only the most famous of many Wilsonian calls for 'dynamic, exciting, thrilling change . . . [in] the direction of our national life'.[17] Warburg had no illusions about the challenges the new government faced (see epigraph above): the recurrent balance of payments problems, the restrictive practices of the trade unions, the 'weak and morbid elements' in the City of London.[18] But he relished the chance to play the 'red' financier, supporting the new government even as the rest of the banking world recoiled from it. Already in February 1964 he had invited

* 'Quite apart from the political aspect there is not so much the question of morality but also of taste and public decency involved. Apparently there have been regular parties of distinguished people, all undressed except for masks and socks! At these parties the most awful orgies of old Roman style were organized by Mr Stephen Ward, all this in the midst of representatives of the dear British upper class': fragment of a letter dated 15 June 1963.

Wilson, along with a select band of businessmen, for a 'frank and relaxed discussion' over dinner at his home in Eaton Square.[19] Eight months later his cultivation of Wilson paid off. Warburg now had a foot in the door of 10 Downing Street.

II

For Warburg the economic key to Wilson's position was simple: another devaluation of sterling must at all costs be avoided. It was, as he put it in a letter to *The Times*, co-authored with Jack Hambro and published on 21 November 1964, 'a measure which means abusing the confidence of those who have placed their trust in sterling; which would be demoralising to the whole nation; which would represent a permanent and substantial movement of the terms of trade against us; and finally which would give, at best, only a very temporary fillip to our competitive position'.[20] There seems little doubt that Warburg had already expressed this view to Wilson before his elevation to the premiership. It is therefore highly significant that Wilson's first act as prime minister, at a meeting with the Chancellor James Callaghan and the Secretary of State for Economic Affairs George Brown on Labour's first day in office, was to rule out devaluation – a decision not even discussed in Cabinet until 1966 and long seen on the left as a fatal error.[21] On 30 November 1964 Warburg had the first of numerous meetings with the new Prime Minister to discuss financial matters. Wilson admitted to being 'very puzzled about the movement of capital away from London in the last few weeks'. In response, Warburg argued that a pre-budget announcement of a new corporation tax had triggered a withdrawal of hot money. He outlined a list of measures he regarded as necessary for the effective defence of sterling: a 'substantial reduction of defence expenditure', a policy Wilson consistently pursued; tax incentives for exports; and – his old hobby horse – 'an Overseas Holding and Development Company . . . by which the foreign exchange burden of finance for underdeveloped countries might be taken off the shoulders of the British Government'.[22] Under the Conservatives this idea had run aground on the sands of civil service suspicion. Inevitably the same mandarins now raised the same objections (the government was pledging valuable assets to attract foreign capital into risky projects that might fail), though officials appear belatedly to have grasped that the real point of the scheme was to bolster Britain's international reserves, not to invest in the Commonwealth.[23] As a former civil servant, Wilson was well versed in the ways of Whitehall. 'I wouldn't underestimate what SW [Siegmund Warburg] suggests can be done,' he scribbled on yet another negative Treasury memorandum. 'He's not unsuccessful at raising international loans.'[24]

Warburg fully expected sterling to 'remain weak for a considerable period of time'.[25] Nevertheless, 'from an economic point of view devaluation of sterling should be and could be avoided'.[26] It was a theme he reverted to in a meeting with the Prime Minister that May, in which he proposed a pre-emptive 'offensive/defensive alliance between the Federal Reserve Board and the Bank of England', another piece of advice Wilson took.[27] There appear to have been several other meetings to discuss the subject of devaluation; on one occasion, Henry Grunfeld was summoned from the City to Westminster to bolster Warburg's arguments. Grunfeld was dismayed by the 'total lack of understanding' on the part of the politicians, who struck him as 'dilettantes' who 'were all spooked by things that had nothing to do with the extant facts, all because of politics'.[28]

Letters to *The Times* had for some time been Warburg's preferred channel for public communications. He and Hambro wrote another in November 1965, adding a further recommendation that restrictions on overseas borrowing by British companies be lifted.[29] However, it was a sign of Warburg's growing commitment to the Wilson government that in October 1966 he composed and published a full-length newspaper article entitled 'The Case for Sterling', intended to counter what he called 'the prevailing atmosphere of uncertainty and currency hypochondria' in Britain. Carefully reviewing the relevant statistics, Warburg reverted to his earlier argument that Britain's overseas defence expenditure was out of proportion to its ability to earn foreign currency. He lamented the continuing burden represented by the sterling balances accumulated by former colonies prior to their independence. Yet he remained optimistic. The country's external assets still exceeded its external liabilities. In any case, the benefits of devaluation would be more than outweighed by the costs in terms of higher import prices, competitive devaluations by other countries and the loss of government credibility.[30] As far as Warburg could see, British officials and politicians ever since the war had been in thrall to what he called 'the sterling complex . . . This was indeed a complex – and is still to some extent a complex – in the psychoanalytical sense of this word, i.e. a combination of a superiority and an inferiority complex.'[31] If anyone kept Wilson committed to the no-devaluation policy, it was Siegmund Warburg, since by late 1966 neither George Brown nor Callaghan still believed in it.

Devaluation was not the only subject Warburg discussed with Wilson. The banker urged the politicians to reduce import duties, to introduce a value added tax so as to reduce the burden of direct taxation, and to counter French pressure on the dollar by converting British gold reserves into US currency. To keep long-term interest rates down, he proposed exempting British government bonds (gilt-edged securities or gilts) from capital gains tax.[32] Perhaps export–import guarantees could be sold overseas for hard currency.[33] Another Warburg proposal was for 'a Corporation to encourage inward investment on a partnership basis to worthwhile schemes to promote the development of knowhow etc.'.[34] The mandarins of the Treasury chafed as usual (though their preference for gold over the dollar would in the end be amply vindicated).[35] So did left-wing economists like Oxford's Thomas Balogh, the official Economic Adviser to the Cabinet, who suspected that Warburg's masterplan was a covert US takeover of the UK economy.[36] Balogh and his Cambridge counterpart (and fellow Hungarian) Nicholas Kaldor had a very different set of policies in mind, including a selective employment tax to discriminate in favour of manufacturing and against services and a 15 per cent import surcharge. These were measures Warburg was powerless to stop. Nevertheless, it was a sign of Wilson's growing confidence in Warburg that, in the wake of Southern Rhodesia's unilateral declaration of independence in November 1965, he was appointed a director of the Reserve Bank of Rhodesia, a measure designed to assert British control over the bank's overseas assets.[37] When other directors contemplated resignation because 'their connection with the Rhodesian Central Bank was prejudicial to their business interests', Warburg declined to do so 'because he thought . . . this would gravely embarrass the Government'.[38]

Warburg and Wilson saw eye to eye on another issue too. Acutely aware of the threat posed to the government by excessive wage demands and strikes, the banker loyally expressed his support for the government's prices and incomes policy, whereby the government sought to slow inflation by reaching agreements with employers and unions through a new National Board for Prices and Incomes – though Warburg also urged the introduction of 'positive incentives' to increase productivity and exports.[39] Indeed, he went so far as to advocate 'some form of permanent control over prices, wages and dividends', an opinion that put him far to the left of nearly all his peers in the City.[40] Not surprisingly, the fact that Warburg had Wilson's ear encouraged other ministers also to seek his advice.[41] Harold Lever, then Financial Secretary to the Treasury, also turned to Warburg, who later recalled 'a certain midnight meeting in March 1968 at the Treasury' (of which no record survives).[42] With Wilson's express permission, Lever and Warburg met again the following month to discuss the perennial problem of the sterling balances.[43]

Wilson was evidently satisfied with advice Warburg gave him. In 1966, almost certainly on the Prime Minister's recommendation, he was awarded a knighthood in the Queen's Birthday Honours (along with the editor of the *Financial Times*, Gordon Newton, the composer Michael Tippett and a batch of captains of industry, including the chairman of Esso Petroleum).[44] Although he was 'not keen on public decorations and honours', Warburg did not decline the honour 'on the grounds of the encouragement it would give to other refugees', and was duly gratified by the quantity of congratulatory letters he received.[45] That, at any rate, was his version of events. Henry Grunfeld had in fact advised him against accepting the knighthood, 'coming as it did from a man who was head of a government which was responsible for 96% taxation* on income in the United Kingdom'. (Grunfeld's own caustic view of Wilson was that he was 'slippery'.)[46] For his part, Charles Sharp found it 'paradoxical' that, after the long years of argument about the restoration of the name Warburg in Hamburg, his boss should wish to become 'Sir Siegmund'.[47] But Warburg ignored such objections, saying simply: 'We all have our private vanities.'[48] Others

---

* The top direct tax rate at that time was in fact 97.5 per cent: 82.5 per cent on wages and salaries plus a 15 per cent surcharge on 'unearned' (investment) income.

in the City felt that the honour should never even have been offered. The Governor of the Bank of England, Lord Cromer, was opposed on the ground that, though Warburg 'had, of course, been very successful in his own affairs', he had 'not . . . made any outstanding contribution to the common weal of the City that calls for public recognition'.[49] It was a source of further adverse comment that no sooner had Warburg received his knighthood than he apparently retired, moving for half the year to his secluded Tuscan holiday house at Roccamare.[50]

In practice, as we have already noted, this was not retirement as it is commonly understood. As Warburg explained, he and Eva intended to spend the period from May until October in Italy:

but of course these months are often interrupted by journeys to London and various places on the Continent. However I find these interruptions do not do any harm to the leisure time but rather enhance it. One of our London secretaries is always staying at a hotel nearby – on a rotation basis – and this helps me to keep in touch with the outside world and to maintain my correspondence as well as work on matters which have nothing to do with my business.[51]

As Warburg well knew, this was a somewhat unusual arrangement. 'Some of my friends', he remarked, 'make jokes about the fact that my holiday was not a proper holiday because I always have a secretary staying at a hotel nearby and dictate to her every morning for a few hours' – to say nothing of multiple telephone calls to London, New York and elsewhere in the course of the day.[52] This pattern continued even after the couple moved on a full-time basis to Blonay in Switzerland in 1973 (Warburg having grown frustrated with the unreliability of communication to and from the Italian coast). He might be physically absent from London, but Warburg's presence continued to make itself felt throughout the year. Judging by what has been preserved in his private papers, the number of business memoranda bearing his name actually increased after his retirement.

The difficulty was that, while Wilson might listen to Warburg, the Treasury had its own ideas about how best to withstand the pressure on sterling – and Treasury officials were in London all the year round, as were the Prime Minister's Hungarian advisers. To Warburg, the conduct of policy leading up to the devaluation of November 1967, which saw the dollar–sterling rate fall from $2.80 to $2.40, evinced 'an almost incredible combination of arrogance and dilettantism'.[53] 'The reasons for the devaluation', Warburg wrote to Paul Mazur, 'were ultimately not of an economic but of a psychological nature, mainly arising from a sort of currency hypochondria which seems to be one of the prevalent sicknesses throughout our Western World of today.' The problem was that the British had 'not given up the sacred cows of old imperialism in many sections of military and economic policy, including the role of Sterling as a so-called reserve currency'. And 'the chief stumbling blocks as regards moving the obsolete remnants of the old imperial status' were none other than 'the British Treasury and the British Foreign Office'.[54] As he later said in an unattributed comment to the *Sunday Telegraph*:

When people enter the superior surroundings of the Treasury . . . they are infected by a strange kind of intellectual arrogance. They're sort of glorified dons, but happy to sit there and not in Oxford or Cambridge, where they really belong.

They are all decent people of complete integrity, first-class and highly able, yet when I look back over the years, I see they have made every mistake they could have made. They have been very thorough, they haven't left out a single one.

For example, some of us have been telling the Treasury people since the end of the war that keeping sterling as a reserve currency made no sense whatever. Yet whenever you said that to them, they looked at you as if they wanted to find an excuse to put you in prison because you might assassinate the Queen.[55]

This was perhaps too harsh. If devaluation had ultimately been forced on Wilson, it was not just the fault of the Treasury. Not only labour unrest but the confiscatory taxation of which Grunfeld complained were hardly calculated to attract capital into Britain. The tax on services was as misconceived as the import duties were at odds with the country's commitments under the General Agreement on Trade and Tariffs, not to mention the European Free Trade Association. Still, Warburg's animus against what a later generation would call the 'Sir Humphreys' of Whitehall was not wholly unjustified. Once the same elite had opposed Keynes and all his works; now, thirty years on, they were mostly Keynesians and greatly underestimated the risks of Wilson's policies.

The obvious antidote to the supposedly dead hand of the civil service was to draw new men into government: ideally, new men from S. G. Warburg & Co. This did indeed happen. In 1966 George Brown recruited Ronnie Grierson to head a new Industrial Reorganization Corporation,* which had a £150 million budget to initiate or support mergers that seemed likely to increase the international competitiveness of British industry.[56] Three years later, in 1969, Ian Fraser left Warburgs to act as director-general of the City Panel on Takeovers and Mergers, established under the Monopolies and Mergers Act to ensure that the ensuing mergers did not restrict competition.[57] The firm stood ready to advise the government not only on currency questions, but also on the finances of nationalized entities like the National Coal Board. At the same time, as we have seen, Warburg did not hesitate to recruit an arch-mandarin, Eric Roll, as an executive director following the latter's retirement from the Department of Economic Affairs.[58] Roll was clearly intended to provide a channel of communication between 30 Gresham Street and Whitehall, to say nothing of the many foreign governments with which he had previously had dealings. Even after his appointment as deputy chairman of S. G. Warburg, he continued to accept official as well as private sector appointments. In May 1968 he was invited by the Chancellor of the Exchequer, Roy Jenkins, to join the Court of the Bank of England (in effect to become a director of the Bank).[59] Three years later, the Heath government appointed him as one of the two independent members of the National Economic Development Council, which had been set up by the Tories in 1962 to show that they too believed in economic planning.[60]

Far from solving Britain's financial problems, devaluation in 1967 (just as Warburg had predicted) offered only a temporary respite.

---

* It was a job Grierson tried hard to avoid. Not wishing to be offered a government job, he hastily decamped to Harvard to participate in Henry Kissinger's renowned International Seminar. However, on his return he was offered the IRC job by George Brown, and encouraged to accept it by Harold Lever and Arnold Weinstock. According to Grierson: 'Siegmund said, "I'll give you advice on this, I think when you're asked to do this sort of thing, you should do it. Even if it's not the prime minister who asked you, it's the deputy prime minister." And I talked to a few other people, and they all said, "This is an absurd organization, the IRC" – and I knew it was absurd – "but if somebody else took it, they might put us in the way of harm, and you could prevent it from doing harm," which is all I ever did – I was there for two years, and I prevented it from doing harm.'

Though the government tightened its fiscal policy, raising taxes and cutting defence spending, nothing could be done overnight to restore the Bank of England's much depleted reserves and it was not long before speculation against sterling resumed. In 1961 the previous government had secured a credit of £2 billion from the IMF. It was a facility Wilson had already had to use to defend the pound in 1965 and he had to seek yet more help from foreign monetary authorities after the devaluation. The trouble was that the IMF now insisted on tough deflationary policies, including a balanced budget and limits on domestic credit expansion – conditions that drove Callaghan to resign the chancellorship. Was there any alternative? Warburg bluntly told Wilson 'that we should borrow more from Germany, particularly for the nationalized industries. The Chancellor . . . agreed and said he would see what could be done about this.'[61] One idea canvassed by Warburg was that public sector bodies like British Steel or the Gas Council should raise money abroad by means of deutschmark-denominated Eurobond issues.[62] The Gas Council did in fact raise around £31 million by this route in 1969.[63] By October 1971 British public sector agencies had raised a total of $122 million (£51 million) through such loans.[64] The trouble, as the Treasury was not slow to point out, was the serious currency risk embedded in such loans. In the event of further devaluation of sterling, or a unilateral appreciation of the deutschmark, the sterling value of the debt would increase overnight. And that was highly likely. In four successive quarters from mid-1967 to mid-1968, the authorities had to spend £2.2 billion in defending the pound's new lower rate – much more than the Bank of England's total reserves, and vastly more than could be raised on the Eurobond market. Only the IMF and other central banks were keeping sterling from yet another devaluation.

By the end of the 1960s, with sterling still under pressure and unemployment and inflation both significantly higher than they had been when Wilson entered 10 Downing Street, the government's grip on power was crumbling. The White Paper *In Place of Strife*, published in 1969, said it all: heady visions of 'dynamic, exciting, thrilling change' had given way to a hungover reality of chronic industrial unrest. It was by now painfully obvious that Britain's economic malaise went much, much deeper than the rate of exchange of (in Wilson's famously hollow phrase) 'the pound in your pocket'. The Labour government had come into office intent on modernizing the British economy with a National Plan. It had created new Ministries for Technology and Economic Affairs. It had increased public sector investment by a massive 29 per cent. And yet the results were distinctly underwhelming. True, between 1960 and 1970 there was a 34 per cent increase in GDP and a 42 per cent increase in productivity. But performance in every other major industrial country was superior, including even Italy, where productivity grew more than twice as fast. Britain led the world in only one respect: nowhere did unit labour costs rise faster. And, partly for that reason, nothing could stop the inexorable retreat of British manufacturing from world markets: Britain's share in world trade in manufactures fell by more than a third.[65] What had gone wrong? Or, as Siegmund Warburg might have put it, why was the patient not responding?

III

While Warburg was more than usually ready to offer macroeconomic prescriptions in the mid-1960s, his principal area of interest remained, in effect, microeconomic practice. Whatever the difficulties of sterling or the defects of the civil service, he retained his faith in the potential of British industrial enterprises. In essence, he saw it as his role to help realize that potential by offering UK companies the best-quality financial advice. In particular, he liked to draw an analogy between his own brand of corporate finance and medicine. It was an analogy he made public in 1970 when he gave a rare and remarkably frank interview to the journalist Patrick Hutber:

The motives of a doctor are a mixture of altruism – the wish to help others – and of the ambition to do a good job. He hopes to obtain both the inner satisfaction arising from well-accomplished achievement as well as material recognition. On this basis a good doctor should in the first place listen with great attention to the problems and complaints of his patient and try to gain a comprehensive picture of his strong and weak points, looking not only at the patient's specific ailments but observing the state of the patient as a whole with its physical and psychological ramifications.

A doctor must neither neglect smaller impairments of the health of his patient nor must he despair over the patient's most critical afflictions nor desert him even on his deathbed. Moreover a good doctor must have the courage to tell the patient unpleasant facts and to oppose the patient when the patient wants to do things which appear to the doctor to be unwise.

Finally, the doctor when looking after his patient should think only how he can give best care to his patient and should not give any thought to the bill which he will send to the patient afterwards. However, once the doctor has performed a good service, he should not be shy about sending proper bills to those who can afford to pay them. The primary point seems to me always to be the quality of the service and the courage to persist in giving well-considered advice, no matter how unpopular that might be at times.[66]

Warburg saw banking as a form of specialized financial consultancy, in which remuneration took the form of fees, as opposed to the traditional model of a lending and deposit-taking business, in which interest and commissions were the main source of revenue.

It was for this reason that Warburg regarded client relationships as the firm's primary concern. The critical thing was that they should be the right clients. 'Our chief interest', Warburg told his colleagues in 1967, 'should be to look after our important industrial clients in this country, in the United States, and on the Continent of Europe.'[67] A year later he sought to persuade them 'that our ambition should not be, as it seems to be with some of my colleagues, to do quantity-wise as much or even more business than our chief competitors. On the contrary, our emphasis should be on making SGW & Co. an elite house, excelling in the service it gives to its industrial clients in this country and abroad rather than on doing business on a mass-production basis.'[68] As far as Ian Fraser could see, Warburg had two tried-and-tested methods of winning and retaining such clients:

For the strong his main instrument of persuasion was logic and originality of thought, for the weak it was flattery, often outrageous flattery; and far too many English industrialists and businessmen fell for it, a treatment for which their often Nonconformist upbringing had not prepared them. I do not think that I am exaggerating in saying that the better part of the merchant bank's English client companies in those years were won over by this extraordinary technique.[69]

Warburg himself had acknowledged this many years before. 'To possess a certain talent for bluffing', he admitted, 'is rather important in the banking profession.'[70] This was an art, not a science. 'Let the client talk,' he explained to one of his protégés. 'Don't try to sell him what you've got to sell. Get him to tell you what his problem is and that will give you time to think about it. Try and give him the answer to his problem in his own words. He'll think "How remarkably clever this man is, he's telling me exactly what I always intended to do anyway." Then you've got to impress him that you're the person who can implement the idea.' And 'never leave a conversation with a prospective client without leaving something on the table that you can get back to him on. You don't say, "Goodbye maybe we'll see each other in a year's time." You say, "Thank you for seeing me. I'll look up that book I referred to ten minutes ago and send you a copy." You [leave] the door slightly open so that you [have] a good natural excuse to go back again.'[71] Eric Roll remembered how Warburg would use self-deprecation to disarm a potential candidate:

When a new client came along, he would say two things to him. He would say, 'Look, we may not always be as competent as we would like to be, but we are tremendously discreet.' He would always say that first. And then he would say a little bit later, after the client had talked about his problem, should we do this, do that, should we grow organically, acquire, merge, what should we do, should we seek new products? He would say, 'Look, when it comes to what products your company should produce, I'm no use to you. You know how your company makes sausages or motorcars. I can help you in explaining the surrounding circumstances and particularly the financial situation, financial aspects of what you have to do and what you may want to do.' And then he would say, 'Supposing you could have it entirely your own way, what would be your ideal solution, before I give you my advice?'[72]

Warburg had many such rules of client engagement, some of them distinctly unconventional. In Warburg's eyes, for example, the customer was not always right. Asked on one occasion 'whether we act like barristers for important clients through thick or thin provided that there is at least a faint chance of winning their case or whether even towards extremely important clients we have the courage to refuse to comply with their wishes or views', Warburg replied that 'it had in fact always been our policy to express our criticisms to our clients, however much they might dislike it, and even to refuse to act for them if we differed from them on important matters.'[73] This precept was acted upon on more than one occasion, and was regarded by Warburg as the difference between his ideal of the financial physician and the (to his mind) less noble approach taken by barristers. Nor should clients in difficulties automatically be deserted: 'We should not behave . . . in accordance with the precept which is unfortunately so frequently followed in the City, namely to bully the weak and to suck up to the bullies.'[74] When things went wrong, there was no other course but 'agonizing self-appraisal'. All this worked extraordinarily well. As Peter Stormonth Darling recalled, Warburg 'wasn't a technical genius, but he was a genius at bringing people into the bank. So what makes a banker? That was banking . . . to bring clients, or potential clients, in.'[75] Bernard Kelly was often privately critical of Warburg in his diary. His definition of 'Warburgundism' – after watching his boss in action with potential Swedish clients at both lunch and dinner – was 'the spinning out of the day, making us sound helpful and positive but really being hot air'. Yet he could not deny that Warburg had a 'magnetic presence'. Years later, when a major Swedish bond issue was on the verge of being pulled, Kelly could only marvel at the way Warburg 'saved the day' with a combination of 'pressure and authority'.[76]

The corollary of Warburg's appetite for major corporate clients was a highly competitive relationship with rival City firms. True, many aspects of City life were still characterized by all kinds of restrictive practices, notably with respect to initial public offerings, which were systematically underpriced throughout the period (essentially because companies had to accept fixed and usually rather steeply discounted prices from the merchant banks doing the underwriting).[77] The battle for British Aluminium had nevertheless marked the dawn of a new era in British finance, when merchant banks would no longer politely leave each other's clients alone. We have already seen how Warburgs won ICI's international business from Schroders. Another change of allegiance came when the Hawker Siddeley Group switched from Philip Hill to Warburgs.[78] As the *Sunday Telegraph* noted, 'The convenient convention that once a client of a particular merchant bank, always a client, has been fractured and is doomed.'[79]

But exactly what kind of advice did British companies need? To Warburg the answer could be summed up in a single word: rationalization. Often used in the inter-war period to describe the tendency towards greater concentration within German industry, rationalization in 1960s Britain meant the elimination of uncompetitive entities and the exploitation of economies of scale. That could be best achieved through mergers and acquisitions (M&A), enabling the strong to take over the weak, the big to consume the small. Warburg's working assumption in this regard was straightforward: 'We will move . . . to still bigger units in the economic life of the Western world which, of course, from a human point of view is very regrettable but in the light of the technical developments of recent decades appears unavoidable.'[80] Again, the takeover of British Aluminium had set an important precedent in this regard, not least because it had so successfully advertised the skills of S. G. Warburg in the field of M&A. Sometimes, however, all that was needed was an injection of new capital (often in the form of a share flotation or a Eurobond issue) and a change of management.

S. G. Warburg's financial general practice (to pursue the medical analogy) boomed in the 1960s. In the wake of the British Aluminium battle, all kinds of industrial companies beat a path to 30 Gresham Street, drawn by the firm's more aggressive style of doing business. Warburg himself did not pretend to have expert knowledge of every sector of the British economy. As he explained to Eric Roll:

He neither knew, nor could hope to know, about making sausages, or motor cars, or about publishing newspapers or running hotels, but that there were certain features of running a business in a modern society – not only specific financial ones, which one had, of course, to master – that were reasonably uniform and that experience and judgement enabled one to advise on.[81]

To Ian Fraser he went further. 'Never visit a factory,' he once warned him. 'You will be too much impressed.'[82] This was no flippant aside. In 1957 Warburg had been among a group of bankers taken on a tour of an Italian steelworks. 'Most members of our visiting delegation including myself,' noted Warburg,

understood nothing whatsoever of the intricacies of the technical aspects of the enterprise but everybody – except me – tried hard to give the impression of being profoundly impressed on the basis of deep knowledge. What a world of hypocrisy and pretence, it would be so much more honest and so much less of an effort to admit one's ignorance towards the experts! The worst pretenders were my banker-colleagues.[83]

Though much involved in the motor industry's travails, Warburg frequently and unashamedly boasted of his ignorance of the workings of the internal combustion engine. (As we have seen, he could not even drive a car, let alone repair one.) Warburg's expertise was that of the generalist: to achieve 'important improvements as regards management teams and structural setups in the enterprises affected' – less euphemistically, the elimination of dead wood.

But just how successful was this remedy for Britain's financial ills? Macroeconomic policy in the Wilson era had been a disappointment: the National Plan scrapped, devaluation reluctantly accepted and stop–go once again the order of the day. Were the microeconomics of the 1960s any better? With an ex-Warburgs man at the IRC, and an ex-Warburgs man at the Monopolies Commission, Britain embarked on an M&A boom. Between 1965 and 1973 a total of 875 proposed mergers were considered by the Board of Trade (later renamed the Department of Trade and Industry). Only eighteen of these were referred to the Monopolies Commission and a mere six were prohibited.[84] Concentration increased in most major economic sectors: textiles, engineering, newspapers and the motor industry. But did performance improve? Was efficiency increased? Or did Wilsonian economics once again generate more white heat than light?

A distinction needs to be drawn here between corporate finance, meaning the provision of advice for fees, and the direct investment of Mercury Securities' own capital (*nostro* business). The latter was a good deal riskier. Indeed, a number of investments exposed all too clearly the limits of the generalist's approach. In 1955, for example, the Mercury subsidiary Brandeis Goldschmidt took control of Elkington & Co., a company that specialized in the manufacture of silver-plated cutlery.[85] The first step towards rationalizing Elkington was to replace its managing director, a man named Baer, who had become mentally unstable (Henry Grunfeld recalled him jumping on Warburg outside

Claridge's Hotel, 'kissing him and not letting go until the porter succeeded in freeing' the doubtless appalled financier). Unfortunately, the man chosen as Elkington's new MD proved little better. Having persuaded Warburgs that Elkington's largest silver-plating plant could be converted into a copper refinery, he turned out to have entered into large, loss-making copper futures contracts. Warburg was desperate to avoid having to announce a loss so soon after floating the company, as is clear from a fragment of a letter to his wife:

something seems to have turned up which – in the eyes of the hypocritical world which to a businessman is so important – may put a black spot on the white waist of the firm which I have built up with so much care. This new blow will not do us any financial damage as such but will set back the general development of the firm and this at a time when I have brought my son into it, thus burdening him as well with this present bad luck period of mine. I know that Henry, Eric and Ernest, my dear three musketeers, when they would hear all this would say that I exaggerate in saying such things, that I see my business matters at present in wrong proportions and that in fact every other respectable and active banking house has had to deal with similar cases of bad luck or mismanagement. I hope that my three musketeers are right and more-over that I can regain a more cheerful attitude.[86]

The three musketeers kept their heads. Grunfeld hastily transferred the loss-making copper-refining business into a subsidiary of Brandeis Goldschmidt, selling the rest of Elkington to Delta Metal, at a slight profit to shareholders.[87] Another equally disastrous investment was in the sports and leisure company Excel Bowling.[88]

Not all such *nostro* investments went wrong. As Mercury acquired additional assets as part of a systematic strategy of diversification, it evolved into something like a financial services conglomerate, embracing insurance (Stewart Smith & Co. and Matthews Wrightson), consulting (Metropolitan Pensions Association), advertising (the Masius Wynne-Williams agency) and opinion polling (Gallup). The oil infrastructure company Trunk Pipelines was also temporarily controlled by Warburgs, with no obvious ill effects.[89] Conversely, Mercury itself was for a time intimately linked to Minerals Separation Ltd (Minseps), a firm which had originally specialized in the extraction of silver, lead and zinc, but which by the late 1950s had evolved into a holding company or investment trust under the direction of John Buchanan, a former financial director of Rio Tinto. Minseps' 15 per cent stake in Mercury was in fact its biggest asset; Buchanan was therefore the Warburg Group's biggest outside shareholder.[90] For years, the two groups had collaborated closely, even sharing office space.[91] By 1963, however, the relationship had broken down. Buchanan had been selling off Mercury shares at a time when financial stocks were weakening, and threw down the gauntlet by resigning from the Mercury board. For his part, Warburg believed that, at seventy-six, Buchanan was now too old and 'stubborn' to continue as Minseps' chief executive.[92] In June 1964 Buchanan got his way as Warburg and another director resigned from the Minseps board.[93] It was just one of the many bad-tempered boardroom battles that would be such a feature of 1960s Britain. Whether either Minseps or Mercury benefited from the relationship, or from its breakdown, seems doubtful.

If there was one sector of the British economy that was ripe for rationalization it was the textile industry. Once at the cutting edge of the country's Industrial Revolution, the cotton and woollen manufacturers of the north of England and central Scotland were in a parlous state by the 1960s, woefully unable to withstand competition from Japan and other cheaper and more efficient producers. Mergers seemed to be the answer. Warburgs advised Courtaulds as it rose under Frank Kearton's leadership from being a specialist in man-made fibres to being the world's largest textile manufacturer by the mid-1970s, acquiring firms like Lancashire Cotton and Fine Spinners and Doublers, fending off a hostile bid from ICI. Warburgs carried out a number of successful mergers for the Glaswegian consumer-credit and mail-order king (and philanthropist) Sir Isaac Wolfson, including companies like Waring & Gillow, Aire Wool and Whittingham.[94] A less happy story was the rise and fall of Viyella, which Joe Hyman built by merging Gainsborough Cornard with William Hollins and other firms. In a single year, Peter Spira and Michael Bentley launched thirteen takeover bids by Viyella (named after the firm's signature blend of wool and cotton). As far as Ian Fraser could see, however, Viyella was no more than 'the rubbish basket into which all the remains of the Lancashire and Midland cotton and viscose industries were stuffed'.[95] The relationship broke down when Hyman had the audacity to propose a bid by Viyella for Mercury Securities itself.[96] Not long after this he was ousted as chairman of Viyella, which in turn was gobbled up by Carrington & Dewhurst.

In the closely related chemical industry, meanwhile, Warburgs not only advised ICI on Eurobonds, but also regularly acted for Fisons, the fertilizer company, notably over the acquisition of stakes in Spencer Chemical and British Drug Houses.[97] It was Warburgs who brokered the sale of its stake in the paper and packaging company Thames Board Mills to the food and household goods multinational Unilever.[98] It was also Warburgs who defended Ellis & Everard against a hostile bid by Unilever.[99] Another important Warburg client was the chemical company Croda.[100]

The net result of all this activity was drastically to reduce both employment in and production of British textiles. Output of cotton spinning slumped from 350,000 tons in the mid-1950s to just over 150,000 tons by the mid-1970s. Germany, France and Italy all performed better. Significantly, concentration was substantially lower in all three continental economies. In 1975 the top three firms in the British textiles business accounted for two-fifths of employment in the sector; for France the figure was 17 per cent, for Italy 8 per cent, for Germany 5 per cent.[101] The evidence gives the lie to the Wilsonian assumption that bigger was necessarily better. On the contrary, the future of European textiles lay in the sophisticated fabrics and fashionable designs that nimble continental firms excelled at producing.

Transportation loomed even larger than textiles at 30 Gresham Street. Among the firm's clients were the shipbuilders Vosper and Cammell Laird,[102] the aircraft manufacturer Fairey Aviation, which Warburg defended against a takeover bid from Bristol & Westland in 1960;[103] and its competitor Hawker Siddeley, which (according to Ian Fraser) defected from its previous bankers only after Warburg agreed to take over the chairman's personal £150,000 overdraft at a knockdown rate of just 3½ per cent.[104] But it was above all the automobile industry that symbolized the challenges facing British industry in the 1960s. It is easy to forget that Britain was once Europe's leading car manufacturer. In 1938 UK motor-vehicle production was well ahead of German, French and Italian and three British companies – Austin, Morris and Ford's English operation – dominated the market, with

Leyland Motors, Rover and Jaguar not far behind. Twelve years later, Britain's share of world car exports was 52 per cent. With the merger of Austin and Morris to form the British Motor Corporation (BMC), Britain appeared to have created its own version of General Motors.[105] When BMC bought Jaguar and Leyland bought Rover in 1966 it signalled the start of another bout of merger mania.

Warburgs already had some experience of the automobile sector, having advised the US car-maker Chrysler on possible European acquisitions since the late 1950s, at a time when Chrysler was seeking to match General Motors' success with Opel, Vauxhall and other European brands.[106] Simca of France and Barreiros of Spain were quickly snapped up. From 1963, however, attention turned to the UK motor industry after the Rootes Group became a Warburg client.[107] As the makers of such forgotten marques as Hillman, Humber, Sunbeam and Talbot, the Rootes Group was in many ways the quintessence of the British problem: still a family-run business, still heavily concentrated on the domestic market, of which it accounted for 12 per cent. Seeking to produce a rival to BMC's seemingly immortal Mini, Rootes designed the Hillman Imp, but they were cajoled by the government into building Imps at a new plant in Linwood, south-west of Glasgow. Eccentric design, abysmal supply chains and industrial strife led by increasingly militant shop stewards resulted in disaster.* Having begun by advising Rootes on possible acquisitions, Warburgs quickly found themselves looking for ways in which the company might itself be acquired. In mid-1964 Chrysler was persuaded to seize the opportunity, offering to buy 30 per cent of the company from the various family members who at that point still controlled 55 per cent of the voting shares.[108]

As in the British Aluminium battle, Warburgs stood ready to assist Chrysler in the purchase of shares on the open market if the formal offer was not accepted by the Rootes board. Warburg tried to resist the idea that the government should have some kind of veto over Chrysler's ultimately securing a majority stake, but in the end persuaded the Americans to accept this sop to economic nationalism.[109] By 1966 Warburg was advising Chrysler that there needed to be a 'first-class Britisher who is good at dealing with problems of industrial organisation' on the

---

* To which I can testify, having experienced as a child many uncomfortable and often incomplete journeys in my parents' Hillman Imp.

1. The Alsterufer Warburgs, with Siegmund's grandfather at the centre of the back row, and his father Georges seated at the far left.

2. The five Mittelweg Warburg brothers: from left to right, Paul, Felix, Max, Fritz and Aby M.

© M. M. Warburg & CO KGa

3. Aby M. Warburg: 'Der liebe Gott steckt im Detail.'

4. Max Warburg: 'Kaiser Max'.

5. Siegmund as a baby with his parents, Lucie and Georges.

6. Schloss Uhenfels, which towered over the farm where Siegmund grew up.

7. Siegmund as a boy: already happiest with book in hand.

8. Felix Warburg with his son Paul ('Piggy') aboard the SS *Aquitania*. Siegmund was repelled by his American cousins' country-club lifestyle.

9. Siegmund's wedding to Eva Philipson, Stockholm, November 1926.

10. The carefree young husband.

11. Siegmund Warburg with his son George: 'There is no question of his tenderness and kindness, but he should have more initiative and more feeling of responsibility.'

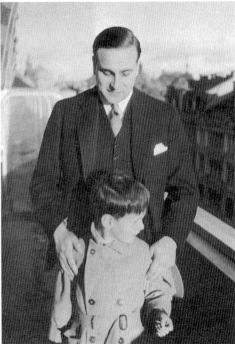

12. The M. M. Warburg & Co. offices in the Ferdinandstrasse, Hamburg.

13. Wall Street looking towards number 40 (now the Trump Building) where Kuhn, Loeb & Co. had its offices.

14. Siegmund with his mother in England, 1934: 'Happiness in life consists in fulfilment of duties and not of desires.'

15. Charles Portal, first Viscount Portal of Hungerford, chairman of British Aluminium.

16. Geoffrey Cunliffe, managing director of British Aluminium.

*"In the years to come, darling,
I shall feel so proud of you when
the children ask what you did in
the British Aluminium war."*

17. The 'Aluminium War' as seen by the cartoonist Nicolas Bentley.

18. Siegmund with Princess Margaret.

19. Siegmund at a 'Saints and Sinners' dinner, March 1951.

20. Theodora Dreifuss, his trusted graphologist and confidante.

21. The Chairman's Committee of
S. G. Warburg & Co., c. 1978: left
to right, Herman van der Wyck,
Oscar Lewisohn, Henry Grunfeld,
David Scholey, Eric Roll, Siegmund
Warburg, Geoffrey Seligman and
Peter Stormonth Darling.

22. Henry Grunfeld, shortly before
his death in 1999. As Siegmund
had said: 'You couldn't have done it
without me and I couldn't have done
it without you.'

Rootes board, reflecting not only his own 'very low opinion of the management of the company', but also his awareness of the allergy to foreign control which afflicted many Cabinet ministers.[110] Arguing that 'it would be inexpedient to allow another major manufacturer to fall under American control', Tony Benn (then Minister for Technology) urged Wilson to back the alternative of 'a BMC/Leyland/Rover merger with Rootes', relegating Chrysler's takeover to a fallback position.[111] However, the financial disadvantages of an all-British solution to the Rootes crisis seemed overwhelming.[112] In the end, the creeping takeover by Chrysler was the line of least resistance, with the last UK shareholders finally being bought out by January 1973. It proved to be the least successful of all the company's foreign acquisitions.

The argument nevertheless still seemed compelling for further consolidation of the British motor industry. One obvious option was for the relatively profitable truck manufacturer Leyland to absorb the loss-making British Motor Holdings (as BMC was renamed after the acquisition of Jaguar). This merger had the blessing of the government and the IRC, but it was Warburg who worked out the details – in particular, the decision to make Donald Stokes of Leyland the CEO of the new company, British Leyland.[113] When BMC proposed having 'a Chairman with three Deputy-Chairmen and no Managing Director or Executive Chairman', Warburg was adamant:

Surely it is recognised nowadays that in a great industrial enterprise there must be a chief executive officer who should delegate his responsibilities on the widest possible basis but who would clearly have the final say on any important decision, subject of course to the overriding authority of the Board, to be taken . . . Divided responsibilities in executive matters are bound to lead to delays and to confused decisions.[114]

The takeover battle was very nearly as acrimonious as that for British Aluminium – and, once again, the result failed to live up to expectations. New models like the Morris Marina, the Austin Allegro and the Rover saloon were at once charmless and unreliable. Industrial relations in the firm's forty or so plants were notoriously bad. As early as February 1970, Warburg found Stokes in 'a state of despair about his inability to cope with the various strikes or strike threats which face his company'.[115] Trying to switch the labour force from piecework to

Ford-style measured day work was a recipe for trouble. Profits were dismal (a mere £4 million on sales in excess of £1 billion in 1970). [116] Nothing better epitomized the decline and fall of the British auto industry than British Leyland's subsequent history – its nationalization in 1975, its transformation into the Rover Group in 1986, the Group's bankruptcy in 2005 and the final, ignominious sale to foreign buyers of historic brand names like MG, Jaguar and Land Rover.[117] Once again, the strategy of rationalization through mergers had abjectly failed. The bankers had promoted it enthusiastically, but when the resulting conglomerate proved unprofitable – because, once again, it could not compete against superior continental or cheaper Japanese imports – they withdrew financial support, leaving the taxpayer to foot the bill. Again it was striking that other countries preserved competition: Volkswagen did not merge with BMW or Daimler-Benz; Peugeot and Renault remained separate, as did Honda and Toyota.

From the mid-1950s onwards, Warburgs also became involved in the less obviously doomed British newspaper industry. As early as 1955, Warburg was advising Cecil King of the *Daily Mirror* group about a possible investment trust for the group's non-newspaper interests.[118] This was at a time when 'the City did not want to touch the *Daily Mirror* which they considered leftish and a second-class paper.'[119] Then, in July 1959, Henry Grunfeld advised the Canadian newspaper baron Roy Thomson during his acquisition of all eighteen of Lord Kemsley's newspapers, including the *Sunday Times* – a £12.5 million deal that would have been beyond Thomson's means* but for Grunfeld's pioneering 'reverse bid' strategy, whereby technically Kemsley acquired Thomson's STV, only to cede control of the merged company to Thomson.[120] Two years later the two clients collided in the so-called Battle of Long Acre, when the Mirror group sought to take control of Odhams Press, publisher of the *People* and the Labour Party's mouthpiece, the *Daily Herald*, with the aim of reducing the number of magazine titles on British newsstands.[121] In a vain attempt to keep Odhams out of King's grasp, the company's chairman Sir Christopher Chancellor had sought to arrange a merger with Thomson Newspapers (in fact another reverse

* Grunfeld was dumbfounded when, as the negotiations were nearing a conclusion, Thomson asked him to advise him on how to raise the necessary money. He later said this was the only time in his career he was ever lost for words.

takeover). This time, however, Thomson could not rely on Grunfeld's ingenuity. Informing Thomson regretfully that they would have to advise King, who had been a client for longer, the Warburg takeover team again joined forces with Lionel Fraser of Helbert Wagg; Thomson turned to Philip Hill (though he later went back to the Warburg fold). As in the case of British Aluminium, the result was a great deal of publicity, ultimate victory for Warburgs' client – and a handsome premium for the former shareholders.[122] The disappearance of Odhams was not only politically controversial, involving frantic lobbying of the Labour Party leadership and prompting questions in Parliament about the future freedom of the press.[123] It was also financially controversial. Although insider trading had yet to be criminalized, the rumour that King intended a bid had led to a surge in Odhams' share price sufficiently large to prompt a Stock Exchange inquiry.[124] Behind King stood the enigmatic figure of Sir John Ellerman, a publicity-shy millionaire who also controlled the newsprint manufacturer Albert E. Reed and the brewers J. W. Cameron & Co. His deep pockets enabled King to raise his offer for Odhams from £32 million to £38 million (63 shillings a share, far above the 40 shilling market price prior to the battle). Here, it might be thought, was a happier story than the decline and fall of the British motor industry. Governments might smile upon monopolies in other sectors, but no responsible politician wanted a single press baron to rule Fleet Street. Yet even the preservation of competition did not prevent the British newspaper business from suffering years of heavy losses as, once again, industrial strife – led by recalcitrant print-workers – eroded profit margins.

The financial physician had no Hippocratic oath; he was perfectly capable of turning away patients, no matter how urgently they required treatment. The notorious rack-renting landlord Peter Rachman was shown the door after just five minutes in Warburg's office.[125] The unscrupulous press baron Robert Maxwell was rebuffed after failing to impress Warburg and three other directors over lunch. Even the distinguished publisher George Weidenfeld did not pass muster at Warburgs, having antagonized Ian Fraser during the latter's time as a journalist; in this case, one black ball sufficed.[126] (The Weidenfeld case illustrates the operation of another Warburg rule, similar to the rule of four; for a client to be taken on, he had to be approved by all the directors at one of the regular 9.15 a.m. meetings.) By contrast, Sir Hugh Fraser, chairman of the House of Fraser department store, was considered *salonfähig*, and became a major client in the early 1970s when he contemplated mergers first with British American Tobacco and then with Boots, as was the hotelier Charles Forte, whom Warburgs helped to take over the Trust House chain of hotels and to see off a hostile bid by Allied Breweries.[127] Another high-profile client was the notoriously ruthless and combative 'Tiny' Rowland, whose company Lonrho (London & Rhodesian Land, Finance and Investment) went on a veritable shopping spree for dormant African mining companies like Hendersons Transvaal Estates, Witwatersrand Coal and Ashanti.[128] However, Warburg severed all ties with Rowland after he paid £12 million for the rights to the Wankel rotary engine without consulting the Lonrho board, at a time when Lonrho's finances were badly over-stretched. (This was before the revelations of tax evasion by Rowland and his chairman, the former Conservative politician Duncan Sandys.)[129] For Warburg, Rowland had always been a dubious character, who Ian Fraser had persuaded him to take on against his own better judgement.[130]

As the preceding paragraphs make clear, the range of Warburgs' interests in the field of corporate finance was remarkably broad. Throughout the 1960s and into the 1970s, Warburg and his colleagues fought aggressively to secure as many mandates as possible to advise and represent larger British firms, repeatedly squeezing out their more sedate competitors, to the latter's great chagrin.[131] Whether it was Grand Metropolitan's acquisition of the London brewer Watneys in 1972 or Sainsbury's initial public offering the year after, Warburgs were the first-choice advisers. Admittedly, more art than science was involved. When it came to picking a share price for an IPO, Peter Spira liked to tell clients that he used the 'Wasserman test', meaning that if Warburg's secretary would buy at a certain price, then that was the right price (not realizing that the Wassermann Test is in fact a medical procedure for establishing if a patient has venereal disease).[132] If there was a discernible trend, it was towards finding international solutions to national problems. Perhaps sensing that the deficiencies of British management were unlikely to be put right by insiders, Warburg increasingly favoured European or American investments or takeovers. ICI plus Bayer, Chrysler plus Fiat, British Leyland plus Volkswagen or

Daimler-Benz – these were the pipedreams of the later 1960s. At the same time, as we have seen, Warburgs were expanding their Eurobond business, offering their established UK clients a new source of offshore finance.[133] The more Warburg himself thought along these lines, the more the daily grind of UK corporate finance was left to Frank Smith and his loyal lieutenant and successor Michael Valentine. Smith was in many ways the true master of the takeover, the man who (in the *Economist*'s words) had 'done more than any man to perfect the techniques of takeovers in the last twenty years'.[134] Repeated exposure to boardroom battles eventually made him too cynical. Asked by Hugh Barton, the former chief executive of Jardine Matheson who had been newly recruited to Warburgs, 'What do you look after here?', Smith coolly replied: 'Myself, mostly.'[135] 'From a management point of view,' Robin Jessel recalled, 'there was one thing and one thing only that mattered, and that was the deal. And it was one deal after another. And it was the problems that showed up in the deals that illuminated the next one, and it was the people you met on the deals that led to the next deal, and it was a continual turnover of new business and new people.'[136] This attitude eventually proved to be Smith's undoing. In 1971 he was publicly castigated for telling an 'untruth' to Lord Shawcross, the chairman of the City Takeover Panel, in connection with a bid by Hay's Wharf (Shawcross could not resist the pun that 'Mr Smith had been less than frank'). To the dismay of his younger colleagues, Smith's resignation was accepted by the Chairman's Committee – because, Peter Spira believed, Smith was 'often too outspoken for [the committee's] tastes'.[137]

In theory, as we have seen, all these microeconomic efforts were supposed to complement the macroeconomic policies of the Wilson government. Successful rationalization would raise British industrial productivity and ultimately make a positive contribution to the balance of payments. That, at any rate, was the thrust of a draft speech Warburg wrote for Wilson in March 1968, which put the most positive gloss possible on the preceding four years:

Throughout the 13 years before we came to power any Government interference in industry was considered as taboo but we have now succeeded in creating a climate in which the problems of industry are having the continuous attention of the Government and are tackled in close co-operation between Government and industry . . . Far be it from me to say that what we have done as regards modernisation of British industry is more than a beginning . . . [But] we are gradually succeeding in introducing into our economy a spirit in favour of change as opposed to the all too widespread atmosphere of complacency and addiction to ingrained bad habits which we found when taking over the Government.[138]

Given what lay ahead for firms like British Leyland, and indeed for the British economy as a whole, this was excessively sanguine. Yet Warburg cannot be accused of naivety. He, more than most, was aware of the deficiencies of British management. He, more than most, was sceptical about the efficacy of government bureaucracies. Indeed, only a month after drafting that speech for Wilson, Warburg found himself face to face with the depressing realities of Britain's managed – or, rather, mismanaged – economy. As advisers to the electronics and telecommunications company Plessey, Warburgs had already suffered a reverse when Tony Benn used (as he put it in his diary) 'strong language in trying to frighten them [Grunfeld and Roll] off' the idea of a takeover of International Computers and Tabulators (ICT):

I [Benn] said that we had devoted three years of effort in trying to establish a viable British computer corporation, that we were determined to get it and that £25–£30 million of Government money was involved in it. I also hinted that there were very large orders involved, and even went so far as to say that we were large purchasers of telecommunications equipment and didn't intend to see Plesseys frustrate our policy in this way. I pointed out that ICT simply wouldn't exist if it hadn't been for Ministry of Technology support in the early days and that I took a most unfavourable view of what they were proposing to do.[139]

When Plessey's next bid – to acquire English Electric – escalated into a hostile takeover, Warburg was dismayed, firstly because his own client had disregarded his advice and, secondly, because the IRC appeared to have 'taken sides' against Plessey, despite having previously favoured similar takeovers by Arnold Weinstock's GEC.[140] In his view, 'the question at issue should be left to the industries concerned to be sorted out between them, and that indeed these industries should look at matters rather from the point of view of what would be profitable for the companies and their shareholders than of what would be in accordance with so-called "industrial logic"' – a term Warburg dismissed as 'a highly dangerous cliché, like so many of the clichés of the theologians of the Middle Ages'.[141] In truth, Warburg had been outmanoeuvred by Weinstock, who was able to acquire English Electric for GEC, just a year after taking over AEI – a wound for the wizards of Gresham Street which at least one commentator saw as 'self-inflicted'.[142] That was certainly the view of Michael Valentine, who regarded Warburg's public criticism of Plessey as a fatal blunder.[143] Stung by such criticism, Warburg reacted by questioning his own fundamental assumptions about rationalization:

1. How far is the assumption justified that the larger a company the better is its organization and efficiency? . . . Indeed there is much to be said against any such assumption . . .
2. It should perhaps be said that if the [American] anti-Trust regulations were to apply in the UK, both Lord Nelson [of English Electric] and Arnold Weinstock would today be in prison for criminal offences . . .
3. The safeguarding of competition – in contradistinction to the encourage-ment of monopolistic enterprises or of enterprises with excessive domination over their markets – is a value which has apparently grown out of fashion in the UK . . .[144]

The row over Plessey was so bitter that Ronnie Grierson had to resign his non-executive directorship of S. G. Warburg, which he had retained when he accepted the IRC post. This time not even he could deny that there was a conflict of interest, since he was now serving as deputy chairman of GEC.[145] Within ten years, however, the irrepressible Grier-son had not only effected a reconciliation with Warburg but also re-established Weinstock as a Warburg client, which he had been on and off since the early 1950s.[146]

'How far is the assumption justified that the larger a company the better is its organization and efficiency?' That was indeed the right question, though it took defeat at the hands of Weinstock to make Siegmund Warburg ask it. The answer was that it was certainly not justified if mergers, with or without government sponsorship, merely lumped together inefficient, poorly run firms and reduced the pressure of competition on management and workforce alike. The problem was that the only realistic alternative – large-scale closures of moribund firms, a frontal assault on the trade unions and shop stewards and an invitation to foreign companies to come and do better – did not become politically feasible until the 1980s.

The question therefore poses itself: was rationalization better for the bankers than for the UK economy? As we have seen, Siegmund Warburg sometimes expressed a preference for corporate finance over Eurobond issuance or investment management – to say nothing of the firm's later unit trusts (as mutual funds were known in the UK), which he ignored altogether. Takeovers, mergers and acquisitions were what he called 'constructive' financial activity, with the client relationship as the key. Giving investment advice to private individuals was to cultivate the wrong kind of relationship. As for selling a bond, that was a mere transaction. Admittedly, there is very little evidence from his surviving correspondence that Warburg cared about the fees that clients were charged. On the contrary, it seems that he very often left it to clients to decide the amount to be paid, counting on them to overshoot rather than undershoot if they had been sufficiently pleased with the Warburg service.[147] Only rarely, as when Arnold Weinstock offered what struck Warburg as a 'stingy' amount in 1977, did he even refer to the subject of fees.[148]

Yet there is no question that corporate finance appealed to Warburg partly because of the fee structure. As he had pointed out in 1967, a single fee from a big industrial client could be worth more than an entire year's earnings from Eurobond issues.[149] In an uncontested takeover, the bank could expect one-half of 1 per cent of the amount paid for the acquisition; in the case of a successful contested bid, 1 per cent.[150] When Bernard Kelly advised Hugh Fraser on the sale of his stake in House of Fraser, the agreed fee was three-quarters of 1 per cent of the deal's total value, plus £75,000, making a 'breathtaking' total of £334,500.[151] As the total value of mergers rose to £2,313 million in 1968 compared with £800 million the previous year, the rewards of corporate finance grew commensurately.[152] Between 1959 and 1969 Mercury net profits rose sixfold after allowing for inflation. The 1960s were the group's golden decade, with the share price surging to a high of £213 in January 1969, twenty times the price of a decade before.

The paradox is that, for all the dynamism suggested by these figures, the reality was that the City of London in the 1960s was as hidebound by archaic practices as any rusty textile mill, car assembly line or newspaper printroom. This was still a world in which bankers were by convention forbidden to visit stockbrokers in their offices; the latter, no matter how venerable, were obliged to call on the former, no matter how lowly. In the same way, bankers were not allowed to communicate directly with the Treasury; all such communications had to go through the Governor of the Bank of England.[153] Bankers, brokers, jobbers and an army of clerks went about their business much as they had before the war. Many of the bankers even dressed as their fathers had, complete with bowler hats and black umbrellas. It was always a little unlikely that British industry would find salvation from this gentleman's club – even if the club had admitted an unabashed player like Siegmund Warburg, who had no qualms about advising a Labour prime minister.

IV

Though he enjoyed his flirtation with the Labour Party – not least in order to *épater les bourgeois* in the City – Siegmund Warburg was never a socialist in any meaningful sense of the word. At heart he was a political agnostic.* Thus, when Edward Heath was elected leader of the Conservative Party in 1965, Warburg was quick to offer his customary flattering congratulations. Here at last was a Tory 'leader who is not hidebound and has a dynamic attitude'.[154] 'Such a radical and un-conservative leader' would never have emerged had it not been for the challenge posed by Harold Wilson, reasoned Warburg; this change on the right might prove to be Wilson's most enduring achievement.[155] At around the same time Warburg was persuaded by Ronnie Grierson to donate money to a new Conservative 'radical pressure group' called Pressure for Economic and Social Toryism (PEST), which they hoped would 'put new life into the Conservative Party'.[156] As that name

---

* As Charles Sharp put it: 'From time to time he may have flirted with Labour, less often with the Tory Party. What I am sure of is that he never voted for the Liberal Party. He believed in leadership and was either "for" or "against" but never for anything in between.' Warburg liked to refer to himself as a 'floating voter'.

suggests, Warburg was drawn to the left of the Tory Party almost as much as to the right of Labour. He had no time for those who, for example, followed Enoch Powell's lead in opposing immigration.[157] Powell's supporters, he told Cecil King, 'resembled the German party that in the 'Thirties was to the right of the Nazis'.[158] By contrast, Warburg was happy to donate £5,000 to the moderate Bow Group in response to an approach by Lord Carrington, the old-school Tory leader in the Lords.[159] By the end of 1968 Warburg was expressing strongly positive views of Conservative plans for tax reform, which aimed to reduce income tax and introduce a value added tax.[160] Two years later, he was even prepared to address the Conservative Finance Committee.[161] The Tory sympathies and political ambitions of John Nott – who had joined Warburgs in 1959, and went on to serve as defence secretary under Margaret Thatcher – may have played a part in this reorientation.[162] Other Conservatives considered as possible recruits to the bank at around this time were Christopher Soames, a Cabinet minister under both Macmillan and Alec Douglas-Home, and the rising star William Waldegrave, whose ministerial career lay in the future.

Yet doubts remained. After lunching with Heath in 1968, Warburg undertook his own graphological and psychological analysis of the Tory leader. The results were damning:

- basically weak – self-indulgent, almost narcissistic.
- subject to influence from people whom he considers able to improve his image.
- very intelligent but without character.
- much too easily influenced by people who fascinate him.
- his own opinions are not founded strongly enough and not fixed in a well constructed pattern with the result that even opponents can reverse his views if his inner weakness[es] – in particular his vanity – are touched at their many sensitive points.
- he is not good at defending himself in face of unexpected and hard difficulties.
- he will change his stand point not because of unreliability as such but because the necessary inner force in him is lacking.
- there are strong aesthetic elements in him and his is an extraordinary ability to react with subtlety and delicate understanding.

- he is like the most refined receiving set for radio waves hence he can assimilate facts and impressions with accurateness and comprehension.
- he could have been a first class scientist, especially in a field where abstract and imaginative ways of thinking have to be done. He could also be a good chief of a publishing firm.
- his strength is in intellectual assessment and analysis but he lacks completely any talent for human contacts and relations.
- he is a circumspect thinker but not fighter.
- to summarize: he is a man with an intellect of high quality but a weak character.
- (not committing himself to others because not committed within himself because of inner uncertainty).[163]

Other senior Conservatives left Warburg equally cold: Anthony Barber, the future Chancellor of the Exchequer, struck him as 'very, very shallow'.[164] Asked for his political prognosis by Cecil King in early 1970, Warburg replied, 'he thought there would be an election in September which Labour would lose. He thought Heath would be a worse P.M. than Wilson and that after an interval – round about 1972–3 – there would be a coalition under Wilson.'[165] He was not far out. Wilson called an election four months earlier than Warburg had expected, but Labour lost all the same.

Not surprisingly, given his assessment of the new premier's character, Warburg was never as close to Heath as to Wilson. True, they did see one another socially.[166] And Warburg did not stop proffering economic advice to Downing Street – for example, urging the new government to permit new hard currency borrowings by public sector bodies like British Steel (which had been renationalized by Wilson).[167] But there is little sign that this suggestion was seriously explored. Another Warburg plan – to sell the government's BP shares to private investors – was killed by the former BP chairman Eric Drake and had to await the return of Labour to power to be realized.[168] Having already ended his firm's relationship with 'Tiny' Rowland in 1971, Warburg resisted the urge to respond when the Prime Minister denounced Lonrho as the 'unacceptable face of capitalism' for its involvement in Rhodesian sanctions-busting, vetoing a riposte his colleagues had wished to send to *The Times*.[169] But he had no sympathy when the government undermined its own economic efforts by unleashing the short-lived 'Barber boom' (see Chapter 11), a debacle which served only to confirm Warburg's low opinion of the Chancellor as 'a sort of half-wit'.[170]

One subject on which Siegmund Warburg and Edward Heath might have been expected to see eye to eye was Europe. Heath was a long-standing proponent of British membership of the European Economic Community, having been the minister responsible for the country's first abortive bid to join. Warburg, as we have seen, had been an ardent European since before the war, and a keen advocate of British accession in the 1950s and early 1960s. In the debates on Europe that had split the Wilson government, he sided with the pro-Europeans led by Roy Jenkins.[171] As in the past, Warburg tended to focus on the economic rationale for integration, proposing (for example) that Heath set up an EEC Industries Fund as 'a financing organization to provide funds for industry in special cases, where the European Investment Bank, which hitherto had confined its activities to the regions, was not necessarily likely to operate [for example] . . . such industries as North Sea oil, the aircraft and aero engine industries and the nuclear power industry'.[172] He eagerly looked forward to a time when 'there would be "European" companies owning holdings in various "national" companies in Europe.'[173]

By the early 1970s, however, Warburg's enthusiasm for the politics of European integration had cooled, not least because of the growing importance of agricultural protectionism under the Common Agricultural Policy adopted in 1962. In Warburg's eyes, the EEC had entered 'a second stage [of development] when the strong European spirit started to evaporate and when the protection of sectional economic interests – above all in agriculture – seemed to step into the foreground'.[174] In October 1972, less than two weeks after the European Communities Act received the royal assent, Warburg confessed to being 'afraid that we are now entering the European Economic Community in circumstances when both Germany and France are economically in a much stronger position than the United Kingdom', making it 'difficult for us to play the kind of guiding role in Brussels to which this country is entitled on the basis of its great international tradition'.[175]

What were the reasons for Warburg's shift towards Euroscepticism?

Mounting European anti-Americanism – not only of the Gaullist variety but also from the radical left – was certainly not to his taste, particularly when it threatened to undermine Western unity in the face of the Soviet Union. By early 1974 he had almost wholly lost patience with the tendency of national governments to put self-interest ahead of the European ideal. Both Britain and France were 'at present guided by particularly bad governments', he complained to his cousin Eric, 'both pretending to be very European but in reality being utterly nationalistic and non-European. Indeed, these two governments involve themselves in courses of action which endanger any constructive development of the European Economic Community – anyhow a very fragile and embryonic organism.'[176] As far as Warburg was concerned, the 'deterioration of transatlantic relations and internal European relations' was 'largely the fault of the British and French Governments'.[177] What was necessary, he argued in a draft statement for Harold Wilson shortly after the latter's return to 10 Downing Street in 1974, was:

a European community which will spread its influence throughout the world, which will look after European interests less by emphasis on opposition to non-Europeans and by insistence on European independence but rather by strengthening co-operation with the actual or potential friends of Europe. Indeed in building up our European community it would be disastrous if we were to permit the development of European institutions which would see parts of their policy in antagonising our friends in America or in throwing spanners into the possibilities of a détente with Russia. Above all Britain's role in Europe must never detract from our old ties with the Commonwealth but rather enhance these.[178]

Equally important was Warburg's sense that the European institutions had fallen victim to bureaucratization. The 'amazing conglomeration of bureaucratic establishments' that had sprung up in Brussels were, he complained to George Steiner, 'almost a prototype of a category of establishments which have become all too common in the economic and political fields of our Western world of to-day on both sides of the Atlantic':

The German word *Selbstzweck*, for which the term 'end in itself' is a poor translation, has become the proper attribute of a continuously increasing number of organisations which have grown too large and which are too much led by mediocrities to produce any constructive decisions or in fact any decisions at all. This certainly applies to the overwhelming majority of today's soi-disant functionaries in Brussels and Luxembourg, who are supposed to be the servants of Europe.

It is symbolic of the institutions to which I have referred that instead of taking actions they incessantly form new committees which postpone decisions and operate as instruments of delay rather than, as they ought to, of progress-chasing. Furthermore it belongs to the characteristics of these *Selbstzweck* institutions that they produce a never-ceasing chain of long and inconclusive reports. It is in turn the fate of such reports that they are rarely read by anyone except their authors and that as soon as the reports are published they disappear into giant archives without being perused again ever after.[179]

Warburg's hopes that Roy Jenkins, in his new role as president of the European Commission, might be able to break the bureaucratic gridlock in Brussels were swiftly (and perhaps predictably) dashed.[180]

As we have seen, Warburg was a man who all his life fell in and out of love – with institutions as much as with people. European integration had been among his first loves. Perhaps it was inevitable that eventually his passion would give way to disenchantment. There is, however, another possible explanation. British membership of the EEC was Edward Heath's principal achievement as prime minister. Yet one unintended consequence of accession was to expose British manufacturing industry to unaccustomed competition. Textile producers and car manufacturers alike had been sheltered by tariffs for more than four decades. Entry into the Common Market swept protection away and revealed the competitive advantage the continental economies had achieved from their earlier embrace of free trade within Western Europe.

V

By the early 1970s a paradox was firmly established: the success of S. G. Warburg as a bank seemed to proceed independently of the failure of the UK economy. The twenty-fifth anniversary of the foundation of S. G. Warburg in January 1971 provided an opportunity for some modest self-congratulation. 'I must admit', Warburg wrote to Henry Grunfeld after a celebratory dinner in London,

that you are right in stating that I have reason to be proud of the achievements of SGW & Co. over the 25 years which have been completed last Saturday. Indeed I feel that I must share this pride with you on a complete partnership basis . . . Above all I shall be grateful from my whole heart and up to my last day for your faithful friendship and for your encouragement and understanding which never failed me. I can certainly say about you: '*Einen besseren Kameraden gibt es nicht.*' [There could not be a better comrade.][181]

Yet even as the Warburg–Grunfeld double act went from strength to strength, matters continued to deteriorate for the UK as a whole. The current account surpluses of 1969–72 flattered to deceive. Symbols of Britain's proud past, ranging from Rolls-Royce to *The Times* newspaper, teetered on the verge of insolvency.[182] The Conservative Chancellor Anthony Barber's solution was a relaxation of the controls on credit. Rather than battle against currency speculators, in June 1972 the government followed the lead of the United States and a number of European countries by allowing the currency to float. The results were disastrous. Inflation surged from below 6 per cent in the summer of 1972 to above 10 per cent in November 1973, an increase that could only partly be blamed on the oil shock following the Yom Kippur War (see next chapter). As so often in post-war British history, a politically motivated stimulus led not to higher growth and lower unemployment but to higher consumer prices, spiralling wage claims, a widening current account deficit and yet more downward pressure on sterling. The inevitable switch from go back to stop – which took the form of hikes in the Bank of England's minimum lending rate from 6 per cent to 9 per cent in the last quarter of 1972, and then again from 9 per cent to 13 per cent in the second half of 1973 – failed to tame inflation. Not much more effectual were the Supplementary Special Deposits (the so-called corset) introduced in December 1973 to check the growth of interest-bearing bank liabilities. The Heath government sentenced itself to electoral defeat in November 1972 when it was driven to revive the Labour policy of wage control. By the time Heath called an election on 7 February 1974, the miners were on strike.[183] 'Who Rules Britain?' was the Conservative election slogan. The answer was: not Heath.

With the return of Harold Wilson to 10 Downing Street in March 1974, following Heath's failure to form a coalition in the wake of the previous month's inconclusive general election, Warburg once again turned his mind to Britain's macroeconomic predicament. This was now dire. The miners were on strike and the entire economy was on a three-day working week (to say nothing of the virtual civil war in Northern Ireland), and Britain had a yawning current account deficit worthy of Argentina. As Warburg put it, Wilson was resuming office 'at a time when the country is facing the most serious economic crisis in its history, a crisis which indeed is not only of a material character but is a crisis of the whole fabric of our society'.[184] Warburg at once recommended a $2–3 billion loan from the International Monetary Fund 'to prevent a further flight from the pound by foreign creditors and to increase the country's foreign exchange reserves with extremely large amounts'.[185] Privately, he could muster only faint praise for the government: 'At least one can say that the Wilson government is not quite as bad as the Heath Government.'[186] When he met Wilson in early June he was struck, not entirely favourably, by the premier's 'unbeliev-ably detached attitude regarding his colleagues, regarding the Opposition, regarding the trade unions, and really regarding everyone and everything of importance'.[187]

Warburg's principal worry was that the new government was still underestimating the inflationary danger.[188] It was. Retail price inflation was running at 8 per cent when Labour returned to power; by mid-1975 it was above 20 per cent. Once again Warburg reverted to his old hobby horse: the possibility of raising hard currency, preferably deutschmarks, either by selling the government's stake in British Petroleum or by borrowing by public agencies like the National Enterprise Board and (in Wilson's phrase) 'the new big national oil company which will contain all the North Sea assets'.[189] But by now there was scant foreign enthusiasm for British public sector securities. The German Chancellor Helmut Schmidt expressed reservations about a mooted sale of BP shares to investors in the Federal Republic.[190] Whereas a $35 million Eurobond issue for British Steel had been successfully placed in 1974,[191] a similar operation for British Gas the following year nearly foundered because of Swiss and American complaints that the yield being offered was too low.[192] Meanwhile, Chrysler UK was placed under the direct control of the American parent company in a last desperate attempt to curtail its losses.[193] Shortly after becoming Chrysler's CEO, Lee Iacocca sold all the company's European subsidiaries to Peugeot for a nominal $1. (Warburgs acted for Chrysler on the sale – and took another fee.)

By 1975 Warburg had all but given up on the government, and particularly on the Trades Union Congress, which he believed had wholly lost control of its own rank-and-file members. Hearing that Roy Jenkins was organizing a 'new group within the Labour Party called "The Social Democratic Alliance"', Warburg expressed his interest in giving it financial support.[194] When, on 16 March 1976, Wilson unexpectedly announced his intention to resign – claiming that he was exhausted but perhaps fearing the consequences of early-onset Alzheimer's disease – Warburg shed no tears.[195] Within months, with the public sector borrowing requirement approaching 10 per cent of GDP, Wilson's successor, 'Lucky Jim' Callaghan, had been forced to turn to the International Monetary Fund for a $3.9 billion loan. It came with stringent fiscal and monetary conditions that heralded a new era of public spending cuts and monetary targeting. The *Wall Street Journal*'s headline of the previous year said it all: 'Goodbye Great Britain'.[196] For Bernard Kelly, with eight children to educate and aristocratic aspirations to own grand houses and fine art, it really was goodbye. Faced with punitive tax rates, he and his colleague Gianluca Salina began to ask themselves 'whether our type of occupation ("really worthless, it doesn't add anything to anything") would last out our lives, and we talked of where we could emigrate'. When he heard Warburg airily 'explaining how Denis Healey was a strong and good Chancellor', Kelly 'exploded, arguing that this could not be said when he was destroying the upper and middle classes by ferocious taxation . . . at one stage I went as far as was polite, saying "we will all come to populate both sides of the lake of Geneva."' In the end he chose to accept a job in Monaco, resigning from Warburgs in the summer of 1976 and not returning to London until 1980.[197]

The Wilson era had ended in failure – from the white heat of technology to the 'cold, grey ash' of stagflation in the space of a dozen years.[198] Its failure was both general and particular. At the macro level, Britain's political economy had been exposed as more Latin American than European. At the micro level, too few British firms or manufacturing sectors had proved themselves capable of meaningful rationalization. For Warburg, who had been more willing than anyone in the City of London to give Wilson his backing, it was a bitter disappointment – and for the Warburg Tories, not least Kelly, unwanted vindication. Small wonder that, when the Conservative Party embraced an altogether more radical economic policy under the leadership of Margaret Thatcher, Warburg felt a certain relief. His verdict on the years 1964 to 1979 was damning: '[The] situation . . . under successive Labour and Conservative governments of the post-War period had continuously deteriorated. The mess which she has inherited is almost unmanageable . . . [They] had encouraged this country to live far beyond its means . . . this reckless course of self-indulgence is long overdue for a radical change.' [199]

This, however, is to anticipate the radical changes that came about in the aftermath of the great global crisis of the 1970s. For, in truth, it is impossible to make proper sense of Britain's economic decline, fall and revival if the story is set in a narrowly national context. Siegmund Warburg certainly liked to think of himself as a financial physician to British firms, as well as a behind-the-scenes adviser to governments which appeared to share his vision of a rationalized UK economy. But the other role to which he aspired in the 1960s and 1970s – and it grew more important as the health of his British patient deteriorated – was altogether more visionary. It is above all as a prophet of globalization that Siegmund Warburg needs to be understood; and it is to his performance in that role, at a time when the odds seemed to be stacked heavily against international economic integration, that we must now turn.

11

The Malaise in our Western World

My opinion is that 1975 will be, probably more than any previous year, a period of 'brinkmanship' . . . In all probability 'brinkmanship' will not lead in the near future to violent and catastrophic explosions but will just stop short of them whilst there will prevail an atmosphere of oppressive and degrading tension. To live in the surroundings and corresponding influences of such an atmosphere will, I think, be the best we can expect in our Western world for the time being. It is our duty as individuals to counteract these dangerous influences by building and preserving wherever possible some small islands of sanity and decency.

Siegmund Warburg, January 1975[1]

Since about 1968 I had expected that some time in the seventies the present international oil emergency would break out. Indeed it had been brewing for several years and even without the war in the Middle East of October 1973 it would by now have been in full swing . . . In this expectation I feared that the consequences of the oil crisis would be serious not only from an economic and financial point of view but that the crisis would lead to a further corruption of Western society. This is now happening in an even worse way than I had anticipated but of course moral corruption – human or national – has a fertile ground whenever there exists a basic core of moral weakness . . .

Siegmund Warburg, February 1975[2]

I

It was a peculiarity of his temperament, as we have seen, that Siegmund Warburg quite regularly fell in and out of love. Usually it was a platonic affection for bright young men whom he had recruited to his bank. Occasionally, as with Harold Wilson, it was a politician. Only once did Warburg fall for an entire country. That country was the state of Israel.

As a young man, Warburg had been no Zionist. Like many members of eminent Jewish banking families that had attained wealth and social status in the nineteenth century, he was wary of the project for a Jewish nation-state, since the existence of such an entity might awaken doubts about the national allegiances of Jews living elsewhere. Jews, he declared in 1942, 'should not be infected by that worst modern epidemic of folly called nationalism'.[3] Indeed, at that time – before the full magnitude of the Holocaust was apparent – he went so far as to call the Zionists 'nearly as free of any moral inhibitions as the Nazis'.[4] As he later recalled,

It seemed to me that the project of a Jewish national home . . . was to offer a home to those Jews who wanted to emigrate from countries in which they had little chance of acquiring citizenship rights equal to those of the other inhabitants. However I thought that those Jews who enjoyed such equal citizen[ship] rights in their homelands should hold on to and enhance, wherever possible, these rights by complete dedication to their countries.[5]

Though Warburg had played some part in the efforts of his relations (notably his uncle Fritz) to facilitate Jewish emigration from Germany to Palestine in the 1930s, he seems to have paid little attention to events in the British Mandate (the euphemism for Palestine's semi-colonial status) in the wake of the Second World War. He certainly knew both Chaim Weizmann and David Ben-Gurion – the former had an affair with his cousin Lola – but no record survives of his reaction to the proclamation of the state of Israel on 14 May 1948. When approached by a Tel Aviv businessman two years later, Warburg stated curtly that the idea of establishing 'a sort of banking pied à terre in Tel Aviv' was 'out of the question', without specifying why.[6]

On the other hand, Warburg certainly had no sympathy with the Arabs at this time, regretting that more 'resolute action' had not been taken by the Western powers following the nationalization of the Suez Canal and deploring 'the extravagant and completely irresponsible ambitions of the Middle East potentates led by [the Egyptian President Gamal Abdel] Nasser and supported by the windfall of their almost excessive oil assets'.[7] Indeed, he came to see the 'appeasement' of Arab nationalism as one of the major blunders of post-war American foreign policy.[8] Nevertheless, throughout the 1950s Warburg continued to concentrate his philanthropic efforts on individual refugees, declining to contribute to the United Jewish Appeal, which raised substantial funds from the American Jewish community to support Jews migrating to Israel.[9] He turned down an invitation from Edmund de Rothschild to put a representative of S. G. Warburg & Co. on the board of the Anglo-Israel Investment Trust.[10] Not until late 1959, more than a decade after the state's foundation, did Warburg visit Israel, accompanied by his wife and daughter.[11]

Though it only lasted twelve days, this first visit was the *coup de foudre*. 'Before I went to Israel,' he told one of his hosts, 'I had, of course, studied many books about it and had been passionately interested in the developments there. However,' he went on,

what I have seen has far surpassed my expectations. I had expected that in view of Israel's precarious position, surrounded by enemies on all sides, I would find there[,] as being only too natural under such emergency conditions[,] much more tension and fanaticism and much less moderation and balance. When I think of the many admirable things I have noticed in Israel, the most admirable one is that the leaders of a people who are, for all practical purposes, in a state of war and faced with such immense problems, can maintain a completely relaxed and peaceful spirit, free from any hate and pretences, concentrating on long-term planning at the highest level and giving at the same time whatever attention is required in regard to the very pressing day-to-day emergencies.[12]

The young state reminded him, he said, of early nineteenth-century Prussia – at first sight an unlikely parallel. The Prussian reformers Wilhelm von Humboldt and Gerhard von Scharnhorst, Warburg reasoned, 'must have been rather similar to the present leaders of Israel in that the former had a deep faith linked with a philosophical attitude in which the chief elements were individual freedom and emphasis on education and the latter had an equally deep faith but combined with less intellectualism and with a more practical approach, of which justice, austerity and discipline were the foundation stones'.[13] He was especially impressed by a visit to the Weizmann Institute of Science in Rehovoth, a research centre established in 1933 by Chaim Weizmann, the distinguished chemist who had gone on to become the first president of Israel.[14] He later had a moving reunion with his uncle Fritz's widow, Anna Warburg.[15] The familial ties to Israel were further strengthened when his daughter Anna met and married the Zionist activist and fundraiser Dov Biegun in 1962.*

For all Warburg's newfound interest in Israel's politics, he was valued by the Israelis primarily for his financial expertise. Just a few months after his visit, a representative of the Israeli Ministry of Development paid a visit to London to seek assistance with the sale of shares in state-owned companies.[16] The most promising candidate for such a privatization appeared to be the Dead Sea Works, which had been set up in 1952 to exploit the rich mineral resources of the Dead Sea, producing potash, bromine and salt.[17] It was decided to float fifteen million of its shares in partnership with Bank Leumi, the successor to the Anglo-Palestine Bank Ltd (and as such the oldest bank in the country), along with N. M. Rothschild, Kuhn Loeb, Bank of America and the World Bank.[18] For the young Joshua Sherman of Kuhn Loeb, the transaction provided a first glimpse of the way business was done at 30 Gresham Street, not least 'the Wykehamist approach to prospectus preparation'.[19] In the following years, Warburgs participated in share issues for Bank Leumi itself as well as for the Israel Discount Bank.[20]

Almost from the outset, however, there were problems with these ventures, particularly the Dead Sea Works.† By the autumn of 1965 Warburg was fretting that the company's erratic performance 'would have a very bad effect on the credit status of Israel'.[21] He was also

* If Warburg had been hoping his daughter would marry a suitable business associate, he was to be disappointed. At one point she announced her engagement to 'Abu' Abraham, the Indian-born cartoonist of the *Observer*. Dov Biegun had been born in Pinsk in 1911. Fluent in no fewer than fourteen languages, he had served during the war with the British Army Intelligence Corps.

† Immortalized by Sherman and Peter Spira in the pseudo-biblical sketch 'Visit of the Boy Joshua to the Land of the Israelites'.

uneasy about the 'bad situation on the Tel Aviv Stock Exchange'.[22] A year later his anxiety was that 'Bank Leumi has over-expanded and the burden of responsibility has become too great for the rather narrow group of the management.'[23] By 1967 his concerns extended to the Israeli economy as a whole. 'The present problems of Israel', he wrote in June of that year, 'are more of an economic than a military character. Every day by which the total mobilization of the Israeli military forces has to be continued, uses up increasing parts of the financial reserves of the country.' To alleviate the pressure Warburg now proposed 'that an international banking syndicate . . . be formed to issue a loan for which Israel should act as borrower and which would not carry a joint but a several guarantee of the USA, UK, France, Germany, Italy and possibly also Canada, Japan, and the Scandinavian countries . . . One might consider to give the loan some such name as "Middle East Peace Loan".'[24] Ironically, this letter was written just three days before the outbreak of the Six-Day War.

Israel had been forged by war; and the threat of war never ceased to hang over it. In 1948 the Arabs' refusal to accept the two-state solution envisaged by the United Nations General Assembly's Resolution 181 had led to the outbreak of war with the new Jewish state at the very moment of its birth. Although no fewer than five Arab countries had attacked Israel – Egypt, Syria, Jordan, Lebanon and Iraq – the Israelis had held them at bay, while at the same time ruthlessly driving hundreds of thousands of Palestinian Arabs from their homes. But low-level hostilities had continued. Palestinian fedayeen launched attacks from the Gaza Strip, occupied by Egypt in 1948. War broke out again in 1956 when Israel joined Britain and France in an attempt to recapture the Suez Canal from Egypt; but the Israeli occupation of the Sinai Peninsula was short lived after the Europeans capitulated to American financial pressure and withdrew.

Warburg had his own ideas about how peace might be achieved in the Middle East. In 1963, hoping to build on the success of the German–Israeli reparations agreement, he proposed Hermann Abs as a possible mediator between Israel and Egypt – a rather unlikely candidate, it might be thought, given Abs's less than heroic role in the Third Reich.[25] A year later, Warburg proposed combining 'a sort of 10-years' plan for the constructive development of Egypt' with 'another 10-years' plan which would provide for a solution of the problem of the Arab refugees' by creating 'a special enclave within the Negev with safeguards of minority rights and the like', as well as 'the creation of a broad neutralised or demilitarised zone between Israel and all its neighbouring states'.[26] None of this could get beyond the drawing board so long as the Arab states continued to dream of a military victory over Israel. Yet Nasser's clumsy preparations for war presented the Israelis with a perfect opportunity for a pre-emptive strike. Warburg was reminded 'of September 1938, the time of Munich, when a small brave country was at the mercy of the big powers and surrounded by cruel and violent bullies with a threatening world conflict in the background' – with the difference that this time the small country took the offensive.[27] Fearful that a third world war might be brewing, Warburg inveighed angrily against the politicians whose insincere posturing at the United Nations brought back memories of the 'criminals of Munich'.[28]

When the Six-Day War broke out on 5 June 1967, Warburg's first thought was naturally for his daughter, who remained in the country throughout the conflict along with her husband and their baby daughter Batya. (Shortly after hostilities ceased, Batya was sent with an au pair to stay at Roccamare, where she was joined by her parents in early July.) It was not long, however, before Warburg threw himself into the public debate about the war's origins, writing a stiff letter to *The Times* in response to remarks by the Conservative MP Ian Gilmour, who had implied a moral equivalence of Israel and the Arab states:

Does Mr Gilmour realize [he asked] that while for years past Arab leaders have indulged in statements of violent hatred and of propaganda for wholesale murder of the Israelis, no Israeli leader has expressed himself in terms of hatred or incitement to murder? Indeed, there is strong evidence of genuine desire on the part of the Israeli leaders to arrive at a fair and durable understanding between Israel and her Arab neighbours.[29]

Israel's military success pleased Warburg, though not as much as the lack of effective Western support displeased him.[30] The crisis, he argued in an unusually splenetic letter, was mainly the fault of the Russians, 'who thought that by brinkmanship short of war, they could conquer the Middle East as Hitler conquered Czechoslovakia in 1938':

What the Russians should have liked best, was, if as a result of a Middle East war, ninety percent of the Arabs and ninety-nine percent of the Jews had been killed and the ensuing vacuum would have been taken over by Russia. Thanks to the fortitude of the Israelis this irresponsible game of Russian power politics has so far failed, but I still would not exclude the possibility of a third world war arising from further exercises in brinkmanship . . . by the Russians.

The United Nations should be renamed 'United Hypocrites'. De Gaulle was also to blame for having undermined the Western military alliance by withdrawing from NATO's integrated command structure. Only the Americans showed any sign of doing the right thing; but they were hampered by their spiralling military commitments in Vietnam.[31]

In this same impassioned mood, Warburg announced to friends that he and Eva had resolved to reduce their private expenditures to the barest minimum in order to 'make it easier to use practically the whole of our capital for the support of Jewish causes'.[32] He racked his brain for practical ways in which to assist 'that brave, young State of Israel' – ranging from the construction of desalination plants to the floating of a $1 billion international loan – and paid a two-day flying visit to Jerusalem in August to attend the first of a series of conferences designed to drum up business interest in the Israeli economy. The fruit of these efforts was a new Industrial Development Bank of Israel, established in late 1967 with the support of Deutsche Bank and a consortium of mainly European houses.[33] So energetically did Warburg work for the Zionist cause that Tony Benn heard that he 'had been the man responsible for coordinating the collection of money from rich millionaire Jews to support Israel during the Six Day War last summer and he had managed to raise £50 million during that period of which about £7 million came from Britain, about £10 million from Germany and the rest from the United States and Canada.'[34] Warburg also sought to broker unofficial talks in London between Arab and Israeli leaders.[35] At the same time, he actively interested himself in the affairs of a pioneering Israeli technology company, Israel Computer Software.[36] His speech at the second Jerusalem Economic Conference in April 1968 called for Israel to focus its economic planning not just on agriculture and tourism but also on the chemical industry and the nascent computer sector.[37] And he gave his support to the new Israel Corporation holding company set up at the conference to increase trade and foreign investment, vainly pressing Harold Lever at the Treasury to ease foreign exchange restrictions so that British investors could put money in it.[38]

This was the high water mark of Warburg's affair with Israel. 'When I compare the head of Prime Minister Eshkol's office, the permanent head of the Israel Finance Ministry and the Governor of the Bank of Israel with their counterparts in the UK,' he wrote to Joshua Sherman:

it is to me significant how much more vitality, perspicacity, courage and thoroughness there is in the Israeli personalities than in the Britishers concerned – notwithstanding the fact that these three Israelis of whom I talk are a selection from 2,300,000 people while the corresponding Britishers are a selection from over 50 million people, but I suppose this has nothing to do with numbers and is a question of the youthful spirit in Israel as against a certain senility . . . here.[39]

He was equally impressed by the Israeli Defence Minister General Moshe Dayan, assuring George Ball (the US ambassador to the United Nations) that Dayan 'really understands the Arab problems almost as well as if he were an Arab and that he only wants to hold on to the occupied territories [Gaza and the West Bank] to the extent to which he considers this necessary from the point of view of Israel's security. Moreover, he is very keen on getting rid of the occupied territories on the widest possible basis as soon as real peace is restored in the Middle East.'[40]

Yet there remained doubts about this newly beloved country. One who knew him well – Paul Ziegler – never quite believed in Siegmund's conversion to the Zionist cause, dismissing it as 'a pseudo-solution and inadequate in any case; not that I disbelieve [his] sincerity, but it does not fit into the picture of the Siegmund whom I know pretty well – it is a *faute de mieux*.'[41] This was astute. When (without consulting him) the Israeli government authorized the merger of the Dead Sea Works into a new chemicals conglomerate, Warburg was incandescent about this 'monstrous behaviour'.[42] Almost from that moment, the object of his affections could do no right. He was infuriated by the 'inefficiency, negligence and sloppiness' of the King David Hotel in Jerusalem when he had difficulty making a reservation.[43] Two business trips to Tel Aviv in 1968 left him so frustrated that he declined an invitation from the Israeli government to participate 'in a full review . . . of economic developments in Israel'.[44] The management of Israel Corporation meanwhile made what Warburg considered 'a sloppy beginning'.[45] The software project was 'delayed in a very unsatisfactory way', though it did ultimately prove possible to attract investment from the Californian-based Computer Planning Corporation.[46] By 1970 Warburg's patience with the Israelis as business partners was all but exhausted. He offered to resign from the board of the Dead Sea Works on the ground that his financial advice was simply being ignored.[47] He berated the government for its 'deficient' treatment of foreign investors like British Leyland.[48] He was irked by the failure of his scheme to get Israel Corporation to invest in the country's principal oil refinery at Haifa.[49] A year later things were no better. Israel Corporation was guilty of managing its money in 'a fourth class way'.[50] Its participation in the Israeli shipping company Zim was too risky.[51] Finally, on 7 September 1971, Warburg resigned from Israel Corporation's board, protesting at the 'totally unacceptable' way in which the firm's managing director, Michael Tzur,* had sought to oust twelve of his fellow directors at the previous week's annual general meeting.[52] Despite his best efforts, Edmund de Rothschild could not persuade Warburg to withdraw his resignation.[53]

To be sure, Warburg never wholly turned his back on the Israeli economy, accepting the Trade Minister Pinchas Sapir's invitation to serve as the co-president of the UK Economic Council for Israel in 1972,[54] and devoting considerable time to the project for setting up a merchant bank in Israel the following year.[55] By this time he had visited the country at least twenty times. But he was now much more ambivalent about 'this community which is inwardly so very unbalanced yet unique in its intensity'.[56] There were, he complained, 'few reliable and thorough men in the Israeli economy'.[57]

---

* Warburg's reservations about Tzur proved to be well founded. In 1975 Tzur was indicted on charges of fraud, bribery and breach of trust. According to the indictment, he withdrew about $16.2 million from Israel Corporation and paid the money into a Liechtenstein credit trust controlled by Tibor Rosenbaum, president of the Geneva-based International Credit Bank. Rosenbaum used the deposits to pay off mounting debts incurred by his other enterprises, mostly real estate ventures. The collapse of the International Credit Bank, which was reputedly also involved in Mafia money laundering, was a major embarrassment for the World Jewish Congress, of which Rosenbaum was treasurer. It was also more than merely an embarrassment for Warburg's son-in-law Dov Biegun, who became embroiled in a lawsuit involving ICB.

A further difficulty was the divergence between Warburg's views of what might be achieved to bring peace to the Middle East and those of most Israeli politicians. 'The ultimate solution of the Arab/ Israeli problem', Warburg wrote in December 1969, 'ought to be the formation of an enlarged Palestine which would consist of an Arab unit and an Israeli unit, with the two units living side by side. The ties between these units would probably at first be somewhat tenuous but might gradually develop into a sort of new Switzerland in the Middle East . . .'[58] This later mutated into a scheme for 'a kind of federation between Israel, Jordan and Lebanon'.[59] He and Victor Rothschild found it difficult to understand why the Israelis were so unwilling to make concessions on the question of the Palestinian refugees. In Rothschild's view, Israel was 'hurtling, like the Gadarene Swine, to perdition' by devoting so much of its foreign exchange to imports of military hardware; he believed it was time for the government to accept the UN Security Council's resolution of November 1967, which called for an Israeli withdrawal from the territories occupied as a result of the Six-Day War.[60] Increasingly disillusioned with the 'deeply ingrown party tactical inclinations' of Golda Meir and the 'mediocrities' in her Cabinet,[61] Warburg found himself drawn to Nahum Goldmann,* the President of the World Jewish Congress, who was prepared as early as April 1970 to countenance a meeting with Nasser as part of a wider initiative to improve relations with Israel's Arab neighbours. Goldmann soon became Warburg's closest adviser on Middle Eastern matters, receiving in return investment advice of a general nature and contributions to the Institute of Jewish Affairs and the Israel Fabian Society.[62] Along with Marcus Sieff, the chairman of Marks & Spencer, Warburg also took an interest in the precarious finances and editorial line of the left-of-centre London-based magazine the *New Middle East*.[63]

A visit to Israel in November 1970 raised Warburg's hopes, not least because of the favourable impression he formed of Shimon Peres, then

---

* Nahum Goldmann, born in a Polish *shtetl* and educated in Germany, was an energetic proponent of Zionism who emigrated to the United States after the Nazis came to power. One of the founders and later the long-serving President of the WJC, Goldmann played an active role in negotiating the post-war reparations agreements between Germany and Israel. Although a citizen of Israel from 1962, he was never permanently resident there.

the minister responsible for improving the housing and infrastructure in the occupied territories.[64] Yet there remained good reason to fear another 'nasty war', especially with the Soviet Union increasing its influence in the Arab countries, notably Egypt.[65] Warburg also worried that Israeli 'military actions [he at first wrote 'aggression'] for the sake of aggrandisement and ruthlessness beyond the requirements of defence would harm Israel's great cause and weaken the spiritual forces within the community'.*[66] It was presumably to diminish the risk of Soviet intervention in the Middle East that Warburg brokered a meeting between the Soviet scientist Grigori Bondarevsky (a Jewish academician known as 'the Professor') and Aharon Yariv, the Russian-born Chief of Israeli Military Intelligence in 1971.[67] Warburg was fleetingly encouraged when King Hussein of Jordan appeared to recognize Israel's legitimacy and right to security in February 1973.[68] But the renewal of hostilities by Egypt and Syria on 6 October (Yom Kippur) that year unleashed the 'nasty war' he had long anticipated. As in 1967, Warburg's first thoughts were for the safety of his daughter and granddaughter.[69] He was relieved that the Israelis were able to mount successful counterattacks in both Sinai and the Golan Heights, but remained pessimistic about the likelihood of a sustainable peace in the absence of major Israeli concessions.[70] The aggression had been against Israel rather than by Israel. The Israelis had suffered proportionately heavier casualties than their enemies. They had succeeded in driving their enemies back, surrounding an Egyptian army east of the Suez Canal and coming within striking distance of Damascus. Yet Warburg continued to argue that 'if Israel in the course of this year and next should give up most of the territories which were occupied after the Six Days' War and would receive only small rectifications of her territory this would be a good solution.'[71] In a draft peace plan dated June 1974, Warburg argued that in return for recognition by the Arab states, Israel should offer:

* Warburg was to have given this speech at a meeting of the Jerusalem Economic Conference in May 1973, but was forced to cancel his trip because of a bout of influenza. A truncated message from him was read aloud by another British delegate, but the passage about 'aggrandisement and ruthlessness' was omitted. Warburg privately admitted that he had not been sorry to miss the event as he regarded 'most of these conferences organised in Israel under the sponsorship of some of the Government departments as bad kinds of a human circus'.

[1] to help in the establishment of . . . a [Palestinian] state, provided satisfactory undertakings can be obtained from the Palestinian leaders as to the liquidation of their terrorist organisations.

[2] . . . [to] go back to the pre-1967 borders, provided that on both sides of these borders demilitarised zones of not less than, say, ten miles will be established.

[3] . . . to transform Jerusalem into a Free City, autonomously administered under multi-national trusteeship, and on the understanding that the holy places of the Arabs are as open to the Arabs as the holy places of the Jews are open to the Jews.[72]

The premise of this approach remained Warburg's pessimism about the internal health of Israel itself. As he privately admitted:

I am more worried than ever about the position in Israel, and that . . . however great may be the dangers . . . of Arab military power and Arab economic power, the greatest threat to Israel comes from within, namely from the lack of inner cohesion in the country. The present situation there reminds me much of the Weimar Republic . . . The opportunities which Israel has missed in the last six years to obtain a peaceful settlement – obviously of a compromise nature – are rather considerable in number and it is very unfortunate that even today too few people in Israel realise that time is working not for them but against them.[73]

Time and again, Warburg lamented that Israelis had succumbed to the 'infectious mental disease' of nationalism.[74] As he put it in a letter to Nahum Goldmann's son Guido: 'In the general world infection caused by a contagious stupidity, the Israelis are indeed very high on the sick list.'[75] By this time Warburg had wholly embraced Goldmann's vision of a two-state solution, in other words the creation of a Palestinian state alongside Israel. 'The Israelis cannot be told often enough', he wrote to the Austrian Chancellor Bruno Kreisky, 'that, just as they justifiably claim for themselves the right of an independent statehood, they should recognize a similar right for the Palestinians and that this recognition should be expressed not only ungrudgingly but with magnanimity.'[76]

II

Ironically, in view of Siegmund Warburg's increasingly critical view of Israel and conciliatory attitude towards the Arab states, it was in the wake of the Yom Kippur War that he became a target for anti-Zionist sentiment. The Arab powers might have failed in their bid to defeat Israel on the battlefield. But they were still able to flex their economic muscles in ways that rocked the world economy. On 15 October 1973 the members of the Organization of Arab Petroleum Exporting Countries announced that they were imposing an oil-export embargo on the United States in retaliation for US arms supplies to Israel during the war. (The plan to do something along these lines had in fact been hatched between Egypt and Saudi Arabia the previous August.) This was later extended to the Netherlands, because some of the American arms had reached Israel via Dutch airfields. With the Arab producers also cutting oil production by 25 per cent, the price of oil more than trebled, rising from $4.12 a barrel before the war to $12.92 by June 1974. This had the effect of driving up inflation in Western economies and exacerbating, if not triggering, a protracted recession. The energy crisis also led to a rapid accumulation of dollar reserves in the oil-exporting countries, so-called petrodollars which Western banks had every incentive to accumulate as deposits and recycle as loans. This provided the Arab states with an additional political lever.

Warburg had long understood that his public support for Israel might have consequences for his personal safety. In 1970, contemplating the risk of his being kidnapped or involved in a hijacking, he circulated a memorandum making it clear what the firm's position should be: 'If subsequent to any hostage manoeuvres my life would be saved as a result of paying ransom of a financial or other nature I would feel ashamed. It is my firm belief that fear is always a bad adviser and that it is better to sacrifice lives than to take an appeasing attitude towards blackmail.'[77] It was not his life that came under threat in 1974, however, but his business. Warburg was not slow to denounce the Arab oil embargo as 'blackmail' and to warn European governments against the temptation to appease OAPEC.[78] The British and French, in particular, he denounced as *Jämmerlingen* ('wretches') for their 'cowardly' responses to the embargo.[79] It was American firmness, he believed, that led to the ending of the embargo in March 1974. Warburg detected similar cowardice in certain quarters of the City of London when it emerged that the name of S. G. Warburg & Co. had been placed on an Arab blacklist of banks sympathetic to Israel, and that the cash-rich Arab banks would not participate in Eurobond issues if Warburgs, N. M. Rothschild or Lazard Frères were among the underwriters.[80]

Here was a direct threat to Warburgs' business, for exclusion from the recycling of petrodollars meant missing the biggest banking bonanza of the 1970s. According to Peter Stormonth Darling, at least one other blacklisted bank elected to 'roll over resignedly and accept the situation', but Warburgs took a very different line. In the words of David Scholey:

There were many occasions when people would say to us in arranging an issue for a borrower whom we knew, 'I'm sure you'll understand that we can't invite you into this because we have Middle Eastern bankers in the management groups.' And we always said: 'We don't understand, we don't think it's right and we don't think you should accept that sort of limitation.'[81]

As Martin Gordon later recalled, 'Any bank which committed a boycott act against us had a vociferously worded protest on its Chairman's desk within an hour of opening of business.' Gordon travelled to Japan to spell out to wavering clients that 'neutrality' was not an acceptable option if it meant accepting the exclusion of Warburgs – the founders of the Eurobond market – from underwriting syndicates.[82] In an interview with the American journalist Cary Reich, Warburg himself gave a similar account. 'Your firm was faced with virtual extinction in the Euromarket because of the Arab boycott,' Reich suggested (which was certainly an exaggeration). 'Yet you managed to stand up to the boycott much better than other blacklisted houses. How were you able to do that?' Warburg replied:

I think we were just tougher. I mean, I would ring up my friends in the important European banks and say, 'I hear you seem to be giving in to this blackmail of the Arabs. I think that is very unfair to us and it's wrong in itself. Shall I interpret that as meaning you sympathise with anti-Semitism? And don't kid yourself, we can – in the end – place just as well as those Arabs.'

REICH: In other words, you personally interceded and asked people why they were boycotting you?

WARBURG: And how I did. I certainly did not hesitate to use all the arguments, even some pretty, how shall I say, almost offensive arguments.

REICH: Do you think those appeals helped you to overcome the boycott?

WARBURG: I wouldn't [say] entirely, but to a large extent they did.

REICH: Did you ever figure out why you were on the blacklist, but Kuhn Loeb for instance wasn't?

WARBURG: It boiled down to the difference between the U.S. State Department and the British Foreign Office. I mean, this is not a question of slight nuances or shades of difference. It simply amounts to the fact that the State Department backed up the American firms while the British Foreign Office didn't do the same for the British ones.

REICH: That was the difference?

WARBURG: Nothing else.[83]

The reality was somewhat more complicated. The blacklist was never rigidly applied by the Arabs. According to one newspaper report, nearly half of $50 million of Eurobonds issued in January 1974 for British Steel Corporation ended up in the hands of Middle Eastern investors, including the Saudis, despite the fact that S. G. Warburg & Co. led the underwriters.[84] In February 1975 the Kuwait International Investment Company itself consented to appear alongside Warburgs and Rothschilds as underwriters for a $25 million Volvo Eurobond issue and a US bond issue for Mexico.[85] Warburg himself had every intention of helping to 'find . . . a home for some of the surplus funds of the oil producing countries which were now accumulating on such a terrifying scale'.[86] In May 1974, for example, he suggested to the chairman of Commerzbank, Paul Lichtenberg, 'that we should try out Prince Karamat Jah [the brother of the erstwhile Nizam of Hyderabad] in connection with possible placings in the Middle East, on the basis that he would be sponsored by Commerzbank'. Warburg noted that 'for obvious reasons our name should not be put into the foreground'.[87] A related idea, also involving Prince Karamat Jah, was for 'the formation of a European advisory group for Saudi Arabia under the chairmanship of Swiss Bank Corporation'.[88] Another way of dealing with the 'delicate matter' was to use the bank's Frankfurt subsidiary Effectenbank-Warburg, which the Arab Boycott Office in Damascus had somehow omitted from its blacklist.[89] In other words, Warburg considered ways of lowering his firm's profile in order to maintain business links with the Middle East. To Bernard Kelly, there was a whiff of hypocrisy here. It had been he who had proposed that Warburgs donate £100,000 to Israel at the time of the Yom Kippur War, a move actuated more by his desire to rehabilitate himself after a spat with the Uncles than by his own hitherto minimal Zionist sympathies. Yet it was also Kelly who first recognized the danger posed by the Arab boycott to the firm's international business if it was cut off from 'the middle East money bags'. He was baffled when Warburg's initial view was 'that we had over-reacted, that there was no real problem, that the [A]rabs really had no spare funds', and indignant when he tried to blame a lost Swedish mandate on negligence by Kelly, as opposed to the boycott.[90]

Nevertheless, Warburg was genuinely indignant when it then emerged that, under pressure from 'friends' in Kuwait, Commerzbank had dropped Warburgs from a Eurobond issue for Autoroutes Paris–Lorraine.[91] He also protested to Hermann Abs when Deutsche Bank requested that the name of Rothschild be omitted from the tombstone advertising a Eurobond issue for the European Investment Bank, again in response to Kuwaiti pressure.[92] When his counterparts at Paribas appeared to be weakening on the same issue, David Scholey took a firm line that clearly echoed Warburg's view of the matter:

We explained that we were fully aware of and sympathetic to the cause of Paribas's embarrassment vis-à-vis SGW & Co. We were all in favour of Paribas maximising their opportunity for profit out of their excellent connections in the Arab world and for this reason had made and would continue to make every effort to introduce to Paribas potential borrowers on a bilateral basis. However the question of publicly advertised Eurodollar issues was entirely different . . . the exclusion of SGW & Co. from underwriting lists was far from being a matter of honour or pride but potentially had a significant effect on our business. As we all know, the competitive instinct in the international investment banking market can at times be demonstrated with some rawness and, far more important than casual gossip between bankers, existing and potential customers may well have it frequently drawn to their attention that SGW & Co.'s effectiveness in the international market is demonstrably diminishing as can be seen from their absence in the underwriting lists.[93]

But the Paribas management would not commit themselves to withdrawing from any issue if Warburgs were excluded because of Arab pressure. Pierre Moussa, the French bank's chief executive, continued to fret that 'the business of Paribas in the Middle East – which . . . is at present about the most profitable part of Paribas' activities – could be endangered by the fact that SGW & Co. is on the Arab black list.'[94] Similar excuses were offered by Kleinwort Benson for excluding blacklisted banks from a $20 million Eurobond issue for the Japanese company Marubeni.[95] When Rolf Diel of Dresdner Bank asked for Warburg's 'understanding' that his firm would have to be excluded from the list of underwriters for a new Eurobond issue in deference to the wishes of the Kuwaiti sovereign wealth fund, Warburg replied that he 'would consider any concessions of Dresdner Bank towards KIIC in an unfavourable light, whatever his explanations might be and I felt that . . . Dresdner Bank's attitude would be picked up by the press with critical comments'. As he reported back to London, 'I feel that we cannot be tough enough in our attitude, i.e. though reserved in a dignified way making our disapproval unmistakably clear.'[96]

The threat of the press was probably a bluff, though Warburg directors were certainly authorized to brief journalists on the subject of the boycott. As Warburg explained to Goldmann, 'nothing has helped the Arabs so much with regard to boycott matters as the undue publicity given to this subject. If we want to do something useful and constructive with regard to the relevant subject the more we act outside the spotlights of the public media the better.'[97] Vindication came in 1976 when an attempt by the consortium bank Orion to exclude Warburgs and Rothschilds from an issue for the UK Electricity Council was quashed after Warburg protested privately to the Bank of England. The Governor, Gordon Richardson, summoned Orion's William de Gelsey and ordered him to stop the issue, stating coldly when Gelsey declared that it was too late: 'I think that you will find that it is not too late.' Orion had to tell the Kuwaitis that the deal was off and find an alternative source of foreign funding in Venezuela, which had no objection to Rothschild and Warburg involvement.[98] But this was one victory among many defeats. For some younger directors at Warburgs, it was a deeply alarming time, when the very future of the bank seemed to be at stake. Kelly repeatedly raised 'the troublesome matter of our lack of presence with the Arabs, and our inability to channel their funds to our clients, or engineer profitable transactions with them'. He and others were most worried that 'as a pro-Zionist bank . . . [the Arab] world is totally closed to us . . . The fearful thought is that there is nothing we can do'.[99] Henry Grunfeld's dry comment – 'You must remember that this is not the first time that difficulties have been placed in my way!' – helped to stiffen resolve.[100] 'At one of the darkest moments,' Martin Gordon later recalled, 'when I was in a black and depressed mood about our loss of business, Siegmund consoled me by saying that he had seen many worse things in his life and I should not allow it to depress me too much. This brought me up sharply.'[101] Grunfeld warned Kelly not to 'demoralise' the younger men with his 'too pessimistic' view that 'we are losing all our business'.[102]

Yet even as Warburg sought to counter the effects of the Arab black-list, he continued to distance himself from Israel. For example, he reduced his financial support for the organization known as Britain and Israel as well as for the Weizmann Institute.[103] In 1977, evidently at Warburg's instigation, Michael Gore – his right-hand man on Israeli matters – resigned from the board of Israel Corporation, ending a decade of association between Warburgs and the holding company.[104] A month later Warburg himself declined the offer of an honorary doctorate from the Weizmann Institute, 'in the light of recent political developments in Israel'.[105] A significant shift in Warburg's attitudes came after he met the Egyptian President Anwar Sadat for the first time in March that year, eight months before his historic visit to Israel. Like Henry Kissinger, Warburg was impressed by Sadat:

I was particularly struck by what I would call a very significant Jewish rhythm in expressing his views and in showing his reactions both by words and physical movements. I found him definitely 'sympathisch' as a human being while from an intellectual angle I observed in him a strange combination of directness and shrewdness on the one hand and a lack of sense for nuances on the other hand.[106]

Sadat had declared himself willing to make peace with Israel on the basis of United Nations Security Council Resolutions 242 and 338 (drawn up after the Six-Day War and the Yom Kippur War, respectively), which called for Israel to withdraw from the territories it had occupied in 1967 and for the Arab states to recognize Israel's right to exist within its pre-war frontiers. This offer had initially been received with scepticism by the Israeli Prime Minister Menachem Begin and with hostility by other Arab leaders. Yet Warburg was hopeful that, if enough American pressure were applied, the Israelis might come round. His advice to Sadat was to be patient, allowing a 'productive pause . . . for the necessary educational process among the many recalcitrant people both in the Arab and in the Israeli camps to make gradual and thorough progress'.[107] He was dismayed by Begin's policy of expanding Israeli settlements in the occupied territories, which he considered 'a breach of undertakings given by previous Israeli governments in regard to U.N. resolutions' as well as an expression of 'an attitude of fanatic nationalism contrary to the tenets of humanitarianism and tolerance which are among the best elements of Judaism'.[108]

For Warburg, Begin was the personification of 'chauvinism . . . unashamed nationalism and militant territorial expansionism'.[109] So negative was Warburg's assessment (he shared Ben-Gurion's view of Begin as a Zionist Hitler) that he underestimated the chances of a successful agreement between Egypt and Israel.[110] He saw Sadat, by contrast, as the man who would 'stand out in the world's history as an example of a leader who had the courage of taking utmost risks for the sake of peace' – as he told the Egyptian leader after their second meeting in February 1978.[111] This meeting prompted Warburg to write a letter to *The Times* exhorting Israel to react 'constructively and generously' to Sadat's peace offer and denouncing in the most emphatic terms the policy of settling the occupied territories:

The creation of a secure existence for a community is not identical with nationalistic opportunism. Safety in this world can never be guaranteed by more barbed wire. It can only result from a condition of reciprocal trust. While every friend of Israel – and I have been such continuously – must be aware of the urgency of providing all possible means for Israel's protection, this is the opposite of striving for the kind of territorial gains which merely increase dangers and risks rather than improve safety. It is one of several significant instances in this context that the present Government of Israel insists on the preservation and even extension of settlements outside the territories legally belonging to Israel. Far from adding to Israel's security, the maintenance and creation of such settlements are bound to expose Israel in general, and the settlers concerned in particular, to risks which are arbitrarily manufactured and senseless from the point of view of those who pray for a strong and forward looking Israel.[112]

Although this letter was hailed for its 'courage and wisdom' by the pro-Arab former Conservative minister Sir Anthony Nutting, it dismayed many British Zionists.[113] Indeed, by this time Warburg's position was so far out of the Anglo-Jewish mainstream that Victor Rothschild seriously wondered if he was having 'some talks with the PLO'.[114] This was prescient. Although Warburg despised the terrorist tactics of Yasser Arafat's organization, in 1981 he did in fact establish contact with the moderate PLO leader Isam Sartawi.[115]

It was not that Warburg was acting this way in order to get his firm taken off the Arab blacklist. On the contrary: his dislike of Begin and admiration of Sadat were both sincere and deeply rooted in his own political *Weltanschauung*, particularly his aversion to the 'nationalist pathology'. It genuinely surprised him that the two men were able to reach an agreement at Camp David in 1978 and to sign a peace treaty the following year (especially as he had a low opinion of President Jimmy Carter, whose one great achievement it was to broker the deal). Nor, however, was Warburg the kind of man to sit idly while other firms profited from his firm's handicap. As he pointed out to Claude de Kemoularia* of Paribas:

Our being on the black list – whilst houses such as Goldman Sachs, Lehmans or Loeb Rhoades are not – is utter nonsense. In this connection it should also be explained to those concerned that whilst several members of the aforementioned three New York houses are active members of the United Jewish Appeal's top organization and vociferous Zionists, no-one in SGW & Co. has ever identified himself with the United Jewish Appeal or with Zionism, but we have only given support for a prosperous, non-nationalistic Israeli homeland, and moreover had in our humble way tried to exercise influence in favour of a Middle East solution which would have to be just as fair to the Arabs as to the Israelis.[116]

* De Kemoularia had served as the UN Secretary-General Dag Hammarskjöld's personal assistant in the 1950s and had worked for Prince Rainier of Monaco in the 1960s.

Warburg was indeed increasingly irritated by those 'American Jews . . . [who] think they can combine the role of good Americans with the role of supporters of an utterly chauvinistic Israeli policy'.[117] As he told de Kemoularia, he had in fact received 'various invitations to visit Sadat in Egypt', but took the view that it 'would no doubt appear strange if a man on the black list' were suddenly to appear in Cairo.[118] On 3 October 1979 Warburg went so far as to offer his firm's services to Sadat 'with a view to reinforcing the international credit of Egypt and helping to develop Egypt's financial relations with the international banking and industrial communities'. This was a joint initiative with Lehman Brothers and Lazard Frères* and was intended to help Egypt address its chronic shortage of modern housing.[119]

Warburg had hoped that de Kemoularia could play the part of Henry Kissinger, conducting shuttle diplomacy between Warburgs and the Arabs.[120] Indeed, if Warburg had got his way, Kissinger himself after stepping down as secretary of state would have been recruited to his firm to play precisely this role (Kissinger opted instead to set up his own consulting firm).[121] However, when a deal was reached in the summer of 1980 it was on less than palatable terms. The Arabs would remove Warburgs from their blacklist provided 'that we would not be involved in any dealings with Israel' for at least two months, and that any future dealings with Israel would be conditional on the Arabs' approval.[122] Warburg would have none of this. From the outset, he told Geoffrey Seligman,

We made it absolutely clear that while we had never done anything and would never do anything to support Zionist nationalism we would not accept to be dictated to by any Arab quarters in our ordinary dealings with Israel and in our philanthropic help to non-political Israeli institutions such as the Weizmann Institute. I think we all agreed that any other attitude on our part would have been highly undignified. For the same reason we feel we should not consult de Kemoularia on whether it is appropriate or inappropriate for us to send members of the firm to Israel or to deal with Israeli business affairs.[123]

* The three firms had formed the so-called Troika in 1975 to advise governments around the world on their international financing requirements. The first such client was Indonesia. Others included Gabon, Gambia, Sri Lanka and Turkey.

Like his continued regular communication with the Israeli ambassador in London, Gideon Rafael, this makes it clear that Warburg's disillusionment with Israel was never total. Though chronically prone to overreact when disappointed by the latest object of his affections, in the case of Israel Warburg was able to forgive a great deal of both economic and political disappointment. The three aphorisms about Israel that Warburg recorded between 1967 and 1980 neatly summarize the trajectory of his disillusionment:

The second worst thing – after the Holocaust – which the Nazis did to the Jews was to force the Jews to make some other people homeless. (July 1967)

Israeli policy is today mainly based on three illusions: first that security depends on obstinacy and not on flexibility; secondly that security depends rather on geographical safeguards than on the support by one's few friends; thirdly that security depends above all on not giving away anything. (October 1975)

The policy pursued at present by Begin is supposed to provide Israel with defence and security positions but in reality creates a chain of hostages who will be at the mercy of Israel's enemies and help those who aim at Israel's destruction to achieve this aim. (August 1980)[124]

Begin remained Warburg's bête noire in the Middle East until the day he died. In one of his last letters on the subject, Warburg bracketed him together with the leader of the Iranian Revolution, Ayatollah Khomeini, as 'equally evil in their power-drunkenness and brutality'.[125] By contrast, as Warburg put it to the Mayor of Jerusalem, Teddy Kollek, he himself had always remained loyal to 'the ideals which in their different ways Chaim Weizmann and David Ben-Gurion have preached and practised'.[126] Or so it seemed to him. Three decades later, it is striking that the debate about future relations between Israelis and Palestinians continues to be couched in terms Warburg would have no difficulty recognizing. With his belief in a two-state solution and his opposition to the settlement of the occupied territories, Warburg was in many ways ahead of his time. What seemed then to be a radical, pro-Palestinian position is now the official policy of the US government.

III

It is impossible to understand the global upheaval precipitated by the Arab–Israeli War of 1973 without setting the Middle Eastern conflict in its Cold War context. But for the indefatigable and deft diplomacy of Henry Kissinger, the Soviet Union might have derived a great deal more advantage from the situation. The 1970s were an intensely difficult time for the United States, beginning with the agonizing withdrawal from South Vietnam and ending with the disaster of the Iranian Revolution. The world – and especially the Third World – appeared to be going the Soviet Union's way.[127] But American statecraft successfully marginalized the Soviet Union in the strategically vital Middle East. The transition of the Egyptian–Israeli relationship from war to peace was brokered almost exclusively by Washington. On the other hand, the consequences of Arab frustration – particularly the oil embargo – were highly disruptive to the economies of the Western world, while at the same time giving the Soviet system a stay of execution, if not a new lease of life.[128] The dramatic increase in oil prices exposed serious economic weaknesses not only in the United States but in a number of West European economies too, notably that of Britain. Policies loosely described as Keynesian, whereby monetary and fiscal policy had been used to maintain full employment (more often in response to impending elections than to actual recessions), had given rise to inflationary pressures which the energy crisis made acute.[129]

Like a number of other Western intellectuals, notably the Harvard economist John Kenneth Galbraith and the Dutch Nobel prizewinner Jan Tinbergen,[130] Siegmund Warburg believed that the United States and the Soviet Union were converging. 'What we are experiencing today', he wrote in April 1967, 'is a strong evolution – on the one hand in Soviet Russia and on the other hand in the old Capitalist countries of the West – in opposite directions' towards the same destination:

namely in Soviet Russia from Socialism to a mercantilist system and in the old Capitalist countries of the West from Capitalism to a mercantilist system. I use the term mercantilist deliberately in the sense of . . . the eighteenth century. It is interesting that the new mercantilism which is in the process of formation is similar in both cases . . . namely containing a mixture between three elements: first, overall government planning, secondly, partial government ownership of the means of production and thirdly, partial private ownership of the means of production.[131]

Such musings suffered a blow when the Soviets sent their tanks into Prague the following year. Warburg promptly reverted to his earlier view that the USSR was 'a ruthless regime which acts counter to any respect for personal values in general and privacy in particular'.[132] As late as 1975 he could envisage 'the Southern flank of Europe from Portugal to Spain in the West to Greece and Turkey in the East' as 'almost an invitation for interference from Russia'.[133]

At the same time, Warburg found himself warming to the man who had – after a long, hard political struggle – fought his way to the White House in 1968. Richard Nixon had always struck Warburg as a 'mediocrity'. His election he had regarded as an 'expected though unhappy shock'.[134] There was little natural rapport when they met for the first time in London in February 1969.[135] But by 1970 Warburg had to acknowledge that the President was 'not without strong elements of courage and dynamic energy'.[136] Fifteen months later he was defending Nixon's 'courage' and 'leadership'.[137] By September 1972, it seemed to Warburg that Nixon was 'next to Truman . . . the best American President so far in this century because, like Truman, he combines common sense and courage although he lacks brilliancy'.[138] Nixon's Vietnam policy was, in Warburg's view, 'the opposition [sic] of the appeasement policies which were practised in the thirties and which led to Hitler's war and to Hitler's atrocities':

I know few things are nowadays as fashionable among international intellectuals as attacks on Nixon and on his policy in Vietnam. However, as we know from historical experience – even going back as far as the period of Athens at the end of the Peloponnesian war – there are certain continuously recurring types of intellectuals who detest straightforward realism and common sense but who love to indulge in . . . wishful non-thinking.[139]

For Warburg, the Watergate scandal represented more than just 'a widespread revulsion against some actual misdeeds committed at a slightly lower level at the White House'; it was a symptom of that 'general hysteria . . . [which] in our time of excessive press activities is a more contagious illness than either cholera or smallpox ever were'.[140] Such views, needless to say, accorded well with those of another Jewish refugee from Nazi Germany whose career in the United States had been even more brilliant than Warburg's in the United Kingdom. So highly did Warburg esteem Henry Kissinger that, even before the latter stepped down as secretary of state, he was being considered as a possible future director of S. G. Warburg & Co. Kissinger struck him as nothing less than 'the greatest hope of our Western world of to-day'.[141]

What vitiated this hope was Warburg's deepening pessimism about the Western economies. Their difficulties could be summed up in a single word coined by the Conservative MP and editor of the *Spectator* Iain Macleod as early as 1965: stagflation. In Britain the annual increase in the retail price index peaked at 27 per cent in August 1975, the worst inflation the country experienced in the entire twentieth century. For the decade as a whole, the average rate was just under 13 per cent, roughly the same as for Greece, Italy, Portugal and Spain. The United States fared better, with an average inflation rate of just over 7 per cent. More serious was the volatility of US growth. The decade saw two recessions: one that lasted from December 1969 to November 1970, the other from November 1973 to March 1975. On average, growth was a full percentage point lower in the 1970s than in the 1960s: real GDP increased at an average annual rate of 3.6 per cent compared with 4.6 per cent between 1960 and 1969. The US unemployment rate rose from 4.6 per cent in October 1973 to a peak of 9 per cent in May 1975. For financial markets, stagflation spelt double trouble. With corporate profits squeezed, returns on stocks turned negative. With inflation surging, bonds offered no protection. Between 1970 and 1979, the average annual return on UK stocks was minus 1.4 per cent, allowing for inflation; on bonds the return was minus 4.4 per cent.[142] In inflation-adjusted terms, the FT-Actuaries All-Share Index – the broadest London index – fell by 74 per cent between 1972 and 1974. As late as 1979 it was still at 43 per cent of its 1972 level.

Warburg was only a little better prepared for this storm than the man in the street. In 1966 he had conveyed his fears of inflation to the journalist Joseph Wechsberg:

He is convinced that money is becoming worth less all the time. He speaks wistfully about the wise law of Solon in Athens that all debts not paid back within seventy years must be cancelled. People who contract debts pay the interest. But . . . the money they pay back [today] is always worth less . . . Warburg's 'painful experience' after the First World War, when bondholders lost nearly everything while shareholders who didn't sell eventually came out all right, has formed his basic investment philosophy.[143]

But what exactly did that 'philosophy' mean in practice? Although he was right to expect 'further heavy falls' both on Wall Street and in the City, his advice to Nahum Goldmann in August 1970 to 'be about half invested in equities and half invested in fixed interest securities' – the latter of which promised 'a really worthwhile income . . . coupled with maximum security' – was woefully inadequate.[144] Goldmann would have done much better to stick to equities, and better still to buy gold. Even in a quicksilver mind like Warburg's, expectations adapt more slowly than in neo-classical economic theory. Henry Grunfeld admitted many years later how completely he too had been taken by surprise by inflation, and how little he and Warburg had been able to do to protect their bank from its ravages.[145] It was not until June 1974 that Warburg saw the need for a new kind of index-linked bond that would offer investors protection against inflation – an idea he immediately proposed to the British government.[146] It was finally adopted in 1981, and has since become a well-established form of investment on both sides of the Atlantic. Meanwhile, inflation and currency depreciation wreaked havoc with Britain's merchant banks, rendering them (as the *Economist* remarked) the 'genteel poor of the international banking community'. The value of Hill Samuel's assets, for example, declined by nearly half in real terms between 1973 and 1977.[147] In 1969 Bernard Kelly's gross salary, including the fees from his various company directorships and extra pension payments, had been £21,000, which equates to around £644,000 in today's money. But by 1975 his nominally higher package of £35,000 was more than a third lower in terms of purchasing power: that equates to around £405,000 in today's pounds.

For Warburg it was obvious as early as 1968 that the system of fixed exchange rates established at Bretton Woods in 1944 was doomed. Unlike the French economist Jacques Rueff, Warburg ruled out a return to the gold standard as likely to 'create conditions almost exactly the opposite to those we desire'. Yet he was also doubtful about the idea of an 'international certificate through a world bank . . . backed up by the leading industrial powers', which seemed unlikely to work in the absence of a government based on global federalism of the sort sketched by Churchill's literary agent, the Hungarian-born writer and publisher Emery Reves, a friend and client of Eric Korner.[148] That left the dollar. Warburg had no illusions about the problems created by American capital exports and unrequited transfers (to Vietnam and other hotspots) in the late 1960s. French dissatisfaction with the 'torrent of dollars' was no secret; nor was the resulting upward pressure on the deutschmark, which forced the German authorities to accept a 10 per cent revaluation in 1969 and to float the mark in 1971. But Warburg agreed with Nat Samuels that the 'torrent of dollars to the world . . . now constitute[s] the major resource of the international market'. The success of the Eurobond market had shown that 'the corporate managers of all countries take convertibility and the increasing financial integration of the world literally, while central bank governors and finance ministers sometimes tremble when the implications become explicit'.[149] This was true as far as it went. The Eurobond market continued to function despite currency uncertainties and stock-market slumps. But investors' preference for deutschmarks and Swiss francs drove up short-term Eurodollar interest rates.[150] As Warburg put it in a letter to Jean Furstenberg in September 1970: 'I expect that the malaise in our Western world will grow from bad to worse before we reach the bottom of the recession which started at the beginning of this year.'[151]

Warburg watched with some impatience the long, lingering death of Bretton Woods. He was dismissive of the 'perverted gold hallucinations' of 'intellectuals who are more brilliant than sound', and urged the United States to sever the link between the dollar and gold sooner rather than later.[152] The 'gold complex', he argued, was one of 'many kinds of superstition which are highly contagious diseases of the mind'.[153] 'Gold somnambulism' was another of the terms of abuse he reserved for proponents of a return to pre-war ways; he was enraged by the French attempt to undermine the paramountcy of the dollar by 'going for gold'.[154] So Warburg could hardly disapprove when Nixon finally ended the (vestigial and limited) convertibility of the dollar into gold on 15 August 1971. He had no faith in the short-lived compromise arrangement, which allowed currencies to fluctuate by up to 2.25 per cent above or below their Bretton Woods rates. Nevertheless, he was dismayed by the onset of 'monetary anarchy', to which he responded from February 1973 by holding 'as much money as possible in Swiss Francs or German Marks' – something his residence in Switzerland allowed him to do, since it removed him from the UK exchange controls.[155] The great 'realignment' of currencies of the early 1970s was indeed more chaotic than he had anticipated. While two major currencies depreciated relative to the dollar – the British pound and the Italian lira – the rest grew markedly stronger, led by the deutschmark and the Swiss franc. Within Europe the moves were dramatic: in deutschmark terms the pound slid from just above 4.00 in 1969 to 1.72 by the end of 1979, more than doubling the cost of German imports to British consumers. The price of gold soared twentyfold from below $36 an ounce in July 1970 to a peak of $850 in January 1980. Yet the pound actually appreciated against the dollar after North Sea oil began to flow in 1975. The oil shock was an ill wind indeed, since the last thing Britain's despairing industrialists needed in the late 1970s was a strengthening pound.

The problem, as Warburg saw it, was that 'the so-called monetary experts . . . are obsessed either consciously or unconsciously . . . [with the idea] that all important countries should have simultaneously favourable balances of trade and favourable balances of payment'. By comparison with more recent times, the US trade deficit in the 1970s seems trivial in size, as do the capital outflows of the early 1970s. The largest trade deficit run by the United States in the 1970s was 1.5 per cent of GDP. Net US assets abroad rose from 0.9 per cent of GDP in 1970 to 2.8 per cent in 1976. Warburg understood that such imbalances were an inevitable consequence of the increasing integration of the global markets for goods and capital. Yet he underestimated the disruptive consequences of economic policies that aimed more at short-run political advantage than at long-run macroeconomic stability. His insistence, in November 1973, that 'viewed in a long-term perspective, the dollar ought to be the strongest currency in the western world' flew in the face of the distinctly different policies being pursued by central banks in Washington, Frankfurt, Zurich and Tokyo.[156] Significantly, he began arguing for restoring fixed parities 'as far as at all possible' as early as May 1974.[157] 'Floating currencies are proving too volatile and too permissive,' he complained in late 1977. 'A new currency system, incorporating fixed parities, is needed to replace Bretton Woods.'[158] The scheme he sketched was for 'an enlargement of the International Monetary Fund into a sort of Central bank of Central bankers' which 'would thereby obviate the necessity of the dollar being the world's reserve currency'.[159] By now he had come to believe that since 'the fundamental causes of the dollar's weakness, namely the trade deficit and particularly the level of oil imports, remained uncorrected . . . the dollar could no longer play the role of a reserve currency now that the U.S. was a substantial debtor nation'.[160] This was an analysis that would come to be shared by more and more economists in the subsequent thirty years, as the US current account deficit grew and the dollar gyrated up and down, along with the price of oil. We are, however, no closer to embracing the radical remedy Warburg proposed.

As with Israel, so with Europe: the crisis of 1973 saw Warburg's love turn to disillusionment. As far as he could see, the Europeans were guilty of ingratitude towards the United States. Was it not time, he half seriously suggested to Cecil King over lunch in May 1971, for a European 'Marshall Aid plan for the U.S. to help them out of their troubles caused by overseas aid and the Vietnam War'?[161] The United States should stop its 'appeasement policy in economic affairs both towards Japan and towards Europe', and remind those who complained about 'excessive American investments in Europe' that 'the large volume of these investments has been one of the main contributory factors in developing the European prosperity of the last two decades'. After a meeting with the American Commerce Secretary Peter Peterson in February 1973, he argued that:

The Americans must in their own interest as well as in the interest of the free world as a whole assume the leadership in regard to international economic measures without however expecting to achieve a unanimous following by the countries of Europe and by Japan . . . I am convinced that the majority of the European nations . . . will join a strong lead from the USA, always provided that such leadership . . . goes forward on the premise that the Dollar is essentially the only really international currency and that the USA will proceed either multilaterally together with those who accept this self-evident premise or otherwise unilaterally without any consideration for those so-called trading partners who have largely made the USA the suckers of Europe and of Japan.[162]

The European leaders, particularly the British Prime Minister Edward Heath and the French President Georges Pompidou, were 'the Munich men of our time and even worse than Chamberlain and Daladier' – a fine example of late-Warburg hyperbole. Europe was losing the 'will to fight for ideals'.[163] His only (ultimately well-founded) consolation was 'that however great the self-destructive tendencies are in the West ultimately the self-destructive tendencies of the Russians will be even greater'.[164] Warburg correctly identified the Russian invasion of Afghanistan at the end of 1979 as a turning point, not least because it would help the Americans to get 'rid of their Vietnam complex' and 'at last [be] prepared to act in certain important directions as an imperialistic power and . . . no longer [be] ashamed to do so'.[165]

Time and again, Warburg's reading of the sequence of international crises in the 1970s was accurate. He saw clearly the geopolitical implications of the currency chaos that followed the breakdown of Bretton Woods, discerning that the volatile new world of unregulated capital flows would ultimately benefit the United States and its allies more than the Eastern bloc. It would be wrong, however, to portray Warburg as infallible. Of all his misjudgements, perhaps none was so wide of the mark as his assessment of the Shah of Iran, whom he repeatedly ranked alongside Kissinger as one of the two world leaders who were not 'utter mediocrities'.[166] Warburg was convinced that Iran was the Middle Eastern country with the brightest future, though he was persuaded by the more sceptical Henry Grunfeld not to open a permanent office there, since hotel rooms were easier to leave in a hurry. The Shah's overthrow and the advent of the Islamic Republic of Iran plunged American foreign policy into a new crisis from which the presidency of Jimmy Carter never recovered. 'Malaise' was a word that came to be associated with Carter, though he did not in fact use it in his famously gloomy speech of 15 July 1979, five months after the Shah's overthrow and the beginning of the Iranian hostage crisis. Instead, he spoke of 'a crisis of confidence . . . that strikes at the very heart and soul and spirit of our national will . . . [and threatens] to destroy the social and political fabric of America'. In Warburg's eyes this crisis was all too legible and extended beyond the United States to afflict the entire Western world.

IV

With all his flaws, Siegmund Warburg was a prophet of globalization. As early as 1969, he took the view that 'Industrialism today demands exchanges between the populations of the five Continents and aims at the free flow of goods and services without any artificial barriers. In short, modern industrialism is an all-powerful, deep-seated, all-encompassing force, the basic characteristic of which is universalism . . .'[167] Yet in practice Warburg was always very cautious about involving his firm in what would later become known as emerging markets. He viewed Latin America with an unyielding suspicion born of recurrent defaults and devaluations. He had almost nothing at all to do with Communist countries, and reacted with scepticism in 1972 to the expressed 'desire of . . . President Ceauşescu to develop Rumania's links with western industry through our intermediary'.[168] Even as late as 1974, by which time there was a veritable scramble by East European countries to raise money on Western capital markets, Warburg still held back, fearing (rightly) that the borrowers might end up defaulting on their debts.[169] Unlike many other bankers, Warburg was never blind to 'the contrast which consists in the Soviet bloc on the one hand of excessive military power and on the other hand of frightful economic weakness throughout that whole conglomerate of nations'.[170] As he later put it, his firm consistently 'tried to concentrate . . . apart from the United Kingdom, on the Continent of Europe and on North America . . . in other parts of the world, without wishing to be rigid, we tried not to get involved with local financial instruments.' Globalization, in other words, essentially meant the integration of Britain, Western Europe, the United States and Canada. The sole exception to this rule was Japan – perhaps the happiest of Warburg's late love affairs.

There was in fact a tradition of Warburg involvement in Japanese finance, dating back to M. M. Warburg and Kuhn Loeb's leading role in the Japanese foreign bond issues around the time of the Russo-Japanese War of 1904–5. This was revived in October 1962 when Warburg and his wife joined Sir Alexander Hood of Schroders, Edmund de Rothschild and others* as part of a City of London delegation invited to visit Japan by Tsunao Okumura, the chairman of Nomura Securities.[171] Significantly, John Schiff had made a similar visit two years previously, representing Wall Street in all its pomp.[172] The aim of the British trip was, as Warburg put it, 'to see . . . to it that Japanese/American financial relations will not entirely overshadow what might possibly be done between Britain and Japan',[173] though the restrictions on British capital export clearly limited what he and his fellow delegates had to offer their hosts. Warburg met with six different Japanese Cabinet ministers during his visit, pronouncing the most enthusiastic verdicts on Hayato Ikeda, the Prime Minister ('clearly a comprehensive "dirigiste"'), and Kiichi Miyazawa, the future Minister of International Trade and Industry and later Prime Minister ('not only a first-class economist but altogether a highly cultivated intellectual' – praise indeed from Warburg). But the only real friendship he made in Japan was with the Cambridge-educated Jiro Shirasu, a close adviser to Prime Minister Shigeru Yoshida and a key Japanese negotiator on constitutional questions during the post-war American occupation. With Shirasu's guidance, Warburg was quick to grasp the distinctive way in which the Japanese economy worked, with the Bank of Japan acting as 'the central executive of the economic planning policy of the Government' and treating the commercial banks 'more or less like departments or branch offices'. The commercial bankers themselves struck him as 'with very few exceptions excessively keen to get foreign loans, and much too optimistic, rather thinking on the lines that an unlimited rise in Japanese economic activity was somewhat inevitable'. Similarly, most of the securities brokers seemed 'rather irresponsible in the way in which they talked about investments, only intent on getting buying orders, and . . . only influenced by day-to-day involvements in the markets'.

On the other hand, the industry and austerity of ordinary Japanese workers were bound to appeal to him. They worked hard. They were

---

* Among the others were representatives of Baring Brothers, M. Samuel & Co., Westminster Bank, the Hongkong & Shanghai Banking Corporation, Panmure Gordon and Scottish United Investors. The delegation had the blessing of the Bank of England.

punctual. They were thrifty and 'extremely restrained both in eating and drinking, and very modest in regard to their housing conditions and the way they live altogether'. Standards of hygiene were superior to those in Europe. To be sure, Warburg struggled with the reluctance of hosts to speak their minds and noted the lack of 'a democratic spirit in the European or American sense'. The system of economic planning meant that too much power was 'being concentrated on a small top of an enormous pyramid' of bureaucrats. Strict labour laws also made it difficult for industrial firms to lay off workers. Yet these were minor concerns compared with the 'enormous industrial opportunities' which Japan was 'in an exceptionally good position to make use of . . . above all, through the high standard of education prevailing on every level, and through the amazingly keen interest which young and adult people alike take in improving their knowledge and their capabilities'.[174] Many of these were qualities the Japanese shared with their wartime allies the Germans, of course, but Warburg could not resist noting that they possessed 'to a remarkable extent, one quality among others which very few Germans have, namely, modesty'.[175] He returned with a real appetite to do business with Japan, and particularly with the Bank of Tokyo, Industrial Bank of Japan, Nomura Securities and Daiwa Securities. Tokyo, he told his uncle Fritz, was like 'a mixture between Berlin in the Twenties and the Detroit of today'.[176]

In the years that followed, Warburg cultivated his new connections in Japan, dining with Okumura when he visited London and employing Shirasu's son at Warburgs.[177] Shirasu, in return, acted as a kind of 'unofficial adviser to Warburgs' in Tokyo, hosting dinners for visitors from 30 Gresham Street – led by Ian Fraser and Peter Spira – and ensuring that they met the right Japanese counterparties.[178] The first major Japanese deal came in 1963 with a loan for the Tokyo city government. A year later Warburgs collaborated with Nomura to arrange a convertible dollar loan for Toyo Rayon (later Toray), the textile firm.[179] Matters were somewhat complicated by turf wars with Wall Street firms – first Dillon Read, then Kuhn Loeb – that regarded themselves as having prior claims to certain kinds of Japanese business.[180] But the increasing efforts of the American authorities to limit US overseas investment gave Warburg an opportunity to pitch the benefits of the Eurobond market as a future source of finance for

Japan.[181] The only constraint (identified by Spira) was that the firm was committing too few senior people to the Japanese market, where 'maturity is especially important'.[182] By contrast, Warburg himself felt strongly that 'two to three visits a year would be about right'.[183] Familiarity, he seemed to fear, might breed contempt. Shirasu agreed, telling Christopher Purvis:

The curious thing about the relationship between him and Siegmund was that over the twenty years between their meeting in 1962 and Siegmund's death in 1982 they rarely wrote to each other and only spent a very small number of hours in total in each other's company whether in Tokyo or in London; but Jiro . . . counted Siegmund as one of his very closest friends.[184]

As was perhaps inevitable, Warburg himself had by 1970 cooled somewhat towards the land of the Asian miracle. Indeed, at times he sounded almost afraid of the prodigious strength of the Japanese economy. 'My prognosis', he told Joshua Sherman, '[is] that in 20 years from now our old earth will probably be dominated by a Chinese–Japanese alliance, once the Japanese have drawn out of the Americans whatever advantages could be derived . . . from that quarter.'[185] Japan's rise was the antithesis of the Western malaise. It seemed inevitable that Japan and China would 'get together by the end of this century'. 'I only hope', Warburg mused, 'that by the time they obtain world domination, they will have become more mellow and civilised than they are now.'[186] Partly for these reasons, and partly out of his customary aversion to risk, Warburg declined a suggestion by Shirasu that he invest in an office building in downtown Tokyo. Fortunately for the firm, his younger colleagues were free from such forebodings. Martin Gordon and Andrew Smithers, in particular, played a crucial role in developing and deepening S. G. Warburg's relations with Japanese business, as did Martin Edelshain, who ran the permanent Warburgs office in Tokyo established in the 1970s. By this time the Bank of Tokyo regarded S. G. Warburg as its principal European partner; indeed, throughout Japan the name of Warburgs now ranked above some of the longer-established British merchant banking names.[187]

As Martin Gordon recalled, some Japanese mores accorded well with the ways of Gresham Street:

Whereas other firms sometimes complained of the excessive interference of MOF [the Ministry of Finance], to us it was second nature to cooperate with MOF, and to make sure that any business we did in Japan followed the spirit and not just the letter of the law and the prevailing guidelines. Our [written] internal communication compared with the highest Japanese standards, and could not fail to earn us respect in Japan. On top of all the above, Siegmund believed in good manners and courtesy and personal communication to the most refined degree and, in a country like Japan, where good manners are an art, even a game – but a serious game – Siegmund's own example caused enormous appreciation in Japanese circles. As a result, those of us involved in our business in Japan regarded it as a hobby, and never as a burden. Interaction with Japanese people was always a pleasure and we took great care never to look unintelligent, or gross, or discourteous in Japanese eyes. Indeed we learnt things from doing business in Japan which could usefully be applied in all other societies.[188]

When the Japanese government bestowed the First Class Order of the Sacred Treasure* on Warburg in 1978 – an honour he travelled to Tokyo to receive – it consummated a decade and a half of sustained engagement.[189] In addition to lavish hospitality,† not to mention multiple opportunities to broker new deals, this second and last visit to Japan provided Warburg with reassurance that, contrary to his fears in 1962, the Japanese had not been 'overawed and over-influenced by the industrialism of the American/European societies and their excessive emphasis on a self-indulgent consumer economy': 'In contrast, I find it highly interesting to observe now that there has been in recent years in many Japanese groups side by side with wide-ranging economic progress a renaissance of old, simple and dignified traditions which are cultivated not only on the surface, and which promise the evolution of a new structure of their society based on high spiritual standards.'[190] They were ascetics like him, after all.

*

* The honour was lower in status than the Order of the Rising Sun and was quite frequently bestowed on foreigners who had been good friends to Japan. It was nevertheless a mark of official esteem that Warburg received the First Class version, since there were eight classes in all. Another recipient of the honour was the economist Milton Friedman.
† Present at one reception were the Governor of the Bank of Japan and the presidents of all the major Japanese banks and securities houses.

Warburg's deep-rooted puritanism made him susceptible to the notion, which became fashionable in the 1970s, that there were real and ultimately insuperable 'limits to growth' (the title of the famous report published by the Club of Rome think tank in 1972).[191] 'Economic and technical growth' were not, he wrote in April 1972, a 'perpetuum mobile'; to believe this was to fall victim to 'a kind of escalation psychosis (Steigerungspsychose)'.[192] For Warburg, the 1970s energy crisis was in fact 'a blessing in disguise':

It will of course in the first place lead to many upsetting changes throughout the economies of the Western world including an avalanche of bankruptcies or similar financial difficulties but it will result in a long overdue purge and after excessive expansion in many wrong directions there is a good chance of more sober attitudes evolving and expressing themselves in constructive actions. It will be a very slow development but I believe sounder conditions may ensue than those from which we have suffered in recent years.[193]

'The growth complex of our Western world' was based on the assumption 'that in the economic sphere – contrary to the sphere of anatomy, biology and psychology and altogether contrary to the laws of the natural sciences – trees can grow into the sky'.[194] This complex, in Warburg's view, was the 'cause of our galloping inflation in the monetary field and the deterioration in our moral, intellectual and aesthetic standards'.

Yet Warburg also understood that lower growth would inevitably be associated with higher unemployment. On this point his views were more than usually heterodox. For Warburg, 'neither fiscal nor monetary nor any other economic measures' could 'deal satisfactorily with the twin problems of inflation and unemployment'. The problem was simply 'the obsolescence of human labour':

For we have to realize that at today's stage of industrial development we are faced in most of the industrialised countries with the dilemma that the more we improve the industrial machinery the more we create unemployment. To fight unemployment by inflation will only have short-term effects followed by crises of still longer duration and further magnitude. Unemployment arises from the saving of labour by the steadily increasing use of industrial technology, and this is an almost automatic process towards more and more industrial unemployment . . .

This was problematic not because of the hardship involved, which had been much reduced by the rise of the welfare state, but only because 'it is generally considered a social stigma to draw unemployment benefits, just as many from the point of view of human dignity assumedly inferior functions – domestic services or manual operations connected with public cleansing are only two instances among a great number of so-called degrading occupations – are looked upon as being afflicted by a similar social stigma'. The only answer was for Western societies to:

arrive at a new direction and division of labour under which the jobs which suffer from a social stigma have to be done by conscripted labour to which every able-bodied human being will have to be subjected for a limited period of time, a system which had been especially advocated by Mao Tse Tung. More important still: many kinds of labour will have to be apportioned over, say, a three-day working week or, say, a five-month working year. Furthermore a large number of additional fringe occupations will have to be created or extended in regard to such work as gardening, or use of leisure time or companionship of the old and ill. Such fringe occupations may have to be carried on without remuneration or with relatively small rewards.[195]

'Perhaps', Warburg reflected in 1977, 'we will try one of these days to copy the old Egyptians who kept people busy by building pyramids. This would in any case be healthier and less harmful than the crazy increase in armaments.'[196] No doubt pyramids would have been preferable to yet more nuclear warheads. The irony of this statement, however, was that Warburg himself was by this time embroiled in the laborious and ultimately deeply frustrating task of building a financial pyramid, at the apex of which S. G. Warburg & Co. was supposed to stand.

12

Expensive Lessons

My feeling is that in the last few years our momentum is some-
what slackening and our style slightly deteriorating through a
proliferation of committees, through excessive tolerance of
mediocrities, and through the tendency towards a hectic prestis-
simo *tempo rather than the maintenance of a steady, streamlined*
rhythm. Here again I blame myself for omitting to retire in a
more decisive way . . . An old man like me should not overstay
his welcome or outlive his usefulness in the surroundings in
which he played at one time a rather decisive role and he must
above all be careful not to add to the problems of those who
come after him.

Siegmund Warburg, December 1977[1]

I

It was not easy to be the son of Sir Siegmund Warburg. Even after
resigning as a director of S. G. Warburg & Co. in 1963, at the age of
thirty-five, George Warburg continued to live in the shadow of his
dominant, demanding father. In 1970 he resolved to emerge into the
light. In partnership with his friend Milo Cripps, the nephew of the
former Labour Chancellor Stafford Cripps,* he set up C.W. Capital

---

* Milo Cripps, fourth Baron Parmoor (1929–2008), was an Ampleforth- and Oxford-
educated Roman Catholic whose early, somewhat eclectic career was marred by
alcoholism. (He gave up drinking after gate-crashing one of his mother's dinner parties,
rugby-tackling the principal guest and vomiting on the floor.) It was his mother who
persuaded Siegmund Warburg – her neighbour in Eaton Square – to give Cripps a job

Ltd – an abbreviation doubtless chosen to avoid a clash with his father over the use of the sacrosanct family name, though also (as Cripps himself joked) because 'W. C. Capital' was not really an option.[2] The firm, George told Henry Grunfeld, was to be a merchant bank, 'active mainly as financial advisers and as investment managers' but perhaps also taking deposits and making loans. With ordinary share capital of £500,000 and thirteen employees, C.W. was conspicuously not backed by S. G. Warburg & Co. Instead, its principal investor was the august banking house of Williams & Glyn.[3] Warburg *père* naturally kept a wary eye on Warburg *fils*, expressing guarded interest in the new firm's agency relationship with New England Merchants National Bank.[4] Dealings with S. G. Warburg were entrusted to a young American, who lost little time in requesting a short-term lending facility of £250,000 from Warburgs. The response from 30 Gresham Street was cool. While it was certainly 'Sir Siegmund's wish . . . to develop a relationship with C.W. Capital', nevertheless the upper bound for such credit would be £100,000 'until such time as we obtain a clearer picture of the nature of their lending'.[5] By March 1972, the desired clarity had been attained. With assets of nearly £9 million, C.W. had made – as Warburg Senior was happy to admit – 'fine progress'.[6] In January 1973 he gave his blessing to a fateful name change: C.W. became Cripps Warburg.[7] Shortly afterwards Warburgs invested £225,000 in the form of partly convertible unsecured bonds (equivalent, if they were converted, to around 2.5 per cent of the firm's equity). With the backing of both the family name and the family firm, Cripps Warburg grew by leaps and bounds. By the end of March 1973, its balance sheet had more than quadrupled to £37 million. It seemed the perfect opportunity to put aside 'former misunderstandings' and begin a new era of harmony between father and son:

---

as a filing clerk in 1960. So impressed was Warburg by Cripps's intellect that by 1964 he had been made a director of the bank and rose to be head of the Investment Department. However, Warburg came to suspect him of 'megalomaniac tendencies' and there was a difficult parting of the ways five years later. To his friends, however, Cripps was an irresistible man, 'exuberant in everything; avid for the next deal, for the sight of a previously unvisited cathedral, for an unusual chocolate cake – avid for life . . . fired at a whiter heat than the rest of us'. A (somewhat) repressed homosexual, he found happiness and success after Cripps Warburg in reinvigorating the antiquarian book dealer Bernard Quaritch, of which he became chairman.

The old English sentence 'all's well that ends well' might often sound rather like a platitude [wrote Warburg to his son]. Still it is frequently true with regard to serious and important matters, and it seems to me to apply definitely to what happened recently between you and me.

After you and I have marched forward for several years on somewhat diverging roads it is doubly satisfying and cheering to know that our two roads – though rightly remaining separate so as to do justice to individual strength and autonomy on both sides – have now become parallel in a very fine sense, namely based on deep mutual friendship and respect and going for similar goals and under similar standards.[8]

The reconciliation, however, was to prove agonizingly short lived.

Cripps Warburg acquired its new name on the eve of one of the greatest banking crises in modern British history. From the vantage point of today, the so-called secondary banking crisis has a distinctly familiar look to it. It had its origins in the relaxation of credit controls by the Conservative Chancellor of the Exchequer Anthony Barber in 1971, which ended the fixing of deposit and lending rates by the cartel of London clearing banks and introduced a new Reserve Asset Ratio rule requiring banks to hold just 12.5 per cent of their liabilities in reserve assets. The results were unintentionally explosive. Bank lending leaped upwards, increasing by 33 per cent in 1973.[9] This, as much as the oil shock, explains Britain's surge to double-digit inflation. But far more dramatic was the increase in house price inflation, as the liberalization of banking regulation and cuts in direct taxation fuelled a classic asset bubble. At their peak in late 1972, existing home prices were rising at an annual rate of more than 40 per cent. On average, the price of British housing doubled in the space of just four years. At the same time, there was a stock-market boom. From its low point in March 1971, the *Financial Times* ordinary share index rose by two-thirds in the space of just fourteen months. Monetary tightening failed to tame inflation, but it did succeed in bringing house price inflation back down to single digits. The least intended consequence of all this was a stock-market crash. By the end of 1974, the FT All-Share index was down a wrenching 69 per cent from its peak. Adjusted for inflation, the losses were even greater – comparable, indeed, with the losses suffered by American investors in the Great Depression. For the new banks that had proliferated in the heady days of the Barber boom, the effects were catastrophic, particularly for those who had lent most enthusiastically to property developers. Around thirty banks had to be bailed out by the Bank of England, most famously Slater Walker (the bank founded in 1964 by the corporate raider Jim Slater and the Tory MP Peter Walker); another thirty required emergency assistance. It is against this backdrop that the demise of Cripps Warburg needs to be understood.

Tensions first arose in early 1973 when George Warburg complained to Henry Grunfeld about his 'unforthcoming attitude' in connection with a transaction that was supposed to be handled jointly by Cripps Warburg and S. G. Warburg.[10] In Siegmund's mind, this exchange vindicated the graphologist* Theodora Dreifuss's earlier warning that 'whenever the reactions of my son made me happy I should always be prepared to be faced a few weeks later with a disappointment because of his neurotic nature.'[11] The real disappointment lay ahead, however. On 19 July 1974 Cripps and Warburg called on David Scholey to confess that they had 'manoeuvred themselves into a rather bad situation through having entered into large commitments in financing real estate propositions of various kinds'. To be more precise, their capital had been very nearly wiped out by multiple bad loans to small property companies – a business strategy inspired by Cripps's naive insight that 'in our era of increasingly galloping inflation the business field which deserved more intensive attention and involvement than any other one was real estate.'[12] The elder Warburg seethed. His son and his partners had committed the ultimate sin of 'wishful non-thinking'. They had committed 'grave errors'. They should have admitted to these 'at a much earlier stage'. The fact that the ailing firm bore the Warburg name 'should . . . not carry any weight with us'. There could be no question of investing more money; that was the responsibility of Williams & Glyn and the other founding shareholders. The most he would recommend was that 'we might assist them with special facilities on a proper business basis.'[13] Even the explanations now offered for the firm's difficulties were marred by 'sloppiness' and 'ambiguities'.[14] It was simply 'false' to regard Cripps Warburg as being 'closely associated with us',

---

* See the Appendix for a full discussion of the role of graphology at Warburgs.

Warburg snapped.[15] His son's abject contrition – 'he blames himself utterly and ruthlessly' – did not change Warburg's mind, nor alter his conviction that Milo Cripps was the sole culprit.* He was willing to offer advice, but not to throw good money after bad.[16]

The refusal of S. G. Warburg to support a recapitalization of Cripps Warburg doomed the firm.[17] In the spring of 1975 it went into voluntary liquidation with losses exceeding £4 million.[18] Despite supportive words from David Scholey and George Blunden, the head of banking supervision at the Bank of England, the younger Warburg was crushed. 'You were right (as usual),' he wrote to his father. 'David Scholey was most kind and helpful. Gently but persistently he tried to stiffen my very weak backbone.'[19] Two years later, Warburg once again proposed that George return to 30 Gresham Street. But when his son suggested to Scholey that he might act as a 'middle-aged filial intermediary between older and younger generations', his father's response was at first a chilly silence and then, as an anguished George described it, a 'bombardment' of 'assertions . . . to show that I am entirely on the wrong track ("such complexes the boy has")'. It was indeed, as the younger man lamented, something like a 'Greek tragedy'.[20]

Siegmund Warburg had many extraordinary qualities, but unconditional fatherly love was not his strong suit – and he knew it. As he once explained to Jacob Rothschild, Goethe's elective affinities mattered more to him than family ties.[21] Rothschild – whose relationship with his own father and other relatives was far from easy – doubtless understood. George Warburg found happiness with his wife Ellie in faraway Waterbury, Connecticut, working for the modest New England regional lender Colonial Bank, and raising their three sons. Even at this distance, his relationship with his father remained fraught. A simple missed telephone call could be the occasion for yet another bout of paternal recrimination and filial contrition.[22]

---

* In reality, George Warburg had failed to restrain his colleagues, as had the equally bullish John Morgan of Williams and Glyn. 'The trouble with you, George,' declared Morgan before the crash, 'is you only like to do business with nice people.'

II

It was not only with his own son that Warburg was becoming increasingly cantankerous. His dissatisfaction extended to nearly every aspect of life at 30 Gresham Street. By December 1970 he was so dismayed by the firm's 'abandonment of high criteria . . . both in moral and intellectual respects' that he proposed that its name be changed to Mercury Bank Ltd to spare him further personal identification with it.[23] A standardized 'terms and conditions' document produced by the personnel department was 'one of the worst products of a fanatically bureaucratic attitude which I have ever seen', characterized by 'meaningless platitudes' and 'a concentration camp attitude'.[24] Meetings of the increasingly important Chairman's Committee* were being contaminated with 'the "me-too", attitude, i.e. the wish to be consulted on relatively secondary matters'.[25] Symptoms of decadence were everywhere to be found – even in the corporate dining room:

In years past . . . the food was . . . absolutely first-class, not in fancy or parvenu style but well prepared, tasty and wholesome. On the other hand the chef whom we now use in this office apparently takes – among several other deviations from good cooking – a particular pleasure in manufacturing elaborate sauces for the purpose of spreading these sauces over meat, fish and vegetables, thus spoiling the natural flavour of the various foods . . . Unless we change the arrangements which we have at present with an obviously second-class firm, I can see only one solution, namely that we no longer serve any hot meals but only a cold buffet. In this way the chef is deprived of the opportunity of contaminating the produce to be cooked . . . I cannot understand why we should not be able to enjoy pleasant genuine English cooking rather than to be treated to a 'cuisine' which tries to apply pseudo-Continental cooking methods without really knowing anything about first-class Continental cooking.[26]

Such lapses, in Warburg's eyes, were symptoms of a deeper malaise: a lowering of 'our previous high standards' attributable to the firm's

---

* Intended to institutionalize the power of the Uncles and other senior directors, the committee in practice was a channel for Warburg's own views, particularly if Roll was in the chair. When Hugh Stevenson became its secretary, he was congratulated by Arthur Winspear on 'having reached the point of indecision'.

expansion.[27] 'With the increasing volume of the firm's business', he complained in a heartfelt memorandum written in 1975 and later circulated to all directors, they had become 'more and more surrounded by mediocre influences':

We have lost some of the *feu sacré* which has been the basis of our progress during our first two decades and we are no longer guided to the same extent as previously by certain ground rules which we developed during our pioneering years. We are no longer as exacting and perfectionist in our attitudes as we used to be . . . We are slowly but definitely descending to a far-diffused level of mediocrity.[28]

Increasingly, Warburg set his face against 'the fashionable race for continuous growth as such and record achievements'.[29] The increase in overheads was 'terrifying'; the increase in staff 'excessive'.[30] By May 1979 he was urging his colleagues to 'plan for shrinkage [rather] than for growth'. 'We have already grown too much,' he wrote. 'Our excessive growth over the last four years or so has had the effect of making the various parts of our firm less and less controllable.'[31] A year later he was lamenting the 'attitude of arrogance and lack of self-criticism', the 'spirit of complacency', the 'trend towards bureaucracy, mediocrity and off-handedness' and 'cheerful passivity'.[32] A typical injunction, frequently repeated, was that the firm needed to 'think *nostro*' more – that is, to focus on managing its own assets rather than clients' assets. As Oscar Lewisohn pointed out in September 1977, more than two-fifths of the firm's gross income in the preceding financial year had come from 'the employment or placing at risk of our capital' – not least a substantial profit from the bond-market rally that followed the IMF's loan to Britain – as opposed to fees, commissions and interest margins arising from advisory and credit services offered to clients. Yet directors spent most of their time on clients' business.[33] This emphasis on managing the bank's own capital not only contradicted Warburg's earlier emphasis on fees; it also ran directly counter to the growing opportunities that were presenting themselves in the field of asset management, which Warburg disparaged as mere 'share-pushing'. Indeed, he was now so hostile to Warburg Investment Management, the firm's semi-autonomous asset-management wing, that he tried to 'get rid of it' in 1979, first to Flemings and then to Lazards, who were foolish not to buy at the absurdly low price Warburg asked: just £10 million. When Merrill Lynch acquired it in 1997 the price paid was $5.3 billion (£3.1 billion).[34]

For the younger directors, such bouts of 'agonising reappraisal' – often communicated by telephone at weekends or in lengthy memoranda dictated in distant Blonay – can only have been intensely irksome, particularly as the firm's financial performance seemed satisfactory to most outside observers.[35] As we have seen, Warburg's retirement from an executive role at the bank that bore his name was a protracted and in some respects imperceptible process that had begun as early as 1954. Sixteen years later he was still not quite off the stage. As the new decade dawned, it was announced that henceforth Warburg would no longer serve as a director of S. G. Warburg & Co. and its parent company Mercury Securities; instead, his title would be president. He intended, he told the *Financial Times*, to act 'in an advisory capacity as the "headmaster" of the younger men in the bank'.[36] He would be 'a kind of constitutional head, i.e. on the one hand to represent identification with and responsibility for the firm's public image and on the other hand to refrain from any executive involvement'.[37] In practice, however, Warburg continued to regard himself privately as 'the managing director of the whole international business of our group' and treated the entire Warburg Group as if it were his personal fiefdom. He constantly interfered in the day-to-day running of the firm, from issues of overall strategy down to the personal problems of the younger directors. In 1973, after a prolonged internal wrangle over the pecking order among the younger directors, a new Executive Committee was set up to represent the most dynamic members of the next generation (Bonham Carter, Darling, Kelly, McAndrew, Scholey and Spira) alongside the old guard of Grunfeld, Roll and Seligman.[38] But the efforts of Kelly and the other young Turks to prevent the promotion of Roll to the chairmanship of Warburgs were thwarted by the Uncles.[39] In October 1975 the Executive Committee, having first been expanded to include more pliable figures, was then unceremoniously disbanded on the ground that it was 'no longer fulfilling its purpose'.[40] Warburg claimed unconvincingly that this was in response to complaints by other young directors who were not members of the body.[41] The losers were dismayed. The winners, Kelly confided to his diary, reminded him of 'the pigs in Animal Farm'.[42]

Predictably, the ambitious began to chafe. Ian Fraser and Gert Whitman left the bank in 1969; in Warburg's eyes they had become 'intriguing elements',[43] and he made no effort to entice Fraser back after his stint at the Takeover Panel.* Four years later, much to Henry Grunfeld's disgust, John Craven quit to join White Weld, returning only briefly as vice-chairman in 1979 – for just long enough to remember why he had left. In 1974, incensed by 'unacceptable behaviour on the part of some of my most senior colleagues', Peter Spira resigned to join the auctioneers Sotheby's.[44] As he later recalled, 'Septuagenarians still ran the place [Warburgs] and, although one was in a position of seniority, it was frustrating to be treated, to a certain extent, like a small boy.'[45] Although Spira remained a non-executive director of Mercury Securities until 1982, his one attempt to challenge the board's 'Kremlinesque' mode of operation elicited multiple pages of invective from Warburg.[46] Thus, when George Warburg offered vainly to act as an intermediary between the older and younger directors, he was quite correctly identifying a 'destructive element' in his father's 'increasing frustrations with the shortcomings of the splendid younger generation'.[47] The feeling of frustration was entirely mutual. Kelly's dislike of Roll and the other 'old men' grew deeper with every year. He particularly resented their habit of dropping in on negotiations, 'which created confusion, for they did not know the issues and tended to make comments in half completed sentences, [which they] ended by looking mystically into the middle distance'.[48] It was this kind of interference, almost as much as Labour's tax policies, that convinced Kelly he had to leave Warburgs after thirteen years in harness. As he grumbled to Nick McAndrew: 'At our age we should form the jolly nucleus of a ruling junta in the bank, with a feeling of partnership.'[49]

Nor did it make any real difference when Grunfeld stepped down from the chairmanships of Mercury and Warburgs. With Eric Roll as his successor and Geoffrey Seligman as his deputy and chief executive, the change was in large measure cosmetic – though David Scholey's

---

*Bernard Kelly speculated in his diary that there had been 'monumental rows with the old men'. Relations were probably not helped by Fraser's view 'that during his tenure as Director General of the Panel, nearly every row in which he had been concerned had involved Jews . . . he had thought of writing an article on the subject but would not do so as he could never come to the City again': Kelly Diary, 15 January 1972; 28 March 1972.

appointment as vice-chairman at least confirmed that there was an heir apparent in the next generation.[50] When Roll resolved that he would follow Grunfeld into retirement in 1978, Seligman simply stepped into his shoes. Now it was agreed that after another year Scholey would take over as chairman of Warburgs.[51] Yet when he finally ascended to the chairmanship in 1980 – having spent two years trying to sort out the bank's tangled relationships in the United States (see below) – he was obliged to share the job with the seventy-two-year-old Roll.[52]

As so often in the past, Warburg periodically threatened to relinquish his remaining ties to the firm. In December 1977 he even offered to resign as president of S. G. Warburg, suggesting at one point that the bank change its name to Warburg Successors Ltd or Mercury Bank or even Scholey, Seligman & Co.* It is hard not to see these proposals as emanating from an old man's vanity. They were put forward in the expectation that Scholey would reject them, and would thereby implicitly affirm Warburg's right to exert power as and when the mood took him. This was indeed what happened. In 1981 a disagreement with Geoffrey Elliott over the management of Brandeis Goldschmidt produced a 'thunderstorm' and 'volcanic frustrations'.[53] As late as September 1982 – less than two months before his death – Warburg was still arranging his 'future activities concerning 30 Gresham Street' under seven distinct headings ranging from 'Teaching of members of the young generation' to 'Bothering chief associates by the introduction of strong nonconformist individuals who should be considered for important positions within the Mercury/SGW group'.[54]

A growing preoccupation of Warburg's later years was the idea of a merger with another City firm.[55] This was not a wholly new idea. According to Edmund de Rothschild, for example, he had first floated the idea of some kind of merger with N. M. Rothschild as early as 1955, saying: 'Si par hasard you would ever like to be joint with me, I would be

---

* The last suggestion gave Scholey a chance to score a point: 'He threw a great tantrum [Scholey recalled], and he said to me, "I don't care what you do. You can change the name of the firm, you can change it to Seligman and Scholey, I'm going to drop my name, I don't want anything more to do with it," and he stormed out. So I thought this was simply irresistible, and I followed him into his room. And his face was like thunder, with his being frustrated, and he was saying "What do you want?" and I said, "You can have your views about anything you want to have, and I can have my views about anything I want to have, but you will never use my family name in that way."'

honoured and delighted.'[56] Four years later Warburg had considered 'joining in some way or other with the Charterhouse group'.[57] 'The number of merchant banking houses in relation to the business to be done is too large,' he had noted in 1960, 'and most of them operate on a remarkably low basis of profitability.'[58] Some kind of merger would clearly be a simple way of acquiring new talent and exploiting economies of scale. With the departure of his son from the family firm, discussions along these lines grew more frequent. As David Scholey later remarked, 'Corporate flirtation was [Siegmund's] constant pastime and pleasure.' In 1968 Kenneth Keith of Hill Samuel approached Warburg with a proposal to create 'the most powerful merchant bank on the London stage', but Warburg demurred, arguing that 'the formation of groups between certain merchant banking houses was much better than mergers', since in most cases 'a merger would not mean that 1 + 1 add up to 2, but only to 1½'.[59] More or less simultaneous advances by Guinness Mahon were spurned for similar reasons.[60] A year later it was the turn of the mercurial Jim Slater of the ill-starred Slater Walker briefly to be considered for a possible union. According to Slater's account, Warburg's suggestion was that, after mutual exchanges of shareholdings, 'the banking and financial services side would then be concentrated in Warburgs and Slater Walker would be responsible for the industrial and overseas interests'. This time it was Slater who felt unenthused, while his board rejected the idea of a full-scale merger when the idea resurfaced in 1972.[61] Yet another idea that surfaced at around the same time was to sell 40 per cent of Mercury Securities to Barclays Bank and Dresdner Bank.[62] White Weld was also considered.[63] A year later it was Jim Wolfensohn at Schroders who was being sounded out,[64] and Wolfensohn came up again in 1982, when he sought to interest the American insurance company Aetna in buying a stake in a UK merchant bank.[65]

It should be emphasized that Warburg himself was nearly always lukewarm about such plans. A merger, he wrote in 1970, would be 'a slightly lesser evil as compared with our going on on our own . . . Almost any combination is better than the other alternative of paddling our own canoe.' The reason for considering such a step was his refusal 'to be the onlooker while the general standard of our services and care for the firm's standing goes downwards'.[66] His alter ego, Henry Grunfeld, was no more enthusiastic. It was he who was sent to discuss the details of Kenneth Keith's proposed merger, and who identified the fundamental incompatibility between the two firms:

> [Keith] said he could not quite understand how we ran our business because in his company, if a manager of a department had a problem . . . he would go to the general manager, the general manager would go to the managing director, the managing director would go to the chief executive and the chief executive would go to the chairman. This, what he called 'the chain of command', was in his opinion absolutely essential to the efficient running of a firm. From what he had heard of Warburgs, people could go from one to another and anyone could see everybody. This he would certainly not approve of . . . I told him that was exactly how we ran our business . . . and that we would not for one moment contemplate changing it.[67]

Keith saw that the merger would be inviable so long as Grunfeld remained at the helm; Grunfeld made it clear that he had no intention of retiring imminently.[68] Old habits died hard. At Warburgs the instinct was to regard other firms as competitors not collaborators. The purpose of a not untypical meeting of the International Department in 1971, for example, was 'like a mafia family carve up, to decide tactics for a meeting tomorrow with . . . Kuhn, Loeb: how could we cooperate with them in Scandinavia, to the detriment of everyone else including them'.[69]

Of all the possible partners Warburg contemplated, Rothschilds seemed to many observers the most plausible – not just because of the long-standing ties between the two illustrious banking dynasties, but also because in Jacob Rothschild he believed he had identified a kindred spirit.[70] Rumours of a Rothschild–Warburg merger began to circulate in earnest in the spring of 1970.[71] The reality, however, was that Warburg was merely considering the possibility of recruiting Jacob's estranged father, Victor Rothschild, whose career in military intelligence and science had given him only minimal experience of banking, but whose political contacts were good.[72] It was Jacob who was the stronger proponent of a merger – the idea even had a Rothschild codename, 'War and Peace'.[73] But when Victor himself proposed a merger, following his appointment as chairman of Rothschilds, Warburg was sceptical. 'To put new life into the traditional assets of that firm would be a task beyond our strength,' he commented, 'quite apart from the many personal complications which would arise with the members of the Rothschild family both here and on the Continent.' The most he would countenance was co-operation in the field of mutual funds, where Jacob's firm Rothschild Investment Trust had blazed a trail.[74]

If the idea of a merger with another merchant bank was a chimera, was there any alternative to merely soldiering on as before? In a memorandum for the Chairman's Committee written in July 1978 Warburg passed a gloomy verdict on the previous four years. The 'deficiencies in our general direction', he wrote, 'derive from the lack of effective management partnership in recent years':

If we are unable to put this right, there would not be sufficient *raison d'être* for the continuation of an independent SGW & Co. and we ought to become a subsidiary of one of the 'Universalbanken' (among whom I do not include the British clearing banks) . . . To surrender our present independence to the control by a 'Universalbank' would be from many human, constructive, and historical points of view a highly regrettable step, but would still be preferable to our becoming a slowly sliding firm which might grow in volume but which would decay on the original, creative side and in its elite character.[75]

At the time, the firm's younger directors may well have rolled their eyes at this latest sign of senescence. Yet these would prove to be prophetic words. As Warburg discerned, the profitability of S. G. Warburg & Co. relative to its traditional London rivals was masking the start of a significant decline in market share relative to new competitors from overseas. 'Particularly on the Continent of Europe, which used to be our most successful battlefield,' noted Warburg, 'we have lost ground compared with such houses as Morgan Stanley, First Boston Corporation . . . Goldman Sachs and Salomon [Brothers].'[76] If the firm failed to rise to this new challenge from across the Atlantic, then Warburg foresaw its likely fate: not to be the equal partner in a merger, but to be the object of a takeover.

III

For all his ambivalence about the core business at 30 Gresham Street, the leitmotif of Siegmund Warburg's later years was expansion. To be precise, while aiming to keep S. G. Warburg & Co. a lean and unbureaucratic firm of 'merchant adventurers who have to act with a high degree of punch and panache', he wanted to make it the nodal point of an ambitious global network of business partnerships.[77] Warburg was convinced, as we have seen, that a process of financial globalization was under way, dating from the birth of the Eurobond market. The greatest challenge of his twilight years was to devise a business structure that would profit from that process without getting too far ahead of it. For the reality was that financial liberalization was gradual and piecemeal in the 1970s. All kinds of regulations remained in place in the City of London that restricted the flow of capital in and out of the United Kingdom, or limited institutional integration within the Square Mile. Exchange controls were not abolished until shortly after Margaret Thatcher became prime minister in 1979. The ancient distinction between stockbrokers and stockjobbers persisted at the London Stock Exchange until the Big Bang of 1986. In any case, Warburg's ambivalence about economies of scale – his distaste for even the quite limited growth of S. G. Warburg itself – ruled out anything resembling a modern financial services conglomerate. Instead, he contemplated something more like a molecular structure, with S. G. Warburg as the nucleus and Mercury Securities the atom. Over time, other atoms became connected by a variety of different bonds, some strong, some weak. The resulting structure was highly complex. It also proved to be highly unstable.

This last chapter of Siegmund Warburg's life as a banker is, in the end, a story of failure. Such stories are generally less pleasurable to read than tales of business success. And yet there is as much to be learned from a debacle as from a coup – and sometimes more.

The entity that came to be known as the Warburg Group included partners or subsidiaries in Hamburg (M. M. Warburg-Brinckmann, Wirtz & Co.), Frankfurt (Effectenbank-Warburg AG), Zurich (Banque de Gestion Financière, later S. G. Warburg Bank AG) and New York (S. G. Warburg & Co. Inc.). None was without its problems. The attempt to build new bridges to the old family firm in Hamburg was never likely to succeed, given the deep-seated differences in temperament between Siegmund and Eric Warburg. In 1970 the latter joined the board of S. G. Warburg, along with Siegmund's protégé Hans Wuttke, as part of a share-swap arrangement that gave M. M. Warburg-Brinckmann, Wirtz (WBW) a stake in S. G. Warburg and vice versa.

Almost immediately there were disagreements about the valuation of WBW's long-term investments and about the winding up of Eric Warburg's American firm. Although the long-running battle over the Hamburg firm's name had ended in a compromise, restoring the original name but retaining the Aryanized name alongside it, Siegmund was dismayed when the Warburg name continued to be used in New York by Eric's ambitious partner Lionel Pincus. Despite Eric's assurances 'that the name of Warburg would finally be dropped altogether by the end of 1972' (later 1974), Pincus made sure that it lived on (and indeed lives on as Warburg Pincus to the present day).[78] Siegmund Warburg's doubts about Pincus were predictable: 'Is he a man of sufficient calibre', he asked his cousin, 'to be the leader of what I would call an *haute banque* firm, i.e. of a firm which is not only going to do profitable deals but to build up an international banking business of wide scope?'[79] In his view, it was 'a kind of prostitution of the name if the living bearer of the name puts his name at the disposal of a firm without any important voice in its conduct'.[80]

For a time, Warburg took a bigger interest in the new entity in Frankfurt, Effectenbank-Warburg AG (EWAG), formed when Warburgs acquired a stake in the Deutsche Effecten- und Wechsel-Bank, a joint venture with the Hamburg bank, the insurer Munich Re and the engineering companies Robert Bosch and J. M. Voith. But it was not long before dissatisfaction manifested itself here, too, and not just in the usual complaints about bureaucracy and complacency.[81] Were the directors up to the job? Should the Bayerische Vereinsbank become involved? Should WBW and EWAG be merged? If so, what structure would the merged firm have? Or should Dresdner Bank acquire an interest in EWAG? Such questions led, predictably, to new and time-consuming wrangles with Hamburg, which only seemed to become more difficult with the accession of a new generation: Eric's son, Max, and Rudolf Brinckmann's son, Christian.[82] The collapse of the EWAG–WBW merger talks in 1975 left Warburg, as he put it in a letter to Eric's sister Lola Hahn-Warburg, 'very sad'.[83] Indeed, a meeting with Christian Brinckmann in January 1976 was described by Warburg as 'one of the three worst business meetings in my whole life'.[84] By March 1977 he was ready to withdraw altogether from the relationship with WBW; only the protests of the Industriekreditbank representatives on the board dissuaded him.[85] A last-ditch attempt to force through the merger foundered once again on the opposition of Christian Brinckmann who, Warburg felt, had 'manoeuvred my group and me into an impossible position, as if we wanted to be uninvited intruders into Ferdinand Strasse', still the location of the Hamburg bank's offices.[86] It had all been in vain, and Warburg could only lament that 'the business of our group in Germany [was now] far weaker than it was even two or three years ago.'[87]

The Swiss story was more straightforward. In 1969 Warburgs had acquired a controlling stake in the Zurich-based Banque de Gestion Financière. This small private bank managed portfolios for wealthy individuals totalling around 300 million Swiss francs by 1973.[88] The aim, as Warburg put it two years later, was 'not . . . to compete against the big Swiss banks but to give first-class service in regard to the administration of investment accounts [and] to develop a few ancillary activities'.[89] As so often, however, Warburg was soon grumbling about the people entrusted with running the subsidiary. 'It is amazing how long it takes them to arrive at decisions even on relatively small matters,' he complained in June 1976:

Every subject which is not entirely clear has to go through long stages of pro and con discussions which are without sense and waste much time . . . I must add here that the power of these gentlemen to decide is further hampered by the fact that they are, in my view, too afraid of criticism from London and indulge far too much in the habit . . . of referring all sorts of problems to London which should really be able to be dealt with without consultation with anybody outside the Bank.[90]

Despite a full-scale reconstruction of the firm's board in 1975 and the initiation of what Warburg called a 'solution and [re]vitalization process' ('Loesungs- und Belebungsprozess'), he continued to complain that most 'members of the management team remained highly overpaid and transparently mediocre'.[91] The decision to change its name to S. G. Warburg Bank AG, Zurich represented just the latest attempt to inject life into the firm's Swiss offshoot. Perhaps surprisingly, the growing amount of time Warburg spent in Switzerland after his move to Blonay did not greatly increase that country's importance in his eyes. It was always a sideshow compared with Germany. From the vantage point of 30 Gresham Street, Banque de Gestion was really 'Bank Indiges-tion': a dumping ground for Eurobonds that could not be placed elsewhere.[92] It faded into insignificance after 1981 when Warburgs bought a stake in Soditic, a Geneva-based investment house led by the Lebanese-born Maurice Dwek, which boldly set out to challenge the dominance of the Swiss bond market by the Big Three (UBS, Credit Suisse and SBC).[93]

Of far greater importance to the long-term future of S. G. Warburg & Co. was New York, the home of the firms that would become its biggest rivals in the 1970s and 1980s. It took some time for Warburg to recover from the disappointment of his failure to turn around Kuhn Loeb. Not until 1965 did he feel ready to 'start a small office in New York under the name of S. G. Warburg & Co. Inc. . . . to advise American industrial companies on their European problems and Euro-pean industrial companies on their American problems and . . . to go in for special situations in America'.[94] The office of S. G. Warburg & Co. Inc. was initially set up by Peter Stormonth Darling and David Scholey and then entrusted to David Mitchell. As far as Warburg was concerned, the function of the office (which was located in the Rockefel-ler Center) was essentially that of an 'embassy'; Mitchell's role was to cultivate and enlarge the existing Warburg network in Manhattan, beginning with David Rockefeller, whose family office Dick Dilworth was now running, and George Love, the former chairman of Chrysler.[95] But the hope that Mitchell would be able to generate deals of the sort Warburg had in mind – major investments by US corporations in Europe, or at least medium-term credits from US banks – was ana-chronistic. This was the era of the Vietnam War, and successive administrations had no desire to see American capital exported to foreign competitors. Mitchell soon became disillusioned with his ambas-sadorial role, complaining that visiting directors from London treated him like 'excess baggage', which in turn prompted Warburg to accuse him of having a 'status complex'.[96]

An alternative strategy – which became known as Project X – was to revamp Ernest Spiegelberg's old firm, American European Associates. AEA had been ticking over profitably under the direction of Kurt Loewenberg, who specialized in what came to be known as value investing (looking for apparently underpriced shares and buying them up). Now, however, AEA was to become something like a prototype private equity partnership, using debt to acquire major stock disposals by US companies – in other words, leveraged buy-outs. On paper it looked supremely gilt-edged. The investors included the Harrimans, the Mellons and the Rockefellers, not to mention the Agnellis; the board was packed with former chief executives of General Motors, General Electric and Du Pont. The small investment house of Laird & Co. came in too, and Carl Hess was recruited from American Securities to become CEO.[97] The man entrusted with supervising this new strategy was once again Darling, who was sent to New York as senior vice-president with orders to work in 'partnership' with Mitchell.[98] The idea, Warburg put it expansively, was to make AEA 'a laboratory of ideas' that would pioneer European-style 'financial engineering' in the US.[99] The investors bought 'participations' totalling $15.4 million.

Almost from the moment of its birth, however, Warburg developed an animus against AEA. Within weeks, he was complaining about the 'extremely cumbersome and slow progress in [its] working machinery'.[100] Hess was 'neurotic'; Sidney Staunton of Laird was 'sloppy'.[101] In an attempt to galvanize the New York office, Ira Wender was brought in from the international law firm of Baker & McKenzie.[102] But no sooner was this done than Laird got into difficulties and had to withdraw from the operation.[103] Then, in late 1970, it began to emerge that one of AEA's first two investments – the acquisition of a stake in the Leisure Group for up to $4.5 million – had been a serious blunder.[104] Warburg's initial response was to merge AEA and Warburg Inc. to reduce overheads.[105] Soon, however, he had persuaded himself of the need to get rid of AEA altogether. Hess, he complained bitterly, was 'euphoric in his approach to many matters, slow to admit mistakes and reluctant to take advice'.[106] The result, as Ronnie Grierson recalled, was 'the most flaming row', in which Warburg behaved 'atrociously'.[107] In the end AEA bought out S. G. Warburg for 10 cents a share, which represented a 'substantial' loss. To compound Warburg's misery, Lionel Pincus stepped in to take his place. The subsequent spectacular success of AEA – by 1998 the shares were worth $250 each – redounded to the benefit of the one firm with the Warburg name over which Siegmund Warburg had no influence at all. The irony was not lost on Vincent Mai, the young Warburgs employee who was a witness of this debacle and who later ended up running AEA.[108]

IV

'The problem for a merchant banking house like SGW & Co.', Warburg reflected in April 1979, was 'to stand up to the continuously increasing position of the universal banks'.[109] It was not just the Wall Street 'bulge bracket'* investment banks that threatened to eclipse the much smaller London merchant banks. Warburg also worried about the emergence of a European 'club des célibitaires' (literally a bachelors' club) of big banks that did not need smaller partners to execute major underwriting transactions: firms like Amro, Creditanstalt, Deutsche Bank, Midland, the French Société Générale and its Belgian namesake.[110] The subsidiaries in Frankfurt, Zurich and New York had been Warburg's first response to these challenges, but their disappointing performance forced him to rethink. Another possible solution was to switch from Warburg-controlled offshoots to joint ventures with one or more of the existing European universal banks. A first tentative step was the discussion in 1971 with Banca di Roma, Commerzbank and Crédit Lyonnais about a possible Warburg stake in their New York subsidiary, EuroPartners.[111] The arguments for such combinations were clear. On one side there was the 'advisability for a merchant banking house of having recourse to the large financial resources and wide-spread placing powers of the big commercial banks'.[112] On the other side Warburgs could offer a continental firm a share of their unrivalled position in London. 'If German banks or French banks or banks in other European countries had the desire to become European institutions in the widest possible sense,' Warburg argued in 1972, 'the only logical procedure to achieve this would be either for these institutions to merge completely with institutions in other countries, or to establish branches of their own in other countries, similarly to the way in which many American banks

---

* The 'bulge bracket' was an allusion to the fact that the name of the lead firm in any major securities flotation – the book-running manager of the underwriting syndicate – appeared in a larger font-size than the rest on the tombstone advertising the issue, and ideally in the coveted Ronaldson Slope font. The membership of the bulge bracket was always in flux. In 1975 it was said to consist of Morgan Stanley, Salomon Brothers, Goldman Sachs, First Boston, Merrill Lynch and possibly Blyth Eastman Dillon, but not Lehman Brothers, Kuhn Loeb, Dillon Read, Dean Witter, E. F. Hutton or Paine Webber.

had expanded in Europe.'[113] The crucial thing was to find a suitable partner among the universal banks. The Eurobond market, with its need for large underwriting syndicates, had made such a combination easy to imagine because of the habits of co-operation it fostered. But marriage was another matter, and clearly any partnership with a universal bank, no matter how it was structured, would be hard to present as an alliance between two equals. As an institution that did not collect deposits but instead devoted much of its energies to advisory services, S. G. Warburg inevitably had a smaller balance sheet than most of the universal banks. A number were considered as possible partners – Barclays, Commerzbank, Deutsche Bank and Dresdner Bank – only to be rejected.

The Banque de Paris et des Pays-Bas (Paribas for short) could trace its roots back to the nineteenth century and was one of the few major French banks to avoid nationalization after the Second World War. Formally a *banque d'affaires* rather than a universal bank, Paribas specialized in long-term investment in French industry and the financing of foreign trade.[114] Warburg was naturally well acquainted with its leading light in the post-war era, Jean Reyre, the bank's chief executive from 1948 and chairman from 1966 until 1969, and took a considerable interest in the establishment and staffing of Paribas' London branch. Reyre, for his part, invested a modest amount in Warburgs' Frankfurt subsidiary.[115] However, relations were more strained with Pierre Haas, the tough former Resistance hero who ran Paribas International.[116] It was not until the 1970s that Reyre's successors, Jacques de Fouchier (chairman from 1969 to 1978) and Pierre Moussa (chairman from 1978 to 1981), became seriously interested in some kind of joint venture with a British merchant bank – part of their own ambitious strategy for global expansion aimed at narrowing the gap between themselves and their principal French rival, the Compagnie Financière de Suez.[117] For more than a year, the French flirted with other possible City partners: Hill Samuel was the leading alternative but, as Moussa later joked, he and his colleagues found it difficult to understand Kenneth Keith's accent. With the cosmopolitan Warburg, by contrast, Moussa gradually established an intimate rapport, regularly dining with him *à deux*, playing the part of the youthful Plato to Warburg's Socrates, sipping Château Haut-Brion while the elder man held forth on his favourite subjects: European politics, nineteenth-century literature, *haute banque* principles, 'human relationships' and, of course, the decline of Western civilization.[118]

The negotiations for 'further co-operation between Paribas and ourselves' at last became earnest in 1972, not coincidentally on the eve of British entry into the European Economic Community. Fouchier's proposal was threefold:

(a) . . . that the two houses should co-operate in the closest way wherever possible, even though they had to recognise that arrangements to this end could not in all cases be exclusive and had to have regard to pre-existing relations, friendships, etc. of the two houses.

(b) That such co-operation, while it was particularly important, perhaps, initially in New York, should not be confined to New York . . .

(c) . . . that an agreement to co-operate in this way should be underpinned by a 'significant' linking, i.e. a cross-participation in Mercury Securities as the holding company on our side, and Compagnie de Paris et des Pays-Bas on their side.[119]

Inevitably, the negotiations that ensued about this *grande alliance* were tortuous. To secure proportionally equal cross-holdings in the two parent companies was itself far from straightforward since the market capitalization of the French firm was larger (£220 million as compared with £70 million), as was its £1 billion balance sheet (more than five times the size of S. G. Warburg's), though the revenues of the two firms were closer (£4.8 million compared with £3 million).[120] As Fouchier saw it, the relationship had to be 'asymmetric', by which he meant that Paribas should be the senior partner. Henry Grunfeld retorted by explaining that the Bank of England and the Accepting Houses Committee would accept no foreign stake higher than 25 per cent. There was a predictable debate about the name: Warburg-Paribas or Paribas-Warburg.[121] The final arrangement was complex – perhaps over-complex.* In essence, there

---

* In April 1973 a new holding company, Paribas-Warburg SA, was set up, which was 50 per cent owned by Warburgs, and which in turn owned 25 per cent of Paribas and 20 per cent apiece of its Belgian, Dutch and Swiss subsidiaries, thereby giving Warburgs a 12.5 per cent stake in Paribas and 10 per cent stakes in its subsidiaries. The Paribas parent company, Compagnie de Paris et des Pays-Bas, meanwhile took a 25 per cent stake in S. G. Warburg & Co. At the same time Warburg Continuation was absorbed into Mercury Securities, ending the direct control wielded over Warburgs by Siegmund and his family.

was to be a partial share swap (and director swap), not a merger. Only in New York would the operations of the two firms be truly merged with the creation of a new Warburg Paribas Corporation.[122]

Just as Fouchier and Warburg had intended, the deal was hailed in the press as a financial expression of the new era of Anglo-European integration.[123] In reality, as in the political sphere, relations between London and Paris came under frequent strain. Warburg's friend Jean Furstenberg was not the only one to regret that the marriage had been to a French rather than German bank.[124] As Fouchier put it in his memoirs, 'Relations between Warburg and Paribas have been punctuated by periods of amicable cooperation followed by [periods of] rancorous chilliness. Such cyclical alterations are typical of long flirtations without any acknowledged end.'[125] He omitted to mention as one of the sources of rancour the embarrassing discrepancy between the buoyant earnings of the Warburg Group and those of the Paribas Group, which were dismal in the first quarter of collaboration.[126] Another was the lack of co-ordination between the two partners in the Eurobond market, which culminated in the exclusion of Warburgs from an EEC issue in which Paribas played a leading role, and which Warburg blamed on Pierre Haas's 'competition passion'.[127] As Michael Valentine saw it, there was simply 'no incentive for either party to present to the other deals which it could do itself'.[128] Bernard Kelly was also suspicious of the way the deal was presented as a fait accompli by the 'old men'. He winced when Jacob Rothschild joked at a lunch for Harold Wilson that 'our merged office in New York was "two old trouts supporting each other"'.[129] A third bone of contention was the reluctance of Paribas to compromise its Middle Eastern connections during the Arab boycott of Warburgs (see Chapter 11). As the *Economist* discerned, there was less to the new partnership than met the eye.[130]

Although the Warburg–Paribas collaboration was intended to be global in scope, from the outset it was agreed between Warburg and Fouchier that 'the New York operation was to be the first priority in that the success of our co-operation would be seen to rest on this'.[131] Having secured priority in nomenclature, Warburg now made it clear that he would be taking a personal interest in precisely this part of the partnership. 'Although in general I tried to withdraw from most business matters,' he explained, 'I looked upon this American project as a

sort of personal challenge to which I would like to devote a considerable part of my time.'[132] The plan was to involve the new firm as much
as possible in underwriting. The challenge now was to choose a suitable American partner with the kind of distribution network that
neither S. G. Warburg nor Paribas possessed in the United States. Candidates included First Manhattan, Blyth Eastman Dillon and White Weld,
as well as Kuhn Loeb, J. Henry Schroder and the brokerage house E.
F. Hutton.[133] But the winner – or, perhaps, the firm most willing to
accept the Europeans' terms – was A. G. Becker, a specialist in commercial paper, certificates of deposit and US bonds, Chicago-based but a
member of the New York Stock Exchange.

Links between Warburgs and Becker in fact dated back to the 1950s
and probably stemmed from the Chicago firm's long-standing links to
the Stinnes family.[134] But it was not until the early 1970s that Warburg
came into contact with Becker's forty-three-year-old chief executive
Paul Judy.[135] When the French head of Warburg-Paribas, Hervé Pinet,
proposed the acquisition of Becker, Warburg was ambivalent. Though
his first impressions of Judy were 'positive', Warburg pointedly reminded
his colleagues 'that his background is Chicago and the Middle West
and not any part of the international banking world'.[136] The negotiations of what became a 50:50 'amalgamation' of Becker and
Warburg-Paribas were no easier than the earlier Warburg–Paribas
preliminaries, with Warburg and Grunfeld repeatedly expressing their
doubts about the dominant position Judy was able to establish ('which
equals almost a dictatorship function').[137] It was, Warburg told Moussa,
'essential that if the desired image regarding WPB was to be created,
the two European shareholders should clearly be seen to play a leading
role not exclusive of Becker but jointly with Becker'.[138] 'Image' was the
crucial word. To a man obsessed with the idea of finance as a higher
calling, the Midwesterner Judy revealed himself to be unacceptably
low. (Warburg was especially offended by Judy's over-enthusiastic
consumption of peanuts at a cocktail party, a flagrant breach of *haute
banque* etiquette.) 'The computer-dominated homunculi of Chicago'
swiftly became objects of loathing.

Even before its launch in September 1974 there were difficulties with
Warburg Paribas Becker (had no one noticed that the acronym was
the standard abbreviation for waste-paper basket?). Warburg had

'considerable misgivings about the limitations of Pinet as regards knowledge of Wall Street and, what is even more important, of feeling for banking problems of the kind which would be of primary importance for WPB'.[139] Judy, on the other hand, was 'the type of man to whom one had to stand up from time to time . . . to counteract any possible impression that Warburg-Paribas Inc. were being taken over by Becker'.[140] The advertisement announcing the new firm in the *Herald Tribune* was 'bad style' and 'exhibitionism which goes all counter to the traditions of our firm' – to say nothing of the 'stupid cocktail parties' organized by Judy.[141] When Warburg visited Judy in October he 'lectured' him on the way S. G. Warburg had built up its corporate finance business, even suggesting he come to Gresham Street for a week 'as a sort of sophisticated trainee'.[142] Becker was all very well for 'mass-production business', but Judy clearly lacked the finesse necessary to win and retain top corporate clients.[143] He and his colleagues at Becker believed 'that the chief task of WPB is to "produce" transactions at almost any price and with as large a number as possible of either existing or new clients rather than to build up gradually a purposely limited number of client relationships which may not immediately lead to transactions but will be worthwhile from a long-term point of view'. Judy, Warburg complained, had an 'almost perplexing lack of elegance and graciousness and above all of appreciation of the overriding importance of human relations'; inexplicably, he attached less importance to 'personal contacts with clients as well as with colleagues' than to 'computer based or statistically motivated working sheets or "Business Development Reviews" or similar pseudo-analytical documentations'. He was 'a technocratic manager of a mechanised army' rather than 'a leader of a team of sound individuals'. He was also inclined to be 'irrationally mean . . . where financial amounts were concerned – especially small ones'.[144]

Yet it was precisely Judy's attention to low prices and high transaction volumes that made Becker such a successful firm in the early 1970s. In pestering him to adopt Gresham Street practices, Warburg was essentially trying to turn a financial factory into a boutique. Wall Street was different, and this Warburg never seemed to grasp. With the hinterland of a vast and homogeneous US economy, American finance was already significantly more commoditized than anything in Europe. Here there really were economies of scale, in the sense that a very wide, very deep capital market allowed all forms of credit and debt to be bought and sold in more standardized forms than in Europe. Big institutional investors like pension funds and foundations played a far more important role in New York than in London, where wealthy individuals still accounted for a significant amount of business. Judy might be over-fond of eating peanuts, but he understood that the kind of business Siegmund Warburg favoured could result in the financial equivalent of peanuts if the transaction costs were too high and the turnover too low.

Almost as a last resort, Warburg suggested yet another partnership – with either Dillon Read or Kuhn Loeb – as a way of putting WPB into the coveted bulge bracket. But this idea dismayed Moussa and his colleagues at Paribas, who justifiably suspected Warburg of flogging an all-but-dead horse.[145] The negotiations with Kuhn Loeb blew apart spectacularly when (to the horror of Scholey and Darling) the newly appointed president and chief executive officer of Kuhn Loeb, Harvey Krueger, demanded that he and his Kuhn Loeb colleagues have all the senior management positions in any merged entity.[146]

It was no good; the differences in business culture were just too great and it only made matters worse when others (like Yves Istel of Kuhn Loeb) pointed them out 'with a sort of smile'.[147] Even the 'nonchalant' way Judy suggested an impromptu visit to Blonay irked Warburg, who detested social spontaneity.[148] By June 1976 he was arguing for a 'new vehicle' or 'liaison office' to represent Warburgs in New York (the later S. G. Warburg North America Ltd).[149] Within a few months he declared that he would 'not be entirely surprised if Judy were to end in a lunatic asylum' (he did not). Indeed, Warburg detected:

a considerable similarity between the Judy group and the [Jim] Slater group: they have the same belief that they are simply incapable of making any mistakes, they have the same lack of readiness to admit mistakes and the same contempt for any members of their own generation and even more of the older generation who might differ from the so-called 'philosophy' that basically computerised brains arrive at better results than common-sense and carefully thinking minds.

I remember so well when I first became more closely acquainted with Slater and was impressed by his dynamic rhythm, and when subsequently I became gradually disenchanted through noticing ominous signs of excessive self-assurance and of a disinclination to answer embarrassing questions. Slater, like Judy, had throughout an important stage of his career many good qualities of will-power and quick arguing and thinking and under the strong influence of sound associates he would probably have achieved considerable long-term success, but at a certain moment he developed from a sober and mechanically competent operator into a megalomaniac dictator. I am afraid we may be faced with similar developments in the case of Judy.[150]

Not for the first time, Warburg wondered if Jim Wolfensohn could somehow be brought in as a replacement, but he assumed (correctly) that he would easily be outbid by Salomon Brothers, which was to WPB what 'a string section of Stradivarius violins' was to 'a brass section of euphoniums of poor quality metal . . . the first instruments being of the right quality to reproduce the best possible compositions and the second instruments being just good enough to record the grating outpourings of the strategy development programmes of Judy'.[151] Not surprisingly, Judy himself could stand only so much of this kind of sniping from the other side of the Atlantic. In November 1976 he announced his intention to resign by the end of 1978 at the latest.[152]

In retrospect, Warburg Paribas Becker was an unstable compound of incompatible elements. Much as Warburg disliked Paul Judy's methods, with their 'one-sided emphasis on meaningless papers and indulgence in formalities', the prospect of his departure can scarcely be said to have helped the firm. Vincent Mai, one of Warburg's favourites in the next generation of Warburg recruits, had become so frustrated at WPB that in January 1977 he quit to join Kuhn Loeb, which was now belatedly transforming itself into a corporation (as opposed to a family-run partnership) and seeking to merge with another Wall Street house.[153] Warburg flailed around trying to resuscitate the idea of a Kuhn Loeb merger with WPB, but these negotiations led nowhere – a failure for which, inevitably, Judy was blamed.[154] Nothing worked: not 'getting rid' of Judy, not a merger of WPB with Loeb Rhoades, Mitchell Hutchins, Blyth Eastman Dillon, Kidder Peabody or Stuart Brothers – nothing.[155] When, after 'many unduly protracted and often utterly irritating conversations', Kuhn Loeb finally accepted merger terms from Lehman Brothers at the end of 1977, Warburg's disappointment was bitter indeed. *Faute de mieux* – or so it seemed – Ira Wender finally took over Judy's mantle, but not even the arrival of Martin Gordon could inject life into WPB.[156] None other than Ronnie Grierson was brought back into the Warburg fold with the specific task of 'working out how Becker' made their money; he professed himself unable to do so and recommended a speedy exit.

What had gone wrong? Warburg blamed 'a combination of poor business with crazy overheads, a wide spread of low intellectual and ethical standards, and a far-going internal demoralisation' (not to mention 'counter-productive mass assemblies in the form of cocktail parties, dinner parties, and similarly low-level festivities').[157] But the reality was that neither he nor any of the senior Warburg people sent to 'sort out New York' fully grasped the fundamental difference between the American and European financial markets. It was left to the recession of 1981–2 to deliver the *coup de grâce*. After a period of what Warburg decried as 'expansionist euphoria', the firm's results in 1981 were 'disastrously bad' and the first quarter of the following year was no better.[158] Soon it was Wender's turn to be accused of 'incipient self-inflicted madness', of 'negligence bordering on irresponsibility' and of running 'a rudderless and paradox dictatorship guided at the top mainly by moods and duplicity'.[159] He left WPB in July 1982 amid threats of litigation. The transatlantic '"they and we" complex' which was at the heart of WPB's unhappy history had claimed yet another victim.[160]

The dream of a global banking structure – molecular in its nature, with S. G. Warburg & Co. as its nucleus – had largely faded by the end of 1978. All that remained was an unwieldy complex of subsidiaries, cross-holdings and joint ventures, with an inverse relation between the amount of time each component consumed and the amount of net revenue it generated. When Pierre Moussa succeeded Fouchier as head of Paribas in 1978, he and Warburg discussed ways of further 'mixing up' or 'linking up' mutual interests, whether by rationalizing the US operation, by working together more closely in other countries such as Germany or Switzerland, or by increasing the Paribas stake in S. G. Warburg. But even Warburg now had to acknowledge the fundamental differences in business culture that had made the previous years so frustrating:

In comparing the hierarchies on the two sides we have to bear in mind that, contrary to London, there are no 'me too' habits at Paribas. Moreover . . . all important decisions in recent years have been taken exclusively by de Fouchier with Moussa as second-in-command, and are now being taken exclusively by Moussa with . . . his two chief deputies. Even as regards those being consulted or informed on the important matters, the circle in Paris is much smaller than in London.

In my view our system is far better in developing teamwork and individual achievements, but Paribas are better in arriving quickly at clear-cut decisions and waste less time in committee meetings.[161]

As the two partners sought to hammer out new terms, 'a gap of views and perspectives and mutual valuations . . . manifested itself' so wide that it 'frankly terrified' Warburg. Even his once intimate relationship with Moussa suffered a crisis as their views 'greatly diverged'.[162] The reality was that, in the eyes of at least some senior Paribas executives, the aim was to turn S. G. Warburg into a 'subsidiary'.[163] This reflected the fact that, under Moussa, the French bank had embarked on an 'almost wild expansion of their commercial banking business', building a national and international branch network and energetically touting for deposits.[164] Paribas, in short, was mutating into a universal bank, at a time when Warburg was resisting almost any kind of expansion in London.

The dream of the partnership with Paribas had been to strike a 'delicate balance between competition and collaboration'.[165] But, as it became clear that even a well-disposed universal bank like Paribas could regard his beloved firm as merely one of many potential overseas acquisitions, an unpleasant question began to play on Siegmund Warburg's mind: if this could be contemplated now – in his own lifetime – how long would S. G. Warburg & Co. be able to postpone absorption by a bigger bank after his death? Might the pioneer of the hostile takeover end up hoist by his own petard?

13

The Education of an Adult

*Warburg is set apart from the ruck of merchant bankers who
pride themselves on hallowed but faded names and who for the
most part stand upon their dignity and little else.*

*Warburg has a seeing eye, great ingenuity and resource plus
an inheritance of honourable skill in money getting. He also
cares for more civilised things than fortune making.*

Brendan Bracken, 1957[1]

*Your father is that highly unusual thing, an artist of finance.
. . . He [is] creative in banking as an artist is in his material. In
some way it is an awful pity that money should have been thrust
upon him as his material – marble, for instance . . . is rather
more attractive – but it's useless to complain about this. The
pity is a real one – it is a howling injustice that your father
should go down in history as just a successful City Banker – he
is it, but with a big difference.*

Paul Ziegler, 1968[2]

*He was pre-eminently a life-long searcher, consciously seeking
more thorough understanding of the complex universe in which
he moved, convinced that life offers us a series of lessons, none
without its cost, each a guide to future action.*

*In the brief intervals afforded throughout an extremely active
business life his mind ranged widely in history, philosophy,
literature and psychology in search of enduring truths; but he
was also a profound believer in the wisdom of the heart, and*

respected intuition and feelings as modes of perception no less
valid than conscious reasoning.

Joshua Sherman, 1984[3]

I

'Foresight, The ability to teach people about themselves, The appreciation of the subtle nuances of people and circumstances, A flair for knowing when people need comfort and help, Sensitivity, Culture': these were the character traits singled out by David Scholey at a dinner to mark Siegmund Warburg's seventieth birthday in 1972.[4] As the 1970s wore on, however, those qualities were less and less in evidence. Warburg was a man on the wane. Not only was he becoming physically weaker. The passage of time was beginning to caricature what had once been sources of strength. The perfectionism was slipping into pedantry, the pessimism into an almost reflexive gloom.[5] 'May I today give you two small but symptomatic examples . . . as to the way in which, in spite of my capacity as founder of the firm and a moderate contributor to its present position, my views are being treated,' he wrote to Henry Grunfeld in May 1978:

You know of the innumerable notes which I have sent . . . to the effect that there should be systematic and regular monitoring of tombstones [the advertisements for bond-underwriting syndicates]. It is quite clear to me that those who should mainly concern themselves with this matter consider my suggestions in the related respects (which to me are important) as having the character of some kind of joke of a gaga man who should obviously not be taken too seriously. The same applies to my insistence *ad nauseam* that we should avoid abbreviations, whether of ordinary words or names of companies, in all cases where it is not absolutely obvious that the abbreviations are understood by everyone (such as ICI). Here again my requests are treated with the negligence which a collectivity of mediocrities likes to practise towards people whose somewhat greater experience and former authority they resent.[6]

'Gaga' was a favourite word of Warburg's, one he had often applied to businessmen or politicians who had passed their prime. But now it applied only too well to Warburg himself. He privately admitted to

Eric Korner that he suffered from 'great general tiredness and . . . frequent failings of . . . memory'. Again and again he spoke of his desire 'to withdraw from any position whatsoever in that firm'; 'to retire completely by 30th June of this year [1980] from every one of my involvements in the affairs of the London firm'; to give up his room in the office and remove all his personal effects.[7] But there was always some new defect that needed to be corrected: the location of the offices of members of the Chairman's Committee, which should not all be on the fifth floor 'as this would create a sort of anti-fifth floor "complex" (in psychoanalytic terms)'; the circulation of 'a rather . . . strange document, containing neither the name or names of whoever it was addressed to nor the name or names of those by whom it was composed . . . [which] certainly represents to me a new departure both in spirit and in style'; 'the habit of letting loose on our clients five or six people when the right number of those present on behalf of SGW & Co. at lunches and meetings should as a rule be two individuals'; the failure of some underling to inform him of an indiscretion by Deutsche Bank in connection with a Swedish Eurodollar issue – not to mention 'the introduction of code names into our internal memoranda . . . at the suggestion of a man whose name I will not mention but whom I consider, in spite of his abilities, a highly destructive character and a person who has dangerously increased the amount of bureaucracy in our firm' – presumably Peter Spira.[8] The wise 'adviser and fatherly comrade' was, it seemed, degenerating into a grandfatherly nuisance.[9] As early as mid-1975 Warburg seemed to Michael Valentine to be 'more often than not a malevolent influence'.[10]

The old man was haunted by a sense of failure. The subsidiaries in Frankfurt, Zurich and New York had been disappointments. The attempt to revive the relationship with the original Hamburg Warburgs had fizzled out. The old tie to Kuhn Loeb had proved impossible to resuscitate. And where he had been most innovative the results had been least satisfactory. The rationale of the partnership with Paribas had been to establish a bulge-bracket institution in the United States. But Warburg Paribas Becker had been a washout. Nor had it proved possible to find a suitable partner for a merger in London. Instead, there was a growing risk that S. G. Warburg & Co. might end up being devoured by Pierre Moussa's rapidly expanding Paribas.

In politics as much as in business Warburg was despondent. He had grown disillusioned with the process of European integration, once so dear to his heart. He had lost faith in the state of Israel. As for Britain, having been knighted by Her Britannic Majesty for his services to the City of London (or, rather, to the government of Harold Wilson), Warburg had moved his domicile to Switzerland, apparently despairing of his adopted country's economic future. The prophet of financial globalization had become a Cassandra, endlessly prophesying the next Great Depression. 'In my opinion,' he wrote in 1980, 'we were moving towards a sort of second 1929 crisis which, however, would be – contrary to 1929 – less of a stock exchange and more of an economic and gradually accelerating social crisis.'[11] Younger colleagues had to listen to such dire predictions over and over again.

It is indeed tempting to attribute these and other forebodings to creeping senescence. And yet we should not forget that there was enough amiss in the late 1970s to justify deep pessimism about business, politics and the world economy. In January 1981, for example, Warburg sent yet another irascible memorandum to the S. G. Warburg Chairman's Committee:

An infectious mental disease seems to have taken hold in certain quarters of our group which has paralysed the ability to visualise negative trends in the future with the result that those suffering from the disease are only able to foresee increases in turnover and furthermore assume that increases in turnover automatically result in proportionate increases in profits. In my view one-sided calculations of this character are not only contrary to experience but are bound to lead to wrongly based deliberations and fallacious decisions.

When we look back on the last ten years or so it is, of course, obvious that turnover and organisational scope have increased enormously but the trend in profits has been generally much slower and in certain sections of our business rather arrested. If we were to substitute for presentations in sterling figures analytical statistics based on inflation accounting we would be bound to arrive at several gloomy conclusions and would find that the return on net assets in our group leaves much to be desired in comparison with some past periods.[12]

The old man was at it again – except that what he said was perfectly true. Nominally, net profits at Mercury Securities had risen by 79 per cent between 1976 and 1981, to just over £12 million (around £68 million in today's terms). Adjusted for inflation, however, they had fallen. They did not regain their 1976 level until 1983, a year after Siegmund Warburg's death (see Figure 3). Not all Warburg's gloom, in short, was 'gaga' hand-wringing. He was absolutely right to be cautious about the 1974 Eurobond issue for British Steel. As he put it in typical Warburgese: 'Now is not the time to be valorous.' It might have galled the young Turks, but it was true. The same applied to Warburg's refusal, a month later, to buy shares in the new Channel Tunnel company for either the bank or its clients. It might have embarrassed Kelly, who had secured a seat on the company's board, but it was prudent given the highly unfavourable macroeconomic climate for the launch of such an ambitious project.[13] Warburg's complaints about Mercury's metal-trading operation, Brandeis Goldschmidt, were also eminently justified.[14] Indeed, its earnings had become so volatile that it was decided to sell the firm to the French aluminium and chemicals group Pechiney Ugine Kuhlmann.[15] Small wonder, then, that the Mercury share price in March 1981 was exactly what it had been in January 1969.

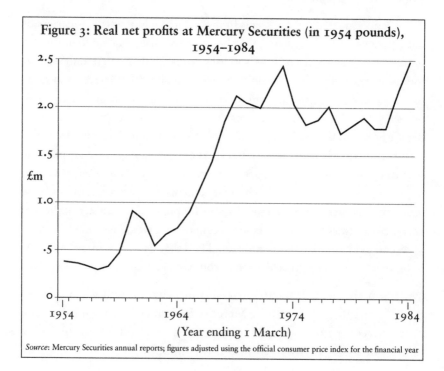

Figure 3: Real net profits at Mercury Securities (in 1954 pounds), 1954–1984

(Year ending 1 March)

Source: Mercury Securities annual reports; figures adjusted using the official consumer price index for the financial year

'What worries me most regarding the firm', Warburg told Henry Grunfeld (in what proved to be their last conversation), 'is complacency.'[16] Was he perhaps right to be worried? 'I certainly do not share the view held in some quarters', declared Eric Roll in 1979, 'that the functions which the merchant banks have been and are performing either are likely to be less needed in future or are increasingly likely to be taken over by other institutions.'[17] Yet the 1974 stock-market crisis, the inexorable slide of sterling and foreign competition had all taken their toll. All the merchant banks had relatively narrow capital bases. The Bank of England prevented them from having assets more than twelve times the size of their capital. The Treasury refused to allow them to hold even a part of their capital in foreign currency. And the Inland Revenue insisted on taxing unrealized foreign exchange gains on currency loans, but denied tax relief on corresponding increases in the cost of repaying foreign borrowings.[18] Even the best of the breed had to be struggling. And Warburgs were only the best in terms of profitability; in terms of their balance sheet, they ranked sixth in the City, while Morgan Grenfell had weathered the inflationary storm significantly better (see Table 1). Sitting in his Blonay office, Warburg knew all this full well, even if the young guns of Gresham Street were in denial about it. In the face of complacency, how could he possibly retire?

Table 1: Merchant bank balance sheets (£ millions), 1973–1977

	Balance sheet 1977–8	Percentage change adjusted for inflation over past four years	Deposits incl. inner reserves and tax provisions	Shareholders' funds	Disclosed net attributable profit
Kleinwort Benson	1,430	-23	1,114	77	7.5
Hambros	1,423	-32	1,048	65	7.1
Hill Samuel Group	1,304	-46	868	63	6.9
Schroders	1,177	-23	944	45	3.5
Morgan Grenfell	863	27	706	31	5.5
Mercury Securities	765	-3	499	66	8.1
Lazard Brothers	569	-17	443	38	3.8
N. M. Rothschild	528	-11	470	20	0.6
Baring Brothers	326	-32	147	20	0.7

Source: *Economist*, 31 March, 1979, p. 58.

Among the large collection of aphorisms Siegmund Warburg left for posterity were four on the subject of leadership, written between February 1977 and October 1978. They help to explain why, even in his seventies, he found it so hard to give up working:

It is one of the preconditions of good leadership to take as little notice as possible of mediocre people.

In order to build a good team of men the head of the team must in critical though rare moments not only support the members of the team when they are right but when they might be wrong.

Too many people manage; too few people lead.

The hardest job for a good boss is to find a suitable successor for himself.

II

The irony was that Warburg's pessimism was perhaps more justified for S. G. Warburg & Co. than it was for the Western world, whose decline he had for so long anticipated with dread. To be sure, the year 1979 brought more than its fair share of disasters. The Iranian Revolution and the Soviet invasion of Afghanistan struck twin blows against the presidency of Jimmy Carter. The following March, as oil prices once again surged upwards, inflation in the United States reached its post-war peak of just under 15 per cent. Britain, meanwhile, began 1979 in the grip of what became known as the Winter of Discontent, the economy paralysed as car workers, truck drivers, ambulance drivers and local authority workers – including refuse collectors and gravediggers – went on strike against the Labour government's 5 per cent cap on pay rises. Here, surely, was ample vindication of Warburg's habitual despondency. Yet at the end of 1980 he felt able to make a startling and highly uncharacteristic admission:

I must confess that, for the first time for more than ten years, I am becoming a *little* bit more optimistic about the political situation in our Western world. It seems likely that the new American President [Reagan] will make fewer mistakes than his predecessor and in Britain Mrs Thatcher, notwithstanding a few rather wrong decisions in the financial field, is as a whole showing great courage in cleaning up a situation which under successive Labour and Conservative governments of the post-War period had continuously deteriorated. The mess which she has inherited is almost unmanageable but she has shown determination to tackle it.[19]

Margaret Thatcher's election victory on 3 May 1979 was without question a turning point in its own right. Exchange controls were scrapped along with the bank corset, tougher monetary targets adopted, government spending slashed and the unions confronted head-on. But this British revolution coincided with a series of other changes in the world that together marked the end of a decade of Western stagnation and the beginning of nearly thirty years of Western resurgence. Already the Chicago-inspired reforms of Augusto Pinochet's dictatorship in Chile had signalled a revival of free-market economics and, in particular, of monetarist solutions to the problem of inflation. In 1978 Deng Xiaoping began China's long march to capitalism, while an anti-Communist Pole, Karol Józef Wojtyła, became Pope John Paul II. The appointment of Paul Volcker as chairman of the Federal Reserve in August 1979 was another step in the same direction, as Volcker soon revealed himself to be an anti-inflation hawk. With the election of Ronald Reagan in November 1980 Americans seemed to regain their faith not only in the free market – summed up in Reagan's declaration that 'Government is not the solution to our problems; government is the problem' – but also in political freedom. Though the United States was powerless to prevent the imposition of martial law in Poland and the prohibition of the Solidarity trade union, the American strategy of increasing military expenditures, combined with Reagan's call on the Soviet leadership to 'tear down' the Berlin Wall, helped speed up the dissolution of Communist rule in Eastern Europe. Another turn came in 1982, when the Christian Democratic leader Helmut Kohl became West Germany's chancellor. Though it was not until three years later that Mikhail Gorbachev became general secretary of the Soviet Communist Party and embarked on the reforms that would wreck Marxist-Leninism and shatter the Soviet Union, the great capitalist-democratic wave of the 1980s was already well under way.

It was symbolic of the close community of interests that linked the Thatcher government to the City of London that on 13 February 1981

Margaret Thatcher herself came to lunch at 30 Gresham Street.[20] Warburg himself had a private meeting with her the following May.[21] As a man who had throughout his life identified much more with the left than with the right – who counted as his political friends Manny Shinwell, Stafford Cripps and Harold Wilson, and who was regarded by Hugh Gaitskell as a 'rather Left-Wing financial man' – Warburg was never likely to be an uncritical Thatcherite, much less a Reaganite.[22] Though he was unstinting in his praise of 'the courageous and positive elements in the policy of the Thatcher Government', and the 'valour and fortitude' of the Prime Minister herself, he was frequently critical of her Chancellor Geoffrey Howe's application of monetarist theory. Publicly he defended Howe's anti-inflation budget of 1981, writing one of his occasional letters to *The Times*.[23] Privately he had doubts. 'Fatal mistakes are in my opinion being made by the Treasury', he wrote apprehensively, 'in trying to manipulate with interest rates a situation which has to be tackled by a delicate mixture of economic and financial steps.' Like a majority of British economists, Warburg believed the appreciation of sterling, in combination with the tighter domestic credit conditions, would drive unemployment up to intolerable heights.[24] Though attracted to the Education Secretary Keith Joseph's desire 'to bring private business into this picture' (the policy that became known as privatization),[25] Warburg worried that the government had 'no proper backing either from industry or from the trade unions or even any of the sound groups in the middle of British politics'.[26] As Joseph put it after a meeting in March 1981, Warburg 'underestimated . . . the extra burdens we face from nationalized industries and trade unionist attitudes'.[27] To the last, indeed, he retained the old Weimar faith in corporatist deals between big business and organized labour. 'Monetary policy is not a sufficiently effective medicine against inflation,' he grumbled, 'unless it is accompanied by an incomes policy of some sort.'[28] On European issues, too, Warburg was not a natural Thatcherite. From a very early stage, he favoured British membership of the European Monetary System, a step Thatcher resisted until very late in her premiership.[29]

In the same way, Warburg approved of Reagan's tougher stance towards the Soviet Union, but was less sure about his economic policy. He found it, he wrote in January 1981, 'very reassuring that throughout the new Washington establishment the old liberal misconceptions and Vietnam guilt complexes have at least disappeared and the Americans seem to be on the point not only of regaining their self-confidence but of being filled with a new wish to give a lead to the world and to turn over a fresh leaf in their domestic policy'.[30] Warburg the veteran Cold Warrior was sincerely 'relieved' to see an American president 'resolutely confronting the Russians'. But Reagan's economic policies struck him as 'much too euphoric, trying to mix soft taxation measures with excessively tough monetary manipulations. In my view [he told his old Japanese friend Jiro Shirasu] he should increase taxes – if not direct taxes at least indirect taxes – and balance his Budget rather than playing with artificial medicines such as excessively high interest rates.' These defects reflected the fact that 'in . . . today's decay of democratic structures even a leader who has been elected with a strong majority is inclined to give preference to his efforts in making himself popular with the voters rather than to serve the actual long-term interests of his country.'[31] What Warburg most admired about Thatcher, by contrast, was her readiness to risk unpopularity. Through two full years of monetary tightening, spending cuts and deep recession, the opinion polls were consistently against her, but – as she famously put it at the 1981 Tory Party conference – the lady was not for turning.

The shortcomings of the Anglophone new right in Warburg's eyes were, however, as nothing compared with those of the Francophone old left. The election of François Mitterrand as French president in May 1981 proved to be the last gasp of an unreconstructed socialism based on the old policy prescription of state control, increased workers' rights, high direct taxation and reduced working hours. Its implications for the financial sector were dire as the government implemented its plan to nationalize the country's biggest banks – including S. G. Warburg's partner Paribas. This was hardly a bolt from the blue. As early as May 1977, anticipating a possible Socialist victory in the elections to the French National Assembly, Warburg had discussed the possible nationalization of Paribas with Moussa, and had indeed suggested a course of action to protect their joint venture in New York from such a measure.[32] Two years later, Warburg once again raised the issue, suggesting that 'active help' to pre-empt nationalization – for example, transferring Paribas' direct holdings in the group's Swiss, Belgian and Dutch subsidiaries to the jointly owned Paribas-Warburg SA (which would not be a target for nationalization). The key point, Warburg emphasized, was to act sooner rather than later, in order to avoid any 'embarrassing situations with the French authorities'.[33] No action, however, was taken, so that Mitterrand's victory in 1981 unleashed an undignified scramble.

In Warburg's eyes, France had embarked on 'a sort of new revolution, not as bellicose and stormy as the previous one at the end of the 18th century, but perhaps even more far going in substance'; the country might end up like Yugoslavia, Communist but not aligned with the Soviet Union.[34] Yet he was very reluctant to risk a frontal confrontation with the new government in Paris. Warburg favoured the speedy creation of a 'new international overall holding and operating company . . . for the purpose . . . of owning the larger part of the non-French assets of the Paribas Group', to be based safely out of the way in Canada. It was a scheme he seemed to have sold to Mitterrand's adviser, the ubiquitous polymath Jacques Attali.[35] However, Moussa argued instead for using a Swiss holding company called Pargesa effectively to smuggle Paribas assets out of France – a gambit Warburg dismissed as *'folie'*, not only because the French authorities were bound to detect it, but also because Moussa insisted on minimizing the Warburg stake in Pargesa.[36] It was now the Frenchman's turn to be cast as the favourite fallen from grace. He had become, Warburg told him shortly after he had been replaced by his former boss Jacques de Fouchier, 'increasingly difficult to comprehend'.[37] The 'Damoclean sword' of nationalization had evidently driven him and his colleagues to 'considerable hysteria'.[38]

Such reproaches were disingenuous. In truth, the nationalization of Paribas was a *deus ex machina* that enabled Warburg to extricate his own firm from a relationship that had become increasingly unbalanced. When de Fouchier proposed that S. G. Warburg & Co. become a shareholder in a new holding company that would acquire the non-nationalized international operations of Paribas, he was politely rebuffed.[39] In meetings with Jean-Yves Haberer – the Mitterrand government's chosen chairman for the state-owned Paribas – Warburg was charming but evasive.[40] He and Scholey made it clear to their French interlocutors that, while they did not rule out a future joint venture in the international capital market (provided it was run from London), they had no further interest in the core relationship with Paribas, which must now be 'dismantled', with Paribas buying the

Warburg stake in Paribas–Warburg SA and Mercury Securities buying the Paribas stake in S. G. Warburg.[41] When heavy losses at Warburg Paribas Becker (totalling £2 million) precipitated Ira Wender's demise in New York, the writing was on the wall. 'Into action we must swing,' was Henry Grunfeld's old call to arms, and never were his skills as a negotiator displayed to better effect than in the dismantling of the Warburg–Paribas relationship – a remarkable feat for a man in his late seventies.[42] The subsequent sale to Paribas of the Warburg stake in WPB for $33 million* marked the end of the affair.[43] The French experiment with socialism did not last much longer. It had sufficed to demonstrate the unsustainability of such policies (not least because capital flight from France brought the franc to the brink of collapse). It had also served to extricate S. G. Warburg from a less than happy cross-Channel entanglement, a venture that had consumed far more time and energy than its meagre financial returns remotely justified.

III

For a man whose idea of exercise was a walk around Eaton Square and whose favourite game was bridge, Siegmund Warburg was remarkably healthy. As we have seen, he had a pet theory that bankers never became ill because of overwork but only because of 'bad organisation or bad business' – or boredom.[44] Certainly, he permitted himself remarkably few days of rest. The telephone calls with which he plagued junior directors on high days and holidays were only the most obvious symptoms of a chronic addiction to business. But it was his mind that was hyperactive, not his body. Even the weekend walks he took with colleagues were intended not as exercise but to discuss the client relationships that were uppermost in his mind. This regime left Warburg vulnerable to periodic bouts of bronchitis, influenza and plain exhaustion. Yet even when he was confined to bed or consigned to a spa, the correspondence and the telephone calls continued.[45]

Although he often likened himself to a physician, Warburg's relationship with real doctors was ambivalent. In 1942, for example, he was

* Paribas was left to weather the heavy losses of the 1987 Wall Street Crash, after which the rump WPB was sold to Merrill Lynch at a loss of $40 million.

plagued by 'everlasting colds', insomnia and low blood pressure. Only after consultations with multiple doctors was he admitted to hospital; he spent several months convalescing from what appears to have been a severe streptococcal throat infection.[46] After the war, this condition necessitated more than one operation. The experience gave him a prolonged suspicion of the medical profession and 'any medicines which end with the two syllables "mycin"'.[47] Doctors and nurses, he observed half seriously in 1962, should be regarded 'more as technical appliances than as friendly fellow humans'.[48] They were certainly no 'demi-gods in white [coats]' (*Halbgötter in weiss*).[49] From 1964 onwards, however, he overcame this prejudice by establishing an enduring and intimate relationship with Dr Heinz Goldman.[50] When Goldman prescribed valium to help Warburg sleep, his patient was delighted. A 'small dose', he told a friend, had a 'wonderful effect' and was 'completely harmless'.[51] By this time, Warburg thought of himself as 'an old man' in a state of semi-retirement, and this naturally increased his interest in doctors.[52] Goldman was one of a succession of favourite practitioners, on each of whom Warburg pinned his hope of indefinite longevity. Their task could only become harder, his disappointments deeper. Not long before his seventieth birthday, a hernia operation laid him low.[53] In 1976 he was twice admitted to hospital, the first time with a slipped disc, the second time with prostate trouble.[54] The deaths of old friends – Edmund Stinnes in 1980, Nahum Goldmann and Marcus Wallenberg in 1982 – gave melancholy intimations of his own mortality.

Yet Warburg refused 'to fall into a kind of hypochondriac mood', insisting on 'remain[ing] active on matters of primary importance while delegating everything else to our friends and comrades in arms'.[55] Indefatigably, he continued to travel on business: to Germany, to England, to America. Indeed, he told Henry Grunfeld he was considering moving out of the house at Blonay and into a hotel suite; he was tired, he said, of being the slave of his possessions.[56] As late as the summer of 1982, he was in New York, vainly endeavouring to salvage the wreck that Warburg Paribas Becker had become, cajoling here, brow-beating there, negotiating for hours at a time.[57] It was his last transatlantic trip; indeed, Peter Stormonth Darling suspected the strain of it precipitated his final illness.[58] On 20 September, shortly after a business meeting in Munich and just five days short of his eightieth birthday, Warburg suffered the first of two debilitating strokes.* The planned celebratory dinner, which was to have been hosted by Jacob Rothschild, had to be cancelled.[59] He was rushed not to Switzerland but back to England, the home he had adopted only to leave. On 18 October 1982 Sir Siegmund Warburg died at the London Clinic in Devonshire Place.

Siegmund Warburg was never a conventionally religious man. He married outside the Jewish faith. He and his wife raised their children to 'revere' both Protestantism and Judaism, but to practise neither. His son was circumcised, but educated in predominantly Anglican institutions.[60] He and his sister were, in their father's words, 'educated with full consciousness' of their 'Jewish roots' but only 'connected in a loose and somewhat more individualistic way with Jewish life and history'.[61] He hardly ever attended a synagogue and never kept kosher. He was a generous donor to a number of Jewish charities and foundations. Yet from as early as the 1920s he sought to distance himself socially from the Jewish communities in Germany and the United States; there were, as he put it, too many parvenus among German and American Jews.[62] Later he felt much the same way about their English counterparts. 'Why', he asked himself, 'must certain rich Jews always advertise their wealth by possessing a Rolls Royce and by living at Claridge's Hotel[?]'[63] Like many products of the German-Jewish elite, Warburg had his own distinctive brand of anti-Semitism, which inclined him to judge Jews more harshly than Gentiles. He disliked the 'professional Jews' (*Berufs-Juden*) at the forefront of Jewish associations.[64] He was also, as we have seen, a highly ambivalent Zionist.[65] The most he would acknowledge as a young man was the existence of 'a kind of genealogical tie, something which does not identify itself with either the religious community or Palestine nationalism'.[66] As he was frequently reminded by the subtle and not-so-subtle social snubs of the Anglo-Saxon elites, he was in their eyes no more than a 'Refugee-Finance-Jew'.[67] His retort was revealing:

The City says about Warburgs that in order to be successful in the firm you have to be one of three things, best of all, all three things, either a Wykehamist,

---

* Hours before, he and Scholey had been discussing a personnel problem relating to an allegedly 'supercilious' employee. 'All right, David,' Warburg at last said wearily, 'it's up to you. I'm sure whatever you decide to do will be for the best.' Scholey had never heard him speak with such resignation.

or an accountant, or a Jew. In my view our greatest danger in the firm is to have too many public school boys . . . I am rather cynical. I think we have too few Jews and we try to bring forward those Jews who have ability.[68]

By birth a 'German citizen of the Jewish faith', Warburg kept a wary eye open for signs of renascent anti-Semitism in the land he had been forced to leave by Hitler.[69] But he was a Jew by fate more than by faith.

Warburg's indifference to Judaism as a religion was part of a wider scepticism about all established systems of belief and worship. He was, as he put it in December 1939, not 'optimistic as to the ethical and religious possibilities of Judaism'.[70] Unlike some highly assimilated Jews, however, he was no more attracted to Christianity, disliking church services in which 'every other word [was] "Jesus" or "the Holy Ghost"'.[71] Raised by his mother to revere Kant above Christ, Warburg once proposed a neat simplification of the Old and New Testaments: 'The two basic sins are intolerance – except against intolerance – and violence – except in self-defence.'[72] A keen admirer of the Austrian historian Friedrich Heer's book *God's First Love*, Warburg was no atheist, insisting that 'we cannot bypass God and mystery by rational considerations and tautological formulae'.[73] As he put it in a letter written in 1964 (to, of all people, his barber):

We are surrounded in this very world by mysterious incursions from another world. Our poor human mind tries to find rational explanations for these incursions and is unable, or unwilling, to proceed with sufficient energy into a field which goes beyond our so-called 'rational' reasonings. The word 'rational', invented by, used and gradually being led ad absurdum by narrowly thinking philosophers . . . in fact covers up in a labyrinth of word games a poverty of imagination – a poverty which has been created largely by loss of genuine faith.[74]

It was not God ('as an abstract force or in [Henri-Louis] Bergson's definition as "élan-vital"')[75] whose existence Warburg questioned, but the value of collective genuflection before Him. 'The most significant element of all churches', he once remarked, 'is the organisation of hypocrisy on a multilateral basis.' He preferred 'the Golden Mean' as 'an alternative to Christian or Judaic religion – a faith in the sanctity of both the spiritual and of the sensual and in the sanctity of the Golden Mean as a combination of spiritual and sensual forces'.[76]

Such sceptical views enabled Warburg to contemplate death with a certain utilitarian relish. 'Life is like a fatal illness,' he once noted, 'and the only open question in regard to this illness is its duration . . . A long life makes sense only in so far as the years of youthfulness are increased but not if the period of senility is extended.'[77] In 1962 he prescribed his own distinctly unsentimental funeral arrangements (or lack thereof):

1) My eyes should be at the disposal of one of the institutes for blind people, where eyes from dead people are used for replacement purposes. I understand that it is very important that the eyes of dead people are transferred as quickly as possible after the death has occurred.

2) The body as such should be put at the disposal of a hospital where proper use of it can be made for investigation purposes.

3) The foregoing dispenses with the necessity of a funeral. Moreover, I do not want any remnants of me to be buried anywhere, nor do I want a memorial service to be held. I consider any such arrangements as expressions of barbaric exhibitionism.[78]

Nearly twenty years later he reiterated this wish, though in gentler terms. There should, he insisted, be no funeral service:

I believe in the old precept that it is better to give flowers to the living than wreaths to the dead. Moreover to the extent to which anything is to be preserved from a dead human being it should be the memory of his or her good deeds and thoughts rather than any physical remnants.

In view of the foregoing my wish is that my body should be suitably used for medical purposes and in particular that, if possible, my eyes may serve a good purpose for others through implantation . . .

Should a cremation be considered the right course I want my ashes not to be preserved but to be scattered as near as possible to the place where I die.

Finally, what I have written here and what I have expressed orally must not be considered as demands on my part but only as humble expressions of my wishes. If these wishes are not followed for good or bad reasons no one should worry as to what my reaction would have been if I had been alive. Altogether the chief criteria should be dignity in style and simplicity in pro-cedures.[79]

*

There were no wreaths, no elaborate funeral rites. There was, however, a tide of tributes. He had been, wrote the obituarist of *The Times*, 'more than any other single person . . . responsible for the change in the City's habits which made it ready to take advantage of the circumstances of the second half of the twentieth century' and 'a principal authority of the rebirth of the effectiveness of the City'. Warburg, 'more than any of his indigenous contemporaries, [had] again made valid the term "London banker" as [a] mark of distinction'.[80] At a secular memorial meeting held at London's Guildhall the following January, his most senior colleagues, Henry Grunfeld and Eric Roll, spoke in similar terms. Warburg had been, said Grunfeld, 'an extraordinary personality'. He had built up the firm that bore his name with a unique combination of an 'intense feeling of personal responsibility', 'hard work . . . originality and imagination', a 'non-conformist spirit', 'courage', 'perfectionism', 'intensity and perseverance', a 'fighting spirit' and 'an uncanny sense – a kind of inbuilt antenna – which told him, before others who were much more closely involved noticed it, that something was going wrong'.[81] For Roll, Warburg had been an 'exceptional man', 'completely devoted to the highest standards of personal behaviour and performance . . . prudent and economical, yet at the same time full of imagination and boldness'. While Grunfeld emphasized his partner's intolerance of sloppiness, complacency and ostentation, Roll saw his defining characteristic as an unsparing capacity for *self*-criticism, 'the essential concomitant of a sense of duty'. The reputation now enjoyed by the firm he had founded was 'more than the result of a business concept: it was his own inner self in action'.[82]

The passing of Siegmund Warburg was not an occasion for humbug. Both Grunfeld and Roll acknowledged their former chief's principal defect. As Roll put it, Warburg had 'an extraordinary capacity for swift and generally accurate judgement of people . . . long before lesser mortals', but 'just now and again, he went astray . . . almost always in overestimating a person, perhaps in expecting too much':

And then, when he felt himself let down, his disappointment knew no bounds and he would suffer real agonies of distress, not only because his own judgement had proved faulty, but because it pained him to discover the feet of clay in those he had so highly esteemed . . . He was very ready to praise, sometimes even extravagantly, but he never held back if he thought criticism was called for. Indeed, he could be formidable when castigating mistakes, even those committed by colleagues for whom he had the greatest respect and affection . . . He was compassionate towards personal problems, forgiving even of grave professional errors except when there was no sign that these were acknowledged. Then his wrath could be terrifying.

Yet for the man who had perhaps suffered the most from Siegmund Warburg's mercurial temperament – his son George – there was no legacy of bitterness. For years, as we have seen, theirs had been a troubled and painful relationship. But his father's death allowed George to express that love which, in life, Siegmund Warburg had struggled to articulate. In verses composed on the night of his father's death, he poured out his feelings in a way that had never been possible before:

> Beloved Sun,
> Your morning rays
> were pure and bright and not to be denied;
> your noontide fire
> ripened, sweetened, chastened and seared;
> your evening glow
> warmed and caressed with infinite tenderness.
>
> Your bounteous gifts,
> your warmth, sweetness and light,
> sustain those whom you loved
> even this night.
>
> . . . finally your strength is spent.
> May your spirit rest in peace.[83]

Now, as George Warburg sent these words to his mourning mother and sister, he knew there could be no last rebuke, no final stylistic correction.[84] The irony is how many of Siegmund Warburg's colleagues and business associates paid tribute to the 'fatherly' role he had played in their own lives: Pierre Moussa, Jacob Rothschild, David Scholey and Hans Wuttke, to name just four.[85] As Eric Roll put it: 'We have all been orphaned.'[86] Two women could not long endure the bereavement. His wife Eva survived him by just over a year. Five years after his death, having already suffered several strokes that left her with aphasia, his devoted graphologist and confidante Theodora Dreifuss committed suicide.

IV

What was Siegmund Warburg really like? Long after his cremation, former colleagues ventured to voice criticisms. To Ian Fraser, the Warburg he had once known – 'inventive, innovative and optimistic, confident of his powers' – had sadly degenerated, his once brilliant personality warped by pessimism, bad temper and a growing contempt for the English.[87] Peter Stormonth Darling allowed that the old man had become a 'control freak'. Even Henry Kissinger, whom Warburg had sought to recruit after his departure from government, commented that he 'was an easy person to get along with if you just said "yes"'.[88]

Judged by his actions alone, Warburg was no more or less than a very successful London banker. In this he was far from unique. Like Nathan Rothschild a century and a half before, he was a German-Jewish immigrant who had made good in the City with a combination of intelligence and industry. Like Rothschild, he had built a new merchant bank from scratch. Like Rothschild, he had made that bank the best in its field. With financial power had come political influence: Warburg was to Harold Wilson what Nathan Rothschild's son Lionel had been to Benjamin Disraeli. And, like so many members of the Rothschild family, Warburg was a philanthropist. Youth Aliyah, the Central British Fund for Jewish Relief and Rehabilitation, the Weizmann Institute in Israel, the Dilworth Chair at Yale University and the Warburg Science School at King Edward's School, Witley – these were just some of the institutions to which he made donations in cash and kind.*

---

* It is impossible to ascertain how much money Warburg donated to charitable causes, but the sums were substantial. As he wrote to his cousin Lola Hahn-Warburg in 1980: 'Two close friends of mine whom I consult continuously on my charitable contributions have been telling me since the beginning of last year that over quite a long period of time I have earmarked too large sums of money for philanthropic purposes and that it would be madness on my part to go further in this respect in the present circumstances when soon new unforeseen emergency situations may require to be tackled. As to some of my recent contributions, I have for instance not long ago arranged for payments to the Weizmann Institute which were in excess of £100,000' – around half a million pounds today.

Yet these and other worldly deeds were by no means the best indicators of Siegmund Warburg's character. He was, to begin with, as much a puritan as a Jew in his own eyes. 'I would have to say', he told George Steiner, 'that the principal features of South German puritanism were the tenets prevailing in the home of my parents and throughout those of the majority of their friends . . . [and] that these principles played a dominant role in forming my outlook on life and my aims':

A definition of what I call the principles of South German puritanism might be that the important values in life are single-minded efforts to serve the community in whatever individual place one occupies and to give to such service the utmost of one's intensity and enthusiasm and that all other elements of life such as aesthetic, material or subjective considerations are to be looked upon as being of inferior quality.[89]

Moreover, Warburg was a financier *faute de mieux*. But for the catastrophe of Hitler, as his friend Paul Ziegler observed, he would almost certainly have remained in Germany as an intellectual or politician. 'You continue to serve Mammon,' Ziegler wrote to Warburg in 1981. 'But you have never truly been a servant of Mammon. Money for you is just raw material, as oil paints were for Cézanne.'[90] Indeed, Warburg himself told the *New Yorker* in 1966 that he might easily have become 'one of the "non-banking" Warburgs . . . a university don, a scientist, a philosopher, or a writer'.[91] Even after he settled in England, his inner life remained that of a thinker, who conducted his business as banker primarily in order to fulfil his own intellectual imperatives, not in order to make money. 'A good human, artistic experience is worth more than any kind of business undertaking,' he noted in his diary in 1934.[92] The primary goal of work was:

Constructive collaboration on a better [form of] education, a powerful new religion, a more just and simple world organisation – inner independence of the ego to the maximum extent, expecting nothing from other people, helping where one can, but never expecting pay or thanks, enthusiastically, strongly and purely sticking with all one's might to one's duty in life.[93]

It became a kind of mantra: 'Human matters are much more important than business affairs.'[94] Those who knew Warburg well appreciated that this was no mere affectation. As Brendan Bracken told Lord

Drogheda, Warburg genuinely 'care[d] for more civilized things than fortune making'.[95] Peter Stormonth Darling, too, discerned that the human factor was Warburg's principal concern: he once told Darling that he felt like 'an observer of human nature from outer space'.[96] Perhaps George Steiner expressed it best:

To his great, great honour, I don't think he gave a damn about wealth . . . All ostentation was beyond words [odious to him]. He didn't even really want a knighthood. Certainly nothing more. To be Lord Warburg [would have been] loathsome to him . . . Yes, [he had] a nice house. Yes, he had a car chauffeured. [But] the idea of a private jet, I think he once . . . said . . . was one of the [hall] marks of vulgarity. And . . . he had a nose for [vulgarity] which was phenomenal . . . [He was] wonderfully ascetic. [He had] the finest sense, not to be seduced by any flimflam of wealth. He simply knew about money. It fascinated him . . . His own [problem] was . . . to bring an especial integrity to the life of high finance . . . I think that was very important. [He had] an integrity so absolute that the merest hint of slipperiness or sleaze left him utterly disgusted.[97]

Warburg's leisure pursuits were those of a don not a merchant prince. Although raised in the Swabian countryside, he did not hunt, shoot or fish. He had no yacht, nor any country estate.[98] He had no interest in sports cars or, for that matter, in sports or in cars of any sort. On Atlantic crossings as a young man, he preferred philosophy to deck tennis.[99] If he ever attended a race meeting or a polo match, no record of the occasion has survived. He played golf – once. The fashionable pastimes of his generation of millionaires – skiing, sunbathing and seducing other men's wives – he eschewed. The fashionable destinations of the era – Antibes, Martha's Vineyard, Saint-Tropez – he avoided altogether, preferring Victorian-era spa towns like Bad Gastein. He attended the cinema seldom and with little enthusiasm, preferring the theatre.[100] He enjoyed playing bridge and gin rummy, but at home with his family and close friends.[101] By comparison with most bankers, then, Warburg was a monk, consciously aspiring to feel 'contempt for possessions, contempt for luxury'.[102] That is not to say that he lived meanly; he was no miser. His suits and shirts were stitched by the finest tailors. He drank – sparingly – only the best French wines. He stayed in only the best hotels (the Ritz, the Savoy and Claridge's). And in London there are, after all, few addresses smarter than Eaton Square. Yet the houses at Roccamare and later at Blonay were modest by Rothschild standards,* with minimal staff, and his collection of art was of negligible importance compared with the gilt-edged private gallery of his counterpart at Lazards, André Meyer, which included works by Cézanne, Degas, Picasso, Renoir and Toulouse-Lautrec.

Strange though it may seem, then, the most celebrated British banker of his generation did not die an especially wealthy man. Though other former Warburgs employees have suggested significantly higher figures, Ian Fraser estimated that Warburg's estate was worth only around £2 million.[103] This does not seem wholly implausible. Warburg's annual salary from the bank was just over £9,000 in the year ending March 1968, supplemented with a bonus of £6,000 – which (allowing for both growth and inflation) equates to just under £540,000 in today's money. The following year the salary was raised to £10,000 but the bonus cut to £4,000. The combined package in 1973 was just over £25,080 – in real terms a reduction since 1968.[104] In 1980 Warburg's salary was still only £15,000.[105] True, his stake in Mercury Securities had grown in that time. But not by very much.† In 1968 it was said to be worth £950,000.[106] Between then and 1982 the shares appreciated by a factor of just one and a half, but prices in the same period rose by a factor of nearly five. Even the huge library of books Warburg

---

* The former consisted of 'one big living and dining room, a study, three large bedrooms with bathrooms (one with two beds and two with large single beds), three servants' bedrooms and a double garage'. The latter was designed, according to Warburg's own instructions, to be 'a reasonably comfortable house which should not be pompous but be arranged in a simple, balanced, tasteful style'. While prepared to be 'financially almost extravagant' about 'the aesthetic side' of 'the rooms on the ground floor . . . the staircase (including the balustrade) and . . . the exterior of the house' he 'opposed . . . undue expenditure in regard to the bathrooms and in regard to a possible lift'. 'I would be entirely happy', he wrote, 'if the bathrooms are up to the standard of a modest Swiss bourgeois family.'

† Mercury Securities shareholders had seen their investment increase by a factor of roughly twenty in the first seven years of the company's existence, an earnings yield of 145 per cent, but in common with most British stocks Mercury did not perform especially well in the 1970s. Ian Fraser calculated that the executive stock options over 62,505 shares of Mercury Securities which he received in 1968 made him very little money in real terms. In 1972, having paid 12s 1od each for the shares, he sold them at an average price of 36s 11d. Had he kept them until 1994 they would have gone up in value by a factor of six, but that would barely have kept pace with the depreciation of sterling.

amassed was not very valuable, since he knew about but did not care about first editions or rare bindings. Unlike the other Uncles, Warburg did not collect. As Charles Sharp put it, 'For him books . . . were reading matter and nothing else.'[107] Even allowing for economic growth and inflation, Henry Grunfeld's estate when he died in 1999 was considerably larger, with a gross value of £35 million (around £11 million in 1982 pounds). The contrast with André Meyer is even more striking. When Meyer died in 1979 his estate was valued at $89.5 million (£40 million), though the true extent of his fortune – taking account of gifts to his family in his later years – was probably closer to $500 million (£226 million). When forty-one of his paintings were auctioned by Sotheby's they fetched $16.4 million.[108] Lazards' operation in New York was certainly a more profitable business than Warburgs' in London. There were always much bigger deals to be done in the United States than in the United Kingdom, and the American economy was not hit nearly as hard as the British by the miseries of stagflation. Yet the real difference lay in the fact that one of these two remarkable men lived to accumulate capital, and the other did not. Throughout his life, Siegmund Warburg had other motives than the profit motive.

There was, Warburg once said of himself, 'unrest in his fragile soul', and probably that was always the case.[109] But the best salve for that inner *Angst* was an intensive engagement with other people – preferably, though not necessarily, potential kindred spirits in the younger generation. 'People are the most multi-faceted and most interesting object of life and of art,' he wrote in his diary in 1934.[110] Having his own bank gave him a kind of psychological laboratory in which to study his favourite species and cultivate new elective affinities. 'The way in which we carry on our lives', Warburg once wrote, 'is a continuous experiment,' and 'the most important field, in which we should do [much more] learning, teaching and research work, is the field of human relationships.'[111] There was indeed something of the laboratory about S. G. Warburg & Co.: the long hours, the meticulous record-keeping and above all the post-mortems when the experiment went wrong. That rigorous commitment to 'agonizing self-appraisal' dated back a long way, to his mother's injunction 'that every night before going to sleep I should ponder hard over all the things during the day which I had not done in the right way and should make a very strong effort to admit all my mistakes to myself and think out how I could learn from them in the future'. The rule was almost masochistically self-critical, as Warburg later recalled: 'If I could not think of at least three mistakes made during the day there was something wrong with me.'[112] The experience of the Second World War only served to reinforce his belief that it was a 'crime to encourage complacency by avoiding ruthless inquests'.[113] It is hardly surprising, then, that some people found him difficult to work with. Warburg agreed with the British historian and journalist E. H. Carr that 'improvement in human affairs is wholly the work of the uncontented characters' – the 'worriers'.[114] He relished the insight that 'paradoxical decisions are often the right decisions'.[115] The more 'wishful non-thinking' he encountered, the more determinedly he challenged the conventional unwisdom of the habitually complacent majority. The striking thing is not that Warburg made a few enemies, but that so many of those who worked for him did so with a loyalty verging on love – an emotion rarely encountered in the realm of finance. But then, as we have seen, Warburg was only outwardly, superficially, a banker.

If, in one of his many lives, Siegmund Warburg was an experimental psychologist using a bank as his lab, in another he was (in David Scholey's phrase) an 'old actor-manager'. The Prussian professor was also the Henry Irving or Laurence Olivier of the City, captivating in performance, with an extraordinary dramatic range that extended from faintly camp charm* to brutal ill-temper – 'Lear one minute . . . Richard the Third another'.[116] Even Ian Fraser had to acknowledge Warburg's ability, in meetings, lunches and dinners, to 'fascinate his guests with the breadth of his reading of contemporary and classical literature [and] his comments on the opera and stage, his considerable knowledge of fine bindings and furniture'. He was, when the mood took him, 'hilariously funny but seldom offensive'.[117] Eric Roll recalled how Warburg 'could be relaxed even in moments of high drama, loving the sporting element which he perceived in a transaction, particularly when it was highly competitive, and the fun – as he put it – that could be experienced

---

* Warburg himself more than once noted that 'the most developed man should have a combination of masculine and feminine qualities with masculine emphasis'. There was generally a faint hint of *Death in Venice* about his relationships with his male protégés.

from it': 'People invariably came to him . . . He acted like a magnet even where taxis were concerned: in the most difficult circumstances such as leaving the Opera on a rainy night, a taxi would turn up. He certainly had a magnetic quality, for people, for problems and, for one who avoided the media, even for news.' Yet the inner man was anything but gregarious. He detested parties and indeed crowds of any description. Roll vividly depicted Warburg 'in a large gathering of important people (say at Number Ten, at a Bilderberg Group meeting or at the annual Siemens banking conference, occasions which often give rise to effusiveness), standing quietly, apparently lost in thought, in a corner while the crowd surged around him'.[118] Charles Sharp recalled that at parties he was either the host or 'in the most remote corner of the room . . . [or] near to the exit'. Parties, he said, were a deeply boring combination of 'too much drink' and 'mouth-gymnastics'.[119] As he told Paul Ziegler, he despised all forms of 'escapism . . . from nowhere to nowhere'.[120] His favourite social occasions were the so-called Reunion Parties for retired Warburgs employees, at which he would 'passionately kiss the retired cook . . . and the retired tea ladies, all on both cheeks and with genuine joy'.[121]

The crucial point about Warburg is that he was above all a man of the word: the spoken word, the handwritten word but above all the printed word. He must be judged and understood as much by what he *read* as by what he did. It is not coincidental that among his best friends was the great French bibliophile Jean Furstenberg.[122] Anyone who contemplates the size and composition of his library* cannot fail to be impressed – not by the number of first editions, but by the intensity of their former owner's engagement with their contents. Around three thousand books bear Warburg's personal bookplate with the motto 'Progress in thinking is progress towards simplicity', as well as his pencilled notes on the cover page. A substantial proportion of the collection is eighteenth- and nineteenth-century English literature, in which he immersed himself after his migration: Gibbon's *Decline and Fall*, Boswell's *Life of Johnson*, George Eliot's *Middlemarch*, Trollope's Palliser novels, and so on. French and Russian authors of the same period are well represented too (Balzac and Stendhal, Dostoyevsky and

---

* After discussions between Warburg's widow, his daughter and his secretary Doris Wasserman, it was decided to donate his library to Anna's *alma mater*, St Paul's Girls' School.

Tolstoy). But the core of Warburg's library is the German and Austrian literature of the Enlightenment, Wilhelmine and Weimar periods. Three writers in particular loomed large in his mind: Friedrich Schiller, whose 'huge dramatic gifts' and 'heaven-storming, enthusiastic idealism' he always revered; Friedrich Nietzsche, whom he began reading at the age of fifteen, 'throw[ing] into the melting pot all my early religious and philosophical concepts'; and Thomas Mann, whose great allegory of the German catastrophe, *Doctor Faustus*, he read almost as often as *Joseph and his Brothers*. Many of his favourite aphorisms (see below) were jotted down from his favourite books as he read them. A typical example (from 1967) was inspired by George Sand:

There are two ways in which human desires can be satisfied; one way, the more superficial one, consists in what the English language calls 'happiness' or 'pleasure' and what the French language calls 'bonheur'; one way, the deeper one, consists in intensity of living – the German language calls this 'erhoehtes Lebensgefuehl' and contains both suffering and joy. Nothing could throw a truer light on these two different ways of living of the soul than George Sand's words: 'Laissez-moi fuir la menteuse et criminelle illusion du bonheur! Donnez-moi du travail, de la fatigue, de la douleur et de l'enthousiasme!' ['Get me away from the mendacious and criminal illusion of happiness. Give me work, fatigue, sadness and enthusiasm.']123

Though the nineteenth century was his first love, Warburg remained throughout his life a literary omnivore, seldom going on business trips with fewer than three books, from Judge Ben B. Lindsey and Wainwright Evans's *Revolt of Modern Youth* in 1927 to Hilaire Belloc's *Oliver Cromwell* in 1934; from Dean Inge's *Vale* in 1935 to the second Earl Lytton's *Antony* the following year; from H. A. L. Fisher's *History of Europe* in 1939 to Alex Kapstein's *Something of a Hero* in 1942; from E. M. Forster's *Virginia Woolf* in 1943 to Hermann Rauschning's *Time of Delirium* in 1948; from Aldous Huxley's *The Devils of Loudon* in 1952 to Lord David Cecil's *Melbourne* in 1955; from Albert Camus' *The Plague* in 1958 to Simone de Beauvoir's *Memoirs of a Dutiful Daughter* in 1959. James Baldwin, Cyril Connolly, Arthur Koestler, Max Frisch, Erich Fromm, Peter Gay, Yasushi Inoue, Aniela Jaffe, Nikos Kazantzakis, Thornton Wilder, Carl Zuckmayer – all had their time in Siegmund Warburg's attaché case.

Warburg believed passionately in sharing literature, constantly sending his friends the books he had most enjoyed. He also regarded some literary knowledge as a *sine qua non* for any new recruit to his firm. Job applicants were startled to be asked at interview what they were reading for pleasure, as we have seen. Joshua Sherman was very reluctant to admit that he was reading Mann and Kafka, fearing it might prejudice a hard-nosed financier against him, little realizing that this was the perfect answer.[124] But Warburg was not content to read and recommend great writers. He also corresponded with many of the living authors he most admired, notably Forster, Fromm and Koestler, as well as Brigitte B. Fischer, the daughter of the German publisher Samuel Fischer. He knew Hermann Hesse, met H. G. Wells, patronized George Steiner and lunched and dined often with Isaiah Berlin. 'Berlin is an outstanding *Causeur* [conversationalist] in the best sense of the word,' he wrote after their first meeting on a transatlantic liner in 1949:

It is a pity that, due to his great social success, he allows himself to be abused as a sort of Falstaff or court jester to rich American ladies and stupid snobs from various countries. Still his powers of mental observation and verbal description are quite extraordinary and I find it practically impossible to understand how he could spend the whole day talking almost without interruption and at the same time reading intensively not only books [but also] newspapers, and writing scientific treatises.[125]

Their relationship nevertheless blossomed in the course of the next thirty years. 'I . . . have the greatest admiration not only for your mind – and who does not?' wrote Berlin to Warburg in 1979, 'but [also for] your moral integrity and courage and sense of reality and insight – and being your own man in all these respects – I am glad of this opportunity of saying all this, and of thanking you for your friendship and your devotion to decency and civilization – of how many bankers can this be said?'[126] Yet Warburg's most important literary relationship – indeed, friendship – was with the Viennese novelist and biographer Stefan Zweig, perhaps best known today as the author of *Chess* and *Beware of Pity*. Warburg knew Zweig for twenty years, shared his vision of peace through European integration and corresponded with him regularly during his Brazilian exile until his suicide in 1942.[127] Though he was fond of Isaiah Berlin, Warburg rated Zweig higher.[128]

Of all of the great thinkers Warburg studied, however, it was probably Sigmund Freud who had the biggest influence on him, though the two men never met. 'Is it possible', Warburg once asked himself, 'to fill the moral vacuum of our time by a religion based on aesthetic and ethical elements but without sin complexes?' – essentially the question posed by Freud in *The Future of an Illusion*.[129] 'From the moment human beings transcend their animal basis', Warburg told George Steiner in 1976, 'by moving from blind instinct to increasing consciousness and from dumbness to linguistic expression, the tendencies towards self-destruction within ourselves become stronger and must be fought with increasing vigour.'[130] That was an unmistakably Freudian insight – though it was typical of Warburg to cite the death instinct rather than the erotic as the prime mover in human affairs. In a way, psychoanalysis was Warburg's lifelong hobby, though he consistently deplored the tendency for professional analysts to regard all moral failings as the excusable results of earlier traumas.

A lifelong immersion in late nineteenth- and early twentieth-century German literature is not likely to make a man an optimist. 'I have been inclined towards pessimism throughout most of my life and especially since 1930,' Warburg once admitted. 'My attitude towards my various activities has been and continues to be based on the assumption that – with extremely few exceptions – matters will not go in accordance with [the] programme and that an unfavourable or unreasonable outcome is more likely than the other way round . . . accompanied on a less conscious level by some irrational hope to the effect that things may not turn out quite as badly as my rational considerations anticipate.'[131] But Warburg's pessimism was not so much a reflection of cultural despair as a hedge against disappointment. In times of crisis, he wrote in 1942, 'the pessimist comes into his own': 'Others, varying from the normally confident to the criminally complacent, are shaken, gloomy, and depressed. We who are habitually apprehensive are only a little more so now and, in comparison both to others now and to ourselves in other times, seem almost optimistic. We haven't so far to fall and, therefore, do not get so bruised.'[132] Warburg's working assumption was always that Western civilization was doomed to be swept away. However, as he told George Steiner many years later,

The overthrow of so many idealistic values which were and still are the foundation of my beliefs has never been felt by me as a disappointment over which I was crying tears or over which I was indulging in strongly articulated complaints but rather as a challenge to fight and to persevere in the directions to which I felt enthusiastically attached. The idealistic values to which I have referred have somehow not changed throughout my life. The floods of modern barbarism which have grown throughout the period of my adulthood have never frightened me and made me despair, but have rather strengthened my resolve to stick to the opposite purposes which were felt by me, and to do so even if this would imply that one cannot often realize these values nowadays except in small islands of solid sanity and fanatic faith in a better world to come.[133]

Given his literary leanings, Warburg might have been expected to write more than mere business letters and memoranda. He did indeed attempt to write a book in the 1920s, but the manuscript has not survived.[134] However, he long resisted suggestions that he write his memoirs, for fear of being accused of 'self-advertising'.[135] There was, as he put it, a dilemma on whose horns the notion of an autobiography was fatally impaled:

The autobiographies produced by others than such historical figures [as Churchill and de Gaulle] suffer in my view from this simple dilemma: either the autobiographies are to be honest. In this case they have to contain details which are essential in order to achieve a comprehensive picture but which are not of general significance; or the autobiographies concentrate on points which are of a character meaningful to a substantial group of people. In this case they can only be of a fragmentary and thereby one-sided nature.[136]

Instead, he proposed to compose two 'short treatises', one to be called 'The Education of an Adult', on the 'cultivation of élan vital as a basic part of adult education', the other 'Expensive Lessons', describing the episodes of 'pain, sorrow and suffering' from which he had gained knowledge of lasting value.[137] Neither saw the light of day. The long interviews Warburg gave to the philosopher and historian of ideas George Steiner at Blonay in 1976 were clearly intended to form the basis of a jointly authored memoir, but that scheme too fizzled out.

(Though a banker's son, Steiner was by his own admission an unlikely choice of ghost writer, and he finally abandoned the project when Warburg gave an almost equally candid interview to a journalist at *Institutional Investor*.)[138] A final literary enterprise, also still-born, was 'An Anthology for Searchers', Warburg's planned compendium of the numerous aphorisms and aperçus he had either devised or transcribed since the 1940s and which he arranged thematically in 1972. After Warburg's death, at the suggestion of his widow, Joshua Sherman finished the job of editing the aphorisms, but it was decided not to proceed with publication.[139]

There was undoubtedly something rather fitting about this final literary bequest: an unpublished mass of partially edited pearls of wisdom, the authorship of nearly all of them unclear. Here was Siegmund Warburg with everything but the great thoughts stripped away. The man was invisible, the lives and loves effaced; only the bons mots and pensées remained, of which the following selection are among the most revealing:

Élan vital's real purpose is to bring the various possibilities of a human being to their highest possible development. (May 1959)

To be in love with another human being, and to be in love with life – these two loves united into one great single love is the greatest gift that can come to us. (January 1963)

The highest degrees of human potency are reached in enthusiasm on the one hand [and] in suffering on the other. (January 1965)

Honesty towards oneself is more important even than honesty towards others. (May 1965)

The ego, this mysterious conception, hypothetical motor of human beings, is a clear unity only in the physical sense but a mixture of many different and contradictory elements in the psychological sense. (July 1965)

The one who accepts supreme challenges and who succumbs ultimately in an all-out effort to live up to the challenges is the real victor in life. (April 1966)

The man who gives his whole self to another human being or to a great cause should expect to be rewarded with more suffering than happiness. But he ought to be grateful for this kind of suffering because it makes him stronger and better. (September 1967)

It is supposed to be good manners not to cry over spilt milk or let sleeping dogs lie, but in fact it is highly educational to cry over spilt milk and not to let sleeping dogs lie. (October 1968)

In our time when faith has [abated] in wide circles in favour of scepticism and cynicism the few who hold on to faith in high and transcendent values far beyond our material existence have a great duty not only to strengthen their faith within themselves but to keep the torch of their faith alight, to confess their faith aloud with determination and enthusiasm – feu sacré in action. (October 1968)

When we listen to other people we should pay as much attention to what they do not say as to what they [do] say. (February 1969)

Whenever you pursue an important or unimportant course – whatever energy you apply to it – you should always have in mind various alternatives for which you are well prepared. (March 1972)

Work is more absorbing, more fascinating, more enjoyable than the best of holidays or the best of games. (July 1972)

For the bulk of human beings fear is the chief adviser and it is always a bad adviser. (July 1977)

We have to be idealists without illusions. (November 1978)

One of the great human problems is how to combine tolerance and discrimination. Tolerance neglects so easily to discriminate, while discrimination leads so often to intolerance. Tolerance without discrimination produces a dangerous lack of standards and a soft indulgence. Discrimination without tolerance makes for fanaticism and injustice. We have to be both tolerant and discriminating: this is a continuous challenge. (undated)

Belief in transcendence based on the experience of great books, great pieces of music, great human achievements in kindness and understanding – I cannot imagine that the spirit in those books, in those pieces of music, in those human achievements will be ever lost even if those books are completely destroyed or the notes containing those pieces of music have completely disappeared or the personal memories of those human achievements have vanished. (undated)

Influence is more important than power. This applies both to nations and individuals. (undated)

Freedom is not simply being allowed to do what you like; it is intensity of will. (undated)

The greatest adventure is thinking. (undated) [140]

A better expression of human deracination than these disembodied *obiter dicta* would be rather hard to imagine, though they reveal a great deal more about Warburg's personality than any previously published study.

Siegmund Warburg was indeed in many ways the personification of the rootless cosmopolitan. 'I consider myself in several places of this world to be both "daheim" and "zuhause", in other words a multi-national,' he said in 1976. 'I know this word is despised by many people nowadays but I am not ashamed nonetheless to admit and even to stress that I am a multi-national.' Yet his friend Paul Ziegler was perhaps closer to the truth when, in a letter to Warburg's son, he defined him as a kind of wandering German. Certainly, the predominant influences in the aphorisms are *mitteleuropäisch*: not only Nietzsche and Freud but also the great Viennese master of the genre, Karl Kraus. As Paul Ziegler rightly remarked, Warburg was a nineteenth-century German trapped in twentieth-century England, who had to make his business his *Heimat*:

Now this is a very terrible thing to happen to anyone . . . I am sure that there is deep suffering in your father's life . . . For behind that highly successful and efficient intelligence and will there is a great romantic depth and simplicity that needs roots somewhere and cannot find the real satisfaction for which it hungers in the highly artificial world in which it has to perform, and that hung up in empty space . . . Your father needs warmth and though he has innumerable friends, I should not think he has had many true friendships, at least since he left Germany – under the surface he is too complex and shy and vulnerable a person for that and with too exacting and idiosyncratic standards.[141]

Perhaps it is not inappropriate that this most insightful assessment of Siegmund Warburg's personality was written by a true ascetic, a Jew by birth and a former banker who had himself become a Benedictine monk.[142]

V

Warburg the perpetual pessimist sensed what lay ahead. Within five years of his death, he told Peter Stormonth Darling on more than one occasion:

Warburgs would break several of his most cherished rules. We would, he said, change the name of the quoted company, Mercury Securities, to incorporate the Warburg name, we would produce glossy annual reports in place of the plain off-white ones we traditionally used (he actually used the word 'glazed'), we would have brochures with photographs of members of the firm, as all our competitors had, we would advertise, we would grow too big, and have too many people, and worst of all, we would join the City establishment and inherit its complacency.[143]

This was more or less exactly what happened. Freed from the restraining hand of the bank's founder, with only Henry Grunfeld as an active representative of the Uncles, the senior executives at S. G. Warburg & Co. embarked on a course of rapid expansion. Their aim was full-blown competition with the Wall Street bulge bracket. Warburgs was to be transformed from a merchant bank into an investment bank. This is a story that has been told elsewhere and lies beyond the scope of this biography.[144] But it must be told briefly, if only because it illustrates Siegmund Warburg's remarkable prescience.

Even before the Big Bang of 1986, S. G. Warburg began to expand aggressively. In 1984 the firm moved from Gresham Street to much larger and more modern offices at 33 King William Street. Almost as soon as the City's traditional distinctions between banking, broking and jobbing were removed, Warburg snapped up the brokers Rowe & Pitman, the jobber Akroyd & Smithers and, with the encouragement of the Bank of England, the Government broker Mullens & Co., moving once again – this time to Finsbury Avenue – to accommodate the new staff.[145] Just how wise these investments were remains debatable.* But the objective of expansion was certainly achieved. In 1984 Warburgs' equity capital exceeded that of Morgan Stanley and was not far behind that of Goldman Sachs, the firm's two most obvious American competitors. Profits in the 1980s soared ahead of the London competition.[146] By 1993 the market capitalization of the firm was £2 billion, compared

---

* Warburgs paid £41 million in cash for 29.9 per cent of Akroyd & Smithers, the equivalent of £42.5 million in Mercury stock for Rowe & Pitman and £8.6 million, also in Mercury shares, for Mullens. On the basis of the firms' most recent profits, those were generous valuations. In effect, Mercury shareholders exchanged 100 per cent ownership of their existing firm for 59 per cent of the new conglomerate. The increase in net asset value (from £170 million to £236 million) did not justify the dilution.

with just £1 million in 1957; the total number of employees worldwide was 6,500, up from 4,900 in March 1990 and half that number in 1985. With investment banking offices in thirty-one locations, S. G. Warburg was the undisputed champion of home-grown British finance. Its Corporate Finance Department had 560 corporations and governments as clients and was universally acknowledged as the European number one. It ranked sixth worldwide in international equity issuance, and consistently topped the league tables for European equity brokerage. It had one of the financial world's largest research departments, with more than 250 analysts, an unrivalled number. And still the old culture seemed to survive intact. Writing in 1992, ten years after Siegmund Warburg's death, one journalist compared the bank's offices to 'Zhongnanhai, the mysterious enclave in Peking from which the Chinese leadership holds sway'. 'There are few holes to be picked in Warburgs' performance,' he noted with appropriate reverence. 'Warburgs . . . has come top of all of [the league tables] at one time or another.'[147]

Yet the results of this headlong expansion proved to be ephemeral. To bolster its bottom line, Mercury Securities came to rely more and more on Mercury Asset Management, in which it had retained a 75 per cent stake after MAM's 1987 stock-market flotation. A crass advertising campaign of the sort Siegmund Warburg would have deplored ('Before you go shopping in Gothenburg, St Petersburg or Salzburg, be sure to visit Warburg'; 'The one thing we'll never merge is into the background') could not paper over the problems. Expenses escalated by nearly a third in 1992–3 and by the same proportion the following year. And still the firm kept growing, with new chief executive Simon Cairns (the sixth Earl Cairns) committing himself to an expansion of the firm's bond operation in February 1994.[148] Too late, in the summer of 1994, Cairns sought to negotiate a merger with Morgan Stanley. It was going to be 'the investment bank of the future', a transatlantic fusion of two of the biggest names in financial history: Morgan and Warburg.[149] But before the deal was done, on 3 October, slumping revenues from investment banking forced Cairns to issue a profits warning.[150] To make matters worse, the negotiations then became public. After a tug of war over the valuation of MAM, John Mack of Morgan Stanley abruptly pulled out.[151] The effect was disastrous. With both profits and the share price slumping, there was a rush for the exits, led by the equity capital markets team, who defected to Morgan Grenfell. Cairns resigned; almost immediately Warburgs announced that they were withdrawing from the Eurobond market – the market Siegmund Warburg had himself created.

In April 1995, just two months after a rogue trader brought low the venerable house of Barings, S. G. Warburg & Co. was bought by Swiss Bank Corporation for £860 million – essentially the net asset value of the investment banking business plus an 8 per cent premium – 'a miserly price', in the words of one former employee. (The stake in MAM was not included but was distributed to the other MAM shareholders.) Those in charge expressed relief that the acquisition had not been by Morgan Stanley or NatWest, since somehow a Swiss bank seemed less of a humiliation than a Wall Street house or, worse by far, a British clearing bank.[152] Momentarily forgetting the travails of the famous car company, Scholey confidently claimed that SBC and Warburgs would fit together 'like the clunk of a Rolls-Royce door'. But perhaps the fit with the WASPs of Morgan Stanley would have been better in the long run for the Warburg brand. On closer inspection, the 'SBC traders in their elegant chinos and £100 shirts' were only marginally more bearable than the NatWest managers with their 'peeping Tom-type mackintoshes'.[153] For a brief period the investment bank operated under the name SBC Warburg, then, following the acquisition of Dillon Read, it became SBC Warburg Dillon Read. A few years later Warburgs became part of a larger Swiss behemoth when chief executive Marcel Ospel merged Swiss Bank Corporation with the larger Union Bank of Switzerland, whereupon the name changed yet again to Warburg Dillon Read and finally to UBS Warburg. But in November 2002, as part of a corporate rebranding exercise, UBS decided to drop the name Warburg, along with that of PaineWebber, another of its recent acquisitions.[154] Ironically, after all Siegmund Warburg's strictures against his less gifted relatives, the Warburg name has survived longer in both Hamburg and New York. Of the firm that he created in London, nothing now remains save memories. Even the name Mercury disappeared not long after Merrill Lynch bought MAM for £3.1 billion in 1997 – a sum that would surely have astonished Warburg.

What caused the downfall of S. G. Warburg & Co.? It could, of course, be argued that none of the British merchant banks could ever have hoped to match the sheer resources of the big foreign firms that invaded London's Square Mile after Big Bang. Between 1990 and 2000, Morgan Grenfell, Barings, Kleinwort Benson, Smith New Court, NatWest Markets, Barclays de Zoete Wedd and finally Schroders all lost their independence to foreign buyers. Only Rothschilds survives today, as a family-owned boutique. There was, in John Jay's vivid phrase, a kind of 'doom loop', in which failure to match the foreign banks' compensation packages led to an exodus of talent, leading in turn to a takeover.[155] Yet Warburgs always had the best shot at the global bulge bracket. What had gone wrong?

Henry Grunfeld blamed Cairns, telling him he had 'destroyed in one year what [Siegmund Warburg and he] had built up over sixty years' – though the last of the Uncles continued stoically coming to work for the next four years, until literally the day of his death at the age of ninety-five.[156] Ian Fraser blamed a combination of 'arrogance' and 'insufficient dedication' that was not confined to Cairns alone.[157] The *Economist* took a similar view:

> Warburg's failure has been not in its vision but in its implementation. It tried to go it alone and from scratch in America. When that strategy failed it waited too late before seeking a rich partner in the form of Morgan Stanley . . . Britain's premier investment bank was [then] . . . compelled by stock-exchange rules to make a premature announcement of merger talks . . . [which] subsequently fell through . . . Sir David Scholey [who had become chairman when Cairns was appointed CEO] . . . must rue the arrogance that led Warburg to go on thinking it could survive by itself even as its profits were collapsing.[158]

An American verdict was that Warburgs had 'become English and City establishment through and through', and the result had been 'a real attitude problem, a cosiness and smugness of mentality which is out of tune with the modern world'.[159] For a veteran insider like Michael Valentine, the bank's distinctive ethos had simply been 'swamped' by the additional personnel from the brokers and jobbers that had been bolted on.[160] David Freud, however, felt the bank's leadership, drawn predominantly from among the corporate financiers like Valentine, had 'failed to adjust to the revolution in handling risk in scale in the securities markets'.[161]

Chances were arguably missed, for example the decision in 1986 not to buy the small US investment bank Wertheim – yet another abortive attempt to secure a New York footing (though Schroders later struggled to make a success of its acquisition of Wertheim). The expansion of the bank's fixed interest business in 1994 was a leap in the dark, as Cairns himself confessed to Freud, and a leap the bank's capital base (£720 million in 1990) simply could not support. There was clearly a loss of control over costs and a waning of that 'employee ownership mentality' which Warburg had striven for so long to inculcate. The old corporate finance model of bespoke deals for long-standing clients was obsolescent, but the old guard 'were extremely reluctant to allow teams to be built which could operate with clients on a volume basis'.[162] As the *Economist* wryly observed, in its later years Warburgs had evinced 'a singular inability to make money for anybody but its employees . . . [which is] perhaps . . . why it is remembered so fondly'.[163] But by the mid-1990s it was no longer making them enough.

Nevertheless, it was Peter Stormonth Darling who gave the simplest answer to the question of why S. G. Warburg disappeared. 'Those at the helm', he wrote, simply 'forgot to follow some of Siegmund's most basic rules. Most of all, he sought to guard against the complacency that followed success and which he sensed could too often lead to what he called "expansion euphoria".'[164]

As we look back on the decade of worldwide 'expansion euphoria' that opened the twenty-first century, an era in which the big Western banks were the principal cheerleaders for unfettered financial markets and the most reckless risk-takers – an era which ended in the greatest financial crisis since the Great Depression – it is hard not to wish that a great many more people in the financial world had followed those same rules. Above all, we must regret that the appetite for making money from 'handling risk in scale in the securities markets' – piling on the leverage and trading at the highest possible frequencies – supplanted Warburg's passionate attention to the psychological factor in financial relationships. As George Steiner rightly said, bringing 'an especial integrity to the life of high finance' was Siegmund Warburg's mission. If this small biographical contribution to modern financial history has one unchallengeable claim to make, it is that we still have much to learn from his lives and time.

Appendix: Graphology

Clients of the merchant bank SG Warburg have been a little perturbed to hear of that institution's unorthodox technique for selecting little merchant bankers. Apparently the young gentlemen are instructed to write out 500 words with pen and ink on stout paper and this is then dispatched to old Siegmund Warburg's Swiss lady graphologist. If the Oracle does not approve of their handwriting, no amount of academic distinction or financial acumen will help the aspirants.

Private Eye, July 1970

Of all the facets of Siegmund Warburg's multi-faceted personality, his faith in graphology – the analysis of handwriting – posed the biggest problem for this biographer. From the outset, I found it inherently implausible that any profound psychological insights into a man's personality could be inferred from a sample of his handwriting. And yet the evidence in Siegmund Warburg's papers and from many other sources made it clear that most of the key decisions about personnel at S. G. Warburg & Co. were based in part on graphological analysis. A candidate for employment would first be interviewed and his credentials scrutinized. Siegmund Warburg had great and not unwarranted faith in his own abilities as a judge of character, and no one proceeded further who fell at this most important fence. However, Warburg also insisted on sending off a handwriting sample for independent analysis by a professional graphologist, for many years the Zurich-based graphologist and psychologist Theodora Dreifuss. As a general rule, the only information the graphologist received was the age, sex and nationality

of the writer. It was exceedingly hard, though not impossible, for someone to be hired by Warburgs if the verdict of the graphologist was very
negative – though it was perfectly possible for a positive verdict to be
ignored if other factors counted against a candidate.* When I began
my research I took the view that this was akin to consulting an astrolo-
gist, a view evidently shared at the time by *Private Eye*. I was surprised
to find that a number of other European firms still follow this practice.[1]
I was even more surprised to find that not a single former Warburgs
director I interviewed shared my scepticism. I began to wonder if I was
writing the history of a bank or of a cult.

The 200 or so graphological reports that have survived in Siegmund
Warburg's papers certainly make for interesting reading, especially as
Warburg also liked to get reports on the handwriting of some of the
more eminent politicians and businessmen he dealt with.[2] Theodora
Dreifuss's analyses of the personalities of well-known public figures
– notably the young Nigel Lawson, who would go on to become chancellor of the exchequer – all ring remarkably true at the first reading.[3]
On close inspection, however, her approach had much in common with
the Freudian psychology in which Warburg also believed, and to which
it was indeed related through interested psychotherapists like Herbert
Binswanger.

Dreifuss had something like a formula, which consisted of asserting
that intelligent men had buried weaknesses of various sorts. She seldom
wrote a report that was categorically negative – though she risked the
phrase 'psychopathic megalomaniac' in at least one case – leaving
Warburg to take what he wanted from her assessment. And her assertions were more or less impossible to falsify, since they concerned
subliminal traits that might or might not surface in the future. Only
occasionally did she make an obviously wrong call. 'Tiny' Rowland,
for example, proved to be anything but 'very careful and circumspect
in his business dealings'.[4] Jim Slater was another who slipped through
Theodora's net ('nothing binding can be said about the writer's human

---

* In 1965, despite a glowing testimonial from Dreifuss, John Goodwin was very nearly
turned down, at Peter Spira's insistence, because he was connected to Joe Hyman, a
client who was giving the firm a good deal of trouble. In the end Spira was overruled
by Warburg, who summoned Goodwin for an interview and offered him a job without
further ado.

integrity and reliability') – though the experience persuaded Slater to employ a graphologist at Slater Walker.[5]

In any case, it is distinctly possible from the intimate tone of their correspondence that Siegmund Warburg's relationship with Theodora Dreifuss was as romantic as it was scientific.[6] It seems clear that he established the European Foundation of Graphological Science and Application in Zurich primarily in order to provide her with an institutional base.[7] She may even have been one of the unspoken reasons for his move to Switzerland. Warburg certainly made no secret of the relationship, even proposing that he and Eva go on holiday *à quatre* with Theodora and her husband Leopold.[8] And Warburg was certainly not insincere in his belief (as he put it when the Zurich institute opened in 1963) that graphology had the potential to become a rigorous science:

I realise [he admitted] that many people still consider graphologists to be cranks and eccentrics. Actually, graphologists pioneer new segments of psychological knowledge. Many sciences have started as myths. The knowledge of the stars began as astrology and only gradually became the accurate science of astronomy. Today no one would call an astronomer a crank. Eventually, I am convinced, graphology will become *hoffähig* – presentable at the court of profound knowledge.[9]

Yet Warburg's relationship with Dreifuss made that less likely, not more. As he himself sought to study graphology with the British practitioner Joan Cambridge – whose Scientific Graphologists company he also supported financially – he began to supply Dreifuss with hints of his own assessments in the covering letters he sent with samples, which naturally raises questions about the objectivity of her subsequent reports.[10] In some cases, he carried out his own handwriting analysis, as in the case of Edward Heath (see Chapter 10) and Kenneth Keith.[11] Soon he had got into the habit of telling Dreifuss precisely why he was interested in an individual, in a way that must surely have marked her cards.[12] By the mid-1960s he had grown so reliant on her opinion that he arranged for Peter Stormonth Darling to meet her in Zurich so that she could study the man behind the handwriting, at a time when he suspected Darling of having 'deteriorated' psychologically.[13] There were times when Warburg would write to her or telephone her on a daily basis, sending an incessant stream of writing samples and badgering her for her views on everyone from the latest Gresham Street trainee to the Prime Minister's wife.[14] On at least two occasions, he even got her to analyse his own son (see Chapters 9 and 12).

In 1972, David Scholey turned the tables by asking a graphologist to analyse Warburg's own hand. With characteristic chutzpah, he read the report aloud as part of a speech at Warburg's seventieth-birthday dinner:

You are a man of great authority and competence and your judgment is based on instinct and a sense of reliability. You are irritated by unpunctuality, sloppiness and superficiality. Facetiousness is the least popular word in your vocabulary. Your timing is perfect which makes you a wonderful negotiator.

Your handwriting is that of a rather unique human being, not so much for outstanding vision, imagination, efficiency, thoroughness and tenacity but for the rare quality of a great man – your complete lack of envy; your readiness to admire the performance of others, their standards and their achievements. You are more proud to see the fruits of your teaching than your own success.[15]

This was not science. It was deft flattery. To do him full justice, Warburg did not pretend that graphology was infallible. 'There have been some anomalies,' he admitted to George Steiner. 'Perhaps in 10–20% of cases my judgement has differed from the graphological analysis. However there have been only rare cases where the graphological analysis has been diametrically opposed to my instinct . . . In this connection it must always be borne in mind that a conscientious graphologist is very afraid that a negative analysis may destroy a person, and is therefore particularly careful to avoid a harshly worded analysis.'[16]

Before writing this appendix, I asked if I could see the analysis of my own handwriting that was carried out before Siegmund Warburg's trustees agreed to entrust me with the task of writing his biography. So accurate was the assessment – not least the discussion of my principal fault – that it did much to dispel my scepticism. It is all too true that I 'lack in practical, hands-on resourcefulness'. I do indeed 'find refuge in ideas, books and artistic endeavours, which do not expose [me] to competitive efforts or people who are emotionally more solid than [I am]'. 'Obviously,' the graphologist wrote in conclusion, 'his fragile and vulnerable emotional structure is not without unresolved conflicts and emotional baggage, which weigh on him (later this could

become more of a problem), but which he is unable to face or tackle
. . . His intellectual work provides a sense of purpose and goal, allowing him to sublimate, integrate and find a place for himself.'[17] (What
a harshly worded analysis would have said I shudder to think.) These
comments may simultaneously help to explain why Siegmund Warburg
attached importance to graphology, and why it was possible for me
– precisely because of my so legible character flaws – to write this
account of his many lives.

The fact nevertheless remains that graphology has not become
hoffähig, as Warburg had hoped. Like eugenics, in fact, it had its best
shot at respectability in the nineteenth and early twentieth centuries,
when writers like Abbé Michon, Jules Crépieux-Jami, Alfred Binet and
Ludwig Klages eagerly promoted it as a 'science of the future'. But the
post-war schism between 'graphoanalysis' and 'holistic graphology',
like the contemporaneous rifts within the Freudian community, was a
harbinger of decline. Today graphology is a pseudoscience of the past.
Degrees are offered in graphology at just four universities in the world,
in Italy, Spain and Argentina. The only American institution ever to do
so was Felician College in Lodi, New Jersey, and it stopped in 2000.
The reason is clear. Numerous studies by experimental psychologists
since the 1960s have demonstrated that graphology has, to quote the
British Psychological Society, 'zero validity' as a method of assessing
aptitude or personality.[18] There are also legal objections to its use in
the United States.* With all due respect to the subject of this book, I
therefore do not propose to start using it to assess my students, my
junior colleagues – or myself.

---

* Handwriting analysis had to be dropped even by the Warburg die-hards at Mercury
Asset Management after it was acquired by Merrill Lynch, because the American bank's
lawyers ruled that handwriting analyses could be construed as discriminatory if they
were obtained under the Freedom of Information Acts by employees in dispute with
the company.

Notes

ABBREVIATIONS

BoE	Bank of England
FW	Felix Warburg papers
GW	George Warburg papers; and George Warburg himself
JS	Joshua Sherman papers
JW	James P. Warburg papers
LSE	London School of Economics
MW	Max M. Warburg papers
NA	The National Archives, Kew
PW	Paul M. Warburg papers
SGW	Siegmund Warburg papers; and Siegmund Warburg himself
UWMRC	University of Warwick Modern Records Centre

PREFACE

1. SGW Box 34, SGW to Goldman, 13 November 1974.
2. Roberts and Kynaston, *City State*, p. 86.
3. SGW Personal Documents, SGW Draft sketch of 'Expensive Lessons', n.d.
4. SGW Personal Documents, Steiner interview, June 1976.
5. SGW VME/MA../ZZ../4, SGW Diary, 11 February 1944.
6. The most significant of these were with Patrick Hutber for the *Sunday Telegraph* in 1970 and Cary Reich for *Institutional Investor* in 1980. He also co-operated with Ernest Bock's article about the firm in *Aspect* (1963) and with the American journalist Joseph Wechsberg when he wrote a profile of Warburg for the *New Yorker* (1966). Generally speaking Warburg insisted on

seeing draft articles in advance of publication and reacted irately if his corrections were not accurately implemented in the published text.

7. Attali, *Man of Influence.*

8. Farrer, *Warburgs* is journalistic and unreliable. Chernow, *Warburgs* is better but still relies much more heavily on interviews than on primary sources. Rosenbaum and Sherman, *M. M. Warburg & Co.* is an authorized history of the original family firm.

9. See my *Ascent of Money.*

10. Warburg [Max], *Aufzeichnungen*; Warburg [James], *Long Road Home*; Warburg [Eric], *Times and Tides*; Warburg Spinelli, *Erinnerungen.*

11. SGW DME/CO../RPBZ/6, SGW to Eric Warburg, December 16, 1971; May 8, 1972; Box 29, SGW to Eric Warburg, May 23, 1972.

12. SGW VME/CL/CZ../2, SGW to Eric Warburg, February 2, 1972; February 3, 1972; February 4, 1972; Box 29, Toby Eady to SGW, June 27, 1972; SGW to Eady, June 28, 1972; VME/CL/CZ../2, SGW to Eady, July 31, 1972; Box 30, David Farrer to Toby Eady, August 10, 1972; VME/CL/CZ../2, SGW to Eric Warburg, October 11, 1972; January 7, 1973; January 10, 1973; Box 31, August 20, 1973; Box 34, SGW to Ziegler, September 11, 1974; Box 35, January 31, 1975.

13. Chernow, *Death of the Banker*, esp. pp. 125–30.

14. See Sherman, 'Left Bank Account'.

15. See e.g. Darling, *City Cinderella*; Fraser, *High Road*; Nott, *Here Today*; Spira, *Ladders and Snakes*; Valentine, *Free Range Ego.*

CHAPTER 1:
SIEGMUND AND HIS COUSINS

1. Mann, *Joseph and his Brothers*, p. v.

2. Attali, *Man of Influence*, pp. 111f.

3. Rosenbaum and Sherman, *M. M. Warburg & Co.*, p. 51.

4. Mosse, *German-Jewish Economic Elite*, p. 168.

5. Jaide, *Generationen eines Jahrhunderts*, p. 44.

6. Evans, *Death in Hamburg*, p. 181.

7. Ibid., pp. 181–226, 403–69.

8. Warburg, *Aufzeichnungen*, pp. 14f.

9. Gombrich, *Aby Warburg*, pp. 117, 128.

10. Ibid., pp. 14–19. See also the genealogies in ibid., pp. 172f.; and the biographical dictionary in Warburg Spinelli, *Erinnerungen*, pp. 442–61.

11. Rosenbaum and Sherman, *M. M. Warburg & Co.*, p. 19.

12. Ibid., pp. 22f. The fact that Moses refused to ransom his brother when he was imprisoned by the French in 1813 suggests that an oath might have been advisable.

13. Ibid., pp. 51f.

14. Warburg, *Aufzeichnungen*, pp. 2ff.

15. Rosenbaum and Sherman, *M. M. Warburg & Co.*, pp. 14–19; Warburg Spinelli, *Erinnerungen*, pp. 442ff.

16. Rosenbaum and Sherman, *M. M. Warburg & Co.*, pp. 32ff.; Warburg, *Aufzeichnungen*, pp. 2f.

17. The Hirsch family were notable Jewish exponents, but non-Jewish families of the Hamburg *Grossbürgertum* did likewise. See Mosse, *German-Jewish Economic Elite*, pp. 161–85.

18. There was only one obvious slip: Marianne's marriage to a swindler by the name of Zagury, who cost the family a great deal in the course of a protracted divorce. Of Siegmund's children, one married a Gunzburg (though this connection also turned sour), and two others married into the Stuttgart Kaullas: Rosenbaum and Sherman, *M. M. Warburg & Co.*, p. 46; Mosse, *German-Jewish Economic Elite*, p. 172.

19. Schnee, 'Hoffaktoren-Familie Kaulla'.

20. Warburg, *Aufzeichnungen*, pp. 3–7.

21. Warburg Spinelli, *Erinnerungen*, pp. 447, 449–51.

22. Warburg, *Aufzeichnungen*, pp. 8–13.

23. Warburg Spinelli, *Erinnerungen*, pp. 445, 456, 458.

24. Ibid., pp. 52f.

25. Ibid., p. 447.

26. Ibid., pp. 458f.; JW, James Warburg, 'Diary', pp. 1–32.

27. Gombrich, *Aby Warburg*, pp. 93–109.

28. See Warburg Spinelli, *Erinnerungen*, pp. 40ff.

29. Mosse, *German-Jewish Economic Elite*, pp. 96f.

30. Ibid., pp. 166, 168, 178.

31. Ferguson, *World's Banker*, pp. 302f.

32. Evans, 'Family and Class in the Hamburg Grand Bourgeosie'.

33. Schramm, *Neun Generationen*, vol. II, pp. 334–77, 401–8.

34. Ibid., p. 425.

35. Mann, *Buddenbrooks*, pp. 47f.

36. Schramm, *Neun Generationen*, vol. II, pp. 445–53.

37. Ibid., p. 401.

38. Warburg, *Aufzeichnungen*, p. 14.

39. Rosenbaum and Sherman, *M. M. Warburg & Co.*, pp. 1–13.

40. Ferguson, *World's Banker*, pp. 302f.

41. Rosenbaum and Sherman, *M. M. Warburg & Co.*, pp. 91–112. Details in the firm's unpublished annual reports, drawn up by Max Warburg himself after 1903.

42. Rothschild Archive London, XI/130A/o, N. M. Rothschild & Sons to de Rothschild Frères, May 7, 1906.

43. Rosenbaum and Sherman, *M. M. Warburg & Co.*, p. 75; MW, M. M. Warburg & Co., 'Jahresbericht 1917'.

44. Pohl, *Hamburger Bankengeschichte*, pp. 96–101.

45. Rosenbaum and Sherman, *M. M. Warburg & Co.*, pp. 29–43. Cf. Mosse, *German-Jewish Economic Elite*, pp. 161–85.

46. Birmingham, *Our Crowd*, pp. 154–87. See also Cohen, *Jacob H. Schiff*; Adler and Schiff, *Jacob H. Schiff*.

47. Ferguson, *Paper and Iron*, pp. 31–92.

48. See in general Freimark and Herzig, *Hamburger Juden*; Zimmermann, *Hamburgischer Patriotismus und deutscher Nationalismus*; Krohn, *Juden in Hamburg*.

49. Lorenz, *Juden in Hamburg*, vol. I, p. lxv.

50. Ibid., p. lxxiv.

51. Ibid., pp. xlii, xlv, li.

52. Warburg, *Aufzeichnungen*, pp. 2f.; Rosenbaum and Sherman, *M. M. Warburg & Co.*, p. 46. See also Warburg Spinelli, *Erinnerungen*, p. 43.

53. See Gombrich, *Aby Warburg*, pp. 25, 81f., 93, 137.

54. Mosse, *German-Jewish Economic Elite*, p. 152.

55. Freudenthal, *Vereine in Hamburg*, pp. 423, 522.

56. Ibid., p. 522.

57. Lorenz, *Juden in Hamburg*, vol. I, p. cxxxvi.

58. Ibid., pp. liii, cxxix.

59. Warburg Spinelli, *Erinnerungen*, p. 446; Schramm, *Neun Generationen*, vol. II, p. 451.

60. Lorenz, *Juden in Hamburg*, vol. I, p. lxv.

61. Ibid., pp. lxvff.; Warburg Spinelli, *Erinnerungen*, p. 43; Schramm, *Neun Generationen*, vol. II, pp. 314, 414.

62. Cecil, *Albert Ballin*, p. 36.

63. Hamel, *Völkischer Verband*, pp. 14–122.

64. See e.g. Evans, *Death in Hamburg*, pp. viii, 88f.

65. Schramm, *Neun Generationen*, vol. II, 305–8, 448.

66. SGW DME/AA../CNZZ/5, Eric Warburg to SGW, June 5, 1969.

67. See in general Hauschild-Thiessen, *Bürgerstolz und Kaisertreu*.

68. Washausen, *Hamburg und die Kolonialpolitik des Deutschen Reiches*, pp. 55–179; Böhm, *Überseehandel und Flottenbau*, pp. 76–130.

69. See Ferguson, 'Max Warburg and German Politics'.

70. Cecil, *Albert Ballin*, p. 118.

71. Vagts, 'M. M. Warburg & Co.', p. 330.

72. Warburg, *Aufzeichnungen*, p. 24.

73. Ibid., pp. 311f., 320–7.

74. Vagts, 'M. M. Warburg & Co.', pp. 342ff.

75. MW, M. M. Warburg & Co., 'Jahresbericht 1911'.

76. Berghahn, *Germany and the Approach of War*, p. 78.

77. Max M. Warburg, 'Die geplante Reichsfinanzreform. Wie vermeiden wir, daß aus der Beseitigung der Reichsfinanznot eine Bundesstaatsfinanznot entsteht?', in PW, Ser. II, Box 8, Folder 118.

78. Warburg, *Aufzeichnungen*, pp. 29–33.

79. MW, M. M. Warburg & Co., 'Jahresbericht 1905'.

80. Vagts, 'M. M. Warburg & Co.', pp. 318f.

81. Reitmayer, *Bankiers im Kaiserreich*, p. 334.

82. MW XIX, Gesammelte Vorträge, Max M. Warburg, 'Finanzielle Kriegsbereitschaft und Börsengesetz', August 5, 1907.

83. Kroboth, *Finanzpolitik des Deutschen Reiches während der Reichskanzlerschaft Bethmann Hollwegs*, p. 56.

84. MW, M. M. Warburg & Co., 'Jahresbericht 1911'.

85. Berghahn, *Germany and the Approach of War*, pp. 68, 78.

86. Warburg, *Aufzeichnungen*, pp. 27ff.; Cecil, *Albert Ballin*, pp. 161–5, 180–200.

87. Pohl, *Hamburger Bankengeschichte*, p. 110.

88. MW, M. M. Warburg & Co., 'Jahresbericht 1914', pp. 1f. This passage was crossed out in pen at a later date, probably when Warburg was preparing to publish his *Aufzeichnungen* in the 1940s. See MW, M. M. Warburg & Co., 'Jahresbericht 1920'; Warburg, *Aufzeichnungen*, p. 29.

89. GW, Worte am Sarge von Herrn Rechtsanwalt Dr Jordan, October 18, 1923.

90. Warburg Melchior, 'Dear Past', p. 171.

91. A year earlier, his sister had married Otto Kaulla.

92. See e.g. GW, Georges Warburg [SGW's father] to Elsa Warburg, November 25, 1901.

93. Warburg Melchior, 'Dear Past'.

94. GW, Uhenfels Visitors' Book.

95. SGW Personal Documents, Steiner interview, June 1976.

96. SGW VME/CL/CZ../2, SGW, 'Lucie L. Warburg 13/03/1866–25/10/1955', December 1, 1955.

97. Ibid.

98. For Siegmund, to 'live like a real Kaulla' meant having the ability 'to savour both what is pleasant as much as what is hard': SGW VME/CL/CZ../2, SGW to Eric Warburg, December 29, 1927.

99. SGW VME/CL/CZ../2, SGW to Edgar Koerner, February 20, 1954.

100. SGW VME/CL/CZ../2, SGW, 'Lucie L. Warburg 13/03/1866–25/10/ 1955', December 1, 1955.

101. Ibid. See also SGW DME/AA../CNZZ/5, SGW to A. E. Smurthwaite, December 21, 1954.

102. SGW VME/CL/CZ../2, SGW, 'Lucie L. Warburg 13/03/1866–25/10/ 1955', December 1, 1955.

103. SGW Personal Documents, Steiner interview, June 1976. See also SGW VME/CL/CZ../2, SGW, 'Lucie L. Warburg 13/03/1866–25/10/1955', December 1, 1955.

104. SGW VME/CL/CZ../2, SGW to Jacob Rothschild, October 1, 1980.

105. SGW Box 37, SGW, 'Preface' to answers to Steiner questions about his life, August 2, 1976.

106. SGW VME/CL/CZ../2, SGW, 'Erinnerung an das Uracher Seminar (1918–20)', *Württembergische Seminar Nachrichten* (1976–7) [*Mitteilungsblatt des Hilfsvereins für die evangelischen Seminare*, Heft 19–20], p. 379.

107. Witness the somewhat muted reunion with a contemporary named Richard Wagner in 1964.

108. SGW Personal Documents, Steiner interview, June 1976.

109. Ibid.

110. Haffner, *Defying Hitler*, pp. 13–23.

111. SGW Personal Documents, SGW Draft sketch of 'Expensive Lessons', June 1976.

112. Ibid.

113. SGW Personal Documents, George Steiner draft interview, June 1976.

114. Gombrich, *Aby Warburg*, p. 206.

115. Warburg Spinelli, *Erinnerungen*, p. 54.

116. Warburg, *Aufzeichnungen*, p. 7.

117. PW, Series I, Box 4, Folder 53, Paul Warburg to President Wilson, May 27, 1918.

118. Ferguson, *Paper and Iron*, pp. 93–151.

119. Warburg, *Aufzeichnungen*, p. 46.

120. MW, M. M. Warburg & Co., 'Jahresbericht 1916', p. 13, Warburg to Ballin, March 10, 1916; Warburg to Wahnschaffe (Under State Secretary at the Reich Chancellery), May 19, 1916.

121. MW, M. M. Warburg & Co., 'Jahresbericht 1914', Anlage IV, 'Gutachten über eine mögliche Kriegsentschädigung', November 26, 1914; MW, M. M. Warburg & Co., 'Jahresbericht 1918', Anlage 13, 'Bemerkungen über die östlichen Friedensverträge und die deutschen Kriegsziele', May 1, 1918.

122. MW, M. M. Warburg & Co., 'Jahresbericht 1914', p. 6; Warburg, *Aufzeichnungen*, pp. 34f.

123. MW, M. M. Warburg & Co., 'Jahresbericht 1915', pp. 2–5; 'Jahresbericht 1916', Warburg to Ballin, February 2, 1916; Warburg, *Aufzeichnungen*, pp. 39–48; Cecil, *Albert Ballin*, pp. 272, 276–84, 295f., 307. See also Haupts, *Deutsche Friedenspolitik*, pp. 113f.

124. MW, M. M. Warburg & Co., 'Jahresbericht 1916', Warburg to Ballin, February 2, 1916. See also Haupts, *Deutsche Friedenspolitik*, p. 119.

125. MW, M. M. Warburg & Co., 'Jahresbericht 1917', Warburg to Langwerth von Simmern, January 26, 1917.

126. MW, M. M. Warburg & Co., 'Jahresbericht 1918', p. 3; Warburg, *Aufzeichnungen*, p. 58; Baden, *Erinnerungen*, pp. 248, 252, 660f.

127. MW, M. M. Warburg & Co., 'Jahresbericht 1918', Anlage 13, Max M. Warburg, 'Bemerkungen über die östlichen Friedensverträge und die deutschen Kriegsziele', May 1, 1918.

128. Haupts, *Deutsche Friedenspolitik*, pp. 103, 119f., 123, 132f.

129. SGW Personal Documents, Steiner interview, June 1976. See also SGW Personal Documents, SGW, 'Expensive Lessons', June 1976.

130. SGW Personal Documents, Steiner interview, June 1976.

131. SGW Personal Documents, SGW, 'Expensive Lessons', June 1976.

CHAPTER 2:
THE FIRST WORLD REVOLUTION

1. SGW Box 37, SGW answer to Steiner question.
2. Ibid.
3. MW, M. M. Warburg & Co., 'Jahresbericht 1918', pp. 12–13a, Anlage 36, Tagebuchnotizen (Fritz Warburg). Cf. Comfort, *Revolutionary Hamburg*, pp. 4, 6f.; Ferguson, *Paper and Iron*, pp. 152–97.
4. See e.g. Schramm, *Neun Generationen*, vol. II, pp. 407, 498.
5. SGW Personal Documents, Steiner interview, June 1976.
6. Ibid.
7. MW, M. M. Warburg & Co., 'Jahresbericht 1918', pp. 4–6, Anlage 1, 5, 8, 9, 21.
8. Ibid., Anlage 5, Max Warburg to Fritz Warburg, October 7, 1918.
9. Warburg, *Aufzeichnungen*, p. 64.
10. MW, M. M. Warburg & Co., 'Jahresbericht 1917', p. 19. Cf. *Hamburger Fremdenblatt*, December 8, 1917, which explicitly attributed his defeat to anti-Semitism.

11. Warburg, *Aufzeichungen*, p. 68; Bundesarchiv Koblenz, R45 II/53, DVP Geschäftsführende Ausschuß, April 19, 1920.

12. MW, M. M. Warburg & Co., 'Jahresbericht 1919', Max Warburg to Alice Warburg, June 20, 1919.

13. MW, M. M. Warburg & Co., 'Jahresbericht 1918', Anlage 6, Warburg to Schiffer [State Secretary at Reich Treasury Office], November 17, 1918.

14. MW, M. M. Warburg & Co., 'Jahresbericht 1919'. Cf. Warburg, *Aufzeichnungen*, pp. 70–78.

15. Ferguson, 'Keynes and the German Inflation'. Cf. Skidelsky, *Keynes*, vol. I, pp. 358–63.

16. See Ferguson, *Paper and Iron*, pp. 198–363.

17. See Krüger, 'Rolle der Banken'. Krüger misleadingly suggests that Warburg 'spoke on behalf of industry'; ibid., p. 572. See also Krüger, *Deutschland und die Reparationen*, pp. 74–82.

18. MW, M. M. Warburg & Co., 'Jahresbericht 1919', Max Warburg to Eric Warburg, April 24, 1919.

19. MW, 34, Politische Correspondenz 1923, [untitled memorandum on currency], August 12, 1923.

20. Ferguson, *Paper and Iron*, chapters 5 to 7.

21. For an overview, see Ferguson, 'Constraints and Room for Manoeuvre'.

22. MW, M. M. Warburg & Co., 'Jahresbericht 1920', p. 31.

23. MW, M. M. Warburg & Co., 'Jahresbericht 1918', Anlage 6, Warburg to Schiffer, November 17, 1918.

24. Ibid., pp. 11, 11a.

25. MW, M. M. Warburg & Co., 'Jahresbericht 1920', pp. 12ff., 25.

26. MW, M. M. Warburg & Co., 'Jahresbericht 1919', Warburg to Schiffer, [day illegible] December 1918.

27. MW XIX, Gesammelte Vorträge, 'Die notwendigen Vorbedingungen für die Gesundung der deutschen Währung' [speech delivered at the 5th Deutsche Bankiertag, October 26, 1920].

28. MW, M. M. Warburg & Co., 'Jahresbericht 1919', Max Warburg to Alice Warburg, June 7, 1919.

29. MW 34, Politische Correspondenz 1923, Melchior Notiz, August 22 1923; Melchior Angabe, May 24, 1923; Warburg to Arndt von Holtzendorff [Hapag director], August 5, 1923; Warburg [untitled memorandum on currency], August 12, 1923.

30. MW 34, Politische Correspondenz 1923, Max Warburg to Alice Warburg, November 21, 1923.

31. SGW Personal Documents, Steiner interview, June 1976.

32. MW 33 contains details of the firm's balance sheet before and after stabiliz-

ation. Although the bank had built up a nest-egg of foreign currency worth around 10 million gold (i.e. pre-inflation) marks, it lost a substantial sum of money as a result of unsuccessful commodity speculation: MW, M. M. Warburg & Co., 'Jahresbericht 1923'.

33. MW, M. M. Warburg & Co., 'Jahresbericht 1920'.

34. SGW Personal Documents, Steiner interview, June 1976.

35. SGW VME/MA../ZZ../4, SGW Diary, February 1933–January 1935.

36. SGW DME/CO../RPBZ/6, SGW to Paul Ziegler, September 29, 1975.

37. SGW Personal Documents, Steiner interview, June 1976.

38. SGW Box 38, SGW to Tony Griffin, January 12, 1977.

39. SGW VME/CL/CZ../2, SGW to Max Warburg, June 6, 1920.

40. SGW VME/CL/CZ../2, Max Warburg to SGW, June 8, 1920.

41. SGW Personal Documents, Steiner interview, June 1976.

42. SGW VME/MA../ZZ../4, SGW Diary, February 1933–January 1935.

43. SGW DME/AA../CNZZ/5, Edmund Stinnes to SGW, May 12, 1972.

44. SGW VME/CL/CZ../2, SGW Draft memoir of Carl Melchior, October 12, 1965.

45. Ferguson, 'Keynes and the German Inflation'. Cf. Keynes, *Two Memoirs*, pp. 11–71.

46. PW, Series 1, Box 4, Folder 56, Benjamin Strong to Paul Warburg, August 9, 1918. See also the material in PW, Series 1, Box 2, Folders 21 and 22; JW, James Warburg 'Diary' MSS, pp. 34–44.

47. Federal Reserve Bank, New York, Benjamin Strong Papers, Paul Warburg to Strong, August 13, 1918.

48. Birmingham, *Our Crowd*, pp. 316f.

49. Details of the Amsterdam memo in PW, Series I, Box 4, Folder 58; Box 5, Folders 59, 60, 61, 62; Series II, Box 8, Folders 93, 96; Federal Reserve Bank, New York, Strong Papers 1000.3, Diary, pp. 94f.

50. SGW Personal Documents, Steiner interview, June 1976.

51. Ibid.

52. Rothschild Archive, London, XI/111/433, Anthony de Rothschild to Max Warburg, August 9, 1926; SGW to Anthony and Lionel de Rothschild, November 1, 1926.

53. SGW Personal Documents, Steiner interview, June 1976.

54. Palin, *Rothschild Relish*.

55. SGW Personal Documents, Steiner interview, June 1976.

56. SGW VME/CL/CZ../2, SGW to Erich Alport, February 21, 1928.

57. SGW VME/MA../ZZ../4, SGW Diary, March 26, 1942.

58. SGW VME/CL/CZ../2, SGW Aphorisms on love and friendship.

59. SGW VME/CL/CZ../2, SGW to his parents-in-law, May 22, 1927.

60. See Chapter 4. On flirtation see SGW, VME/MA../ZZ../4, SGW Diary, February 1933–January 1935.

61. Grunfeld interview.

62. SGW Box 36, SGW to Pierre Moussa, May 3, 1976.

63. SGW VME/MA../ZZ../4, SGW Diary, December 28, 1935.

64. GW to the author, September 7, 2004.

65. GW, SGW to Philipson, n.d., c. 1927.

66. SGW VME/CL/CZ../2, SGW to Eva Warburg, 'To be opened after my death', August 16, 1937.

67. GW interview.

68. GW, SGW to Philipson, March 5, 1927.

69. SGW VME/CL/CZ../2, SGW to Aby Warburg, October 26, 1927.

70. SGW VME/CL/CZ../2, SGW to Aby Warburg, June 29, 1927.

71. SGW VME/CL/CZ../2, SGW to Marie-Louise Spiegelberg, 28 June 1927.

72. SGW VME/CL/CZ../2, SGW to Eric Warburg, July 1, 1927.

73. SGW VME/CL/CZ../2, SGW to Mr Maurice, August 8, 1927.

74. SGW VME/CL/CZ../2, SGW to Emma and Oskar Warburg, July 7, 1927.

75. SGW VME/CL/CZ../2, SGW to Aby Warburg, December 26, 1927.

76. SGW VME/CL/CZ../2, SGW to Max Warburg, July 6, 1927.

77. SGW VME/CL/CZ../2, SGW to Herr Dufour, June 20, 1927.

78. SGW VME/CL/CZ../2, SGW to Magda and Eduard Goldschmidt, August 12, 1927.

79. SGW VME/CL/CZ../2, SGW to Erich Alport[?], December 29, 1927.

80. SGW VME/CL/CZ../2, SGW to Aby Warburg, December 6, 1927.

81. SGW VME/CL/CZ../2, SGW to Aby Warburg, December 26, 1927.

82. SGW VME/CL/CZ../2, SGW to Walter, February 13, 1928.

83. GW, SGW to Philipson, December 15, 1927.

84. GW, SGW to Philipson, August 23, 1927.

85. SGW VME/CL/CZ../2, SGW to Max Warburg, December 8, 1927.

86. SGW VME/CL/CZ../2, SGW to Eric Warburg, December 19, 1927.

87. SGW VME/CL/CZ../2, SGW to Max Warburg, January 11, 1928. See also SGW to Kocherthaler, January 13, 1928.

88. SGW VME/CL/CZ../2, SGW to Brinckmann, March 31, 1928.

89. Ibid.

90. GW, SGW to Philipson, December 15, 1927. See also February 19, 1928; SGW to Ludwig Rosenthal, March 17, 1928.

91. SGW VME/CL/CZ../2, SGW to Max Warburg, January 11, 1928.

92. SGW VME/CL/CZ../2, SGW to Karl [surname unidentifiable], January 3, 1927; SGW to Herr Hamlet, August 17, 1927.

93. SGW VME/CL/CZ../2, SGW to Max Warburg, November 11, 1927.

See also SGW to Aby Warburg, November 11, 1927; SGW to Hans Meyer, March 24, 1928.

94. SGW VME/CL/CZ../2, SGW to Kocherthaler, January 13, 1928.

CHAPTER 3:
THE DEGENERATION OF A REPUBLIC

1. GW, SGW to Philipson, May 8, 1927.

2. Balderston, *German Economic Crisis.*

3. Ritschl, *Deutschlands Krise und Konjunktur.*

4. See in general James, *German Slump.*

5. Significantly, his uncles had wanted him to stay there longer than the year they had originally agreed: SGW VME/CL/CZ../2, SGW to Aby Warburg, January 28, 1928.

6. SGW VME/CL/CZ../2, SGW to Hamlet, August 17, 1927.

7. SGW VME/CL/CZ../2, SGW to Erich Warburg, December 29, 1927.

8. SGW VME/CL/CZ../2, SGW to Kurt A. Salomonsohn, September 18, 1928.

9. SGW VME/CL/CZ../2, SGW to Philipson, August 20, 1928.

10. SGW VME/CL/CZ../2, SGW to Karl, August 17, 1927.

11. SGW VME/CL/CZ../2, SGW to Herr Solmitz, November 12, 1927.

12. SGW VME/CL/CZ../2, Max Warburg to SGW, December 31, 1929; SGW to Max Warburg, January 2, 1930.

13. GW, SGW to Philipson, May 8, 1927.

14. GW, SGW to Philipson, May 23, 1927.

15. SGW VME/CL/CZ../2, SGW to Ludwig Rosenthal, March 17, 1928.

16. SGW VME/CL/CZ../2, SGW to Brinckmann, March 31, 1928.

17. SGW VME/CL/CZ../2, SGW to Karl, August 17, 1927.

18. SGW VME/CL/CZ../2, SGW [in Eva Warburg's hand] to Nachmann, September 30, 1930.

19. SGW VME/CL/CZ../2, SGW to Samuel Stephany, December 26, 1927.

20. SGW VME/CL/CZ../2, SGW to Wilhelm [surname unidentifiable], December 26, 1927.

21. SGW VME/CL/CZ../2, SGW to Erich Warburg, December 29, 1927.

22. SGW VME/CL/CZ../2, SGW to Walter [surname unidentifiable], February 13, 1928. See also SGW to Herr Winkler, February 18, 1928.

23. PW, Series I, Box 5, Folder 65, Paul Warburg to H. M. Robinson, May, 6 1929. See also Paul Warburg to Andrew Mellon, March 8, 1929; Paul Warburg to Sir Henry Strakosch, May 25, 1930.

24. SGW Personal Documents, Steiner interview, June 1976.

25. Born, *Bankenkrise.*

26. Balderston, 'German Banking between the Wars', p. 564.

27. Schnabel, 'German Twin Crisis'. See also the same author's 'Great Banks' Depression'.

28. Hardach, *Weltmarktorientierung und relative Stagnation*, pp. 126–31.

29. James, 'German Banking Crisis of 1931'.

30. Ferguson and Temin, 'Made in Germany', esp. p. 36.

31. Schnabel, 'German Twin Crisis', p. 10.

32. SGW VME/CL/CZ../2, SGW to Nachmann, October 23, 1930. Warburg asked Nachmann to tear this letter up after reading it.

33. Ibid.

34. Ibid.

35. GW, SGW Diary, September 1, 1930.

36. Pohl, *Hamburger Bankengeschichte*, p. 147.

37. JW, Box I, 'Skizze zu den Richtlinien für eine Reorganisation', May 31, 1931; James Warburg to Paul Warburg, June 8, 1931, June 9, 1931, June 10, 1931, June 15, 1931; James Warburg, 'A Book for Jimmy', pp. 52–6.

38. JW, Box I. Cf. Rosenbaum and Sherman, *M. M. Warburg & Co.*, pp. 133–56; James, *German Slump*, p. 311; Büttner, *Staats- und Wirtschaftskrise*, pp. 217–33; Pohl, *Hamburger Bankengeschichte*, pp. 145–9.

39. James, *German Slump*, p. 311.

40. Ibid., pp. 315, 387f.

41. JW, James Warburg, 'A Book for Jimmy', pp. 55–60.

42. Warburg, *Long Road Home*, p. 93.

43. JW, James Warburg, 'A Book for Jimmy', p. 65.

44. SGW VME/MA../ZZ../4, SGW Diary, February 25, 1934.

45. Ibid.

46. Ibid.

47. Ibid.

48. James, 'German Banking Crisis', p. 82.

49. Borchardt, 'Zwangslagen und Handlungsspielräume'.

50. The arguments are reviewed in Borchardt and Ritschl, 'Could Brüning Have Done It?'

51. SGW Personal Documents, Steiner interview, June 1976.

52. These memoranda do not appear to have survived.

53. GW, SGW Diary, September 30, 1930.

54. GW, SGW Diary, October 1, 1930.

55. SGW Personal Documents, Steiner interview, June 1976.

56. GW, SGW to Philipson, October 21, 1930.

57. SGW Personal Documents, Steiner interview, June 1976.

58. SGW VME/MA../ZZ../4, SGW Diary, July 7, 1942.

59. SGW Box 34, SGW to Freddie Rubinski, October 12, 1974.

60. GW, SGW Diary, October 2, 1930. See also SGW 4, SGW Diary, March 1, 1933.

61. GW, SGW Diary, October 2,1930.

CHAPTER 4: EXILE

1. SGW Personal Documents, Steiner interview, June 1976.

2. SGW VME/MA../ZZ../4, SGW Diary, March 4, 1933. Interestingly, the next five lines of the entry were subsequently cut out.

3. See esp. Ritschl, *Deutschlands Krise und Konjunktur*.

4. Lohalm, *Völkischer Radikalismus*; Krause, 'Hamburger NSDAP'.

5. For the press attacks against Warburg in July 1919, MW, Warburg 'Aufzeich-nungen' MS, June 23, 1919; Jochmann (ed.), *Nationalsozialismus und Revolution*, pp. 5–10, 25–8.

6. Bundesarchiv Potsdam, RKÜöO 67174, Bl. 329, Deutschvölkische Schutz-und Trutzbund Abschrift 1922; Warburg, *Aufzeichnungen*, pp. 107, 120–25; Vagts, 'M. M. Warburg & Co.', p. 377.

7. MW, Allgemeines 1922, Max Warburg to Paul Warburg, July 1, 1922; MW, M. M. Warburg & Co., 'Jahresbericht 1922', Warburg, Diktat (1940).

8. Jochmann (ed.), *Nationalsozialismus und Revolution*, pp. 49ff. See also Krause, 'Hamburger NSDAP', p. 32.

9. MW 34, Politische Correspondenz 1923, Warburg Notiz, November 5, 1923; Max Warburg to Alice Warburg, November 9, 1923; Aufzeichnungen MS, p. 311; Warburg, *Aufzeichnungen*, pp. 120–25.

10. MW 34, Politische Correspondenz 1921, Max Warburg to Alice Warburg, August 28, 1921.

11. Politisches Archiv des Answärtigen Amts R1010, Rechenberg to Auswär-tiges Amt, August 29, 1919; Jochmann (ed.), *Nationalsozialismus und Revolution*, pp. 5–10, 25f. See also Lorenz, *Juden in Hamburg*, vol. II, p. 1005.

12. Bundesarchiv Koblenz, von Loebell NL, Max Warburg to von Loebell, December 23, 1919; MW, Politische Correspondenz 1920, von Loebell to Max Warburg, August 17, 1920.

13. Lorenz, *Juden in Hamburg*, vol. II, pp. 1014f.; Vagts, 'M. M. Warburg & Co.', pp. 378ff.

14. MW, M. M. Warburg & Co., 'Jahresbericht 1919', Max Warburg, 'Rede gehalten vor den hamburgischen kaufmännischen Vereinen am 5. März 1919';

Max Warburg to Hermann Samson, July 13, 1920; Max Warburg to von Loebell, August 7, 1920.

15. MW, Allgemeines 1922, Max Warburg to Lili du Bois-Reymond, July 15, 1922; Fritz Warburg to Max Warburg, July 20, 1922; Lili du Bois-Reymond, to Max Warburg, July 21, 1922; Max Warburg to Melchior, July 25/28, 1922; Lili du Bois-Reymond to Max Warburg, July 30, 1922; Max Warburg to Fritz Warburg, August 12, 1922. Cf. Lorenz, *Juden in Hamburg*, vol. II, p. cxli.

16. MW, Allgemeines 1922, 'Aufruf' [draft], August 1922.

17. Lorenz, *Juden in Hamburg*, vol. II, p. cxlviii.

18. Details in Ferguson, *Paper and Iron*, pp. 137–43.

19. See in general Krause, 'Hamburger NSDAP'.

20. Hamilton, *Who Voted for Hitler?*, pp. 101–28.

21. Jochmann (ed.), *'Im Kampf um die Macht'*.

22. Büttner, *Politische Gerechtigkeit*, pp. 82n, 135f., 192, 198–206.

23. Kohlhaus, 'Hapag', p. 176.

24. Kraus, 'Hamburger NSDAP', pp. 202–8.

25. Ibid., pp. 208–10; Büttner, *Politische Gerechtigkeit*, pp. 266f.; James, *German Slump*, p. 140.

26. On the idea of the Nazi seizure of power as a 'restoration' see Johe, 'Institutionelle Glechschaltung in Hamburg'.

27. Büttner, 'Ende der Weimarer Republik'; Büttner, 'Rettung der Republik oder Systemzerstörung'.

28. GW, SGW to Philipson, September 15, 1930.

29. GW, SGW to Philipson, October 21, 1930.

30. SGW Personal Documents, Steiner interview, June 1976.

31. SGW VME/MA../ZZ../4, SGW Diary, February 27, 1933.

32. SGW VME/MA../ZZ../4, SGW Diary, February 28, 1933.

33. SGW VME/MA../ZZ../4, SGW Diary, March 6[?], 1933.

34. SGW VME/MA../ZZ../4, SGW Diary, March 2, 1933.

35. SGW VME/MA../ZZ../4, SGW Diary, March 6[?], 1933.

36. Ibid.

37. Ibid.

38. SGW VME/MA../ZZ../4, SGW Diary, March 11, 1933.

39. SGW VME/MA../ZZ../4, SGW Diary, March 19, 1933.

40. SGW VME/MA../ZZ../4, SGW Diary, March 8, 1933.

41. SGW VME/MA../ZZ../4, SGW Diary, March 9, 1933.

42. For the first expression of unease about anti-Semitism, see SGW VME/MA../ZZ../4, SGW Diary, March 12, 1933.

43. SGW VME/MA../ZZ../4, SGW Diary, March 21, 1933.

44. Noakes and Pridham (eds.), *Nazism*, vol. I, p. 130.

45. Jochmann, 'Gesellschaftliche Gleichschaltung', p. 95.

46. He was obliged to give up 18 of his 108 supervisory-board seats in 1933: Warburg, *Aufzeichnungen*, pp. 147ff.; Rosenbaum and Sherman, *M. M. Warburg & Co.*, pp. 157f.

47. Warburg Spinelli, *Erinnerungen*, pp. 95ff.

48. Rosenbaum and Sherman, *M. M. Warburg & Co.*, p. 158.

49. Lester, *Suicide and the Holocaust*, p. 87.

50. SGW Personal Documents, Steiner interview, June 1976.

51. SGW VME/MA../ZZ../4, SGW Diary, March 27, 1933.

52. Ibid.

53. SGW VME/CL/CZ../2, SGW Fragment, March 31, 1933.

54. SGW VME/CL/CZ../2, SGW to Philipson, March 31, 1933.

55. SGW VME/CL/CZ../2, SGW, Fragment, April 4, 1933.

56. Columbia University Oral History Collection, James P. Warburg Diary, pp. 382f.

57. Ibid., pp. 709–32.

58. Ibid.

59. SGW VME/CL/CZ../2, Philipson to SGW, May 15, 1933.

60. SGW VME/CL/CZ../2, SGW to 'Mein Bestes', May 25, 1933.

61. SGW VME/CL/CZ../2, SGW to Philipson, May 25, 1933.

62. SGW VME/CL/CZ../2, SGW to James Warburg, October 20, 1935.

63. SGW VME/MA../ZZ../4, SGW Diary, March 24, 1934.

64. Ibid.

65. SGW VME/CL/CZ../2, SGW to James Warburg, October 9, 1934.

66. SGW VME/CL/CZ../2, SGW to James Warburg, October 20, 1935.

67. SGW VME/CL/CZ../2, SGW Memorandum, London April 1, 1939.

68. SGW VME/CL/CZ../2, SGW to James Warburg, October 9, 1934.

69. Ibid.

70. SGW VME/CL/CZ../2, SGW to Philipson, October 8, 1934.

71. SGW VME/CL/CZ../2, SGW to Eva Warburg, September 16, 1933. Also 'interested' in the new firm, according to Siegmund, were Rothschilds and Barings.

72. SGW VME/CL/CZ../2, SGW to James Warburg, October 20, 1935. See e.g. SGW VME/CL/CZ../2, SGW to Kohn-Speyer, February 18, 1935. Founded with a capital of £84,000, it grew quite rapidly, thanks principally to the investment of profits from Warburg's new financial mediation business.

73. SGW VME/CL/CZ../2, SGW to James Warburg, October 9, 1934. It was obligatory to publish the nationality of directors of UK companies and for obvious reasons Warburg had no desire to broadcast his German origins. See also SGW Personal Documents, Agreement between SGW and

the New Trading Company Ltd, November 12, 1934. His role was defined as being to 'render to the Company services of an advisory nature . . . and [to] use his best endeavours to promote the placing of business with the Company by the Dutch Group which he represents'. He would 'take part in the deliberations of the Board' but would not be entitled to a vote.

74. Oscar Lewisohn papers, 'Selected Reminiscences of Henry Grunfeld', October 1999.

75. SGW VME/CL/CZ../2, James Warburg to SGW, October 3, 1938.

76. SGW VME/CL/CZ../2, SGW to James Warburg, October 20, 1934.

77. Jacob Rader Marcus Center of the American Jewish Archives, Cincinnati, Felix Warburg Collection, SGW to Felix M. Warburg, July 23, 1936.

78. Wake, *Kleinwort Benson*, pp. 472f.

79. Figures courtesy of a document in the private possession of John Goodwin. Cf. SGW VME/CL/CZ../2, SGW to James Warburg, November 8, 1937.

80. SGW VME/CL/CZ../2, SGW Fragment, July 6, 1933.

81. SGW VME/CL/CZ../2, SGW to James Warburg, October 20, 1935.

82. SGW VME/MA../ZZ../4, SGW Diary, December 28, 1935.

83. See e.g. SGW Abs Correspondence, SGW to Abs, September 13, 1937; VME/CL/CZ../2, SGW to Abs, August 1, 1939. For visits to Germany see FW, SGW to Felix Warburg, March 1, 1936.

84. SGW VME/CL/CZ../2, SGW 'Entwurf', September 1941.

85. Details in Bajohr, *'Aryanization' in Hamburg*, pp. 24, 35, 53, 125f.; Köhler, *'Arisierung'*, p. 141, table 12.

86. SGW VME/CL/CZ../2, SGW to James Warburg, January 6, 1938. See also James Warburg to SGW, January 18, 1938. Cf. Bajohr, *'Aryanization' in Hamburg*, pp. 208ff.; Köhler, *'Arisierung'*, pp. 330ff.

87. SGW VME/CL/CZ../2, SGW to James Warburg, April 2, 1938.

88 Ibid.

89. GW interview.

90. See Mosse, *German-Jewish Economic Elite*, p. 293; Vagts, 'M. M. Warburg & Co.', p. 387.

91. Warburg, *Aufzeichnungen*, pp. 146f.

92. Feldman, *Allianz*, pp. 67, 71; Bajohr, *'Aryanization' in Hamburg*, pp. 127f.; Barkai, 'Max Warburg im Jahre 1933'.

93. SGW DME/AA../CNZZ/5, Dr Joseph Walk, Yad Vashem, Jerusalem, to Eric Warburg, April 30, 1975, citing Wagener's post-war testimony. Siegmund Warburg disbelieved this story: Eric Warburg to SGW, May 26, 1975; SGW to Eric Warburg, June 2, 1975. Cf. Wagener's memoir, *Hitler aus nächster Nähe*.

94. Bajohr, *'Aryanization' in Hamburg*, pp. 128f.

95. Ibid., pp. 131f.

96. Köhler, 'Arisierung', pp. 106, 320.

97. Bajohr, 'Aryanization' in Hamburg, p. 130; Dippel, Wheel of Fire, pp. 174f. Cf. Rosenbaum and Sherman, M. M. Warburg & Co., p. 161.

98. Dippel, Wheel of Fire, p. 175. See also Bajohr, 'Aryanization' in Hamburg, p. 125.

99. Warburg Spinelli, Erinnerungen, pp. 150f.

100. SGW VME/CL/CZ../2, 'Memorandum, London, April 1939'.

CHAPTER 5:
TRADING AGAINST THE ENEMY

1. SGW VME/CL/CZ../2, SGW to Erich Alport, February 21, 1928.

2. SGW VME/CL/CZ../2, SGW to Philipson, May 25, 1933.

3. SGW VME/CL/CZ../2, SGW to Louis Golding, April 26, 1937.

4. SGW VME/MA../ZZ../4, SGW Diary, December 31, 1939.

5. SGW VME/MA../ZZ../4, SGW Diary, March 20, 1942.

6. SGW VME/MA../ZZ../4, SGW Diary, May 26, 1940.

7. SGW VME/MA../ZZ../4, SGW Diary, May 31, 1940.

8. SGW VME/MA../ZZ../4, SGW Diary, April 7, 1942.

9. SGW VME/MA../ZZ../4, SGW Untitled memorandum, July 8, 1941.

10. SGW VME/MA../ZZ../4, SGW Notes for Emanuel Shinwell, October 2, 1942.

11. SGW VME/MA../ZZ../4, SGW to Shinwell, October 2, 1942.

12. Darling, City Cinderella, p. 117.

13. SGW VME/MA../ZZ../4, SGW Diary, June 13, 1940. McFadyean was not uncritical of Warburg on occasion: see e.g. LSE McFadyean papers, McFadyean to SGW, May 1, 1941.

14. SGW VME/MA../ZZ../4, SGW Diary, February 1–May 8, 1940; SGW VME/CL/CZ../2, Minutes of the board meeting, November 11, 1940.

15. SGW VME/MA../ZZ../4, SGW Diary, October 14, 1943.

16. Oscar Lewisohn papers, 'Selected Reminiscences of Henry Grunfeld', October 1999.

17. Oscar Lewisohn papers, 'Henry Grunfeld', reflections on his eightieth birthday, 1981.

18. Oscar Lewisohn papers, Grunfeld, 'How Siegmund Warburg and I Met', December 13, 1993.

19. Oscar Lewisohn papers, 'Selected Reminiscences of Henry Grunfeld', October 1999.

20. Oscar Lewisohn papers, Grunfeld, 'Speech on the Occasion of his 90th Birthday', 1991.

21. Oscar Lewisohn papers, Grunfeld to SGW, September 28, 1971.

22. Oscar Lewisohn papers, Grunfeld to SGW [draft letter], c. August 1, 1971.

23. Oscar Lewisohn papers, SGW to Grunfeld, May 27, 1974.

24. Oscar Lewisohn papers, SGW to Grunfeld, May 25, 1954.

25. Oscar Lewisohn papers, SGW to Grunfeld, July 28, 1971.

26. Oscar Lewisohn papers, 'Selected Reminiscences of Henry Grunfeld', October 1999. See also *The Times*, October 28, 1980, for Korner's obituary.

27. SGW VME/CL/CZ../2, Thalmann to SGW, undated fragment, summer 1943.

28. See Oscar Lewisohn papers, Charles Sharp, 'Sir Siegmund Warburg: Some Recollections'.

29. SGW VME/MA../ZZ../4, SGW Diary, December 28, 1935.

30. SGW VME/CL/CZ../2, SGW to Carl T. Keller, May 26, 1942.

31. SGW VME/CL/CZ../2, SGW to Hans Fabry, November 18, 1940; SGW to Edmund H. Stinnes, November 28, 1940.

32. Eva had put George's name down for Westminster at the suggestion of a kindly housemaster's wife some years before. It was a school of which his father had formed a positive impression: GW, SGW to GW, February 28, 1940.

33. SGW VME/MA../ZZ../4, SGW Diary, September 30, 1939.

34. SGW VME/MA../ZZ../4, SGW Diary, December 31, 1939.

35. SGW VME/CL/CZ../2, SGW to Lewis V. Randall [the former Ludwig Rosenthal of M. M. Warburg], September 10, 1941.

36. SGW VME/CL/CZ../2, SGW to Fritz Warburg, April 28, 1942.

37. SGW VME/CL/CZ../2, SGW to Philipson, September 29, 1945.

38. SGW VME/CL/CZ../2, SGW to Keller, June 10, 1940.

39. SGW VME/CL/CZ../2, SGW to Fritz Warburg, April 28, 1942.

40. SGW VME/CL/CZ../2, SGW to Philipson, September 29, 1945.

41. SGW VME/MA../ZZ../4 SGW Diary, September 5, 1944.

42. SGW VME/CL/CZ../2, SGW to Philipson, September 29, 1945.

43. SGW VME/MA../ZZ../4, SGW Diary, December 31, 1943.

44. Anna Biegun interview.

45. Anna Biegun, private communication, September 21, 2009.

46. Chernow, *Warburgs*, p. 413. Cf. London, *Whitehall and the Jews*, pp. 16–32.

47. SGW VME/CL/CZ../2, SGW Memorandum to Lucas, February 15, 1938.

48. SGW VME/CL/CZ../2, SGW to Lucas, October 7, 1938.

49. Newton, *Profits of Peace*. See also Ferguson, *War of the World*, pp. 336–44, 370–72.

50. SGW VME/MA../ZZ../4, SGW Diary, September 30, 1939.

51. SGW VME/MA../ZZ../4, SGW Diary, October 6, 1939.

52. SGW VME/MA../ZZ../4, SGW Diary, September 20 and 23, 1939.

53. SGW VME/MA../ZZ../4, SGW Diary, May 10, 1940; Oxford University, Margot Asquith papers MS Eng. d.3275 47, SGW to Chamberlain, enclosure in SGW to Lady Oxford, May 13, 1940.

54. SGW VME/CL/CZ../2, SGW to Kurt Neu, June 5, 1940.

55. Churchill Archive Centre, Cambridge, Amery papers, AMEL 7/34, Amery Diary, June 13, 1940; SGW VME/MA../ZZ../4, SGW Diary, June 13 and 18, 1940. See also Memorandum of April 23, 1941; Memorandum of May 8, 1941; Memorandum of February 17, 1942.

56. SGW VME/MA../ZZ../4, SGW Diary, February 1–May 8, 1940.

57. See e.g. SGW VME/CL/CZ../2, SGW Memorandum, May 13, 1943.

58. Churchill Archive Centre, Cambridge, Amery papers, AMEL 7/33, Amery Diary, September 19, 1939.

59. SGW VME/MA../ZZ../4, SGW Diary, October 13, 1939.

60. SGW VME/MA../ZZ../4, SGW Diary, October 18, 1939.

61. SGW VME/MA../ZZ../4, SGW Diary, February 1–May 8, 1940, and SGW to Sinclair (two letters), May 6, 1940.

62. SGW VME/MA../ZZ../4, SGW Diary, May 28, 1940.

63. SGW VME/MA../ZZ../4, Secretary of the Offices of the War Cabinet to SGW, January 4, 1941, and SGW Diary, January 7 and 8, 1941; SGW to James Warburg, January 8, 1941.

64. SGW VME/CL/CZ../2, SGW Memorandum, June 10, 1941. They met again the following year: SGW VME/MA../ZZ../4, SGW Diary, May 1, 1942.

65. SGW VME/CL/CZ../2, D. A. C. Dewdney, October 9, 1941.

66. SGW VME/MA../ZZ../4, Draft for letter by Lucas to Eden, June 3, 1941; Draft for letter by Lucas to Eden, February 17, 1942.

67. SGW VME/MA../ZZ../4, SGW to Cripps, February 9, 1942; Memorandum, July 13, 1942.

68. SGW VME/MA../ZZ../4, SGW Diary, September 27, 1939. See also October 21 for Max Warburg's argument in favour of accepting Hitler's disingenuous peace offer to Britain.

69. See e.g. SGW VME/MA../ZZ../4, SGW Diary, September 11, 1939; 'Some Thoughts for a Speech on a New Magna Carta', enclosure in SGW to Lady Oxford, August 27, 1940; SGW Memorandum, November 22, 1940; SGW Memorandum [sketch for a broadcast to the German people], December 30, 1940; SGW, 'Fragments of a speech which might make every bomb dropped on Germany twice as effective as it would otherwise be', January 7, 1941; 'Special points of propaganda', March 10, 1941; 'A Few Points on Propaganda', June 20, 1941; 'Notes Concerning Propaganda', December 7, 1943.

70. SGW VME/MA../ZZ../4, SGW Diary, September 12, 1939. See also enclosure: Sofort Programm (for a post-war Germany).

71. SGW VME/CL/CZ../2, Demuth to Notgemeinschaft Deutscher Wissenschaftler im Ausland, October 12, 1939; SGW to Leith-Ross, October 20, 1939, and accompanying 'Notes on Measures against German Foreign Trade'. Henry Grunfeld was also a member of the economic committee.

72. SGW VME/MA../ZZ../4, SGW Diary, September 4, 1939, and enclosure.

73. SGW VME/MA../ZZ../4, SGW Diary, September 7 and 8, 1939.

74. SGW VME/CL/CZ../2, Anonymous memorandum, probably by SGW, October 25, 1938; Undated memorandum, probably by SGW in early 1940. See also diary entry of September 14, 1939.

75. Violet Bonham Carter, Diary, May 15, 1940, in Pottle (ed.), *Champion Redoubtable*, pp. 213f.

76. SGW VME/CL/CZ../2, SGW to Max Warburg, April 4, 1940.

77. SGW VME/MA../ZZ../4, SGW Undated memorandum, *c.* November 1939. See also enclosure to diary, January 26, 1940.

78. SGW VME/CL/CZ../2, D.H. to W., January 14, 1940.

79. Klemperer, *German Resistance*, pp. 397f.

80. SGW VME/CL/CZ../2, SGW Memorandum, November 22, 1941.

81. SGW VME/MA../ZZ../4, SGW Diary, enclosure, January 5, 1940.

82. SGW VME/MA../ZZ../4, SGW Diary, Memorandum for Dansey, May 6, 1940.

83. SGW VME/MA../ZZ../4, SGW Diary, May 21, 1940.

84. SGW VME/MA../ZZ../4, SGW Diary, September 9, 1939. See also entry for November 17, 1939.

85. SGW VME/CL/CZ../2, SGW to Keller, June 10, 1940.

86. SGW VME/MA../ZZ../4, SGW Diary, June 16, 1940.

87. SGW VME/MA../ZZ../4, SGW Diary, May 18, 1940.

88. SGW VME/CL/CZ../2, SGW to Edmund Stinnes, November 28, 1940.

89. SGW VME/CL/CZ../2, Memorandum, enclosure in SGW to Lady Oxford, June 25, 1940. Not the least of these was Erich Körner of New Trading.

90. Ibid.

91. See the fascinating memorandum he sent to Leo Amery: VME/CL/CZ../2, SGW to Amery, June 18, 1940.

92. SGW VME/CL/CZ../2, SGW to W. P. Barrett, Treasury Chambers, September 4, 1941; Lucas to SGW, October 7, 1941.

93. SGW VME/CL/CZ../2, SGW Memorandum, February 17, 1942.

94. SGW VME/MA../ZZ../4, SGW Memorandum, April 23, 1941. See also VME/MA../ZZ../4, SGW Diary, September 19, 1939 and October 27, 1939; 'Notes of a conversation with L. S. Amery', April 5, 1940.

95. See e.g. SGW VME/CL/CZ../2, SGW 'Memorandum on Trade Possibilities in the Middle East', August 9, 1940.

96. SGW VME/MA../ZZ../4, SGW Diary, June 10, 1940.

97. SGW VME/MA../ZZ../4, SGW, 'Battle of the Atlantic', April 23, 1941.

98. SGW VME/CL/CZ../2, SGW Memorandum, May 7, 1941. The offensive was launched on June 22.

99. SGW VME/MA../ZZ../4, SGW Diary, May 8, 1943; Memorandum, August 30, 1943; Memorandum, May 1944.

100. SGW VME/MA../ZZ../4, SGW Diary, May 14, 1942; June 20, 1942. The setbacks of 1942 made Warburg for the first time critical of Churchill: see the letter he sent to *The Times*, published under the name of the journalist and Liberal MP T. L. Horabin, June 24, 1942.

101. SGW VME/MA../ZZ../4, SGW Diary, April 9, 1942; Memorandum, May 13, 1943; October 13, 1943.

102. SGW VME/CL/CZ../2, SGW to Fritz Warburg, July 30, 1945.

103. SGW VME/MA../ZZ../4, SGW Diary, June 5, 1940.

104. SGW VME/CL/CZ../2, SGW Memorandum, June 18, 1940.

105. SGW VME/CL/CZ../2. SGW, 'Draft for August 4th, 1941', July 25, 1941; 'Fragmentary Thoughts on British Foreign Policy', April 14, 1942. See also 'Problems of British Foreign Policy towards Europe', December 2, 1943.

106. SGW VME/MA../ZZ../4, SGW Diary, December 31, 1944.

107. SGW VME/CL/CZ../2, SGW to Max Warburg, February 15, 1940.

108. SGW VME/CL/CZ../2, SGW to Edmund Stinnes, March 13, 1942.

109. Oscar Lewisohn papers, Grunfeld, 'Speech on the Occasion of his 90th Birthday', 1991. See also SGW VME/CL/CZ../2, SGW to Gero von Schulze-Gaevernitz, February 17, 1940.

110. SGW VME/CL/CZ../2, SGW to Max Warburg, March 15, 1941.

111. SGW VME/CL/CZ../2, SGW to Randall, September 10, 1941.

112. For a complete listing of companies, see SGW VME/CL/CZ../2, SGW to Fritz Warburg, December 11, 1944.

113. SGW VME/CL/CZ../2, SGW, 'Business Rules of NTC', May 21, 1940.

114. SGW VME/MA../ZZ../4, SGW Diary, March 21, 1942.

115. SGW VME/CL/CZ../2, Lucas to E. Holland Martin, April 1, 1941.

116. SGW VME/CL/CZ../2, SGW to [Aunt] Agnes Warburg, April 24, 1941; SGW to Lady Oxford, May 20, 1941.

117. Oscar Lewisohn papers, 'Selected Reminiscences of Henry Grunfeld', October 1999.

118. SGW VME/MA../ZZ../4, SGW Diary, May 15, 1942; June 4, 1942; October 21, 1943.

119. SGW VME/CL/CZ../2, SGW to Spiegelberg, July 3, 1943.

120. SGW VME/CL/CZ../2, SGW to Max Warburg, December 15, 1942.

121. SGW VME/CL/CZ../2, SGW to Max Warburg, February 13, 1943.

122. SGW VME/MA../ZZ../4, SGW Diary, November 23, 1939.

123. SGW VME/CL/CZ../2, SGW to Edmund Stinnes, March 12, 1943.

124. SGW VME/CL/CZ../2, SGW Memorandum, February 23, 1943.

125. Oscar Lewisohn papers, 'Henry Grunfeld', reflections on his eightieth birthday, 1981.

126. SGW VME/CL/CZ../2, SGW to Spiegelberg, July 3, 1943.

127. SGW VME/MA../ZZ../4, SGW Diary, November 6, 1943.

128. SGW VME/CL/CZ../2, Chairman's Speech to 11th Annual Meeting [draft], August 17, 1945.

129. SGW VME/MA../ZZ../4, SGW Diary, September 5, 1944.

130. SGW VME/CL/CZ../2, SGW to the Dutch Minister for Trade and Justice, November 1, 1944.

131. SGW VME/CL/CZ../2, SGW to Fritz Warburg, December 11, 1944; SGW to Spiegelberg, June 8, 1945.

132. SGW VME/MA../ZZ../4, SGW Diary, June 10, 1940.

133. Anna Biegun interview.

134. SGW VME/CL/CZ../2, SGW to Philipson, October 2, 1947.

CHAPTER 6: RESTORING THE NAME

1. SGW VME/CL/CZ../2, Ernest Bock, 'Companies with a future: Warburg', draft article, corrected by SGW, 1963.

2. SGW DME/CO../RPBZ/6, Eric Faulkner to SGW, January 8, 1970.

3. Thomas Lamont papers, Baker Library, Harvard Business School, 136–12, Max Warburg to Lamont, October 2, 1940; Max Warburg [memorandum of conversation with Lamont], April 3, 1942.

4. Warburg Spinelli, *Erinnerungen*, pp. 445, 454.

5. Ibid., pp. 454ff.

6. Ibid., pp. 449–51. See also Birmingham, *Our Crowd*, pp. 383f.

7. Warburg Spinelli, *Erinnerungen*, pp. 150–266.

8. SGW VME/CL/CZ../2, SGW to Spiegelberg, August 30, 1945.

9. SGW VME/CL/CZ../2, SGW to Spiegelberg, June 8, 1945; SGW to Fritz Warburg, July 5, 1945.

10. SGW VME/CL/CZ../2, Eric Warburg to SGW, July 1, 1945; Max Warburg to. SGW, July 3, 1945.

11. SGW VME/CL/CZ../2, SGW to Max Warburg, July 9, 1945. See also McFadyean to Max Warburg, July 11, 1945; Max Warburg to SGW, July 12 and July 17, 1945; Louis Sterling to SGW, July 17, 1945.

12. SGW VME/CL/CZ../2, SGW to van Biema, September 19, 1945.

13. SGW VME/CL/CZ../2, SGW to Philipson, undated fragment *c.* August 1945; SGW to Eric Warburg, August 2, 1945; McFadyean to Max Warburg, August 8, 1945; SGW to Fritz Warburg, August 10, 1945; SGW to Spiegelberg, August 30, 1945; Eric Warburg to SGW, December 1, 1945; McFadyean to Eric Warburg, December 5, 1945; Eric Warburg to SGW, December 19, 1945; SGW to Eric Warburg, December 27, 1945 [telegram and letter]; Eric Warburg to SGW, January 3, 1946; SGW to Eric Warburg, January 4, 1946 [two unsent drafts]; SGW to Philipson, January 11, 1946; SGW to Eric Warburg, January 22, 1946.

14. SGW VME/CL/CZ../2, SGW to W. H. Schubart, January 18, 1946.

15. SGW VME/CL/CZ../2, SGW to Fritz Warburg, July 30, 1945.

16. SGW VME/CL/CZ../2, SGW to Philipson, September 29, 1945.

17. SGW VME/CL/CZ../2, SGW to Philipson, January 17, 1946.

18. Wake, *Kleinwort Benson*, p. 321.

19. SGW VME/CL/CZ../2, SGW to Fritz Warburg, July 30, 1945.

20. SGW VME/MA../ZZ../4, SGW Diary, September 19, 1945.

21. SGW VME/CL/CZ../2, SGW to van Biema, September 19, 1945.

22. SGW VME/MA../ZZ../4, SGW Diary, August 31, 1949.

23. SGW VME/CL/CZ../2, SGW to Abs, December 1, 1947.

24. SGW VME/MA../ZZ../4, SGW, 'Notes for my Diary', January 2, 1947.

25. SGW VME/CL/CZ../2, SGW Memorandum, August 24, 1949.

26. SGW VME/CL/CZ../2, SGW to Jakob Goldschmidt, August 31, 1949. See also SGW, 'Thoughts on the Present Economic Situation', October 15, 1949.

27. See e.g. Barnett, *Audit of War*. But see also Edgerton, *Warfare State*.

28. See Tomlinson, 'Balanced Accounts?'

29. SGW DME/AA../CNZZ/5, SGW to Amery, February 12, 1954.

30. SGW Box 6, SGW to Richard McConnell, August 21, 1961.

31. SGW Box 2, SGW to Mrs Josette Aubrey, January 19, 1959.

32. SGW VME/CL/CZ../2, SGW, 'A Few Fragmentary Thoughts on the Present Political Situation', May 26, 1950.

33. SGW VME/CL/CZ../2, SGW to Thalmann, March 12, 1952.

34. SGW VME/MA../ZZ../4, SGW, 'Note for my Diary', March 12, 1948.

35. BoE C48/51, [D.E.B.] to the Chief Cashier, May 22, 1951.

36. BoE C48/291 45, Memorandum to Sir Kenneth Peppiatt, July 20, 1953.

37. BoE C48/51, Memorandum [probably by Hilton Clarke], September 8, 1953.

38. BoE C48/149 66, H. A. S[ieppmann] Memorandum, November 17, 1948.

For a more hostile assessment, see BoE C48/149 82, Memorandum, December 2, 1949.

39. SGW Box 63, SGW Half Weekly Notes No. 1, January 3, 1951.

40. SGW Box 63, SGW Half Weekly Notes No. 7, January 29, 1951; BoE C48/51, [R.C.B.] Memorandum, May 17, 1951; J. V. Bailey to W. H. J. Cooper, June 5, 1951; SGW to D. E. Johns, June 28, 1951. For the Bank's initially negative reaction to this proposal, see BoE C48/51, Note, December 15, 1949.

41. BoE C48/51, Bolton to Deputy Governor, January 20, 1951. See also SGW Box 63, SGW Half Weekly Notes No. 13, March 31, 1952.

42. SGW VME/CL/CZ../2, SGW to Thalmann, April 18, 1952.

43. Grierson interview.

44. SGW Box 63, SGW Half Weekly Notes No. 10, March 19, 1952.

45. BoE C48/51, O'Brien to Peppiatt, November 10, 1955; Clarke to Peppiatt, February 29, 1956; SGW Box 64, SGW Daily Report, March 20, 1956; BoE C48/51, Clarke to Peppiatt, December 14, 1956.

46. BoE C48/51, H.S.C. to Chief Cashier, April 12, 1957; L.K.O'B. Note, April 17, 1957; F.C.H. Note, April 18, 1957. Formally, the bank now became known as S. G. Warburg & Co. Ltd (incorporating Seligman Brothers).

47. *Economist*, April 27, 1957.

48. Kynaston, *City of London*, vol. IV, p. 107.

49. SGW VME/CL/CZ../2, SGW to Eric Warburg, February 9, 1958.

50. BoE C48/51, Note for the Record, December 17, 1959.

51. SGW VME/CL/CZ../2, SGW to Griffin, September 1, 1955.

52. SGW Box 64, SGW Daily Report, February 23, 1956.

53. SGW Box 64, SGW Daily Report, February 28, 1956.

54. SGW Box 64, SGW Daily Report, April 5, 1956.

55. SGW DME/AA../CNZZ/5, SGW to Hailsham, February 28, 1957.

56. SGW Box 64, SGW Daily Report, July 15, 1957.

57. 'Food for Thought', *Investors Chronicle*, September 21, 1961.

58. SGW Box 63, SGW Half Weekly Notes No. 11, March 24, 1952. See also SGW VME/CL/CZ../2, SGW to Grierson, May 13, 1952.

59. SGW DME/AA../CNZZ/5, SGW to Robinow, July 3, 1953.

60. SGW Box 64, SGW Daily Report, February 19, 1955.

61. SGW Box 2, SGW to John Foster, April 20, 1959.

62. SGW VME/CL/CZ../2, Special Letters, Lola Warburg to SGW, September 25, 1948.

63. 'Warburg's Record', *Sunday Times*, July 30, 1961.

64. *Economist*, August 3, 1947, p. 349.

65. See e.g. BoE C48/149 1, H.A.S. to Mr Bull, August 22, 1946, and notes by H.B.C.Y. and A.C.B.

66. BoE C48/149 4, H.A.S. Memorandum, August 28, 1946; C48/149 14, Memorandum, September 30, 1946; C48/149 25, Memorandum, December 5, 1946.
67. See Kynaston, *City of London*, vol. IV, p. 270.
68. SGW Box 24, SGW to R. H. Fry, draft article, November 8, 1969 and letter of November 12, 1969. See also later drafts of January 15, 1970.
69. SGW Box 62, SGW Journey to Switzerland, February 13, 1948.
70. SGW Box 64, SGW Half Weekly Notes No. 14, March 29, 1952.
71. SGW VME/CL/CZ../2, SGW to Marga and Edmund Stinnes, December 31, 1945.
72. SGW VME/CL/CZ../2, SGW to van Biema, June 1, 1949.
73. SGW VME/MA../ZZ../4, SGW, 'Notes for my Diary', January 2, 1947.
74. SGW VME/CL/CZ../2, Abs to SGW, July 8, 1947.
75. SGW VME/CL/CZ../2, SGW to Abs, July 15, 1947.
76. James, *Deutsche Bank and the Nazi Economic War against the Jews*. Cf. Simpson (ed.), *War Crimes of the Deutsche Bank and the Dresdner Bank*; Nicosia and Huener (eds.), *Business and Industry*, pp. 56–9.
77. James, *Nazi Dictatorship and the Deutsche Bank*, pp. 119ff.
78. Steinberg, *Deutsche Bank and its Gold Transactions*, esp. pp. 59–66.
79. SGW VME/CL/CZ../2, SGW to Abs, December 1, 1947.
80. SGW Box 45, SGW Journey to Switzerland, February 21, 1948.
81. SGW Box 62, SGW Journey to Switzerland, February 23, 1948.
82. SGW Box 63, SGW Half Weekly Notes No. 9, March 15, 1952.
83. See e.g. SGW VME/CL/CZ../2, SGW to Bücher, November 2, 1949.
84. SGW VME/CL/CZ../2, SGW to van Biema, September 19, 1945.
85. SGW VME/CL/CZ../2, SGW to Brinckmann, December 17, 1949.
86. SGW VME/CL/CZ../2, SGW to Fritz Warburg, December 12, 1949.
87. SGW Box 63, SGW Half Weekly Notes No. 26, May 28, 1951; BoE C48/51, Memorandum to the Governor, July 16, 1952.
88. Köhler, 'Arisierung', pp. 515ff.
89. SGW Box 64, Internal memorandum, August 21, 1950.
90. GW, SGW and Eva Warburg to GW, November 18, 1950.
91. SGW Box 63, SGW Half Weekly Notes No. 19, April 30, 1951; see also No. 10, March 19, 1952.
92. SGW Box 62, SGW's journey to North America, May 31, 1952.
93. SGW DME/AA../CNZZ/5, SGW to Spiegelberg, July 14, 1952.
94. SGW Box 63, SGW Half Weekly Notes No 2, January 7, 1953.
95. SGW Box 63, SGW Daily Report, April 16, 1954.
96. SGW DME/AA../CNZZ/5, SGW Daily Report, August 31, 1954; September 4, 1954; SGW Box 63, SGW Daily Report, November 1, 1954; Box 64, SGW Note, December 7, 1954.

97. SGW Box 64, SGW Daily Report, February 7, 1955; March 5, 1955; March 15, 1955; May 27, 1955; DME/AA../CNZZ/5, SGW Note, September 9, 1955; DME/AA../CNZZ/5, SGW Daily Report, September 14, 1955.

98. SGW Box 64, SGW Daily Report, February 8, 1956.

99. SGW DME/AA../CNZZ/5, SGW Note, June 3, 1957; VME/CL/CZ../2, SGW to Fritz Warburg, June 11, 1957.

100. SGW Box 63, SGW Daily Report, September 10, 1957; September 13, 1957; November 5, 1957.

101. SGW Box 1, SGW to Eric Warburg, September 12, 1958; VME/CL/CZ../2, SGW to Fritz Warburg, May 22, 1959; Box 64, SGW Daily Report, September 18, 1959.

102. SGW DME/AA../CNZZ/5, SGW to Brinckmann, March 21, 1960.

103. SGW DME/AA../CNZZ/5, SGW to Spiegelberg, June 7, 1960. See also Spiegelberg to SGW, July 6, 1960.

104. SGW DME/AA../CNZZ/5, SGW to Spiegelberg, July 16, 1960. There was an extremely bitter row on the finance committee on this subject later that year: SGW to Fritz Warburg, December 5, 1960; SGW to Brinckmann, December 7, 1960.

105. DME/AA../CNZZ/5, SGW Memorandum, September 3, 1960. See also Spiegelberg to SGW, September 27, 1960.

106. SGW Box 5, SGW to Eric Warburg, 1961; SGW to Spiegelberg, January 5, 1961.

107. SGW Box 6, SGW to Eric Warburg, October 7, 1961.

108. SGW DME/AA../CNZZ/5, SGW to Fritz Warburg, April 26, 1962; SGW to Marie-Louise Spiegelberg, July 6, 1963.

109. SGW Box 9, SGW to Marie-Louise Spiegelberg, March 9, 1963.

110. SGW Box 6, SGW to Eric Warburg, September 4, 1961.

111. SGW DME/AA../CNZZ/5, SGW to Eric Warburg, October 28, 1967; Eric Warburg to SGW, November 28, 1967.

112. 'From Wagons to Banking', *Economist*, March 6, 1954, pp. 727f.

113. Grunfeld interview.

114. SGW DME/AA../CNZZ/5, SGW to Spiegelberg, July 16, 1960.

115. SGW VME/CL/CZ../2, Grunfeld to SGW, January 13, 1956.

116. SGW DME/AA../CNZZ/5, SGW to Eric Warburg, June 4, 1968.

117. SGW VME/CL/CZ../2 SGW, 'Lucie L. Warburg', December 1, 1955.

118. SGW Box 63, SGW Half Weekly Notes No. 30, June 9, 1951.

119. SGW Box 63, SGW Half Weekly Notes No. 15, April 7, 1952.

120. SGW Box 64, SGW Daily Report, February 3, 1954; July 15, 1954.

121. SGW Box 63, SGW Daily Report, September 1, 1954; November 17, 1954.

122. See e.g. SGW Box 64, SGW Daily Report, March 24, 1956; October 15, 1956.

123. SGW Box 63, SGW Daily Report, October 30, 1956; SGW Box 64, SGW Note, November 30, 1957.

124. SGW Box 63, SGW Daily Report, September 13, 1957. Cf. Kynaston, *City of London*, vol. IV, p. 107.

125. SGW Box 1, SGW to Abs, January 6, 1958. For a good example of the range of their common business interests, see Box 2, SGW Note, October 22, 1959.

126. SGW DME/AA../CNZZ/5, Stinnes to SGW, December 11, 1970.

127. SGW Box 2, SGW Note, September 19, 1959.

128. SGW Box 64, SGW Daily Report, September 24, 1959; Box 2, SGW to Ernest Spiegelberg, November 28, 1959.

129. SGW Box 2, SGW to John S. Guest, December 14, 1959; Box 3, Minutes of group management meeting, February 11, 1960; VME/CL/CZ../2, Spethmann to SGW, October 8, 1970. See also 'Mr Warburg Laughs Last', *Daily Mail*, October 10, 1960.

130. SGW Box 3, SGW Note, June 21, 1960.

131. SGW Box 12, Sharp note to SGW, Grunfeld, Whitman and Dixon, September 29, 1964.

132. SGW Box 13, SGW to Furstenberg, January 11, 1965.

133. SGW DME/AA../CNZZ/5, SGW to Marie-Louise Spiegelberg, August 14, 1964.

134. The crisis seems to have caused Whitman to panic: DME/AA../CNZZ/5, Whitman to SGW, November 18, 1965; SGW to Whitman, November 23, 1965 and November 24, 1965.

135. 'S. G. Warburg's links with Germany intensified', *Financial Times*, January 3, 1966.

136. SGW Box 22, SGW to Policy Committee, Korner, Whitman and Sharp, July 15, 1968. See also SGW Box 13, SGW Note to Whitman, Sharp, Stheeman et al., February 24, 1965; SGW DME/AA../CNZZ/5, SGW to Daus, October 9, 1966; SGW to Wuttke, January 4, 1967; Wuttke to SGW, January 6, 1967; Box 18, SGW to Whitman, April 7, 1967 and April 10, 1967.

137. SGW Box 22, SGW to Sharp, Policy Group, Korner, Whitman and Lewisohn, November 11, 1968, and November 13, 1968; SGW to Grunfeld, Whitman, Sharp, Daus, Wuttke and Lewisohn, January 6, 1969; SGW DME/AA../CNZZ/5, SGW to Wuttke, January 6, 1969; SGW to Daus, March 5, 1969; Box 23, SGW to Grunfeld, Korner, Roll, Sharp and Lewisohn, enclosing draft letter to George Bolton, June 20, 1969; SGW to Grunfeld, Korner, Roll et al., July 27, 1969; Memorandum, July 28, 1969; SGW to Policy Group, September 29, 1969.

138. SGW DME/AA../CNZZ/5, SGW to Franz Schuette, January 10, 1967.

139. SGW Box 63, SGW Daily Report, April 8, 1954.

140. SGW DME/AA../CNZZ/5, SGW to Eden, January 17, 1955.

141. SGW VME/CL/CZ../2, SGW Fragment, November 8, 1957.

142. SGW VME/CL/CZ../2, SGW Aphorisms, n.d.

143. SGW Box 32, SGW to Mazur, November 24, 1973.

144. SGW DME/AA../CNZZ/5, SGW to Nigel Law, April 25, 1956.

145. SGW Box 2, SGW to Spiegelberg, September 3, 1959.

146. SGW DME/AA../CNZZ/5, SGW to Kurt Birrenbach, February 15, 1960.

147. SGW DME/AA../CNZZ/5, SGW to Fromm, March 23, 1967.

148. SGW Box 2, SGW to Kurt Krueger, June 8, 1959.

149. GW, SGW to GW, August 7, 1960.

150. See e.g. SGW DME/AA../CNZZ/5, SGW to Eric Warburg, August 17, 1977; VME/CL/CZ../2, SGW to Kurt Reissmueller, December 9, 1978; SGW to Goetz A. Blankenfeld, February 19, 1981.

151. GW, SGW to GW, September 27, 1980.

152. SGW DME/AA../CNZZ/5, SGW to Hans Meyer, August 18, 1960. See Meyer to SGW, August 22, 1960; SGW to Meyer, August 29, 1960; SGW to Meyer, September 19, 1960.

153. GW, Paul Ziegler to GW, April 24, 1968.

154. SGW DME/AA../CNZZ/5, Eric Warburg to SGW, May 29, 1968; SGW to Eric Warburg, June 4, 1968.

155. SGW DME/AA../CNZZ/5, Eric Warburg to SGW, January 6, 1970; SGW to Eric Warburg, January 19, 1970.

156. SGW DME/AA../CNZZ/5, SGW to Pfarrer Paul Werner, January 1, 1969.

157. SGW VME/CL/CZ../2, SGW to Kurt Reissmueller, December 9, 1978.

158. SGW DME/AA../CNZZ/5, SGW to Mayer-List, May 5, 1969.

159. SGW DME/AA../CNZZ/5, SGW to von Hase, February 13, 1973.

160. SGW DME/AA../CNZZ/5, Stinnes to SGW, February 3, 1970.

CHAPTER 7: ATLANTIC UNIONS

1. SGW VME/CL/CZ../2, SGW to Keller, December 15, 1952.

2. SGW VME/CL/CZ../2, Steiner interview with SGW, n.d.

3. GW, SGW to Philipson, August 23, 1927. See also SGW VME/CL/CZ../2, SGW to Hamlet, August 17, 1927.

4. SGW VME/CL/CZ../2, SGW to Max Warburg, January 11, 1928.

5. SGW VME/CL/CZ../2, SGW to Kocherthaler, January 13, 1928.

6. SGW Box 62, SGW Report, February 13, 1946.

7. SGW Box 62, SGW Report, March 1, 1946.

8. SGW Box 62, SGW Report, May 19, 1947.

9. SGW Box 62, SGW Report, November 14, 1947.

10. SGW Box 62, SGW Report, January 1, 1949.

11. SGW Box 62, SGW Report, September 28, 1946.

12. SGW Box 62, SGW Report, November 5, 1947.

13. SGW Box 62, SGW Report, January 4, 1949.

14. SGW VME/CL/CZ../2, SGW to Spiegelberg, October 1, 1947.

15. SGW Box 62, SGW Report, January 4, 1949.

16. SGW VME/CL/CZ../2, SGW to van Biema, January 16, 1950. See also SGW to Spiegelberg, May 30, 1951.

17. SGW Box 64, SGW Note, July 24, 1950.

18. SGW VME/MA../ZZ../4, SGW Diary, August 1, 1941.

19. SGW VME/MA../ZZ../4, SGW Diary, June 17, 1940.

20. SGW VME/MA../ZZ../4, SGW Diary, March 31, 1942.

21. See e.g. SGW VME/MA../ZZ../4, SGW Diary, February 5, 1944.

22. SGW VME/CL/CZ../2, SGW to Otto Benzinger, August 15, 1944. See also VME/CL/CZ../2, 'Security and a Future Order for Europe', n.d. 1945.

23. SGW VME/CL/CZ../2, SGW to Otto Kaulla, September 25, 1948.

24. SGW Box 62, SGW Report, January 15, 1949; DME/AA../CNZZ/5, SGW to Ziegler, October 9, 1949.

25. See e.g. SGW Box 63, SGW Note, May 21, 1951.

26. SGW VME/CL/CZ../2, SGW to Schubart, October 10, 1949.

27. SGW DME/AA../CNZZ/5, SGW to Liddell Hart, March 3, 1955.

28. SGW VME/CL/CZ../2, SGW to Randall, December 29, 1950.

29. SGW VME/CL/CZ../2, SGW to Lamm, January 13, 1951. See also SGW to Keller, August 14, 1951.

30. SGW VME/CL/CZ../2, SGW to Lamm, January 13, 1951.

31. SGW VME/CL/CZ../2, SGW to van Biema, May 8, 1950.

32. SGW Box 64, SGW Note, January 9, 1951; Box 63, SGW Note, June 9, 1951; SGW Note, August 1, 1951.

33. SGW DME/AA../CNZZ/5, SGW to Shinwell, May 25, 1951; June 4, 1951.

34. SGW VME/CL/CZ../2, SGW to Mazur, March 20, 1951.

35. SGW Box 63, SGW Note, August 7, 1951; Box 62, SGW Note, September 24, 1951. For a list of the initial members of the group, see *The Times*, September 25, 1951, p. 5.

36. *The Times*, July 9, 1952, p. 7.

37. SGW VME/CL/CZ../2, Friends of Atlantic Union, Statement of Policy, July 1952. For Warburg's later involvement in the International Atlantic Committee and the Atlantic Treaty Association, see SGW VME/CL/CZ../2,

SGW to Eppstein, March 10, 1955. When the new organization seemed to lose momentum, Warburg became frustrated: SGW Box 1, SGW to Donald McLachlan, July 29, 1958. By 1961, however, he was once again active in trying to form a high-level Advisory Council of the International Movement for Atlantic Union: SGW Box 6, Streit to Shawcross, June 23, 1961.

38. SGW DME/AA../CNZZ/5, SGW to Liddell Hart, August 3, 1954.

39. SGW Box 63, SGW Report, September 1, 1954.

40. SGW DME/AA../CNZZ/5, SGW to Spiegelberg, June 7, 1960. See also SGW to Fritz Oppenheimer, December 28, 1964.

41. SGW Box 64, SGW Report, May 28, 1955.

42. SGW Box 1, SGW to Miss Ovington, April 7, 1958.

43. SGW DME/AA../CNZZ/5, SGW to Spiegelberg, May 23, 1960.

44. SGW DME/AA../CNZZ/5, SGW to Hans Arnold, January 4, 1962.

45. SGW DME/AA../CNZZ/5, SGW to Fromm, October 31, 1966.

46. See his illuminating letter to Edmund Stinnes, drawing a parallel with the outbreak of the First World War: SGW DME/AA../CNZZ/5, SGW to Stinnes, June 4, 1967.

47. SGW VME/MA../ZZ../4, SGW Diary, September 19, 1944.

48. SGW DME/AA../CNZZ/5, SGW to Spiegelberg, May 23, 1960.

49. SGW VME/CL/CZ../2, SGW to Fritz Warburg, November 16, 1946.

50. SGW Box 62, SGW Report, September 28, 1946.

51. SGW Box 62, SGW Report, October 5, 1946.

52. SGW VME/CL/CZ../2, SGW to René H. Thalmann, December 31, 1949.

53. SGW VME/MA../ZZ../4, SGW Diary, February 5, 1942; February 11, 1944.

54. See e.g. SGW VME/CL/CZ../2, 'Initial Main Activities of New Corporation' and other draft memoranda on the same subject, May 4, 1942.

55. SGW VME/CL/CZ../2, SGW to Keller, May 26, 1942; SGW to Spiegelberg, June 8, 1945.

56. SGW VME/MA../ZZ../4, SGW Diary, December 31, 1943.

57. SGW VME/MA../ZZ../4, SGW Diary, September 5, 1944.

58. SGW VME/CL/CZ../2, SGW to Stinnes, September 13, 1945.

59. SGW Box 62, SGW Report, February 10, 1946.

60. SGW DME/AA../CNZZ/5, SGW to Ziegler, January 9, 1954.

61. SGW Box 62, SGW Report, February 18, 1946.

62. SGW Box 62, SGW Report, May 30, 1947.

63. SGW VME/MA../ZZ../4, SGW Notes for Diary, n.d., c. July 1947.

64. SGW VME/CL/CZ../2, SGW to Abs, December 1, 1947.

65. SGW Box 62, SGW Report, September 28, 1946.

66. SGW VME/CL/CZ../2, SGW to Fritz Warburg, November 16, 1946.

67. Oscar Lewisohn papers, Grunfeld, 'Speech on the occasion of his 90th

birthday', June 6, 1994. The man in question, Lewis Randall, had (when he was known as Ludwig Rosenthal) been head of foreign exchange at M. M. Warburg & Co.

68. The principal shareholders were S. G. Warburg, Helbert, Wagg & Co., Kuhn Loeb and Lehman Brothers: *Daily Telegraph*, July 7, 1953; *Economist*, November 7, 1953.

69. *Daily Telegraph*, October 4, 1955; *Economist*, August 10, 1955.

70. SGW Box 29, SGW to Darling, Grunfeld, Korner et al., May 6, 1972.

71. SGW Box 64, SGW Report, May 31, 1955.

72. SGW Box 62, SGW Report, February 16, 1948.

73. SGW VME/MA../ZZ../4, SGW Notes for Diary, December 18, 1948.

74. SGW VME/CL/CZ../2, SGW Notes on meetings with W. H. Schubart, February 6, 1949. See also Box 62, SGW to Sir Oliver S. Franks, March 19, 1949; VME/CL/CZ../2, SGW, 'A Few Fragmentary Thoughts on the Present Political Situation' [for Eden], May 26, 1950.

75. SGW Box 62, SGW Report, February 20, 1949.

76. SGW Box 62, SGW Report, February 26, 1949.

77. Maddison, *World Economy*, Table A1-d.

78. SGW VME/CL/CZ../2, SGW to Schubart, September 26, 1949.

79. SGW DME/AA../CNZZ/5, SGW to Ziegler, December 19, 1949.

80. SGW VME/CL/CZ../2, SGW to van Biema, January 16, 1950.

81. SGW VME/CL/CZ../2, SGW to Keller, November 3, 1951.

82. SGW VME/CL/CZ../2, SGW to Griffin, September 1, 1955.

83. SGW Box 64, SGW Report, February 23, 1956.

84. See Dimsdale, 'British Monetary Policy', p. 108.

85. SGW VME/CL/CZ../2, SGW Memorandum, May 24, 1950.

86. SGW VME/CL/CZ../2, SGW to Furstenberg, October 26, 1950.

87. SGW VME/CL/CZ../2, SGW Proposal for an International Defence Loan, December 24, 1951.

88. SGW Box 63, SGW Note, April 7, 1952; Box 64, SGW Note, April 9, 1952.

89. SGW Box 64, SGW Report of conversation with US Treasury Secretary Robert Anderson, June 3, 1958.

90. SGW DME/AA../CNZZ/5, Eden to SGW, February 27, 1959; SGW to Eden, March 4, 1959.

91. SGW DME/AA../CNZZ/5, SGW to Eden, July 27, 1954; October 21, 1954.

92. SGW DME/AA../CNZZ/5, SGW to Nigel Law, July 31, 1956.

93. SGW Box 64, SGW Report, November 8, 1956.

94. SGW DME/AA../CNZZ/5, SGW to Eric Warburg, December 28, 1956.

95. SGW Box 1, SGW to Vogelstein, July 19, 1958.

96. SGW Box 63, SGW Note, July 30, 1951.

97. SGW VME/CL/CZ../2, SGW to Schiff, July 1, 1952; Box 63, SGW Note, November 29, 1952. See also Memorandum for the New York Stock Exchange, November 7, 1952; BoE C48/51, Note to the Governors, November 19, 1952.

98. SGW Box 63, SGW Note, November 29, 1952.

99. Ibid.

100. SGW Box 62, SGW Note, February 20, 1953.

101. SGW Box 62, SGW, 'Thinking Aloud about a Ten-years' Plan for K.L. & Co.', April 24, 1953.

102. SGW VME/CL/CZ../2, Coordination Plan, November 30, 1953.

103. BoE C48/51, September 8, 1953.

104. JS Kuhn Loeb file, Condensed statement, May 31, 1952; Profit and loss statement for the eleven months to November 1953.

105. SGW VME/CL/CZ../2, SGW to Eva Warburg, April 4, 1954.

106. SGW VME/CL/CZ../2, SGW, 'Thinking Aloud about Some of the Present Problems of KL & Co.', November 1, 1954.

107. SGW Box 64, SGW Report, May 31, 1955.

108. SGW VME/CL/CZ../2, Schiff to SGW, December 22, 1954; Box 4, SGW Report, March 19, 1955, March 30, 1955 and April 8, 1955.

109. SGW VME/CL/CZ../2, SGW Report, May 26, 1955.

110. SGW VME/CL/CZ../2, SGW to Wiseman, January 30, 1956 and February 1, 1956; SGW VME/CL/CZ../2, SGW to Bolton, March 27, 1956.

111. SGW VME/CL/CZ../2, SGW to Wiseman, May 17, 1957.

112. SGW Box 1, SGW to Wiseman, January 9, 1958.

113. Chernow, *Warburgs*, pp. 617–20. Cf. his obituary in the *New York Times*, July 11, 1973.

114. SGW Box 1, SGW to Wiseman, March 5, 1958.

115. SGW VME/CL/CZ../2, SGW to Eva Warburg, March 20, 1958. See also SGW Draft note for partners, March 25, 1958.

116. SGW VME/CL/CZ../2, SGW to Schiff, April 15, 1958.

117. SGW VME/CL/CZ../2, SGW to [Eva Warburg?], April 16, 1958.

118. SGW VME/CL/CZ../2, SGW to [Eva Warburg?], April 17 and May 1, 1958; DME/AA../CNZZ/5, SGW to Wiseman, June 10, 1958.

119. SGW DME/AA../CNZZ/5, SGW to Wiseman, September 10, 1958.

120. SGW VME/CL/CZ../2, SGW to Schiff, December 6, 1958.

121. SGW Box 1, SGW Note to members of 9.15 Meeting, July 24, 1958; SGW to Jessel, July 28, 1958.

122. SGW VME/CL/CZ../2, SGW to Schiff, December 6, 1958.

123. SGW VME/CL/CZ../2, Schiff to SGW, April 30, 1959; SGW to Schiff, June 12, 1959; SGW to Schiff [draft], November 23, 1959; SGW to Schiff,

December 11, 1959; SGW VME/CL/CZ../2, SGW Draft, February 25, 1960; SGW Note for Swatland, March 1, 1960.

124. SGW VME/CL/CZ../2, SGW Memorandum, February 1, 1959; Yale University Library Manuscripts and Archives, Wiseman Papers, Box 19, f. 1, Wiseman to SGW, March 9, 1959.

125. SGW VME/CL/CZ../2, SGW to Schiff, June 12, 1959.

126. Yale University Library Manuscripts and Archives, Wiseman Papers, Box 19, f. 150, SGW to Wiseman, December 11, 1959; SGW Box 2, SGW to Grunfeld, December 16, 1959.

127. SGW VME/CL/CZ../2, SGW to Wiseman, March 16, 1960; DME/AA../CNZZ/5, Schiff to SGW, May 14, 1960.

128. SGW VME/CL/CZ../2, SGW Undated fragment, 1960; Box 6, SGW to Grierson, August 21, 1961; SGW to Grunfeld, October 25, 1961.

129. See e.g. SGW Box 8, Grierson to Schiff, August 20, 1962.

130. SGW DME/CO../RPBZ/6, Dreifuss Note, September 10, 1961.

131. SGW Box 9, SGW to Duschnitz, February 5, 1963.

132. SGW DME/AA../CNZZ/5, Dilworth to SGW, October 30, 1964. Cf. Box 12, SGW to Schiff, November 13, 1964; SGW Note, November 24, 1964; SGW to Jessel, December 5, 1964.

133. SGW Box 13, Nott Note to Steering Committee, January 29, 1965; Box 18, SGW to Jessel [cable], January 31, 1967. For the deterioration of this arrangement, see Box 22, SGW to Policy Committee, Korner, Whitman and Kelly, July 8, 1968.

134. SGW VME/CL/CZ../2, SGW to Eva Warburg, January 30, 1965.

135. SGW Box 64, SGW Report, February 15, 1956.

136. SGW Box 64, SGW Report, May 1, 1956.

137. Kynaston, *City of London*, vol. IV, p. 115.

138. Fraser, *All to the Good*, pp. 280f.

139. Courtney and Thompson, *City Lives*, p. 151. See also Spira, *Ladders and Snakes*, pp. 101ff.

140. SGW VME/CL/CZ../2, Steiner interview with SGW, n.d.

141. BoE G1/179 44, Governor's Note, December 22, 1958.

142. BoE G1/179 48, Governor's Note, December 31, 1958.

143. NA T 231/1287, Simon Note, January 2, 1959.

144. Kynaston, *Cazenove*, p. 237.

145. Kynaston, *City of London*, vol. IV, pp. 110–15. For a slightly different account, see Chernow, *Warburgs*, pp. 647–53.

146. Chernow, *House of Morgan*, p. 526.

147. Kynaston, *City of London*, vol. IV, p. 116.

148. Thompson, 'Pyrrhic Victory', p. 287.

149. SGW VME/CL/CZ../2, Steiner interview with SGW, n.d.

150. SGW Box 64, SGW Report, March 3, 1956.

151. SGW Box 64, SGW Report, May 1, 1956, May 27, 1956 and November 8, 1956.

152. SGW Box 64, SGW Report, May 1, 1956.

153. SGW Box 63, SGW Report, January 2 and 4, 1957.

154. SGW Box 63, SGW Report, January 7 and 8, 1957; February 4, 1957.

155. SGW VME/CL/CZ../2, Steiner interview with SGW, n.d.

156. SGW Box 63, SGW Report, January 10, 1957. See also February 5, 1957, for his conversation with André Meyer of Lazards.

157. SGW Box 63, SGW Report, February 14, 1957.

158. SGW Box 63, SGW Report, February 18, 1957. See also Yale University Library Manuscripts and Archives, Wiseman Papers, Box 19, f. 136, SGW to Wiseman, February 28, 1957.

159. SGW Box 1, SGW to Wiseman, September 25, 1958.

160. SGW Box 64, SGW Report, June 20, 1957.

161. SGW Box 64, SGW Report, October 25, 1957.

162. SGW Box 64, SGW Report, September 17, 1957.

163. SGW Box 1, SGW to Wiseman, January 14, 1958.

164. GW interview.

165. SGW Box 1, SGW Memorandum, July 1, 1958. See also Box 64, SGW Memorandum, September 12, 1958.

166. SGW Box 64, SGW Report, September 10, 1958. For evidence of Warburg's impatience with Stedeford, see SGW Report, September 17, 1958.

167. SGW Box 64, SGW Report, September, 11, 1958.

168. SGW Box 64, SGW Report, September 18, 1958; Box 1, SGW to Wiseman, September 20, 1958.

169. SGW Box 1, SGW Note, September 20, 1958.

170. SGW Box 64, SGW Report, September 23, 1958.

171. SGW Box 64, SGW Report, October 23, 1958.

172. SGW Box 64, SGW Report, November 1–5, 1958.

173. Ibid.

174. SGW Box 64, SGW Report, November 6, 1958.

175. NA T 231/1285, Sir Frank Lee Note, November 10, 1958.

176. See SGW DME/AA../CNZZ/5, Viscount Bridgeman to SGW, January 10, 1958; SGW to Bridgeman, January 13, 1958.

177. NA T 231/1285, Heathcoat-Amory to Macmillan, November 24, 1958.

178. NA T 231/1287, Simon to Macmillan, January 3, 1959.

179. NA T 231/1285, Heathcoat-Amory to Macmillan, November 24, 1958.

180. NA T 231/1285, Rickett to Makins, November 25, 1958.

181. BoE G1/179, HCBM Note, November 26, 1958.

182. NA T 231/1286, Makins to Economic Secretary to the Treasury, December 3, 1958; BoE G1/179 27, Note for the Deputy Governor, December 3, 1958.

183. NA T 231/1286, Makins to Economic Secretary, December 4, 1958.

184. NA T 231/1286, Makins Note, December 4, 1958. The offer was conditional, subject to the various stipulations imposed by the government, and for a 50:50 combination of cash and TI shares.

185. BoE G1/179 21, Makins, Record of conversation, December 2, 1958.

186. NA T 231/1286, Makins to Glaves-Smith, December 4, 1958.

187. NA T 231/1286, Anson Note, December 11, 1958; Economic Secretary Note, December 31, 1958.

188. Kynaston, *City of London*, vol. IV, pp. 111ff.; SGW VME/CL/CZ../2, Steiner interview with SGW, n.d. See also Drogheda, *Double Harness*, p. 149.

189. BoE G1/179 37, CRPH to Deputy Governor, December 9, 1958.

190. Yale University Library Manuscripts and Archives, Wiseman Box 19, f. 144, SGW to Wiseman, December 1, 1958.

191. SGW Box 1, SGW to Schiff, December 6, 1958.

192. SGW Box 2, SGW to J. H. McConnell, January 9, 1959.

193. Oscar Lewisohn papers, 'Selected Reminiscences of Henry Grunfeld', pp. 24–8.

194. As pointed out by Ernest Bock, 'Companies with a Future: Warburg', undated draft article, *c.* 1963 (in SGW VME/CL/CZ../2).

195. *News Chronicle*, January 19, 1959.

196. NA T 231/1285, Draft minute to the Prime Minister, December 2, 1958.

197. BoE G1/179, HCBM Note, November 25, 1958.

198. BoE G1/179 20, HCBM Note, December 1, 1958.

199. NA PREM 11/2670 122–6, Economic Secretary to the Cabinet, December 2, 1958.

200. NA T 231/1286, Macmillan to Heathcoat-Amory, December 3, 1958.

201. NA T 231/1285, Draft minute to the Prime Minister, December 2, 1958. For Stedeford's assurances on this score see T 231/1287, Stedeford to Simon, January 2, 1959.

202. NA T 231/1285, Rickett to Makins, November 14, 1958. The American company had offered shares rather than cash, allowing the Treasury to veto the deal 'on the ground that we did not allow UK residents to acquire dollar securities'.

203. NA T 231/1286, Minister of Transport and Civil Aviation to Macmillan,

December 4, 1958; Draft note, December 29, 1958; PREM 11/2670 71, Economic Secretary to Macmillan, December 31, 1958.

204. NA T 231/1286, Wilson to Heathcoat-Amory, December 4, 1958. Cf. Glaves-Smith Minute, December 8, 1958.

205. NA T 231/1286, Draft Cabinet paper by Economic Secretary, December 15, 1958.

206. NA T 231/1286, Macmillan to Economic Secretary, December 15, 1958; PREM 11/2670 76-7, Economic Secretary to Macmillan, December 16, 1958.

207. BoE G1/179 48, Governor's Note, December 31, 1958; G1/179 51, Makins Note, December 31, 1958.

208. GW, 'Rough Note for Ron [Chernow]', January 6, 1993.

209. BoE G1/179 55, Makins Note, January 1, 1959.

210. NA PREM 11/2670 65-6, Financial Secretary to the Treasury [J. E. S. Simon] Note, January 2, 1959; T 231/1287, Simon to Macmillan, January 3, 1959; PREM 11/2670 37-9, Macmillan to Portal, January 5, 1959; T 231/1287, Note, Secret, January 6, 1959; PREM 11/2670 43-43A, Portal to Macmillan, January 6, 1959.

211. NA T 231/1287, FJE to Macmillan, January 1, 1959.

212. Hence Warburg's short-lived suggestion to the Bank of England that the head of Barings be consulted 'to express a view on the ethics of the present position': BoE G1/179 22, Note to the Deputy Governor, December 2, 1958. Warburg later told Wiseman that the Barings senior partner, Sir Edward Reid, had 'indicate[d] to me in various ways their sympathy and support, which in the case of these reserved people means especially much': SGW Box 2, SGW to Wiseman, January 17, 1959.

213. Kynaston, *Cazenove*, pp. 234ff. Cf. Kynaston, *City of London*, vol. IV, pp. 108ff.

214. SGW Box 2, SGW to Frederick Warburg, January 8, 1959.

215. SGW Box 2, SGW to Wiseman, January 17, 1959.

216. NA T 231/1287, Makins to Financial Secretary, January 6, 1959; Macmillan to Financial Secretary, January 7, 1959; Makins Note, January 8, 1959; BoE G1/179 76, Governor's Note, January 7, 1959. Cf. SGW Box 2, 'Control of B.Al.', January 7, 1959.

217. SGW Box 2, SGW to Wiseman, January 10, 1959; DME/AA../CNZZ/5, SGW to Ovington, January 10, 1959. See also GW, GW to Michael Verey, April 15, 1996.

218. NA T 231/1287, Draft minute to Macmillan, n.d. [January 8, 1959]; Tony Phelps to C. S. Bennett, January 9, 1959; Draft minute to Macmillan, n.d. [January 16, 1959]; Minute by Macmillan, January 19, 1959.

219. NA T 231/1287, Order paper, January 20, 1959.

220. BoE G1/179 71, Governor's Note, January 2, 1959; NA T 231/1287, Makins Note, February 2, 1959.

221. NA PREM 11/2670 19–20, Macmillan Note for the record, January 17, 1959.

222. Darling interview.

223. Kynaston, *City of London*, vol. IV, p. 220.

224. Bramsen and Wain, *Hambros*, p. 432. Cf. SGW Box 2, SGW to Lionel Fraser, January 12, 1959; SGW Letter to *The Times*, draft, January 12, 1959.

225. SGW Box 2, SGW to Donald B. Macurda, January 5, 1959.

226. SGW Box 2, SGW to Grunfeld and GW, August 10, 1959.

227. SGW Box 3, SGW to Guest, February 1, 1960.

228. Fraser, *All to the Good*, p. 281; Chernow, *Warburgs*, p. 653.

229. Roberts, *Schroders*, p. 408.

230. Courtney and Thompson, *City Lives*, p. 153. See also Spira, *Ladders and Snakes*, p. 103.

231. Oscar Lewisohn papers, 'Selected Reminiscences of Henry Grunfeld', p. 28.

232. 'Catto, Stephen Gordon, second Baron Catto', *Dictionary of National Biography*.

233. SGW Box 2, SGW to Ovington, January 10, 1959.

234. SGW Box 2, SGW to Spiegelberg, January 5, 1959.

235. SGW Box 64, SGW Report, September 11, 1958.

236. SGW Box 2, SGW to Sir Findlater Stewart, January 8, 1959.

237. SGW Box 2, SGW to Schaeffer, August 10, 1959.

238. Hatch and Fores, 'Struggle for British Aluminium', p. 485.

239. SGW Box 4, SGW to Sir James Helmore, July 4, 1960.

240. SGW Box 2, SGW to Spiegelberg, March 12, 1959.

241. SGW Box 3, SGW Note, April 14, 1960. According to Warburg's account at the time, Olaf described as 'absolute nonsense' the rumour that Hambros no longer wished to do business with Warburgs. The outcome of the Aluminium War had been an example of 'sound competition in the City'. Later, Warburg recalled Hambro saying: 'Have we not been awful fools?': VME/CL/CZ../2, Steiner interview with SGW, n.d.

242. SGW DME/AA../CNZZ/5, SGW to Spiegelberg, August 30, 1960; SGW to Schiff, November 1, 1960.

243. SGW Box 8, SGW to Mazur, July 21, 1962. Cf. Box 5, SGW to James Meade, January 3, 1961; SGW to Mazur, January 18, 1961; SGW to Furstenberg, June 30, 1961; Box 8, SGW to Leonard Keesing, August 27, 1962.

244. SGW DME/AA../CNZZ/5, SGW to Randall, June 20, 1967; SGW Box 20, SGW to Dilworth, November 24, 1967.

245. SGW DME/AA../CNZZ/5, SGW to Coudenhove-Kalergi, November 12, 1951.
246. SGW Box 64, SGW to 'members of S. G. Warburg & Company Limited', December 31, 1959.

CHAPTER 8: THE FINANCIAL ROOTS OF EUROPEAN INTEGRATION

1. SGW DME/AA../CNZZ/5, Fritz Oppenheimer to SGW, May 24, 1966. A version of this chapter appeared as Niall Ferguson, 'Siegmund Warburg, the City of London and the Financial Roots of European Integration', *Business History*, 51, 3 (May 2009), pp. 362–80.
2. See e.g. Burn, 'State, City and Euromarkets'.
3. Milward, *European Rescue of the Nation-State*.
4. Richebächer, 'Problems and Prospects', p. 337.
5. Schenk, 'Sterling, International Monetary Reform and Britain's Applications', p. 359.
6. Ibid., p. 360.
7. See e.g. Hitchcock, *Struggle for Europe*.
8. Schenk, 'Sterling, International Monetary Reform and Britain's Applications', p. 348. See in general Schenk, *Britain and the Sterling Area*.
9. Schenk, 'Sterling, International Monetary Reform and Britain's Applications', p. 366. See Ellison, *United States, Britain and the Transatlantic Crisis*.
10. Schenk, 'Sterling, International Monetary Reform and Britain's Applications', p. 355.
11. For the claim that Warburg was not the progenitor of the Eurobond markets, see Kerr, *History of the Eurobond Market*, p. 11. It is clear, however, that the multiple-currency loan raised in 1957 for the Belgian oil company Petrofina was not a true Eurobond. It was a privately placed, short-term (three-year) loan.
12. Orluc, 'Wilhelmine Legacy?'.
13. SGW VME/CL/CZ../2, SGW to Ernst Kocherthaler, July 20, 1927.
14. SGW VME/CL/CZ../2, SGW to Coudenhove-Kalergi, July 26, 1927.
15. SGW VME/CL/CZ../2, SWG to Lilly Melchior-Roberts, February 16, 1940.
16. SGW VME/MA../ZZ../4, SGW Diary, February 5, 1942.
17. SGW VME/MA../ZZ../4, SGW Diary, February 18, 1942.
18. SGW VME/CL/CZ../2, SGW, 'A Few Fragmentary Thoughts on British Foreign Policy', April 14, 1942.

19. SGW VME/CL/CZ../2, SGW, 'The Principles of Federal Union Applied to British Foreign Policy', December 7, 1942. An edited version was published under the pseudonym 'Simplificator' in the *Federal Union News*, 95 (January 1943), pp. 4–5. These ideas were further developed by Warburg in a memorandum entitled 'Problems of British Foreign Policy towards Europe', December 2, 1943. Interestingly, Warburg envisaged the break-up of Germany into 'a separate Austria, Bavaria, Württemberg, Baden and Rhineland/Westphalia, Prussia, etc. within a Central and West European Federation': SGW to Otto Benzinger, August 15, 1944.

20. SGW VME/CL/CZ../2, SGW, 'Notes on [a visit to] France', July 1945.

21. SGW VME/MA../ZZ../4, SGW Diary, draft memorandum, April 27, 1942. See also the diary entry for April 30, 1942 on the subject of European railways.

22. SGW VME/MA../ZZ../4, SGW Diary, September 20, 1944. See also VME/MA../ZZ../4 SGW, 'Notes for my Diary', January 2, 1947, for Warburg's vain efforts to persuade Stafford Cripps; and 'Note for my Diary', March 12, 1948 on a conversation with Bob Boothby arguing for 'a two-party motion of various members of the Labour Party and the Conservative Party in favour of a federation of Western Europe'.

23. SGW VME/CL/CZ../2, SGW Memorandum, enclosed in a letter to Lionel Fraser, February 2, 1947.

24. Among them the Action Committee for a United States of Europe, the United Kingdom Council of the European Movement and the European Foundation.

25. SGW DME/AA../CNZZ/5, SGW Note, July 26, 1950.

26 SGW Box 64, SGW Note, March 29, 1952. Cf. DME/AA../CNZZ/5, SGW to Anne-Marie Kaulla, February 17, 1955.

27. Grierson interview.

28. SGW DME/AA../CNZZ/5, SGW to Julian Amery, April 27, 1951; Box 2, SGW to Mrs Josette Aubrey, January 19, 1959. Indeed, Warburg argued (with the French model in mind) that 'nothing would do more to strengthen the cohesion of the Commonwealth than the adherence of the United Kingdom to the Common Market, whilst nothing would do more harm to the cohesion of the Commonwealth than if the United Kingdom were excluded from the Common Market': Box 2, SGW to Sir Alexander Spearman, February 7, 1959.

29. SGW VME/CL/CZ../2, SGW to E. G. Thompson, September 10, 1956. He was one of over fifty 'prominent persons' who signed a pro-membership letter to the press published in most major newspapers on October 8.

30. SGW Box 64, SGW Report, September 23, 1958.

31. SGW Box 3, SGW to Max Kohnstamm, June 23, 1960; DME/AA../CNZZ/5, Birrenbach to SGW, July 12, 1960.

32. SGW DME/AA../CNZZ/5, SGW to Birrenbach, August 2, 1960.

33. SGW DME/AA../CNZZ/5, SGW to Coudenhove-Kalergi, November 12, 1951.

34. SGW Box 8, SGW to Nicholas Kaldor, November 13, 1962.

35. SGW Box 62, SGW to Grierson, November 30, 1953.

36. DeLong and Eichengreen, 'Marshall Plan'.

37. SGW Box 62, SGW Report, June 14, 1947.

38. SGW Box 64, SGW Report, March 3, 1956. There are numerous letters in Warburg's papers on the subject of the ECSC's finances. Of particular importance in this regard was his friendship with Hans Skribanowitz, the Director of the ECSC's Finance Division.

39. Yale University Library Manuscripts and Archives, William Wiseman Papers, Box 19, f. 137, SGW to Wiseman, April 15, 1957.

40. SGW Box 1, SGW to Edmund Stinnes, May 24, 1958; Box 64, SGW Report, June 2, 1958; DME/AA../CNZZ/5, SGW to Wiseman, June 10, 1958; Box 8, SGW to Valéry Giscard d'Estaing, November 5, 1962.

41. SGW Box 1, SGW to Skribanowitz, July 3, 1958.

42. Michie, 'Insiders, Outsiders and the Dynamics of Change', esp. p. 557. See also Thompson, 'Pyrrhic Victory', pp. 287, 290ff., 295.

43. SGW Box 41, SGW to H. R. Hutton, June 11, 1979.

44. At least one participant considered Abs, rather than Warburg, 'the father of the Eurobond market'.

45. See Hinrichsen, *Ratgeber*.

46. SGW Box 64, SGW Report, April 23, 1955.

47. SGW Box 64, SGW Report, September 2, 1957.

48. SGW DME/AA../CNZZ/5, SGW to Birrenbach, December 4, 1957. See also Box 63, SGW Report, September 7, 1957.

49. Krozewski, 'Sterling, the "Minor" Territories, and the End of Formal Empire'. See also Tomlinson, 'Balanced Accounts?'

50. For Warburg's discussion of the idea with John Stevens, a Bank of England director, see SGW Box 64, SGW Note, September 15, 1958.

51. SGW DME/AA../CNZZ/5, SGW to Coudenhove-Kalergi, September 15, 1960.

52. See on this point Altman, 'Integration of European Capital Markets'.

53. American investors accounted for, respectively, 38 per cent, 38 per cent, 37 per cent and 57 per cent of the four loans; in other words, a majority of the dollar-denominated bonds ended up in European hands: SGW Box 8, SGW to Giscard d'Estaing, November 5, 1962.

54. SGW Box 1, SGW to Schiff, October 30, 1958.

55. SGW Box 2, I. J. Fraser, 'SGW and I. J. Fraser's visit to Brussels', April 17, 1959; Box 3, SGW Report, February 16, 1960.

56. Schenk, 'Origins of the Eurodollar Market', p. 232.

57. Ibid., p. 222.

58. Burk, 'Witness Seminar', p. 76.

59. Schenk, 'Origins of the Eurodollar Market', pp. 224f. Midland then sold these dollars spot for sterling and bought them back forward at a premium, so that it could obtain sterling at a rate 50 basis points below Bank Rate.

60. Schenk, 'Origins of the Eurodollar Market', p. 230.

61. Wake, *Kleinwort Benson*, pp. 344f.

62. Roberts and Kynaston, *City State*, p. 88. See also Burk, 'Witness Seminar', p. 66.

63. Schenk, 'Crisis and Opportunity', p. 208.

64. SGW Box 2, SGW to Stinnes, April 23, 1959.

65. SGW Box 2, SGW to Max Kohnstamm, April 23, 1959; SGW to René Sergent, May 21, 1959.

66. SGW Box 5, SGW to Sir Richard Jessel, June 22, 1961.

67 SGW Box 6, SGW to Lord Gladwyn, August 22, 1961; see also SGW to Gladwyn, October 31, 1961.

68. Schenk, 'Sterling, International Monetary Reform and Britain's Applications'.

69. SGW Box 5, SGW to Jessel, June 22, 1961.

70. SGW Box 8, SGW to Gladwyn, September 26, 1962.

71. SGW Box 9, SGW to Lord Avon, February 1, 1963.

72. Hence his support for the organization Britain In Europe: Cambridge University, Churchill Archive Centre, Gladwyn Papers GLAD 1/3/6, SGW to Gladwyn, May 30, 1963. Typically, Warburg pressed Britain In Europe to merge with the European Atlantic Group, which he also supported.

73. SGW Box 22, Roll to SGW, Policy Committee, Korner, Whitman, Sharp and Hopper, November 6, 1968.

74. SGW Box 10, SGW to Randall, September 6, 1963.

75. SGW DME/AA../CNZZ/5, SGW to Randall, December 11, 1967.

76. SGW Box 21, SGW to Whitman, Roll, Kelly et al., April 27, 1968.

77. SGW Box 12, SGW Note, December 1, 1964. See in general Parr, *Britain's Policy towards the European Community*.

78. SGW DME/AA../CNZZ/5, SGW to Gladwyn, October 20, 1964.

79. SGW Box 23, SGW to Fritz Karsten, August 13, 1969.

80. Patrick Hutber, 'Sir Siegmund Warburg Speaks', *Sunday Telegraph*, January 21, 1970.

81. Mendelson, 'Eurobond', p. 113.

82. Burk, 'Witness Seminar', p. 67.

83. Schenk, 'Origins of the Eurodollar Market', p. 228.

84. Ibid., p. 235.

85. Anon., 'To What Extent Did the City Determine that No Restrictions were Placed on the London Eurodollar Market in the Period 1960–3?'

86. The Swiss, French and West German authorities all introduced regulations to limit the influx of hot money, while currency instability prompted West Germany to reintroduce capital controls in 1961: Schenk, 'Origins of the Eurodollar Market', p. 234.

87. Ibid., pp. 223f.

88. Burk, 'Witness Seminar', p. 80.

89. Grierson interview.

90. Kynaston, *City of London*, vol. IV, p. 276; Burn, 'State, City and Euromarkets', p. 233.

91. Kynaston, *City of London*, vol. IV, p. 276.

92. Schenk, 'Origins of the Eurodollar Market', p. 232.

93. SGW Box 8, SGW to Grunfeld, Korner, Whitman et al., August 2, 1962. See also SGW Circular to Grunfeld, Korner, Grierson et al., draft, 'European Issues of Multiple Currency Loans', to be sent to Bolton for Bank of England scrutiny, August 8, 1962. Cf. Courtney and Thompson, *City Lives*, pp. 88f. In the words of one participant, the Stock Exchange truly 'missed the boat': Burk, 'Witness Seminar', p. 78.

94. SGW Box 9, Stheeman to SGW, Korner, Grierson, Whitman and Sharp, April 1, 1963.

95. Gordon, 'Autostrade'.

96. SGW Box 9, Gurney to Grierson, Whitman and Sharp, May 13, 1963.

97. For details see Chapter 10.

98. BoE OV47/6 64, C.R.P.H. Note, April 25, 1963. Warburgs later qualified this assurance. 'It is expected', the Bank was informed, 'that no more than a nominal amount will be purchased in the U.K. . . . there will be no circulation offering the Bonds but . . . a few "friends" in the U.K. will subscribe with "switch" dollars, and it is for this reason they are being quoted in London and a prospectus issued to meet Stock Exchange requirements': NA T 295/885, R. G. Gillings to Blacker, June 18, 1963.

99. BoE OV47/6 66, J. M. Stevens to Roll, April 26, 1963.

100. NA T 295/885, J. G. Owen to Roll, April 26, 1963; BoE OV47/6 67, D. P. Reilly to Roll, Treasury, April 30, 1963; NA T 295/885, G. B. Blaker to Radice, May 8, 1963; BoE OV47/6 68, Blaker to J. M. Stevens, May 9, 1963.

101. BoE OV47/6 69, Stevens Note, May 21, 1963. Skribanowitz preferred to stick to the tried-and-tested method of issuing dollar bonds in New York.

102. Kynaston, *City of London*, vol. IV, p. 277.

103. Fraser, *High Road*, pp. 259–62; Spira, *Ladders and Snakes*, pp. 115–24; Burk, 'Witness Seminar', p. 68.

104. Gordon, 'Autostrade'. Banque Internationale à Luxembourg handled the Luxembourg listing.

105. Mendelson, 'Eurobond', p. 111.

106. Gordon, 'Autotrade'

107. 'Dollars to Lend', *Economist*, June 8, 1963, p. 1048.

108. Burk, 'Witness Seminar', p. 70.

109. Fraser, *High Road*, p. 262.

110. The measure essentially imposed a 15 per cent tax on US investment in long-dated foreign issues. On its effects, see Cooper, 'Should Capital Controls be Banished?' The US government's intentions in this regard had, admittedly, been signalled in a speech by Secretary of the Treasury Douglas Dillon in May 1962. But the tax was not actually enacted until September 1964. Some American observers erroneously interpreted the Eurobond market as resulting from the introduction of the IET: Scott, 'Problems and Prospects of Integrating European Capital Markets', p. 350. See also Griffith, 'Effect of the Interest Equalization Tax Act', pp. 538f.

111. Mendelson, 'Eurobond', p. 119.

112. Kynaston, *City of London*, vol. IV, p. 284.

113. Richebächer, 'Problems and Prospects', p. 344.

114. Roberts and Kynaston, *City State*, p. 89.

115. Schenk, 'Crisis and Opportunity', p. 211. For a list of Eurobond issues managed by Warburg, see SGW Box 16, 'List of Some Issues in Chronological Order', May 13, 1966.

116. Mendelson, 'Eurobond', p. 122.

117. Ibid., p. 124.

118. SGW Box 12, SGW Note, July 9, 1964.

119. Burk, 'Witness Seminar', p. 82.

120. Kelly Diary, July 13, 1972; August 2, 1971; August 5, 1971.

121. Burk, 'Witness Seminar', p. 81.

122. Fraser, *High Road*, pp. 271f.

123. Schenk, 'Crisis and Opportunity', p. 209. For 1966, the top seven banks in the Eurobond market (ranked by issues initiated and managed) were: White Weld ($141 million), Deutsche Bank ($106 million), Kuhn Loeb ($94 million), S. G. Warburg ($92 million), First Boston and Morgan Stanley ($85 million each) and N. M. Rothschild ($72 million): Kynaston, *City of London*, vol. IV, p. 326. Deutsche Bank was consistently in first place every year from 1968 to 1971.

124. Roberts and Kynaston, *City State*, p. 89.

125. SGW Box 20, SGW to all executive directors, October 31, 1967.

126. Burk, 'Witness Seminar', p. 82.

127. SGW Box 13, SGW, 'London as an International Capital Market', April 13, 1965.

128. SGW Box 12, SGW Note, October 5, 1964.

129. Richebächer, 'Problems and Prospects', p. 343.

130. SGW Box 10, SGW, 'Bank of England', December 31, 1963. See also SGW Box 11, SGW to Whitman, Grierson, Fraser et al., January 21, 1963; SGW to Whitman, Korner, Grierson et al., January 27, 1963.

131. SGW Box 11, SGW Note, 'Sterling/Mark loans', February 27, 1964; SGW Draft memorandum on sterling loans to the Italian government, March 13, 1964; SGW, 'Bank of England', March 18, 1964; Fraser Note to SGW, Grunfeld, Korner et al., April 7, 1964; SGW to Fraser and Spira, April 28, 1964.

132. SGW, 'Double Currency Clause', *The Times*, March 19, 1964; SGW, 'London as a Market for Foreign Bonds', *The Times*, March 20, 1964.

133. SGW Box 11, SGW to Samuels, April 10, 1964.

134. Burk, 'Witness Seminar', p. 83.

135. Fraser, *High Road*, p. 274; Spira, *Ladders and Snakes*, pp. 111, 146f.

136. SGW Box 8, SGW Note, December 29, 1962; Box 10, SGW Note, December 10, 1963.

137. SGW Box 9, SGW Note, May 30, 1963.

138. SGW Box 23, SGW to Policy Group, Korner et al., January 25, 1969.

139. SGW Box 28, SGW to Spira, Grunfeld, Korner et al., July 6, 1971; Roll to SGW, Grunfeld, Korner et al., July 6, 1971.

140. SGW Box 13, Fraser and Kelly, 'Note to the Bond Team', February 4, 1965. See also SGW to Roll, February 22, 1965.

141. J. H. Hambro and SGW, 'Action That Must be Taken Now', *The Times*, November 20, 1965. See also 'Crisis Warning from City Bankers', *Daily Telegraph*, November 22, 1965.

142. SGW Box 13, SGW, 'London as an International Capital Market', April 13, 1965.

143. Richebächer, 'Problems and Prospects', p. 346.

144. Larre, 'Facts of Life about the Integration of National Capital Markets', pp. 325, 327.

145. SGW, 'Indigestion on European Capital Market, B.I.S. to Control Queue?', *The Times*, March 29, 1966.

146. Ibid. The *Economist* disagreed: 'Don't Cartelise Euro-bonds', April 2, 1966.

147. SGW Box 26, SGW to Korner, Craven, Lewisohn et al., June 17, 1970; SGW to Korner, Craven and members of Policy Committee, June 29, 1970.

148. SGW Box 26, SGW & Co. Draft memorandum, 'Establishment of

Machinery for the Coordination of Euro-issues', August 3, 1970; Draft memorandum, August 21, 1970.

149. SGW Box 43, SGW to Roll, Scholey, members of the Monday meeting, directors and International Department, August 26, 1981.

150. SGW Box 19, SGW to Whitman, text of possible announcement, June 16, 1967.

151. SGW Box 16, SGW, 'Transatlantic Bond Fund', May 25, 1966.

152. SGW Box 25, Martin Gordon to SGW, Kelly, Korner et al., April 29, 1970.

153. SGW Box 29, Roll to SGW, Grunfeld, G. C. Seligman et al., January 6, 1972.

154. 'Sir Siegmund Warburg, Interview', *Investors Chronicle*, April 13, 1973.

155. Schenk, 'Crisis and Opportunity', p. 212; Roberts and Kynaston, *City State*, p. 90. On the case of the consortium bank Orion, see Roberts and Arnander, *Take your Partners*.

156. Not to mention the help he had offered to give Roy Jenkins in his new role as president of the European Commission, for which this seemed scant reward. SGW Box 38, SGW to Roll, Grunfeld, Korner et al., May 23, 1977 and May 25, 1977; SGW to Salina, Roll, Gordon et al., June 2, 1977; Salina to SGW, Korner, Roll et al., June 30, 1977.

157. Mendelson, 'Eurobond', table 1.

158. Kynaston, *City of London*, vol. IV, p. 338. See also Roberts and Arnander, *Take your Partners*.

159. Kynaston, *City of London*, vol. IV, p. 339.

160. 'Birth of a Hybrid', *Economist*, April 11, 1970, p. 83; May 2, 1970, p. 85. Cf. Spira, *Ladders and Snakes*, pp. 164f.

161. For discussions of other ways to insure British borrowers against the exchange rate risk, see SGW Box 22, SGW Enclosure to Grierson, Fraser paper, 'Exchange Guarantees for UK Borrowers', October 11, 1968. As Warburg noted, offering some kind of insurance against sterling depreciation in return for a percentage commission would simply make the effective interest rate of any loan too high.

162. SGW Box 28, Salina to SGW, Roll, Korner et al., September 28, 1971.

163. SGW Box 21, Kelly to SGW, Korner, Whitman et al., January 8, 1968; Box 21, SGW to Whitman, Roll, Kelly et al., April 27, 1968.

164. SGW Box 26, SGW & Co. Draft memorandum, August 21, 1970.

165. Patrick Hutber, 'Sir Siegmund Warburg Speaks', *Sunday Telegraph*, January 21, 1970.

166. 'Sir Siegmund Warburg, Interview', *Investors Chronicle*, April 13, 1973.

167. The idea was to create 'a private sector, i.e. non-governmental, international financing instrument to support major new initiatives involving the industries of more than one EEC country with medium and long-term finance': SGW Box

31, Bonham Carter to SGW, Roll, Spira, Kelly and O'Neill, February 22, 1973; SGW to Guth, February 28, 1973.

168. SGW Box 30, SGW to Gladwyn, October 20, 1972.

169. SGW Box 37, Steiner interview with SGW, August 2, 1976.

170. SGW Box 23, Draft of article/letter to Poole with amendments by SGW, January 7, 1969.

171. For Warburg's continuing dissatisfaction with the EEC, see SGW Box 33, SGW to Roll, 'Rough draft', April 1, 1974.

172. Roberts and Kynaston, *City State*, p. 114.

173. Claes, De Ceuster and Polfliet, 'Anatomy of the Eurobond Market'. It is worth noting that since 1980 European countries have accounted for around a third of all issuance. Around 40 per cent of the face value of Eurobonds issued in that period was dollar-denominated. It seems likely, however, that euro-denominated issues will soon overtake dollar-denominated issues.

174. David Clementi, 'The City and the Euro: Innovation and Excellence', speech at the City Seminar on 'London in the 21st Century', Palace Hotel, Tokyo, February 13, 2001.

175. Roberts and Kynaston, *City State*, p. 72.

CHAPTER 9:
THE RHYTHM OF PERFECTION

1. SGW Personal Documents, Steiner interview, n.d.

2. SGW Box 2, SGW Note, April 10, 1959.

3. SGW Box 64, Note to members of the 9.15 Meeting, June 15, 1964.

4. Quoted in Kynaston, *City of London*, vol. IV, p. 6.

5. Courtney and Thompson, *City Lives*, p. 9.

6. 'The Invisible Banker behind That Take-over', *News Chronicle*, January 19, 1959.

7. 'Mr Warburg Laughs Last', *Daily Mail*, October 10, 1960; Diana Mallory, 'Who are the Men behind the Men Who Mean Money?', *Queen*, August 2, 1961; 'Banks Help to Plug That Trade Gap', *Sun*, December 7, 1964.

8. Ferris, *Gentlemen of Fortune*, pp. 196ff.

9. Darling, *City Cinderella*, p. 3. See also Moussa, *Roue de la fortune*, p. 176.

10. Courtney and Thompson, *City Lives*, p. 9.

11. Cary Reich, 'Probing the Mystique of Warburgs', *Institutional Investor*, February 1977, p. 31.

12. Darling, *City Cinderella*, p. 3.

13. Joseph Wechsberg, 'Profiles: Prince of the City', *New Yorker*, April 9, 1966.

14. Craven interview; Wechsberg, *Merchant Bankers*, p. 165.

15. Ferris, *Gentlemen of Fortune*, p. 196.

16. Cary Reich, 'Probing the Mystique of Warburgs', *Institutional Investor*, February 1977, pp. 28f.

17. Stevenson interview.

18. SGW, Charles Sharp, 'Semi-Retirement', January 1960.

19. Ibid.

20. SGW, Charles Sharp, 'Report A.D. 5000 of the Archaeological Society on Excavations of Buildings in the City of London Believed to Belong to the Twentieth Century of the Christian Era', n.d., *c.* 1965.

21. Ibid.

22. Ibid.

23. Ibid.

24. SGW, Charles Sharp, 'A Minority Participation', February 8, 1967.

25. SGW, Charles Sharp, 'Parsnip and Pickles', January 1968.

26. Ibid.

27. SGW, Charles Sharp, 'Expansion', October 1969.

28. SGW, Charles Sharp, 'The Economy Drive', February 1970. After joining Warburgs in 1967, Eric Roll became a member of the boards of the Bank of London and South America, the Austrian paper manufacturer Bunzl, Chrysler UK, the Commonwealth Development Finance Corporation, the American insurance company Dominion Lincoln and Times Newspapers. See Roll, *Crowded Hours*, pp. 193–207.

29. SGW, Charles Sharp, 'Report by Vice-President Jackson D. Jackson', April 1, 1965.

30. SGW, Charles Sharp, 'Expansion', October 1969.

31. Fraser, *High Road*, p. 203.

32. Scholey interview.

33. See for example Kelly Diary, August 1, 1971; December 14, 1972.

34. Private communication, September 6, 2009.

35. SGW Box 62, SGW, 'Thinking Aloud about a Ten-years' Plan for K.L. & Co.', April 24, 1953.

36. SGW Box 62, SGW Journey Report 10, February 22, 1946.

37. SGW VME/CL/CZ../2, SGW to Fritz M. Warburg, November 16, 1946.

38. Darling, *City Cinderella*, pp. 112f.

39. SGW Box 64, SGW Daily Report, March 24, 1956; April 20, 1956; Bank of England C48/51, [H. S. Clarke?] to Sir Kenneth Peppiatt, December 14, 1956.

40. Quoted in Courtney and Thompson, *City Lives*, p. 87. See also Spira, *Ladders and Snakes*, p. 109.

41. Wechsberg, *Merchant Bankers*, pp. 222f.

42. Stevenson interview.

43. Oscar Lewisohn papers, Martin Gordon, 'Mr Henry Grunfeld and Sir Siegmund Warburg: Addendum and Epilogue', October 8, 1997, p. 4.

44. Joseph Wechsberg, 'Warburg: The Nonconformist', *Sunday Times*, November 13, 1966.

45. SGW Box 64, SGW Half Weekly Notes No. 18, April 30, 1951.

46. SGW VME/CL/CZ../2, SGW to Spiegelberg, October 1, 1947.

47. Fraser, *High Road*, p. 272.

48. Kelly Diary, September 17, 1971; December 22, 1971; March 3, 1975.

49. Grunfeld interview.

50. Oscar Lewisohn papers, 'Selected Reminiscences of Henry Grunfeld', p. 30.

51. Kynaston, *City of London*, vol. IV, p. 334.

52. Cary Reich, 'Probing the Mystique of Warburgs', *Institutional Investor*, February 1977, p. 31.

53. SGW Box 62, SGW Journey Report 5, November 5, 1947.

54. SGW Box 64, SGW Daily Report, June 14, 1958.

55. Wechsberg, *Merchant Bankers*, pp. 167, 218f.

56. SGW VME/CL/CZ../2, SGW, 'Business Rules of New Trading Co.', May 21, 1940.

57. Darling, *City Cinderella*, p. 61. A quirk arising from Warburg's dalliance with Kuhn Loeb was that the board of S. G. Warburg had no permanent chairman. In practice, Warburg chaired meetings. In his absence, Andrew McFadyean played the role or, after 1962, Henry Grunfeld: LSE McFadyean papers, McFadyean to SGW, February 9, 1962; SGW to McFadyean, February 12, 1962.

58. SGW Box 2, SGW Memorandum, December 7, 1959.

59. Fraser, *High Road*, pp. 270f.; Courtney and Thompson, *City Lives*, pp. 88f.

60. Fraser, *High Road*, p. 200.

61. Darling interview.

62. SGW Box 2, SGW to 9.15 Meeting, May 13, 1959.

63. SGW Box 2, SGW Draft note to 9.15 Meeting, June 2, 1959.

64. SGW Box 2, SGW to 9.15 Meeting, June 17, 1959.

65. SGW Box 2, SGW Note for C. Lippmann, September 7, 1959.

66. SGW Box 2, SGW to 9.15 Meeting, October 22, 1959.

67. SGW Box 11, SGW Circular to all staff, January 7, 1964.

68. SGW Box 62, SGW Journey Report 11, May 30, 1947.

69. For his heartfelt tribute to Meyer when she retired, see SGW DME/AA../CNZZ/5, SGW to Meyer, November 30, 1961.

70. SGW VME/CL/CZ../2, Sharp to SGW, September 29, 1972.

71. Wasserman interview.

72. Quoted in Kynaston, *City of London*, vol. IV, p. 336.

73. Oscar Lewisohn papers, Sharp, 'Sir Siegmund Warburg: Some Recollections', pp. 2ff.

74. SGW Box 15, SGW to Whitman, February 22, 1966.

75. SGW VME/CL/CZ../2, SGW Memorandum, July 27, 1942.

76. SGW Box 64, SGW Daily Report, February 19, 1955.

77. SGW Box 64, SGW Note for general circulation in the office, September 25, 1957.

78. SGW Box 2, SGW to Sharp, November 11, 1959.

79. Kynaston, *City of London*, vol. IV, p. 334.

80. SGW Box 11, SGW Draft note to members of the 9.15 Meeting, April 22, 1964; Box 64, SGW Note to members of the 9.15 Meeting, June 15, 1964.

81. SGW Personal Documents, Steiner interview, n.d.

82. Roll interview.

83. Darling, *City Cinderella*, pp. 35f.

84. GW interview.

85. Roll interview.

86. SGW Box 62, SGW Journey Report 8, n.d. [November 1947].

87. SGW Box 63, SGW Half Weekly Notes No. 21, May 8, 1951.

88. SGW Box 63, SGW Half Weekly Notes No. 25, May 22, 1951.

89. SGW VME/CL/CZ../2, SGW to Eva Warburg, March 28, 1954. It is of course possible that Warburg was equally charming to Bowater's face, and Bowater equally scathing about Warburg behind the latter's back.

90. SGW VME/MA../ZZ../4, SGW Diary, May 22, 1944.

91. SGW VME/MA../ZZ../4, SGW Diary, September 23, 1944.

92. SGW DME/AA../CNZZ/5, SGW to Seligman, May 23, 1960.

93. SGW Box 6, SGW Note to all directors and executives, July 12, 1961; Box 11, SGW Note to directors, executives and secretaries, February 4, 1964.

94. SGW Box 13, SGW to Korner, Whitman, Sharp, Fraser and directors who are members of the Steering Group, February 27, 1965.

95. SGW Box 21, SGW Circular to executive directors and senior directors, March 19, 1968.

96. Wasserman interview.

97. Fraser, *High Road*, p. 203.

98. Darling, *City Cinderella*, p. 56.

99. Fraser, *High Road*, p. 205.

100. See Nott, *Here Today*, p. 121.

101. SGW VME/MA../ZZ../4, Martin Gordon, 'Siegmund Warburg 1902–1982: A Personal Perspective', October 30, 1992.

102. Valentine, *Free Range Ego*, pp. 91f.

103. SGW DME/AA../CNZZ/5, Grierson to SGW, January 22, 1951.

104. Quoted in Kynaston, *City of London*, vol. IV, p. 5.

105. SGW Box 2, SGW to John Noble, September 7, 1959.

106. Valentine, *Free Range Ego*, pp. 46f.

107. Fraser, *High Road*, pp. 224ff.

108. Oxford University, Bonham Carter papers MS 198 162, SGW to Violet Bonham Carter, December 28, 1966.

109. Fraser, *High Road*, p. 234.

110. Cary Reich, 'Probing the Mystique of Warburgs', *Institutional Investor*, February 1977, p. 32.

111. Kelly Diary, June 17, 1971; October 11, 1971; November 12, 1971.

112. SGW DME/AA../CNZZ/5, SGW to Gladwyn, June 2, 1964; Gladwyn to SGW, June 2, 1964.

113. SGW DME/CO../RPBZ/6, Jellicoe to SGW, November 22, 1966.

114. 'The Warburg Roll-call', *Financial Times*, November 13, 1973.

115. See Roll, *Crowded Hours*.

116. SGW Box 16, SGW to Roll, June 26, 1966; SGW DME/AA../CNZZ/5, SGW to van der Beugel, August 2, 1966.

117. Fraser, *High Road*, p. 277. When chairing a morning meeting, Roll was once heard to postpone a decision by saying: 'There is someone whose opinion I particularly admire and whom I should like to consult before we minute this decision.' This elicited derisive laughter from his younger colleagues. See also Valentine, *Free Range Ego*, pp. 83f.; Goodwin interview.

118. Scholey interview.

119. Kelly Diary, March 21, 1974.

120. See e.g. 'Banker Who Made Takeovers his Art', *Daily Express*, October 21, 1968.

121. SGW VME/CL/CZ../2, SGW to Olaf H. Lamm, January 13, 1951.

122. SGW DME/AA../CNZZ/5, SGW to Spiegelberg, June 14, 1955.

123. SGW VME/MA../ZZ../4, SGW to the editor of the *Daily Mail*, February 20, 1942.

124. Drogheda, *Double Harness*, p. 149.

125. SGW VME/MA../ZZ../4, SGW Diary, February 11, 1944.

126. SGW Box 2, SGW to Samuels, June 12, 1959.

127. See e.g. SGW Box 9, SGW to Seligman, June 14, 1963.

128. See e.g. SGW VME/CL/CZ../2, Ernest Bloch to SGW, November 9, 1963.

129. SGW Box 2, SGW to Laurence Meynell, October 28, 1959.

130. See e.g. SGW, 'Double Currency Clause Would Aid Europe Investment',

The Times, March 19, 1964; SGW, 'London as a Market for Foreign Bonds', *The Times*, March 20, 1964; SGW, 'The Case for Sterling', *Sunday Times*, October 2, 1966.

131. Darling, *City Cinderella*, p. 53.

132. SGW Box 9, SGW to Sidney Simon, June 11, 1963.

133. SGW DME/AA../CNZZ/5, SGW to Boothby, May 5, 1958.

134. SGW DME/AA../CNZZ/5, SGW to Randall, December 11, 1967.

135. SGW Personal Documents, Steiner interview, n.d.

136. SGW Box 1, SGW to V. Bloch, October 6, 1958. See also Box 39, SGW to Roll, February 6, 1978.

137. SGW DME/AA../CNZZ/5, SGW to Jakob Goldschmidt, June 25, 1953.

138. SGW Box 64, SGW Daily Report, October 29, 1958.

139. SGW VME/CL/CZ../2, Ziegler to SGW, December 14, 1959.

140. SGW Personal Documents, Steiner interview, n.d.

141. Oscar Lewisohn papers, Sharp, 'Sir Siegmund Warburg: Some Recollections', pp. 2ff.

142. Jessel interview.

143. Darling, *City Cinderella*, p. 52; Fraser, *High Road*, p. 195.

144. Fraser, *High Road*, pp. 271f.

145. Ibid., p. 360.

146. Ibid., p. 285.

147. Darling, *City Cinderella*, pp. 112f. See also Andrew Smithers, private communication, February 18, 2010.

148. SGW Box 2, SGW to Sharp, November 26, 1959. See also DME/AA../CNZZ/5, Arnheim to SGW, May 20, 1966.

149. SGW DME/AA../CNZZ/5, SGW to Cripps, Policy Committee, Korner et al., May 25, 1968.

150. *Economist*, September 13, 1969, p. 95.

151. SGW Box 64, SGW Daily Report, September 30, 1959.

152. SGW Box 12, Note to members of 9.15 Meeting, October 5, 1964.

153. SGW to Sharp, Policy Group, Korner et al., November 11, 1968.

154. Cary Reich, 'Probing the Mystique of Warburgs', *Institutional Investor*, February 1977, p. 34.

155. See SGW Box 1, SGW Note for members of the 9.15 Meeting, January 31, 1958.

156. Fraser, *High Road*, p. 251. For the allegation that Warburg himself proposed insider trading in the shares of a Canadian company in 1977, see Darling, *City Cinderella*, p. 109.

157. Courtney and Thompson, *City Lives*, pp. 88f.

158. Valentine, *Free Range Ego*, pp. 75f.

159. See e.g. SGW Box 64, Bi-weekly notes No. 62, August 9, 1950.

160. SGW DME/AA../CNZZ/5, SGW to Grunfeld, May 25, 1954.

161. SGW Box 63, SGW Daily Report, October 15, 1954.

162. SGW VME/MA../ZZ../4, SGW Diary, August 28, 1945.

163. SGW Box 1, SGW to Grierson, April 25, 1958.

164. SGW DME/AA../CNZZ/5, SGW to Wiseman, September 10, 1958.

165. SGW Box 2, SGW to Thalmann, June 17, 1959.

166. SGW Box 64, SGW to members of S. G. Warburg & Company Limited, December 31, 1959.

167. SGW Box 64, SGW to Grunfeld, November 16, 1963.

168. SGW Box 8, SGW Draft 'to, say, eight of the Junior Executives of the Firm', February 20, 1962.

169. SGW VME/CL/CZ../2, SGW to Spira, March 28, 1964.

170. Joseph Wechsberg, 'Warburg: The Nonconformist', *Sunday Times*, November 13, 1966.

171. Courtney and Thompson, *City Lives*, pp. 104ff.

172. SGW VME/CL/CZ../2, Transcript of Patrick Hutber's interview with SGW, January 19, 1970.

173. SGW Box 64, SGW to Grunfeld, November 16, 1963. See also Box 10, SGW Draft note to Grunfeld and Seligman, December 12, 1963.

174. SGW Box 40, SGW to Roll, Chairman's Committee, October 20, 1978.

175. SGW Box 12, Grierson to Grunfeld, August 20, 1964; SGW to Grierson, September 1, 1964; Grierson note to SGW, September 10, 1964; DME/AA../CNZZ/5, Grierson to SGW, March 26, 1965. Cf. 'Mr Warburg Steps Down', *Guardian*, July 11, 1964.

176. SGW DME/AA../CNZZ/5, SGW to Randall, September 14, 1966.

177. Joseph Wechsberg, 'Warburg: The Nonconformist', *Sunday Times*, November 13, 1966.

178. SGW DME/AA../CNZZ/5, van der Beugel to SGW, March 14, 1966.

179. SGW Box 13, SGW to Korner, Whitman, Sharp et al., February 27, 1965; Box 18, SGW Circular to Steering Group, January 26, 1967 and March 14, 1967; Box 19, SGW to Steering Group, June 2, 1967.

180. Courtney and Thompson, *City Lives*, p. 106.

181. Kelly Diary, April 13, 1971; July 28, 1971; September 14, 1972; September 15, 1972; May 21, 1975.

182. SGW Box 16, SGW to Grunfeld and Spira, July 7, 1966.

183. SGW Box 16, SGW to Grunfeld, June 29, 1966.

184. SGW Box 19, SGW to Steering Group and New Business Group, July 7, 1967.

185. SGW Box 23, SGW to Marlow, Policy Committee, September 20, 1969.

186. Fraser, *High Road*, p. 275.

187. SGW VME/MA../ZZ../4, Gordon, 'Siegmund Warburg 1902–1982: A Personal Perspective', October 30, 1992.

188. Quoted in Kynaston, *City of London*, vol. IV, pp. 6f.

189. SGW DME/AA../CNZZ/5, Richards to SGW, June 16, 1951; SGW to Richards, June 18, 1951.

190. SGW VME/CL/CZ../2, Spira to Warburg, December 22, 1961.

191. Courtney and Thompson, *City Lives*, p. 89.

192. Cary Reich, 'Probing the Mystique of Warburgs', *Institutional Investor*, February 1977, p. 32.

193. SGW VME/CL/CZ../2, SGW to Eric Warburg, December 27, 1945.

194. SGW VME/CL/CZ../2, SGW to Keller, January 8, 1951.

195. GW, GW to his parents, January 13, 1963.

196. SGW DME/CO../RPBZ/6, GW to SGW, January 20, 1966; SGW to GW, January 24, 1966.

197. SGW DME/CO../RPBZ/6, SGW to Theodora Dreifuss, February 2, 1966.

198. SGW Box 20, SGW to Anna Biegun, November 22, 1967.

199. GW, Paul Ziegler to GW, April 24, 1968.

200. SGW VME/CL/CZ../2, Grunfeld to SGW, February 11, 1970.

201. See SGW VME/CL/CZ../2, SGW to Jacob Rothschild, October 1, 1980.

202. Wasserman interview.

203. Spira, *Ladders and Snakes*, pp. 108f., 225, 255; Spira interview.

204. Wasserman interview.

205. SGW Box 19, SGW to Wuttke, May 15, 1967. Cf. Wolfensohn interview. See also Mallaby, *World's Banker*, pp. 30f.

206. Grierson interview.

207. SGW Box 19, SGW to Grunfeld, September 30, 1967.

208. Darling, *City Cinderella*, p. 40.

209. SGW Box 24, SGW to Policy Committee, October 13, 1969.

210. SGW Box 24, SGW Draft statement, October 25, 1969. For Spira's proposal that Warburg retain a place 'on the letterhead of SGW & Co. either as President or Senior Adviser', see Spira to SGW, November 3, 1969. For Scholey's vain attempt to delay his resignation until the publication of the end-of-year results, see Scholey to SGW, November 3, 1969. For Seligman's outright opposition to Warburg's resignation, see Seligman to SGW, November 4, 1969. See 'Sir Siegmund Makes Way for Young Warburg Men', *Financial Times*, January 1, 1970.

CHAPTER 10:
BRITAIN'S FINANCIAL PHYSICIAN

1. SGW Box 16, SGW to Stinnes, August 1, 1966.
2. LSE Hetherington papers 14 (14), Points from a meeting with Joe Hyman, February 15, 1968.
3. Scholey interview.
4. SGW VME/CL/CZ../2, SGW Aphorisms.
5. Crossman, *Backbench Diaries*, pp. 606f.
6. Hansard, November 3, 1960. The *Daily Telegraph* described this as 'a fine ranting performance'.
7. SGW Box 22, SGW to Policy Committee, Korner, Whitman and Sharp, August 10, 1968; NA PREM 13/2020, Halls Note, August 5, 1968.
8. O'Hara, *Dreams to Disillusionment*, p. 42. See in general Cairncross, *British Economy since 1945*, pp. 139-61.
9. NA T 312/1115, S. G. Warburg & Co., 'Proposal for a New Instrument for Commonwealth Financing', November 29, 1960.
10. SGW, Box 9, SGW Note to Korner, Whitman and members of Steering Group, February 13, 1963; SGW Note to Korner and Whitman, February 16, 1963; SGW Note, February 27, 1963; SGW to Korner, Grierson, Whitman and Fraser, March 12, 1963; SGW to Reinhardt, Credit Suisse, April 9, 1963; Fraser to SGW, Korner and Steering Group, April 10, 1963; SGW to Grierson, Korner and Fraser, April 10, 1963.
11. NA PREM 11/4200, Macmillan to Maudling, March 28, 1963.
12. NA T 312/1115, Stevens to Rickett, November 2, 1960; Rickett to Milner-Barry, November 9, 1960; Milner-Barry to Rickett, November 15, 1960; Milner-Barry to Sir Frank Lee, November 17, 1960; Stevens to Milner-Barry, December 30, 1960; Bottomley to Milner-Barry, January 2, 1961; Sandys to Grierson, February 17, 1961; Warburg's & Co. (Grierson, Fraser), meeting with Treasury (Rickett, Milner-Barry, Mackay, Bennett), CRO (Sir Algernon Rumbold) and Bank of England (R. J. Cunnell), March 7, 1961; Hayes to Mackay, March 29, 1961. The scheme was revived two years later: NA PREM 11/4200, Grierson to Philip de Zulueta, February 5, 1963; de Z[ulueta] to Bligh, February 6, 1963; Bligh to Mitchell, February 8, 1963; de Z[ulueta] to Bligh, February 14, 1963; Bligh to Mitchell, February 15, 1963; Note on Financial Policy, March 11, 1963; Macmillan to Maudling, March 11, 1963; Maudling to Macmillan, March 28, 1963. For details of the second Warburg proposal see Grierson, 'Proposed Mobilisation of Treasury Portfolio of International Securities', April 24, 1963. For the Bank of England's counter-proposal,

see Cromer to Maudling, May 30, 1963. Cf. Kynaston, *City of London*, vol. IV, pp. 266f.

13. Lamb, *Macmillan Years*, p. 98.
14. SGW DME/AA../CNZZ/5, Tony Griffin to SGW, October 26, 1963.
15. SGW DME/AA../CNZZ/5, SGW to Edward Heath, July 30, 1965.
16. SGW DME/CO../RPBZ/6, SGW to Dreifuss, February 27, 1967.
17. O'Hara, '"Dynamic, Exciting, Thrilling Change"', p. 79.
18. SGW Box 16, SGW to Stinnes, August 1, 1966.
19. SGW DME/AA../CNZZ/5, SGW to Lord Tangley, February 24, 1964.
20. J. H. Hambro and S. G. Warburg, 'The Economic Problem: Devaluation Not a Solution', *The Times*, November 21, 1964. Cf. SGW DME/AA../ CNZZ/5, SGW to James Callaghan, November 20, 1964.
21. O'Hara, *Dreams to Disillusionment*, p. 43. Cf. Cairncross, *British Economy since 1945*, pp. 163–71.
22. SGW Box 12, SGW Note, December 1, 1964.
23. NA PREM 13/278, Mitchell to Bancroft, December 1, 1964; Hubback to Rickett, December 10, 1964; Bancroft to Mitchell, December 17, 1964. T 312/1115, Rickett to Armstrong and Bancroft, December 14, 1964.
24. NA PREM 13/278, Bancroft to Mitchell, December 17, 1964; T 312/1849, Bancroft Note, March 24, 1965.
25. SGW Box 13, SGW to Furstenberg, March 23, 1965.
26. SGW Box 13, SGW to Dilworth, March 26, 1965.
27. NA PREM 13/278, Wilson Note, May 18, 1965. See also Bancroft to Mitchell, May 28, 1965.
28. Grunfeld interview. Wilson insisted that records of meetings relating to devaluation be destroyed. In some cases, minutes were simply not kept.
29. J. H. Hambro and S. G. Warburg, 'The Economic Problem: Action that Must be Taken Now', *The Times*, November 20, 1965. See also 'Crisis Warning from City Bankers: Export Incentive Need', *Daily Telegraph*, November 22, 1965.
30. SGW, 'The Case for Sterling', *Sunday Times*, October 2, 1966.
31. SGW VME/CL/CZ../2, SGW to R. H. Fry, November 12, 1969.
32. NA T 312/1849, Bancroft Note for the record, January 18, 1965; EW 24/19, Secretaries' memorandum to Fiscal Incentives Committee, February 3, 1965; PREM 13/278, Wilson Note, May 18, 1965.
33. NA T 312/1727, Bancroft to Goldman, September 8, 1965; Grierson to Lord Brown, November 25, 1965; Brown to Grierson, December 31, 1965.
34. NA PREM 13/2024, Halls Note, March 11, 1967.
35. NA PREM 13/278, Treasury memorandum, 'Mr Warburg's suggestion', May 28, 1965. See also UWMRC MSS 200C/3/P1/3/10, Callaghan to Maurice Laing, November 26, 1965.

36. NA PREM 13/2024, Balogh to Wilson, March 22, 1967.

37. NA T 295/42, S. Goldman Note, December 1, 1965. Cf. Percie Nash, 'Bank Chiefs', *Daily Telegraph*, December 4, 1965; 'Rhodesia Defaults on Loan Interest', *Sunday Telegraph*, December 5, 1965.

38. NA PREM 13/1150, Balogh to Wilson, May 13, 1966.

39. SGW, 'The Case for Sterling', *Sunday Times*, October 2, 1966.

40. SGW DME/AA../CNZZ/5, SGW to Boothby, December 6, 1966.

41. Roll, *Crowded Hours*, p. 195.

42. SGW Box 33, SGW to Roll, Grunfeld, Korner et al., March 1, 1974.

43. NA PREM 13/2024, Note, April 30, 1968.

44. *London Gazette*, November 18, 1966. Cf. *Daily Telegraph*, June 11, 1966.

45. SGW VME/MA../ZZ../4, SGW to Joseph Wechsberg, June 29, 1966; Darling, *City Cinderella*, p. 117. Legend had it that all the letters were sent away for graphological analysis: 'Albany at Large', *Sunday Telegraph*, November 18, 1973.

46. Grunfeld interview.

47. Oscar Lewisohn papers, Sharp, 'Sir Siegmund Warburg: Some Recollections', p. 13.

48. Oscar Lewisohn papers, Gordon, 'Mr Henry Grunfeld and Sir Siegmund Warburg: Addendum and Epilogue', October 8, 1997, p. 4.

49. Kynaston, *City of London*, vol. IV, p. 317.

50. Fraser, *High Road*, p. 285.

51. SGW DME/AA../CNZZ/5, SGW to Randall, September 14, 1966.

52. SGW Box 17, SGW to Graham Blaine, October 24, 1966.

53. SGW Box 20, SGW to Boothby, November 23, 1967.

54. SGW Box 20, SGW to Mazur, December 9, 1967.

55. Graham Turner, 'Whitehall at its Wits' End', *Sunday Telegraph*, April 24, 1977.

56. Grierson, *Truant Disposition*, pp. 28ff. See also Young and Lowe, *Intervention in the Mixed Economy*, pp. 41–9.

57. Fraser, *High Road*, p. 280.

58. Roll, *Crowded Hours*, pp. 190, 193ff.

59. SGW DME/CO../RPBZ/6, Roy Jenkins to SGW, May 31, 1968; DME/AA../CNZZ/5, SGW to Jenkins, June 5, 1968; VME/CL/CZ../2, Roll to SGW, June 6, 1968.

60. Roll, *Crowded Hours*, p. 207.

61. NA PREM 13/3153, Le Cheminant note, September 19, 1968. See also PREM 13/2670, Note of a meeting, December 10, 1969.

62. Warburg suggested arranging such a loan for the Commonwealth Development Finance Co., the Central Electricity Generating Board or the National Coal Board: SGW Box 19, SGW to Whitman, Fraser, Kelly et al., May 20,

1967; SGW to Steering Group, September 27, 1967; Box 20, SGW to Steering Group, October 3, 1967; Box 22, SGW to Spira, Policy Committee, Korner et al., October 5, 1968; SGW to Roll, Grunfeld, Korner et al., October 21, 1968; Spira to SGW, Policy Committee, Bonham Carter et al., November 4, 1968; Roll to Roy Jenkins, November 6, 1968. Such loans were also contemplated for British Steel, the Atomic Energy Authority, the Gas Council, the Post Office and the Greater London Council. Despite considerable reservations in Whitehall, the Treasury was willing to contemplate such loans, and indeed to offer an exchange rate guarantee for maturities of less than ten years.

63. 'DM's at 6½ pc for Gas Council', *Daily Telegraph*, March 18, 1969.

64. SGW Box 28, SGW & Co. Memorandum, 'UK Balance of Payments: Long-term Borrowing', October 15, 1971.

65. Cairncross, *British Economy since 1945*, p. 175.

66. Patrick Hutber, 'Sir Siegmund Warburg Speaks', *Sunday Telegraph*, January 25, 1970. Cf. SGW VME/CL/CZ../2, Transcript of Patrick Hutber's interview with SGW, January 19, 1970.

67. SGW Box 20, SGW to all executive directors, Korner, Whitman and Sharp, October 31, 1967.

68. SGW Box 22, SGW Draft note to executive directors, Korner, Whitman and Sharp, October 21, 1968.

69. Fraser, *High Road*, p. 284.

70. SGW VME/CL/CZ../2, SGW to Karl [?], January 3, 1927.

71. Quoted in Courtney and Thompson, *City Lives*, p. 9.

72. Roll interview.

73. SGW Box 22, SGW to executive directors, Korner, Whitman and Sharp, September 8, 1968. Cf. Fraser, *High Road*, p. 206.

74. SGW Box 2, SGW Daily Report, September 7, 1959.

75. Darling interview.

76. Kelly Diary, February 15, 1972; December 14, 1972; April 24, 1975.

77. Chambers, 'Gentlemanly Capitalism Revisited'.

78. SGW Box 9, Seligman to SGW and Helmore, January 22, 1963.

79. Kenneth Fleet, 'Modern Attitudes in Merchant Banking', *Sunday Telegraph*, n.d.

80. SGW DME/AA../CNZZ/5, SGW to Gert Whitman, November 24, 1965.

81. Roll, *Crowded Hours*, pp. 196f.

82. Fraser, *High Road*, p. 280.

83. SGW VME/CL/CZ../2, SGW Fragment, November 9, 1957.

84. Cairncross, *British Economy since 1945*, p. 173.

85. *Economist*, September 24, 1955.

86. SGW VME/CL/CZ../2, SGW to Eva Warburg, fragment, March 18, 1955.

87. Oscar Lewisohn papers, Grunfeld, 'Speech on the occasion of his 90th birthday', June 6, 1994, pp. 7f.

88. SGW Box 14, SGW to Grunfeld, Korner, Whitman et al., June 19, 1965; Box 22, SGW to executive directors, Korner, Whitman and Sharp, September 8, 1968. Cf. Spira, *Ladders and Snakes*, p. 132.

89. SGW DME/AA../CNZZ/5, SGW to Spiegelberg, July 16, 1960. Cf. *Economist*, August 28, 1965, p. 817; *Daily Telegraph*, September 26, 1968; *Economist*, May 27, 1978, p. 106.

90. *Economist*, June 18, 1960, p. 1279.

91. 'A Separation Plan for Warburgs', *Daily Telegraph*, May 28, 1964.

92. See e.g. SGW Box 10, SGW to John Buchanan, Minseps, September 28, 1963; Box 11, SGW to Prain, May 15, 1964.

93. SGW Box 21, SGW to executive directors, Korner and Whitman, February 27, 1968. *Sunday Telegraph*, June 7, 1964.

94. Nott, *Here Today*, pp. 104f.

95. Fraser, *High Road*, p. 281.

96. Private communication from Peter Spira to the author.

97. See e.g. SGW Box 64, SGW Daily Report, March 2, 1955; Box 5, Grierson Note, June 30, 1961. Cf. Fraser, *High Road*, p. 238.

98. See e.g. SGW Box 6, SGW to Friedman, July 21, 1961; Box 8, SGW to Friedman, January 18, 1962.

99. Valentine, *Free Range Ego*, pp. 78–83.

100. Ibid., pp. 62 and 113–17 for a detailed chronicle of Warburgs' defence of Croda against a bid by Burmah.

101. Owen, *Empire to Europe*, pp. 68–78, 83.

102. See e.g. BoE C48/51, Clarke to Chief Cashier and Deputy Governor, September 15, 1961.

103. See e.g. SGW Box 3, SGW Note, February 2, 1960; Fraser to SGW, February 2, 1960; Box 8, Fraser Note, February 26, 1962. Cf. 'A Famous Victory', *Evening Standard*, February 28, 1962. On this occasion, Lionel Fraser of Helbert Wagg was on the other side, along with Lazards, who also advised Bristol & Westland.

104. Fraser, *High Road*, p. 282.

105. Owen, *Empire to Europe*, pp. 212, 215, 218.

106. SGW Box 63, SGW Daily Report, December 31, 1957.

107. SGW Box 10, SGW Note to Dixon, November 1, 1963.

108. Oxford University, Wilson papers m.883 (econ.2), Labour Party Research Department, June 1, 1964.

109. SGW Box 12, SGW Note, June 15, 1964; SGW Note, June 25, 1964; SGW Draft note, July 7, 1964; SGW to Grierson, July 23, 1964.

110. SGW Box 17, SGW to Louis Warren, November 16, 1966.

111. NA CAB 128/41 part 3, Cabinet minutes, December 20, 1966.

112. NA CAB 128/41 part 3, Cabinet minutes, December 22, 1966; SGW Box 19, SGW to Fraser and Steering Group, May 5, 1967.

113. SGW Box 20, SGW to Grunfeld and Fraser, November 10, 1967; Horne to SGW, Grunfeld, Roll et al., November 21, 1967; SGW to Grunfeld, Roll, Fraser et al., November 30, 1967; Horne to SGW, Grunfeld, Roll, Berry and Policy Committee, December 5, 1967. Cf. Graham Turner, 'How Stokes Got the Top Job', *Sunday Telegraph*, April 18, 1971.

114. SGW Box 20, Draft letter, December 13, 1967. See also Box 21, SGW to Richard Clarke, January 11, 1968; Berry to SGW, Grunfeld, Horne and Roll, February 16, 1968. Cf. Kynaston, *City of London*, vol. IV, p. 373.

115. SGW Box 25, SGW to Roll, Korner, Horne et al., February 25, 1970.

116. Owen, *Empire to Europe*, p. 232.

117. Fraser, *High Road*, p. 282.

118. SGW Box 64, SGW Daily Report, February 17, 1955. Cf. *Economist*, September 3, 1955, p. 801; December 20, 1958, p. 1119.

119. SGW VME/CL/CZ../2, Steiner interview with SGW, n.d., 1976.

120. Details in Braddon, *Roy Thomson*, pp. 250–63. According to Geoffrey Elliott, 'We kept [Thomson] solvent. We blanketed that account. We lived with them.' For an amusing account of the initial negotiations (with the wrong Lord Astor), see Fraser, *High Road*, pp. 237f.

121. SGW Box 5, Draft statement, January 27, 1961; Draft statement, January 30, 1961. Odhams' magazine titles included *Woman, Ideal Home, Horse and Hound* and *Wham!* See *Economist*, February 11, 1961, p. 582.

122. See e.g. SGW Box 5, SGW to Grierson and Fraser, March 2, 1961. Details in Braddon, *Roy Thomson*, pp. 291–8. Cf. Chernow, *Warburgs*, p. 653; Wechsberg, *Merchant Bankers*, pp. 214f.

123. SGW VME/CL/CZ../2, Ernest Bock, 'Companies with a Future: Warburg', draft article, *c.* 1963.

124. Roberts, *Schroders*, pp. 407f.; Fraser, *High Road*, p. 249.

125. Steiner interview.

126. Fraser, *High Road*, p. 340.

127. SGW Box 8, SGW to Grierson and Fraser, February 26, 1962.

128. Fraser, *High Road*, p. 258.

129. *Economist*, October 16, 1971, p. 104. Cf. Bower, *Rowland*.

130. Kelly Diary, April 17, 1976.

131. See e.g. SGW Box 21, SGW to Grunfeld, Roll, Fraser et al., March 15, 1968.

132. Spira, *Ladders and Snakes*, pp. 170f., 175.

133. See e.g. SGW Box 21, Fraser to Policy Committee and SGW, May 14 and 15, 1968.

134. *Economist*, December 23, 1967, p. 1251.

135. Valentine, *Free Range Ego*, p. 62.

136. Jessel interview.

137. Spira, *Ladders and Snakes*, pp. 160f.

138. SGW Box 21, SGW Draft speech for Harold Wilson, March 5, 1968.

139. Benn, *Office without Power*, pp. 18f.

140. See 'Warburgs Statement on Plessey and English Electric', *The Times*, June 28, 1968; SGW DME/AA../CNZZ/5, SGW to Grunfeld, August 26, 1968. On the IRC's bias in favour of GEC, see Hills, 'Industrial Reorganization Corporation'; Owen, *Empire to Europe*, p. 195.

141. SGW Box 22, SGW to Grunfeld, Winspear, Bentley and Smith, September 3, 1968.

142. 'English Electric–GEC: Why and How Much', *Sunday Telegraph*, September 8, 1968.

143. Valentine, *Free Range Ego*, pp. 60ff.

144. SGW Box 22, SGW to Grunfeld, Roll and Winspear, September 21, 1968.

145. SGW DME/AA../CNZZ/5, Grierson to SGW, September 29, 1968. Cf. Grierson interview; Grierson, *Truant Disposition*, p. 59.

146. SGW Box 40, SGW to Scholey, Grunfeld, September 22, 1978.

147. See e.g. SGW Box 21, SGW to Grunfeld, Roll, Fraser et al., June 18, 1968. In this case, British Leyland paid Warburgs £75,000 for their 'invaluable help' in the merger negotiations with BMH.

148. SGW Box 38, SGW to Grunfeld, Scholey, Orr et al., May 4, 1977.

149. SGW Box 20, SGW to all executive directors, October 31, 1967.

150. Kenneth Fleet, 'Modern Attitudes in Merchant Banking', *Sunday Telegraph*, n.d.

151. Kelly Diary, March 15, 1974.

152. 'What Next for Merchant Banks', *Economist*, June 21, 1969, p. xlv.

153. Grierson interview.

154. SGW Box 14, SGW to Mitchell, July 31, 1965. Cf. SGW DME/AA../CNZZ/5, SGW to Heath, July 30, 1965.

155. SGW VME/CL/CZ../2, SGW to Stinnes, n.d.

156. SGW DME/AA../CNZZ/5, SGW to Grierson, December 13, 1965. See also SGW DME/AA../CNZZ/5, Grierson to SGW, November 4, 1970; SGW to Grierson, November 21, 1970.

157. SGW Box 21, SGW to Nott, February 28, 1968.

158. Kynaston, *City of London*, vol. IV, p. 413.

159. SGW Box 22, SGW to Jellicoe, September 21, 1968; SGW DME/AA../CNZZ/5, Jellicoe to SGW, October 15, 1968; Christopher Brocklebank-Fowler to SGW, October 23, 1968; SGW to Brocklebank-Fowler, December 12, 1968. Cf. Barr, *Bow Group*, p. 108.

160. SGW DME/AA../CNZZ/5, SGW to Jellicoe, December 30, 1968.

161. SGW DME/AA../CNZZ/5, Piers Dixon to SGW, December 17, 1970; Wasserman to SGW, April 6, 1971.

162. SGW VME/CL/CZ../2, Nott to SGW, October 5, 1964.

163. SGW DME/CO../RPBZ/6, SGW Note, June 25, 1968.

164. King, *Diary: 1970-1974*, pp. 106f.

165. Kynaston, *City of London*, vol. IV, p. 413.

166. See e.g. SGW Box 29, SGW to Heath, April 21, 1972; Box 31, SGW to Heath, April 17, 1973.

167. SGW Box 28, SGW & Co. Memorandum, October 15, 1971; SGW to Spira, Grunfeld, Korner et al., October 19, 1971.

168. *Sunday Telegraph*, December 5, 1976; Valentine, *Free Range Ego*, pp. 94-9.

169. SGW Box 32, Draft letter to *The Times*, July 23, 1973; SGW to Spira, Grunfeld and Seligman, July 23, 1973; SGW to Spira, Grunfeld, Roll, Seligman and Scholey, August 10, 1973.

170. SGW Box 34, SGW to Scholey, July 17, 1974.

171. SGW DME/AA../CNZZ/5, SGW to Roy Jenkins, July 26, 1971.

172. SGW Box 31, Bonham Carter to SGW, Roll, Spira, Kelly and O'Neill, February 22, 1973; SGW to Guth, February 28, 1973.

173. 'Sir Siegmund Warburg Interview', *Investors Chronicle*, April 13, 1973.

174. SGW VME/CL/CZ../2, Transcript of Patrick Hutber's interview with SGW, January 19, 1970.

175. SGW Box 30, SGW to Gladwyn, October 30, 1972.

176. SGW Box 33, SGW to Eric Warburg, January 13, 1974.

177. SGW Box 33, SGW to Freddie Rubinski, February 17, 1974.

178. SGW Box 33, SGW to Roll, 'Rough draft', April 1, 1974.

179. SGW Box 37, Steiner interview with SGW, August 2, 1976.

180. SGW Box 37, SGW to Roll, September 13, 1976.

181. SGW VME/CL/CZ../2, SGW to Grunfeld, January 28, 1971.

182. King, *Diary: 1970-1974*, pp. 106f.

183. Cairncross, *British Economy since 1945*, pp. 182-191.

184. SGW Box 33, SGW to Wilson, March 5, 1973. See also the draft of a speech by Warburg, intended for Wilson's use, n.d., *c.* June 1973. Warburg gave Wilson the draft when they met on June 10: see SGW to Roll, June 11, 1973.

185. SGW Box 33, SGW to Roll, Grunfeld, Korner et al., March 1, 1974.

186. SGW Box 33, SGW to Freddie Rubinski, April 6, 1974.

187. SGW Box 33, SGW to Roll, June 11, 1974.

188. SGW Box 35, SGW to Roll, Grunfeld, Korner et al., January 21, 1975.

189. SGW Box 35, SGW to Roll, Grunfeld, Seligman and Scholey, February 26, 1975.

190. SGW Box 35, SGW to Roll, Grunfeld, Korner et al., August 1, 1975; Box 36, SGW to Roll, Korner, Scholey et al., November 27, 1975.

191. 'Business Diary: Steel Bond', *The Times*, January 16, 1974.

192. SGW Box 36, Gordon to SGW, Grunfeld, Korner et al., December 5, 1975.

193. Wilson, *Final Term*, p. 195.

194. SGW Box 35, SGW to Roll, August 11, 1975.

195. SGW Box 36, SGW to Steiner, March 18, 1976.

196. See Burk and Cairncross, *Goodbye, Great Britain*.

197. Kelly Diary, January 2, 1975; May 20, 1975; April 3, 1976; June 21, 1976; July 19, 1976.

198. Hennessy, *Muddling Through*, p. 267.

199. SGW Box 42, SGW to Doris Levy, December 9, 1980; SGW to Spira, December 18, 1980.

CHAPTER 11:
THE MALAISE IN OUR WESTERN WORLD

1. SGW DME/CO../RPBZ/6, SGW to Ziegler, January 31, 1975.

2. SGW Box 35, SGW to Rubinski, February 22, 1975.

3. SGW VME/MA../ZZ../4, SGW Diary, May 29, 1942.

4. SGW VME/MA../ZZ../4, SGW Diary, July 22, 1942.

5. See SGW Box 37, SGW interview with Steiner, August 2, 1976.

6. SGW Box 64, SGW Bi-weekly notes No. 52, July 3, 1950.

7. SGW Box 1, SGW to Vogelstein, July 19, 1958; DME/AA../CNZZ/5, SGW to Fromm, March 23, 1967.

8. SGW Box 30, SGW to Lord Avon, October 3, 1972.

9. SGW DME/AA../CNZZ/5, SGW to J. Edward Sieff, April 15, 1957. Cf. Box 1, SGW to Edmund de Rothschild, December 4, 1958.

10. SGW Box 2, SGW Daily Report, September 3, 1959.

11. SGW Box 2, SGW to Yeshiahu Foerder, November 30, 1959.

12. SGW Box 3, SGW to Foerder, January 21, 1960.

13. SGW VME/CL/CZ../2, SGW to Ziegler, March 28, 1960. Cf. Box 3, SGW to Spiegelberg, February 8, 1960.

14. SGW DME/AA../CNZZ/5, SGW to Josef Cohn, January 25, 1960. Cf. VME/CL/CZ../2, SGW, 'Weizmanns guter Schüler', Weizmann Institute of Science, December 1964, pp. 9f.

15. SGW DME/AA../CNZZ/5, SGW to Anna Warburg, December 15, 1964.

16. SGW Box 3, Korner Note, April 11, 1960.

17. SGW Box 5, Seligman Note, April 14, 1961.

18. SGW Box 5, SGW to Samuels, April 10, 1961. Cf. SGW to Spira, April 21, 1961; Box 6, SGW to Lolli, August 10, 1961.

19. SGW DME/AA../CNZZ/5, Sherman to SGW, August 10, 1961.

20. SGW Box 8, SGW to Samuels and Friedman, December 6, 1962; SGW Note, December 10, 1962. Cf. Kenneth Fleet, 'Investing in Israel', Daily Telegraph, May 10, 1964. See also Aharoni, Israeli Economy, pp. 232f., and Halevi, Bank Leumi.

21. SGW Box 14, SGW to Seligman and Spira, October 6, 1965.

22. SGW Box 14, SGW Note to Spira, Seligman, Jessel et al., October 26, 1965.

23. SGW Box 17, SGW to Korner, Jessel et al., October 3, 1966.

24. SGW Box 19, SGW to Korner and Steering Group, June 2, 1967.

25. SGW Box 10, SGW to Dov Biegun, September 30, 1963. See also Box 19, SGW Note, August 21, 1967. The idea was to set up, under the auspices of the Red Cross, a committee of neutral experts to devise some sort of Arab–Israeli peace settlement: VME/CL/CZ../2, SGW to Marcus Sieff, June 2, 1969.

26. SGW VME/CL/CZ../2, SGW to Biegun, January 3, 1964.

27. GW, SGW to GW, June 2, 1967.

28. SGW DME/AA../CNZZ/5, SGW to Stinnes, June 4, 1967.

29. SGW, 'Arabs' Lack of Tolerance', The Times, June 9, 1967.

30. SGW DME/AA../CNZZ/5, SGW to Wechsberg, June 13, 1967; SGW to Eric Warburg, June 13, 1967. Cf. Box 19, SGW to Mazur, June 11, 1967.

31. SGW DME/AA../CNZZ/5, SGW to Randall, June 20, 1967.

32. SGW Box 19, SGW Note, July 12, 1967.

33. SGW Box 19, SGW to Krueger, September 25, 1967.

34. Benn, Office without Power, p. 24. This was not wholly inaccurate: see SGW VME/CL/CZ../2, Minutes of the meeting of the UK Central Committee, February 20, 1968.

35. SGW DME/AA../CNZZ/5, King to SGW, March 4, 1968.

36. SGW VME/CL/CZ../2, SGW to Soroker, March 8, 1968.

37. SGW Box 21, Draft speech, March 16, 1968. See 'Wave of Emotion at Trade Talks', Israel Today, April 12, 1968.

38. SGW Box 21, SGW to Hans Baer, May 6, 1968; Box 22, S. W. O. Seligman to SGW, October 8, 1968. Cf. Box 23, SGW to Aharon Remez, January 21, 1969.

39. SGW DME/AA../CNZZ/5, SGW to Sherman, May 6, 1968.

40. SGW VME/CL/CZ../2, SGW to Ball, June 19, 1968.

41. GW, Ziegler to GW, April 24, 1968.

42. SGW Box 21, SGW to Korner, Sharp, Spira, Seligman and D. M. C. Warburg, January 3, 1968.

43. SGW Box 21, SGW to Soroker, February 8, 1968; February 12, 1968.

44. SGW Box 22, SGW to Herzog, September 4, 1968.

45. SGW Box 22, SGW to Foerder, December 23, 1968.

46. SGW Box 24, SGW to Prof. Estrin, October 1, 1969; SGW to Zeev Sharef, Minister for Commerce and Industry, October 1, 1969. For attempts by Warburg to increase the subsidy paid to the company by the Israeli government, see Box 25, Seligman to SGW and Smith, February 4, 1970.

47. SGW Box 25, SGW to Israel Gal-Edd, March 10, 1970.

48. SGW VME/CL/CZ../2, SGW amendment to 'Papers and Proceedings' of the Economic Conference Praesidium, April 22, 1970.

49. SGW Box 25, S. W. O. Seligman to SGW and Gore, June 1, 1970. See also Box 26, SGW to Astorre Mayer, August 12, 1970.

50. SGW Box 27, Gore to SGW, S. W. O. Seligman and G. C. Seligman, April 22, 1971.

51. SGW Box 27, SGW to Edmund de Rothschild, June 21, 1971.

52. SGW Box 28, Gore to SGW, G. C. Seligman, S. W. O. Seligman and Goodwin, September 10, 1971; SGW telex to Harvey Krueger, September 15, 1971.

53. SGW Box 28, Gore to SGW, Grunfeld, G. C. Seligman, S. W. O. Seligman and Goodwin, November 18, 1971; SGW to Grunfeld, G. C. Seligman, S. W. O. Seligman and Goodwin, January 11, 1972. See also Box 32, SGW to Gore, Grunfeld, G. C. Seligman et al., August 30, 1973; SGW to Gore, September 13, 1973.

54. SGW VME/CL/CZ../2, Sapir to SGW, January 20, 1972.

55. SGW Box 32, SGW Gore to Japhet, 'Proposed Merchant Bank in Israel', December 28, 1973.

56. SGW DME/AA../CNZZ/5, SGW to Marie von Bluecher, March 20, 1972.

57. SGW Box 30, SGW to Gore, November 17, 1972.

58. SGW DME/AA../CNZZ/5, SGW to Nutting, December 1, 1969.

59. SGW Box 25, SGW to Coudenhove-Kalergi, February 13, 1970.

60. SGW DME/AA../CNZZ/5, Victor Rothschild to SGW, December 8, 1969; Box 24, SGW to Rothschild, December 13, 1969. Cf. Box 25, SGW to Victor Rothschild, June 10, 1970.

61. SGW Box 25, SGW to Sherman, May 4, 1970.

62. SGW Box 25, SGW to Goldmann, February 6, 1970; VME/CL/CZ../2, SGW to Goldmann, April 14, 1970; Goldmann to SGW, May 15, 1970; SGW to Goldmann, May 18, 1970; Goldmann to SGW, August 3, 1970; SGW to Goldmann, August 6, 1970; Goldmann to SGW, December 22, 1970; SGW

to Goldmann, December 29, 1970. Cf. DME/AA../CNZZ/5, SGW to Lola Hahn-Warburg, August 3, 1970.

63. SGW Box 27, SGW to Lord Goodman, February 9, 1971; SGW to Jon Kimche, April 14, 1971; George Weidenfeld to SGW, May 5, 1971; Box 28, SGW to Ehud Avriel, August 19, 1971; Kimche to SGW, October 6, 1971; Kimche to SGW, October 22, 1971; Box 29, SGW to Weidenfeld, April 21, 1972; Weidenfeld to SGW, October 4, 1972, December 21, 1972.

64. SGW Box 26, SGW to Ernst van der Beugel, October 26, 1970; DME/ AA../CNZZ/5, SGW to Eric Warburg, November 16, 1970.

65. SGW VME/CL/CZ../2, Goldmann to SGW, January 8, 1971; SGW to Goldmann, January 12, 1971.

66. SGW VME/CL/CZ../2, Goldmann to SGW, April 11, 1971; Box 31, SGW, 'Draft skeleton of a speech to be made in Jerusalem towards the end of May 1973', February 20, 1973; Third draft, March 19, 1973; VME/CL/CZ../2, Fourth draft, May 11, 1973; SGW to Kleeman, June 13, 1973.

67. SGW VME/CL/CZ../2, Kimche to SGW, July 13, 1971.

68. SGW, Marcus Sieff and Lord Goodman, 'King Husain [*sic*] on Israel', *The Times*, February 8, 1973.

69. SGW Box 32, SGW to Doris Levy, October 7, 1973; SGW to Edmund de Rothschild, October 7, 1973; SGW to Anna Biegun, November 21, 1973.

70. SGW DME/AA../CNZZ/5, SGW to Stinnes, November 12, 1973.

71. SGW Box 33, SGW to Rabbi Shlomo Lorincz, March 20, 1974.

72. SGW VME/CL/CZ../2, SGW, 'Peace in the Middle East?', June 10, 1974. This document was described by Warburg himself as one 'which, for the time being should not be published but only be handed by a small group of Jews from the Diaspora to a small group of Israeli political leaders'. As he confessed to Goldmann, the document 'represent[ed] only thinking aloud by way of paper of certain worries, dreams, illusions and hopes': SGW to Goldmann, June 12, 1974; Goldmann to SGW, June 17, 1974.

73. SGW Box 34, SGW to Rubinski, October 12, 1974.

74. SGW Box 37, Steiner interview with SGW, August 2, 1976.

75. SGW VME/CL/CZ../2, SGW to Goldmann, October 8, 1976.

76. SGW VME/CL/CZ../2, SGW to Kreisky, February 24, 1977. By 1980, however, he had changed his position once again: Box 42, SGW to Ernst Cramer: 'the creation of a Palestinian state would in present circumstances be in fact a deadly danger to Israel.'

77. SGW Box 26, SGW to executive directors, September 10, 1970.

78. SGW VME/CL/CZ../2, SGW draft letter to *The Times*, 'Appeasement of Blackmail is Both a Crime and a Mistake', November 8, 1973. See also DME/ AA/CMZZ/5, SGW to Lever, November 15, 1973.

79. SGW DME/AA../CNZZ/5, SGW to Stinnes, November 21, 1973. See also Box 32, SGW to Skribanowitz, November 30, 1973; SGW to Sam Hamburger, December 17, 1973.

80. *Economist*, February 15, 1975, p. 82.

81. Darling, *City Cinderella*, pp. 54f.

82. SGW VME/MA../ZZ../4, Gordon, 'Siegmund Warburg 1902–1982: A Personal Perspective', October 30, 1992.

83. Kynaston, *City of London*, vol. IV, pp. 526f.

84. See the report in the *Evening Standard*, January 21, 1974. Cf. 'The Arab Return to Eurobonds', *Financial Times*, January 22, 1974.

85. 'Three Blacklisted Banks in Kuwaiti-managed Issue', *Financial Times*, February 11, 1975.

86. SGW Box 33, SGW to Roll, Grunfeld, Korner et al., May 1, 1974.

87. SGW Box 33, SGW to Grunfeld, Korner, Roll et al., May 1, 1974; Box 34, SGW to Korner, Grunfeld, Roll and Lewisohn, July 29, 1974.

88. SGW Box 34, SGW to Grunfeld, Korner, Roll et al., August 6, 1974.

89. Cary Reich, 'Probing the Mystique of Warburgs', *Institutional Investor*, February 1, 1977, p. 30.

90. Kelly Diary, October 12, 1973; October 15, 1973; January 14, 1974; January 17, 1974; December 5, 1974; January 16, 1975; March 19, 1975; March 26, 1975; April 6, 1975.

91. SGW Box 34, SGW to Grunfeld, Korner, Roll et al., November 11, 1974.

92. SGW Box 35, SGW to Roll, Grunfeld, Korner et al., January 21, 1975; Gordon to SGW, Grunfeld, Korner et al., January 28, 1975; Gordon to SGW, Grunfeld, Korner et al., January 29, 1975.

93. SGW Box 35, Scholey to SGW, Gordon and members of the Executive Committee, January 29, 1975.

94. SGW Box 35, SGW to Grunfeld et al., February 10, 1975. See also SGW to Seligman, Grunfeld, Roll and Scholey, July 25, 1975.

95. SGW Box 35, SGW to Grunfeld, Korner, Gordon and members of the Executive Committee, February 11, 1975.

96. SGW Box 36, SGW to Grunfeld, Korner, Roll et al., December 13, 1975.

97 SGW VME/CL/CZ../2, SGW to Goldmann, December 29, 1975.

98. Kynaston, *City of London*, vol. IV, p. 527. For further details, see Roberts and Arnander, *Take your Partners*, pp. 106ff.

99. Kelly Diary, May 12, 1974.

100. Stevenson interview.

101. SGW VME/MA../ZZ../4, Gordon, 'Siegmund Warburg 1902–1982: A Personal Perspective', October 30, 1992.

102. Kelly Diary, February 13, 1975.

103. SGW Box 35, SGW to G. C. Seligman, Gore, S. W. O. Seligman et al., September 22, 1975. But see also Box 42, SGW to Jacob de Rothschild, February 6, 1980.

104. SGW Box 38, Gore to Krueger, July 6, 1977; Box 39, SGW to Gore et al., December 9, 1977; Box 40, Gore to Edmund de Rothschild, December 22, 1978.

105. SGW VME/CL/CZ../2, SGW to Michael Sela, August 29, 1977.

106. SGW Box 39, SGW to Gideon Rafael, March 27, 1977.

107. Ibid.

108. SGW VME/CL/CZ../2, SGW Draft letter to *The Times*, May 21, 1977.

109. SGW VME/CL/CZ../2, SGW to Michael Sela, August 29, 1977.

110. See e.g. SGW VME/CL/CZ../2, SGW Draft letter to *The Times*, February 8, 1978; Box 39, SGW to Birrenbach, February 13, 1978; SGW to Gideon Rafael, February 13, 1978; VME/CL/CZ../2, SGW to Goldmann, May 10, 1978; Box 40, SGW to Mazur, December 15, 1978.

111. SGW VME/CL/CZ../2, SGW to Sadat, February 14, 1978. Cf. 'Goldmann praises Sadat', *Jewish Chronicle*, February 17, 1978.

112. SGW, 'Israel's Stance in the Peace Talks', *The Times*, February 18, 1978.

113. Nutting's letter was published in *The Times* on February 23. For a Zionist complaint, see SGW VME/MA../ZZ../4, George Garai, Director of the Zionist Federation Information Office, to SGW, February 23, 1978. See also Anthony Lewis, 'Americans and Israel', *New York Times*, March 27, 1978.

114. SGW VME/CL/CZ../2, Rothschild to SGW, March 8, 1978; April 10, 1978.

115. SGW VME/CL/CZ../2, Sartawi to SGW, February 18, 1981; March 17, 1981; SGW to Sartawi, March 20, 1981.

116. SGW DME/CO../RPBZ/6, SGW to Gordon, Greenhill, Gore et al., May 19, 1978.

117. SGW Box 40, SGW to Mazur, November 11, 1978; December 15, 1978. Cf. Box 41, SGW to Rafael, July 2, 1979. See also Box 42, SGW to George Ball, March 3, 1980.

118. SGW DME/CO../RPBZ/6, SGW to Gordon, Greenhill, Gore et al., May 19, 1978; SGW Box 30, SGW to Gordon and Chairman's Committee, October 3, 1978.

119. SGW Box 41, SGW to Sadat, October 3, 1979; SGW to Craven and van der Wyck, October 8, 1979; Box 42, SGW to van der Wyck, January 2, 1980; SGW to Salina and van der Wyck, January 7, 1980.

120. Oscar Lewisohn papers, Gordon, 'Mr Henry Grunfeld and Sir Siegmund Warburg: Addendum and Epilogue', October 8, 1997.

121. SGW Box 42, SGW to Seligman, July 11, 1980.

122. SGW Box 42, Seligman to Lewisohn and Chairman's Committee, July 4, 1980.

123. SGW Box 42, SGW to Seligman, July 11, 1980; Seligman to SGW, July 14, 1980.

124. SGW VME/CL/CZ../2, SGW Aphorisms.

125. SGW Box 44, SGW to Ball, September 1, 1982.

126. SGW Box 44, SGW to Kollek, August 12, 1982.

127. See in general Andrew, *The World was Going our Way*.

128. Kotkin, *Armageddon Averted*.

129. For a different view, see Tomlinson, 'Why Was There Never a "Keynesian Revolution"?'

130. See e.g. Galbraith, *New Industrial State*.

131. SGW Box 18, SGW to Louis Warren, April 22, 1967.

132. SGW Box 32, SGW to Rubinski, October 13, 1972.

133. SGW Box 35, SGW to Birrenbach, October 17, 1975.

134. SGW VME/CL/CZ../2, SGW Fragment, November 20, 1968.

135. SGW SGW DME/AA../CNZZ/5, Bruce to SGW, February 21, 1969; DME/CO../RPBZ/6, Nixon to SGW, March 5, 1969.

136. SGW Box 26, SGW to van der Beugel, October 2, 1970.

137. SGW Box 28, SGW to McConnell, December 29, 1971.

138. SGW Box 30, SGW to Rubinski, September 4, 1972.

139. SGW Box 31, SGW to Dreifuss, January 2, 1973.

140. SGW Box 31, SGW to Rubinski, May 14, 1973.

141. SGW VME/CL/CZ../2, SGW to Goldmann, May 17, 1979.

142. Dimson, Marsh and Staunton, *Triumph of the Optimists*, p. 303, table 32-2.

143. Wechsberg, *Merchant Bankers*, p. 220.

144. SGW VME/CL/CZ../2, SGW to Goldmann, August 5 and 6, 1970.

145. Grunfeld interview.

146. SGW Box 33, SGW & Co. Memorandum, 'Index Linked Bonds', June 10, 1974; SGW to Harold Lever and Robert Armstrong, June 11, 1974; SGW to Roll et al., June 11, 1974. See also Lewisohn to SGW et al., June 17, 1974; SGW to Roll, Grunfeld, Seligman et al., June 26, 1974; DME/CO../RPBZ/6, Armstrong to SGW, August 9, 1974.

147. 'Merchant Banking Renaissance', *Economist*, March 31, 1979, pp. 50–65.

148. SGW Box 23, SGW amendments to an article by Emery Reves, January 7, 1969.

149. SGW Box 25, SGW to Samuels, April 6, 1970.

150. SGW Box 26, SGW & Co. Draft memorandum for Christopher Fildes at *Euromoney*, August 21, 1970.

151. SGW DME/AA../CNZZ/5, SGW to Furstenberg, September 1, 1970.
152. SGW Box 27, SGW to Dilworth, April 30, 1971. See also Box 28, SGW to Mazur, November 13, 1971; SGW to McConnell, December 29, 1971; DME/AA../CNZZ/5, SGW to Furstenberg, December 31, 1971.
153. SGW Box 29, SGW to Mazur, March 25, 1972.
154. NA T 312/1849, Bancroft Note, January 18, 1965.
155. SGW Box 29, SGW to Roll, Kelly, Spira et al., April 10, 1972.
156. SGW DME/AA../CNZZ/5, SGW to Stinnes, November 21, 1973. See also SGW Box 33, SGW to McAndrew, January 2, 1974.
157. SGW Box 33, SGW to Roll, Grunfeld, Korner et al., May 1, 1974.
158. SGW Box 39, Darling to SGW, Grunfeld, Roll et al., December 14, 1977.
159. SGW Box 40, SGW to Margaret Scarborough Wilson, August 29, 1978.
160. SGW Box 40, Edelshain to SGW, November 24, 1978.
161. King, *Diary: 1970–1974*, pp. 106f.
162. SGW Box 31, SGW to Mazur, February 26, 1973. See also DME/AA/CMZZ/5, SGW to Rubinski, February 27, 1973.
163. SGW Box 33, SGW to Rubinski, February 17, 1974.
164. SGW Box 41, SGW to Skribanowitz, November 19, 1979.
165. SGW Box 42, SGW to Furstenberg, January 12, 1980.
166. SGW Box 32, SGW to Skribanowitz, November 30, 1973.
167. SGW Box 23, SGW amendments to an article by Emery Reves, January 7, 1969.
168. SGW Box 30, Jackson to SGW, Grunfeld, Roll et al., December 19, 1972.
169. SGW Box 34, SGW to Grunfeld, August 28, 1974; Box 36, SGW to Roll, Grunfeld, Korner et al., February 5, 1976.
170. SGW DME/CO../RPBZ/6, SGW to Stinnes, March 8, 1976.
171. Rothschild, *Gilt-Edged Life*, pp. 193f.
172. SGW DME/AA../CNZZ/5, Schiff to SGW, May 14, 1960.
173. SGW Box 8, SGW to Jessel, July 16, 1962.
174. SGW VME/CL/CZ../2, SGW, 'Report on Trip to Japan', October 7–26, 1962.
175. SGW Box 8, SGW to McConnell, October 30, 1962.
176. SGW DME/AA../CNZZ/5, SGW to Fritz Warburg, November 7, 1962.
177. SGW Box 8, SGW to Korner et al., October 29, 1962; LSE McFadyean papers, SGW to McFadyean, October 29, 1962.
178. Courtney and Thompson, *City Lives*, p. 90. On the unpaid services rendered by Shirasu, see SGW Box 38, SGW to Gordon, Grunfeld, Roll et al., January 27, 1977.
179. SGW Box 10, SGW to Okumura, October 28, 1963; Box 11, SGW to Okumura, January 21, 1964; Box 12, SGW to Okumura, June 18, 1964. See

also VME/MA../ZZ../4, Gordon, 'Siegmund Warburg 1902–1982: A Personal Perspective', October 30, 1992.

180. See e.g. SGW Box 13, Spira to SGW, Korner, Whitman et al., April 22, 1965.

181. SGW Box 23, SGW to Murai, Ministry of Finance, December 23, 1968.

182. SGW DME/AA../CNZZ/5, Spira to SGW, May 29, 1969.

183. SGW Box 23, SGW to Adams, June 26, 1969.

184. Purvis interview.

185. SGW VME/CL/CZ../2, SGW Fragment, n.d.

186. SGW DME/AA../CNZZ/5, SGW to Carl Derenberg, February 23, 1970.

187. SGW DME/CO../RPBZ/6, SGW to Stinnes, September 3, 1976.

188. SGW VME/MA../ZZ../4, Gordon, 'Siegmund Warburg 1902–1982: A Personal Perspective', October 30, 1992.

189. SGW Box 39, Roll to Kato, December 19, 1977; VME/CL/CZ../2, *Nihon Keizai Shimbun*, November 5, 1978; Box 40, Gordon to Chairman's Committee, November 27, 1978.

190. SGW DME/CO../RPBZ/6, SGW to Ziegler, November 11, 1978.

191. Meadows, Meadows, Randers and Behrens, *Limits to Growth*.

192. SGW DME/AA../CNZZ/5, SGW to Stinnes, April 5, 1972; February 15, 1973.

193. SGW Box 33, SGW to Mazur, January 14, 1974.

194. SGW Box 33, SGW to Rubinski, February 17, 1974.

195. SGW Personal Documents, Steiner interview, n.d.

196. SGW Box 38, SGW to Anna Halperin, September 20, 1977. See also SGW Box 39, Darling to SGW, Grunfeld, Roll et al., December 14, 1977; Box 42, SGW to Pierre Haas, May 23, 1980.

CHAPTER 12: EXPENSIVE LESSONS

1. SGW Box 39, SGW to Roll, Grunfeld, Seligman, Scholey and Darling, December 9, 1977.

2. Kelly Diary, September 15, 1971.

3. SGW VME/CL/CZ../2, Grunfeld to SGW, February 11, 1970. The original firm of Glyn, Mills & Co. could trace its history back to the eighteenth century, but since 1939 it had been owned by Royal Bank of Scotland. In 1970 it had been merged with Williams and Deacon's Bank to form Williams & Glyn.

4. SGW VME/CL/CZ../2, to Grunfeld, Korner, Seligman et al., February 24, 1971; P. J. Mann Note, April 2, 1971.

5. SGW VME/CL/CZ../2, Mann Note, June 9, 1971.

6. SGW VME/CL/CZ../2, SGW to GW, March 17, 1972.

7. SGW VME/CL/CZ../2, Grunfeld to Roll, January 10, 1973.

8. SGW Box 31, SGW to GW, January 26, 1973.

9. Dimsdale, 'British Monetary Policy', pp. 114–20. See also Cairncross, *British Economy since 1945*, p. 191.

10. SGW Box 31, GW to Grunfeld, March 6, 1973; Grunfeld to GW, March 6, 1973.

11. SGW Box 31, SGW to Dreifuss, March 13, 1973.

12. SGW Box 34, SGW to Scholey, Grunfeld, Roll et al., August 27, 1974.

13. SGW Box 34, SGW to Scholey, Grunfeld, Roll et al., July 20, 1974. See also VME/CL/CZ../2, Scholey to SGW, July 22, 1974; Scholey to SGW, Grunfeld and Seligman, July 22, 1974; July 23, 1974.

14. SGW Box 34, SGW to Scholey, Grunfeld, Roll et al., July 23, 1974; VME/CL/CZ../2, SGW to Scholey, July 24, 1974.

15. SGW VME/CL/CZ../2, SGW Note, July 29, 1974.

16. SGW Box 34, SGW to Scholey, Grunfeld, Roll et al., August 27, 1974; VME/CL/CZ../2, GW to SGW, February 20, 1975; SGW to GW, February 20, 1975; Box 36, SGW to Roll, Grunfeld, Seligman et al., May 6, 1976.

17. SGW VME/CL/CZ../2, Scholey to SGW, Grunfeld and Seligman, July 29, 1974.

18. SGW VME/CL/CZ../2, Dalton to SGW and Scholey, May 28, 1976.

19. Scholey to SGW, Grunfeld, Roll and Seligman, March 11, 1975; SGW DME/CO../RPBZ/6, GW to SGW, July 4, 1975.

20. GW, GW to his mother, March 4, 1977; GW to Anna Warburg, March 4, 1977; GW to SGW, March 4, 1977; March 10, 1977; March 11, 1977; SGW to GW, March 15, 1977.

21. SGW VME/CL/CZ../2, SGW to Jacob Rothschild, October 1, 1980.

22. See, for example, GW, SGW to GW, March 8, 1982; SGW DME/CO../RPBZ/6, GW to SGW, March 11, 1982; SGW to GW, March 28, 1982; GW to SGW, April 4, 1982.

23. SGW Box 26, SGW to Grunfeld, Roll and Seligman, December 7, 1970.

24. SGW Box 31, SGW to Marlow, Grunfeld, Roll et al., January 11, 1973.

25. SGW Box 39, SGW to Roll, Grunfeld, Scholey et al., November 7, 1977. See also Box 41, SGW to Roll and Grunfeld, May 21, 1979.

26. SGW Box 29, SGW to Grunfeld, Roll, Seligman et al., May 10, 1972.

27. SGW Box 34, SGW to Marlow, Grunfeld and Arnheim, July 25, 1974.

28. SGW Box 37, SGW to Grunfeld, Roll, Seligman et al., May 27, 1975.

29. SGW Box 38, SGW to Roll, Grunfeld, Korner et al., September 21, 1977.

30. SGW DME/CO../RPBZ/6, SGW to Seligman, April 19, 1978.

31. SGW to Gore, Underwood, Seymour et al., May 2, 1979.

32. SGW Box 42, SGW to Chairman's Committee, May 20, 1980.

33. SGW DME/CO../RPBZ/6, Lewisohn to Chairman's Committee, September 5, 1977; SGW to Lewisohn, Grunfeld, Roll et al., September 6, 1977. Cf. Darling, *City Cinderella*, p. 85.

34. SGW Box 42, SGW to Chairman's Committee, September 22, 1980. The story of Mercury Asset Management, as it became known, is told in Darling, *City Cinderella*; see esp. pp. 106f., 112f. Cf. Kynaston, *City of London*, vol. IV, p. 564; Fraser, *High Road*, p. 285.

35. 'Mercury Securities: Justifying a Premium Rating', *The Times*, July 6, 1976; 'Warburg Sets a Fast Pace', *Daily Telegraph*, July 5, 1977; 'The Two Who've Made It', *Economist*, March 31, 1979, p. 54.

36. 'Sir Siegmund Makes Way for Young Warburg Men', *Financial Times*, January 1, 1970; 'Sir Siegmund is Mercury President: Evolution at S. G. Warburg', *The Times*, January 1, 1970.

37. SGW Box 39, SGW to Roll, Grunfeld, Seligman et al., December 9, 1977.

38. Kelly Diary, May 10, 1973; January 16, 1974.

39. Ibid., June 5, 1974; June 28, 1974; July 1, 1974; July 2, 1974; July 3, 1974; July 8, 1974; July 9, 1974; July 18, 1974.

40. Valentine, *Free Range Ego*, p. 84.

41. SGW Box 25, SGW to Policy Group, January 19, 1970.

42. Kelly Diary, October 2, 1975.

43. SGW VME/CL/CZ../2, SGW Fragment, *c.* January 1, 1970.

44. Spira, *Ladders and Snakes*, pp. 163, 185.

45. Courtney and Thompson, *City Lives*, p. 89.

46. SGW Box 38, SGW to Scholey, Grunfeld, Roll et al., March 2, 1977; Roll Memorandum, April 18, 1977; SGW to Spira, May 3, 1977; June 13, 1977; SGW to Roll, June 13, 1977. Cf. Spira, *Ladders and Snakes*, pp. 212ff., 223.

47. GW, GW to SGW, March 4, 1977; March 9, 1977; March 10, 1977.

48. Kelly Diary, February 22, 1974.

49. Ibid., November 5, 1975.

50. 'Warburg's Chairman to Retire', *The Times*, July 20, 1974. See also SGW Box 34, Roll, 'Note to Directors and Executives', July 26, 1974; Seligman to directors and executives, August 15, 1974.

51. SGW Box 37, SGW to Grunfeld, Roll and Seligman, August 3, 1976.

52. SGW Box 39, SGW to Roll, Grunfeld, Seligman et al., January 30, 1978; Box 41, SGW to Scholey, December 17, 1979; Scholey to SGW, December 31, 1979.

53. SGW Box 43, SGW to Grunfeld, Roll and Scholey, February 16, 1981;

SGW to Chairman's Committee, March 12, 1981; Elliott to SGW, March 16, 1981.

54. SGW Box 44, SGW to Roll, September 2, 1982.

55. SGW Box 39, SGW to Roll, Grunfeld, Seligman and Darling, December 9, 1977.

56. Rothschild, *Gilt-Edged Life*, pp. 182f.

57. Bank of England C48/51, Note for record, December 17, 1959. See also HSC memorandum of conversation with S. Warburg, June 18, 1963; SGW Box 24, SGW Note, October 2, 1969.

58. SGW DME/AA../CNZZ/5, SGW to Spiegelberg, July 16, 1960.

59. SGW Box 22, SGW to Policy Committee, Korner, Whitman and Sharp, July 16, 1968. See also 'Merger Moves in Merchant Banking', *Daily Telegraph*, May 8, 1971.

60. SGW Box 22, SGW to Scholey, Grunfeld, Smith et al., July 18, 1968.

61. Slater, *Return to Go*, pp. 167f. Cf. Kynaston, *City of London*, vol. IV, pp. 411, 457f.

62. SGW Box 30, SGW to Grunfeld, Korner, Roll et al., September 5, 1972.

63. SGW Box 29, Grunfeld to SGW, May 19, 1972.

64. SGW Box 32, Roll to Grunfeld, September 6, 1973.

65. SGW Box 44, SGW, 'Some Fragmentary Thoughts', May 17, 1982; Weiss to SGW, Scholey, Garmoyle et al., July 22, 1982; SGW to Chairman's Committee, July 28, 1982.

66. SGW Box 26, SGW to Grunfeld, Roll and Seligman, December 7, 1970.

67. Oscar Lewisohn papers, 'Selected Reminiscences of Henry Grunfeld', p. 29.

68. Fraser, *High Road*, p. 324.

69. Kelly Diary, November 30, 1971.

70. Rose, *Elusive Rothschild*, p. 200.

71. SGW DME/AA../CNZZ/5, SGW to Stinnes, April 18, 1970; Stinnes to SGW, April 22, 1970.

72. SGW DME/AA../CNZZ/5, van der Beugel to SGW, October 26, 1970.

73. Ferguson, *World's Banker*, p. 1021.

74. SGW Box 36, SGW to Roll, Grunfeld, Seligman et al., April 28, 1976; Box 38, SGW to Evelyn de Rothschild, June 9, 1977.

75. SGW Box 40, SGW to Roll, July 24, 1978.

76. SGW Box 42, SGW to Chairman's Committee, May 20, 1980.

77. SGW Box 40, SGW to Roll, July 24, 1978.

78. SGW DME/AA../CNZZ/5, SGW to Eric Warburg, December 12, 1967; December 29, 1967; Eric Warburg to SGW, May 29, 1968; SGW to Eric Warburg, June 4, 1968; October 1, 1968; SGW to Grunfeld, October 21, 1968; Whitman to SGW, October 22, 1968; Box 22, SGW to Eric Warburg,

November 25, 1968; DME/AA../CNZZ/5, SGW to Eric Warburg, June 2, 1969; Box 25, Lewisohn to SGW, Grunfeld, Hanks et al., January 20, 1970; DME/AA../CNZZ/5, Grunfeld to SGW, February 23, 1970; Eric Warburg to Grunfeld, February 27, 1970. See also SGW Box 27, SGW to Lewisohn, Grunfeld and Sharp, June 24, 1971; Box 28, SGW to Eric Warburg, August 24, 1971; DME/AA../CNZZ/5, Eric Warburg to SGW, August 30, 1971; SGW to Eric Warburg, September 6, 1971; Eric Warburg to SGW, June 12, 1972; Box 30, Roll to Pincus, November 30, 1972; DME/AA../CNZZ/5, SGW to Eric Warburg, December 12, 1973; February 13, 1974; Eric Warburg to SGW, May 22, 1974; SGW to Eric Warburg, June 3, 1974; Eric Warburg to SGW, June 13, 1974; Eric Warburg to Lionel Pincus, November 13, 1974; Eric Warburg to SGW, November 13, 1974; SGW to Eric Warburg, December 1, 1974.

79. SGW DME/AA../CNZZ/5, SGW to Eric Warburg, December 29, 1967.

80. SGW DME/AA../CNZZ/5, SGW to Eric Warburg, June 16, 1972; SGW Box 30, SGW to Grunfeld, Roll, Scholey et al., August 8, 1972.

81. SGW Box 25, SGW to Korner, Sharp, Lewisohn and Wuttke, March 2, 1970; DME/AA../CNZZ/5, Eric Warburg to SGW, March 26, 1970; Box 25, SGW to Wuttke, Grunfeld, Korner et al., March 31, 1970; SGW to Grunfeld and Wuttke, May 7, 1970.

82. SGW Box 25, SGW to Korner, Sharp, Wuttke et al., May 20, 1970; Box 26, SGW to Eric Warburg, June 16, 1970; SGW to Wuttke, Grunfeld, Korner et al., August 10, 1970; SGW to Wuttke, Gunfeld, Korner et al., August 14, 1970; Wuttke to SGW, Grunfeld, Korner et al., September 2, 1970; Box 29, SGW to Grunfeld, Korner, Roll, Seligman et al., March 20, 1972; June 17, 1972; Box 30, SGW to Lewisohn, Grunfeld and Sharp, November 8, 1972; SGW to Grunfeld, December 11, 1972; SGW to Wuttke, December 13, 1972; SGW to Kelly and Grunfeld, December 20, 1972; Box 31, SGW to Brinckmann, January 8, 1973; Box 32, SGW to Grunfeld, Korner, Roll et al., July 29, 1973; SGW to Eric Warburg, August 28, 1973; SGW to Eric Warburg, December 15, 1973; Box 33, SGW to Max Warburg, February 4, 1974; March 1, 1974; SGW to Sharp, Lewisohn, Petschek and Grunfeld, March 25, 1974; Framhein to SGW, Grunfeld, Roll et al., May 23, 1974; Petschek to SGW, Korner, Grunfeld et al., June 21, 1974; SGW to Petschek and Grunfeld, June 21, 1974; Box 34, SGW to Grunfeld, Korner, Roll, et al., July 5, 1974; Framhein to SGW, Grunfeld, Korner et al., August 5, 1974; September 25, 1974; SGW to Grunfeld, Korner, Roll et al., November 5, 1974; November 11, 1974; Box 35, SGW to Grunfeld, Korner, Roll et al., January 30, 1975; February 19, 1975; February 27, 1975.

83. SGW Box 35, SGW to Lola Hahn-Warburg, March 6, 1975. Cf. DME/AA../CNZZ/5, Eric Warburg to SGW, March 7, 1975; SGW to Grunfeld, Korner, Roll, Seligman and Scholey, March 10, 1975; DME/AA../CNZZ/5, SGW to Eric

Warburg, March 12, 1975; Box 35, SGW to Grunfeld, Sharp, Lewisohn et al., May 4, 1975; DME/CO../RPBZ/6, Max Warburg to SGW, March 5, 1976; Box 36, SGW to Grunfeld, Petschek, Korner et al., June 22, 1976.

84. SGW DME/AA../CNZZ/5, SGW to Eric Warburg, May 3, 1977.

85. SGW Box 38, SGW to Grunfeld, Korner, Roll et al., March 3, 1977; March 9, 1977; DME/AA../CNZZ/5, SGW to Eric Warburg, May 3, 1977; SGW to Marie-Louise Spiegelberg, May 16, 1977; SGW to Eric Warburg, June 30, 1977; SGW to Petschek, Grunfeld and Framhein, July 29, 1977; Box 39, March 15, 1978; DME/AA../CNZZ/5, Max Kreifels to SGW, April 12, 1978; June 20, 1978; Box 41, SGW to Eric Warburg, June 5, 1979; SGW to Grunfeld, Hutton, Petschek et al., September 10, 1979.

86. SGW Box 42, Grunfeld to Chairman's Committee, January 22, 1980.

87. SGW Box 41, SGW to Roll, April 28, 1979; Box 42, SGW to Eric Warburg, June 23, 1980; Box 43, [draft], June 16, 1981; SGW to Scholey, Darling and Lewisohn, October 14, 1981.

88. SGW Box 32, SGW to Sharp, Grunfeld, Korner et al., July 12, 1973.

89. SGW Box 35, SGW to Grunfeld, Roll, Sharp et al., October 4, 1975; Box 36, Lewisohn to SGW, Grunfeld, Korner et al., November 17, 1975.

90. SGW Box 36, SGW to Lewisohn, Grunfeld, Korner et al., June 14, 1976.

91. SGW Box 38, SGW to Lewisohn, Grunfeld, Korner et al., January 9, 1977; March 14, 1977.

92. Cary Reich, 'Probing the Mystique of Warburgs', *Institutional Investor*, February 1977, p. 29.

93. *Financial Times*, March 13, 1981. Cf. Kevin Muehring, 'Soditic's Assault on Swiss Tradition', *Institutional Investor*, February 1986.

94. SGW Box 14, SGW to Curtis J. Hoxter, June 14, 1965.

95. SGW Box 17, SGW to Korner, Whitman, Fraser et al., November 14, 1966; Box 20, SGW to Seligman, Grunfeld, Roll et al., October 28, 1967.

96. SGW Box 22, SGW to Policy Group, December 3, 1968.

97. SGW Box 18, SGW to Carl Hess, April 21, 1967; Box 20, SGW to Seligman and members of Policy Committee, November 18, 1967; DME/AA../CNZZ/5, SGW to Grunfeld, Korner, Whitman et al., December 12, 1967; Box 22, SGW to G. C. Seligman, Roll, Bonham Carter and Darling, August 12, 1968. See Darling, *City Cinderella*, pp. 77ff.

98. SGW Box 23, SGW to Mitchell, Darling and Policy Group, January 10, 1969.

99. SGW Box 28, Spira to SGW, Roll, Seligman et al., July 8, 1971; SGW to Mark Littman, August 11, 1971.

100. SGW Box 23, SGW to Seligman, Roll, Grunfeld et al., June 20, 1969; June 23, 1969.

101. SGW Box 25, SGW to Wender, Roll, Seligman and Darling, March 11, 1970.

102. SGW DME/AA../CNZZ/5, Darling to SGW, December 18, 1969; Mitchell to SGW, March 23, 1970; Box 26, SGW to Korner, Darling, Gore et al., June 20, 1970; DME/AA../CNZZ/5, SGW to Hess, January 18, 1971.

103. SGW Box 25, Seligman to SGW, Darling, Gore et al., June 12, 1970; August 3, 1970; Gore to SGW, Roll, Seligman et al., August 7, 1970.

104. SGW Box 26, SGW to Seligman, Grunfeld, Roll et al., December 15, 1970; Mai to SGW, Grunfeld, Roll et al., December 23, 1970; SGW to Mai, Grunfeld, Roll et al., December 29, 1970; Box 28, Darling to SGW, Grunfeld, Roll et al., October 4, 1971.

105. SGW Box 27, Mai to SGW, Grunfeld, Roll et al., March 10, 1971.

106. SGW Box 29, Darling to SGW, Grunfeld, Roll et al., March 14, 1972; SGW to Roll, Grunfeld, Seligman et al., March 20, 1972; Box 32, SGW to Roll, Grunfeld, Seligman et al., September 6, 1973; Roll to Grunfeld, Seligman, SGW et al., September 18, 1973.

107. Grierson interview. Grierson had been made a director of AEA.

108. Darling, *City Cinderella*, p. 80. Cf. SGW Box 33, Darling to SGW, Grunfeld, Roll et al., June 14, 1974.

109. SGW Box 41, SGW to Spira, April 21, 1979.

110. The phrase was Hermann Abs's: SGW Box 29, SGW to Grunfeld, Korner, Roll et al., June 17, 1972.

111. SGW Box 27, SGW to Darling, Grunfeld, Korner et al., May 2, 1971; Box 28, Lewisohn to SGW, Grunfeld, Korner et al., October 20, 1971.

112. SGW Box 29, SGW to Grunfeld, Korner, Roll et al., March 11, 1972.

113. SGW Box 29, SGW to Grunfeld, Korner, Roll et al., April 29, 1972.

114. In general, see Bussière, *Paribas*.

115. See e.g. SGW Box 8, SGW Note, February 7, 1962; Box 14, Grierson to SGW, Korner, Whitman et al., March 18, 1965; Box 16, SGW to Grierson and Sharp, June 29, 1966; Box 21, SGW to Barton, Seligman, Kelly et al., February 22, 1968; Box 24, SGW to Policy Committee, September 22, 1969; October 10, 1969.

116. Haas was a shrewd judge of Warburg: Oscar Lewisohn papers, Pierre Haas, 'Sir Siegmund Warburg et S. G. Warburg & Co. Ltd.', February 20, 1984.

117. For the view from Paris, see Fouchier, *Banque et la vie*, pp. 229–33. Cf. Robert Mauthner, 'Banque de Paris et des Pays-Bas: Fears of Relegation', *Financial Times*, April 6, 1973. Fouchier had created in the Union Bancaire a nationwide network of deposit-taking banks. After its takeover by Paribas, he emerged as the dominant figure. Cf. Bussière, *Paribas*, pp. 162f.

118. Moussa, *Roue de la fortune*, pp. 175–8. Cf. SGW Box 31, SGW to

Moussa, February 12, 1973; Box 32, SGW to Moussa, September 25, 1973.

119. SGW Box 30, Roll to SGW, Grunfeld, Korner et al., November 30, 1972.

120. 'Common Market: A Stock Swap Links Two Powerful Bankers', *Business Week*, April 14, 1973.

121. SGW Box 30, SGW to Roll, Grunfeld, Korner et al., December 1, 1972; Roll to SGW, Grunfeld, Korner et al., December 5, 1972; Box 31, January 9, 1973; SGW to Roll, Grunfeld, Korner et al., January 16, 1973; Roll to SGW, Grunfeld, Seligman et al., January 17, 1973; February 14, 1973; Hobley to SGW, Grunfeld, Roll et al., March 5, 1973; March 6, 1973; Roll to SGW, Grunfeld, Seligman et al., March 7, 1973; SGW to Fouchier, April 5, 1973.

122. SGW Box 31, SGW & Co./Paribas meeting, April 13, 1973.

123. See e.g. 'Setting a Trend', *Guardian*, April 6, 1973; 'Warburgs and Paribas in £15m share exchange', *Daily Telegraph*, April 6, 1973; 'Warburg and Paribas Form New Holding Company as European Trading Link', *The Times*, April 6, 1973; 'An Elegant Solution', *Sunday Telegraph*, April 8, 1973. See also 'Sir Siegmund Warburg Interview', *Investors Chronicle*, April 13, 1973.

124. SGW DME/AA../CNZZ/5, Furstenberg to SGW, April 17, 1973.

125. Fouchier, *Banque et la vie*, p. 229.

126. SGW Box 34, SGW to Grunfeld, Roll, Seligman et al., August 20, 1974; Box 35, February 10, 1975.

127. SGW Box 36, SGW to Roll, Seligman, Gordon et al., December 16, 1975; Box 37, SGW to Roll, Seligman, Grunfeld et al., September 14, 1976; Box 38, SGW to Salina, Roll, Gordon, Lewisohn et al., June 2, 1977; SGW to Haas, June 9, 1977.

128. Valentine, *Free Range Ego*, pp. 99f.

129. Kelly Diary, February 12, 1972; April 5, 1972; May 2, 1972.

130. 'Paribas–Warburg: Less than Meets the Eye', *Economist*, April 4, 1973. Cf. Sagou, *Paribas*, pp. 31–6.

131. SGW Box 31, Stewart-Roberts to SGW, Grunfeld, Roll et al., June 27, 1973.

132. SGW Box 32, SGW to Grunfeld and Wuttke, August 30, 1973.

133. SGW Box 30, Roll to SGW, Grunfeld, Korner et al., November 30, 1972.

134. SGW Box 2, SGW to Frederick Warburg, December 4, 1959. See also Box 35, SGW to Grunfeld, Roll, Seligman et al., February 10, 1975.

135. SGW Box 33, Stewart-Roberts to SGW, Grunfeld, Roll et al., January 31, 1974.

136. SGW Box 33, SGW to Roll, Seligman, Scholey et al., February 17, 1974.

137. SGW Box 33, Seligman to SGW, Grunfeld, Korner et al., April 25, 1974;

Paribas/SGW & Co. Steering Committee minutes, May 10, 1974; SGW to Wender, May 16, 1974; SGW to Seligman, Grunfeld, Korner et al., May 23, 1974.

138. SGW Box 34, SGW to Seligman, Grunfeld, Korner et al., August 2, 1974.

139. Ibid. See also October 5, 1974.

140. SGW Box 34, SGW to Seligman, Grunfeld, Korner et al., August 20, 1974.

141. SGW Box 34, SGW to Grunfeld, Roll, Seligman et al., September 28, 1974; October 5, 1974; October 10, 1974.

142. SGW Box 34, SGW to Grunfeld, Korner, Roll et al., October 22, 1974; Ward to SGW, Grunfeld, Korner et al., October 31, 1974.

143. SGW Box 35, SGW to Grunfeld, Korner, Roll et al., March 28, 1975.

144. SGW Box 35, SGW to Seligman, Grunfeld, Roll and Scholey, April 14, 1975; October 18, 1975; Box 37, September 18, 1976.

145. SGW Box 35, SGW to Seligman, Roll, Darling and Brooke, July 1, 1975; SGW to Seligman, Grunfeld, Roll and Scholey, July 25, 1975; SGW to Seligman, Grunfeld, Roll, Scholey and Darling, July 29, 1975; DME/CO../RPBZ/6, August 26, 1975; Box 36, SGW to Seligman, Grunfeld, Roll et al., November 11, 1975; Box 37, September 14, 1976.

146. Darling interview.

147. SGW Box 37, SGW to Seligman, Grunfeld, Roll et al., September 18, 1976.

148. SGW Box 36, SGW to Seligman, Grunfeld, Roll et al., June 15, 1976.

149. SGW Box 36, SGW to Elliott, Grunfeld, Roll et al., June 30, 1976.

150. SGW Box 37, SGW to Seligman, Grunfeld, Roll et al., September 18, 1976.

151. SGW Box 37, SGW to Scholey, Grunfeld, Roll and Seligman, November 9, 1976.

152. SGW Box 37, SGW Draft letter to Judy, November 10, 1976; Brooke to SGW, Grunfeld, Roll et al., November 10, 1976; Box 38, SGW to Seligman, Grunfeld, Korner et al., January 11, 1977.

153. SGW Box 38, SGW to Seligman, Grunfeld, Korner et al., January 14, 1977.

154. SGW Box 38, SGW to Seligman, Grunfeld, Roll et al., January 21, 1977; February 24, 1977; SGW to Roll, Grunfeld, Korner et al., March 9, 1977; SGW to Roll, Grunfeld, Seligman et al., March 22, 1977; March 23, 1977; SGW to Scholey, July 31, 1977; August 1, 1977; Judy to SGW, August 9, 1977; Wender to SGW, August 23, 1977; SGW to Seligman, Scholey, Darling et al., August 30, 1977.

155. SGW Box 38, SGW to Roll, Grunfeld, Seligman et al., January 26, 1977; SGW to Grunfeld, Seligman, Scholey et al., October 28, 1977; Box 40, SGW to Scholey, November 30, 1978; Box 41, SGW to Scholey, Craven and Chairman's Committee, April 25, 1979.

156. SGW VME/MA../ZZ../4, Gordon, 'Siegmund Warburg 1902–1982: A Personal Perspective', 30 October 1992.

157. SGW Box 39, SGW to Roll, Grunfeld, Seligman et al., March 25, 1978; DME/CO../RPBZ/6, SGW to Chairman's Committee, April 17, 1978; DME/CO../RPBZ/6, SGW to Chairman's Committee, April 25, 1978; SGW to Seligman, May 2, 1978; Box 40, SGW to Scholey, August 15, 1978; DME/CO../RPBZ/6, SGW to Chairman's Committee, October 2, 1978.

158. SGW Box 43, SGW to Roll, Scholey and Monday meeting, October 5, 1981; SGW to Haas and Scholey, March 15, 1982.

159. SGW Box 44, SGW to Scholey and Chairman's Committee, April 27, 1982; May 28, 1982; June 28, 1982; SGW to Scholey, July 2, 1982; SGW to Haas and Scholey [draft], July 5, 1982.

160. SGW Box 44, SGW to Elliott, August 12, 1982.

161. SGW Box 40, SGW to Chairman's Committee, October 16, 1978; DME/CO../RPBZ/6, SGW to Scholey, November 17, 1978; Box 41, SGW to Roll, Scholey, Elliott et al., January 15, 1979; February 13, 1979. On Moussa's role at Paribas, see Baumier, *Galaxie Paribas*, pp. 82–99.

162. SGW DME/CO../RPBZ/6, Moussa to SGW, December 8, 1981.

163. SGW Box 41, SGW to Moussa [draft], February 13, 1979; SGW to Scholey, Elliott and Chairman's Committee, March 1, 1979; Moussa to SGW, June 21, 1979; SGW Note, June 25, 1979; SGW to Roll and Chairman's Committee, October 7, 1979; Box 42, SGW to Roll, Scholey and Chairman's Committee, May 27, 1980.

164. SGW Box 42, SGW to Roll, Scholey and Chairman's Committee, December 5, 1980; Box 43, March 16, 1981; DME/CO../RPBZ/6, Elliott to SGW, Grunfeld, Roll et al., March 16, 1981; SGW to Elliott and Chairman's Committee, March 19, 1981.

165. SGW Box 42, Elliott to Chairman's Committee, June 3, 1980.

CHAPTER 13:
THE EDUCATION OF AN ADULT

1. Drogheda, *Double Harness*, p. 150.

2. GW, Paul Ziegler to GW, April 24, 1968.

3. SGW VME/CL/CZ../2, Sherman Draft introduction to 'An Anthology for Searchers', March 26, 1984.

4. SGW VME/CL/CZ../2, Scholey to Eva Warburg, March 29, 1973.

5. See Fraser, *High Road*, pp. 284f.

6. SGW Box 40, SGW to Grunfeld, May 10, 1978.

7. SGW Box 42, SGW to Scholey and Chairman's Committtee, March 17, 1980; SGW to Korner, May 29, 1980.

8. SGW Box 41, SGW to Roll and Chairman's Committee, January 2, 1979; DME/CO../RPBZ/6, SGW to Grunfeld, May 15, 1980; Box 42, SGW to Roll, Scholey and Chairman's Committee, May 20, 1980; SGW to Grunfeld, Roll, Scholey et al., October 1, 1980; Box 43, SGW to Grunfeld, Roll and Scholey, September 4, 1981.

9. SGW Box 41, SGW to Scholey, Korner and Chairman's Committee, May 25, 1979.

10. Kelly Diary, July 14, 1975.

11. SGW Box 42, SGW to Darling, Roll, Scholey et al., March 28, 1980.

12. SGW Box 43, SGW to Roll, Scholey and Chairman's Committee, January 14, 1981.

13. Kelly Diary, January 8, 1974; February 5, 1974.

14. SGW Box 43, SGW to Grunfeld, Roll and Scholey, February 16, 1981; SGW to Stevenson and Chairman's Committee, March 12, 1981.

15. *The Times*, February 16, 1981.

16. SGW VME/MA../ZZ../4, Grunfeld Speech, January 12, 1983.

17. 'The Two Who've Made It', *Economist*, March 31, 1979, p. 54.

18. 'Merchant Banking Renaissance', *Economist*, March 31, 1979, p. 50.

19. SGW Box 42, SGW to Doris Levy, December 9, 1980.

20. SGW DME/AA../CMZZ/5, Scholey to Thatcher, February 16, 1981.

21. SGW Box 43, SGW to Joseph, May 5, 1981.

22. Williams (ed.), *Diary of Hugh Gaitskell*, p. 524.

23. SGW Box 43, SGW to Fisher, Smithers and Chairman's Committee, March 16, 1981.

24. SGW Box 42, SGW to Spira, December 18, 1980. See also Box 43, SGW to Roll, Scholey and Chairman's Committee, January 14, 1981.

25. SGW Box 43, SGW to Grunfeld, Fisher, Garmoyle et al., January 15, 1981.

26. SGW Box 43, SGW to Sir Edwin Leather, January 15, 1981.

27. SGW DME/CO../RPBZ/6, Keith Joseph to SGW, March 10, 1981.

28. SGW Box 43, SGW to James Leigh Pemberton, June 1, 1981.

29. SGW Box 43, SGW to Roll, Scholey and members of the Monday meeting, August 26, 1981.

30. SGW Box 43, SGW to Sir Edwin Leather, January 15, 1981.

31. SGW Box 43, SGW to Shirasu, August 5, 1981.

32. SGW Box 38, SGW to Chairman's Committee, May 4, 1977.

33. SGW Box 41, SGW to Roll and Chairman's Committee, October 7, 1979.

34. SGW Box 43, SGW to Tony Griffin, August 10, 1981.

35. SGW Box 43, SGW to Roll, Scholey and members of the Monday meeting, June 23, 1981; SGW to Roll, Scholey and Chairman's Committee, June 29, 1981; SGW to Moussa, July 15, 1981; SGW to Roll, Scholey, Gore et al., October 26, 1981. See also SGW to Roll, Scholey and members of the Monday meeting, November 30, 1981.

36. SGW Box 43, SGW to Eskenazi, November 19, 1981.

37. SGW Box 44, SGW to Moussa, November 23, 1981. See also Box 43, SGW to Furstenberg, November 24, 1981.

38. SGW Box 44, SGW to Scholey, Roll, Darling et al., July 14, 1982.

39. SGW Box 43, SGW to members of the Monday meeting, December 21, 1981; SGW to Fouchier, December 31, 1981; Lewisohn to SGW, Grunfeld, Roll et al., January 6, 1982.

40. SGW Box 44, SGW to Fouchier, January 19, 1982.

41. SGW Box 44, Scholey to Gore, Hobley, Leathes et al., January 20, 1982; Roll to Fouchier, January 20, 1982; DME/CO../RPBZ/6, Haberer to SGW, February 18, 1982; SGW to Scholey, Grierson, Sanders et al., May 24, 1982; SGW to Roll, Scholey, Brooke et al., June 15, 1982; SGW to van der Wyck, Kaempfer, Sanders et al., September 8, 1982; SGW DME/CO../RPBZ/6, van der Wyck and Sanders to Kaempfer and Chairman's Committee, September 17, 1982.

42. Oscar Lewisohn papers, Gordon, 'Mr Henry Grunfeld and Sir Siegmund Warburg: Addendum and Epilogue', October 8, 1997.

43. *The Times*, March 24, 1983; April 30, 1983. Cf. Fouchier, *Banque et la vie*, p. 233.

44. SGW VME/CL/CZ../2, SGW to Spiegelberg, October 1, 1947.

45. SGW Box 16, SGW to Steering Group, April 14, 1966.

46. SGW VME/MA../ZZ../4, SGW Diary, April 14, 1942; July 15, 1942; July 16, 1942; July 23, 1942; July 27, 1942; August 4, 1942; August 7, 1942; May 4, 1943; November 2, 1943; February 12, 1944; VME/CL/CZ../2, Lady Oxford to SGW, April 22, 1942; SGW to Lady Oxford, April 27, 1942.

47. SGW DME/AA../CNZZ/5, Warburg to Keller, February 7, 1955; Box 1, SGW to Vogelstein, January 22, 1958.

48. SGW DME/AA../CNZZ/5, SGW to Anna Warburg, August 24, 1962.

49. SGW Box 41, SGW to Skribanowitz, May 12, 1979.

50. SGW Box 18, SGW to Dilworth, February 28, 1967. See also Box 34, SGW to Heinz Goldman, November 13, 1974; VME/CL/CZ../2, Goldman to SGW, November 16, 1974.

51. SGW Box 18, SGW to James Helmore, March 11, 1967.

52. SGW VME/MA../ZZ../4, SGW to Hans Wuttke, September 30, 1967; DME/AA../CNZZ/5, SGW to Tony Korner, June 8, 1970.

53. SGW Box 30, SGW to Lord Avon, October 3, 1972; SGW to Alfred

Romney, October 20, 1972; DME/AA../CNZZ/5, SGW to Furstenberg, November 21, 1972.

54. SGW Box 37, SGW to Paul von Saanen, October 20, 1976; DME/CO../RPBZ/6, SGW to Marga Stinnes, November 11, 1976.

55. SGW Box 41, SGW to Eric Warburg, March 6, 1979.

56. Grunfeld interview.

57. SGW to Haberer, August 4, 1982.

58. Darling interview.

59. Oscar Lewisohn papers, Gordon, 'Mr Henry Grunfeld and Sir Siegmund Warburg', October 8, 1997, p. 1.

60. GW, SGW to Philipson, n.d., *c.* 1927; September 27, 1927.

61. SGW VME/CL/CZ../2, SGW Speech at the wedding of Anna Warburg and Dov Biegun, August 13, 1962.

62. GW, SGW to his Philipson, December 15, 1927.

63. SGW VME/MA../ZZ../4, SGW Diary, June 6, 1940.

64. SGW VME/MA../ZZ../4, SGW Diary, May 12, 1943.

65. For early traces of this, see Jacob Rader Marcus Center of the American Jewish Archives, Cincinnati, Felix Warburg papers, SGW to Felix Warburg, May 26, 1936. See also SGW VME/MA../ZZ../4, SGW Diary, November 27, 1939; May 29, 1942.

66. SGW VME/CL/CZ../2, SGW to Max Warburg, July 16, 1938.

67. SGW VME/CL/CZ../2, SGW to Eva Warburg, January 15, 1949.

68. SGW VME/CL/CZ../2, SGW interview with Steiner, n.d.

69. SGW DME/AA../CNZZ/5, SGW to Eric Warburg, August 17, 1977; Eric Warburg to SGW, August 29, 1977; September 5, 1977; January 30, 1978.

70. SGW VME/MA../ZZ../4, SGW Diary, December 29, 1939.

71. SGW VME/MA../ZZ../4, SGW Diary, November 3, 1943; January 15, 1944.

72. SGW VME/CL/CZ../2, SGW Aphorisms, February 1960.

73. SGW DME/AA../CNZZ/5, SGW to Edmund Stinnes, June 16, 1970.

74. SGW DME/AA../CNZZ/5, SGW to F. Mullet, January 8, 1964.

75. SGW VME/CL/CZ../2, SGW to Eva Warburg, November 10, 1968.

76. SGW VME/CL/CZ../2, SGW Aphorisms, June 1967 and October 1963.

77. SGW VME/CL/CZ../2, SGW Aphorisms, November 1972 and April 1974.

78. SGW VME/CL/CZ../2, SGW Memorandum, August 27, 1962.

79. SGW VME/CL/CZ../2, SGW Memorandum, August 13, 1980.

80. *The Times*, October 19, 1982.

81. SGW VME/MA../ZZ../4, Grunfeld Speech, January 12, 1983.

82. SGW VME/MA../ZZ../4, Roll Speech, January 12, 1983.

83. GW, GW verses, October 18, 1982.

84. GW, GW to Eva and Anna Warburg, October 18, 1982.

85. Doris Wasserman papers, 'Some Extracts from Letters of Condolence'.

86. Doris Wasserman papers, Oscar Lewisohn to Eric Warburg, October 24, 1983.

87. Fraser, *High Road*, pp. 284f.

88. Darling, *City Cinderella*, p. 42.

89. SGW Personal Documents, Steiner interview, June 1976.

90. SGW DME/CO../RPBZ/6, Paul Ziegler to SGW, January 13, 1981.

91. Joseph Wechsberg, 'Profiles: Prince of the City', *New Yorker*, April 9, 1966.

92. SGW VME/MA../ZZ../4, SGW Diary, October 13, 1934.

93. SGW VME/MA../ZZ../4, SGW Diary, December 31, 1934.

94. SGW DME/AA../CNZZ/5, SGW to Peter Fleck, June 11, 1957.

95. Drogheda, *Double Harness*, p. 150. Cf. SGW VME/CL/CZ../2, Eva Warburg Note, *c.* 1954.

96. Darling, *City Cinderella*, p. 37. See also pp. 51f.

97. Steiner interview.

98. See Joseph Wechsberg, 'Warburg: The Nonconformist', *Sunday Times*, November 13, 1966.

99. SGW VME/CL/CZ../2, SGW to his parents-in-law, May 22, 1927.

100. Darling, *City Cinderella*, p. 51.

101. George and Ellie Warburg interview.

102. SGW VME/CL/CZ../2, SGW Aphorisms, September 1963.

103. Fraser, *High Road*, p. 283. Robin Jessel believed that Warburg 'retired with £30 million': Jessel interview.

104. SGW Personal Documents, Salary statements, April 5, 1968; March 31, 1969.

105. Wasserman interview.

106. *Daily Telegraph*, September 26, 1968.

107. Oscar Lewisohn papers, Sharp, 'Sir Siegmund Warburg: Some Recollections', p. 4.

108. Reich, *Financier*, pp. 350f. See also Cohan, *Last Tycoons*, p. 179.

109. SGW VME/CL/CZ../2, SGW Fragment 'about himself', *c.* 1927.

110. SGW VME/MA../ZZ../4, SGW Diary, October 12, 1934.

111. SGW VME/CL/CZ../2, SGW Aphorisms, n.d. and September 1965.

112. SGW DME/AA../CNZZ/5, SGW to A. E. Smurthwaite, December 21, 1954.

113. SGW VME/CL/CZ../2, SGW Note, February 17, 1942.

114. SGW VME/MA../ZZ../4, SGW Diary, March 17, 1942; VME/CL/CZ../2, SGW Aphorisms, n.d.

115. SGW VME/CL/CZ../2, SGW to Keller, November 3, 1951.

116. Scholey interview.

117. Fraser, *High Road*, p. 284.

118. SGW VME/MA../ZZ../4, Roll Speech, January 12, 1983.

119. SGW Box 45, SGW Note, November 13, 1948; VME/CL/CZ../2, SGW Undated fragment, *c.* 1949.

120. SGW Box 1, SGW to Ziegler, March 17, 1958.

121. Oscar Lewisohn papers, Sharp, 'Sir Siegmund Warburg: Some Recollections'.

122. Breslauer, *Furstenberg*.

123. SGW VME/CL/CZ../2, SGW Aphorisms, September 1967.

124. SGW VME/CL/CZ../2, Samuels to SGW, November 28, 1977.

125. SGW Box 62, SGW Note, January 11, 1949.

126. SGW DME/CO../RPBZ/6, Isaiah Berlin to SGW, June 15, 1979.

127. Leo Baeck Institute, New York, AR7277, Zweig–SGW correspondence (seventy-two letters and postcards from Zweig to SGW as well as copies of SGW's replies to Zweig).

128. SGW VME/CL/CZ../2, SGW Memorandum on Zweig, March 9, 1942.

129. SGW VME/CL/CZ../2, SGW Aphorisms, October 1962.

130. SGW Personal Documents, Steiner interview, June 1976.

131. SGW DME/AA../CNZZ/5, SGW to Randall, March 5, 1968.

132. SGW VME/MA../ZZ../4, SGW Draft letter from Harry Lucas to Anthony Eden, February 18, 1942.

133. SGW Personal Documents, Steiner interview, June 1976.

134. SGW VME/CL/CZ../2, SGW to an unidentifiable female friend, August 15, 1927.

135. SGW DME/AA../CNZZ/5, George Weidenfeld to SGW, September 21, 1971; SGW to Weidenfeld, September 25, 1971.

136. SGW DME/AA../CNZZ/5, SGW to Frederic Warburg, July 14, 1967; SGW Personal Documents, SGW Draft sketch of 'Expensive Lessons', June 1, 1976.

137. SGW VME/CL/CZ../2, SGW Note to executors, November 16, 1972.

138. SGW VME/MA../ZZ../4, Steiner to SGW, March 18, 1980.

139. SGW VME/CL/CZ../2, Joshua Sherman, draft Table of Contents, March 1984; Lewisohn to Roll, March 17, 1984; Sherman, draft introduction to 'An Anthology for Searchers', March 26, 1984. See also Grunfeld interview; JS, SGW Aphorisms file.

140. SGW VME/CL/CZ../2, SGW Aphorisms.

141. GW, Paul Ziegler to GW, April 24, 1968.

142. See Marnham, *Wild Mary*, for further details on Ziegler.

143. Darling, *City Cinderella*, p. 115.

144. See especially Augar, *Death of Gentlemanly Capitalism*. See also Pettigrew and Whipp, *Managing Change*; Smith, *Comeback*.

145. Plender and Wallace, *Square Mile*, pp. 125–7; Ferris, *Master Bankers*, p. 224; Courtney and Thompson, *City Lives*, p. 91.

146. Augar, *Death of Gentlemanly Capitalism*, pp. 67, 141.

147. Martin [Vander] Weyer, 'Inside the Forbidden City', *Spectator*, October 4, 1992.

148. Augar, *Death of Gentlemanly Capitalism*, p. 231.

149. The abortive deal is dissected brilliantly in Kotchen and Sebenius, 'Morgan Stanley and S. G. Warburg', (A) and (B).

150. Patrick Weever, 'Fear Stalks the Square Mile', *Sunday Telegraph*, October 9, 1994.

151. 'Jilted', *Economist*, December 17, 1994.

152. See Oscar Lewisohn papers, Grunfeld to members of S. G. Warburg Group PLC, May 1, 1995. Cf. Kynaston, *City of London*, vol. IV, pp. 770f.

153. David Freud, 'Hubris Followed by Nemesis: How Poor Leadership led to Warburg's Collapse', *Independent*, May 9, 2006.

154. *Financial Times*, November 13, 2002; 'Name Theory', *Economist*, June 14, 2003.

155. John Jay, 'Doom Loop Claims Schroders at Knockdown Price', *Sunday Times*, January 23, 2000; Kirstie Hamilton, 'Surrender in the City', ibid.

156. Oscar Lewisohn papers, Gordon, 'Mr Henry Grunfeld and Sir Siegmund Warburg', October 8, 1997, p. 4.

157. Fraser, *High Road*, p. 272. John Craven agreed: Craven interview.

158. 'The Cruel Fate of Small Fry', *Economist*, May 6, 1995.

159. Kynaston, *City of London*, vol. IV, p. 770.

160. Valentine, *Free Range Ego*, pp. 191–4.

161. David Freud, 'Hubris followed by Nemesis: How poor Leadership Led to Warburg's Collapse', *Independent*, May 9, 2006.

162. Ibid.

163. 'Name Theory', *Economist*, June 14, 2003.

164. Darling, *City Cinderella*, p. 56.

APPENDIX: GRAPHOLOGY

1. See Bangerter, König, Blatti and Salvisberg, 'How Widespread is Graphology?'

2. SGW DME/CO../RPBZ/6, Index to graphological analyses.

3. SGW DME/CO../RPBZ/6, Dreifuss Report, December 21, 1964.

4. SGW DME/CO../RPBZ/6, SGW to Korner, October 21, 1968.

5. DME/CO../RPBZ/6, Dreifuss Report, July 7, 1969; SGW to Theodora

Dreifuss, July 28, 1969. Cf. Slater, *Return to Go*, p. 167f.; Kynaston, *City of London*, vol. IV, p. 411.

6. See e.g. SGW DME/CO../RPBZ/6, SGW to Dreifuss, August 8, 1961; August 8, 1962; July 27, 1963.

7. SGW Box 8, SGW to A. H. Webber, Bank of England, September 11, 1962. On the subsequent financing of the institution, to which he contributed several thousand pounds a year, see DME/AA../CNZZ/5, E. Reinhardt to SGW, January 10, 1967; SGW to Reinhardt, January 11, 1967; Box 25, SGW Draft letter to Chadwick, May 11, 1970.

8. SGW DME/AA../CNZZ/5, SGW to Leopold Dreifuss, February 26, 1966.

9. Joseph Wechsberg, 'Profiles: Prince of the City', *New Yorker*, April 9, 1966. Cf. Wechsberg, *Merchant Bankers*, pp. 221f.

10. See e.g. SGW DME/CO../RPBZ/6, SGW to Dreifuss, September 20, 1962.

11. See e.g. DME/CO../RPBZ/6, SGW Notes on Kenneth Keith, June 24, 1968.

12. SGW DME/CO../RPBZ/6, SGW to Dreifuss, September 17, 1965.

13. Darling, *City Cinderella*, pp. 38f.

14. SGW Box 29, SGW to S. A. Constance, February 15, 1972.

15. SGW VME/CL/CZ../2, Scholey to Eva Warburg, March 29, 1973.

16. SGW VME/CL/CZ../2, Steiner interview, n.d.

17. I am grateful to Hugh Stevenson for showing me the document in question.

18. See for example Ben-Shakhar et al., 'Can Graphology Predict Occupational Success?'

Bibliography

PRIMARY SOURCES

Archives Used

Great Britain

Bank of England, London
Churchill Archive Centre, Cambridge
  Leopold Amery papers
London School of Economics
  Andrew McFadyean papers
Rothschild Archive, London
Sir Siegmund Warburg's Voluntary Settlement, London
  Sir Siegmund Warburg papers
University of Warwick Modern Records Centre, Coventry
  Confederation of British Industry papers

Germany

Bundesarchiv Koblenz
Bundesarchiv Potsdam
M. M. Warburg-Brinckmann, Wirtz & Co., Hamburg
  Max M. Warburg papers
Politisches Archiv des Answärtigen Amts, Bonn

United States

Baker Library, Harvard Business School
  Thomas W. Lamont papers
Columbia University Oral History Collection
  James P. Warburg Diary

Franklin D. Roosevelt Library, New York
  Alexander Sachs papers
Federal Reserve Bank, New York
  Benjamin Strong papers
Herbert Hoover Library, Iowa
  Lewis L. Strauss papers
Jacob Rader Marcus Center of the American Jewish Archives, Cincinnati
  Felix Warburg papers
John F. Kennedy Memorial Library, Boston
  James P. Warburg papers
Leo Baeck Institute, New York
  Hermann Rauschning collection; Hans Schaeffer collection
Sterling Library, Yale University
  Paul M. Warburg papers
Yale University Library Manuscripts and Archives
  Sir William Wiseman papers

Private papers

John Goodwin
Bernard Kelly
Oscar Lewisohn
Joshua Sherman
George Warburg
Doris Wasserman

SECONDARY SOURCES

Adler, Cyrus, *Felix M. Warburg: A Biographical Sketch* (New York, 1938)
—— and Mortimer L. Schiff, *Jacob H. Schiff: His Life and Letters* (Garden City, NY, 1928)
Aharoni, Yair, *The Israeli Economy: Dreams and Realities* (London/New York, 1991)
Altman, Oscar L., 'The Integration of European Capital Markets', *Journal of Finance*, 20, 2 (May 1965), 209–21
Andrew, Christopher, *The World was Going our Way: The KGB and the Battle for the Third World – Newly Revealed Secrets from the Mitrokhin Archive* (New York, 2006)

Anon. [Candidate No. 16188], 'To What Extent Did the City Determine that No Restrictions were Placed on the London Eurodollar Market in the Period 1960–3?', unpublished Modern History Final Honours School thesis (University of Oxford, 2002)

Attali, Jacques, *A Man of Influence: Sir Siegmund Warburg, 1902–1982* (London, 1986)

Augar, Philip, *The Death of Gentlemanly Capitalism: The Rise and Fall of London's Investment Banks* (London, 2001)

Baden, Prinz Max von, *Erinnerungen und Dokumente* (Stuttgart/Berlin/ Leipzig, 1927)

Bajohr, Frank, *'Aryanisation' in Hamburg: The Economic Exclusion of Jews and the Confiscation of their Property in Nazi Germany, 1933–1945* (Oxford/New York, 2002)

Balderston, Theo, 'German Banking between the Wars: The Crisis of the Credit Banks', *Business History Review,* 65, 3 (Autumn 1991), 554–605
——, *The Origins and Course of the German Economic Crisis, 1923–1932* (Berlin, 1993)

Bangerter, Adrian, Cornelius J. König, Sandrine Blatti and Alexander Salvisberg, 'How Widespread is Graphology in Personnel Selection Practice? A Case Study of a Job Market Myth', *International Journal of Selection and Assessment,* 17, 2 (June 2009), 219–30

Barkai, Avraham, 'Max Warbug im Jahre 1933. Missglückte Versuche zur Milderung der Judenverfolgung', in Peter Freimark, Alice Jankowski and Ina S. Lorenz (eds.), *Juden in Deutschland. Emanzipation, Integration, Verfolgung und Vernichtung* (Hamburg, 1991), 390–405

Barnes, John and David Nicholson (eds.), *The Empire at Bay: The Leo Amery Diaries, 1929–1945* (London, 1988)

Barnett, Correlli, *The Audit of War: The Illusion and Reality of Britain as a Great Nation* (London, 1986)

Barr, James, *The Bow Group: A History* (London, 2001)

Baumier, Jean, *La Galaxie Paribas* (Paris, 1988)

Ben-Shakhar, Gershon, Maya Bar-Hillel, Yoram Bilu, Edor Ben-Abba and Anat Flug, 'Can Graphology Predict Occupational Success? Two Empirical Studies and Some Methodological Ruminations', *Journal of Applied Psychology,* 71, 4 (November 1986), 645–53

Benn, Tony, *Office without Power: Diaries, 1968–1972* (London, 1988)

Berghahn, Volker R., *Germany and the Approach of War in 1914* (London, 1973)

Birmingham, Stephen, *Our Crowd: The Great Jewish Families of New York* (New York/Evanston/London, 1967)

Böhm, Ekkehard, *Überseehandel und Flottenbau. Hanseatische Kaufmann-schaft und deutsche Seerüstung, 1879–1902* (Hamburg, 1972)

Borchardt, Knut, 'Zwangslagen und Handlungsspielräume in der großen Wirtschaftskrise der frühen dreißiger Jahre. Zur Revision des überlieferten Geschichtsbildes', *Jahrbuch der Bayerischen Akademie der Wissenschaften* (1979), 87–132

―― and Albrecht Ritschl, 'Could Brüning Have Done It? A Keynesian Model of Interwar Germany, 1925–1938', *European Economic Review*, 36 (1992), 695–701

Born, Karl Erich, *Die deutsche Bankenkrise 1931* (Munich, 1967)

Bower, Tom, *Maxwell: The Outsider* (London, 1992)

――, *Tiny Rowland: A Rebel Tycoon* (London, 1993)

Braddon, Russell, *Roy Thomson of Fleet Street* (London, 1965)

Bramsen, Bo and Kathleen Wain, *The Hambros, 1779–1979* (London, 1979)

Breslauer, Bernard H., *Jean Furstenberg, 1890– 1982: Portrait of a Bibliophile* (n.p., *c.* 1983)

Burk, Kathleen, 'Witness Seminar on the Origins and Early Development of the Eurobond Market', *Contemporary European History*, 1, 1 (1992), 65–87

―― and Alec Cairncross, *Goodbye, Great Britain: The 1976 IMF Crisis* (New Haven, 1992)

Burn, Gary, 'The State, the City and the Euromarkets', *Review of International Political Economy*, 6, 2 (1999), 225–61

Bussière, Éric, *Paribas, 1872–1992: Europe and the World* (Paris, 1992)

Büttner, Ursula, 'Das Ende der Weimarer Republik und der Aufstieg des Nationalsozialismus in Hamburg', in Ursula Büttner and Werner Joch-mann, *Hamburg auf dem Weg ins Dritte Reich. Entwicklungsjahre 1931–1933* (Hamburg, 1983), 7–37

――, *Hamburg in der Staats- und Wirtschaftskrise, 1928–1931* (Hamburg, 1982)

――, *Politische Gerechtigkeit und sozialer Geist. Hamburg zur Zeit der Weimarer Republik* (Hamburg, 1985)

――, 'Rettung der Republik oder Systemzerstörung?', in Ursula Büttner and Werner Jochmann (eds.), *Zwischen Demokratie und Diktatur. National-sozialistische Machtaneignung in Hamburg. Tendenzen und Reaktionen in Europa* (Hamburg, 1984), 41–65

Cairncross, Alec, *The British Economy since 1945: Economic Policy and Performance, 1945–1990* (Oxford/Malden, Massachusetts, 1995)

Cecil, Lamar, *Albert Ballin: Business and Politics in Imperial Germany* (Princeton, 1967)

Chambers, David, 'Gentlemanly Capitalism Revisited: A Case Study of the Underpricing of Initial Public Offerings on the London Stock Exchange, 1946–86', *Economic History Review*, 62, S1 (2009), 31–56

Chapman, S. D., 'Aristocracy and Meritocracy in Merchant Banking', *British Journal of Sociology*, 37, 2 (June 1986), 180–93

Chernow, Ron, *The Death of the Banker: The Decline and Fall of the Great Financial Dynasties and the Triumph of the Small Investor* (New York, 1997)

——, *The House of Morgan* (London, 1990)

——, *The Warburgs: A Family Saga* (London, 1993)

Claes, Anouk, Marc J. K. De Ceuster and Ruud Polfliet, 'Anatomy of the Eurobond Market, 1980–2000', *European Financial Management*, 8, 3 (2002), 373–86

Cohan, William D., *The Last Tycoons: The Secret History of Lazard Frères & Co.* (New York, 2007)

Cohen, Naomi Wiener, *Jacob H. Schiff: A Study in American Jewish Leadership* (Hanover, NH, 1999)

Comfort, Richard A., *Revolutionary Hamburg: Labor Politics in the Early Weimar Republic* (Stanford, 1966)

Cooper, Richard N., 'Should Capital Controls be Banished?', *Brookings Papers on Economic Activity*, 1 (1999), 89–141

Courtney, Cathy and Paul Thompson, *City Lives: The Changing Voices of British Finance* (London, 1996)

Crossman, Richard, *The Backbench Diaries of Richard Crossman* (London, 1981)

Darling, Peter Stormonth, *City Cinderella: The Life and Times of Mercury Asset Management* (London, 1999)

DeLong, J. Bradford and Barry Eichengreen, 'The Marshall Plan: History's Most Successful Structural Adjustment Programme', in Rüdiger Dornbusch, Wilhelm Nölling and Richard Layard (eds.), *Postwar Economic Reconstruction and Lessons for the East Today* (Cambridge, MA, 1993), 189–230

Dimsdale, N. H., 'British Monetary Policy since 1945', in N. F. R. Crafts and N. W. C. Woodward (eds.), *The British Economy since 1945* (Oxford, 1991), 89–140

Dimson, Elroy, Paul Marsh and Mike Staunton, *Triumph of the Optimists: 101 Years of Global Investment Returns* (Princeton, 2002)

Dippel, John V. H., *Bound upon a Wheel of Fire: Why So Many German Jews Made the Tragic Decision to Remain in Nazi Germany* (New York, 1996)

Drogheda, Lord [Charles Garrett Moore, Earl of], *Double Harness: Memoirs* (London, 1978)

Edgerton, David, *Warfare State: Britain, 1920–1970* (Cambridge, 2006)

Ellison, James, *The United States, Britain and the Transatlantic Crisis: Rising to the Gaullist Challenge, 1963–68* (Basingstoke, 2007)

Evans, Richard J., *Death in Hamburg: Society and Politics in the Cholera Years, 1830–1910* (Oxford, 1987)

——, 'Family and Class in the Hamburg Grand Bourgeosie, 1815–1914', in David Blackbourn and Richard J. Evans (eds.), *The German Bourgeoisie: Essays on the Social History of the German Middle Class from the Late Eighteenth to the Early Twentieth Century* (London, 1991), 118–26

Farrer, David, *The Warburgs: The Story of a Family* (New York, 1974)

Feldman, Gerald D., *Allianz and the German Insurance Business, 1933–1945* (Cambridge, 2001)

Ferguson, Niall, *The Ascent of Money: A Financial History of the World* (London, 2008)

——, 'Constraints and Room for Manoeuvre in the German Inflation of the Early 1920s', *Economic History Review*, New Series, 49, 4 (1996), 635–66

——, 'Keynes and the German Inflation', *English Historical Review*, 110, 436 (1995), 368–91

——, 'Max Warburg and German Politics: The Limits of Financial Power in Wilhelmine Germany', in Geoff Eley and James Retallack (eds.), *Wilhelminism and its Legacies: German Modernities, Imperialism and the Meanings of Reform, 1890–1930* (New York/Oxford, 2003), 185–201

——, *Paper and Iron: Hamburg Business and German Politics in the Era of Inflation, 1897–1927* (Cambridge, 1995)

——, 'Siegmund Warburg, the City of London and the Financial Roots of European Integration', *Business History*, 51, 3 (May 2009), 362–80

——, *The War of the World: History's Age of Hatred* (London, 2006)

——, *The World's Banker: The History of the House of Rothschild* (London, 1998)

Ferguson, Thomas and Peter Temin, 'Made in Germany: The German Currency Crisis of July 1931', Massachusetts Institute of Technology Department of Economics Working Paper 01-07 (February 2001)

Ferris, Paul, *The City* (London, 1960)

——, *Gentlemen of Fortune: The World's Merchant and Investment Bankers* (London, 1984)

——, *The Master Bankers* (London, 1984)

——, *The Money Men of Europe* (New York, 1969)

Fouchier, Jacques de, *La banque et la vie* (Paris, 1988)

Fraser, Ian, *The High Road to England* (Norwich, 1999)

Fraser, William Lionel, *All to the Good* (London, 1963)

Freimark, Peter and Arno Herzig, *Die Hamburger Juden in der Emanzipationsphase, 1780–1870* (Hamburg, 1989)

Freud, David, *Freud in the City* (London, 2006)

Freudenthal, H., *Vereine in Hamburg* (Hamburg, 1968)

Galbraith, John Kenneth, *The New Industrial State* (New York, 1967)

Gall, Lothar, *Der Bankier. Hermann Josef Abs – Eine Biographie* (Munich, 2004)

Goldman, Nahum, *Mein Leben als deutscher Jude* (Munich, 1980)

Gombrich, Ernst H., *Aby Warburg: An Intellectual Biography* (Oxford, 1970)

Gordon, Martin, 'Autostrade and the Dawn of the Eurobond', unpublished MS (n.d.)

Grierson, Ronald, *A Truant Disposition: Pages from my Diary* (London, 1992)

Griffin, Tony, *Footfalls in Memory* (Toronto, 1998)

Griffith, John R., Jr, 'The Effect of the Interest Equalization Tax Act and the Interest Equalization Tax Extension Act on Purchases of Long-Term Bonds of Selected Countries Marketed in the United States: 1959 to March 1966', *Journal of Finance*, 24, 3 (June 1969), 538–9

Haffner, Sebastian, *Defying Hitler* (New York, 2000)

Halevi, Nadar, with Nahum Gross, Ephraim Kheiman and Marshall Sanat, *The History of Bank Leumi Le-Israel* (Jerusalem, 1981)

Hamel, Iris, *Völkischer Verband und nationale Gewerkschaft. Die Politik des Deutschnational-Handlungsgehilfenverband, 1893–1933* (Frankfurt, 1967)

Hamilton, Richard F., *Who Voted for Hitler?* (Princeton, 1982)

Hardach, Gerd, *Weltmarktorientierung und relative Stagnation. Währungspolitik in Deutschland, 1924–1931* (Berlin, 1976)

Hatch, Stephen and Michael Fores, 'The Struggle for British Aluminium', *Political Quarterly*, 31, 4 (October 1960), 477–87

Haupts, Leo, *Deutsche Friedenspolitik. Eine Alternative zur Machtpolitik des Ersten Weltkrieges* (Düsseldorf, 1976)

Hauschild-Thiessen, Renate, *Bürgerstolz und Kaisertreu. Hamburg und das Deutsche Reich von 1871* (Hamburg, 1979)

Hennessy, Peter, *Muddling Through: Power, Politics and the Quality of Government in Post-war Britain* (London, 1997)

Hills, Jill, 'The Industrial Reorganization Corporation: The Case of the AEI/GEC and English Electric/GEC Mergers', *Public Administration*, 59, 1 (1981), 63–84

Hinrichsen, Hans-Peter, *Der Ratgeber. Kurt Birrenbach und die Aussenpolitik der Bundesrepublik Deutschland* (Berlin, 2002)

Hitchcock, William I., *The Struggle for Europe: A History of Europe since 1945* (London, 2003)

Jaide, W., *Generationen eines Jahrhunderts. Wechsel der Jugendgeneration im Jahrhunderttrend. Zur Sozialgeschichte der Jugend in Deutschland, 1871–1985* (Opladen, 1988)

James, Harold, 'The Causes of the German Banking Crisis of 1931', *Economic History Review*, New Series, 37, 1 (February 1984), 68–87

——, *The Deutsche Bank and the Nazi Economic War against the Jews: The Expropriation of Jewish-Owned Property* (Princeton, 2001)

——, *The End of Globalization: Lessons from the Great Depression* (Cambridge, MA, 2001)

——, *The German Slump: Politics and Economics, 1924–1936* (Oxford, 1986)

——, *The Nazi Dictatorship and the Deutsche Bank* (Cambridge, 2004)

Jochmann, Werner, 'Gesellschaftliche Gleichschaltung in Hamburg 1933. Freiheit des Individuums oder Sicherheit und Schutz der Gemeinschaft?', in Ursula Büttner and Werner Jochmann (eds.), *Zwischen Demokratie und Diktatur. Nationalsozialistische Machtaneignung in Hamburg. Tendenzen und Reaktionen in Europa* (Hamburg, 1984), 91–114

—— (ed.), '*Im Kampf um die Macht*'. *Hitlers Rede vor dem Hamburger Nationalklub von 1919* (Frankfurt am Main, 1960)

—— (ed.), *Nationalsozialismus und Revolution: Ursprung und Geschichte der NSDAP in Hamburg 1922–1933. Dokumente* (Frankfurt am Main, 1963)

Johe, Werner, 'Institutionelle Glechschaltung in Hamburg 1933. Revolutionäre Umgestaltung oder Wiederherstellung traditioneller Ordnungen?', in Ursula Büttner and Werner Jochmann (eds.), *Zwischen Demokratie und Diktatur. Nationalsozialistische Machtaneignung in Hamburg. Tendenzen und Reaktionen in Europa* (Hamburg, 1984), 66–90

Katz, Gabrielle, *Madame Kaulla, 1739–1806. Die erste Unternehmerin Süddeutschlands und die reichste Frau ihrer Zeit* (Filderstadt, 2006)

Kerr, Ian M., *A History of the Eurobond Market* (London, 1984)

Keynes, John Maynard, *Two Memoirs: Dr Melchior, a Defeated Enemy; and, My Early Beliefs* (New York, 1949)

King, Cecil, *The Cecil King Diary: 1965–1970* (London, 1972)

——, *The Cecil King Diary: 1970–1974* (London, 1975)

Klemperer, Klemens von, *German Resistance against Hitler: The Search for Allies Abroad, 1938–1945* (Oxford, 1994)

Klessmann, Eckart, *M. M. Warburg und Co. Die Geschichte eines Bankhauses* (Hamburg, 1998)

Köhler, Ingo, *Die 'Arisierung' der Privatbanken im Dritten Reich. Verdrängung, Ausschaltung und die Frage der Wiedergutmachung*, Schriftenreihe zur Zeitschrift für Unternehmensgeschichte, vol. 14 (Munich, 2005)

Kohlhaus, H.-H., 'Die Hapag, Cuno und das Deutsche Reich, 1920–1933', unpublished PhD thesis (University of Hamburg, 1952)

Kopper, Christopher, 'Nationalsozialistische Bankpolitik am Beispiel des Bankhauses M. M. Warburg & Co. in Hamburg', unpublished Magister thesis (University of Bochum, 1988)

Kotchen, David T. and James K. Sebenius, 'Morgan Stanley and S. G. Warburg: Investment Bank of the Future (A)', Harvard Business School Case N9-898-140 (6 January 1998)

——, 'Morgan Stanley and S. G. Warburg: Investment Bank of the Future (B)', Harvard Business School Case N9-898-141 (6 January 1998)

Kotkin, Stephen, *Armageddon Averted: The Soviet Collapse, 1970–2000* (Oxford, 2001)

Krause, Thomas, 'Von der Sekte zur Massenpartei. Die Hamburger NSDAP von 1922 bis 1933', in Maike Bruhns, Claudia Preuschoft and Werner Skrentny (eds.), *'Hier war doch alles nicht so schlimm'. Wie die Nazis in Hamburg den Alltag eroberten* (Hamburg, 1984), 18–49

Kroboth, Rudolf, *Die Finanzpolitik des deutschen Reiches während der Reichskanzlerschaft Bethmann Hollwegs und die Geld- und Kapitalmarktverhältnisse (1909–1913/14)* (Frankfurt am Main, 1986)

Krohn, Helga, *Die Juden in Hamburg. Die politische, soziale, kulturelle und politische Entwicklung einer judischen Großstadtgemeinde nach der Emanzipation, 1848–1918* (Hamburg, 1974)

Krozewski, Gerold , 'Sterling, the "Minor" Territories, and the End of Formal Empire, 1939–1958', *Economic History Review*, New Series, 46, 2 (May 1993), 239–65

Krüger, Peter, *Deutschland und die Reparationen, 1918/19. Die Genesis des Reparationsproblems in Deutschland zwischen Waffenstillstand und Versailler Friedensschluß* (Stuttgart, 1973)

——, 'Die Rolle der Industrie und Banken in den reparationspolitischen Entscheidungen nach dem Ersten Weltkrieg', in Hans Mommsen, Dietmar Petzina and Bernd Weisbrod (eds.), *Industrielles System und politische Entwicklung in der Weimarer Republik*, vol. II (Düsseldorf, 1974), 568–81

Kynaston, David, *Cazenove & Co.: A History* (London, 1991)

——, *The City of London*, vol. IV: *A Club No More, 1945–2000* (London, 2001)

——, *Siegmund Warburg: A Centenary Appreciation* (London, 2002)

Lamb, Richard, *The Macmillan Years, 1957–1963* (London, 1995)

Larre, René, 'Facts of Life about the Integration of National Capital Markets', *Journal of Money, Credit and Banking*, 1, 3 (August 1969), 319–27

Lester, David, *Suicide and the Holocaust* (New York, 2005)

Lohalm, Uwe, *Völkischer Radikalismus. Die Geschichte des Deutsch-völkischen Schutz- und Trutzbundes, 1919–1923* (Hamburg, 1970)

London, Louise, *Whitehall and the Jews, 1933–1948: British Immigration Policy, Jewish Refugees and the Holocaust* (Cambridge, 2000)

Lorenz, Ina, *Die Juden in Hamburg zur Zeit der Weimarer Republik*, 2 vols. (Hamburg, 1987)

Lowe, Jacques, Sandy McLachlan and Fiona Pilkington, *The City: The Traditions and Powerful Personalities of the World's Greatest Financial Centre* (London, 1980)

Maddison, Angus, *The World Economy: A Millennial Perspective* (Paris, 2001)

Mallaby, Sebastian, *The World's Banker: A Story of Failed States, Financial Crises, and the Wealth and Poverty of Nations* (New York, 2004)

Mandelbrote, G. (ed.), *Out of Print and into Profit: A History of the Rare and Second-hand Book Trade in Britain in the 20th Century* (London, 2006)

Mann, Thomas, *Buddenbrooks. Verfall einer Familie* (Berlin, 1901)

——, *Joseph and his Brothers*, trans. H. T. Lowe-Porter (New York, 1945 [1934])

Marnham, Patrick, *Wild Mary: The Life of Mary Wesley* (London, 2006)

Meadows, Donella H., Dennis L. Meadows, Jørgen Randers and William W. Behrens III, *The Limits to Growth* (New York, 1972)

Mendelson, Morris, 'The Eurobond and Capital Market Integration', *Journal of Finance*, 27, 1 (March 1972), 110–26

Michaelis, Anthony R. and Hugh Harvey (eds.), *Scientists in Search of their Conscience. Proceedings of a Symposium on 'The Impact of Science on Society'*, organized by the European Committee of the Weizmann Institute of Science, Brussels, 28–29 June 1971 (Berlin/Heidelberg/New York, 1973)

Michie, R. C., 'Insiders, Outsiders and the Dynamics of Change in the City of London since 1900', *Journal of Contemporary History*, 33, 4 (October 1988), 547–71

Milward, Alan S., *The European Rescue of the Nation-State*, 2nd edn (London, 2000)

Mosse, Werner E., *The German-Jewish Economic Elite, 1820–1935: A Socio-cultural Profile* (Oxford, 1989)

Moussa, Pierre, *La roue de la fortune: souvenirs d'un financier* (Paris, 1989)

Newman, Peter C., *Establishment Man: A Portrait of Power* (Toronto, 1982)

Newton, Scott, *Profits of Peace: The Political Economy of Anglo-German Appeasement* (Oxford, 1996)

Nicosia, Francis R. and Jonathan Huener (eds.), *Business and Industry in Nazi Germany* (New York/Oxford, 2004)

Noakes, Jeremy and Geoffrey Pridham (eds.), *Nazism, 1919–1945*, vol. I: *The Rise to Power, 1919–1934: A Documentary Reader* (Exeter, 1983)

Nott, John, *Here Today, Gone Tomorrow: Memoirs of an Errant Politician* (London, 2002)

O'Hara, Glen, '"Dynamic, Exciting, Thrilling Change": The Wilson Government's Economic Policies, 1964–70', in Glen O'Hara and Helen Parr (eds.), *The Wilson Governments 1964–1970 Reconsidered* (London/New York, 2006), 79–98

——, *From Dreams to Disillusionment: Economic and Social Planning in 1960s Britain* (Basingstoke/New York, 2007)

Orluc, Katiana, 'A Wilhelmine Legacy? Coudenhove-Kalergi's "Paneuropa" as an Alternative Path towards a European (Post-)Modernity, 1922–1932', in Geoff Eley and James Retallack (eds.), *Wilhelminism and its Legacies: German Modernities, Imperialism, and the Meanings of Reform, 1890–1930* (Oxford/New York, 2003), 219–34

Owen, Geoffrey, *From Empire to Europe: The Decline and Revival of British Industry since the Second World War* (London, 1999)

Palin, Ronald, *Rothschild Relish* (London, 1970)

Parr, Helen, *Britain's Policy towards the European Community, 1964–7: Harold Wilson and Britain's World Role* (London, 2006)

Pettigrew, Andrew and Richard Whipp, *Managing Change for Competitive Success* (Oxford, 1991)

Plender, John and Paul Wallace, *The Square Mile: A Guide to the New City of London* (London, 1985)

Pohl, Manfred, *Hamburger Bankengeschichte* (Mainz, 1986)

Pottle, Mark (ed.), *Champion Redoubtable: The Diaries and Letters of Violet Bonham Carter, 1914–1945* (London, 1998)

Reich, Cary, *Financier: The Biography of André Meyer – A Story of Money, Power, and the Reshaping of American Business* (New York, 1998)

Reitmayer, Morten, *Bankiers im Kaiserreich. Sozialprofil und Habitus der deutschen Hochfinanz* (Göttingen, 1999)

Richebächer, Kurt, 'The Problems and Prospects of Integrating European Capital Markets', *Journal of Money, Credit and Banking*, 1, 3 (August 1969), 336–46

Ritschl, Albrecht, *Deutschlands Krise und Konjunktur, 1924–1934. Binnenkonjuktur, Auslandsverschuldung und Reparationsproblem zwischen Dawes-Plan und Transfersperre* (Berlin, 2002)

Roberts, Richard, *Schroders: Merchants and Bankers* (London, 1992)

—— and Christopher Arnander, *Take your Partners: Orion, the Consortium Banks and the Transformation of the Euromarkets* (Basingstoke, 2001)

—— and David Kynaston, *City State: A Contemporary History of the City of London and How Money Triumphed* (London, 2001)

Roll, Eric, *Crowded Hours* (London/Boston, 1985)

Rose, Kenneth, *The Elusive Rothschild: The Life of Victor, Third Baron Rothschild* (London, 2003)

Rosenbaum, Eduard and A. J. Sherman, *M. M. Warburg & Co., 1798–1938: Merchant Bankers of Hamburg* (London, 1979)

Rothschild, Edmund de, *A Gilt-Edged Life* (London, 1998)

Sagou, M'hamed, *Paribas: anatomie d'une puissance* (Paris, 1981)

Schenk, Catherine R., *Britain and the Sterling Area: From Devaluation to Convertibility in the 1950s* (London, 1994)

——, 'Crisis and Opportunity: The Policy Environment of International Banking in the City of London, 1958–1980', in Youssef Cassis and Éric Bussière (eds.), *London and Paris as International Financial Centres in the Twenteeth Century* (Oxford, 2004), 207–28

——, 'Decolonisation and European Economic Integration: The Free Trade Area Negotiations, 1956–58', *Journal of Imperial and Commonwealth History*, 24, 3 (1996), 444–63

——, 'The Market vs. the State: Capital Market Integration in the 1960s', in R. Perron (ed.), *The Common Market: Towards the European Integration of Industrial and Financial Markets? (1958–1968)* (Paris, 2004), 141–59

——, 'The "New" City and the State, 1959–1971', in Ranald Michie (ed.), *The British Government and the City of London in the Twentieth Century* (Cambridge, 2004), 322–39

——, 'The Origins of the Eurodollar Market in London, 1955–1963', *Explorations in Economic History*, 35 (April 1998), 221–38

——, 'Sterling, International Monetary Reform and Britain's Applications to Join the European Economic Community in the 1960s', *Contemporary European History*, 11, 3 (2002), 345–69

——, 'The UK, the Sterling Area and the EEC 1957–63', in A. Deighton and A. S. Milward (eds.), *Widening, Deepening and Acceleration: The EEC, 1957–63* (Baden-Baden, 1999), 123–37

Schnabel, Isabel, 'The German Twin Crisis of 1931', Sonderforschungsbereich 504, 02–48 (September 2002)

——, 'The Great Banks' Depression: Deposit Withdrawals in the German Crisis of 1931', Sonderforschungsbereich 504, 03–11 (March 2003)

Schnee, Heinrich, 'Die Hoffaktoren-Familie Kaulla an süddeutschen Fürsten-höfen', *Zeitschrift für Württembergische Landesgeschichte*, 20, 2 (1962), 238–67

Schramm, Percy Ernst, *Neun Generationen: 300 Jahre deutscher 'Kultur-geschichte' im Lichte der Schicksale einer Hamburger Bürgerfamilie*, 2 vols. (Göttingen, 1963, 1965)

Scott, Ira O., Jr, 'The Problems and Prospects of Integrating European Capital Markets: Comment', *Journal of Money, Credit and Banking*, 1, 3 (August 1969), 350–53

Sherman, Joshua, 'Left Bank Account', *Times Literary Supplement* (May 23, 1986), 550

Simpson, Christopher (ed.), *War Crimes of the Deutsche Bank and the Dresdner Bank: Office of Military Government (U.S.) Reports*, Part 810 (Teaneck, NJ, 2002)

Skidelsky, Robert, *John Maynard Keynes*, vol. I: *Hopes Betrayed, 1883– 1920* (London, 1983)

Slater, Jim, *Return to Go: My Autobiography* (London, 1978)

Smith, Roy C., *Comeback: The Restoration of American Banking Power in the New World Economy* (Boston, 1993)

Somary, Felix, *The Raven of Zurich: The Memoirs of Felix Somary*, trans. A. J. Sherman, (London, 1986)

Spira, Peter, *Ladders and Snakes: A Twist in the Spiral Staircase* (Chichester, 1997)

Steinberg, Jonathan, *The Deutsche Bank and its Gold Transactions during the Second World War* (Munich, 1999)

Thompson, Paul, 'The Pyrrhic Victory of Gentlemanly Capitalism: The Financial Elite of the City of London, 1945–2000', *Journal of Contemporary History*, 32, 3 (June 1997), 283–304

Tomlinson, Jim, 'Balanced Accounts? Constructing the Balance of Payments Problem in Post-war Britain', *English Historical Review*, 124 (2009), 863–84

——, 'Why Was There Never a "Keynesian Revolution" in Economic Policy?', *Economy and Society*, 10 (1981), 72–87

Vagts, Alfred, 'M. M. Warburg & Co. Ein Bankhaus in der deutschen Weltpolitik, 1905–1933', *Vierteljahresschrift für Sozial- und Wirtschafts-geschichte*, 45 (1958), 289–398

Valentine, Michael, *Free Range Ego* (London, 2006)

Wagener, Otto, *Hitler aus nächster Nähe. Aufzeichnungen eines Vertrauten, 1929–1932* (Frankfurt am Main/Berlin/Vienna, 1978)

Wake, Jehanne, *Kleinwort Benson: A History of Two Families in Banking* (Oxford, 1997)

Warburg, Eric, *Times and Tides: A Log-Book* (Hamburg, n.d.)

Warburg, Frederic, *An Occupation for Gentlemen* (London, 1959)

Warburg, James P., *The Long Road Home* (New York, 1964)

Warburg, Max M., *Aus meinen Aufzeichnungen* (Hamburg, 1952)

Warburg Spinelli, Ingrid, *Erinnerungen, 1910–1989. Die Dringlichkeit des Mitleids und die Einsamkeit, nein zu sagen* (Hamburg, 1990)

Warburg Melchior, Elsa, 'That Dear Past', ed. Ruth Fleck, unpublished MS, n.d.

Washausen, H., *Hamburg und die Kolonialpolitik des Deutschen Reiches, 1880–1890* (Hamburg, 1968)

Wechsberg, Joseph, *The Merchant Bankers* (Boston/Toronto, 1966)

Williams, Philip M. (ed.), *The Diary of Hugh Gaitskell* (London, 1983)

Wilson, Harold, *Final Term: The Labour Goverment, 1974–1976* (London, 1979)

Young, Stephen C. and A. V. Lowe, *Intervention in the Mixed Economy: The Evolution of British Industrial Policy, 1964–72* (London, 1974)

Zimmermann, Mosche, *Hamburgischer Patriotismus und deutscher Nationalismus. Die Emanzipation der Juden in Hamburg* (Hamburg, 1979)

Index

The abbreviation SGW stands for Siegmund Warburg.